OXFORD MODERN LANGUAGES
AND LITERATURE MONOGRAPHS

Editorial Committee

The Poetry of
Hugo von Hofmannsthal
and French Symbolism

ROBERT VILAIN

CLARENDON PRESS · OXFORD

OXFORD
UNIVERSITY PRESS

Great Clarendon Street, Oxford, OX2 6DP
Oxford University Press is a department of the University of Oxford.
It furthers the University's objective of excellence in research, scholarship,
and education by publishing worldwide in

Oxford New York

Athens Auckland Bangkok Bogotá Buenos Aires Calcutta
Cape Town Chennai Dar es Salaam Delhi Florence Hong Kong Istanbul
Karachi Kuala Lumpur Madrid Melbourne Mexico City Mumbai
Nairobi Paris São Paulo Singapore Taipei Tokyo Toronto Warsaw

and associated companies in Berlin Ibadan

Oxford is a registered trade mark of Oxford University Press
in the UK and certain other countries

Published in the United States
by Oxford University Press Inc., New York

British Library Cataloguing in Publication Data

Data available

Library of Congress Cataloging in Publication Data

Data available

ISBN 0-19-816003-8

1 3 5 7 9 10 8 6 4 2

Typeset by Regent Typesetting, London
Printed in Great Britain
on acid-free paper by
T.J. International Ltd.,
Padstow, Cornwall

For my parents

ACKNOWLEDGEMENTS

THIS book is a revised and extended version of a D.Phil. thesis submitted to the University of Oxford. It has benefited greatly from the advice of friends and colleagues, and I thank in particular my supervisors, David Constantine and Margaret Jacobs. Geoffrey Chew read large portions of the original thesis and patiently weeded out many errors and infelicities, and the revisions have been facilitated by the meticulous and sensible comments of the Press's anonymous reader. The careful scrutiny of my examiners, Ray Ockenden and Gar Yates, prompted important corrections and improvements, for which I am very grateful. Mike Holland, Rudolf Hirsch, Simon Hyde, David Luke, Niall Livingstone, Peter Pütz, Jim Reed, Christopher Robinson and Dugald Sturges all gave food for thought at various stages of my work. If any of this good advice has been ignored or misapplied, it is my fault.

Parts of Chapter 4 first appeared in the *Deutsche Vierteljahrsschrift* and I am grateful to the editors and to the Metzler Verlag for permission to include these here in revised form. I should like to thank the Stefan George-Stiftung in the Württembergische Landesbibliothek, Stuttgart, for permission to reproduce the jacket illustration. For financial assistance I am indebted to the British Academy, the Governing Body of Christ Church, Oxford, the University of Oxford Faculty of Medieval and Modern Languages, the Stiftung FVS (Hamburg), and Royal Holloway, University of London. The efficiency of the staff of the Taylorian Institute Library (Oxford), the Founder's Library at Royal Holloway, the Houghton Library (Harvard), the Freies Deutsches Hochstift (Frankfurt) and the Deutsches Literaturarchiv (Marbach-am-Neckar) has also been very much appreciated. I should like to thank my friends and colleagues at Royal Holloway for their support, encouragement and advice. My greatest debt is to my parents, to whom this book is dedicated with love and gratitude.

R.V.

CONTENTS

ABBREVIATIONS

Hofmannsthal's works are quoted from the Critical Edition (*SW*) or from the ten-volume paperback edition. References to these editions are by abbreviation (see below), volume-number (where appropriate) and page-number, and are usually incorporated into the main body of the text. Hofmannsthal's letters are cited with the name of the correspondent, *BW*, and a page number. All quotations preserve the orthography of the source. Italics are from the original unless otherwise stated.

BW	*Briefwechsel*
D	Hugo von Hofmannsthal, *Gesammelte Werke in zehn Einzelbänden*, ed. Bernd Schoeller in consultation with Rudolf Hirsch (Frankfurt am Main: Fischer Taschenbuch Verlag, 1979), vols. i–vi: *Dramen I–Dramen VI*
EGB	Hugo von Hofmannsthal, *Gesammelte Werke in zehn Einzelbänden*, ed. Bernd Schoeller in consultation with Rudolf Hirsch (Frankfurt am Main: Fischer Taschenbuch Verlag, 1979), vol. vii: *Erzählungen, Erfundene Gespräche und Briefe. Reisen*
OC	*Œuvres complètes*
OP	*Œuvres poétiques*
RA	Hugo von Hofmannsthal, *Gesammelte Werke in zehn Einzelbänden*, ed. Bernd Schoeller with Rudolf Hirsch (Frankfurt am Main: Fischer Taschenbuch Verlag, 1979–80), vols. viii–x: *Reden und Aufsätze*
SW	Hugo von Hofmannsthal, *Sämtliche Werke. Kritische Ausgabe veranstaltet vom Freien Deutschen Hochstift*, ed. Rudolf Hirsch, Clemens Köttelwesch, Christoph Perels, Heinz Rölleke, and Ernst Zinn (Frankfurt am Main: S. Fischer, 1975–).

NOTE ON TRANSLATIONS

Translations from French and German are my own. They are deliberately plain, intended only as simple props for accurate comprehension, and have no pretensions to elegance or beauty. Verse quotations are rendered into prose, fairly literally and with a minimum of interpretative elaboration. All quotations are translated at their first appearance only. Quotations in footnotes are not translated, being of interest primarily to the specialist academic reader.

Von meiner Poesie hängt mein Ich ab; ist jene ein Irrthum, so bin ich selbst einer!

Friedrich Hebbel, *Tagebücher*, 3 October 1839

To influence someone is to give him one's own soul. He does not think his natural thoughts, or burn with his natural passions. His virtues are not real to him. His sins, if there are such things as sins, are borrowed. He becomes an echo of someone else's music, an actor of a part that has not been written for him.

Oscar Wilde, *The Picture of Dorian Gray*

Schädlicher als Beispiele sind dem Genius Prinzipien. Vor ihm mögen einzelne Menschen einzelne Teile bearbeitet haben. Er ist der erste, aus dessen Seele die Teile, in Ein ewiges Ganzes zusammen gewachsen, hervortreten. Aber Schule und Principium fesselt alle Kraft der Erkenntnis und Tätigkeit.

Johann Wolfgang von Goethe,
'Von deutscher Baukunst', quoted from
Hofmannsthal's *Deutsches Lesebuch*

INTRODUCTION

There can hardly be a book or an article about Hofmannsthal's early work that does not mention somewhere the influence of French Symbolism on his poetry. Most take it for granted that there was such an influence and that it was beneficial. A few study the question in detail and reach broadly the same conclusion; others play down the matter of influence and prefer to see Hofmannsthal as a unique, almost magical creative talent, vastly well-read but fundamentally original. Some of Hofmannsthal's admirers react defensively to the suggestion that his most celebrated, most magical writing is indebted to others, and they overstate their case for his originality. Rudolf Borchardt, for example, writes of his earliest works, 'sie zeigten keinerlei Einfluß seiner Lektüre; was er gelesen hatte, hatte er in sich verbrannt und nur Wärme, nicht Stoff daraus gewonnen' [they displayed no influence from his reading; what he had read, he had consumed within himself and derived only warmth, not substance from it].[1] He is particularly keen to discredit any rumour of an influence from George, and exaggerates somewhat when he writes, 'er hat nie eine Strophe Georgeschen Stiles geschrieben' [he never wrote a stanza in George's style].[2] Hilde Burger is similarly prickly, maintaining that 'the French influence has a different effect in the case of Stefan George and it is as though it were grafted on—while in the case of Hofmannsthal these influences of form and thought belong to his blood stream. They are wholly assimilated.'[3]

The pedigree of this view of Hofmannsthal's response to Symbolism can be traced to Rilke:

Loris hat gewiß von Frankreich her manche Geste übernommen, und er träumte manchen Farbentraum einem Baudelaire oder einem Mallarmé nach; aber diese verschiedenen romanischen Erbstücke waren seinem reichen, ursprünglichen Besitz so verwandt, daß man sie kaum mehr zu sondern vermag.[4]

[1] Rudolf Borchardt, 'Hofmannsthals Lehrjahre', in *Gesammelte Werke in Einzelbänden*, ed. Marie-Luise Borchardt (Stuttgart: Klett-Cotta, 1957–90), v: *Prosa I* (1957), 140.

[2] Ibid. 145.

[3] Hilde Burger, 'French Influences on Hugo von Hofmannsthal', in W. P. Friedrich (ed.), *Comparative Literature 2: Proceedings of the Second Congress of the ICLA* (Chapel Hill: University of North Carolina Press, 1959), 697.

[4] Rainer Maria Rilke, *Sämtliche Werke*, ed. Rilke-Archiv and Ruth Sieber-Rilke, with Ernst Zinn (Frankfurt a.M.: Insel, 1955–97), v. 387.

[Loris certainly derived many a gesture from France, and dreamed many a colourful dream in the manner of Baudelaire or Mallarmé; but these various Romantic
legacies were so closely related to his own rich and original talent that they are now
hardly distinguishable from it.]

In such matters one cannot dispute the opinion of an authority such as
Rilke without misgivings. The authority of this judgement derives not
only from his own supreme creative talent and poetic understanding,
but also from his own familiarity with the French literary heritage.
They are the words of a poet fully qualified to assess the influence of
France on a contemporary, but they smack of the complimentary
rather than the analytical. Wallace Stevens made a similar point about
French Symbolist influence on his verse in 1941:

I have read something, more or less, of all [these] poets . . . but if I have picked up
anything from them, it has been unconsciously. It is always possible that where a
man's attitude coincides with your own attitude, or accentuates your own attitude,
you get a great deal from it without effort.[5]

This, too, sounds a little defensive, almost as if to profess a continued,
conscious indebtedness to something that sounds as mysterious and
thrilling as French Symbolism is to have clung on too long to a fashion
that is now out of date.

   This book takes quite a different line, and aims to show instead that
the influence of Symbolism was real and crucial, not subconsciously
formative, but a continuous, often conscious component of Hofmannsthal's poetic thinking in the 1890s and beyond. It was imperfectly
assimilated, only partially re-formed by his own original talent, and
ultimately inimical to the survival of his early lyric style. It was partly
responsible for Hofmannsthal's famous 'farewell to poetry' after about
1899 and also, therefore, for some of the agonies revealed in the
Chandos Letter. Despite his precocious, 'altklug' confidence, the disorienting social, psychological and cultural conditions of *fin-de-siècle*
Vienna exacerbated the instability of Hofmannsthal's emerging
literary identity. Encouraged by contemporaries, especially Stefan
George, he sought the support of French Symbolism, which offered
the attractions simultaneously of stability within the Romantic tradition and of originality as a modern movement overtly desirous of
extending the capacities of literary language. Being part of any tradition may hamper the emergence and sustaining of a characteristic lyric

---

   [5] Letter to Hi Simons, *Letters of Wallace Stevens*, ed. Holly Stevens (London: Faber, 1966),
391.

voice, but a tradition like Symbolism that culminates in the sort of writing that suppresses individuality and highlights the problems of epigonism was doubly inhibiting.

Hofmannsthal's situation in 1890s Vienna was privileged but precarious. He was living in a period extraordinarily rich in cultural activity but amongst a class largely detached from social and political concerns, the combination contributing to an air of irresponsibility and a sense on the part of many writers of an increasingly tenuous hold on their artistic identity. In a letter to Richard Beer-Hofmann written in 1895, Hofmannsthal raises the question of how he is to deal with the multiplicity of stimuli to which he is subject, and proposes a bizarre solution. He refers to the story of Grigori Potemkin, who erected mock villages to impress Catherine the Great, and suggests that he, too, can set up 'Potemkin villages' on his intellectual horizon, partially suspending his disbelief in their substantiality (thus sacrificing himself to the illusion), yet maintaining a level of scepticism and therefore control. Crucial to the success of the procedure is learning how to cut out the influence of the majority of external inspirations, focusing on a few significant elements on the horizon, and balancing the factors of 'Herrschaftlichkeit' and 'Abhängigkeit', mastery and dependence, with which the psychological device operates.

Chapter 1 explores the implications of this device—which itself has an interesting antecedent in the literature of Symbolism and Decadence—and maps the terrain on which Hofmannsthal's 'Potemkin villages' were laid out in the early 1890s, the terrain of Symbolism. It looks at the dissemination of French Symbolism in Vienna in the 1890s in journals and elsewhere, and at the contemporary discussion, analysis, debate, recital and performance of Symbolist literature. There is a sense in which the influence of the French Symbolists must be presupposed for any Modernist poet,[6] but in Hofmannsthal's case the influence was particularly great. Chapter 1 therefore also assesses in some detail the extent of Hofmannsthal's own knowledge both of Symbolism and of French literature in general, via his education, his reading and in connection with his friends' interests. Chapter 2 traces the development of Symbolism from Romanticism in France and Germany and examines Hofmannsthal's selective individual understanding of that development mainly using notes and essays, some so far unpublished. A monograph on the early poetry of a single author is

---

[6] See Graham Hough, 'The Modernist Lyric', in Malcolm Bradbury and James McFarlane (eds.), *Modernism 1890–1930* (London: Pelican, 1976), 239–40.

not perhaps the ideal place for a disquisition on nineteenth-century European literary history, but I have presented my reading of it in more detail than one might expect because an understanding of the twists and turns in how the various poetic movements supersede, foster, oppose and interrogate each other is essential for an understanding of Hofmannsthal's appreciation of Symbolism, and because I have not so far found an account that presents this quite as I see it. For Hofmannsthal studies in particular, it is important to appreciate how and why Impressionism has more in common with Naturalism than with Symbolism.

The third and fourth chapters are close readings and detailed analyses of selected texts, mostly verse and prose poems by Hofmannsthal, although some are by Stefan George, who was one of Hofmannsthal's mentors in Symbolism. Chapter 3 concentrates on the works that Hofmannsthal explicitly called Symbolist, but Chapter 4 looks at some of the other poems, beginning with 'Erlebnis' and 'Psyche', including a number of the neglected prose poems, and concluding with 'Manche freilich', which represents the point at which I think Hofmannsthal most successfully managed the confusing elements in the literary traditions to which he belonged naturally or in which he was trying to find a place. All the poems have affinities with, or are in part directly inspired by, recent and contemporary French literature, and they articulate Hofmannsthal's complex response to it. They are not perhaps commentaries in the traditional sense, because the analyses are so explicitly angled to bring out the major issue at hand, but they are intended also to stand independently as coherent readings of some of Hofmannsthal's most dense and beautiful poems.

Chapters 5 and 6 are accounts of Hofmannsthal's retrospection from 1903 and 1906–7. By 1900 Hofmannsthal had more or less stopped writing poetry, and by 1903 had written his famously eloquent account of the incapacity to write, the Chandos Letter, so often used as a paradigm of Modernism. For Hofmannsthal himself, however, it does not present quite as definitive a statement on poetry as is often assumed. Chapter 5 analyses *Das Gespräch über Gedichte*, the moving post-crisis statement of Hofmannsthal's faith in the genre of lyric poetry that takes fully into account the confusion into which Symbolism had led him in the previous decade. Chapter 6 is a tentative postscript, looking at what was virtually Hofmannsthal's last lyric poem, 'Vor Tag', and suggesting how its structure and imagery might betray a renewed, or nostalgic, interest in Symbolism in the person of

Arthur Rimbaud. Rimbaud seems to feature hardly at all amongst the influences on Hofmannsthal's lyrical decade, but I suspect he was vestigially present none the less, surfacing only later, in about 1906, in a 'Vorspiel für ein Puppentheater' and the poem.

Ultimately, the closeness of Hofmannsthal's attention to the Symbolists made the effect of their poetry ambiguous. His consciousness of its being a model to imitate prevented his ever assimilating it into what Rilke called his own 'ursprünglicher Besitz', indeed impeded the formation of his own poetic voice. Hofmannsthal recognized that there were new attitudes to poetry and new manners of writing, but recognition is not the same as incorporation. These new ideas are kept largely at arm's length, discussed, reflected upon—utilized also, but more as curiosities discovered than as revelations fully annexed into his own repertoire. It is of course legitimate for poets to respond critically to their predecessors' work, and to do so consciously, but if the response is in its turn to become poetry it must become a new impulse, and it is this process that caused Hofmannsthal difficulties that would perhaps not have occurred were he less conscious of his assimilations. The appropriate balance of critic and creator in Hofmannsthal was often not maintained, and the result is sometimes a disturbing sense of the critic's objectivity and distance within the poetic work. If it is characteristic of Symbolist and other modern poetry 'to talk about itself to itself',[7] the self talking must be secure in its relationship to the language it uses, even if this relationship is one of distrust, and not hide behind its appreciations of others' talk. Harold Bloom warns of the dangers of being too critical of one's own creativity: 'if any poet knows too well what causes his poem, then he cannot write it, or at least will write it badly.'[8] T. S. Eliot—to choose a dramatically contrasting example—remarks on the dangers of this in 'After Strange Gods': 'I doubt whether any poet has ever done himself anything but harm by attempting to write as a "romantic" or as a "classicist".'[9] In his attention to Symbolism, Hofmannsthal sometimes exposed himself to these dangers.

This study is not, of course, the first to argue for or document the presence of Symbolism behind Hofmannsthal's early work. The importance of French literature to Hofmannsthal has been so widely

[7] Seamus Heaney, ' "The Fire i' the Flint": Reflections on the Poetry of Gerard Manley Hopkins', *Proceedings of the British Academy*, 60 (1974), 415.

[8] Harold Bloom, *Poetry and Repression* (New Haven: Yale University Press, 1976), 5.

[9] T. S. Eliot, *Selected Prose*, ed. John Hayward (Harmondsworth: Penguin, 1953; repr. Peregrine, 1963), 30.

recognized as to be virtually axiomatic. There is a wide range of articles that treat individual aspects and debts to particular authors, from the Pléiade and Molière to Stendhal, Proust and Valéry. The *Hofmannsthal-Gesellschaft* devoted its Pont-à-Mousson conference in 1986 to the subject of Hofmannsthal and France, and its proceedings were published as volume ix of the *Hofmannsthal-Forschungen*. Geneviève Bianquis, Hilde Burger, Claude David and Helmut Fiechtner have given overviews of the variety of Hofmannsthal's interests; but only Francis Claudon's *Hofmannsthal et la France* attempts to investigate the full range at any length and in detail.[10] Next to the influence of Molière, perhaps the area of French influence that has received most attention is Symbolism, with articles by Steffen and Böschenstein as well as two monographs by Sondrup and Kovach.[11] Walter Perl's was one of the earliest studies to make the association, contrasting Hofmannsthal with George in 1936, and summarizing gently, 'Baudelaire wirkte in seiner formalen Strenge und Gebundenheit am stärksten auf die Frühzeit Stefan Georges ein, während das lyrisch gelöste Wesen Paul Verlaines der Hofmannsthalschen Mentalität näher steht' [it was Baudelaire's formal strictness and constraint that had the greatest effect on Stefan George's early years, whilst the lyrically relaxed nature of Paul Verlaine was closer to Hofmannsthal's mentality].[12] But there has been surprisingly little flesh put upon those bones between this and Helmut Fiechtner's brief comment to the effect that 'Verlaine hat Hofmannsthal sehr geschätzt, und ohne ihn sind einige . . . Gedichte nicht zu denken' [Hofmannsthal valued Verlaine very highly and some poems are inconceivable without him].[13] Despite the number of attempts, and despite also the relatively clear delimitation of the period in which Symbolism interested and affected Hofmannsthal, the topic has not been illuminated as thoroughly as the presence of Molière behind the comedies and opera libretti. The exception here is the influence of Maeterlinck, on Hofmannsthal's Symbolist lyrical dramas. I have attempted to investigate Hofmannsthal's debt to Symbolist

[10] Francis Claudon, *Hofmannsthal et la France*, European University Studies, Series XVIII: Comparative Literature 21 (Berne: Peter Lang, 1979).

[11] Steven P. Sondrup, *Hofmannsthal and the French Symbolist Tradition*, Utah Studies in Literature and Linguistics 4 (Berne: Herbert Lang, 1976), and Thomas A. Kovach, *Hofmannsthal and Symbolism: Art and Life in the Work of a Modern Poet*, American University Studies, Series III: Comparative Literature 18 (New York: Peter Lang, 1985)—both originally Harvard Ph.D. theses.

[12] Walter H. Perl, *Das lyrische Jugendwerk Hugo von Hofmannsthals* (Berlin: Dr Emil Ebering, 1936), 50.

[13] Helmut Fiechtner, 'Hofmannsthal und Frankreich', *Literatur und Kritik*, 135 (1979), 274.

poetry in much more detail, and, more importantly, to trace its consequences.

One of the problems that have bothered commentators is the question of what Symbolism is, and I have answered it relatively simply, despite its very complex history. Jean Moréas started to define the term Symbolism in 1885 and in 1891 produced a volume of his own poetry to which he intended it to be applied. In 1899 Arthur Symons had sidelined Moréas and established Mallarmé, Villiers de l'Isle-Adam, Rimbaud, Laforgue and above all Verlaine as the representatives of the movement whose great precursor was Baudelaire. In 1928, T. S. Eliot wrote that when 'Mr Symons and his friends' compared Baudelaire with Verlaine they were misguided: 'we no longer find much in common.'[14] In 1939, more than fifty years after the first flush of Symbolist manifestos in France, Paul Valéry argued that the movement never really existed and that the phenomenon had no real substance at all:

plus on y regarde de près, plus voit-on apparaître entre nos futurs symbolistes, des différences totales, des incompatibilités de style, de moyens, de parti pris, d'idéal esthétique, et nous serons contraints à cette double conclusion qu'il n'y eut guère d'unité de théories, de convictions, de techniques entre tous ces artistes; mais ensuite, qu'ils n'en sont pas moins assemblés les uns aux autres, attroupés par quelque chose qui ne se voit pas encore, car ce quelque chose ne ressort pas du tout de l'examen seul de leurs œuvres, lequel au contraire nous montre qu'elles sont incomparables.[15]

[The closer you look, the more you notice amongst our future Symbolists the emergence of fundamental differences, incompatibilities of style, means, presuppositions, aesthetic ideals; we are constrained to reach the dual conclusion, first that there was hardly any unity of theory, conviction and technique amongst all these artists, and then that they are no less a group for that, herded together by something that is no longer perceptible, because this something does not emerge from a mere examination of their works, which show on the contrary that they are not to be compared with each other.]

He calls the poets in question 'nos futurs symbolistes' because he contends that the term is meaningfully applied only retrospectively, and that the unity of the movement was thereby created retroactively. But it appeared to exist at the time, and one of the characteristics of Symbolism that made it a suitable object of Hofmannsthal's interest

---

[14] T. S. Eliot, 'Baudelaire in our Time', in *For Lancelot Andrewes* (London: Faber, 1970), 69.
[15] Paul Valéry, 'Existence du symbolisme', in *Œuvres*, ed. Jean Hytier (Paris: Gallimard, 1957), i. 690.

was paradoxically the fact that it seemed to possess on one level an 'identity': for all its amorphousness, in the form in which Hofmannsthal came upon Symbolism it had a distinct presence on the literary horizon and even a label, which made it easier for the mind to grapple with and more effective as a literary stabilizer.

The term 'Symbolism' may be vague and disputed, but except at the periphery there is not much doubt as to which writers the word now designates: they are principally Mallarmé, Verlaine, Rimbaud and Villiers de l'Isle-Adam in France, and Maeterlinck in Belgium. Baudelaire is sometimes included as a precursor, Valéry himself as a direct descendant. Henri de Régnier, Gustave Kahn, Francis Vielé-Griffin, Georges Rodenbach, Emile Verhaeren, Charles Van Lerberghe, Max Elskamp and others are amongst the Symbolists of slightly less lasting importance; there were many dozens more minnows. Hofmannsthal's own use of the word 'Symbolists' remains within these borders. Alongside the major names he would have included Baudelaire (with reservations), and several of the less well-known figures: the Belgian Charles Van Lerberghe, for example, was to feature in *Das Gespräch über Gedichte* as the final example of a successful Symbolist poet. This inclusive historical-biographical definition of Symbolism is accordingly the one adopted here as a basis for an investigation of how the movement influenced Hofmannsthal.

As for 'influence', it is investigated here not in the narrow and usually disparaged sense limited to source-tracing and the detection of specific verifiable word- or image-borrowings by one author from another. Writers may be influenced profoundly by someone who never wrote a word and so can never be quoted; they may never quote or identifiably paraphrase the writings of an author who has been of the utmost importance to their own poetic development; they may continually lift telling phrases and ideas from their major influences only to reject or criticize them all; they may quite deliberately and self-consciously set out to continue a line of thought or a style of writing that an influential predecessor has begun. There are a thousand more possibilities, all of which are valid forms of 'influence'. Associations or oppositions of outlook, value, presupposition, manner, style, belief or feeling may be much simpler to identify and write about than borrowings of phrase and image; they may also be much more elusive. Here I have attempted to take both these types of potential influence into account, to trace empirically Hofmannsthal's knowledge of the Symbolists and his quotation of their works, but also to identify the points at which his thinking and writing moves in their orbit. Further-more, I have attempted to evaluate the effects of such contiguities and congruences.

It is questionable whether a lyric poet can afford to be influenced to any very great degree, and Harold Bloom's categories of strength and weakness are useful in this context.[16] A strong poet is 'one who will not tolerate words that intervene between him and the Word, or pre-cursors standing between him and the Muse',[17] and the central idea of the strong poet's search for the original, undistorted (pre-existential) expressive power from which he is separated by others' words is clearly appropriate in Hofmannsthal studies. For Bloom, the history of poetry is a struggle between poets and that new imaginative space is mostly dependent on 'misprision' or *mis*reading. This view is limited in that it reduces poetry by assuming that a poet is a poet only, and that the shaping energies of his creativity come exclusively from within the closed system of poetic history. But a struggle does takes place, within the poet, between his desires and what he perceives to be his abilities, and past poets may inhibit the emergence of talent. Hofmannsthal was aware of the need to preserve his poetic identity from the pressures of his influences, and himself set out the urgent need to resist in the speech 'Poesie und Leben':

der eigene Ton ist alles; wer den nicht hält, begibt sich der inneren Freiheit, die erst das Werk möglich machen kann. Der Mutigste und der Stärkste ist der, der seine Worte am freiesten zu stellen vermag; denn es ist nichts so schwer, als sie aus ihren festen, falschen Verbindungen zu reißen. (*RA* iii. 17)

[one's own voice is all-important; anyone who does not preserve that forgoes the inner freedom that alone can make possible a work of art. The most courageous and the strongest writer is the one who can dispose his words most freely, for there is nothing so difficult as ripping them from their fixed and false combinations.]

---

[16] The vigour and intellectual breadth of Harold Bloom's *The Anxiety of Influence* (1973) and *Poetry and Repression* (1976) have very much encouraged this study, even influenced it, but it is obviously far from being Bloomian in execution.

[17] Bloom, *Poetry and Repression*, 10.

I

MAPPING THE TERRAIN: SYMBOLISM
IN VIENNA IN THE EARLY 1890s

In both published works and private letters, Hofmannsthal had a tendency to slip into a distinctive 'manifesto' mode, characterized by categorical statements describing himself and his function as a poetically creative individual in relation to the world. There is one such passage in a letter to Richard Beer-Hofmann written in the mid-1890s:

Ich glaub immer noch, daß ich im Stand sein werde, mir meine Welt in die Welt hineinzubauen. Wir sind zu kritisch um in einer Traumwelt zu leben, wie die Romantiker . . . Es handelt sich freilich immer nur darum ringsum an den Grenzen des Gesichtskreises Potemkin'sche Dörfer aufzustellen, aber solche an die man selber glaubt. Und dazu gehört ein Centrumsgefühl, ein Gefühl von Herrschaftlichkeit und Abhängigkeit, ein starkes Spüren der Vergangenheit und der unendlichen Durchdringung aller Dinge . . . Nur eins glaub ich muß man bis zu einem dämonischen Grad lernen: sich um unendlich viele Angelegenheiten und Dinge nicht zu bekümmern.[1]

[I still believe that I shall be in a position to construct for myself a world of my own within the real world. We are too critical to live in a dream-world like the Romantics. Of course, it is always only a case of setting up Potemkin villages around us on the edges of the horizon, but they are of the kind in which one actually believes oneself. And to achieve this it is necessary to have a feeling of poise, a feeling both of mastery and of dependence, a strong sense of the past and of the way things are endlessly interrelated. But there is one thing that I think one has to master to a diabolically high degree, and that is how to shut one's eyes to all manner of things and affairs.]

Not only does this passage demonstrate an awareness of the gap between an individual's private world and a world independently existing outside, 'meine Welt' and 'die Welt', but Hofmannsthal insists that clear-sightedness on this point is necessary and inevitable. To be oblivious is to live a dream, and the presence or absence of this critical relationship to one's own perceptions is what for Hofmannsthal here constitutes the difference between Modernism and Romanticism, to

---

[1] Hugo von Hofmannsthal and Richard Beer-Hofmann, *Briefwechsel*, ed. Eugene Weber (Frankfurt a.M.: S. Fischer, 1972), 47–8; letter of 15 May 1895.

which a value-judgement is attached: Romanticism is implicitly criticized for self-delusion.

Hofmannsthal proceeds almost immediately, however, to advocate precisely what he criticizes. His means of dealing with the onslaught of external influences, he says, is to set up a selection of points on which to focus his attention. These are the 'Potemkin'sche Dörfer': the phrase is a Russian idiom meaning unreal achievements, and refers to the legend that in 1787 Grigori Potemkin erected a string of mock-up villages and populated them with hired peasants in order to impress Catherine the Great when she visited his province. Hofmannsthal's Potemkin villages form an artificial horizon and distract from the true, more miserably dilapidated and uncontrolled state of affairs beyond. They may not represent a dream-world exactly, but they remain merely a makeshift. Potemkin's villages were erected to deceive someone else, but for Hofmannsthal the deception is introverted and they end up suspending the self-critical faculty that distinguishes modern man from the Romantic dreamer. They function by effecting a kind of psychological bluff: an artificial structure is necessary to control the mass of information from outside, but for it to fulfil its function its artifice must be forgotten.

Selectively disregarding an infinity of possible stimuli is the method of rendering these stimuli manageable. The prerequisite is 'Centrumsgefühl', the presence within one's self of a sifting agent. The definition of this feeling of poise with two contradictory elements ('Herrschaftlichkeit' and 'Abhängigkeit', mastery and dependence) matches the contradictions of clear-sightedness and self-deception that were the means of mastering the material: dominance is a function of the artifice, and dependence a function of the necessary self-forgetting. '[E]in starkes Spüren der Vergangenheit und der unendlichen Durchdringung aller Dinge' also suggests confidence, whereas the need to learn how to exclude much of the totality suggests vulnerability again. This also corresponds to the partnership of 'das Auflösen und das Bilden von Begriffen' [the dissolution and formation of concepts; *RA* iii. 373] that I shall argue underlies Hofmannsthal's conception of poetry. Finally, the ability to control all this is recognized as in a sense *unnatural*, daimonic—and it is only on this level, the non-rational, that the poise of awareness and ignorance can be maintained.

This is Hofmannsthal's own statement of his hopes for himself, coming after the most intense period of his interest in Symbolism, but well before *Ein Brief*, traditionally seen as a watershed in his poetic career, and *Das Gespräch über Gedichte*, which should be seen alongside the Chandos Letter. It is subject to the caveats that must always attend self-analysis, but by being more contemporary with the poetry to be analysed in this study at least escapes those that necessitate scepticism for the categories of *Ad me ipsum*, where the steeply retrospective stance is distortive. The Potemkin villages letter is useful, however, as an introduction into a study of Hofmannsthal's relationship to French Symbolism, since it is a succinct and discriminating presentation of some of the complex issues that dominate this relationship, and moreover a presentation whose own subtlety and ambivalence are characteristically at odds with the cut-and-dried manifesto tone. The object of this study—to take Hofmannsthal's metaphor a little further—is to assess the nature of the terrain of Symbolism, to look at what kind of 'villages' appeared on Hofmannsthal's poetic horizon and who built them, and to test how solid they proved to be. The first 'village', ironically, is Vienna.

In 1891, when he was 17 years old, Hugo von Hofmannsthal wrote a review of *Die Mutter*, a new play by the critic and dramatist Hermann Bahr. One of his complaints was that the language in the play was inauthentic, an ill-considered hotch-potch of registers and local dialects, 'bald die schmiegende, vibrierende Sprache Bahrs, bald ein wolkenlyrisches Pathos, gewolltes falsches Theaterpathos . . . dann wieder Berliner und Wiener Lokalismen von beängstigender Plattheit' [here Bahr's own seductive, quivering language, there a soaring lyrical pathos, false, mannered theatrical pathos; then more Berlin and Viennese dialect expressions of quite alarming banality; *RA* i. 104]. He conceded that this was excusable, however, given the conditions in which Bahr was writing: 'Zugegeben, wir haben keinen allgemeingültigen Gesprächston, weil wir keine Gesellschaft und kein Gespräch, wie wir keinen Stil und keine Kultur haben' [It is true, we have no universal tone for conversation because we have no society and no conversation, just as we have no style and no culture]. Yet the residents of Vienna in the 1890s were amongst the most culturally privileged in Europe, and to say that they lacked style and culture is ostensibly scandalous. Every major city had its theatres and galleries, some had orchestras and opera houses, all would have been able to follow the literary fashions in magazines, periodicals and the *feuilleton* sections of newspapers—and every capital housed particularly high concentrations, in quantity and quality, of cultural activity. And Vienna, far from having 'no style' and 'no culture', seems to have been receptive to the arts at the turn of the century to a uniquely high degree.

Much later Hofmannsthal was to define style as 'unzerteilte Einheit des höheren Menschen' [the unfragmented unity that characterizes superior humanity],[2] and what he missed in the review of *Die Mutter*, with his usual *altklug* condescension, was unity and consistency. 'Style', or more precisely 'a style', was important to Hofmannsthal. As a 21-year-old he was to boast of his 'Stilverdrehungsmanie', a mania for twisting styles around, for plucking stories and characters from works of one period and imaginatively redesigning them with the stylistic attributes of another. The example he gave to Andrian was of the story of Nausicaa from the *Odyssey*, which was buzzing around his head in March 1894, and which he had mentally recast, quite wildly as it seems to more pedestrian critical taste, as 'ganz trecentistisch gobelin-mäßig' [just like *trecento* Gobelins]. Hofmannsthal's involvement with Symbolism was not a whim of 'Stilverdrehungsmanie', and not merely a flirtation with the latest style; it was, however, an attempt to find *a* style, to appropriate for himself *the* style in which his precocious, restless, fantastically intelligent creativity could begin to express itself comfortably and to lasting effect.

This chapter will outline the ways in which Hofmannsthal became familiar with Symbolism and will begin to suggest some reasons why he developed this particular interest. It starts with the widest perspective, the unique cultural atmosphere of Vienna during Hofmannsthal's childhood and adolescence, and then looks at exactly what printed sources of critical comment on Symbolist literature were available at the time. Then it focuses more closely on Hofmannsthal's circle of friends and the specific influence they had on his reception of Symbolism. Finally, in an attempt to derive as clear a picture as possible of his familiarity with the writers and critical issues involved in the movement, it finishes with a detailed account of what we know of the poet's reading of French literature in general and of the Symbolist poets in particular, of his own individual temperament, familial predispositions, personal likes and dislikes, the unique cast of his mind and his special abilities.

The atmosphere in Vienna in the 1880s and 1890s was partly responsible for Hofmannsthal's dilemmas. What Hofmannsthal and others saw as an absence of style and culture was due to the voracious eclecticism of that city. Looking back in the 1940s, Stefan Zweig judged

---

[2] 'Vorrede', *Deutsches Lesebuch* (1922), p. xii (also in *RA* ii. 174).

that the high density of artistic activity in Vienna derived from her position as the only intact point in a crumbling empire, and from her self-aware role as custodian of a massive cultural tradition.[3] Autobiography is a notoriously distorting medium, but these general conclusions are plausibly supported. In an influential study, Carl Schorske has explained that role in terms of the political history of Austria. The theme of his *Fin-de-Siècle Vienna* is the replacement of traditional 'rational man' by twentieth-century 'psychological man', 'a creature of feeling and instinct' that emerged from the political crisis of Viennese liberal culture.[4] Schorske interprets the final liberal defeat in the 1890s (when a government with a weak social base succumbed to increasing demands for representation by new social groups) as the key to the supervening mood of anxious impotence. This mood prompted self-reflectiveness in an attempt at self-understanding, and did so most forcefully amongst the Austrian bourgeoisie, who were in a socially ambiguous position. Their failure to gain a monopoly of power had left them outsiders, ambitious for integration with the aristocracy—and this trend was strengthened by the assimilative drive of a large Jewish element in the population. The highly aesthetic traditional culture of the aristocracy seemed to promise the bourgeoisie 'a surrogate form of assimilation',[5] particularly through architecture and the theatre. Zweig considered that for the Jews the aim of this adopted culture was not merely assimilation but sublimation: 'Der eigentliche Wille des Juden, sein immanentes Ideal ist der Aufstieg ins Geistige, in eine höhere kulturelle Schicht' [the true will of the Jew, his immanent ideal, is the ascent into the spiritual realm, on to a higher cultural stratum].[6] Art offered an escape from the threats of political reality, and 'as his sense of what Hofmannsthal called *das Gleitende*, the slipping away of the world, increased, the bourgeois turned his appropriated aesthetic culture inward to the cultivation of the self, of his personal uniqueness'.[7] Political motivation does not preclude genuine aesthetic enthusiasm, but the tension in the relationship between bourgeois and aristocracy certainly helps to explain why the arts became so centrally important in Vienna in the late nineteenth century.

This tension accounts also for the odd combination of alienation and integration of the artistic community itself. Despite its variety, it

[3] Stefan Zweig, *Die Welt von Gestern* (Frankfurt a.M.: Fischer Taschenbuch, 1970), 26–7.
[4] Carl E. Schorske, *Fin-de-Siècle Vienna: Politics and Culture* (New York: Vintage, 1981), esp. 3–23.   [5] Ibid. 8.
[6] Zweig, *Die Welt von Gestern*, 25.
[7] Schorske, *Fin-de-Siècle Vienna*, 9.

was small and unusually tight-knit, and whereas in London, Paris or Berlin 'the intellectuals in the various branches of high culture, whether academic or aesthetic, journalistic or literary, political or intellectual, scarcely knew each other',[8] this was not the case in the much smaller capital city of Vienna. Publication, performance and exhibition were catalysts there for mutual acquaintance; cafés and salons could still realistically function as 'common rooms' where intellectuals from different disciplines gathered together. Peter Altenberg famously gave his address in Vienna simply as 'Café Central'; Stefan George knew that Hofmannsthal could most easily be approached in the Café Griensteidl; the title of Karl Kraus's satirical pamphlet attacking the aesthetes, 'Die demolirte Litteratur' (1897), metonymically links the demolition of literature with the demolition of the café without putting the rhetorical device under undue pressure.

Edward Timms has designed a diagram punningly labelled 'The Vienna Circles' after the group of logical positivists active during the 1920s.[9] The names of fifteen of the major thinkers or literary, artistic and musical figures of the period are each at the centre of a circle. Otto Wagner is at the centre of a group of architects, Herzl with the Zionists, Hoffmann is associated with the artists of the Wiener Werkstätte, Schoenberg surrounded by musicians. The circles interlock or touch—in the case of Kraus's and Schnitzler's they just fail to touch— and the intersections are marked by the names of other significant contemporaries who were satellites of the central figure. Thus Kraus and Schoenberg are linked by Berg; Schoenberg and Mahler by Alma Mahler; Mahler and Schnitzler by Bruno Walter; Schnitzler and Hofmannsthal by Salten and Bahr, and so on. The diagram, whilst not claiming to be exhaustive, offers a rapidly assimilable snapshot of 'creative interaction in Vienna around 1910'. By 1910 this community was sufficiently detached from the political reality of its age to feel isolated amongst its class, but the situation was more ambiguous in the 1890s.[10] In that decade writers, actors, musicians and the visual artists mostly did not suffer from the sense of isolation they were later to suffer elsewhere in Europe, and which is a characteristic of the artist figures

[8] Ibid., p. xxvii.

[9] Originally in Edward Timms, *Karl Kraus: Apocalyptic Satirist: Culture and Catastrophe in Habsburg Vienna* (New Haven: Yale University Press, 1986), 8; reprinted in the same author's 'Die Wiener Kreise: Schöpferische Interaktionen in der Wiener Moderne', in Jürgen Nautz and Richard Vahrenkamp (eds.), *Die Wiener Jahrhundertwende: Einflüsse, Umwelt, Wirkungen* (Vienna: Böhlau, 1996), 130, and then considerably expanded to show the situation in 1920 ('Die Wiener Kreise', 140).

[10] Cf. also Schorske, *Fin-de-Siècle Vienna*, p. xxvii.

in, say, Thomas Mann's early works. On the contrary, the Viennese lionized them, and gave pride of place to the actors:

Der erste Blick eines Wiener Durchschnittsbürgers in die Zeitung galt allmorgend-lich nicht den Diskussionen im Parlament oder den Weltgeschehnissen, sondern dem Repertoire des Theaters, das eine für andere Städte kaum begreifliche Wichtigkeit im öffentlichen Leben einnahm.[11]

[Every morning, the average citizen of Vienna did not turn first in his newspaper to parliamentary debates or international events but to the theatre programme, something that assumed a degree of importance in public life hardly comprehen-sible for other cities.]

What Zweig called the ' "Theateromanie" der Wiener', their obsessive passion for the theatre, was by no means restricted to the theatre-going classes: Zweig recounts, for example, the grief of his family's cook, an old, semi-literate woman, who had never once been to the smart Burgtheater herself, at the death in 1897 of the tragedienne Charlotte Wolter—the originator of the famous 'Wolterschrei'.[12] Zweig doubt-less exaggerates at some points, but he is a representative of the culture he describes, and his over-enthusiasm is as much authenticating as dis-tortive. The Burgtheater actors Adolf von Sonnenthal, Josef Lewinsky, Josef Kainz and Alexander Girardi were cult figures: Sonnenthal, the incarnation of the Burgtheater tradition, was eventually ennobled, and Hofmannsthal broke his lyric silence to commemorate Kainz in 1910. Alexander Girardi's success has been attributed to the critical distance he had because of his non-Viennese birth. This meant he was able to 'parade the image of the typical Viennese through the town, on and off the stage'.[13] According to Felix Salten, Girardi did not so much act Viennese roles as induce Vienna to act Girardi-roles:

Zuletzt war denn auch jeder zweite junge Herr, den man auf der Straße traf, jeder Fiakerkutscher, jeder Briefträger, jeder Spießbürger eine Girardi-Rolle. Eine Zeitlang lief halb Wien herum und spielte Girardi und wußte nicht, daß es damit sich selbst aufgab, daß es auf seine Echtheit verzichtete und an deren Stelle die besondere Echtheit eines einzelnen annahm.[14]

---

[11] Zweig, *Die Welt von Gestern*, 29.

[12] Ibid. 33 and 30. Wolter was possibly the model for Hermann Bahr's novel *Die Rahl* (1908), which focuses on an actress's transformational abilities and the discrepancy between her heady existence on the stage and the lifeless periods between performances. For Wolter's performances at the Burgtheater, see W. E. Yates, *Theatre in Vienna: A Critical History 1776–1995* (Cambridge: Cambridge University Press, 1996), 76–81.

[13] Ilse Barea, *Vienna: Legend and Reality* (London: Secker & Warburg, 1966), 320.

[14] Felix Salten, 'Girardi', in *Geister der Zeit: Erlebnisse* (Berlin: Paul Zsolnay, 1924), 98 (and, identically, in 'Kainz-Girardi', *Geister der Zeit*, 120).

[Eventually every other young gentleman you met in the street, every coachman, every postman, every petit bourgeois was a Girardi part. For a while half Vienna was running around acting out Girardi, without realizing that in doing so it was betraying itself, giving up its own true identity and taking on in its place the particular identity of an individual.]

Salten contested the over-eager belief amongst the Viennese that Girardi had encapsulated the very essence of the city and challenged his capacity to provide a secure prop for the city's cultural identity:

Aber wenn wir den Begriff Wien als ein Ganzes nehmen . . . dann werden wir finden, daß Girardi weder der Spiegel noch der Ausdruck des Wienertums ist; nicht der Wiener, sondern unter wenigen erlesenen Wienern: Auch einer.[15]

[But if we take the concept of Vienna as a whole, we will find that Girardi is neither the mirror nor the expression of Viennese identity; he is not the Viennese *per se*, but just one of a few select Viennese: one amongst others.]

Vienna was too complex to be mirrored so straightforwardly, and Girardi was ultimately a tool in the population's attempts to grasp at its own identity, the equivalent of the Potemkin villages for Hofmannsthal.

Timms points out that 'as a means of coming to terms with a changing world the Girardi cult had regressive implications',[16] and the popularity of art could not stifle a feeling of unease, what Schorske called the 'mood of impotence'. The result is a 'sense of cultivated artifice' in Vienna, and an awareness amongst artists in particular 'of the discrepancy between official ideology and inner identity, between private self and public role'.[17] Under the heading 'Vereinsamung und Selbstentfremdung' [isolation and alienation from the self], Manfred Diersch also shows how the cultural activity of the artists of *Jung Wien* was a symptom of social alienation. Bahr, Schnitzler, Hofmannsthal, Salten and the others were from what Hofmannsthal referred to as the 'gehobene Bourgeoisie':

Ihre Herkunft erlaubte ein Leben im sozialen Abseits. Daraus entstand das Unbehagen ihres Selbstgefühls, dem sie mit einer Selbstdisziplin zu begegnen trachteten, die die Unrealisierbarkeit eines schrankenlosen und absoluten Individualismus respektiert.[18]

[15] Ibid. 98–9 and (slightly modified) 121.
[16] Timms, *Karl Kraus*, 26.
[17] Ibid. 26–7.
[18] Manfred Diersch, *Empiriokritizismus und Impressionismus: Über Beziehungen zur Philosophie, Ästhetik und Literatur um 1900 in Wien* (Berlin: Rütten & Loening, 1973), 127–33.

[the elevated bourgeoisie: their origins permitted them a life in the social margins. From this arose an unease in their attitude to themselves that they strove to counter with the kind of self-discipline that respects the impossibility of boundless, absolute individualism.]

Such self-discipline was by no means an obvious or straightforward course for the individuals involved.

The personal reminiscences that punctuate Ilse Barea's analysis of this period ruefully exemplify the insubstantiality to which the art and artists seem sometimes to have been reduced, and which was in part the consequence of a lack of self-discipline. Barea writes of an aged relative, 'the unreal trappings of her room, the Makart décor, helped the lonely old woman by making her feel safely sheltered in a dream world',[19] which is just the kind of spurious shelter that Hofmannsthal rejects as inadequate for the critically aware writer in the 'Potemkin letter' to Beer-Hofmann. Hofmannsthal had earlier noted, 'wir reden gern von hübschen Einrichtungsgegenständen, wir sind alle . . . ein bißchen verdorben durch Sensitivität' [we like to talk of pretty things, we are all a little spoilt by our sensitivity].[20] In its context, this remark is countered by an assertion of the potential benefits of saturation in art for the individual creative imagination,[21] and art may also function cohesively for a wider social group. None the less, there was a high risk of its reinforcing rather than exploding individuals' self-absorption, and if the liberal era 'made room for intellectual Jewish salons in Vienna, "in which no longer the aristocracy but an enlightened bourgeoisie mixed with poets and artists" ',[22] that bourgeoisie remained inward-looking.

Ilse Barea's example is the salon frequented by Hofmannsthal himself in 1893 and 1894, that of Frau Wertheimstein. By the end of the nineteenth century, the salon as an institution was becoming dated, but in the 1890s, the suburb of Döbling, north-west of Vienna, still

[19] Barea, *Vienna*, 290.
[20] Hofmannsthal, *Briefe 1890–1901* (Berlin: S. Fischer, 1935), 57; letter to Felix Salten, 27 July 1892.
[21] The context is Hofmannsthal's account of a story in the Koran: the Prophet has murdered his beloved for her infidelity and tries to escape from the reproachful spectacle of her corpse by putting his head into a pitcher of water. His soul escapes and flies through heaven and earth, witnessing battlefields and rose-gardens, shepherds' songs and Sinbad in the valley of diamonds, before returning to the reality of his beloved's dead body: 'Bitte, benützen Sie die Poesie und ihr Talent als Wasserschaffel; es geht ganz gut' (*Briefe 1890–1901*, 57–8).
[22] Barea, *Vienna*, 297, quoting from Hilde Spiel, *Fanny von Arnstein oder die Emanzipation* (Frankfurt a.M.: S. Fischer, 1962), 492.

housed two noted hostesses in the tradition of Rahel Varnhagen, Henriette Herz or Fanny von Arnstein: these were Bertha Zuckerkandl and Josephine von Wertheimstein, with the salon of the former perhaps the more glamorous. The journalist Frau Zuckerkandl received Hermann Bahr, Alexander Girardi, Arthur Schnitzler, Otto Wagner, Gustav Klimt, Max Burckhard (the director of the Burgtheater) and Gustav Mahler.[23] The dominant atmosphere *chez* Frau von Wertheimstein was of 'patrician assurance',[24] and socially the salon was impeccably constituted: Leopold, her husband, worked with the Rothschilds; Josephine was a Gomperz and related to the Todescos, both distinguished Viennese families; her brother Theodor was a professor of philosophy and a Greek historian. The artists and musicians she received and befriended included Franz von Lenbach— who painted a number of portraits of the family—Moritz von Schwind, Adolf von Wilbrandt, Moritz Hartmann and Anton Rubinstein. The most distinguished of the literary habitués, besides Hofmannsthal, were the dramatist Eduard von Bauernfeld, best known for his light *Konversationsstücke*, playwright and sometime Director of the Burgtheater Adolf Wilbrandt, and the poet and novella-writer Ferdinand von Saar. Saar referred to her home as 'das goldene Haus', lived for a while in the garden house, and became almost one of the family.[25]

After being introduced to the Wertheimsteins in August 1892, Hofmannsthal became deeply attached to Josephine and her daughter Franziska. At the age of 19 he wrote to Frau von Wertheimstein, 'daß ich das, was ihr Haus für mich einschließt, als ein großes wahres Glück lebendig und dankbar empfinde' [that I sense vitally and gratefully that what your house represents for me is a thing of great and genuine happiness].[26] According to Barea he was for a while spiritually more at ease there than anywhere else in Vienna, 'an alien in the fusty café [Griensteidl], and even in Schnitzler's bachelor rooms; he was, however, truly at home in Josephine von Wertheimstein's salon that gave an illusion of being outside time and remote from loud reality'.[27] Comfort is inextricably bound up with isolation, and it was perhaps

[23] Cf. Jens Malte Fischer, *Fin-de-siècle: Kommentar zu einer Epoche* (Munich: Winkler, 1978), 26.

[24] Barea, *Vienna*, 293.

[25] Cf. Werner Volke, *Hugo von Hofmannsthal mit Selbstzeugnissen und Bilddokumenten* (Reinbek bei Hamburg: Rowohlt, 1967), 46.

[26] Rudolf Holzer, *Villa Wertheimstein: Haus der Genie und Dämonen* (Vienna: Bergland, 1960), 113; letter from spring 1893.

[27] Barea, *Vienna*, 297.

fortunate for Hofmannsthal that he only attended the salon for two years, and that he was probably not quite so exclusively devoted to it as Barea suggests. Too much devotion to the closed circle risked allowing dreams to encroach too far upon reality. Nevertheless, being exposed to new and wide-ranging thought was important in sustaining Hofmannsthal's interest in contemporary literature, and characteristically he was as aware of this kind of advantage as he was of the potentially claustrophobic effect of the social location in which it was offered.

The artist in Vienna at the turn of the century, therefore, was the product of innumerable tensions. He was socially integrated—yet into a social class that, although governing, was increasingly out of touch with the world it governed. Aesthetic values were recognized and celebrated in his world, yet the high status of art gave society the unselfconscious irresponsibility of a spinning top, and to be caught in the spin was a dubious privilege. In *Hofmannsthal und seine Zeit*, and influenced by Karl Kraus, Hermann Broch deprecates the excitement of this society in the face of approaching collapse, and describes the parallel loss of the moral and aesthetic centres of Viennese society. Timms's diagrams complement Broch's analysis of the so-called 'Wert-Vakuum' of the period by offering the alternative explanation that there was not so much a void of values but a superfluity of competing ideologies.[28] Art in such an atmosphere risked becoming *Kitsch*, and for Hofmannsthal to seek a tradition with some 'Centrumsgefühl' was a natural impulse.

The tradition to which Hofmannsthal first turned was French Symbolism, very much in vogue in Vienna in the late 1880s and early 1890s and accessible in a variety of forms. Symbolist literature and its accompanying critical furore became widely known in Germany and Austria during this period as the works of its more famous exponents— Verlaine, Mallarmé, Maeterlinck and their precursors Baudelaire and Poe—were translated into German or published in French in a large number of cultural periodicals and reviews. Some of the broad issues that dominated French critical debate were also reported in the same publications as being of immediate relevance to the development of contemporary German-language literature; above all these issues concerned the aesthetic relevance of Realist or Naturalist writing. Finally, several modern German writers, including Hermann Bahr and Stefan George, had first-hand experience of the Paris literary scene and enthusiastically reported on it at home. It is clear from Manfred Gsteiger's comprehensive general survey of the reception of

---

[28] Timms, 'Die Wiener Kreise', 128.

Symbolism in German-speaking countries that it was for a while the
subject of the most intense interest and debate in Vienna, and that by
1895 it was no longer a novelty.[29] Articles and essays appearing after
that date 'either explicitly state or tacitly assume that readers are
generally acquainted with the fundamental characteristics of symbolism'.[30] Anthologies of modern French poetry in translation began to
appear in the early 1900s in response to a need for looking back, taking
stock of what was by then so familiar a part of the literary landscape
that the critical distance for selection and summation had been
achieved.[31]

   To begin with the widest angle, Hofmannsthal will have been
swamped with information from the leading papers and journals.[32]
The field was dominated by the liberal daily, the *Neue Freie Presse* in
competition with the *Wiener Zeitung* and the *Neues Wiener Tagblatt* (which
was edited by Moritz Szeps, Berta Zuckerkandl's father).[33] Amongst
the journals, some were like the *Wiener Literatur-Zeitung* founded in
1890, packed with information on contemporary literature and enjoy-
ing a reputation for being varied and in the main non-partisan. It took
a while for the *WLZ* to embrace Symbolism, but after it was refounded
as the *Neue Revue* in 1893 it was more well disposed and published works
by Maeterlinck and Schnitzler as well as critical essays by Bahr, Salten
and Hofmannsthal.[34] Even wider-ranging in its publications of literary
works was Michael Georg Conrad's Munich-based monthly *Die
Gesellschaft* (founded in 1885). Conrad was initially a staunch defender
of Naturalism in its south German manifestations, but he adopted a
hostile stance towards Berlin and *Die Gesellschaft* came round to

---

[29] Manfred Gsteiger, *Französische Symbolisten in der deutschen Literatur der Jahrhundertwende
(1896–1914)* (Berne: Franke, 1971).

[30] Steven Sondrup, *Hofmannsthal and the French Symbolist Tradition* (Berne: Herbert Lang,
1976), 23 (cf. also 19–23).

[31] The earliest anthologies of translations are Sigmar Mehring, *Die französische Lyrik im 19.
Jahrhundert. Mit eigenen Übertragungen* (Großenhain: Baumert & Ronge, 1900) and Otto Hauser,
Die belgische Lyrik von 1880–1900: Eine Studie und Übersetzungen from the same publishers in 1902.
Stefan George's translations, *Zeitgenössische Dichter*, including Verlaine, Mallarmé, Rimbaud
and Régnier, appeared in 1905.

[32] For an outline of the status and role of the press in disseminating literary developments
see Sigurd Paul Scheichl, 'La Place des revues et journaux dans la vie littéraire à Vienne', in
François Latraverse and Walter Moser (eds.), *Vienne au tournant du siècle* (Paris: Albin Michel,
1988), 333–57.

[33] Cf. Karlheinz Rossbacher, *Literatur und Liberalismus: Zur Kultur der Ringstraßenzeit in Wien*
(Vienna: J. & V. Edition, 1992).

[34] Cf. Fritz Schlawe, *Literarische Zeitschriften 1885–1910* (Stuttgart: Metzler, 1961), 40–1. Its
earliest name was *Neue Wiener Bücherzeitung* and it carried the subtitle *Organ für Literaturkunde der
Gegenwart*.

supporting Impressionism and Symbolism by the late 1880s. Amongst Hofmannsthal's circle Peter Altenberg, Arthur Schnitzler, Richard Schaukal and Hermann Bahr wrote for it, and of the Symbolists and their predecessors it featured Baudelaire, Verlaine, Maeterlinck, Rimbaud and Poe. The list of modern German and Austrian contributors is enormous, and it was for a while the most distinguished organ for contemporary writing in German.[35] Across the range of periodicals, works by Mallarmé and Villiers de l'Isle-Adam are rarer, but they appeared occasionally in *Die Zeit* (originally *Wiener Wochenschrift für Politik, Volkswirtschaft und Kunst* and later the *Österreichische Rundschau*), which was at one point edited by Hermann Bahr. Also in *Die Zeit* there were contributions from Altenberg, Andrian and Schnitzler, besides Hofmannsthal's *Märchen* and *Der weiße Fächer*.

Periodicals thrived on disagreement in their rivalry to influence the prevailing taste and Hofmannsthal himself quickly became a counter in the wrangles. Hermann Bahr praised him in the *Freie Bühne* of January 1892 as the very incarnation of 'die Moderne': 'er enthält den ganzen Zusammenhang ihrer Triebe, von den Anfängen des Zolaismus bis auf Barrès und Maeterlinck' [he embraces the whole range of the energies of Modernism, from the beginnings of Zolaism as far as Barrès and Maeterlinck].[36] Marie Herzfeld's sympathetic review of *Gestern* in May 1892 also located him in the Barrès tradition.[37] In the *Wiener Literatur-Zeitung* Edmund Wengraf ('VIVUS') ridiculed the performance of Maeterlinck's *L'Intruse* in which Hofmannsthal had been involved (as co-translator), also in May, and in June Friedrich M. Fels reviewed the same performance more generously, albeit noting that Hermann Bahr's pre-performance lecture did not make the audience acquainted with Maeterlinck and Symbolism in quite the manner they had anticipated.[38] Bahr apparently claimed in this lecture that Symbolism was the very essence of the age, 'die "Quintessenz der Zeit"', and the natural heir to Naturalism; an art not for the common

[35] Fritz Schlawe, *Literarische Zeitschriften 1885–1910*, 18–19. See also the chapter on *Die Gesellschaft* in Albert Soergel, *Dichtung und Dichter der Zeit*, 5th edn. (Leipzig: Voigtländer, 1911), 31–66.

[36] Hermann Bahr, 'Loris', *Freie Bühne für den Entwicklungskampf der Zeit*, 3.1 (Jan. 1892), 97; later in *Studien zur Kritik der Moderne* (Frankfurt a.M.: Rütten & Loening, 1894), 128. Also in Gotthart Wunberg (ed.), *Das junge Wien: Österreichische Literatur- und Kunstkritik 1887–1902* (Tübingen: Niemeyer, 1976), i. 297.

[37] Marie Herzfeld, 'Ein junger Dichter und sein Erstlingswerk', *Allgemeine Theater-Revue für Bühne und Welt*, 1.3 (15 May 1892), 21. Also in Wunberg (ed.), *Das junge Wien*, i. 325.

[38] VIVUS, 'Literatur und Leben', *Wiener Literatur-Zeitung*, 3.5 (May 1892), 1–3; also in Wunberg (ed.), *Das junge Wien*, i. 318–21. Friedrich M. Fels, 'Maeterlinck in Wien', *Freie Bühne für den Entwicklungskampf der Zeit*, 3.6 (1892), 671. Also in Wunberg (ed.), *Das junge Wien*, i. 327.

herd but one calculated to tempt the palates of gourmets.[39] At almost exactly the same time Bahr's essay entitled 'Symbolismus' appeared; it is largely devoted to Hofmannsthal's poetry and quotes 'Die Töchter der Gärtnerin' and 'Mein Garten' because they show the core of what the Symbolists are about. The latter in particular, 'enthält rein, und deutlich, den ganzen Symbolismus und nichts, das nicht Symbolismus wäre' [contains purely and clearly the whole of Symbolism, and nothing that is not Symbolism].[40] The editors of *Die Nation*, in which the essay appeared, felt compelled to add a footnote in their own name, distancing themselves from the movement:

Dieser Aufsatz wird unseren Lesern einen Einblick in jene Absichten gewähren, welche die Künstlergruppe der Symbolisten verfolgt. Herr Hermann Bahr, der selbst dieser Bewegung sehr nahe steht, ist besonders kompetent, Aufschluß zu geben. Ausschließlich um die Ziele der Symbolisten klarzustellen, veröffentlichen wir diese Darlegungen, nicht aber weil wir glaubten, daß der Symbolismus selbst als eine verheißungsvolle und innerlich gesunde Phase der Kunstentwicklung zu betrachten sei. Er ist eine künstlerische Erscheinung, die von symptomatischer Bedeutung ist, und darum beachtet werden will; eine erfreuliche Erscheinung ist er nicht.[41]

[This essay will afford our readers an insight into the intentions of the group of artists known as Symbolists. Mr Hermann Bahr, who is himself closely associated with this movement, is particularly qualified to give an explanation. We are publishing this presentation exclusively in order to clarify the Symbolists' objectives, and not because we believe that Symbolism in itself is to be regarded as a promising and wholesome phase in the development of art. It is an artistic phenomenon important because it is symptomatic, and it therefore demands attention; a pleasant phenomenon it is *not*.]

They were not alone in their disapproval: Oskar Panizza witheringly criticized Hofmannsthal's and George's Symbolist manner in *Die Gegenwart* in 1895.[42] By late 1891 or early 1892, therefore, the general climate of interest in Symbolism had publicly focused on Hofmannsthal himself, amongst others.

The most important source of information on the latest in French literature was probably the *Magazin für die Literatur des Auslandes*, founded in 1832. From October 1890 its title was simply *Magazin für*

---

[39] Quoted by VIVUS, 'Literatur und Leben', 2; Wunberg (ed.), *Das junge Wien*, i. 320–1.
[40] Hermann Bahr, 'Symbolismus', *Die Nation*, 9.38 (18 June 1892), 577; later in *Studien*, 31–2, under the title 'Symbolisten'. Also in Wunberg (ed.), *Das junge Wien*, i. 332.
[41] 'Anmerkung der Redaktion', *Die Nation*, 9.38 (18 June 1892), 576.
[42] Panizza had a very sharp tongue: he was later prosecuted for blasphemy and *lèse-majesté*. See Gsteiger, *Französische Symbolisten*, 270 nn. 151 and 153.

Literatur, and has been called 'the most distinguished mediator of "Weltliteratur" in Germany in the two decades following the Franco-Prussian War'.[43] The bulk of its copy comprised samples of the latest imaginative literature, foreign and domestic, and critical essays, and of the wide range of literatures it sampled, French was distinctly the most favoured. It had correspondents resident in Paris to report the latest sensations, and it also continually returned to the classics. 'The coverage of French literature was comprehensive enough to include the major authors of both past and present and, in addition, many contemporary minor figures, whose works were never translated into German.'[44] Hermann Bahr published one of his contributions to the Naturalism debate there, and this alone would have guaranteed Hofmannsthal's interest in the journal.[45]

Bahr also wrote for *Die Gegenwart* which had been founded by the high-profile novelist and critic Paul Lindau.[46] Lindau was an influential reviewer, passionately devoted to French literature, and was himself often heavily involved in literary controversy. He had entered the lists in the Naturalism debate when criticized for his translations of Zola. Zola himself was called in, and adjudicated against Lindau and for the *Magazin*'s correspondent. Extracts from Zola's *Les Poètes contemporains* had been published in *Die Gegenwart* in 1881, and Germany's first scholarly article on Symbolism appeared there on 14 and 21 June 1890. This was Paul Remer's 'Die Symbolisten: Eine neue literarische Schule in Frankreich'. It identifies the origins of Symbolism in a reaction against Naturalism and places it as the heir to Romanticism. Remer discusses the characteristic traits of Mallarmé, Verlaine, Laforgue, Kahn and Barrès, and those of its immediate predecessor Paul Bourget. Remer quotes Verlaine's 'Il pleure dans mon cœur' at the end of the first instalment of his article, and in the second he includes a glance at the theoretical statements of Gustav Kahn and describes the metrical innovations and high musicality of Symbolist verse. Remer's distinction between Decadents and Symbolists is one of quality: the former were hacks responding to a journalistic fad, trying to make a name for themselves by applying the paraphernalia of the

---

[43] Siegfried Mews, 'Information and Propagation: A German Mediator of "Weltliteratur" in the Late Nineteenth Century', *Revue de littérature comparée*, 42 (1968), 57–8.

[44] Ibid. 60.

[45] Bahr, 'Die Krisis des französischen Naturalismus,' *Magazin*, 59. 36 (6 Sept. 1890), 562–4.

[46] Hofmannsthal includes an anecdote about Lindau and Bismarck in his *Buch der Freunde* from 1921 (*RA* iii. 238).

Déliquescences with a trowel; the latter, he concludes, are true individualists concerned with the exploration of the self.[47]

This account is important not because Hofmannsthal might have read it, which is possible, even though he was a schoolboy at the time, but because it is by a German living in Paris at about the same time as Bahr and George. It is a more formal summary of just the kind of experience and information that will have formed the subject of the unrecorded discussions between Hofmannsthal and his two colleagues. Their value-judgements will have differed, since Hofmannsthal rarely annexed opinions along with information, as comparison of his reviews with Bahr's indicates. Furthermore, Gsteiger's survey of the critiques of Symbolism in contemporary periodicals confirms that Remer's article contains very little that is unique, except perhaps in his substantial sections on Laforgue and Mallarmé.

These were periodicals that strove for maximum readership, but Hofmannsthal belonged also to the elite groups that read *Pan* and *Die Blätter für die Kunst*. Exclusivity was their deliberate aim, so they were expensive and elegant, even though *Pan* was still theoretically available to the public. Its first volume (April/May 1895) contains Verlaine's 'Mon Apologie' under the title 'Prologue pour Varia',[48] a manuscript reproduction of Mallarmé's 'A la nue accablante tu' with a drawing by Khnopff, and three Maeterlinck poems from the *Quinze Chansons*—as well as three *Terzinen* by 'Loris'. Kessler's essay on Henri de Régnier and Symbolism is in the same volume, and he expressly compares Régnier with Hofmannsthal:

> Er liebt es durch Umstellungen der Wörter und Satzteile, durch Auseinanderziehen des Zusammengehörigen, durch Isolieren eines besonders suggestionskräftigen oder melodiösen Wortes die Satzbedeutung zu verwischen, um den Geist ganz den Sinnen, ganz dem Reiz der Klänge und dem Spiel flüchtiger Bilder hingegeben träumen zu lassen. Wie in so vielem Andren gleicht Régniers Poesie auch hierin der von Loris.[49]

> [In order to let the mind dream, given over entirely to the senses or the charm of sounds and the play of fleeting images, he loves to obscure the meaning of a sentence by changing the positions of words and clauses, by separating what belongs together, by isolating a particularly suggestive or melodious word. As in so many other respects, Régnier's poetry here resembles that of Loris.]

[47] Henri Beauclair and Gabriel Vicaire, *Les Déliquescences d'Adoré Floupette* (1885), a volume parodying the Symbolists' and Decadents' characteristic vocabulary and diction.

[48] *Varia* was to be the title of a collection of Verlaine's late lyrics that was never completed. 'Mon Apologie' was first published in the *Revue littéraire et critique* in 1893.

[49] Kessler, 'Henri de Régnier', *Pan*, 1.4 (1895), 247.

The essay is a sensitive evocation of Symbolism, based on the premiss that the suggestive implication and the symbol are the appropriate techniques for one like Régnier, who 'empfindet sein Selbst nicht als Einheit' [does not feel his identity as a unity]. There can hardly be a clearer statement of what Hofmannsthal found of interest in Symbolism and why. The second volume of *Pan* has a facsimile of Verlaine's manuscript of 'Gaspard Hauser chante' and Cäsar Flaischlen's German versions (hardly translations) of Verlaine's 'Sérénade' from *Poèmes saturniens* and two poems from *Sagesse*, 'Un grand sommeil noir' and 'Le ciel est, par-dessus le toit'. These accompany an essay by Magnus von Wedderkop entitled 'Paul Verlaine und die Lyrik der Décadence in Frankreich'. Hofmannsthal's 'Der Jüngling in der Landschaft' is also published there. With extracts from Hofmannsthal's *Das kleine Welttheater* in volume 3 are Franz Blei's translations of two more ballads from Maeterlinck's *Quinze Chansons* and an essay on Maeterlinck by Anna Brunnemann. Brunnemann's essay on Rodenbach appeared in the fifth and last volume in 1900, with Karl Klammer's Verlaine translations, his version of Rimbaud's 'Les Effarés', and finally two of Maeterlinck's *Serres chaudes*. By 1895, when *Pan* was started by Bierbaum and Meier-Graefe, essays like Kessler's and Brunnemann's were most probably Hofmannsthal's first serious introduction to Régnier and Rodenbach. On 8 December 1892 he had written to George, 'Rodenbach, Henri Mazel, Montesquiou und viele andere mit den scheuen Symbolen der flüchtigen Fledermaus, des verschlossenen Fauns, der alten verblichenen Seide, sind mir leider fast nur Namen und Wappen' [... and many others with the shy symbols of the flitting bat, the diffident faun and faded old silk are for me sadly only names and emblems].[50] The longer pieces on Verlaine and Maeterlinck must have served to maintain an established interest.

This list goes some way towards indicating how Hofmannsthal and Symbolism were placed side by side, even treated as synonymous by *Pan*. The essay by Julius Hart, 'Die Entwicklung der neueren Lyrik in Deutschland', makes this explicit, if disapprovingly.[51] Hart traces the family tree of Symbolism back to German Romanticism:

Unmittelbare Schüler der deutschen Romantik sind Coleridge und Poe, ein unmittelbarer Schüler Poes aber ist Baudelaire, und Baudelaire der Urheber und

[50] *Briefwechsel zwischen George und Hofmannsthal*, 2nd, extended edn. (Munich: Küpper-Bondi, 1953), 50–1.

[51] Julius Hart, 'Die Entwicklung der neueren Lyrik in Deutschland', *Pan*, 2 (1896–7), 33–40. Gsteiger (*Französische Symbolisten*, 83) is rather hard on this essay, which if partisan against Symbolism is at least fair to the formal advances involved.

Begründer der Dekadenten- und Symbolistenlyrik Verlaines, Mallarmés, Maeterlincks u.s.w. . . . . Da wo unsere naturalistisch-ästheticistische Lyrik unter den Einflüssen der französischen Dekadenten steht, ist sie eine lebensunfähige und modische vorübergehende Erscheinung.[52]

[Coleridge and Poe are students of German Romanticism at first hand, but a firsthand student of Poe is Baudelaire, and Baudelaire is the originator and founder of the Decadent and Symbolist poetry of Verlaine, Mallarmé, Maeterlinck etc. Where our Naturalist-Aestheticist poetry is under the influence of French Decadence, it is an unviable, modish and transient phenomenon.]

It is in the revivification of elements of Romanticism that he sees the modern poets' virtues:

Etwas Wichtiges und Grosses aber bedeutet die Wiedererweckung des elementaren romantischen Aestheticismus, und die Aufgabe dieser Schule liegt nach der formalen Seite darin, den etwas derberen und stofflicheren Naturalismus der Objektivitätslyrik zu verfeinern, luftiger und aetherischer zu gestalten und ihn auf die rein künstlerischen Erfordernisse strenger hinzuweisen.

[However, the reawakening of elemental Romantic aestheticism is something great and important, and on the formal side, the task of this school is to refine the somewhat crude and earthy Naturalism of the poetry of objectivity, to make it more airy and ethereal and bring it more firmly in line with purely artistic requirements.]

Hofmannsthal, an Austrian in an essay on the poetry of Germany, is given only a brief mention, but his delicate formal gifts are singled out. Hart judges that Hofmannsthal is very closely associated with the French Symbolists, but in a primal spiritual relationship that will always be present in poets who flourish in the same age, which reduces the relationship to little more than mere contemporaneity.

Stefan George never published in *Pan*, although he was invited to, but Karl Wolfskehl did write about him in the last volume. Richard Dehmel, a founder member of the editorial committee, wrote of George in his diary, 'er hat uns aber nicht nur keine Beiträge geliefert, sondern hat bei seinen Pariser Freunden unser Unternehmen sogar zu diskreditieren versucht, als eine Brutstätte des deutschen Naturalismus' [he has not only sent us no contributions' but has even attempted to discredit our enterprise with his friends in Paris, calling it a breeding ground for German Naturalism].[53] The direction of *Pan*

---

[52] Hart, 'Die Entwicklung', 38, col. 1. His use of 'naturalistisch' in conjunction with 'ästheticistisch' is an idiosyncrasy.

[53] Quoted by Karl H. Salzmann, ' "Pan": Geschichte einer Zeitschrift', in Jost Hermand (ed.), *Jugendstil* (Darmstadt: Wissenschaftliche Buchgesellschaft, 1971), 197.

was hardly Naturalist, but George saw it as vulgar competition for his *Blätter für die Kunst*. The *Blätter* were founded in 1892, inspired by the French periodicals *La Plume*, *Le Mercure de France* and *L'Ermitage*, and influenced later by Gérardy's Belgian paper *Floréal*. It is possible that Hofmannsthal subscribed to these Symbolist papers, whose information was as up to date with the latest writing as any in the German-language press, but he may only have seen copies of those with poems by George. On one occasion George wonders why Hofmannsthal has not yet received the latest papers; this and his assumption in April 1893 that Hofmannsthal has the latest *Floréal* may speak for a subscription. In 1895 Hofmannsthal wrote disparagingly to George of 'die analogen französischen Hefte' [the equivalent French papers], which presupposes familiarity—although since the remark is in response to George's insistence that he write for the *Blätter*, the tone is probably simulated.[54]

George's dealings with the French periodicals illustrate the mutual awareness of German and French writers, but relations were more fraught than he might have preferred. The February number of *Mercure de France* praised translations of Verlaine by Richard Dehmel, 'l'un des meilleurs poètes de la toute jeune Allemagne' with a 'subtil talent de lyrique qui excelle aux nuances et aux caressantes intonations du "Lied"'[one of the best of the most recent German poets with a subtle lyrical talent that excels in the nuances and the lulling intonations of the German *Lied*].[55] George drafted a stinging reply damning Dehmel and complaining that his own translations had been incomprehensibly ignored. He immediately sent a 'Report from Berlin' to *La Plume* with a complaint about the quality of literary journals in Germany and a piece of unsolicited publicity for the *Blätter*:

Seit letztem Jahr hat sich bei uns eine Bewegung gebildet, die von Grund auf deutsch und idealistisch ist. Junge Künstler, die von einer neuen dichterischen Blüte träumen, von einer künstlerischen Literatur, haben sich um die 'Blätter für die Kunst' geschart.[56]

[Since last year a movement has formed here that is fundamentally German and idealist. A mass of young artists who dream of poetry flourishing anew have flocked together around the *Blätter für die Kunst*.]

---

[54] George, *BW*, 49, 62 and 82; letters of 17 Nov. 1892, 3 Apr. 1893 and 7 Dec. 1895.

[55] *Mercure de France*, 7 (1893), 186–7. Quoted from Werner Paul Sohnle (ed.), *Stefan George und der Symbolismus: Eine Ausstellung der Württembergischen Landesbibliothek* (Stuttgart: Württembergische Landesbibliothek, 1983), 94.

[56] Sohnle (ed.), *George/Symbolismus*, 95, editor's translation.

This was only partially effective, however, since within less than two years, *La Plume* itself published a certain Clodomir's 'Bericht aus Dresden' entitled 'Verlaine en Allemagne':

Karl Sachs a publié en 1892 son discours SUR LES DÉCADENTS. A la même époque paraît l'étude de Stéphane Waetzold intitulée PAUL VERLAINE, UN POÈTE DE LA DÉCADENCE. Il existe des traductions de Verlaine, voire des imitations, celles, par exemple, de Dehmel. Une école de décadents s'est constituée dans l'Allemagne du nord et en Autriche, les recrues sont nombreuses.[57]

[In 1892 Karl Sachs published his essay 'On the Decadents'. Stephen Waetzold's study entitled 'Paul Verlaine: A Poet of Decadence' appeared at the same time. There are translations of Verlaine, even imitations, such as those of Dehmel. A school of Decadents has formed in northern Germany and in Austria, and it has many new recruits.]

The 'school' had been recognized and advertised, but George himself and the *Blätter* had not, and there is further irony here. The study by Waetzold that 'Clodomir' mentions was an important early German essay on Verlaine, both detailed and balanced, presenting Verlaine alongside Mallarmé as 'Führer und Meister' for '[das] jüngste Geschlecht der französischen Dichter, [die] Décadents, Symbolisten und Impressionisten' [leader and master for the youngest generation of French poets, the Decadents, Symbolists and Impressionists].[58] It also lists a number of secondary works on Verlaine and his contemporaries. Waetzold himself had a position at the Berliner Universität from 1889—and in the summer semester of 1890 taught a seminar on modern French that was attended by Stefan George.[59]

Hofmannsthal's participation in the work of the *Blätter* repeatedly brought him into contact with publications on the Symbolists such as *Le Tombeau de Charles Baudelaire*, eventually published by *La Plume* in 1896 with two of George's translations from *Les Fleurs du mal*.[60] By 1896, though, Hofmannsthal was out of his literary teens and disenchanted with the *Blätter*, which he called 'blöd' [silly],[61] and indeed the first flush of Symbolist verse published there was over. The second volume of the

---

[57] *La Plume*, 137 (1895), 25. Quoted by Gsteiger, *Französische Symbolisten*, 81.

[58] Stephan Waetzold, 'Paul Verlaine, ein Dichter der Décadence', in Julius Zupitza (ed.), *Festschrift zur Begründung des fünften allgemeinen deutschen Neuphilologentages zu Berlin, Pfingsten 1892* (Berlin: Weidmann'sche Buchhandlung, 1892), 168.

[59] Cf. Robert Boehringer, *Mein Bild von Stefan George*, 2 vols., 2nd, extended edn. (Düsseldorf: Küpper-Bondi, 1968), i. 35.

[60] George, *BW*, 46 and 52; letters from Hofmannsthal to Klein, 10 Oct. 1892, and to George, 19 Dec. 1892.

[61] *Briefe 1890–1901*, 207; letter to Clemens Franckenstein, 9 Nov. 1896.

Blätter für die Kunst had contained translations of Mallarmé, Verlaine, Moréas and de Régnier (alongside five poems by Hofmannsthal); Vielé-Griffin, Merrill, Rimbaud and Verhaeren were to appear in later volumes, sometimes in the original, mostly translated. But the *Blätter* grew in the shadow of Mallarmé's artistic elitism—which under George was not so much aristocratic as autocratic—and Hofmannsthal's literary development led him away from this stance.[62] At the outset of the *Blätter* enterprise, Hofmannsthal declared that he was at their disposal willingly and without reservation and claimed to be delighted by their exclusiveness.[63] But George was possessive and suggested that the poems by Hofmannsthal that Bahr published in his 'Loris' essay ought to have been saved for the *Blätter*.[64] Hofmannsthal seemed to vacillate over the undertaking. He wrote to Marie Herzfeld on 29 August 1892 justifying the inclusion of her name on the list of invited subscribers with his belief 'daß die Zeitung ein interessanteres cachet haben wird als die gewöhnlichen Jugendlitteraturblätter' [that the journal will have a more interesting cachet than the usual papers devoted to contemporary literature], and again just after Christmas assuring her that 'hinter der ganzen manierierten und sonderbaren Unternehmung doch etwas "anderes" und "wirkliches" steckt' [behind the whole rather mannered and peculiar undertaking there is something 'different' and 'genuine'].[65] But he was later to complain to Andrian (a much closer friend), 'sie sind so pedantisch manierierte und gleichzeitig manierlose Leute' [these people are so pedantically mannered, yet at the same time with no manners at all].[66] Irritated that he could get no clear guidelines from George about what he was to write, he announced in December 1892 that his essays on foreign literature related to their own work would appear in the popular press. Amongst these he counted Verlaine, Swinburne, Wilde and the Pre-Raphaelites—but not Mallarmé.[67]

Periodicals and journals presented Symbolist works and criticism in

---

[62] Cf. Gsteiger, *Französische Symbolisten*, 71.

[63] George, *BW*, 22; letter of 26 June 1892.

[64] It is interesting that, according to Hofmannsthal, Bahr wanted to quote George's *Hymnen* as examples of Symbolist verse instead of Hofmannsthal's two poems, which further reinforces the terminological link that Hofmannsthal and others perceived between himself and George.

[65] Hugo von Hofmannsthal, *Briefe an Marie Herzfeld*, ed. Horst Weber (Heidelberg: Stiehm, 1967), 31 and 34.

[66] Hugo von Hofmannsthal and Leopold von Andrian, *Briefwechsel*, ed. Walter H. Perl (Frankfurt a.M.: S. Fischer, 1968), 23; letter of 21 Feb. 1894.

[67] George, *BW*, 53; letter of 19 Dec. 1892.

small if regular doses. Occasionally more substantial boosts would appear in the form of books such as Jules Huret's *Enquête sur l'évolution Littéraire*, which Hofmannsthal read and noted in some detail,[68] or Charles Morice's *La littérature de tout à l'heure*, the title of which, at least, was known to him.[69] Another book that dealt in detail with the phenomenon of Symbolism, Max Nordau's *Entartung*, seems also to have excited Hofmannsthal's attention. He cited Nordau as an example of one guilty of a 'tactlose Geringschätzung' of the *Blätter*, 'beiläufig formuliert' in *Entartung* [tactless denigration . . . casually uttered].[70] The book enjoyed a *succès de scandale*, the first volume published in 1892, the second in 1893; both were reprinted in that year and again in 1896; translations into Italian, French and English had appeared by 1895. Nordau sought to debunk the pretensions to quality of nineteenth-century literature from Baudelaire onwards, characterizing it as the outpourings of physical and mental degenerates, misinterpreted as genius by a public whose values had become corrupt.[71] One of his major targets in the first volume is Symbolism. His knowledge of French literature was very detailed and he used it to attack not only the French authors themselves but also the tendencies that the Viennese writers had inherited from the Symbolists. Melancholy, emotionality, mysticism, dream, contemplative inactivity and narcissism all indicated degeneration (the term is borrowed from Nordau's mentor, Cesare Lombroso) and all supposedly characterized *fin-de-siècle* Viennese writing.

There was no question of Hofmannsthal's accepting the positivist criteria of this attack: Verlaine was condemned famously as 'ein abschreckender Entarteter mit asymmetrischem Schädel und mongolischem Gesicht' [a repulsive degenerate with an asymmetrical skull and a Mongolian face],[72] and for his alcoholism as much as for his poetry; there is no tolerance of the imaginative scope of Baudelaire's abyss, merely a charge of insanity and Satanism; Nordau consistently subordinates mood to clinical empiricism; the musicality of poetry so prized by Symbolist writers is dismissed as echolalia.[73] But it caused a

---

[68] See below, pp. 102–12.

[69] *Nachlaß*, H VA 113.6⁴.

[70] George, *BW*, 52; letter of 19 Dec. 1892.

[71] Cf. Max Nordau, *Entartung*, 2 vols. (Berlin: Duncker, 1892), and Jens Malte Fischer, 'Dekadenz und Entartung: Max Nordau als Kritiker des Fin de siècle', in Roger Bauer et al. (eds.), *Fin de Siècle: Zu Literatur und Kunst der Jahrhundertwende* (Frankfurt a.M.: Klostermann, 1977), 98. [72] Nordau, *Entartung*, i. 228.

[73] This was noted in Pius Pauli's review of *Entartung* in the *Neue Revue* of Oct. 1896; quoted from Wunberg (ed.), *Das junge Wien*, i. 633.

stir, and its sheer volume and scope demanded serious refutation. Hofmannsthal evidently did take it seriously and was still concerned enough by it to lend it to Edgar Karg von Bebenburg in 1896.[74]

Michaud says that interest in Symbolism in France came to a head in 1891, 'l'heure du Symbolisme'.[75] In Vienna, the substantial interest in Symbolism from the press and critics was delayed a little, at its height between 1891 and 1895, and it was a general part in the literary atmosphere in which Hofmannsthal grew up. The public literary debate was also linked with Hofmannsthal personally, and as part of the discussion the characteristics of Hofmannsthal's own poetry were challenged or championed, directly and indirectly, under the name of Symbolism.

If the debate thus influenced Hofmannsthal's self-image, his many contacts with other writers and journalists reinforced the effect. One of the most obvious fora was the Café Griensteidl on the Michaelerplatz, and as a kind of commercial salon it functioned most effectively for the younger generation of writers—who, with the exception of Hofmannsthal, were not usually guests at the salons proper. Hermann Bahr held court there and gathered around him Hofmannsthal, Arthur Schnitzler, Leopold von Andrian, Richard Beer-Hofmann, Salten, Richard Specht, Felix Dörmann, Leo Feld and Ferry Bératon.[76] The popular identification of *Jung Wien* with the Café Griensteidl alone is certainly over-simplified—the Cafés Scheidl and Central were literary meeting places, too, and Hofmannsthal's correspondence with Schnitzler also mentions the Pfob, Union and Pucher.[77] But if the locality changed occasionally, whether in the Griensteidl or elsewhere, many of the literary exchanges of Hofmannsthal's early years were conducted semi-publicly with a hugely varied group of participants.

One of the major advantages of the literary cafés was highly practical. Not only did the Griensteidl provide pen and paper for its customers, it possessed a full set of *Meyers Konversationslexikon* and subscribed to so many newspapers and journals for their use that Karl Kraus commented bitterly, 'wer gedenkt nicht der schier erdrückenden Fülle von Zeitungen und Zeitschriften, die den Besuch

[74] Karg's reaction was, 'Ich lese langsam die Entartung u. täte sie gern rasch, rasch durch': Hugo von Hofmannsthal and Edgar Karg von Bebenburg, *Briefwechsel*, ed. Mary E. Gilbert (Frankfurt a.M.: S. Fischer, 1966), 126; letter of 8 Nov. 1896.

[75] Guy Michaud, *Message poétique du symbolisme* (Paris: Nizet, 1947; repr. 1961), 399.

[76] Cf. Alfred Zohner, 'Café Griensteidl', in Eduard Castle (ed.), *Deutsch-österreichische Literaturgeschichte. Ein Handbuch zur Geschichte der deutschen Literatur in Österreich-Ungarn*, iv: *1890–1918* (Vienna: C. Fromme, 1927), 1715–16.

[77] Diersch, *Empiriokritizismus*, 97 n. 61.

unseres Kaffeehauses . . . zu einem wahren Bedürfnis gemacht hatte?'
[who does not recall the sheer, stifling mass of newspapers and journals
that made a visit to our café a real necessity?].[78] When habitués were
not privileged with advance readings they had reviews and notices at
their fingertips. Felix Salten wrote nostalgically of famous visitors to
the café, of Otto Erich Hartleben, the translator of *Pierrot Lunaire*,
eccentrically dressed; the staunch defender of German Naturalism,
Michael Georg Conrad from Berlin, who was accused by the young
Hofmannsthal in public of writing boring articles.[79] Stefan Zweig
recalls the essentially democratic character of the institution:

Es ist eigentlich eine Art demokratischer, jedem für eine billige Schale Kaffee
zugänglicher Klub, wo jeder Gast für diesen kleinen Obolus stundenlang sitzen,
diskutieren, schreiben, Karten spielen, seine Post empfangen und vor allem eine
unbegrenzte Zahl von Zeitungen und Zeitschriften konsumieren kann. In einem
besseren Wiener Kaffeehaus lagen alle Wiener Zeitungen auf und nicht nur die
Wiener, sondern die des ganzen deutschen Reiches und die französischen und
englischen und italienischen und amerikanischen, dazu sämtliche wichtigen
literarischen und künstlerischen Revuen der Welt, der 'Mercure de France' nicht
minder als die 'Neue Rundschau', der 'Studio' und das 'Burlington Magazine'.[80]

[It is in fact a kind of democratic club, accessible to all for the price of a cheap cup
of coffee, where for this tiny outlay any customer can sit for hours, debate, write,
play cards, receive his post and above all devour a limitless number of newspapers
and journals. In the best Viennese coffee houses all the Vienna papers were available, and not only these but papers from the whole of Germany, the French ones,
the English, the Italian and the American, and on top of all that all the most
important literary and artistic reviews in the world, the *Mercure de France* no less
than the *Neue Rundschau*, the *Studio* and the *Burlington Magazine*.]

Not all the denizens of the Griensteidl were Francophile, of course, but
Hofmannsthal's taste was none the less well supported and Kraus
complained that 'Griensteidl stand im Zeichen des Symbolismus' [the
Griensteidl was under the aegis of Symbolism].[81] Symbolism was
certainly discussed there in the early 1890s. Hofmannsthal's diary
records a conversation there on the evening of 28 May 1891, for
example. It arose in response to a report of a 'Symbolist evening' in

    [78] Kraus, 'Die demolirte Literatur', in *Frühe Schriften 1892–1900*, ed. J. J. Braakenburg
(Munich: Kösel, 1979), ii. 277.
    [79] Felix Salten, 'Aus den Anfängen. Erinnerungsskizzen', *Jahrbuch deutscher Bibliophiler und
Literaturfreunde*, 18/19 (1933); repr. in Petra Neumann (ed.), *Wien und seine Kaffeehäuser. Ein
literarischer Streifzug durch die berühmtesten Cafés der Donaumetropole* (Munich: Heyne, 1997), 79–
84.
    [80] Zweig, *Die Welt von Gestern*, 56.
    [81] Kraus, 'Die demolirte Literatur', 278.

Paris, which took him and his friends on to the topic of Maeterlinck and led Bahr to recount the plot of *Les Aveugles*.[82] The report was of a benefit evening for Verlaine and Paul Gauguin held at the Théâtre de l'Art on 21 May. It included Verlaine's short play *Les Uns et les autres*, Charles Morice's *Chérubin*, settings of Catulle Mendès's *Soleil de minuit* and Maeterlinck's *L'Intruse*—this last the only piece to find favour with the audience.[83]

Hofmannsthal's literary friends and acquaintances met frequently to read and discuss literature, and in a sense, literature was the very medium of communication between them:

[ich] rede mit Bahr, Hofmann und Poldy Andrian fast immer über dasselbe, das uns im tiefsten reizt und erregt: Stil, Stil der Seele, der Landschaft, der Kunst, und die damit zusammenhängenden Begriffe: Kultur, innere und äußere, Zusammen-hang von Form und Inhalt in der Kunst und im Leben.[84]

[With Bahr, [Beer-]Hofmann and Poldy Andrian I almost always talk about the same thing, something that stimulates and arouses us so deeply: style, the style of the soul, of the landscape, of art and the concepts associated with it: culture, inner and outer, the relationship of form and content in art and in life.]

Schnitzler notes in his diary for 2 January 1892, for example, that he spent the evening at Dörmann's, who read his *Sensationen*—'Kein Fort-schritt gegenüber Neurotica' [no advance on *Neurotica*]. Bahr, 'Loris' and Salten were also present.[85] But friendship within this circle was tense and beset by jealousy, and Andrian records freer comments on Dörmann and this reading that were made by Hofmannsthal later during one of their own private *soirées*:

aufrichtig gestanden, er ist mir ein bisserl grauslich—er wascht sich nie recht. Und dann,—ich finde seine Gedichte so unsinnlich—so — — — voriges Jahr—das war gemein, da hat er mir seine Gedichte vorgelesen—Wie liest er denn—Er sperrt's Zimmer zu, daß man nicht fortkann, und dann schwitzt er.[86]

[to be quite honest, he makes me feel a little peculiar—he doesn't wash properly. And then I find his poems so nonsensical—so — — — last year—that was awful, he read his poems to me—How is that he reads?—He locks the door of the room so that you can't get away, and then he sweats.]

[82] *Nachlaß*, H VII 17.76ᵇ and *SW* ii. 296–7.

[83] Cf. Kenneth Cornell, *The Symbolist Movement* (New Haven: Yale University Press, 1951), 104.

[84] *Briefe 1890–1901*, 102; letter of 24 May 1894 to Elsa Bruckmann-Cantacuzène.

[85] Schnitzler, *Tagebuch 1879–1892*, ed. Werner Welzig et al. (Vienna: Verlag der Öster-reichischen Akademie der Wissenschaften, 1987), 361.

[86] 'Leopold Andrian über Hugo von Hofmannsthal: Auszüge aus seinen Tagebüchern', ed. Ursula Renner, *Hofmannsthal-Blätter*, 35/6 (1987), 6. A good idea of the tensions is given in Olga Schnitzler's *Spiegelbild der Freundschaft* (Salzburg: Residenz Verlag, 1962).

Hofmannsthal divided his acquaintances into the 'literary' and the 'personal', and after they met in October 1893 Andrian was one of the most intimate circle.[87] In January 1894 Andrian's diary records, 'Hugo Hofmannsthal und ich, die wir uns den ganzen Abend lyrische Gedichte—eigene und fremde—vorlesen' [Hugo Hofmannsthal and I, reading poems aloud all evening—our own and others'].[88] His own poetry reflects his reception of Baudelaire and of Paul Bourget.[89] Andrian knew Henri de Régnier and Maeterlinck—reading *Pelléas et Mélisande* in the spring of 1894 he noted 'man müsste den Symbolismus auch auf den Roman ausdehnen' [one ought to extend Symbolism to the novel],[90] which thought played a part in the genesis of his own novel, *Der Garten der Erkenntnis* (1895), which provoked a flood of praise, not least from Hofmannsthal.[91] The novel dissects the world outside the delicate soul of its hero Erwin for the sole purpose of finding images of that soul in its mirror: Salten described the novel as actionless, 'nur ein staunendes Verweilen bei den wichtigen Augenblicken der Seele' [merely a lingering in amazement around the soul's important moments].[92] Most of all, Andrian loved Verlaine, who fostered his own meticulous narcissism. He sent copies of *Der Garten der Erkenntnis* to him and Barrès in Paris via Hans Schlesinger. Both had less German than was necessary for a proper appreciation, and Verlaine's response was, 'que c'est malheureux de ne pas savoir toutes les langues, mais qu'il s'en rendra compte quand même' [that it is unfortunate not to know every language, but that he will none the less take note of it]. Barrès wrote that he had 'deciphered' this elegant work with great pleasure:

[87] The terms are Hofmannsthal's own, noted in Andrian's diary. See Jens Rieckmann, *Aufbruch in die Moderne* (Königstein/Ts.: Athenäum, 1985), 91.

[88] Entry for 19 Jan. 1894 (so dated in *Leopold von Andrian und die Blätter für die Kunst*, ed. Walter H. Perl (Hamburg: Verlag Dr Ernst Hauswedell, 1960) 116; 'Andrian über Hofmannsthal' heads this entry 'zwischen 20. und 22. Jan.').

[89] On Baudelaire see Andrian, *BW*, 16 and 20 (letters from Jan. 1894) and 'Andrian über Hofmannsthal', 7, where Hofmannsthal is more dismissive of Baudelaire. On Bourget see 'Andrian über Hofmannsthal', 7, and H. R. Klieneberger, 'Hofmannsthal and Leopold Andrian', *Modern Language Review*, 80 (1985), 621–2.

[90] Quoted in *Correspondenzen: Briefe an Leopold von Andrian 1894–1950*, ed. Ferruccio Delle Cave (Marbach am Neckar: Deutsche Schiller-Gesellschaft, 1989), 112.

[91] Cf. Jens Rieckmann, 'Narziss und Dionysos: Leopold von Andrians *Der Garten der Erkenntnis*', *Modern Austrian Literature*, 16.2 (1983), 65–7, and more positively, *Aufbruch*, 136–44.

[92] *Wiener Allgemeine Zeitung* (1895), quoted from Leopold von Andrian, *Der Garten der Erkenntnis*, ed. Walter H. Perl (Frankfurt a.M.: S. Fischer, 1970), 85. Bahr's review notes an obvious debt to Barrès (ibid. 80).

Il ne m'appartient de juger un jardin où j'ai pénétré avec la gêne et la gaucherie d'un étranger qui dans un lieu si nouveau distingue mal les fleurs des légumes et s'y sent un maladroit.[93]

[It is not for me to make a judgement on a garden that I have found my way into with the awkwardness and clumsiness of a foreigner who, in such a new place, can hardly tell the flowers from the vegetables and feels himself out of place there.]

Schlesinger's letters to Andrian show that he was perfectly in tune with the literary life there, the personnel and the papers. Although not a direct influence at this point, Schlesinger was later to become Hofmannsthal's brother-in-law.

Another of the group, Hermann Bahr, was the motivating force behind the *Verein für modernes Leben*, formerly the *Freie Bühne*, a literary society involving many of the *Jung Wiener* whose first and only production, planned for 11 April 1892, was of two plays by Maeterlinck, *Les Aveugles*, translated by Hofmannsthal and Ferry Bératon, and *L'Intrus* [*sic*], translated by Bératon.[94] Bahr had suggested these plays rather than an excerpt from Schnitzler's *Anatol* and Beer-Hofmann's *Pierrot Hypnotiseur* because of a 'Symbolistenabend' in Paris. After delays caused by Bahr's financial difficulties and police intervention (the theatre was closed because the texts had not been submitted to the censors), *L'Intruse* was eventually performed on 2 May. Bahr lectured on Symbolism, and, according to reports in the *Magazin für Literatur* five days later, encountered a mixed reception. His lecture was also reported in the *Freie Bühne*, because, they said, it was characteristic of Vienna and of the newest artistic trends in Vienna.[95]

Amongst the other *Caféhaus-Poeten* (virtually the only one to merit Karl Kraus's approval) was Peter Altenberg, and he, too, was taken up by the wave of interest in Symbolism. From its second printing in 1898, his collection of prose writings *Wie ich es sehe* was headed by a quotation from chapter XIV of *A rebours* where Huysmans details Des Esseintes's relationship to contemporary French literature, Flaubert, the Goncourts, Zola, and also Mallarmé, Verlaine, Villiers and Corbière. This list may hint at the range of Altenberg's literary interests. He was a devotee of Baudelaire's *Le Spleen de Paris* (a poem from which adorns the

[93] Cf. Andrian, *Correspondenzen*, 23–4.

[94] The same gender-change is evident in the title of Otto Erich Hartleben's translation of the play as *Der Ungebetene* (Berlin: Theater-Verlag Eduard Bloch, 1898).

[95] Quoted from Wunberg (ed.), *Das junge Wien*, i. 326. For a fuller description of the evening see Marie Herzfeld's reminiscences in Helmut Fiechtner (ed.), *Hugo von Hofmannsthal: Der Dichter im Spiegel der Freunde*, 2nd edn. (Berne: Franke, 1963), 53–4, and Rieckmann, *Aufbruch*, 63–5.

mantelpiece of Huysmans's Des Esseintes) and his regular *feuilleton* writing has been seen as late participation in the idiosyncratic genre of the prose poem.[96] Altenberg's borrowings from Maeterlinck's *Pelléas et Mélisande* have been traced in the study called *Seeufer-Nachmittag*,[97] and a case may be made for seeing the prose poems as a possible extreme extension of Maeterlinck's *tragédie immobile* as explained in *Le Trésor des humbles* (1896). Hofmannsthal's review ('Ein neues Wiener Buch', 1896) certainly fixes on the Maeterlinckian motifs of the pool and the coloured stones as similes to express Altenberg's technique:

Seine Geschichten sind wie ganz kleine Teiche, über die man sich beugt, um Goldfische und bunte Steine zu sehen, und plötzlich undeutlich ein menschliches Gesicht aufsteigen sieht. So ist das Gesicht des Dichters schattenhaft in die hundert Geschichten eingesenkt und schwebt empor. (*RA* i. 226)

[His stories are like very small pools that one leans over looking for goldfish and coloured stones, and suddenly sees a human face rising from the depths. Thus is the face of the poet, sunk shadow-like into the hundreds of stories, soaring out above them.]

His closing appreciation again suggests parallels with Maeterlinck, focusing on the value of the different kinds of silence ('Le Silence' is the first chapter of *Le Trésor des humbles*) and asserting, 'immerhin ist von diesen geheimnisvollen Mächten dieses kleine Buch irgendwie beherrscht, wie der zierliche Magnet von ungeheuren, im Ungewissen gelagerten Kräften' [this book is none the less somehow in thrall to mysterious powers, as the delicate magnet is to monstrous forces stored up in the unknown; *RA* i. 229]. And of another strand of his writing, the erotic, Altenberg has been described as 'das Bindeglied zwischen der Dirnenromantik der französischen Literatur und der Literatur des Jungen Wien' [the link between the romanticized prostitution in French literature and the literature of *Jung Wien*].[98]

Verlaine was a decisive influence on one more writer of the period, Richard Schaukal, born in 1874 and thus an exact contemporary of Hofmannsthal's; they both also studied law at the University of Vienna. Schaukal, too, made a name for himself when only a student, partly with his own verse (*Gedichte*, 1893, and *Tristia*, 1898), but most notably for his translations of all the Symbolist poets. He began with Verlaine's Pierrot poem from *Jadis et naguère* in 1893 (Pierrot was a

[96] Cf. Franz Norbert Mennemeier, *Literatur der Jahrhundertwende* (Frankfurt a.M.: Peter Lang, 1985–8), ii. 113–15.
[97] Fischer, *Fin-de-siècle*, 159–61.
[98] Ibid. 165.

popular figure at the time—Hofmannsthal and Beer-Hofmann worked on a pantomime called *Pierrot Hypnotiseur* in 1893[99]), and published more Verlaine translations in the *Neue Deutsche Rundschau* and the *Magazin für Literatur* in 1896. He revised his translations constantly and a collected Verlaine volume appeared in 1906. After the turn of the century he turned to Mallarmé, translating *Hérodiade*, amongst many other poems, in 1903.[100]

Andrian shared the young Hofmannsthal's fascination with Baude-lairean gems and metal: *Der Garten der Erkenntnis* attributes 'sinnreiche Schönheit', sensuous beauty, to a long list including amber, coral, onyx, jasper, chrysoprase, precious metals, diamonds, agates, turquoises, sapphires, aquamarines and 'die schwarzen, grünen, blaß-gelben, rosigen, milchfarbenen Perlen' [the black, green, pale yellow, pink, milky pearls].[101] The most passionate disciple of Baudelaire in the circle, however, was Felix Dörmann. Dörmann, properly Felix Bieder-mann, was some four years older than Hofmannsthal and an obsessive devotee of Huysmans and Baudelaire. He translated 'Le Balcon' and four prose poems for the *Moderne Rundschau* in 1891, 'L'Amour et le crâne' and five others for Bierbaum's *Moderner Musenalmanach*.[102] Dörmann was (and is) widely regarded as 'ein lyrischer Poseur' because of his lack of originality and authenticity. The second 'Intérieur' poem from *Neurotica* (1891), for example, owes its details of decor and sensation directly to 'Une martyre' from *Les Fleurs du mal*.[103] Kraus also noted Dörmann's debt to the French poet in 'Die demolirte Litteratur': 'Die Kritik glaubte indess, den Sitz seines Leidens in der Lectüre Baudelaire's gefunden zu haben' [in the meantime critics thought they had discovered the origin of his suffering in his reading of Baudelaire],[104] and may have been prompted by Bahr, who had claimed four years earlier, 'er redet nicht aus dem Leben: er redet immer aus fremden Literaturen. Seine Schmerzen sind von Baude-laire und seine Wünsche sind von Swinburne. Sich verkündet er nirgends' [he does not speak from within life: he always speaks from within the literatures of foreign countries. His pains are Baudelaire's

---

[99] Cf. Robert Vilain, 'An Innocent Abroad: The Pierrot Figure in German and Austrian Literature at the Turn of the Century', *Publications of the English Goethe Society*, ns 67 (1997), 69–99.

[100] For details of the translations see Gsteiger, *Französische Symbolisten*, 42–3 and 254 nn. 64–9.

[101] Andrian, *Der Garten*, 28 (cf. also 13).

[102] Cf. Gsteiger, *Französische Symbolisten*, 40, and 253 nn. 50 and 57.

[103] Cf. Fischer, *Fin-de-siècle*, 123.

[104] Kraus, 'Die demolirte Literatur', 292–3.

and his desires are Swinburne's. He never promotes his real self any-where].[105] Bahr also emphasized the typical Decadent imagery drawn from Baudelaire, eerie flora and icy gems, and indeed praised Dörmann's 'hektische schlanke Narzissen mit blutrothem Mund' [hectic, slender narcissi with their blood-red mouths] and the 'herzlose grüne Smaragde' [heartless green emeralds] as elegant formulations. But he sees them as functionless within their poetic context, decorative and meaningless, 'wie eine Sammlung der besten Citate aus allen Stilen der Gegenwart. . . . Er redet mit fremden Worten, und so reden die fremden Worte für ihn' [like a collection of the best quotations from every contemporary style. He speaks with others' words, and so the words of others speak on his behalf].[106]

Further general conclusions may be drawn from this concerted attack on Dörmann. The influences that overload contemporary poets (Dörmann is not alone) are principally French and, to a much lesser extent, English (Swinburne is the most frequently recurring name). The influence of the German literary tradition was much less con-scious than that from France. Furthermore, it was not merely the use of borrowed images and phrases that was noted by the writers of *fin-de-siècle* Vienna, but also sensations and feelings, habits of mind and poetic forms. There was another view, however, propounded by Emil Rechert in *Charles Baudelaire und die Modernen* (1895), where Baudelaire is seen as the founding father of Modernism, the poet of the ugly, of the common man and the modern city, 'der Dichter des Gemeinen schlechthin' [the quintessential poet of the ordinary]. Dörmann's translations, however—none of them of the metropolitan poems, none treating the external underprivileged world—display a tendency to abstraction or 'Entkonkretisierung' and to the smoothing out of Baudelaire's prominent dissonances:

Mit nervöser Penetranz übernimmt Dörmann all das, was böse ist und das Ich bedroht, nicht jedoch das, was auf der Gesellschaft lastend die Entfaltung des Individuums bedroht. Dörmanns Text begreift nur das sprechende Ich als das beklagenswerte Opfer der Isolation.[107]

[With nervous assertiveness Dörmann borrows everything that is evil and

---

[105] Hermann Bahr, 'Das junge Österreich', in *Studien*, 90. Marie Herzfeld says much the same, listing Baudelaire, Poe, Swinburne and Bourget in 'Felix Dörmann: Eine vorläufige Studie', *Moderne Dichtung*, 2.6 (1 Dec. 1890), 750; also in Wunberg (ed.), *Das junge Wien*, i. 138.

[106] Bahr, 'Das junge Österreich', 89.

[107] Wendelin Schmidt-Dengler, 'Französischer Symbolismus und Wiener Dekadenz', in Mark Ward (ed.), *From Vormärz to Fin de Siècle* (Blairgowrie: Lochee Publications, 1986), 83 and 85.

threatening to the self, but nothing that is oppressive to society and thereby threatens the development of the individual. Dörmann's text comprehends the voice of the self only as the miserable victim of isolation.]

But his own original work brings out more familiar Baudelairean motifs (ugliness, sexuality, criminality), albeit only to reject them again. Dörmann was the mediator of a domesticated *Fleurs du mal*, as the Viennese environment required, sensitized as it was to the threats of the subconscious but wishing to suppress them in public.

Dörmann is perhaps an epigone of a special kind, representing not so much superficiality of response as a missed opportunity in Baudelaire reception, his literary instincts suppressed by the force of his social circumstances. But he is in other respects characteristic of Viennese literature of the time, '[die] mithilfe des Rekurses auf die französischen Vorbilder *sich ihrer Identität bewußt geworden war*' [which had become aware of its own identity by turning to French models].[108] Wendelin Schmidt-Dengler treats this search for identity essentially in a social context, the attempts—whether or not ending in failure—of modern man to come to terms with the growth of the city, greater awareness of the subconscious, the aesthetic function of the ugly. To imply, however, that Hofmannsthal's reception of Baudelaire was comparable to the general trend in the 1890s, less a thoughtful response to the implications of *Les Fleurs du mal* than the use of Baudelaire's name as a shibboleth of culture, is to underestimate Hofmannsthal's depth of feeling about the French tradition.[109]

What makes Hofmannsthal's circumstances exceptional is partly his particularly close dealings with Hermann Bahr and Stefan George, who performed an important mediating function in the development of his ideas on Symbolism. The circumstances of George's sudden appearance in Vienna in December 1891 provide material for a brief assessment here of the more general effect on Hofmannsthal of his experience of Symbolism. George had been familiar with Paris since March 1889, living in the quarter favoured by the Symbolists, and through Albert Saint-Paul he had rapidly gained an entrée into literary circles.[110] He attended some meetings and dinners of the writers' group

---

[108] *From Vormärz to Fin de Siècle*, 78; my italics.

[109] Adopting the term 'Stilverdrehungsmanie' highlighted by Hoppe, Schmidt-Dengler applies it indiscriminately to all the *Jung Wien* writers.

[110] Saint-Paul collaborated on the most important symbolist periodicals, *La Wallonie*, *Écrits pour l'art*, *L'Ermitage* and *Mercure*. *La Wallonie* was the work mainly of Albert Mockel, but on its editorial committee were such as Mallarmé, Moréas, Merrill, Vielé-Griffin, Louÿs, Gide and Valéry.

La Plume where he met Moréas, Régnier, Merrill, and Verlaine, who signed a copy of *Sagesse* for him. At Mallarmé's famous *mardis* in the Rue de Rome he was introduced to Vielé-Griffin, Gustave Kahn and Pierre Louÿs, but apparently he remained reverentially silent at these gatherings. Before leaving Paris in August, he attended the burial of one of Verlaine's 'Poètes maudits', Villiers de l'Isle-Adam, where Mallarmé read a two-and-a-half-hour homily.[111]

Albert Saint-Paul claims to have introduced George to *Les Fleurs du mal* and encouraged him to transport the ethos of Symbolism to Germany. George's transcriptions of some of the French poems that most impressed him have been preserved, and as well as the Romantics Lamartine and Leconte de Lisle, and Parnassian poets such as Coppée and Hérédia, they include selections from Verlaine, Mallarmé, Gustave Kahn, Laforgue, Moréas, Rimbaud and Verhaeren, many poems by de Régnier, some from Bertrand's *Gaspard de la nuit*, and some excerpts from Maeterlinck's *Serres chaudes*. In his *Nachlaß* there is a sheet of notes on literature, made about 1892, which contains the following, apparently hasty, remarks on Symbolism:

Es giebt zwei getrennte arten von Symbolismus einer für das ganze bild und ein anderer für das einzelne wort. Es giebt noch eine dritte art. In den versen steht mehr als sie beim ersten anblick vermuten lassen. Es ist noch ein lesen zwischen den zeilen erforderlich. Das nebenherlaufen eines andern was nicht unbedingt nötig ist.[112]

[There are two separate kinds of Symbolism, one for the image as a whole, and another for the single word. There is also a third kind. In the poetry there is more than at first meets the eye. It is necessary to read between the lines. Something else, something not strictly essential, runs alongside.]

The last sentence is surprising, as it denies a dimension of Symbolism important to Mallarmé in particular and far from being not strictly essential. George goes on to distinguish the different poets: Mallarmé's new 'frisson' is reached 'durch einen sinnverachtenden fluss von gewählten klingenden worten' [by a flow of carefully selected, resonant words that pay no attention to the sense]; Verlaine's by a combination of simplicity and extreme refinement, enchantment, 'Bezauberung', in form and meaning; Maeterlinck's 'durch eine sehr ersonnene schauerverursachende einfachheit' [by a most carefully considered

[111] Cf. Cornell, *The Symbolist Movement*, 88–9; Friedrich Wolters, *Stefan George und die Blätter für die Kunst* (Berlin: Bondi, 1930), 22; Boehringer, *Mein Bild*, i. 201–6 (for George's correspondence with Mallarmé).

[112] Sohnle (ed.), *George/Symbolismus*, 91–2.

simplicity that sends a shiver down the spine]. These descriptions all share a propensity for the non-rational. Saint-Paul saw George unambiguously as the Symbolists' heir, 'er scheint unter den Gestirnen Baudelaires... Mallarmés und Verlaines zu stehen. Der Symbolismus übt seine Anziehungskraft auf ihn aus' [seems to stand under the star of Baudelaire, Mallarmé and Verlaine. Symbolism is exercising its powers of attraction over him].[113]

On 9 January 1892 George gave Hofmannsthal a handwritten transcript of Mallarmé's 'L'Après-midi d'un faune' from Paris as a souvenir. It was between visits to Paris, troubled by nostalgia for his happiness there, that George began his translations of Baudelaire, the first thirty-seven of which appeared in a limited edition on 21 December 1891.[114] Hofmannsthal's diary for the same date reads,

Stefan George. (Baudelaire, Verlaine, Mallarmé, Poe, Swinburne.)
'Unsere Classiker waren nur Plastiker des Stils, noch nicht Maler u. Musiker.'[115]

That the last phrase—'our classic authors were merely stylistic sculptors, not yet painters and musicians'—is one of George's formulations is suggested by the quotation marks; Saint-Paul's early essay also focuses on 'une expression plus claire et plus plastique' [a clearer and more plastic form of expression] as George's heritage from Baudelaire, and Mockel recalls that George himself said as much.[116] Hofmannsthal quotes the phrase again in July 1892 (*RA* iii. 349), and Andrian reports a related comment made by Hofmannsthal early in 1894: 'Wir die Wiener Dichter von heute, wir werden einmal eine Stelle in der Literatur haben wie die "parnassiens"—weil wir in der Form sehr vollendet sind' [we, the Viennese poets of today, will one day have a place in literary history like the Parnassians—because we are so formally perfect]—which in the light of George's lapidary opinion will have been regarded both as an achievement and as a deficiency.[117]

---

[113] *L'Ermitage*, 2 (1891), 585. Quoted from Sohnle (ed.), *George/Symbolismus*, 96, editor's translation.

[114] In the 'Vorrede zu Saint-John Perse "Anabasis"' Hofmannsthal notes 'auch Baudelaire ist nie übersetzt worden, trotz sich immer wiederholender Versuche' (*RA* iii. 146), which is almost a snub to George.

[115] *RA* iii. 340. Orthography from the manuscript, *Nachlaß*, H VII 17.110.

[116] Albert Saint-Paul, 'Stefan George et le Symbolisme français', *Revue d'Allemagne et des pays de langue allemande*, 13/14 (1928), 403; Albert Mockel, 'Quelques Souvenirs sur Stefan George', *Revue d'Allemagne*, 2 (1928), 392. Cf. also Carl August Klein, 'Über Stefan George: Eine neue Kunst', *Blätter für die Kunst*, 1.2 (1892), 46.

[117] 'Andrian über Hofmannsthal', 8.

Less permanent but equally immediate were the conversations about George's friends and acquaintances, their works and George's own works. Such conversations must have provided a fuller stock of personalities and literary guidelines than Hofmannsthal could have gained from any number of critical essays. And then at a third level of familiarity are the echoes of the French poets in George to which Hofmannsthal must now have been alert, 'translations' in a broader sense. *Algabal*, for example, is for Franz Norbert Mennemeier nothing short of an attempt at translating French Decadence into the alien territory of German literature.[118] More precisely, Mallarmé's 'Ouverture ancienne', Baudelaire's 'Rêve parisien' (from *Les Fleurs du mal*) and 'L'Invitation au voyage' (from *Le Spleen de Paris*) supply several features of Algabal's 'Unterreich'[119]—the metallic landscapes, for example, magically studded with jewels and punctuated with mysterious lakes, all organized by an omnipotent poet-creator, who lurks also behind Hofmannsthal's Emperor of China.[120]

George's personal relationship with Hofmannsthal has been thoroughly analysed and the various stages of its disintegration presented and explained. It is clear that George hoped for a close personal and poetic collaboration that Hofmannsthal was unwilling to entertain, personally most probably because he was unwilling to respond in kind to George's homosexual advances, poetically because he was disinclined to take the role of permanent acolyte. That Hofmannsthal was confused and ambivalent about aspects of his sexuality that George made him aware of, or confirmed, is also very probable. 'Einem, der

[118] Mennemeier, *Literatur der Jahrhundertwende*, 56.

[119] First indicated at the time by Richard M. Meyer, 'Ein neuer Dichterkreis', *Preußische Jahrbücher*, 88 (1897), 35. See also H. J. Meessen, 'Stefan Georges *Algabal* und die französische *Décadence*', *Monatshefte für Deutschunterricht*, 39 (1947), 309–10; Enid Duthie, *L'Influence du symbolisme français dans le renouveau poétique de l'Allemagne* (Paris: Champion, 1933), 231–4, and Ursula Franklin, 'The Quest for the Black Flower: Baudelairean and Mallarméan Inspirations in Stefan George's *Algabal*', *Comparative Literature Studies*, 16 (1979), 131–40.

[120] There are Baudelaire echoes in George's later work, too. For example, the litany of paradoxes in 'Ich bin der Eine und bin Beide' (*Der Stern des Bundes*, in Stefan George, *Werke. Ausgabe in zwei Bänden* (Düsseldorf: Küpper-Bondi, 1958), i. 359) compared with Baudelaire's 'Je suis la plaie et le couteau! | Je suis le soufflet et la joue' from 'L'Héautontimorouménos' in *Les Fleurs du mal* (Baudelaire, *Œuvres complètes*, ed. Claude Pichois, 2 vols., Bibliothèque de la Pléiade (Paris: Gallimard, 1975–6), i. 79), noted by Werner Vordtriede, 'Direct Echoes of French Poetry in Stefan George's Works', *Modern Language Notes*, 60 (1945), 462. Manfred Durzak also suggests persuasively that 'L'Albatros' (i. 9–10) is part of the inspiration for 'Der Herr der Insel' (i. 69–70): cf. *Der junge Stefan George* (Munich: Fink, 1968), 59–60 Despite this, Ockenden is right to say that with *Hymnen*, *Pilgerfahrten* and *Algabal* 'George's evident debt to the Symbolists is largely paid': cf. 'Stefan George and the Heritage of Romanticism', in Hanne Castein and Alexander Stillmark (eds.), *Deutsche Romantik und das 20. Jahrhundert* (Stuttgart: Heinz, 1986), 42.

vorübergeht', the poem that Hofmannsthal sent him on 21 December
1891, begins, 'Du hast mich an Dinge gemahnet | Die heimlich in mir
sind' [you have urged me to recognize things that are secretly present
within me], and the secret, unacknowledged aspects to which
Hofmannsthal refers may very well have been sexual.[121] But there is
also an overtly artistic dimension to this poem and it is certainly in part
a grateful homage to the man who most immediately stimulated
Hofmannsthal's poetic production with the example of his own and
the French Symbolists' poetry.[122]

As long as George's own interest in Symbolism could remain intellectual and distant, he was prepared to acknowledge his Parisian
friends, as 'Franken' from *Der Siebente Ring* and the fulsome praise of
Mallarmé and Verlaine in *Tage und Taten* indicate.[123] But when it
appeared to be threatening his reputation, he began to repudiate his
artistic ancestry, and when Merrill planned an article for *La Plume*
indicating George's debt to Baudelaire in *Algabal*, George wrote:

autrefois on appelait tout ce qu'on ne comprenait pas 'décadent' maintenant on dit
'symboliste' demain ce sera autre chose. Ainsi autrefois on m'a appelé disciple de
Baudelaire, aujourd'hui je suis disciple de Verlaine demain je serai disciple de
Mallarmée [*sic*]! Petites ignorances qui m'amusent.[124]

[people used to call everything they did not understand 'Decadent'; now they call
it 'Symbolist'; tomorrow they will call it something else. In the same way, people
used to call me a disciple of Baudelaire, now I am the disciple of Verlaine, and
tomorrow I shall be the disciple of Mallarmé! I am amused by such trivial manifestations of ignorance.]

George was embarrassed to implicate his poetry in petty debates over
unstable terminology—'Decadence' and 'Symbolism' were not robust
enough terms to contain him—and he was reluctant to accept the
implications of the word 'disciple'. But there is arrogance, too, in his
implicit disdain for the judgements of others and in his refusal to accept
masters. In the first volume of the *Blätter* Klein wrote about George's
'neue Kunst', denying any influence from France and insisting on 'das
grundverschiedene seines verfahrens von dem der Franzosen' [the

[121] For a reading that stresses this possibility, see Jens Rieckmann, '(Anti-)Semitism and
Homoeroticism: Hofmannsthal's Reading of Bahr's Novel "Die Rotte Korah"', *German
Quarterly*, 66 (1993), 218–20.
[122] For other aspects of this poem and the closely related sonnet 'Der Prophet', see
Chapters 3 and 4 below.
[123] George, *Werke*, i. 235–6 and ii. 285–91.
[124] Sohnle (ed.), *George/Symbolismus*, 103. Probably from 1893 or 1894, and probably a draft
reply to Merrill's proposal (see ibid. 117–18).

fundamental differences between the way George and the French write].[125] The article was certainly influenced by George himself. Contrast this with the views of Mockel and Saint-Paul adumbrated above and both opinions are transparently partisan, the French anxious to see their contribution recognized and their developments disseminated, the Germans equally anxious to defend George's originality. It was defiant attitudes such as this that also infected George's personal dealings, and finally wrecked his all-too-shaky friendship with Hofmannsthal.[126] The infection was passed, as it were, to Hofmannsthal: Alewyn writes of their correspondence that Hofmannsthal is nowhere else less characteristically himself, 'nirgends läßt er sich in der Wortwahl und dem Tonfall mehr von der Diktion des Partners beeinflussen, die wie aus dem Französischen übersetzt klingt' [nowhere else does he allow himself to be so influenced in his vocabulary and tone by his correspondent's diction, which sounds as if it has been translated from French].[127] French Symbolism, to which Hofmannsthal and *Jung Wien* turned in a search for identity, inhibited the development of identity when combined with the personal presence of George. This pattern is repeated on the literary level, as Chapters 3 and 4 will show.

The situation with Hermann Bahr was rather different, however. He was the victim of relentless animosity from many contemporaries—such as Kraus, who consistently despised him for being guilty of a 'sell-out of ethical integrity' for the sake of journalistic popularity[128]—and he was for many years seen as merely chameleon-like in his ability to adopt the new colours of whatever was the most recent literary style. Bahr is more respected now for his 'uncanny percipience of *future* trends',[129] and although his contribution to the development of Austrian literature at the turn of the century has been extensively assessed,[130] his influence on the young Hofmannsthal was probably greater than is generally assumed. Hofmannsthal was occasionally given to overestimating the literary capabilities of his friends—he often

[125] *Die Blätter für die Kunst*, 1. 2 (1892), 46.

[126] Cf. Adorno's concept of 'Haltung' in this context: Theodor W. Adorno, 'George und Hofmannsthal: Zum Briefwechsel', in *Prismen: Kulturkritik und Gesellschaft* (Frankfurt a.M.: Suhrkamp, 1955), 238–41.

[127] Richard Alewyn, *Über Hugo von Hofmannsthal* (Göttingen: Vandenhoeck & Ruprecht, 1967), 31.

[128] Cf. Timms, *Karl Kraus*, 52.

[129] Cf. Andrew Barker, ' "Der große Überwinder" ', *Modern Language Review*, 78 (1983), 625; my italics.

[130] See in particular the works by Barker, Daviau, Chastel and Streim in the Bibliography.

declared, for example, that Andrian was a far greater artist than he would ever be—but those to whom he was most attached were usually worthy of serious respect, never merely hawkers of catch-phrases. This was the case with Bahr, and not even Schnitzler, who sometimes had pangs of jealousy, could write more negatively in his diary than, 'ueber Andrians Buch, das Hugo überschätzt und über Bahr, den er mindestens ethisch überschätzt' [about Andrian's book, which Hugo overestimates, and about Bahr, whom he at least ethically over-estimates].[131] Not even this was wholly true, however, for one of Hofmannsthal's diary notes from the period reads 'Bahr spielt mit den Weltanschauungen der Menschen, wie die Meerkatzen in der Hexenküche mit der gläsernen Welt' [Bahr plays with people's world-views as the monkeys in the witch's kitchen play with the glass globe].[132] Toying kittenishly with delicate viewpoints—which are hollow inside, as the Monkey's commentary in *Faust* explains—was Bahr's speciality, and his uncomplicated enthusiasm is why Hofmannsthal took him seriously.[133] Making notes in 1917 for *Ad me ipsum*, Hofmannsthal puts under the heading 'Youth', 'Frühe Berühmtheit. Hermann Bahr, George. Das frühere Wien' [early fame. Hermann Bahr, George. Vienna as it was; *RA* iii. 616]. Much later in the list come Beer-Hofmann, Andrian and Frau von Wertheimstein, and for Bahr even to have a place amongst, let alone to head, such company gives him exceptional personal significance. Hofmannsthal even planned a biography of Bahr.[134]

Their friendship began promisingly. When they met in the Café Griensteidl on 27 April 1891, Hofmannsthal noted the meeting in his diary as a privilege: 'Heute im Caféhaus Hermann Bahr vorgestellt' [introduced to Hermann Bahr in the Café today]. This contrasts with Schnitzler's note for the same day, which, without lacking warmth, suggests less immediate intimacy and more measured observation: 'Hermann Bahr im Kfh. kennen gelernt. Liebenswürdig freier Mensch; im Gesicht Roheit, Geist, Güte, Schwindelhaftigkeit' [met

---

[131] Schnitzler, *Tagebuch 1893–1902*, ed. Werner Welzig et al. (Vienna: Verlag der Öster-reichischen Akademie der Wissenschaften, 1989), 131–2; entry for 25 Mar. 1895.

[132] *RA* iii. 368; cf. J. W. von Goethe, *Werke. Hamburger Ausgabe in 14 Bänden*, ed. Erich Trunz (Munich: Beck, 1981), iii. 77.

[133] Whilst it is fair not to assume that interest was always matched by commitment in Bahr, it is exaggerated to claim, as Daviau does, that Bahr was 'never an advocate of any particular artistic method or style': 'The Misconception of Hermann Bahr as a "Verwand-lungskünstler"', *German Life and Letters*, 11 (1957–8), 191.

[134] *Nachlaß*, H VII 6 (a few loosely structured scribbles on the back page of a journal note-book).

Hermann Bahr in the Café. An amiably easygoing person; his face
has traces of coarseness, wit, goodness and guile].[135] Bahr for his part
was keenly interested in Hofmannsthal, albeit not for the same reasons
as George was to be, even if his own description of that first meeting
is distinctly coquettish: 'Er lacht, gibt mir die Hand, eine weiche,
streichelnde, unwillkürlich caressante Hand der großen Amourösen,
wie die leise, zähe Schmeichelei verblaßter Seide, und sagt
beruhigend: ich bin nämlich Loris' [He laughs, holds out his hand, the
soft, stroking, involuntarily caressing hand of the great lovers, like
the soft and tender flattery of faded silk, and says reassuringly: *I
am Loris*].[136] The following day Hofmannsthal and Bahr fell into a
lively, even intimate conversation, and Hofmannsthal felt that even
when Bahr was talking to everyone, he was really addressing him
alone (flattered no doubt that Hofmannsthal had read the recently
published volume of his essays, *Zur Kritik der Moderne*).[137] 'Beim Aus-
einandergehen vor seinem Haus', concludes Hofmannsthal, 'ver-
sprach er unaufgefordert, mich zu besuchen' [when we parted
company at the door of his house, he spontaneously promised to visit
me]. Their motives seem obvious and well matched. Bahr wished to
cultivate the rising star, who had already reviewed one of his plays very
stylishly; Hofmannsthal was an impressionable 17, eager to associate
with an influential and controversial critical figure with experience
that matched and exceeded his own interests in France and French
literature.

Bahr had gone to Paris in November 1888 after military service and
turbulent years at university, and on being told that his father would
finance only one more year of study. 'Mein ganzes Wesen schrie:
Paris!' [my whole being screamed 'Paris!'], he wrote in his autobiography.[138] This was not initially for reasons of unthinking Francophilia,
but because he realized that Germany was unable to provide the
impetus to *progress* that was being offered then by France and its culture
(in the narrow sense of the word):

Ich hatte in Berlin zunächst Zola, Daudet und überhaupt die französischen
Naturalisten, nebenher auch Musset, die George Sand und Rousseau gelesen; wir
holten uns ja damals aus Frankreich die Merkworte der Erneuerung, auf die wir
selber hofften.

[135] *RA* iii. 328; Schnitzler, *Tagebuch 1879–1892*, 327. 'Kennen gelernt' instead of 'vorgestellt'
is less deferential, perhaps because they were closer in age.
[136] Bahr, 'Loris', *Die Freie Bühne*, 3.1 (Jan. 1892), 96, then in *Studien*, 125–6.
[137] Cf. *RA* iii. 328; note from 28 Apr. 1891.
[138] Hermann Bahr, *Selbstbildnis* (Berlin: S. Fischer, 1923), 215.

[In Berlin I had read first Zola, Daudet and the French Naturalists in general, then Musset, too, George Sand and Rousseau; at that time we found in France the tokens of the renewal that we were hoping for ourselves.]

Once installed in a café near Verlaine's favourite haunt, *La Vachette*, Bahr borrowed from the *bouquinistes* and read Balzac, Flaubert, the Goncourts, Villiers de l'Isle-Adam, and above all Huysmans and Barrès.[139] The central experience was of the place and function of form: 'das war mein Pariser Erlebnis, entscheidend für alle Zukunft: das Geheimnis der Form ging mir auf' [that was my Parisian experience, and it was decisive for the rest of my life: the secret of form was revealed to me],[140] a secret lost to German literature, he claims, since the Baroque. It is summarized in Zola's famous aphorism from *Le Roman expérimental*, 'une phrase bien faite est une bonne action' [a well-made sentence is a good deed].[141] The sensation of reversing the Duchess's dictum, of taking care of the sounds and letting the sense take care of itself, was new and exciting for him. It led to a complete reinterpretation of French Naturalism—the understanding that it was a reaction against Romanticism and as much a part of *literary* tradition as Classicism.[142]

Bahr's novel *Die gute Schule* (1890) describes the effect of Paris on a young Austrian provincial clearly modelled on himself, and a letter to his father describes a social life that could have been modelled on a novel by Balzac:

Die lustigste und geistreichste Gesellschaft von Paris, junge Maler, Musiker, Dichter, Bildhauer . . . Schauspieler und Schauspielerinnen . . . alle bereits ein wenig verlebt und darum begierig nach irgend einer ganz neuen Art der Unterhaltung und der Tollheit, nach dem 'Inconnu'.[143]

[The jolliest and wittiest Parisian society, young painters, musicians, poets, sculptors, actors and actresses, all of them already a little dissipated and therefore thirsty for a brand new form of entertainment and madness, for the 'Unknown'.]

'L'Inconnu' is the destination of the travellers in 'Le Voyage', the last poem of Baudelaire's *Les Fleurs du mal*, and is where 'le nouveau' is to be found. Bahr describes his life in literary terms because literature was the focus of his Parisian experience. Baudelaire was important: '[er]

---

[139] Cf. Émile Chastel, *Hermann Bahr: Son Œuvre et son temps* (Lille: Champion, 1977), 253.
[140] Bahr, *Selbstbildnis*, 221.
[141] Quoted in Bahr, *Prophet der Moderne: Tagebücher 1888–1904*, ed. Reinhard Farkas (Vienna: Böhlau, 1987), 40; entry for 7 Jan. 1889.
[142] Bahr, *Selbstbildnis*, 224. Cf. Barker, 'Der große Überwinder', 621.
[143] Bahr, *Tagebücher*, 32 (undated). Cf. also Fischer, *Fin-de-siècle*, 100–14.

war's, der mir zunächst die Bahn der Schönheit wies, und in Théophile Gautiers Vorwort zu den Fleurs du Mal fand ich sozusagen das Vokabular meines Glaubens an die Kunst' [it was Baudelaire who first showed me the path that beauty took, and in Théophile Gautier's preface to *Les Fleurs du mal* I found so to speak the vocabulary of my faith in art].[144] Bahr describes what Baudelaire and modern writers had in common:

Ein einziges Gemeinsames war es, das sie zusammenhielt ... die Liebe zur Schönheit der Form, la phrase bien dite, der Cultus der reinen Form . . . . Aber außer [Baudelaire], diese echt künstlerische Leidenschaft charakterisiert überhaupt die moderne Literatur der Franzosen, seit dem Ausgang der Romantik.[145]

[They were held together by a single thing that they had in common, by a love for the beauty of form, the well-crafted phrase, the worship of pure form. But apart from Baudelaire, this genuinely artistic passion characterizes all of modern French literature since the end of Romanticism.]

Comparing the diaries with *Selbstbildnis*, it is easy to see how the ardour is preserved. Bahr quotes extensively from Gautier's introduction to *Les Fleurs du mal*, clearly having reread it for the purpose, and becomes so carried away in his response that he forgets to paragraph. The style is repetitive and crudely incantatory, but the prose glows with commitment:

Jedes Wort ist zunächst eine Lautgemeinschaft von Vokalen und Konsonanten: Laute ziehen einander geheimnisvoll an, stoßen einander geheimnisvoll ab, und aus diesem Liebesleben von einander suchenden und fliehenden Lauten entsteht die Sprache, zunächst mehr Gebärde, mehr Gestalt als Sinn, den sie später erst, gleichsam um sich vor sich selber zu rechtfertigen, zögernd und ungewiß heranzieht. Dieses Urleben der Sprachen wiederholt sich in den Dichtern; der Dichter hört den Worten ihr geheimes, noch nicht in den Dienst der Verständigung gezwängtes, noch von Zwecken unberührtes Wesen ab.[146]

[Every word is first and foremost a phonetic community of vowels and consonants: sounds mysteriously attract each other, mysteriously repel each other, and it is out of the courtship of sounds seeking and avoiding each other that language itself emerges, at first more as gesture, more as shape than as meaning—which it only later draws in, tentatively and uncertainly, in order to justify itself to itself. The primal life of language is repeated in poets; the poet taps into the secret essence of words, the essence that has not yet been pressed into the service of comprehension, and is not yet tainted by functionality.]

---

[144] Bahr, *Selbstbildnis*, 227.   [145] Bahr, *Tagebücher*, 47.   [146] Bahr, *Selbstbildnis*, 229.

This is what Bahr will have passed on to Hofmannsthal from his experiences in Paris.

From May 1890 until March 1891 Bahr was in Berlin as co-editor of the *Freie Bühne für Modernes Leben* with Otto Brahm and Arno Holz—and found the German capital dull and backward.[147] By April 1891 he was in Vienna again, and slipped easily back into the coffee-house habits of his student days. He attempted to gain a posting as literature correspondent for the *Neue Freie Presse* in Paris, but settled for Vienna after all, and from November lived there until 1912. His journalism expanded rapidly, and he worked with E. M. Kafka on *Moderne Dichtung* whilst simultaneously diverting the newly refounded *Freie Bühne* away from its previous Naturalist course. He raised his social profile by joining the groups in the Café Griensteidl, meeting Salten and Beer-Hofmann as well as Hofmannsthal and Schnitzler. In 1892 he joined the *Deutsche Zeitung* and from February 1893 became the reviewer for Burgtheater performances. His reviews of both art and the theatre consolidated his popularity—and notoriety. By December, when he fell out with Leo Auspitzer (co-proprietor of the *Deutsche Zeitung*), he had established contact with Isidor Singer and Heinrich Kanner, and with them later co-founded *Die Zeit*, of whose *feuilleton* he was editor until 1899: as such he is said to have been the one responsible for introducing the most recent manifestations of Western European culture to Vienna.[148] Meanwhile, of course, he continued to write for the *Wiener Mode, Neue Revue* and *Neues Wiener Tagblatt*. Persistent and vociferous, Bahr was extraordinarily important in Hofmannsthal's Vienna. He had first-hand experience of France, the French and their literature and had developed his tastes with considerable integrity. His championship of France derived not from a rejection of things German or Austrian (on the contrary, he was often the first to recognize and foster native talent) but from the conviction that France had found the way forward first.[149]

Hofmannsthal's review of Bahr's play *Die Mutter* appeared in the *Moderne Rundschau* for 15 April, less than a fortnight before they were introduced. Despite his relative inexperience, the review contains some fierce artistic challenges to Bahr. To judge by this piece, their first

---

[147] Cf. letter to Alois Bahr, 6 July 1890, quoted in *Tagebücher*, 33–4.

[148] Cf. Reinhard Urbach, 'Hermann Bahrs Wien', *Literatur und Kritik*, 199/200 (1985), 404.

[149] Daviau locates the consistent core underlying Bahr's rapidly changing opinions as a concern for 'Alt-Österreich', which is confirmed by Bahr's own claims later in life (Daviau, 'Verwandlungskünstler', 182). In the early years, however, cosmopolitanism was his hallmark.

public 'engagement' and thus in a sense the real beginning of their acquaintanceship, the balance of the relationship must have been at best precarious, and from the first Hofmannsthal seems to have called the tune. He begins with an account of Bahr's earlier volume, *Zur Kritik der Moderne*, and writes of his admiration for his robust commitment to the business of living, portraying him as a figure who does not limit his vision and activity with aims less than life for life's sake: 'er lebt sein Leben, wie man ein entdecktes, erworbenes, teuer erkauftes genießt, er trinkt es, langsam schlürfend, vollbewußt' [he lives his life in the way that one enjoys something one has discovered, acquired, bought dearly, he drinks it, in slow draughts, fully aware; *RA* i. 100]. The life that is so energetically pursued—'dieses Leben, mit seinen starren Formen und Formeln, dies System gedankenlos ineinandergreifender Räder und Rädchen, diese selbstverständliche Aufeinanderfolge entseelter Erscheinungen' [this life with its rigid forms and formulae, this system of mindlessly interlocking wheels and cogs, this sequence of soulless phenomena that we take for granted]—is lived in the conviction that there is behind it 'etwas Großes, Wirkliches, ein unbegreiflich hohes Wunder' [something great, real, an unimaginably lofty miracle]. Hofmannsthal agrees that Bahr, to his credit, has experienced this. But this rhetorically exaggerated goal is brutally deflated in the next clause: 'und seitdem hat er nichts erfahren' [and since then he has experienced nothing]. From then on, Bahr's experiences are reduced to the level of intellectual playthings: 'er sieht allerlei Besonderes, aber er sieht es nicht besonders' [he sees all sorts of exceptional things, but he does not see them in an exceptional way]. His attitude is described as 'kokettier[en] mit der Lebensbejahung' [flirting with the affirmation of life], such that a discrepancy is implied between seriousness of undertaking and frivolity of approach, and this is seen as a phase of development that was eminently suitable for the young Bahr but one which he should now have outgrown. The *coup de grâce* for *Zur Kritik der Moderne* is delivered in the last sentence of the first paragraph: ' "Choses vues" hat Victor Hugo auf sein Lebensausgangs-buch geschrieben' [Victor Hugo's last book was called 'Things Seen'] —implying that such a nobly understated achievement might poten-tially be true of Bahr, too. Instead, Hofmannsthal suggests that ' "Choses entrevues" könnte auf diesem erwartungsreichen Lebens-eingangsbuch stehen' ['Things Glimpsed' might serve for this expec-tant first book], which is downright rude.

Hofmannsthal thinks that Bahr has failed to confront the central artistic problem that should have engaged him in *Die Mutter*, namely a synthesis of brutal reality and lyrical refinement, the transition from mere Naturalism to a new literature of great mystical unity (*RA* i. 104). This echoes Bahr's own Ibsen essay, recently reprinted in *Zur Kritik der Moderne*, which asserts that 'die Synthese von Naturalismus und Romantik ist die gegenwärtige Aufgabe der Litteratur' [the task that faces modern literature is the synthesis of Naturalism and Romanticism].[150] But *Die Mutter* does not tackle the problem head-on, according to Hofmannsthal. Bahr's play attempts too much, is too naturalistically detailed but fails to construct a sense of organic unity. Its milieux and characters are not genuine, but are products of a dilettantish spirit—which Hofmannsthal at one point calls 'Baude-lairismus' or '[die] Darstellung des Angelebten' [Baudelaireism: the depiction of things lived vicariously; *RA* i. 103]—and the play is mere vulgar Romanticism. And for Hofmannsthal at this point, Romanti-cism has no intrinsic worth: 'sie ist Krankheit der reinen Kunst' [it is a disease of pure art; *RA* i. 102]. There is a brief note of encourage-ment, for example, as both Bahr and German Naturalism are described as 'noch so jung, sehr, sehr jung—hoffentlich' [still so young, so very, very young—I hope], but this is rather lordly for a 17-year-old tyro. And there is some genuine enthusiasm for Bahr's virtuosic presentation of the enervated atmosphere of Paris, the harder and crueller mood in Berlin and the exoticism of Romania, but the mixture is a cocktail of too many tastes that clash rather than blend.[151] This is the heart of the problem, and illustrative at least as much of Hofmannsthal's literary situation in the 1890s as of Bahr's: there is no core, no centre to hold together the various centrifugally spinning individual features.

Bahr may have felt the common ground, too, for otherwise it is odd that under these circumstances a personal meeting less than a fortnight later turned out so positively. Bahr's public reaction in his essay 'Loris' (published in the *Freie Bühne* for January 1892) was favourable, too: 'mit so viel Grazie wurde ich von ihm zerzaust und zerzupft, dass ich es vielmehr wie eine Liebkosung empfand' [I was ruffled and plucked at with such grace that I took it more as a caress].[152] He wrote that he thought the review was either by a Frenchman or a middle-aged

---

[150] Bahr, *Zur Kritik der Moderne*, 59–79.

[151] Cf. the negative 'Exkurs 2' in Wunberg, *Der frühe Hofmannsthal* (Stuttgart: Kohlhammer, 1965), 131. Wunberg even suggests, 'ob er [Bahr] überhaupt dichterischen und künst-lerischen Geschmack besessen hat, ist noch nicht erwiesen' (129).

[152] Bahr, *Studien*, 123.

Viennese. Bahr's description of their first meeting is slightly different from Hofmannsthal's in the note quoted above, but the whole essay is so obviously a sentimentalized version of their relationship that it has little value as documentary evidence of the events. Perhaps Bahr was thick-skinned or generously willing to let a young man have his head; perhaps he had an eye to the main chance, for if Hofmannsthal was to be a major figure, it was as well to be associated with him from the outset. The fact that the play of styles over an ever-receding core was also Hofmannsthal's problem may also explain how the review came to have no appreciable negative effect on the incipient friendship of the two men: if they were both circling round a common difficulty, both at the mercy of the ups and downs of a complex art/society, style/object relationship, a critical review may not have had the same force as it does in retrospect.

The relationship between Hofmannsthal and Bahr was at first certainly one of friendship, even if it deteriorated as they grew older. Wunberg presents it as disastrous from the start, ending in frustration and mutual suspicion, but Hofmannsthal's diary notes and the few published letters suggest that initially there was almost no frustration to suppress. After their meeting his diary notes many visits, conversations and excursions, and he and Bahr even lived in the same house in the Salesianergasse for a while.[153] While tension with George forced its way into almost all the letters he and Hofmannsthal sent to each other, Hofmannsthal's to Bahr are cheeky, light-hearted and relaxed. He banters, shows off, scatters his notes with literary allusions and references to art, society and history. They became comfortably intimate—enough so for Schnitzler to complain privately, 'Hugo ist dem Bahr zu nah' [Hugo is too close to Bahr].[154]

Sondrup mentions the importance of Bahr in the development of Hofmannsthal's literary tastes, and attempts to demonstrate this by showing how closely Bahr's own views paralleled 'the essence of symbolist theory'.[155] But this is to confuse the object of Bahr's studies with his cast of mind. Bahr's early summaries and appreciations of French literature are unified by a distinctly un-Symbolist and often critical examination of how works of literature treat *life*.[156] He says, for

[153] See the dedicatory epistle to Andrian and Hofmannsthal in *Renaissance*, [n.p.]. Reprinted in Gotthart Wunberg (ed.), *Hofmannsthal im Urteil seiner Kritiker* (Frankfurt a. M.: Athenäum, 1972), 46–7.
[154] Schnitzler, *Tagebücher 1893–1902*, 165; entry for 21 Dec. 1895.
[155] Sondrup, *Hofmannsthal and the French Symbolist Tradition*, 24.
[156] Cf. Chastel, *Bahr*, 256–8.

example, that Edmond Goncourt's stage adaptation of Zola's *Germinie Lacerteux* is spoiled by its being just that, an adaptation of something essentially too novelistic: none the less its specific virtue is that it strives to represent a typically French attachment to life. French Naturalism is not theory-bound and precept-ridden, but directly concerned with the business of realistic presentation. Even though his stay in France alerted him to the importance of form and to the magic of language, Bahr never allowed these perceptions to divert him into characteristic Symbolist other-worldliness, and the suggestion that Bahr was himself in any sense a Symbolist should be resisted. In any case, an attempt to demonstrate influence by positing agreement is not a fruitful line of argument. In almost all their published work on similar topics Hofmannsthal and Bahr disagree, often apparently fundamentally. Certainly, Hofmannsthal's taste in French literature was directed, enriched, and refined by conversation and disagreement with his older friend, but Bahr's function was essentially to provide some of the raw material. His service to Hofmannsthal was not one of conversion to a set of principles that he espoused, rather it was to introduce him to a series of valued works, and these were at first not Symbolist but Decadent.

Bahr's opening claim in 'Die Überwindung des Naturalismus', that 'die Herrschaft des Naturalismus ist vorüber . . . sein Zauber ist gebrochen' [the reign of Naturalism is over, its spell is broken],[157] is precisely accurate: it registers not a break in tradition but a shift of attention that Bahr had been proclaiming since September 1890:

Die Neugierde der Lesenden und die Neigung der Schreibenden kehren sich von draußen wieder nach innen, vom Bilde des rings um uns zur Beichte des tief in uns, von dem *rendu de choses visibles* nach den *intérieurs d'âmes*—(das Wort gehört Stendhal).[158]

[Readers' curiosity and writers' inclinations are both turning back inwards again, away from showing what is around us to confessing what is deep within us, from giving an 'account of visible things' to revealing our 'innermost souls' (to use Stendhal's expression).]

The shift was taking place in France—as the 1889 essay 'Von deutscher Litteratur' pessimistically notes, surveying modern German authors of note and deciding, 'die Liste ist kurz; und ich fürchte sie ist

---

[157] Bahr, *Die Überwindung*, 152.
[158] 'Die Krisis des französischen Naturalismus', first published on 6 Sept. 1890, quoted from *Die Überwindung* (under the title 'Die Krise des Naturalismus'), 65.

vollständig' [the list is short, and I fear that it is complete].[159] By 1890, according to Bahr, Zola had given way to Decadence, analysed and criticized by Bourget:

Bourget, an dessen Beispiel sich der moderne Geschmack erst auf sich selbst besann, vereitelt uns den Frieden im Naturalismus. Der Naturalismus, aus dessen Gewohnheit sich der moderne Geschmack eine Serie von Bedürfnissen entnahm, vereitelt uns den Frieden im Bourget. Es gilt, allen beiden zu genügen, und dadurch alle beide zu überwinden.[160]

[Bourget, whose example first helped modern taste think about itself, is spoiling our peaceful enjoyment of Naturalism. Naturalism, familiarity with which gave rise to many of the necessities of modern taste, is spoiling our peaceful enjoyment of Bourget. We must satisfy both, and thereby overcome both.]

This represents a challenge to German-language authors to overcome Naturalism *and* Decadence, and one that Hofmannsthal took up. He probably owed his awareness of Paul Bourget to Bahr, who described Bourget's *Essais de psychologie contemporaine* in 'Die neue Psychologie' (August and September 1890). Hofmannsthal read at least some of these, as a note to the essay on Baudelaire confirms.[161] In the third section of this essay, 'Théorie du Décadence', Bourget posits a possible defence of the condition of cultural fragmentation, because the dissolution of social and mental structures has as its corollary a sharp heightening of sensibility. But this fails to answer 'le grand argument contre les décadences', namely 'qu'elles n'ont pas de lendemain' [the most important argument against Decadent movements, that they have no future]: the corollary is that 'ces littératures non plus n'ont pas de lendemain' [these forms of literature have no future either], which amounts to an accusation of epigonism for Baudelaire's successors.[162]

Hofmannsthal was interested, too, in the *Physiologie de l'amour moderne*, which he reviewed in *Die Moderne* in February 1891, before meeting Bahr but having read the earlier article, which is acknowledged in a footnote. He evidently associated Bourget and Bahr closely, since in a diary note, written within a fortnight after publishing the review, he contrasts the characteristics of the two writers:

---

[159] 'Von deutscher Litteratur', first publication unknown, reprinted in *Zur Kritik der Moderne*, 121–4.

[160] Bahr, *Die Überwindung*, 72.

[161] See Chapter 2, pp. 139–41, for the quotation and assessments of aspects of Hofmannsthal's attitude to Decadence.

[162] Bourget, *Œuvres complètes: Critique 1: Essais de psychologie contemporaine* (Paris: Plon, 1899), 17.

Hermann Bahr 'Kritik der	Bourget 'Essais de
Moderne'	psychologie'
polemisch teilnehmend	kritisch analysierend
geht vom Allgemeinen aus	läuft ins Allgemeine aus
sieht das Werdende,	sieht das Absterbende,
Gärende	Faulende[163]

[Hermann Bahr, *Critique of Modernism*, polemically engaged, starts out from generalities, focuses on things that are developing, fermenting. Bourget, *Essays on Psychology*, critically analytical, ends up with generalities, focuses on things that are dying, decaying.]

Bahr is firmly on the side of living and doing rather than watching and decaying, and as Tarot points out, Hofmannsthal's reading of Bourget in the review is nourished by his perception of Nietzsche in the background.[164] Bahr admires Bourget for having trumped Naturalism by formulating the psychological needs of the age,[165] and thereby getting closer to modern life: these were inexpressible in Naturalist works, he says, and Bourget returns to, and derives his literary authority from, pre-Naturalist styles. At root, Hofmannsthal agrees with Bourget's critique of fragmentation and his proposition that 'Einheit der Seele' [unity of soul] be cultivated instead of 'Zweiseelenkrankheit' [the disease of the divided soul; *RA* i. 96]. Ulrich Schultz-Buschhaus comments in this context that both authors are concerned with the same, or at least a similar ideal image of tradition as something fostering commitment, and that they are both opposed to the 'dilettantism' of the aesthetes and sceptics—a dilettantism that is both modern and symptomatic of a tradition in decline.[166] Hofmannsthal adds his own jab, too, when remarking on the high sales figures for the *Physiologie de l'amour moderne*. Most will have missed the point, he says, buying it in snobbish delight at the evocative skill with which Bourget sets up his aristocratic targets; but there is a place for him in the hearts of the tiny proportion of his readers who *are* the targets, 'ein paar Dilettanten—im alten hübschen Sinn dilettanti— . . . die darin nichts suchen als eine

---

[163] *RA* iii. 323; note of 23 Feb. 1892.

[164] Rolf Tarot, *Hugo von Hofmannsthal: Daseinsformen und dichterische Struktur* (Tübingen: Niemeyer, 1970), 40. Poems such as 'Verse auf einer Banknote geschrieben' (Oct. 1890), 'Gedankenspuk' (Dec. 1890) and 'Sünde des Lebens' (Jan. 1891) also show clear signs of Nietzsche's influence. Hofmannsthal also refers to Nietzsche as one of Bourget's sources in his review (*RA* i. 96).

[165] Bahr, *Die Überwindung*, 67.

[166] Ulrich Schulz-Buschhaus, 'Der Tod des "Dilettanten": Über Hofmannsthal und Paul Bourget', in Michael Rössner and Birgit Wagner (eds.), *Aufstieg und Krise der Vernunft* (Vienna: Böhlau, 1984), 192.

Seele, qui aiment à sentir sentir, wie der arme Claude so hübsch sagt'
[a few dilettanti—in the nice old sense of the word—who are looking
for nothing more than a soul, who love to feel themselves feeling, as
poor Claude says so nicely; *RA* i. 97]. Without the last clause and the
mocking repetition of 'hübsch', this might almost have been praise;
indeed there is something of the Dilettant's pleasure detectable in
Hofmannsthal's rich and self-indulgent style here and throughout his
review.[167] Schulz-Buschhaus considers that he adapted Bourget's
concerns, which were predominantly sociological, and applied them
to questions of a more subjective or psychological nature. But the fascination with Bourget's presentation of Dilettantism that Hofmannsthal
betrays suggests also, ironically, that Bourget actually contributed to
the sense of fragmentation felt by the Austrian, exacerbating the condition as well as providing a model for its critique.

Barrès oriented Hofmannsthal's appreciation of the change in
literary styles slightly differently from Bourget, in that Bahr's major
essays on Barrès are a response to Hofmannsthal's views and not vice
versa. Bahr first referred to Barrès's *Un homme libre* as early as August
1890, and he used it as ammunition in an attack on traditional notions
of truth in 1891. He reviewed Barrès's work to date in October 1892,
reported on a visit to the author in December 1892, and discussed him
yet again in February 1894.[168] On one occasion when they talked about
Barrès, Hofmannsthal records, 'er sprach, ich hörte zu' [he spoke, I
listened],[169] but this was early on, probably before he had read the
novels, and after a summer reading *Un homme libre*, *Sous l'œil des Barbares*
and *Le Jardin de Bérénice*,[170] Hofmannsthal had come to an independent
judgement.

Hofmannsthal reviewed Barrès's trilogy in a review published in
the *Moderne Rundschau* on 1 October 1891 and admired it, he said,
because it taught one how to live. He saw its analysis of the situation
of modern man precisely in the terms of his own criticisms of late

[167] Joëlle Stoupy writes merely of 'verarbeiten' as Hofmannsthal's mode of approach
to Bourget's ideas: 'Hofmannsthals Berührung mit dem Dilettantismusphänomen', in
Wolfram Mauser (ed.), *Hofmannsthal-Forschungen*, ix: *Hofmannsthal und Frankreich* (Freiburg
i.Br.: Hofmannsthal-Gesellschaft, 1987), 243.

[168] The essays are, respectively: 'Die neue Psychologie', in *Moderne Dichtung*, 1 Aug. 1890
and 1 Sept. 1890 (reprinted in *Zur Überwindung*, 101–17); 'Wahrheit! Wahrheit!', in *Die Nation*,
1891 (*Zur Überwindung*, 141–51); 'Maurice Barrès II', Oct. and Dec. 1892 (place unknown;
reprinted in *Studien*, 162–73); 'Maurice Barrès III', Feb. 1894 (origin unknown; *Studien*, 173–7).

[169] *RA* iii. 330; note of 25 May 1891.

[170] Cf. *SW* iii. 309. Some of this time was spent in Salzburg with Bahr (cf. diary entry for 16
July 1891, *SW* iii. 310).

nineteenth-century Vienna in the Bahr review, as lacking culture and style: 'ein Mittelpunkt fehlt, es fehlt die Form, der Stil' [there is no centre, there is no form, no style; *RA* i. 118]. The artistic and psychological consequences of this lack are serious:

erstarrte Formeln stehen bereit, durchs ganze Leben trägt uns der Strom des Überlieferten. . . . Wir denken die bequemsten Gedanken der andern und fühlens nicht, daß unser bestes Selbst allmählich abstirbt. Wir leben ein totes Leben. Wir ersticken unser Ich. (*RA* i. 118–19)

[petrified formulae stand ready, we are carried through the whole of our lives on the flood of tradition. We think the most comfortable thoughts of others and do not realize that our selves, the best part of us, is gradually dying away. We are living a dead life. We are stifling our very selves.]

For him Barrès's novels thus constituted a philosophy for living and he felt that the other's fame was that of a philosopher (*RA* i. 118). Bahr, in his essay of October 1892, was more blasé, regarding Barrès's combination of psychological insight and philosophical commonplace as the typical egocentrism of the lyric writer: 'es ist nur eine Marotte des Barrés [*sic*], sich philosophisch zu vermummen' [it is only a foible of Barrès's to get himself up as a philosopher]. As for Barrès's narcissistic self-contemplation, 'das hat man immer Lyrik genannt' [that has always been called poetry]. Instead of a system, Bahr saw mere poetic rhetoric:

Seine Lyrik . . . singt die Gefühle der künstlerischen Schöpfung, das Wehe und die Lust des Künstlers um die Kunst, allen Stolz, die vielen Entmuthungen und den Sieg. Und sie hat dazu eine neue Technik, ihre besondere Rhetorik, die ungewohnt leicht trägt: sie sagt Alles in Gleichnissen und Symbolen. Darum wird sie verkannt.[171]

[His poetry celebrates the feelings involved in artistic creation, the artist's pain and exaltation for the sake of his art, all his pride, the many discouragements and his triumph. And it has a new technique for doing this, its own particular rhetoric, one which is deceptive in an unusually gentle fashion: it says everything in allegories and symbols. That is why it is misjudged.]

Hofmannsthal might have thought this warning gratuitous; the loss of self became a component of the view of lyric that Hofmannsthal was to develop. But his inclination to interpret what he rejected in Barrès in systematic or philosophical terms, rather than to recognize its congruity with lyric creation, may have been in part defensive, to ward off the implications of this rejection for his own craft. George and the

---

[171] Bahr, *Studien*, 165.

debate over Symbolism ('Symbolistenstreit') were to initiate a development that brought this home more forcefully.

Perhaps in order to recapture the attention that George seemed to
monopolize, Bahr published his essay on Hofmannsthal ('Loris') in the
Freie Bühne in January 1892. It is flattering, anecdotal, and tinged with a
light eroticism. Hofmannsthal not only belongs to 'die Moderne', he
embraces it completely, from its earliest stirrings in the works of Zola
right up to the latest manifestations in Barrès and Maeterlinck;[172] he
will also initiate a new phase of modern writing, beyond dry experimentation, full of life and its pleasures. Meanwhile, however—and this
is a vital reservation, held back until the antepenultimate paragraph:

seine grosse Kunst hat kein Gefühl; es gibt in seiner Seele keine sentimentale
Partie. Er erlebt nur mit den Nerven, mit den Sinnen, mit dem Gehirne; er
empfindet nichts. Er kennt keine Leidenschaft, keinen Elan, kein Pathos. Er sieht
auf das Leben und die Welt, als ob er sie von einem fernen Stern aus sähe; so sehen
wir auf Pflanzen oder Steine. Daher jenes Maass, die vollkommene Anmuth, die
edle Würde, daher aber auch die Kälte, die *sécheresse*, der ironische Hochmuth
seiner Verse.[173]

[his magnificent art has no feeling; there is no area of his soul for sentiment. He
only experiences with his nerves, with his senses, with his brain; he does not *feel*
anything. He knows no passions, no exaltation, no emotion. He looks upon life and
the world as if he were seeing them from a distant star, in the way we look at plants
or rocks. That is the reason for the moderation, the perfect grace, the noble dignity
of his poems—but also for their coldness, their dryness, and their ironic disdain.]

Is this 'der ganze Symbolismus, und nichts, das nicht Symbolismus
wäre' [the whole of Symbolism, and nothing that is not Symbolism]?
In Bahr's eyes, Symbolism feels merely with its fingertips and intellec-
tualizes sensations without receiving them into the heart. It is a young
man's art, an art of virtuosic display. This judgement should be borne
in mind when Hofmannsthal's own response to Symbolism is analysed.

Bahr's importance in Hofmannsthal's early literary development
was thus twofold. He introduced new French authors, or confirmed
their significance in conversation and debate, and he was the principal
advocate of the shift in styles from Naturalism to a Modernism
influenced by Romanticism, where the unity of the perceiving subject
was sacrificed to the nuances of the sensations themselves. But this is
what Hofmannsthal saw as Decadence, and he hoped for rather more
from Symbolism proper.

[172] Ibid. 128.   [173] Ibid. 128–9.

Bahr's reservations concerning Hofmannsthal are strikingly justified from the latter's diary. The evening of 28 May 1891 was spent with
Gustav Schwarzkopf and other friends in the Griensteidl; Hofmannsthal records the drift of the conversation and his own reactions. Bahr
recommended imagining their circle of acquaintances from the
Café during a revolution, whilst Hofmannsthal favoured filling in a
questionnaire designed by a psychoanalyst:

> Korff wirft ein, dass wir einander zu wenig kennen, um einander richtig zu
> characterisieren. Streit. Bahr und ich stehen auf Seite der Halbbekanntschaft, der
> Anticipation, die andern wollen gründliches Studium.[174]

> [Korff objects that we do not know each other well enough to capture each other's
> character properly. Debate. Bahr and I are in favour of imperfect acquaintance, of
> anticipation, the others want a more serious investigation.]

There is a manner of seeing things, writes Hofmannsthal, 'in der
plastischen, darstellungsreifen Beleuchtung... die ebenso lügt, wie die
zu genaue Bekanntschaft [täuscht und] verwischt' [in a plastic light
suitable for accurate representation, but one that is none the less
deceptive, just as too close an acquaintance (misleads and) confuses].[175]
No sooner does he begin to consider human friendship than he fights
shy of ethical commitment: the word 'darstellungsreif' shuffles the
question on to the level of mere representation.

A much later exchange between Schnitzler and Bahr in 1904 shows
an uncanny consistency. Bahr had apparently claimed that Hofmannsthal was 'ein Mensch, der das Gesicht seiner Frau nicht kennt' [a man
who does not know his wife's face], to which Schnitzler responded:

> Nein. Er [Hofmannsthal] wird vielleicht einmal etwas schreiben; *aus diesem Werk
> wird ihm eine Gestalt entgegentreten,* —es wird seine Frau sein, so scharf umrissen, als
> hätte er sie ein Leben lang studiert. Menschen dieser Art sehen gerade so gut wie
> andre, aber sie bewahren die Sinneseindrücke sofort, oft, in irgend welchen
> Tiefen, von wo sie zu rechter Zeit (Production) hervorgeholt werden—und wären
> wir im Stande, in eine solche Seele bis in jeden Winkel hinein zu leuchten, so
> würden wir sehen, dass alle Eindrücke bewahrt sind—Landschaften, an denen sie
> anscheinend vorbeigegangen sind, ohne sie zu sehen.[176]

> [No. He will perhaps write something one day, and a figure will rise out of this work
> towards him—it will be his wife, depicted as clearly as if he had spent a lifetime

---

[174] *Nachlaß*, H VII 17.77ᵃ, an entry only partly published in *RA* iii. 330–1, more completely
in *SW* ii. 297.

[175] Ibid. ('täuscht und' is struck through).

[176] Schnitzler, *Tagebuch 1903–1908*, ed. by Werner Welzig et al. (Vienna: Verlag der Öster-
reichischen Akademie der Wissenschaften, 1991), 82–3; entry for 7 Aug. 1904; my italics.

studying her. People like him see just as well as other people, but they store up their sense-impressions at once, often in some deep place whence they are brought forth at the right time (artistic production)—and if we were capable of illuminating the darkest corners of such a soul we would see that all the impressions are stored up— landscapes they have apparently passed by without noticing.]

But this hardly answers Bahr's criticism, even when that is stripped of its rhetorical exaggeration. Hofmannsthal's putative re-creation of his wife's face as he is immersed in the composition of prose is made to seem a more or less accidental procedure. The exercising of Hofmannsthal's creative talent may or may not result in the evocation of his wife's face—the initiative is left to the language, not the poet's intentions. The relationship of the writer to his subject is felt to be of almost no importance as long as the relationship of the writer to his language is untroubled. A reservoir of impressions can be summoned up according to the particular demands of the linguistic situation; and even at the point when these impressions are collected, the importance of personal response to the outside world is attenuated to the vanishing point. The whole process has about it a coldness that Schnitzler else- where in the diaries regards distastefully, even if here he appears to think he is defending or praising Hofmannsthal.

The man at the centre of the web of influences, stimuli and encouragement that *fin-de-siècle* Vienna provided seems to have been regarded by his friends and acquaintances as curiously insubstantial. Although Schnitzler writes of 'Sinneseindrücke', summoned from a repertoire collected gradually, to judge by diaries, letters and poems Hofmannsthal's early impressions were predominantly those of litera- ture not the senses. Whilst these were not exclusively of French culture, a leaning towards the Romance languages was recognizable very early.[177] Whether he was thus predisposed by the Italian blood of his paternal grandmother, Petronilla Antonia Cecilia (1815–98), is debatable, although she certainly taught him to speak and read Italian. Hofmannsthal himself considered his interests partly inherited, for the *curriculum vitae* submitted in 1901 with his *Habilitation* includes the following passage of self-description:

[ich entschloss mich] dem Studium der romanischen Philologie zuzuwenden, hierin sowohl einer lebhaften Neigung folgend als auch von einer zum Theile schon durch die Abstammung bestimmten, durch frühzeitige Reisen und eine

---

[177] For a greater range of examples, cf. Manfred Hoppe, *Literatentum, Magie and Mystik im Frühwerk Hugo von Hofmannsthals* (Berlin: de Gruyter, 1968), 20–65, and Fiechtner, 'Hofmannsthal und Frankreich', 261–4.

fast leidenschaftliche Lectüre geweckten Anlage zu dieser Bethätigung hin-getrieben.[178]

[I decided to devote myself to the study of Romance philology, both following an inclination and also motivated by a predisposition to this activity determined already in part by my family background and stimulated by travel in my youth and by voracious reading.]

Not content with modern French, he chose a Provençal grammar as holiday reading when he was 17.[179]

Modern European languages were not taught at the Akademisches Gymnasium in Vienna where Hofmannsthal went to school, so a private tutor was engaged. The tutor was a remarkable man called Marie-Gabriel Dubray.[180] Born in Saint-Denis in 1846,[181] Dubray came from a family of considerable artistic talent: an uncle, Gabriel-Vital Dubray, was a sculptor who made his name with an exhibit in the Salon of 1840; one cousin, Ernest Hémet, was a painter, and another was Albert Piot, sometime architect to the Rothschilds. Gabriel had been a schoolfellow of the Parnassian poet François Coppée (who visited him in Vienna in August 1885, some three years after his arrival there) and seems also to have been for a while a neighbour of Flaubert's in the Vexin, north-west of Paris. In Vienna, Dubray was first tutor to the two sons of Baron Jean de Bourgoing and his wife, a Countess Kinsky. He also taught the ill-fated Mary Vetsera, the tragic victim of an infamous suicide pact with Crown Prince Rudolf at Mayerling in 1889. Dubray was mentioned in the memoirs of Georg von Francken-stein, the last ambassador of the First Austrian Republic to the Court of St James, as 'a very distinguished-looking, intellectual and eloquent man'.[182] The de Bourgoing children, Paul and Jean, affectionately called their teacher 'Papa Dubray', and this easygoing intimacy seems to have characterized his relationships with all his charges, Hofmanns-thal included.

Dubray published a number of textbooks on French grammar and style, although textbooks is perhaps too dry a term for works of such humour and gentleness.[183] They give some insight into what must have

[178] Rudolf Hirsch, 'Hofmannsthal und Frankreich', in *Beiträge zum Verständnis Hugo von Hofmannsthals*, ed. Matthias Mayer (Frankfurt a.M.: S. Fischer, 1995), 304.

[179] Cf. Beer-Hofmann, *BW*, 3.

[180] The source of all the details in this paragraph is a remarkable piece of detective work by Hilde Burger, 'Marie-Gabriel Dubray (1846–1915): Professeur de français de Hofmannsthal', *Études danubiennes*, 2. 1 (1986), 49–62.

[181] Not Switzerland, as is suggested in *Briefe 1890–1901*, 342 n. 39.

[182] Georg von Franckenstein, *Facts and Figures of my Life* (London: Cassell, 1939), 11.

[183] *Fautes de français* (Vienna: Gerold, 1894), a pamphlet that eventually became a book of

been his teaching methods, drawing all their linguistic examples either from the classics—Rousseau, Molière, Beaumarchais and Coppée, for example—or from contemporary journals such as *Le Journal des débats, Le Petit Journal, Le Petit Parisien, Le Temps* and *Le Figaro*. He clearly had a special gift for satisfying Hofmannsthal's voracious appetite for literature.[184] Linguistically, the demands must have been high, since they began to translate Nietzsche's *Jenseits von Gut und Böse* in May 1891 (*RA* iii. 329). Hofmannsthal translated André Chénier's 'L'Aveugle' in 1887 or 1888 (*SW* ii, 11). One of the earliest entries in Hofmannsthal's diary lists 'E. A. Poe. Poetry, novels. Tennyson. Poems. Béranger. Chansons'.[185] Then there is a brief note headed 'Franz. Litt.' opposing the Southern Troubadours ('cynisch') and the Northern Trouvères ('episch'). On the next page is a checklist of English literature, including Sir Thomas Browne's *Religio Medici* and Arnold's *Lectures on Modern History*, Shakespeare, Byron, Moore, Pope, Sheridan and Goldsmith. Then Hofmannsthal returns to French literature ('Lectüre: Musset, Hugo, Mérimée, Béranger') and more detailed notes on medieval epic. These read like notes from, or for, his lessons with Dubray or his English teacher. His reading schedule for the summer holidays of 1889 included Wilkie Collins's *The Woman in White*, Ovid's *Ars amatoria*, Pushkin's *Boris Godunov* and Alphonse Daudet's *Le Nabab*, which suggests a taste for the sensational. Mérimée and Gautier were 'freie Lektüre' in September 1889.[186]

The second volume of diaries in Harvard lists *La Princesse de Clèves, Femme de quarante ans* (presumably an error for Balzac's *La Femme de trente ans*), Sedaine, Beaumarchais, and Nisard's *Histoire de la littérature française* (1855–61).[187] There are regular references in the diaries to Balzac, and we know that he was reading *Illusions perdues* in August 1889, *Les Chouans* in July or August 1891. He noted 'Balzac gibt die Symptome, Goethe den Sinn des Lebens' [Balzac gives the symptoms of life, Goethe the meaning] on 3 November in the same year.[188] In the middle of reflections on Amiel from January 1891, we find 'Bau-

---

212 pages, reviewed in the *Journal des débats*, 344 (13 Dec. 1899), 1; *Les Gentillesses de la langue française* (Vienna: Gerold, 1897), reprinted many times, translated and expanded in 1940 by Gertrud Gräfin Helmstatt; *Le Roman des mots* (n.d.), of which Hofmannsthal possessed a copy; *Tel peuple, tel verbe* (n.d.); *L'Allemand a son français que le français ne connaît pas* (1911).

[184] Cf. *SW* xxxi. 253 and Fiechtner, 'Hofmannsthal und Frankreich', 260 and 263.

[185] *Nachlaß*, H VII 1.2; 29 Dec. 1888. The first two names are struck through, perhaps indicating that Hofmannsthal had read them.

[186] *Nachlaß*, H VII 1.3 ff.

[187] *Nachlaß*, H VII 2.12.

[188] *Nachlaß*, H VII 2.176.

delaire' deleted, as if he had changed his mind after intending to start notes on him. Diaries for summer 1891 have extended notes on Pascal,[189] Flaubert—'Grausamkeit, Lust am Quälen sehen' [cruelty, love of watching torture][190]—Victor Hugo—'vage, allgemeine Liebe, Pantheismus, universelle Demokratie' [vague, general love, pantheism, universal democracy]—and Poe—'die feuchte moorige Mulde' [the damp, boggy hollow]—as well as jottings on Kleist and quotations from Taine.[191]

At about this time, Hofmannsthal also made a sustained attempt to find out more about Symbolism by reading and noting Jules Huret's *Enquête sur l'évolution littéraire*.[192] The *Enquête* was a collection of sixty-four interviews held by the journalist Jules Huret with the leading literary figures of the day, a series published first in the paper that employed him, *L'Écho de Paris*, from 3 March to 5 July 1891, then again in the same year by Charpentier as a book and many times reprinted. These notes also include recent works of secondary literature, some, like Charles Morice's *La Littérature de tout à l'heure* (1889), referred to in Huret, the others not connected with the *Enquête*. These include the *Répertoire de la comédie humaine* by Anatole Cerfberr and Jules Christophe (published by Calman Lévy with an introduction by Paul Bourget in 1887), the *Histoire des œuvres de Balzac* by Charles de Spoelberch de Lovenjoul (a third, revised edition was issued by the same publisher in 1888). The name Vapereau is mentioned, too: he was the author of reference works, *L'Année littéraire et dramatique* and *Dictionnaire universel des contemporains contenant toutes les personnes notables de la France et des pays étrangers*.[193]

In late 1891 Hofmannsthal wrote to Bahr,

ich habe MM. de la Rochefoucauld, de la Bruyère, de St. Simon, de Montaigne, de Montesquieu, de Buffon, sowie die Herren Chamfort, Courier, Chateaubriand, Voltaire, La Mettrie, Louvet, Jean Jacques, Diderot, Prévost, Gresset, Mably und (hélas!) Volney auch gelesen. Hein?[194]

---

[189] *Nachlaß*, H VII 2.122.

[190] *Nachlaß*, H VII 9.4ᵃ. Probably a reference to the soldiers' joking at the crucified lions on the road to Sicca in chapter 2 of *Salammbô*. The theme is picked up several times in the early 1900s: see Ritchie Robertson, 'The Theme of Sacrifice in Hofmannsthal's *Das Gespräch über Gedichte*', *Modern Austrian Literature*, 23.1 (1990), 19–33, and Chapter 5 below.

[191] *Nachlaß*, H VII 9.4ᵃ. Partly given in *SW* ii. 278.

[192] *Nachlaß*, H VA 113.6ᵃ⁻ᶜ. These notes have been published in full by Roland Spahr, 'Hugo von Hofmannsthals Aufzeichnungen zu Jules Hurets *Enquête sur l'évolution littéraire*', *Wirkendes Wort*, 45 (1994), 432–3.

[193] The 5th edition came out in 1886 (the 6th not until 1893, too late to be the one referred to here). The notes from Huret are examined in Chapter 2, pp. 102–12.

[194] *Briefe 1890–1901*, 33; undated.

The juxtaposition of so many minor figures with the great names of French literary history from the sixteenth to the nineteenth century suggests that one of Dubray's textbooks was an anthology and that Hofmannsthal was showing off.[195] More reliable are the notes of his reading in the letters sent to friends during his holidays in the Salzkammergut. Maupassant is a favourite, especially *Mont-Oriol, Une vie*, and *Fort comme la mort*.[196]

In July 1892 he announced to Marie Herzfeld that his room is 'mit Poesie möblier[t]', and he lists Sophocles, Shelley, Swinburne, Verlaine, Horace, Maeterlinck's *Pelléas et Mélisande*, Moréas's *Pèlerin passionné*, fragments by Otto Ludwig, Renan's *drames philosophiques*, Parsifal, the history of Joan of Arc by Michelet, the stories of Poe and Hawthorne's *Scarlet Letter*: 'Ich habe die Empfindung, daß Ihnen bei dieser Aufzählung ist, als hätte ich hübsche und bunte Farben aufgezählt: matt gold, lapisblau, mauve, silberlila, feuilles mortes, moosgrün, blaß corail u. so f.' [I have the impression that this will make you feel as if I had reeled off a list of pretty coloured stones: dull gold, lapis blue, mauve, silver-pink, dead leaves, moss-green, pale coral, etc.].[197] Hofmannsthal's transposition of his sensations into colours upon reading reflects his conviction that literature enlivens a dull world. Literature is like a drug, and Hofmannsthal is following Baudelaire's invocation, 'enivrez-vous; enivrez-vous sans cesse! De vin, de poésie ou de vertu, à votre guise' [get drunk! get drunk all the time! on wine, on poetry or on virtue, just as you please].[198]

Dubray wrote a book entitled *Gentillesses de la langue française* and

[195] Geneviève Bianquis, 'Hofmannsthal et la France', *Revue de littérature comparée*, 27 (1953), 308; Hilde Burger, 'French Influences on Hugo von Hofmannsthal', in W. P. Friedrich (ed.), *Comparative Literature 2: Proceedings of the Second Congress of the ICLA*, University of North Carolina Studies in Comparative Literature 24 (Chapel Hill: University of North Carolina Press, 1959), 692; Francis Claudon, *Hofmannsthal et la France* (Berne: Peter Lang, 1979), 12; Claude David, 'Hofmannsthals Frankreich-Bild', *Arcadia*, 5 (1970), 164; Fiechtner, 'Hofmannsthal und Frankreich', 262; and Walter H. Perl, *Das lyrische Jugendwerk Hugo von Hofmannsthals* (Berlin: Dr Emil Ebering, 1936), 107 n. 10. All quote this passage; that almost all take it at face value is characteristic of the earlier studies of Hofmannsthal and France. Only Fiechtner qualifies somewhat, with 'wenn es auch nicht die Opera omnia waren'.

[196] *Briefe 1890–1901*, 90; letter of 12 Aug. 1893. *Fort comme la mort* is listed on 6 Nov. 1891 alongside Andersen's fairy tales, Turgenev's *The Nest of Gentlefolk*, Nietzsche's *Menschliches Allzumenschliches*, Strindberg's 'Vater' and the *Blackwoods Magazine* that contained an article on telepathy by 'Reginald Courtenay D(octor) D(ivinitatis), late bishop of Jamaica' (*RA* iii. 335). See also Beer-Hofmann *BW*, 3; *Briefe 1890–1901*, 23 and 59. Hofmannsthal is still making comparisons with Maupassant in May 1896 (*Briefe 1890–1901*, 58–9). It is interesting that alongside Maupassant, Prévost's *Manon Lescaut* and Flaubert's *Trois Contes* appeal more solidly than Bourget (who is 'flach und fast verlogen', *Briefe 1890–1901*, 90).

[197] Herzfeld, *BW*, 28.

[198] Baudelaire, *OC*, i. 337.

Hofmannsthal reviewed it for *Die Zeit* in 1897.[199] 'Review' is perhaps too clinical a term, for the essay is a beautiful homage to Hofmanns-thal's mentor. Opposing philologist and teacher, it brings out the inimitable mixture of experience and love out of which Dubray dis-tilled his work. There is not a hint of patronage or condescension, which cannot be said of all Hofmannsthal's compliments. It is difficult to draw conclusions about the influence on Hofmannsthal of a man about whom we know so little,[200] but it is probable that Dubray was ultimately responsible for Hofmannsthal's special love of French.

As a reward for his excellent school report, Hofmannsthal's parents funded a journey to the Ain and Provence with Dubray in September and October 1892, visiting Dubray's cousins in Lélex on their travels. The holiday was evidently an important experience in revealing or confirming how little spontaneity Hofmannsthal possessed: 'Reise durch Südfrankreich und Oberitalien. Reflexion: mir fehlt Unmittel-barkeit im Erleben' [journey through the south of France and northern Italy. Reflection: I lack immediacy in experiencing things].[201] A letter to Edgar Karg, written during this journey, makes the same equation of poeticization and colouring as in the letter to Marie Herzfeld:

Ich fühle mich während einer Reise meist nicht recht wohl: mir fehlt die Unmittel-barkeit des Erlebens; ich sehe mir selbst leben zu und *was ich erlebe ist mir wie aus einem Buch gelesen*; erst die Vergangenheit verklärt mir die Dinge und gibt ihnen Farbe und Duft. Das hat mich wohl auch zum 'Dichter' gemacht, dieses Bedürfnis nach dem künstlichen Leben, nach Verzierung und poetischer Interpretation des gemeinen und farblosen.[202]

[When I am travelling, I usually don't feel quite right: I lack the immediacy of experience; I watch myself living and what I experience seems to me as if it has been read in a book; things are only transformed for me, given colour and scent, when they are in the past. That is probably what has made me into a 'poet', this need for artificial life, for decoration and the poetic interpretation of what is ordinary and colourless.]

Hofmannsthal began his essay 'Südfranzösische Eindrücke' with a similar point, comparing his memories of the journey to a Chinese picture book whose illustrations had deliberately been disorganized,

---

[199] 'Französische Redensarten', *RA* i. 236–41.

[200] Hofmannsthal's last reference, apart from 'Französische Redensarten', seems to be a diary note of 2 Sept. 1893 with a quotation from a letter of Dubray's (*RA* iii. 366); see also below, pp. 267–8.

[201] *RA* iii. 352; note from Sept./Oct. 1892.

[202] Karg, *BW*, 19; my italics.

and which possessed 'den seltsamen, sinnlosen Reiz der Träume' [the odd, meaningless charm of dreams; *EGB*, 589]. He goes on, 'Reise-erinnerungen [haben] nachher für uns selbst diesen sonderbar traum-haften Charakter, so fremd, wie nicht wirklich gewesen' [memories of travelling afterwards take on a peculiarly dreamlike character even for those of us who were there; so alien, as if they had not been real], and indeed the essay, structured by literary and artistic allusions, is more of a cultural guide than the account of a personal experience. His habitual filtering of experience through the printed word and painted image began early—the only really lively descriptive passage that is not literature-based is his account of what he calls an orgy of colours on his dinner table (*EGB*, 593). 'Es ist keine zufällige Besonderheit, daß ich soviel von Farben spreche' [it is not a coincidence that I am talking so much of colours], is how he begins that paragraph, and one senses that the word 'Literatur' could be substituted for 'Farben' without the sense of the essay being radically altered. The two are at this point sub-consciously interdependent.

Scattered throughout Hofmannsthal's notes and diaries are references to further reading in French. There are transcripts of sections from 'Regards' and 'Attouchements' from Maeterlinck's *Serres chaudes* in the diary for January 1892, and a note in November to 'symbolistische Schule' [the Symbolist school].[203] Hofmannsthal seems to have studied Baudelaire in the latter half of 1892, since there are references to Gautier's essay on him in June or July, to Baudelaire's 'amour du mensonge' [love of lying] in November and to Bourget's essay on Baudelaire in December.[204] A note probably from 1893 lists 'Pierrotpoesie (Gautier, Verlaine, Giraud)',[205] another from early January 1893 or late December 1892 plans an essay on Verlaine:

Aufsätze.
Paul Verlaine.
Viele Franzosen pflegen diesen Dichter durch eine einfache Besprechung die höchste Ehre zu erweisen
Schönheit[206]

---

[203] *Nachlaß*, H VII 4.23–36. Maurice Maeterlinck, *Poésies complètes*, ed. Joseph Hanse (Brussels: La Renaissance du Livre, 1965), 157–60 and 169–73. Sometimes the quotations from Maeterlinck are only single lines.

[204] *SW* xxxi. 7; *Nachlaß*, H VII 4.33; *Nachlaß*, H VII 4.37.

[205] *Nachlaß*, H VB 10.95. The dating is suggested by the reference to Giraud, and by another to Franz Stuck: Hofmannsthal wrote his Stuck essay in 1893.

[206] *Nachlaß*, H VII 5.18 (most of the note is in shorthand). 'Schönheit' is a separate essay title.

[Essays: Paul Verlaine. The French often show this poet the greatest honour in a simple discussion. Beauty.]

Andrian noted of Hofmannsthal on 12 December 1893, 'Baudelaire ist zu rhetorisch, Musset, Swinburne, Verlaine seine Ideale. "Den (d. Verlaine) such ich so viel als möglich nachzumachen—leider gelingt mir sehr wenig" ' [Baudelaire is too rhetorical for him, Musset, Swinburne, Verlaine are his ideals. 'I try to imitate him (Verlaine) as much as possible—unfortunately very rarely am I successful'].[207] Andrian recalled this in his essay on Hofmannsthal in Fiechtner's *Die Gestalt des Dichters im Spiegel der Freunde*, 'Keats, Shelley und Swinburne und insbesondere Verlaine, von dem er im Scherz zu sagen pflegte: "Dem mache ich soviel nach, als ich kann" ' [Keats, Shelley and Swinburne, and in particular Verlaine, of whom he used to say jokingly, 'I imitate him as much as I can'].[208] A jotting from 1899 is explicitly labelled 'Nach Verlaine' ['after Verlaine'], a response to 'Spleen' from *Romances sans paroles*.[209]

On 3 January 1893, Hofmannsthal had noted down some quotations from Jules Lemaître's *Les Contemporains* on Banville and Zola. Of Banville he notes, 'par cette magie des mots on peut dire qu'il a "polychromé" les dieux grecs, qu'il a animé la noblesse de leurs contours et qu'il leur a soufflé une ivresse' [through his magical use of words one may say that he has 'coloured in' the Greek gods, animated the nobility of their outlines and given them a touch of intoxication], referring to Banville's tendency to allow his vocabulary of colour and emotion to develop an almost self-propelling impetus of enthusiasm. The Zola criticism cited also focuses on Zola's accumulations of brutality, which develop a momentum virtually autonomous and independent of any perceptible authorial control. Both passages are about the processes of liberating language from straightforward discursive meaning.[210] Lemaître's seven sets of essays went into many editions in the last fifteen years of the nineteenth century, and according to Gsteiger, it was Lemaître who fostered the popular equation of Symbolists and Decadents in the German-speaking world. Particularly important was the essay entitled 'M. Paul Verlaine et les poètes

[207] 'Andrian über Hofmannsthal', 7.

[208] Andrian, 'Erinnerungen an meinen Freund', in Fiechtner (ed.), *Hofmannsthal im Spiegel der Freunde*, 75.

[209] Cf. *SW* ii. 148 and 440. The poem had already been quoted by Hofmannsthal in a letter to Andrian of 21 Feb. 1894, *BW*, 23.

[210] *Nachlaß*, H VII 5.20–1, cited from Lemaître, *Les Contemporains* (Paris: Lecène & Oudin, 1885), i. 25 and i. 268 ('J'ai beau m'en défendre . . . par leur masse').

"symbolistes" et "décadents" ' for the *Revue bleue* of 1888 that was cited in Anna Brunnemann's influential *Die neueren Sprachen*.[211] There is an essay on Huysmans in the same volume as the critiques of Banville and Zola, whose conclusion will have struck Hofmannsthal: 'Il a la mémoire trop pleine; les impressions ne lui arrivent plus qu'à travers une couche de souvenirs littéraires' [his memory is too encumbered; he now only receives impressions through a layer of literary memories].[212]

At almost exactly the same time Hofmannsthal also mentions Otto Hartleben's translation of Albert Giraud's *Pierrot Lunaire* both to George and in his review of the year's 'Moderner Musenalmanach' published on 2 February:

Die bizarr-phantastische Note gibt Otto Erich Hartleben mit ein paar Gedichten aus dem 'Pierrot lunaire'.

Das ist das morbide und hübsche Buch eines französischen Symbolisten, von dem Berliner mit sehr viel Geschmack, man darf kaum sagen übersetzt. Es liest sich nicht wie Zweite-Hand-Stil.[213]

[The bizarre and fantastical touch is given by Otto Erich Hartleben with a few poems from *Pierrot Lunaire*. This is a pretty, morbid book by a French Symbolist, translated, if this is the right word here, by the Berliner with great taste. It does not read as if the style were second-hand.]

The 'Pierrotpoesie' note also refers to 'A une Madone', a poem from *Les Fleurs du mal*, in the phrase 'Madonna mit den 7 Schwertern' [Madonna with the seven swords], which are the Seven Deadly Sins that the speaker plans to plunge into the Madonna's heart in a frenzied attack.[214] At about the same time he was considering essays on the relationship of poetry and the visual arts in Chénier, Hugo and Verlaine.[215] By 1895 he had read Huysmans's *En route* and works by Villiers de l'Isle-Adam, perhaps the famous *Axël* with its notorious dictum about life: 'vivre? les serviteurs feront cela pour nous' [live? the servants will do that for us].[216]

French remained one of the dominant foci of Hofmannsthal's varied literary experience. He went to Paris from 10 February to 2 May

---

[211] Cf. Gsteiger, *Französische Symbolisten*, 262 n. 9 and 272 nn. 203 and 205. Lemaître's essay was later republished in *Les Contemporains*, iv. 63–111.

[212] Lemaître, *Les Contemporains*, i. 334.

[213] *RA* i. 171 and letter to George of 11 Jan. 1893, *BW*, 56.

[214] *Nachlaß*, H VB, 10.95; cf. Baudelaire, *OC*, i. 59.

[215] *Nachlaß*, H VB 12.73.

[216] *Nachlaß*, H VII 10 and H VB 15.4. The dating is suggested in each case by a reference to Andrian's *Garten der Erkenntnis*. Cf. Villiers de l'Isle-Adam, *Axël*, ed. Pierre Mariel (Paris: La Colombe, 1960), 249.

1901 and was introduced to the literary and artistic circles there by
Hans Schlesinger, his future brother-in-law, meeting Maeterlinck,
Verhaeren and Rodin, and to diplomatic circles by Georg von
Franckenstein. His academic career had already turned in this
direction. After studying law for four semesters at the University of
Vienna, at his father's wish, he transferred in October 1895 to
Romance philology, attending Wilhelm Meyer-Lübke's courses on
Romance philology, the history of French drama and on fifteenth- and
sixteenth-century French literature, and those of Adolf Mussafia on
medieval literature, Provençal, Dante, and the history of the French
language.[217] Hofmannsthal was awarded his doctorate of philosophy
on 20 March 1899 for a philological thesis, *Über den Sprachgebrauch bei den
Dichtern der Plejade*, since lost.[218] For this he wrote to Andrian that he had
had to read all six volumes of the complete works of Ronsard.[219] He
completed a *Habilitationsschrift* in May 1901, *Studie über die Entwickelung
des Dichters Victor Hugo*, but withdrew it whilst the examiners were considering it, ostensibly because of a nervous illness that made him un-
suitable for the academic profession. Volke suggests that the real
reason was his decision to devote himself to poetry, which is possible,[220]
although one might speculate further that the detailed study of a poet
with such a strong grasp of his art and such confidence in his relationship with his tradition confronted Hofmannsthal sharply with his own
difficulties with lyric poetry.

A flat diagram, similar to Timms's Kraus-centred 'Vienna Circles',
might easily be constructed to show Hofmannsthal's social location in
the 1890s. But an attempt to modify such a diagram to take into
account Hofmannsthal's position in his literary and intellectual tradition, to illustrate the specific influences of his environment, his own
family, his education and his abilities and interests, is inconceivable:
the complex interlocking circles quickly exhaust the available repre-

[217] See Franz Hadamowsky (ed.), *Ausstellung Hugo von Hofmannsthal: Katalog* (Salzburg: Amt
der Salzburger Landesregierung, 1953), 71–4 and Rudolf Hirsch, 'Hofmannsthal und Frankreich', in *Beiträge*, 305 and 311 n. 3.
[218] Part of the introduction is published by Hirsch, 'Hofmannsthal und Frankreich' in
Beiträge, 306–7; Meyer-Lübke's report—mostly positive, noting a few philological inaccuracies—is published in Fiechtner (ed.), *Hofmannsthal im Spiegel der Freunde*, 9–10.
[219] Andrian, *BW*, 76–7; letter of July 1897. Cf. correction to the dating by Hirsch,
'Hofmannsthal und Frankreich', in *Beiträge*, 311 n. 5.
[220] Volke, *Hofmannsthal*, 54. Fiechtner, 'Hofmannsthal und Frankreich', 264 and 267–8,
hesitantly inclines to the view that the Faculty was unconvinced of his suitability and
discreetly warned him off; Bianquis describes the work as 'synthèse brillante, et peut-être trop
brillante' ('Hofmannsthal et la France', 310).

sentational dimensions.[221] Hofmannsthal felt the need to do exactly this, however, to represent to himself the material to be controlled for fear of succumbing to its quantity and assortment. His search for controlling devices was predominantly an attempt at *representation*, situating himself in a mental plan of his surrounding atmosphere, and for this he needed both to act and to observe himself acting. Socially there was already a map available, involving marriage, children and a career. The career was difficult to settle, as evinced by his vacillation over the *Habilitationsschrift*. Diersch suggests that he shied away from the responsibilities of starting a family of his own, but undertook them eventually none the less, perhaps in an attempt to give his inner uncertainties something concretely social on to which they might become anchored.[222] Bahr's comment, already reported, that Hofmannsthal would not have recognized the face of his own wife is to be taken seriously.

A poet either pursues dominant tendencies and develops them, or opposes them with something new. Hofmannsthal was in the fortunate position in the fragmented German tradition of having the opportunity to do both, in a sense, by taking part in the 'Überwindung des Naturalismus' and representing Symbolism in German. Sondrup says that 'the ultimate origin of Hofmannsthal's interest in symbolism is unclear',[223] but this suggests he is searching for a single decisive point. No single event 'converted' Hofmannsthal to Symbolism, but around the end of 1891 there was a concentration of external personal, social and literary stimuli, in the light of which a strong interest is not surprising, and which persisted until the mid-1890s.

The range of possibilities presented here for Hofmannsthal's reception of Symbolism is large, and it is unlikely that he was aware of every one or acted upon all those he did know. Of the range of stimuli open to Stefan George, in a similar situation in Paris in 1889, Durzak writes that to assimilate them all,

würde bedeuten, daß er nicht nur über eine ungewöhnliche Rezeptionsfähigkeit verfügte, sondern auch ohne den Ansatz einer eigenen Dichtungskonzeption diese Mannigfaltigkeit literarischer Impulse in sich aufnahm und zu einer Dichtung verarbeitete, die zwar als Substrat der vielen Einflüsse von Interesse sein könnte, aber jeden eigenen Ton vermissen lassen würde. Man wird jedoch sowohl

[221] Claudon's positivistic desire to apply 'les schèmes tainiens pour montrer à quelles influences l'existence de Hofmannsthal était, dès le début, vouée' (*Hofmannsthal et la France*, 11) is doomed.

[222] Diersch, *Empiriokritizismus*, 85.

[223] Sondrup, *Hofmannsthal and the French Symbolist Tradition*, 26.

Georges große Rezeptionsfähigkeit einschränken müssen, wie man auch zugeben wird, daß Georges dichterisches Bewußtsein keineswegs eine *tabula rasa* darstellte, sondern bereits von einer spezifischen Dichtungskonzeption geprägt war.[224]

[would mean not only that he possessed an unusual capacity for reception, but also that he took in this multiplicity of literary impulses without starting to develop his own conception of poetry, working them into a kind of poetry that might be interesting as the product of the many influences but would be fatally lacking in any kind of individual tone. However, we must concede both that George's degree of receptiveness was not so great as that, and that his poetic consciousness was by no means a *tabula rasa*, being instead already imbued with a specific conception of poetry.]

These two final reservations do not apply to Hofmannsthal. First, the receptiveness of the 17-year-old Hofmannsthal was indeed extraordinary, and continued to be so until his death. And secondly, he did not have so solid a poetic conception as George, who was 21 in 1889, and he lacked the temperament to proclaim so magisterially the one he gradually developed.

Hofmannsthal was conscious of this even in his early literary life, and suffered anxiety on that account. This self-conscious attempt to locate himself is not the issue: it is a critical truism to observe that he was unusually self-aware. Schnitzler noted this of him, but the advice he received from Hofmannsthal hints at the depths that this tendency reached:

[Hofmannsthal] sprach von seiner frühesten Jugend, die ihm sehr unheimlich sei, kam sich selbst abjekt vor, wie etwas sehr schlechtes . . . . Ersatz der Gefühle: 'Wenn die Leute wüßten, wie schlecht ich eigentlich bin.'—Ich sprach von meiner Faulheit, Bequemlichkeit, die mich hindert, das zu thun, was ich selbst in einem gewissen Zeitpunkt als das mir gemäße und nützliche empfinde. Hugo sagte; es bilde sich was starres in mir—ich sei der A[rthur] im Verhältnis zur Familie, der A. mit seiner Geliebten, der A. im Café Griensteidl . . . sollte wo anders hin, wo ich rein menschlich gelten und sein kann, statt eine Maske zu tragen.[225]

[Hofmannsthal spoke about his earliest youth, which he thought was quite uncanny, he felt himself to be abject, like something bad. Substitute for feelings: 'if people only knew how bad I really am.' —I mentioned my laziness and complacency, which stops me doing what I myself feel at a given moment is appropriate and useful for me. Hugo said that something lifeless was building up in me—that I was the Arthur of the family, or the Arthur with his lover, the Arthur of the Café Griensteidl, and should aim for somewhere different, where I can exist and make myself felt in a purely human way, instead of wearing a mask.]

[224] Durzak, *Der junge Stefan George*, 63–4.
[225] Schnitzler, *Tagebuch 1893–1902*, 184–5; entry for 17 Apr. 1896.

First Hofmannsthal's sense of a division between observing self and acting self is noted, but Schnitzler, too, is interpreted as splitting into two selves, one in fixed roles, observed, the other watching, and Hofmannsthal's advice is to reunite them. This is a case (at least in part) of projecting his own symptom on to a more truly external object of analysis, moulding the outside world into his own image and articulating his own hope for a solution. Socially and geographically even the vague 'wo anders' was impossible. In literature it took time to achieve, and was manifested in the almost total farewell to lyric, the mask of the decade, borrowed at first from the Symbolists. The task now is to see how neatly the borrowed mask fitted and where it gives signs of melting into a face of Hofmannsthal's own. Alternatively, to return to the terms of the metaphor with which I began, the task is to scrutinize the Potemkin villages that are the Symbolist poets and see how far it was possible to have an artificial horizon of points 'an die man selber glaubt'.

2

FORM AND IDENTITY: HOFMANNSTHAL
AND THE SYMBOLIST AESTHETIC

Amidst the welter of definitions and prescriptions that the Symbolist movement produced is a rich and beautiful statement by Mallarmé that encapsulates in its deceptively innocent directness the cardinal presuppositions of Symbolist poetics:

La poésie est l'expression, par le langage humain ramené à son rythme essentiel, du sens mystérieux des aspects de l'existence: elle doue ainsi d'authenticité notre séjour et constitue notre seule tâche spirituelle.[1]

[Poetry is the expression, restored by human language to its essential rhythm, of the mysterious sense of the aspects of existence: thus it grants authenticity to our time on earth and constitutes our sole spiritual task.]

Poetry is the validation of human existence: the supreme duty of mankind is to attempt contact with its mysterious dimension, and poetry is what makes the merely human authentic and valuable. Language has to be stripped down to an essence before it will be fit for uncovering the mystery. This essence comprises the spiritual, the mysterious, the authentic and the poetic, and is opposed to the empirically observable. Contact between the two dimensions of existence is, to use Baudelaire's term, *correspondance*.

Hebbel, too, provided a definition of poetry, written almost half a century before Mallarmé's, but with several elements in common:

Die lyr. Poesie soll das menschliche Gemüth im Tiefsten erschließen, sie soll seine dunkelsten Zustände durch himmelklare Melodien lösen, sie soll es durch sich selbst berauschen und erquicken.[2]

[The function of lyric poetry is to open up the depths of human nature, to resolve its darkest states with melodies of heavenly clarity, to exhilarate and refresh it through human nature itself.]

[1] Originally in a letter of 27 June 1884 to Léo d'Orfer: Mallarmé, *Correspondance*, ii. 266; published by d'Orfer in *La Vogue*, 2 (18 Apr. 1886), 70–1; repr. in Michaud's *La Doctrine symboliste (documents)* (Paris: Nizet, 1947), 715. Not in Mallarmé, *Œuvres complètes*, ed. Henri Mondor and G. Jean-Aubry, Bibliothèque de la Pléiade (Paris: Gallimard, 1945).

[2] From a letter to Elise Lensing, 24 Feb. 1839; Friedrich Hebbel, *Sämtliche Werke*, Historisch-kritische Ausgabe, ed. Richard Maria Werner (Berlin: Behr, 1904), iii/i: *Briefe 1829–1839*, 401.

There are not so much precise overlaps as intimations of shared thinking patterns: Mallarmé aims at the expression of mystery, Hebbel at
opening up depth and darkness; Mallarmé's spirituality is linked to
the aspirations of Hebbel's 'himmelklar'; the French poet refers to
the rhythms of human language, and the German to melodies, both
instinctively reaching for musical metaphors. The key difference is that
for Hebbel the human temperament is the medium and the *object* of the
action of poetry, whereas Mallarmé appears to have finessed the individual out of primary significance and to be using him as the medium
only, as the means to attain something greater beyond.

Mallarmé's succinct definition was elicited by Léo d'Orfer and
published as part of an inquiry, similar to Jules Huret's, conducted for
La Vogue in 1886.[3] Its substance is not unique, but it is one of the most
succinct available statements of Symbolist poetics, which were the
object of Hofmannsthal's interest in the early 1890s. Nor is Hebbel's
definition especially idiosyncratic, and it has nothing untypical of
Romantic poetic thought—Novalis, for example, also saw poetry as
'offenbarte[s] Gemüth' [the human temperament revealed].[4] But
Hofmannsthal had been reading Hebbel's diaries since Christmas
1890, and had read a volume of his letters a week before that, noting
specifically that 'der hauptsächliche Nutzen solcher Bücher [ist]
vielleicht der, daß wir auf den Wert dessen aufmerksam werden, was in
uns dämmert' [the principal use of such books is perhaps that they
make us aware of the value of what is slumbering within us].[5] He
referred to the very passage from Hebbel's letters quoted above on 13
July 1892 in a note about Symbolism.[6] In 1903 he was to choose Hebbel
to illustrate what he called 'lyrische Grundbedürfnisse' [fundamental
lyric necessities] in *Das Gespräch über Gedichte* in order to show the

---

[3] *La Vogue* was one of the most influential Symbolist journals, publishing much original
verse, and publicizing the theorists' work (notably Téodor de Wyzewa's 'Notes sur
Mallarmé' and Verlaine's self-study in the *Poètes maudits*). It secured the manuscript of the
Illuminations and published *Une saison en enfer* in 1886, making Rimbaud widely available for
the first time.

[4] Novalis, *Schriften: Die Werke Friedrich von Hardenbergs*, ed. Paul Kluckhohn and Richard
Samuel, 2nd extended edn. (Stuttgart: Kohlhammer, 1960–88), iii. 683.

[5] *RA* iii. 315. In Jan. 1890 he contrasts the diaries favourably with Amiel's journal; see *RA*
iii. 321.

[6] *RA* iii. 349. So many of Hofmannsthal's diary jottings quote or resemble Hebbel's that a
detailed study of this relationship is needed. It is quite possible, for example, that Hebbel's
diary sowed the seed for the pivotal scene in *Der Schwierige* where Hans-Karl recalls dreaming
during his burial in the trenches that he was married to Helene: 'Träume . . . Da könnte es
sich wirklich treffen, daß man in demselben Augenblick Hochzeit machte und begraben
würde' (10 Mar. 1838). See Friedrich Hebbel, *Sämtliche Werke: Tagebücher*, i. 222; entry 1031.

manner in which Symbolism fulfils these needs, and much earlier, in March 1893, he had already noted the same connection: ' "Symbolismus" Form des künstlerischen Grundtriebes' [Symbolism: a form of the fundamental poetic impulse; *RA* iii. 357].

That Symbolism and Romanticism are intimately linked is a standard critical view. Edmund Wilson calls Symbolism 'the second flood of the same tide as Romanticism', and Lloyd Austin confirms: 'le Symbolisme, tel qu'ils [Baudelaire, Mallarmé and Valéry] le conçoivent et qu'ils le mettent en œuvre, ne fait que porter jusqu'à leur conclusion logique les prémisses du Romantisme européen' [Symbolism, as they conceive of and practise it, merely brings the premisses of European Romanticism to their logical conclusion].[7] This view was propounded by contemporaries of the Symbolists themselves, notably in Jean Thorel's article 'Les Romantiques allemands et les Symbolistes français'.[8] Stefan George's editor Carl August Klein noted, albeit in an attempt to distance George from the French tradition, 'uebrigens liegen die urquellen der "Nouvelle Poesie" . . . in Deutschland, in der deutschen Romantik: man denke an Hardenberg's hellsichtige aussprüche' [moreover, the deepest roots of the 'New Poetry' lie in Germany, in German Romanticism: think of Hardenberg's perspicacious aphorisms].[9] And even the most determined and spiteful opponents of Symbolism such as Max Nordau use the same point in their critique: 'wir haben schon längst Alles, was die französischen Dichter erst mit Barrikaden und Straßengemetzel erringen wollen' [we have long since possessed everything that the French poets only now wish to achieve with barricades and carnage in the street].[10] Whilst this perspective tends to smudge the fundamental discontinuities between the two movements that other scholars stress,[11] the strength and nature of Symbolism's European pedigree are decisive factors in Hofmannsthal's response to the movement. This chapter begins therefore with an account of the genesis of Symbolism to serve as a framework for a consideration of Hofmannsthal's views on poetry in the 1890s.

[7] Edmund Wilson, *Axel's Castle: A Study of the Imaginative Literature of 1870–1930* (New York: C. Scribner's Sons, 1931), Lloyd James Austin, *L'Univers poétique de Baudelaire* (Paris: Mercure de France, 1956), 11.

[8] Published in *Entretiens politiques et littéraires*, 3.18 (Sept. 1891), 95–105.

[9] Carl August Klein, 'Über Stefan George: Eine neue Kunst', *Blätter für die Kunst*, 1.2 (1892), 47.

[10] Nordau, *Entartung*, i. 214.

[11] See for example Hiltrud Gnüg, *Entstehung und Krise lyrischer Subjektivität* (Stuttgart: Metzler, 1983), 125–9.

There are many aspects of the general term Romanticism, all applicable to some of the creations that go under this name, few true of them all. They include forms of sensibility deliberately distinct from those of the Enlightenment; new attitudes to the self and the fore-grounding of an individual's personal and private characteristics over his social functions; the rejection of any notion of objectivity in the realms of morals, aesthetics and politics; the belief in the universality of art; new stress on the importance of nature and its capacity to reflect the intimacies of humanity and to articulate a sense of man's unity with his surroundings; the need felt for the regeneration and adaptation of art-forms that were becoming stale and rigid; the central importance of the poetic imagination in communicating revivified perceptions of the world; a longing for a realm of greater significance than that empirically (and thus superficially) observable; a conception of the uni-verse as organic, living, unfathomable and without a rationally dis-cernible structure; a preference for the disordered, even chaotic, over the clear and harmoniously ordered, which was often seen as 'neutral-ized'; and a mystical, quasi-religious tone that was often characteristic of the Romantic style.

The balance of these elements, or their dilution and supplementa-tion by other local features, varied greatly from country to country. The Germans leaned towards mysticism and philosophical idealism, explained by René Wellek in terms of the social background of those writing at the time: 'German Romanticism, more so than English and French, was the movement of an intelligentsia which had loosened its class ties and hence was particularly apt to create a literature remote from ordinary reality and social concerns.'[12] The strength of Neo-classicism meant that, after some stirrings in Rousseau, Chateau-briand and Senancour, French Romanticism came as more of a jolt and had much less of a pedestal in theoretical writings upon which to rest. Albert Béguin distinguishes Germany and France in terms of the status of the self:

En Allemagne, des esprits tout pénétrés de science et de philosophie s'étaient en-gagés sur la voie au terme de laquelle ils espéraient tout ensemble aboutir à la véritable connaissance objective et retrouver l'harmonie primitive de l'homme avec son ambiance. . . . On conférait au poète une mission d'ordre métaphysique et mystique: en saisissant le réel, il espérait préparer la réintegration finale de l'humanité dans l'unité originelle.

[12] René Wellek, 'The Concept of Romanticism in Literary History', *Comparative Literature*, I (1949), 167.

Les romantiques français, au contraire, ne semblaient apercevoir aucun au-delà du pur subjectivisme: une littérature de confession lyrique ne prétendait bouleverser les lois traditionnelles et les formes consacrées de l'art d'écrire que pour donner libre cours à l'expression des sentiments, des tourments, des malaises du poète lui-même. Sans doute ces mélancolies et ces nostalgies n'étaient-elles pas sans accompagnement d'inquiétude métaphysique; mais aucune affirmation de magie ne proclamait que le subjectivisme sentimental était le premier temps d'une démarche dont le second mouvement... pouvait atteindre à ce lieu secret où nous ne sommes plus 'nous-mêmes', mais où nous connaissons par analogie ce qui autrement demeure inconnaissable.[13]

[In Germany, intellects steeped in science and philosophy had set out on the way that they hoped would end with their achieving together true objective understanding and with their discovery of the primitive harmony of man with his surroundings. The poet was entrusted with a mission of metaphysical and mystical significance: by grasping what was real, he hoped to prepare the ultimate reintegration of humanity in its original wholeness. By contrast, the French Romantics did not seem to perceive anything beyond pure subjectivism: lyrically confessional literature only claimed to overturn the traditional laws and the forms devoted to the art of writing in order to give free rein to the expression of the emotions, the sufferings, the malaises of the poet himself. Doubtless these forms of melancholy and nostalgia were themselves not without the accompaniment of metaphysical unease; but no affirmation of magic announced that sentimental subjectivism was the first stage of a process whose second stage might attain that secret place where we are no longer our 'selves', but where we understand by analogy things that otherwise remain unknowable.]

French Symbolism can be seen as a more intimate version of 1830s Romanticism. But an international perspective identifies elements that have more in common with the search of the German Romantics for the secret place 'ou nous ne sommes plus "nous-mêmes" '. According to Béguin, French Romanticism was founded on what he calls a secret tradition, hidden beneath triumphal Romanticism, in which are to be found analogues to Novalis, Achim von Arnim and Hoffmann. It is this layer, veiled during Romanticism proper,

[qui] ne parviendra à son plein épanouissement que dans les illuminations de Nerval luttant contre la démence et la mort, de Hugo vieux penché sur le gouffre, de Baudelaire poursuivant la possession de l'Éternité, de Rimbaud adolescent envahi par la vision.

[which will not reach its full flowering until the effulgences of Nerval struggling with madness and death, of the late Hugo leaning over the abyss, of Baudelaire pursuing the conquest of Eternity, of the adolescent Rimbaud possessed by vision.]

[13] Albert Béguin, *L'Âme romantique et le rêve* (Paris: Corti, 1946), 328.

The poetry of the early Symbolists, says Béguin, is 'étrangement voisine de celle que voulut saisir, que ne saisit pas toujours le romantisme allemand' [strangely similar to what German Romanticism wished to grasp, but was not always able to grasp].[14]

This map of the ancestry of Symbolism shows not only how the deeper layer in France is analogous to the thinking of the German Romantics, but also how by the 1880s its development was directly influenced and encouraged by increasing familiarity with the works of such as Novalis and Hoffmann, either in the original or in translation. Maeterlinck's version of the opening of *Les Disciples à Sais*, to which he added *Fragments* when it was published in book form in 1895, represents merely the most visible tip of the French writers' deeper familiarity with the German Romantics.[15] In *Counterparts*, Lilian Furst proposes a view of two intertwined strands that accommodates the mutual influence of the French and German traditions. Both strands begin in the *Sturm und Drang*, a sort of pre-Romanticism that shares with Romanticism proper the attempt to work out what it meant to be modern: the first strand crossed the border, expanding very conspicuously and becoming French Romanticism; the second derivative of the *Sturm und Drang* remained beyond the Rhine, turning inward and becoming German Romanticism; the two joined eventually in Symbolism, and were ultimately picked up by the so-called Neo-Romantics, Hofmannsthal, George and Rilke. Familiar with their own Romantic heritage, they had a subconscious affinity with aspects of it submerged in French Symbolism that partly accounts for the impact of the latter.

In Symbolism, the confidence that imbued Romanticism is largely missing, and crucially this meant a lack of confidence in the capacity of traditional literary language to express their relationship to the world. Why it should have reached crisis-pitch at the point it did is of course impossible to say precisely. But there are features in the historical

---

[14] Ibid. 328–9.
[15] Maeterlinck's translation was published in *Le Réveil* in May 1894. For details relating to Novalis, cf. Werner Vordtriede, *Novalis, und die französischen Symbolisten: Zur Entstehungsgeschichte des dichterischen Symbols* (Stuttgart: Kohlhammer, 1963), 34–97. Baudelaire's frequent quotation of Hoffmann in the *Salons* immediately confirms this. Cf. Baudelaire, *OC*, ii. 425–6; also Jonathan Culler, 'Intertextuality and Interpretation: Baudelaire's "Correspondances"', in Christopher Prendergast (ed.), *Nineteenth-Century French Poetry* (Cambridge: Cambridge University Press, 1990), 120 and 126–7; A. G. Lehmann, *The Symbolist Aesthetic in France 1885–1895* (Oxford: Blackwell, 1968), 208; Austin, *L'Univers poétique de Baudelaire*, 148, 261 and 263; Rosemary Lloyd, *Baudelaire's Literary Criticism* (Cambridge: Cambridge University Press, 1981), 49–50.

ambience that, with hindsight, give it a certain inevitability. One of the effects of a social climate of increasing specialization, perceived by some as fragmentation, is the individual's sense of his merely marginal importance. It is a commonplace to point out that the developing industrialization of the century meant for some the mistaken relocation of value in the superficial, contingent and pragmatic, resulting in the neglect of less tangible concepts of worth and the erosion of the spiritual dimensions of man's interest and activity. There was an anxiety amongst those who were aware that this had not always been so and that it need not necessarily be so, but who felt powerless to effect a change in the prevailing positivism. One response was retreat into a world that had long been recognized as a repository of significance beyond the here-and-now, or as a means of access to such a dimension, the world of art. If society is perceived as hostile, art at bay fortifies itself with egocentrism and indifference. But placing poetry under such strain brings a heightened awareness of the tolerances of its raw material, language, and in particular the knowledge that it is of a kind with the language of its base surroundings. If language is complicit in the problems, it has to be cleansed and renewed, however adequate it has proved in the past. Poetic language must always be one step ahead of non-poetic to preserve the sanctity of its perceptions, and as soon as the suspicion sets in that its difference is being lost, it must move on and be made strange. This is the feeling that dominated the Symbolists' relations with their society, and however un-Symbolist the martial metaphors, they convey something of the vulnerability that underlies Symbolist writing and something of its tactical defiance, and they reflect aspects of the aggressiveness with which it was greeted by some contemporaries.

For the Symbolists, the vocabulary and techniques of previous generations were no longer adequate to express the different types of perception brought into relief by their embattled position *vis-à-vis* their surroundings. And this is especially—crucially—true if all the new perceptions are from the standpoint of men who have lost their linguistic innocence. The very success of previous authors condemns new generations either to epigonism or innovation. When epigonism is conscious it becomes itself a source of new creativity: part of Heine's originality, for example, lies in his ironic and satiric reaction to the old age and death of Romantic sentiment and vocabulary. But even if there is a trace of this jaundice in Baudelaire's attitude to his tradition, he, like Heine, combines it with an attempt at revitalization.

Convention can be reanimated without its ceasing to be convention. His defiant championship of the poetic beauty of ugliness, for example, is in part reaction against the worn clichés of beauty, but the major element is the desire to establish a distinction between the aesthetic construction and the aesthetic object. His service here is to rid poetry of the habit of thinking that existing convention in the matter of the relation of form and content represents the *ne plus ultra* and has the status of an absolute. By means of a consciously traditional poetic form and diction skilfully manipulated around unpoetic subjects, he encourages us to an untraditional perception. In this way he can, as it were, recharge tradition instead of having to invent a new one. Mallarmé's search for the literary absolute is a version of this attempt to escape the perspectivism imposed by the traditional.

One of the origins of the Romantic temperament had been a profound dissatisfaction with Enlightenment rationalism, and the outlook of both the Symbolists and their counterparts the Neo-Romantic German-language writers was similarly motivated in part by a rejection of their immediate literary past. In this case it was the superficial empiricism of the extreme form of Realism known as Naturalism. In France, parallel to the development outlined above, there was a strong Realist tradition in the novels of Stendhal and Flaubert that moved almost imperceptibly into the Naturalism of Maupassant and Zola. But Zola was also very strongly affected by the trends that culminated in Symbolism, and some of his Naturalist works such as *Germinal* or *La Terre* partake too of an intensely symbolic atmosphere. Its ancestor in the novel is the fantastic and mystical in Balzac. Zola's *La Faute de l'abbé Mouret*, for example, is by no stretch of the imagination a Naturalist novel: it is to *Nana* what *Und Pippa tanzt* is to *Die Weber*. But *Und Pippa tanzt* was written in 1906, *Die Weber* in 1892, whereas the two novels by Zola appeared in 1875 and 1880 respectively, the 'Symbolist' work five years earlier than the novel that became the *locus classicus* of Naturalism. For the poets of turn-of-the-century Vienna, German Naturalism, associated with Berlin, was a far more substantial bulkhead to be breached than it had been in France, and so they turned to the French for inspiration. France offered an accessible literary style, opposing the positivistic approach of Naturalism, which was itself an alternative heir of post-Romantic self-alienation—an alternative that betrays its Romantic roots, namely Symbolism.

Even if Hermann Bahr's report of the death of Naturalism was premature in 1891, it did articulate Vienna's decisive rejection of that movement's presuppositions. There was some snobbery involved in Hofmannsthal's participation in this—which one might dignify by calling it an ideological component—but more fundamentally he rejected Naturalism's disregard for the whole issue of personal identity. Both Naturalism and Impressionism are fundamentally anti-Romantic in outlook, despite the fact that Symbolism, Neo-Romanticism and Impressionism are so often considered together as if they were indistinguishable synonyms. Impressionism could not present an attractive alternative, for it too concentrated on sense-perceptions and refused to propound a coherent identity behind them. Whilst it is true that the Impressionists' sensory refinement is a vital precursor of Symbolist poetry, it is so only as a technique and not as a *Weltanschauung*.[16] Paul Hoffmann's view is a common one, namely that Symbolism is a kind of Impressionism 'with depth', as it were, expressed with greater linguistic fluency, and that the former is a necessary development of the latter. Impressionism is essentially a kind of sensibility, Symbolism is characterized by a strong sense of form.[17]

However, Impressionism has much less in common with Symbolism than this suggests. Hofmannsthal attended Ernst Mach's lectures in 1897, and had already noted a response to the *Beiträge zur Analyse der Empfindungen* (1886) as early as April 1892.[18] Mach's philosophical impressionism, his unwillingness to entertain metaphysical speculation on sense-impressions or on the self perceiving was alien to Hofmannsthal's thinking. Mach reduced symbolic effect to a conceit:

Die Empfindungen sind auch keine 'Symbole der Dinge'. Vielmehr ist das 'Ding' ein Gedankensymbol für einen Empfindungskomplex von relativer Stabilität. Nicht die Dinge (Körper), sondern Farben, Töne, Drücke, Räume, Zeiten (was wir gewöhnlich Empfindungen nennen) sind die eigentlichen Elemente der Welt.[19]

[Sensations are not 'symbols for things' either. Rather the 'thing' is a mental symbol for a relatively stable complex of sensations. It is not things (bodies), but colours, tones, pressures, spaces, times (which we usually call sensations) that are the real elements of the world.]

Impressionism takes the dissolution of the self to an extreme without putting anything else in its place. It remains content with 'Farben,

[16] See Paul Hoffmann, *Symbolismus* (Munich: Fink, 1987), 35.

[17] 'Zur Vertiefung und Sublimierung der Impression im Symbol und zur Lockerung der mimetischen Fixierung in der Freisetzung der sprachlichen Potenzen kommt die Bindung der impressionistischen Sensibilität an den strengen Formsinn des Symbolismus' (ibid.).

[18] *Nachlaß*, H VII 4.4.

[19] Ernst Mach, *Mechanik* (3rd edn., 1883), 473; quoted by Richard Hamann and Jost Hermand, *Impressionismus*, 2nd edn. (Berlin: Akademie-Verlag, 1966), 208.

Töne, Drücke', and 'there is nothing the impressionist dreads more than an epistemological interpretation of the sense data he has assembled'.[20] But literature ought not to be so content, with the consequence that Robert Musil trenchantly noted: 'niemals gab es in den höheren Regionen der Dichtung einen Impressionisten' [there has never been an Impressionist in the higher echelons of literature].[21] Clive Scott suggests that the Impressionists 'wish us to look at reality without prejudice' and that literary Impressionism is 'a matter of linguistic techniques, the attempt to make language the act of perception rather than analysis of the act, to make language experiential activity rather than a description of activity',[22] but for Symbolism 'prejudice', in the form of aspiration and valorization, or rejection and dissatisfaction, was perfectly legitimate.

Because of its rejection of the adequacy of rationalism, the literature that emerged from the Romantic sensibility relied on the intuitive rather than the intellectual faculties and developed means of expression appropriate to these. It was underpinned by a feeling of the mutual correspondence of man and world. Novalis's *Die Lehrlinge zu Sais* opens with a statement of this belief:

Mannigfache Wege gehen die Menschen. Wer sie verfolgt und vergleicht, wird wunderliche Figuren entstehen sehen; Figuren, die jener großen Chiffrenschrift zu gehören scheinen, die man überall, auf Flügeln, Eierschalen, in Wolken, im Schnee, in Kristallen und in Steinbildungen, auf gefrierenden Wassern, im Innern und Äußern der Gebirge, der Pflanzen, der Tiere, der Menschen . . . erblickt. In ihnen ahndet man den Schlüssel dieser Wunderschrift, die Sprachlehre derselben.[23]

[Mankind moves along paths that are many and various. Whoever traces and compares them will see marvellous figures forming, figures that seem to belong to the great symbolic script that we glimpse everywhere, on wings and eggshells, in clouds, in the snow, in crystals and in rock-formations, on freezing waters, within and on the surface of mountains, plants, animals and human beings. In these we sense the key to that marvellous script, its very grammar.]

The writing metaphors are not incidental: poetry was a necessary part of the relationship, an instrument both of perception and of expression. For Romantic writers, symbolism was both the relationship of man to the world and the central process of art, representing the link of

---

[20] Ulrich Weisstein, 'Impressionism', *Encyclopedia of Poetry and Poetics* (London: Macmillan, 1975), 381.
[21] Robert Musil, *Tagebücher*, ed. Adolf Frisé (Reinbek bei Hamburg: Rowohlt, 1976), i. 475.
[22] Clive Scott, *A Question of Syllables* (Cambridge: Cambridge University Press, 1986), 222.
[23] Novalis, *Schriften*, i. 79.

the one and the many,—or 'the finite embodiment of the infinite'.[24] Hebbel noted in his diary for 19 October 1839:

Novalis hatte die wunderliche Idee, weil die ganze Welt poetisch auf ihn wirkte, die ganze Welt zum Gegenstand seiner Poesie zu machen. Es ist ungefähr eben *so*, als wenn das menschliche Herz, das sein Verhältnis zum Körper fühlt, diesen ganzen Körper *einsaugen* wollte.[25]

[Because the whole world had a poetic effect upon him, Novalis had the fantastic idea of making the whole world into the object of his poetry. It is approximately the same as if the human heart, aware of its relationship to the body, wished to *consume* this body entirely.]

A. W. Schlegel put it more succinctly: 'Dichten . . . ist nichts andres als ein ewiges Symbolisieren' [writing is nothing other than eternal symbolizing].[26]

This process of symbolization involves both security and risk. If it is secured by man's participation in the divinely created universe, the totality exposes the self to possible annihilation. *Heinrich von Ofterdingen*, for example, shows a figure whose predisposition to poetic creativity is established as he opens up to every new stimulus, whether locality, person or *Märchen*, allowing his individual identity to be subsumed into the outside world: Heinrich and the Merchants (where poetic and non-poetic disposition are counterposed) listen attentively to the conversation:

und der ersterer fühlte besonders neue Entwickelungen seines ahndungsvollen Innern. Manche Worte, manche Gedanken fielen wie belebender Fruchtstaub, in seinen Schoß, und rückten ihn schnell aus dem engen Kreise seiner Jugend auf die Höhe der Welt. . . . Er glaubte nie anders gedacht und empfunden zu haben.[27]

[and Heinrich, full of anticipation, felt quite new developments within him. Some of the words, some of the thoughts fell like invigorating pollen into his lap and quickly shook him out of the narrow orbits of his youth and up on to the pinnacles of the world. . . . He believed he had never thought and felt any other way.]

Earlier, after Heinrich has been given permission to accompany the old man underground, his self-definition evaporates into the moonlit evening:

[24] Ernest Stahl, 'The Genesis of Symbolist Theories in Germany', *Modern Language Review*, 41 (1946), 315.
[25] *Tagebücher*, i. 386; entry no. 1711; Hebbel's italics. See below, p. 86, for the rest of this entry.
[26] In the *Vorlesungen über schöne Literatur und Kunst*, quoted by Stahl, 'Symbolist Theories', 315.
[27] Novalis, *Schriften*, i. 263.

In Heinrichs Gemüt spiegelte sich das Märchen des Abends. Es war ihm, als ruhte die Welt aufgeschlossen in ihm, und zeigte ihm, wie einem Gastfreunde, alle ihre Schätze und verborgenen Lieblichkeiten. . . . Die Worte des Alten hatten eine versteckte Tapetentür in ihm geöffnet.[28]

[The fairy-tale evening was reflected within Heinrich. He felt as if the world had been unlocked and were resting within him, and was showing him all its treasures and secret charms as if he were an honoured guest. The old man's words had opened a hidden door within him.]

This is the kind of identity that Novalis feels is necessary for the production of poetry. Such a view was not confined to the German Romantics and may be said to constitute one of the pillars of Romantic poetics. John Keats's famous letter to Richard Woodhouse defines the 'poetical Character itself' in terms that overlap with Novalis's:

it is not itself—it has no self—it is everything and nothing—It has no character—it enjoys light and shade; it lives in gusto, be it foul or fair, high or low, rich or poor, mean or elevated—It has as much delight in conceiving an Iago as an Imogen. . . . What shocks the virtuous philosop[h]er, delights the camelion Poet. . . . A Poet is the most unpoetical of any thing in existence; because he has no Identity—he is continually in for—and filling some other Body—The Sun, the Moon, the Sea and Men and Women who are creatures of impulse are poetical and have about them an unchangeable attribute—the poet has none; no identity—he is certainly the most unpoetical of all God's creatures.[29]

This is the condition in which he can 'take part in' the existence of a sparrow pecking about in gravel before his window.[30] Again parallel to Heinrich von Ofterdingen, absorbent to the point of self-destruction, Keats makes a radical assertion of the transformations that the Poet must of his nature undergo:

When I am in a room with People if I ever am free from speculating on creations of my own brain, then not myself goes home to myself: but the identity of every one in the room begins [so] to press upon me that, *I am in a very little time an[n]ihilated.*[31]

As Steve Rizza points out, this letter was the subject of considerable and varied interest at the turn of the century. Otto Weininger cites the passage in full in *Geschlecht und Charakter* (1903) as part of an argument

---

[28] Ibid. 252.
[29] *Letters of John Keats: A Selection*, ed. Robert Gittings (Oxford: Oxford University Press, 1987), 157.
[30] Ibid. 38.
[31] Ibid. 158; my italics.

about genius.[32] Rudolf Kassner translates extensively from it in *Die Mystik: Über englische Dichter und Maler im 19. Jahrhundert* (1900) and interprets it as 'the first statement of a particularly modern poetic psychology': 'So hat niemand vor Keats gesprochen. Der Dichter, wie er einer ist, sei da, Eindrücke zu empfangen; seine Seele müsse sich den Dingen um ihn herum verschenken, und er verliere sein Wesen' [no one before Keats had spoken like that. According to him, the poet, as such, is there in order to receive impressions; his soul must give itself up to the things around him and he will lose his self].[33]

The quotation from Hebbel's diary noted above continues, 'Jean Paul nennt Nov. mit Recht einen poetischen Nihilisten' [Jean Paul rightly calls Novalis a poetic nihilist]. Evaporation, loss or annihilation of identity are one part of poetic creation, but Keats and Novalis both undergo or propound self-forgetfulness in the full confidence of its counterpart. Poetry for them is an aesthetic (although not merely aesthetic) equivalent of Christ's paradox, 'he that findeth his life shall lose it: and he that loseth his life for my sake shall find it' (Matthew 10: 39). The Romantics' humanized poetic folly—sacrificing the unpoetic attributes of personality, a superficial level of coherence and consistency in external aspects such as behaviour and value-judgement—has similar rewards for the self. Poetry, as intuitive perception, is able to put together what dry science dissects with sharp knives: 'Unter [den] Händen [der Naturforscher] starb die freundliche Natur, und ließ nur tote, zuckende Reste zurück, dagegen sie vom Dichter, wie durch geistvollen Wein, noch mehr beseelt . . . zum Himmel stieg' [in the hands of scientists, benevolent nature died and left only remnants behind, quivering or dead, but after being animated by the poet, as if after drinking a glorious wine . . . it rose up to the heavens].[34] Keats writes similarly about Newton in 'Lamia': 'Philosophy will clip an Angel's wings, | Conquer all mysteries by rule and line, . . . | Unweave a rainbow.'[35]

The redintegrative component of poetry is no less important and is found in fragments such as 'je persönlicher, localer temporeller,

---

[32] See Otto Weininger, *Geschlecht und Charakter*, repr. (Munich: Matthes & Seitz, 1980), 535–6 and Jacques Le Rider, *Hugo von Hofmannsthal: Historicisme et modernité* (Paris: Presses Universitaires de France, 1995), 117–18.

[33] Rudolf Kassner, *Die Mystik, die Künstler und das Leben: Über englische Dichter und Maler im 19. Jahrhundert* (Leipzig: Diederichs, 1900), 113; Steve Rizza, *Rudolf Kassner and Hugo von Hofmannsthal: Criticism as Art* (Frankfurt a.M.: Peter Lang, 1997), 196.

[34] *Die Lehrlinge zu Sais*; Novalis, *Schriften*, i. 84.

[35] John Keats, *The Complete Poems*, ed. John Barnard (Harmondsworth: Penguin, 1973), 431.

eigenthümlicher ein Gedicht ist, desto näher steht es dem Centro der Poesie' [the more personal, local, temporal or individual a poem is, the nearer it is to the very centre of poetry itself], or 'in eigentlichen Poëmen ist keine als die *Einheit* des *Gemüths*. . . . Poësie = offenbarten Gemüth—*wircksamer* (produktiver) *Individualität'* [in true poems there is nothing but unity of disposition. Poetry = the revelation of human nature—effective (productive) individuality].[36] Both of these presuppose a considerable degree of self-possession, or at least the confidence in the existence of a central core of selfhood. In *Die Lehrlinge zu Sais* the two elements are combined: 'Es ist ein geheimnisvoller Zug nach allen Seiten in unserm Innern, aus einem unendlich tiefen Mittelpunkt sich rings verbreitend' [deep inside us we are mysteriously drawn in all directions by a force that spreads in circles from an infinitely deep centre]. The full reciprocity of inner and outer worlds evoked in this work promotes the dissipation of the self:

Auf alles, was der Mensch vornimmt, muß er seine *ungeteilte* Aufmerksamkeit oder *sein Ich* richten . . . und wenn er dieses getan hat, so entstehn bald Gedanken, oder eine neue Art von Wahrnehmungen, die nichts als zarte Bewegungen eines färbenden oder klappernden Stifts, oder wunderliche Zusammenziehungen und Figurationen einer elastischen Flüssigkeit zu sein scheinen, auf eine wunderbare Weise in ihm. Sie verbreiten sich von dem Punkte, wo er den Eindruck feststach, nach allen Seiten mit lebendiger Beweglichkeit, und nehmen sein Ich mit fort.[37]

[Man must focus his *undivided* attention or his *self* on everything that he undertakes, and if he does this, there will soon arise within him, in a marvellous manner, thoughts or new sorts of perception, which seem to be nothing but the delicate movements of a coloured or scratching pencil, or the fantastic collocations and figurations of an elastic liquid. They spread out in all directions and with the agility of living things from the point at which he fixed the impression, taking his self away with them.]

But this dissipation depends on concentration: 'ungeteilte Aufmerksamkeit' again presupposes some unity of self.

Goethe's conception of symbolism anticipated elements of Romanticism, notably the idea that symbolic expression reproduces not only the totality of which the symbol, work of art or individual is a part, but also something higher, the Idea or essence. According to his most famous definition, in *Maximen und Reflexionen*, 'die Symbolik verwandelt die Erscheinung in Idee, die Idee in ein Bild, und so, daß die Idee im Bild immer unendlich wirksam und unerreichbar bleibt und,

---

[36] Novalis, *Schriften*, iii. 664 and 683.
[37] Novalis, *Schriften*, i. 85 and 96–7; my italics.

selbst in allen Sprachen ausgesprochen, doch unaussprechlich bliebe'
[Symbolism transforms the external appearance into an idea, and
the idea into an image, and does so in such a way that the idea always
remains infinitely effective and unattainable within the image, and
would remain ineffable even if translated into any other language].[38]
But for Goethe, the symbolic process, 'wo das Besondere das
Allgemeinere repräsentiert' [where the particular represents the
general] is closely confined and controlled, and even if the ideas
expressed were unfathomable, they were identifiable and not incomprehensible: symbolism was not a representation 'als Traum und
Schatten' [in dreams and shadows] as it was for his Romantic contemporaries.[39] The Romantic view was altogether more daring, view-
ing the unconscious and dream as gateways to the infinite (Nerval uses
the image of the Gate of Ivory from the *Odyssey*) and encouraging a
more private and less accessible symbolism that was unpalatable to
Goethe. Novalis celebrates the potentially liberating effect of dream in
poetry: 'Der Traum ist oft bedeutend und prophetisch, weil er eine
Naturseelenwirkung ist—und *also* auf Associationsordnung beruht—
Er ist, wie die Poësie bedeutend—aber auch darum unregelmäßig
bedeutend—*durchaus frey*' [a dream is often meaningful and prophetic,
because it is a phenomenon of a natural soul—and therefore depends
on the order of association—It is meaningful in the same way as
poetry—but for the same reason therefore only irregularly meaningful—*completely free*].[40]

Hofmannsthal's own use of the term Romanticism does not correspond at all with that of modern literary historians. Hofmannsthal's
recorded comments during the early 1890s on what he called
Romanticism are largely negative, but—influenced by Georg
Brandes—they refer to only one aspect of what we now understand by
the term. The 'Potemkin letter' to Beer-Hofmann, for example, dis-
misses the Romantics' world as a dreamworld; Hofmannsthal's
first essay on D'Annunzio approvingly cites Brandes's view that
Romanticism is a tendency, 'sich nach dem "Naiven" zu sehnen' [to
hanker after naivety; *RA* i. 176]; a note from April 1891 on Schiller,

---

[38] Goethe, *Werke*, xii. 470. See also below, p. 302. This formulation is echoed in *Ein Brief*,
when Chandos says there is no language in the world that is adequate for the expression of
what he has to say: 'die Sprache, in welcher nicht nur zu schreiben, sondern auch zu denken
mir vielleicht gegeben wäre, weder die lateinische noch die englische noch die
italienische und spanische ist, sondern eine Sprache, von deren Worten mir auch nicht eines
bekannt ist, eine Sprache, in welcher die stummen Dinge zu mir sprechen' (*SW* xxxi. 54).

[39] Goethe, *Werke*, xii. 471.

[40] Novalis, *Schriften*, iii. 452.

Beethoven and Byron claims 'sie scheitern am Wollen des Übergroßen wie die Romantiker am Wollen des Übertiefen' [they come to grief because of their desire to be excessively great, as the Romantics wanted to be excessively deep; *RA* iii. 326]. Hofmannsthal linked dilettantism with Romanticism in equally negative terms, calling the latter a diseased form of true art in the same way that dilettantism is 'das Anempfindungsvermögen, Krankheit des Empfindungs-vermögens' [the capacity to feel at second hand, a disease of the capacity for sensation; *RA* i. 102]. Both are seen as degenerate. A year later, on 19 April 1892, Romanticism is identified with 'neurasthenische Poesie ... Poesie der langen Fieber, wo Traum und Realität ineinanderrinnt' [neurasthenic poetry ... poetry of a slow fever, where dream and reality merge into each other; *RA* iii. 344]. In the essay on Ibsen, to give a final example, the objects of his dramatic characters' longings (Greece, the sea, America) are deprecated as

alles nur symbolische Namen für irgendein 'Draußen' und 'Anders' . . . nichts anderes als das verträumte Verlangen der Romantiker nach der mondbeglänzten Zauberwildnis . . . nach irgendeiner niegeahnten Märchenhaftigkeit des Lebens. (*RA* i. 151)

[all just symbolic names for something 'beyond' and 'other', nothing more than the Romantics' dreamy desire for a magical wilderness illuminated by moonlight, for some sort of hitherto unsuspected fairy-tale dimension to life.]

In general, Hofmannsthal seems to regard the term Romanticism as a synonym for reprehensible escapism or the search for spurious pro-fundity. His attitudes mellow with time, such that by 1903 and *Das Gespräch über Gedichte* he is happy to talk of 'Draußen' and 'Anders', the Beyond and the Other, but in the early 1890s 'Romanticism' was a deeply suspect term.

Two poets that we would nowadays not hesitate to call Romantic, Keats and Novalis, were clearly not included within the range of Hofmannsthal's strictures, and both were central in shaping his early ideas about poetry. Echoes from other Romantic poets, English, German and French, appear now and then, and yet more names are mentioned in Hofmannsthal's essays and notes, but Keats and Novalis dominate.[41] A note from 1920 laments the fragmentation of the German tradition:

[41] Hanna Lewis notes references to Byron and Coleridge, and more extensive debts to Shelley, notably to 'The Witch of Atlas'. Cf. 'Hofmannsthal, Shelley, and Keats', *German Life and Letters*, 27 (1973–4), 256–8. Her mention of De Quincey (232) should perhaps be placed in the context of Hofmannsthal's reading of Baudelaire.

Die Franzosen, die Spanier, die Engländer, alle andern haben, was wir nicht haben: eine literarische Tradition, eine Entwickelung des Urteils von einer Generation zur anderen, kurz eine wirkliche Literatur. Wir haben nur Ansätze und immer wieder Ansätze.[42]

[The French, the Spanish and the English, all the other nations have something that we do not, a literary tradition, a development in judgement from generation to generation, in short a true literature. We only have a series of starting-points.]

One of these 'Ansätze'—'genialer als die Werke der andern' [of greater genius than the others]—is identified as Novalis. As for Keats, Hofmannsthal's famous letter to Walther Brecht about his meeting with George and the early influences on his poetry recalls that Keats was the lodestar for his ambition to produce for German literature 'etwas . . . , was mit den großen Engländern von Keats an sich auf einer poetischen Ebene bewegte und andererseits mit den festen romanischen Formen zusammenhieng' [something that operated on the same poetic level as the great English poets from Keats onwards, and on the other hand something that was consistent with solid Romance forms; *SW* iii. 387], which is no mean goal. Hofmannsthal's academic research was equally ambitious, with theses on the Pléiade poets, who virtually reinvented poetic language in French, and on Victor Hugo, 'who set his sights not on the poem but on poetry, not on the novel but on fiction making'.[43]

In *Ad me ipsum* Hofmannsthal identified his early influences similarly, juxtaposing the Symbolist poets (and their immediate predecessors) and the Romantics:

Zeitpunkt 1892. Frühe Einflüsse: Edgar Poe—Baudelaire—Verlaine—Mallarmé (Georges Kopie des 'Après-midi d'un faune'). Der Zeitgeist: das Musikhafte.
ferner: Novalis, die englischen Dichter, besonders Keats. (*RA* iii. 620)

[1892. Early influences: Edgar Poe—Baudelaire—Verlaine—Mallarmé (George's copy of 'L'Après-midi d'un faune'). The temper of the age: musicality. Furthermore: Novalis, the English poets, especially Keats.]

These references are retrospective and a purely positivist 'head-count' of the names cited during the 1890s would not identify Keats and Novalis as so important.[44] There appears to be only one direct

---

[42] *RA* iii. 557. This was to become one of the leading arguments of 'Das Schrifttum als geistiger Raum der Nation' (1926; *RA* iii. 24–41).

[43] Victor Brombert, *Victor Hugo and the Visionary Novel* (Cambridge, Mass.: Harvard University Press, 1984), 5–6.

[44] Annette Simonis notes 'die erste Erwähnung im Hofmannsthalschen Werk findet Keats, soweit ich sehe, in dem 1903 entstandenen (fiktiven) *Gespräch über Gedichte*', which is technically correct, but it means that the early notes are not taken into account: 'Hofmanns-

reference to Novalis during the lyric decade, six lines of poetry quoted in a notebook.[45] Novalis's works were certainly known to Hofmannsthal then and several motifs from *Die Lehrlinge zu Sais* are taken up in 'Weltgeheimnis', for example.[46] Keats was a slightly more obvious influence: Hamburger records the urgent jotting 'Keats kaufen!!!' [buy Keats!!!] from 1891, and the edition Hofmannsthal in fact bought was from 1892.[47] He judges that Hofmannsthal first read the shorter poems, but a letter to Stephan Gruss from 1907 recalls the 'chameleon poet' from the famous letter from Keats to Woodhouse, and how 'dieser Brief hat mich sehr entlastet, als er mir vor Jahren das erstemal in die Hand kam' [when it first came into my hands years ago, this letter was a great consolation to me].[48] Finally, a letter to John Drinkwater written in English on 10 September 1924 claims that Hofmannsthal had been very fond of English poetry 'almost from my fifth or sixth year', and Keats heads the list of poets cited (although Milton is retrospectively given pride of place).[49]

French Symbolism is a development of Romanticism that undermines the stability in the relationship of symbol and value. Hugo Friedrich's thesis in *Die Struktur der modernen Lyrik* is that modernity is characterized by what he calls 'Entpersönlichung', depersonalization:

in dem Sinne, daß das lyrische Wort nicht mehr aus der Einheit von Dichtung und empirischer Person hervorgeht, wie dies, zum Unterschied von vielen Jahrhunderten früherer Lyrik, die Romantiker angestrebt hatten.[50]

[in the sense in which the lyric word no longer proceeds from the unity of poetry and the real person, which is what the Romantics had aspired to, in contrast to many centuries of earlier lyric poetry.]

thal und die englische Tradition—Rezeption und Adaptation englischsprachiger Literatur in den Schriften Hugo von Hofmannsthals', *Arcadia*, 30 (1995), 294–7.

[45] 'Hätten die Nüchternen | Einmal gekostet, | Alles verließen sie, | Und setzten sich zu uns | An den Tisch der Sehnsucht, | Der nie leer wird.' *Nachlaß*, H VII 5.26 (Novalis, *Schriften*, i. 168). Noted c.Jan. 1893.

[46] Cf. Claudia Abrecht, 'Hofmannsthals "Weltgeheimnis" und *Die Lehrlinge zu Sais* des Novalis', *Hofmannsthal-Blätter*, 16 (1976), 201–8, and Nicholas Saul, 'Hofmannsthal and Novalis', in G. J. Carr and Eda Sagarra (eds.), *Fin de siècle Vienna: Proceedings of the Second Irish Symposium in Austrian Studies* (Dublin: Trinity College, 1985), 26–62.

[47] Michael Hamburger, 'Hofmannsthals Bibliothek: Ein Bericht', *Euphorion*, 55 (1961), 50.

[48] *Briefe: 1900–1909* (Vienna: Bermann-Fischer, 1937), 254. See below, pp. 146–7, for Hofmannsthal's misreading of the image. Steve Rizza suggests plausibly that the 'vor Jahren' refers to the first time Hofmannsthal read Kassner's *Die Mystik*, namely Dec. 1901. He wrote to Kassner immediately, 'Während ich las und las, war mir, als wären Lasten von meiner Brust abgewälzt': see 'Hugo von Hofmannsthal. Briefe an Freunde', 966 and Rizza, *Rudolf Kassner and Hugo von Hofmannsthal*, 198.   [49] Quoted in *SW* ii. 467.

[50] Hugo Friedrich, *Die Struktur der modernen Lyrik* (Hamburg: Rowohlt, 1956), 26.

This development was initiated outside France by Poe, was mediated by Baudelaire, and culminated in the work of T. S. Eliot. 'Entpersön-lichung' was accompanied by 'Entrealisierung', a rejection of repre-sentational writing, and as both self and outside world became unreliable, Symbolists invested the imagination, beauty and language with the capacity for truth. Poe's major innovation—the real argu-ment that lies behind the absurdity that 'The Philosophy of Composi-tion' appears *prima facie* to contend, namely that 'The Raven' is the only possible poem—was to acknowledge the function of form. Form is not a result of writing the poem, it is its origin. Content, or meaning, is a product of the formal, deliberated use of language. In his cham-pionship of the formal autonomy of art, Poe moves almost to the point of *l'art pour l'art*. The calculation depends in part on the sound of the words, and in modern poetry this non-rational, mystical, magical aspect becomes primary: 'ein schwebender, unbestimmter Sinn, dessen Rätselhaftigkeit weniger von den Kernbedeutungen der Worte verkörpert wird als vielmehr von ihren Klangkräften und semantis-chen Randzonen' [an unspecific, floating sense, whose mysteriousness is embodied less by the core meanings of the words than by the power of their sounds and by their semantic fringes].[51] What ultimately dis-tinguishes Symbolism from Impressionism is an awareness that language consists of both 'Kernbedeutungen' and 'Klangkräfte und semantische Randzonen', and a deliberate attempt to harness the tensions between the two.

Post-Romantic writing questions the reliability of the evidence of man's natural senses, instead looks within and explores the possibilities of the individual mind, the imagination and intuition in an attempt to attain knowledge of the universe. A clear individual identity and the possibility of secure self-knowledge are by no means to be assumed.[52] The Romantic assumptions that direct utterance and intimacy with the poet's feelings provide insight into the true nature of the self, and that the self is stable enough to be exposed to dissolution into the natural world as part of the poetic quest for self-knowledge—these come to be seen either as deceptively naive or as enviably innocent. Responses were varied. At one extreme, Rimbaud felt the dissociation of self and world and the insights of dream and intoxication to be true freedom. Uniquely (and only temporarily) he threw out the evidence of

[51] Hugo Friedrich, *Die Struktur der modernen Lyrik*, 37.

[52] See the chapter entitled 'Subjective Reality' in Christopher Robinson, *French Literature in the Nineteenth Century* (Newton Abbot: David & Charles, 1978), 108–70 (the foregoing is a summary of the questions tabulated on p. 111).

his senses and the rhetoric of his tradition altogether, wholly dissatisfied both with the available resources of imagery and the limitations of the normally perceiving individual. His was a massively energetic determination, completely unselfconscious, to recreate reality via visionary experience, the degree of self-alienation involved being encapsulated in the phrase from the *lettres du voyant*, 'Je est un autre' ['I' is someone else].[53] Baudelaire was less meteoric, and since his originality did not constitute wholesale rejection of the past, he manifests problems more akin to those of Hofmannsthal. The opening of Baudelaire's *Mon cœur mis à nu* sets out a poetic programme in terms comparable to the Romantics', namely 'de la vaporisation et de la centralisation du moi' [the vaporization and centralization of the self][54]—although by this time one of the prerequisites for the realization of such a plan, a unified self, had been destabilized. The self for Baudelaire is split, experiencing both integration with the world and alienation from it. It knows of the risks to identity of its Romantic heritage, complete integration with the world, but is caught between that and fragmentation as it becomes more completely dissociated from the structures and contexts (social, psychological and literary) traditionally used to define it. Only at special symbolic moments is the original harmony still perceptible, as Baudelaire writes in *Fusées*, 'dans certains états de l'âme presque surnaturels, la profondeur de la vie se révèle tout entière dans le spectacle, si ordinaire qu'il soit, qu'on a sous les yeux. Il en devient le symbole' [in certain almost supernatural states of mind, the profundity of life is revealed in its entirety in what is happening beneath one's very eyes, however banal that might be. This spectacle becomes the symbol of life].[55] The verb *devenir* highlights the shift from a belief in the permanence of such correspondent possibilities to the more cautious view that these are rare and dependent on peculiar personal states of mind, when the symbolic potential must either be coaxed out of the world or received as a sudden gift. This eventually becomes the phenomenon known by the name James Joyce gave it in *Stephen Hero*, the 'epiphany', often taken as paradigmatic of Modernist artistic practice, and equivalent to the key moments evoked in the Chandos Letter.[56] What differentiates Romantic vision from

---

[53] Arthur Rimbaud, *Poésies, Une saison en enfer, Illuminations*, ed. Louis Forestier, 2nd, rev. edn. (Paris: Gallimard, 1984), *OC*, 200 and 202. See also below, Chapter 6.

[54] Baudelaire, *OC*, i. 676.

[55] Ibid. 659.

[56] For German parallels cf. Theodore Ziolkowski, 'James Joyces Epiphanie und die Überwindung der empirischen Welt in der modernen deutschen Prosa', *Deutsche Viertel-*

epiphanic revelation is that, whilst both presuppose the existence of greater significance behind the constitutive materials of life and the world, during an epiphany there is no interpenetration of self and world, and the distinctness of the individual is preserved alongside his anonymity.[57]

The divided self is symbolized by Baudelaire in 'Le Cygne', and the swan is the symbol *par excellence* of nagging alienation: 'comme les exilés, ridicule et sublime, | Et rongé d'un désir sans trêve' [like exiles, ridiculous and sublime, tormented by ceaseless wishing], it is torn between longing for the renaissance of an irrecoverable past where its identity was not in doubt, and the desire and inability to forget this past.[58] It is no coincidence that the swan is a motif frequently used in literature, for the past that Baudelaire cannot leave behind is more literary than historical. This is clear from the key poem 'Correspondances', simultaneously a summation of a key Romantic topos and a decisive first move beyond Romanticism to Symbolist poetic theory.[59]

> La nature est un temple où de vivants piliers
> Laissent parfois sortir de confuses paroles;
> L'homme y passe à travers des forêts de symboles
> Qui l'observent avec des regards familiers.
>
> Comme de longs échos qui de loin se confondent
> Dans une ténébreuse et profonde unité,
> Vaste comme la nuit et comme la clarté,
> Les parfums, les couleurs et les sons se répondent.

jahrsschrift, 35 (1961), 594–616. He concludes: 'Diese Technik hat James Joyce als erster und einziger die Epiphanie genannt, aber sein Begriff deckt sich völlig mit der Technik, die man bei Hofmannsthal, Musil, Rilke und anderen . . . findet' (616).

[57] In both vision and epiphany, 'die faktische Wirklichkeit des Dinges [steigert sich] zu metaphysischer Symbolhaftigkeit. Das Ding wird gleichsam aus seiner empirischen Starre zu poetischem Leben erweckt' (Ziolkowski, 'James Joyces Epiphanie', 603); but in the epiphany, as Joyce writes in *Stephen Hero*, the object's 'soul, its whatness leaps to us from the vestment of its appearance', *objectively* perceived and not subjectively absorbed (601). Goethe had also mooted the idea that certain objects were in themselves symbolic, 'eminente Fälle, die, in einer charakteristischen Mannigfaltigkeit, als Repräsentanten von vielen andern dastehen, eine gewisse Totalität in sich schließen' (Stahl, 'Symbolist Theories', 311). Neither vision nor epiphanic revelation is prompted by such objects, however; they are merely representative. [58] Baudelaire, *OC*, i. 86.

[59] See also Felix W. Leakey, 'The Originality of Baudelaire's "Le Cygne": Genesis as Structure and Theme', in E. M. Beaumont et al. (eds.), *Order and Adventure in Post-Romantic French Poetry* (Oxford: Oxford University Press, 1973), 38–55. Extensive reference will be made in what follows to Jonathan Culler's 'Intertextuality and Interpretation' which, if not original in every detail, is the most stimulating and convincing analysis available of an interpretative dimension of Baudelaire's 'Correspondances' crucial to an assessment of the shift between Romantic and Symbolist poetic assumptions.

Il est des parfums frais comme des chairs d'enfants,
Doux comme les hautbois, verts comme les prairies,
—Et d'autres, corrompus, riches et triomphants,

Ayant l'expansion des choses infinies,
Comme l'ambre, le musc, le benjoin et l'encens,
Qui chantent les transports de l'esprit et des sens.[60]

[Nature is a temple where living pillars sometimes allow (*or* cause) confused words to be uttered; man walks there through forests of symbols which observe him with familiar expressions. Like long echoes blending in the distance, in a profound and shadowy unity that is as vast as night and light, scents, colours and sounds answer each other. There are scents as fresh as a child's flesh, as sweet as the oboe, as green as the prairie, and there are others that are corrupt, rich and triumphant, having the expansiveness of infinite things, like amber, musk, benzoin resin and incense, which sing of the transports of the mind and the senses.]

'Correspondances' evokes a world whose sensations are all inter-related (horizontal correspondences) and where these interrelations also suggest further significance, or analogy with a mysterious infinity (vertical correspondences). The 'longs échos qui de loin se confondent' (a phrase itself dense with phonetic echoes), where echo is to be understood as synaesthetically embracing colour and perfume, too, are ultimately the harmony 'qui chante[nt] les transports de l'esprit et des sens'. *Sens* of course has the double semantic suggestiveness of *sense-perceptions* on the one hand, and *meanings* or *things signified* on the other. The latter picks up the link with verbal constructs, poetry, hinted at in 'confuses paroles' and in the linguistic overtones of the antiphony of 'se répondent'. The sensuous transports produced by perfect synaesthesia are analogous to, or metonymically overlap with, the riot of signifi-cance of the verbal arts. 'Transports de l'esprit' also cuts in two direc-tions, as *esprit* can mean *spirit* as well as *intellect*.

There is a third dimension of 'Correspondances', where the echoes are understood as literary echoes, and where the sonnet states the dangers to a poem of too dense an intertextual network. Baudelaire is implicitly aware of this. The very word *correspondances* is borrowed, as he acknowledges, from Swedenborg, and many of the images of the sonnet are not original either. Baudelaire's Romantic predecessors Hugo, Lamartine, Constant, Nerval and Chateaubriand have all been adduced as sources for the metaphor of nature-as-temple (or vice versa) and for the harmonious correspondence of sound, light, colour and shape. Baudelaire himself cites another source, E. T. A.

---

[60] Baudelaire, *OC*, i. 11.

Hoffmann's *Kreisleriana*, in the *Salon de 1846*.[61] Austin summarizes Baudelaire's originality *vis-à-vis* these sources by noting that his addition was to have secularized what since time immemorial had been a theological or metaphysical attitude and doctrine. Culler objects: 'the absence of God is not the issue . . . so much as the way Baudelaire's signs function intermittently', and he focuses on the line 'laissent *parfois* sortir de confuses paroles', making the moments of comprehension epiphanically unpredictable and special.[62] One might reconcile the two positions: the intermittence is perhaps a consequence of secularization and self-confidence, the loss of an external goal or frame of reference in which one may trust.

The sonnet therefore echoes an established rhetoric and makes use of a stock of images and ideas already familiar in the poetic repertoire. There is another set of echoes, however, that resound between the sonnet and Baudelaire's own prose works—the Hugo essay and the Gautier essay, as well as the *Salons* and an essay on the Universal Exhibition of 1855.[63] In this last-mentioned essay we read:

Tout le monde conçoit sans peine que si les hommes chargés d'exprimer le beau se conformeraient aux règles des professeurs-jurés, le beau lui-même disparaîtrait de la terre, puisque tous les types, toutes les idées, toutes les sensations se confondraient dans une vaste unité, monotone et impersonnelle, immense comme l'ennui et le néant.[64]

[Everyone can easily see that if those charged with expressing beauty conformed to the rules of the official professors, beauty itself would disappear from the face of the earth, since all types, all ideas, all sensations would blend together in one vast, monotonous and impersonal unity, as immense as ennui and nothingness.]

Culler points out the links between 'se confondraient dans une vaste unité . . . immense comme l'ennui' and the poem's formulations, 'se confondent | Dans une ténébreuse et profonde unité | Vaste comme la nuit', where the last two words are an approximate homonym of 'l'ennui'. The prose works themselves adapt images from Romantic predecessors, and one might add to Culler's list the suggestion that the

[61] Baudelaire, *OC*, ii. 425–6. See Culler, 'Intertextuality and Interpretation', 126–7; Felix W. Leakey, *Baudelaire and Nature* (Manchester: Manchester University Press, 1969),176 and 195–217; Austin, *L'Univers poétique de Baudelaire*, 52, and Robert Vivier, *L'Originalité de Baudelaire* (Brussels: Palais des Académies, 1926; repr. 1952), *passim*.

[62] Austin, *L'Univers poétique de Baudelaire*, 54; Culler, 'Intertextuality and Interpretation', 121.

[63] Baudelaire, 'Victor Hugo', *OC*, ii. 133, 'Théophile Gautier', ii. 117, *Salon de 1846*, ii. 437. See Culler, 'Intertextuality and Interpretation', 122–8, for a summary of the details.

[64] Baudelaire, *OC*, ii. 578.

'immense clavier des *correspondances*' in this essay derives from Hugo's 'Pan', which ends 'Car, ô poètes saints! l'art est le son sublime, | Simple, divers, profond, mystérieux, intime. . . . Que sous vos doigts puissants exhale la nature, | Cet immense clavier!' [because—O sacred poets!—art is the sublime simple, varied, profound, mysterious and intimate sound . . . that the immense keyboard that is nature exhales beneath your mighty fingers!].[65]

The striking repetition of images and phrases between the various Baudelaire texts articulates his ambivalence dramatically. It is at the very least disconcerting that such closely echoing formulations are used in the poem to promote a sense of unity, and in the prose text to damn it, but the consequences are extreme.[66] 'L'ennui et le néant' are the opposites of the spiritualizing effects that the sonnet promotes; and within the interpretative context that establishes correspondence as linguistic, determining the relation between one text and others prior to it, they negate the possibility of creation for a new poet. In the *Salon de 1846*, a quotation from Hoffmann describes nature as 'un tonton qui, mû par une vitesse accélérée, nous apparaît gris, bien qu'il résume en lui toutes les couleurs' [a spinning top moving at great speed, which seems grey to us even though it consists of all different colours][67]— which is a nightmare for the new poet if one reads *poetry* for *nature*. This is exactly what Baudelaire does metaphorically in the *Salon de 1859*, where he raises the possibility of being 'perdu dans une forêt d'originalités' [lost in a forest of originalities].[68] 'Forests of symbols may well evoke, above all, the eerie condition of the poet who, arriving on the scene after romanticism, finds that the world is indeed a forest of symbols, marked by prior poetic discourse,'[69] and the forest 'l'observe avec des regards familiers'.

The transference of the symptoms of being lost from those of the personal psyche in the real world to the textual identity in literary tradition is a key element in the self-conscious development of poetry between Romanticism and Symbolism. Mallarmé voices this sense in

[65] Hugo, *Œuvres poétiques*, ed. Pierre Albouy, Bibliothèque de la Pléiade, 3 vols. (Paris: Gallimard, 1964–74), i. 805.

[66] The sense of unity is already problematic: Paul de Man, taking to one of their possible conclusions the implications of 'se confondent', sees as inherent in the poem's own images the implication that its vast night is one 'of confusion in which distinctions disappear . . . in which infinity is homogeneity': *The Rhetoric of Romanticism* (New York: Columbia University Press, 1984), 45.

[67] Baudelaire, *OC*, ii. 423.

[68] Ibid. 608.

[69] Culler, 'Intertextuality and Interpretation', 122.

the famous opening of 'Symphonie littéraire', a eulogy of Gautier, Baudelaire and Banville: 'Muse moderne de l'Impuissance, qui . . . me condamnes (aimable supplice) à ne faire plus que relire . . . les maîtres inaccessibles dont la beauté me désespère' [modern Muse of Impotence, you condemn me (a pleasant torture) to do nothing more than re-read those inaccessible masters whose beauty makes me despair].[70] Disorientation and desperation are akin to the sense of haunting that pervades much of Mallarmé's verse. Barbara Johnson has shown how even poems such as 'L'Azur', which attempt to affirm the poet's originality in an escape from 'l'éternel azur', eternal blue, or the perfection of poetic masters ('donne, ô matière, | L'oubli de l'Idéal cruel' [O matter, let me forget the cruel Idea][71]) end with a frustrated acceptance of the inescapability of models: '*Je suis hanté*. L'Azur ! l'Azur ! l'Azur ! l'Azur.' Johnson translates, 'I am haunted: cliché, cliché, cliché, cliché.'[72] Her analysis of 'Le vierge, le vivace et le bel aujourd'hui' is a model characterization of Symbolism's anxiety of intertextuality: the failure to sing of the 'cygne d'autrefois' nevertheless haunts the present; it is a symbol of the poetic precursor, one who in this case (Baudelaire, in 'Le Cygne') already represents a divided self; Baudelaire's poem is dedicated to Hugo, whose *Contemplations* are divided into 'Autrefois', yesteryear, and 'Aujourd'hui', today, the constituents of the very tension that structures Mallarmé's poem; and—in Hugo's words—'un abîme les sépare, le tombeau' [an abyss separates them, the tomb].[73] The specific reference here is to the death of Hugo's daughter, but this does not invalidate Mallarmé's response to what Johnson calls 'the temporality of intertextuality', the permanent need to supersede dead predecessors.[74]

The same need is manifested in a text by Hofmannsthal that represents one of his earliest poetological reflections, couched not in theoretical terms but in verse. This is the sonnet 'Was ist die Welt?' (June 1890). It was his first published poem, perhaps his first ever sonnet, and the form alone almost guarantees that he was inspired by others' works. Reading it as a response to Baudelaire's 'Correspondances' accounts more coherently for its characteristics and peculiari-

[70] Mallarmé, *OC*, 261.

[71] Ibid. 38, ll. 21–2.

[72] Barbara Johnson, '*Les Fleurs du mal armé*: Some Reflections on Intertextuality', in Harold Bloom (ed.), *Stéphane Mallarmé* (New York: Chelsea House, 1987), 216.

[73] Hugo, *OP*, ii. 482.

[74] Johnson, '*Les Fleurs du mal armé*', 219. The article very interestingly goes on to examine how Mallarmé sexualizes the problems of intertextual relations, a line of enquiry potentially very fruitful in the context not only of Hofmannsthal but of *fin-de-siècle* Vienna as a whole.

ties than comparison with Hofmann von Hofmannswaldau's 'Die Welt' (suggested in the Critical Edition) which merely begins with the same few words.[75]

> Was ist die Welt? Ein ewiges Gedicht,
> Daraus der Geist der Gottheit strahlt und glüht,
> Daraus der Wein der Weisheit schäumt und sprüht,
> Daraus der Laut der Liebe zu uns spricht
>
> Und jedes Menschen wechselndes Gemüt,
> Ein Strahl ist, der aus dieser Sonne bricht,
> Ein Vers, der sich an tausend andre flicht,
> Der unbemerkt verhallt, verlischt, verblüht.
>
> Und doch auch eine Welt für sich allein,
> Voll süß-geheimer, nie vernomm'ner Töne,
> Begabt mit eigner, unentweihter Schöne,
>
> Und keines Andern Nachhall, Widerschein.
> Und wenn du gar zu lesen drin verstündest,
> Ein Buch, das du im Leben nicht ergründest. (*SW* i. 7)

[What is the world? An eternal poem from which the spirit of the deity radiates and shines, from which the wine of wisdom bubbles and sparkles, from which the sounds of love speak to us, and the changing nature of every human being is a ray that breaks from this sun, a line of verse that is interwoven with a thousand others, and which—unnoticed—dies away, is extinguished, fades. But it is also a world of its very own, full of sweet and mysterious sounds never heard before, endowed with its own undefiled beauty, and not the echo or reflection of anything Other. And even if you could read from it, it is a book that you could never fully fathom as long as you lived.]

Hofmannsthal's sonnet turns Baudelaire's inside out, for the idea of world-as-poem was the remotest of Baudelaire's metaphorical layers and is the core of Hofmannsthal's. That the two elements are mutually reflective is a Romantic idea—Heinrich von Ofterdingen says that 'das Gewissen . . . dieser Keim aller Persönlichkeit, erscheint mir, wie der Geist des Weltgedichts' [the conscience, the seed of every personality, seems to me to be the spirit of the poem of the world][76]— but by the time Hofmannsthal uses them all that is left is the theory, a series of abstractions rather than evocative Romantic conjurations of the interdependence of 'Welt' and 'Gedicht'. Baudelaire, for example,

---

[75] See *SW* i. 115. There is no external evidence for Hofmannsthal's having been reading Baudelaire at the time, either, but it is inconceivable that the poem was unfamiliar to a pupil of Dubray's.

[76] Novalis, *Schriften*, i. 331.

generates mystery by adding the suggestions of temple to those of nature, increasing the reverence with amber, musk, benzoin and incense; even if these are exotic and unfamiliar they have the tangibility of nouns. Hofmannsthal's basic metaphor, 'die Welt [ist] ein Gedicht', already tends to the abstract, and his mystery is expressed in the vague verbs 'strahlen' and 'glühen'.

Hofmannsthal's poem attempts to be altogether more Apollonian than Baudelaire's and he shies from the confusion and shadow present in his model, choosing only the sunshine (l. 6) from the oxymoronic pair in 'vaste comme la nuit et comme la clarté'. The mingling echoes, 'de longs échos qui de loin se confondent', become 'ein Vers, der sich an tausend andre flicht, | Der unbemerkt verhallt' as echoes will. 'Verhallt' is modulated to 'verlischt' and then to 'verblüht' (which one could render 'loses its scent') as if in a deliberate attempt to accommodate 'les parfums, les couleurs et les sons' in reverse. The play of metaphorical possibilities in 'Gemüt, Strahl, Vers'—the variations in human temperament, rays of sunlight and lines of verse all combining to make a whole—are brought to a more sensuous synaesthetic level than the abstractions of the first quatrain by these verbs, but the synaesthetic effect is still forced, described rather than evoked. Finally, each of the verbs indicates not 'l'expansion' or 'les transports' of Baudelaire, but decline and eventual death. The cheerful suggestions of the first quatrain have given way very quickly to a deeply negative reflection—the subject of these *ver-* verbs is after all 'jedes Menschen wechselndes Gemüt'—and the fact that the decline is so inconspicuous ('unbemerkt'), is perhaps the chief source of anxiety: being part of the 'Weltgedicht' is a lurking threat to identity.

The reversal that traditionally takes place between the octave and sestet of a sonnet is present in 'Was ist die Welt?', although not as emphatically as it might be. The first tercet begins 'Und doch auch' rather than more straightforwardly 'Doch auch'. The nervousness is perhaps also rhythmic, for the opening can be read both as an iamb and, if the first two syllables are taken as unstressed, as an anapaest. The assertion of individual distinctiveness gathers force, the importance of 'das Andere' is reduced, and the pre-eminence accorded to 'Geist der Gottheit' earlier is effectively retracted. By finishing the sonnet with the remark that one only has a lifetime to appreciate the book-of-the-world, Hofmannsthal calls attention to the priority of horizontal over vertical correspondences. It is less 'l'expansion des choses infinies' than the internal relations, 'süß-geheime, nievernommne Töne' that hint at what there is to understand—'wenn du gar zu lesen drin verstündest', supposing one knows how to decipher the text. The 'Welt für sich' is also 'ein Gedicht für sich'—'keines [a]ndern Nachhall, Widerschein'—and the book of the last line is a metaphor for itself. There is an inexhaustible reservoir of significance contained in the internal relations of a text if only we are receptive to their patterns. Its beauty is 'eigen' and 'unentweiht', and this insistence is an affirmation of the poem's need to be original and self-reliant.

But, since 'undesecrated' is the language of religious ritual, it reads, as does the whole sonnet, as a response to the suggestions of 'temple' in Baudelaire and his Romantic predecessors. The crucial paradox is that the terms of the poem in which the affirmation of its self-sufficiency is made are derived if not from a reading of another poem—although I think Baudelaire's sonnet is too clearly visible behind it for coincidence— then at least from a receptiveness to the Romantic tradition and above all to its rhetoric. It may be impossible to write a poem that is '*keines* andern Nachhall', and there is an air in Hofmannsthal's sonnet of protesting too much. Analysis of Baudelaire's poem has shown how the question of poetic originality is implicit in its images, apparent perhaps only subconsciously to Baudelaire himself, but more obvious if they are read with the yet more self-conscious literary awareness of a later generation. 'Was ist die Welt?' indicates how Hofmannsthal may immediately have responded to the intertextual resonances of 'Correspondances'. He conjures up Romantic dreams of a world beyond in 'das Andere', and first supplements, then replaces them with Symbolist interest in the status of the text itself. The text both discusses and enacts the problematic situation of a poem *vis-à-vis* the rest of literature. In proposing that significance is derived from the relations internal to the poem, it articulates one of Symbolism's chief preoccupations; and by attempting—not entirely successfully—to assert its own distinctiveness, it raises an anxiety that Hofmannsthal's reception of Symbolism encouraged.

Baudelaire's experience of alienation included the turn away from organic nature to the city, or the recreation of a quasi-natural world out of mineral and metal, the anorganic garden, symbols of his displaced status, which emphasize the non-natural or literary consciousness of his poetry. The bejewelled landscape of Baudelaire's 'Rêve parisien' has a predecessor in Romanticism, too—it was indirectly inspired by the magical underground world in the fifth chapter of

Novalis's *Heinrich von Ofterdingen*.[77] Metallic landscapes have been found in literature from all ages but it was Novalis who first made the journey into the mineral underworld symbolic of the poet's progress, and in *Heinrich* the revelation of the magical world beneath the surface of the earth itself symbolizes the relationship between surface truth and the deeper truth that the symbol articulates. The motif is most strongly associated, however, with the French Symbolists, who, quite unlike Novalis, used it as a substitute for the real natural world. Most famously Mallarmé's Hérodiade guarantees her purity, and the purity of Mallarmé's poetry, in the reflections of her metallic hair and the jewelled garden. By this time the reflections are of an isolated and wholly alienated self, symbolic of the situation of art; where natural phenomena appear (as they do consistently in Maeterlinck's verse, for example), they are very often seductive, hostile or poisonous. Baudelaire needed to state 'Ses yeux polis sont faits de minéraux charmants' and 'cette nature [est] étrange et symbolique' [her polished eyes are made of charming minerals; this nature is strange and symbolic].[78] But for his successors the assumption of symbolism is implicit in the use of the metals and minerals. Vordtriede summarizes: 'Unterreich und künstlicher Garten sind also nicht irgendwelche beliebigen Symbole, sondern jeweils das eigentliche Existenzsymbol des Dichters' [nether world and artificial garden are thus not symbols chosen at random, but in each case the poet's true symbol of existence].[79] By the time Hofmannsthal uses the same motifs, the implication is not only that the landscape is symbolic, but that it is intended to be so in the Symbolists' manner.

Huret's *Enquête*, in which Maeterlinck made the cardinal point about the passivity of the poet, represents without doubt one of the most important stages in Hofmannsthal's thinking about Symbolism and merits a substantial excursus here. Someone even remotely interested in the topic was almost bound to happen upon it at some point in 1891, since it was one of the hottest pieces of literary journalism of the year. Hermann Bahr mentions it later in *Studien zur Kritik der Moderne*:

Jules Huret, ein junger Reporter . . . hat das vorige Jahr die Schriftsteller von Paris über die Zukunft der Litteratur interviewt; man kennt seine 'Enquête sur

---

[77] Novalis, *Schriften*, i. 239–43. See Vordtriede, *Novalis und die französischen Symbolisten*, 43–8. Vivier, *L'Originalité de Baudelaire*, 186–7, shows how the similarities may not have been coincidental.   [78] From 'Avec ses vêtements ondoyants et nacrés'; Baudelaire, *OC*, i. 29.
[79] Vordtriede, *Novalis und die französischen Symbolisten*, 98.

l'évolution littéraire' (Paris, Charpentier), von der alle Zeitungen Europas drei Monate sprechen.'[80]

[Last year, Jules Huret, a young reporter, interviewed Parisian writers about the future of literature. His 'Inquiry on Literary Evolution' (published in Paris by Charpentier) is well known since all the journals in Europe have been talking about it for three months.]

Sokal's influential article on Verlaine owes much to Huret, and the book was influential enough to merit a disappointed comment in *Kritische Studien zur Psychologie der Litteratur* (1895) by the Viennese *Neue Freie Presse* journalist Rudolf Lothar.[81] The notes Hofmannsthal made suggest that he knew the whole work but read only part of it carefully. They indicate that he was at least aware of all the major figures and many of the minor ones, and that he had gained an intimate knowledge of the state of the Symbolism debate sometime late in 1891.[82]

Huret was interested in what best represented the future of modern French literature in the eyes of its contemporary practitioners and took as his starting-point the dispute in France about the relative merits and likely lasting value of two very different types of work, Maurice Barrès's *Le Jardin de Bérénice* and Jean Moréas's *Le Pèlerin passionné*.[83] The former found favour with what Huret calls 'les Psychologues' and the latter with the 'Symbolistes-Décadents'.[84] Huret is restrained and prescient, often very witty, noting that the period he has studied is not like Romanticism and Naturalism, which already have readily identifiable general characteristics, but suggesting that Symbolism, too, might one day fall into this category.

Huret's line of questioning, outlined in his introduction, was designed to find out how far the 'Psychologues' (including Barrès, Anatole France, Édouard Rod and Paul Hervieu) are the heirs to Naturalism, and how far the Symbolists (including Mallarmé, Verlaine, Moréas, Morice, de Régnier) are the descendants of

[80] Bahr, *Studien*, 14. First publication unknown, but Wunberg supposes some time in 1892 (*Das junge Wien*, i. 289).

[81] Cf. Gsteiger, *Französische Symbolisten*, 68. Lothar detected mostly quarrel and animosity amongst the interviewees, and saw its consistency only in a hatred of Naturalism, but this is at least partly the result of the idiosyncratic perspective of late 19th-century Vienna. Michaud, with the benefit of distance, is rightly more generous towards the coherence of views represented (*Message poétique*, 394–9).

[82] The notes are not dated, but the book appeared in or soon after Aug. 1891.

[83] The title is nearly always spelt thus, although the first edition unexpectedly has *Pélerin* both on the title page and throughout. Cf. also n. 26 in Chapter 4.

[84] Jules Huret, *Enquête sur l'évolution littéraire* (Paris: Charpentier, 1891). Quotations and references are from the 1913 reprinting, here 'Avant-propos', p. ix.

Parnassianism. He also suggests in the introduction that Naturalism (represented here by Zola, Huysmans, Maupassant) and Parnassianism (Leconte de Lisle, Mendès, Prudhomme, Coppée) have in common a degree of objectivity in observation. Of the Symbolists he asks,

si contrairement aux écoles parnassienne et réaliste, qui traduisaient la vie par des directes sensations imagées, ils voulaient s'en tenir à en interpréter, par des métaphores ésotériques, *vulgo* des symboles, les abstractions essentielles.[85]

[if, in contrast to the Parnassian and realist schools, which translate life by means of direct sensations made into images, they wished to confine themselves to interpreting life's essential abstractions by means of esoteric metaphors, or, to put it crudely, by means of symbols.]

Huret also undertakes a count of the number of times the contributors refer to each other and to the works of other writers not included in the survey, and hilariously demonstrates how utterly inconclusive this is. One point of significance, however, is that almost all of them—with a few notable exceptions such as Maeterlinck—ignore completely the greatest names of nineteenth-century literature such as Goethe, Heine, Shelley, Lamartine, Nerval, Musset and Dostoevsky, which speaks volumes about contemporary French writers' self-absorption.

Some of Hofmannsthal's notes from the *Enquête* are merely lists of names. 'Viellé-Griffin' is noted,[86] as are de Hérédia and Laforgue, who is praised by Maeterlinck (alongside Swinburne, Rossetti, William Morris, Burne-Jones, Puvis de Chavannes, Baudelaire, Gide and Poe). This is incidentally the only reference to Laforgue traceable in Hofmannsthal's writings other than a mention in loose connection with the prose poems. The reference to Vapereau might suggest that he took the *Dictionnaire universel des contemporains* as a reference work to find out more about the names he did not know.[87] Also listed are some of the French reviews mentioned in the book: 'contemporaine, indépendante, la plume, le Mercure de France, Art et critique', all regular publishers of Symbolist writings, the most important being the *Mercure de France* described by Cornell as 'the richest source of published poetry and critical comment on verse during [the] period'.[88] Other notes are

---

[85] Jules Huret, *Enquête sur l'évolution littéraire*, p. xii.

[86] *Sic*, but often spelt thus in Huret.

[87] Gustave Vapereau, *Dictionnaire universel des contemporains: contenant toutes les personnes notables de la France et des pays étrangers*, 5th edn. (Paris: Hachette, 1880). The 6th edition did not appear until 1893.

[88] Cornell, *The Symbolist Movement*, 203. Cf. André Barre, *Le Symbolisme*, ii. *Bibliographie de la poésie symboliste* (New York: Franklin, [n.d.]), esp. 10–14, 18–22 and 30–3. The article

the titles of poems or books mentioned in the *Enquête*. These include: Mallarmé's 'L'Après-midi d'un faune', René Ghil's *Les Écrits pour l'Art*, and Joseph Caraguel's *Les Barthozouls*.[89] Caraguel was cited by Morice as the only enemy of Symbolism whose work merited attention. Hofmannsthal also notes Morhardt's *Hénor*, which Adrien Remacle considers the only example (besides himself) of a true practitioner of Symbolism. Van Lerberghe's recent prose drama *Les Flaireurs* is noted, recommended as admirable by Maeterlinck (128) and less cordially by Kahn (406).

The book of interviews is divided into eight sections amongst which the participants were distributed according to their own literary tendencies: 'Parnassiens', 'Symbolistes et Décadents' and 'Naturalistes' are familiar groupings, but 'Mages' and 'Psychologues' have since vanished from literary taxonomies. The sections that most interested Hofmannsthal were the first, 'Les Psychologues' (the response by Barrès in particular), the third, 'Symbolistes et Décadents', and the sixth, 'Les Parnassiens'. The fourth page of Hofmannsthal's notes is headed 'Franz. Litteratur' and is effectively a reading list compiled from the 'psychological' response by Maurice Barrès. Barrès mentions 'les pages de Jules Soury sur la *Délia de Tibulle* ou les *Rêveries d'un païen mystique*, de Louis Ménard' and Paul Hervieu's *Diogène le chien* (although not *Flirt*, which also features on Hofmannsthal's list and which will have been noted from the introduction to the response by Hervieu himself). He writes of Anatole France's positive review of André Maurel's *Candeur*, the articles of Georges Bonnamour, 'chroniqueur brillant' and the author of *Fanny Bora* and *Représailles*, and Maurice Beaubourg's *Contes pour les assassins*, who is recommended very highly by Hervieu, too. The other names from Hofmannsthal's list that are taken from Barrès are Emile Hinzelin's *André Marsy* and Maurice Quillot's *L'Entraîne*—which was to appear in 1892. Barrès ends with a hymn of praise to Charles Maurras and Francis Chevassu (20–2), and the following article on Camille de Saint-Croix gives Hofmannsthal his reference to the novel *Mauvaise Aventure* (25). There is little or no evidence that Hofmannsthal made anything of this reading list, and it was perhaps overshadowed by the more substantial points he noted from other sections. He does quote an idea from the response of

on Remacle (see below, pp. 108–9) contains most of the names on this list (Huret, *Enquête*, 106).

[89] Huret, *Enquête*, 110, 355 and 90. Henceforth references to the *Enquête* will usually be by page-number in parentheses in the text.

another of the 'Psychologues', Édouard Rod. Rod believes that Naturalism has had its day, but had its uses, not least the introduction of precision into the novel and vivacity into narrative. He links it to 'psychologism', and links that in turn to Symbolism, which he sees as its twin, distinguished principally by differences of temperament and imagination. The distinction is the sentence that Hofmannsthal quoted: 'les poètes sont symbolistes; les esprits précis se contentent d'être psychologues' [the poets are Symbolists, more exact minds are content to be psychologists; 15]. Symbolism may well be the salvation of literature, he suggests, if it helps it to be rid of classical abstraction. Rod is very tentative, however, and refuses to offer any kind of prediction for the future of letters.

Hofmannsthal seems not to have been much interested in 'Les Mages', the second section, and of the four poets in this category he notes only the name of Paul Adam in the list he took down from de Régnier's response to the *Enquête* as examples of the diversity of Symbolism (92). The response he quoted or referred to most extensively in his notes is from Charles Morice, the author of the much praised *La Littérature de tout à l'heure* (1889), and listed amongst the Symbolists and Decadents. Morice is an opponent of the psychological novel, and maintains that it is in no sense Symbolist. Hofmannsthal quoted this opinion: 'La psychologie n'est pas de la littérature pas plus que la physiologie la géographie, l'histoire' [psychology is not literature any more than physiology, geography or history; 84], and Morice goes on to explain cattily that the confusion has arisen merely because all these disciplines use the same tool, the pen. Poetry, however, has nothing to do with the aims of psychology: 'La poésie n'a pas d'autre essentiel et naturel objet que la Beauté' [poetry has no other essential and natural object than beauty], which Hofmannsthal also quotes. Poetry is concerned essentially with the evocation of the special, timeless moment, not with the scientific description of a state or a process: 'l'art est intuitif, instantané . . . et simultané' [art is intuitive, instantaneous and simultaneous]. For this reason, claims Morice, Naturalism has never produced any poets, which is a judgement very similar to Musil's on Impressionism.

Morice's elegant definition of the symbol is also quoted by Hofmannsthal:

[Le] symbole, c'est le mélange des objets qui ont éveillé nos sentiments et de notre âme, en une fiction. Le moyen, c'est la suggestion: il s'agit de donner aux gens le souvenir de quelque chose qu'ils n'ont jamais vu. (85)

[The symbol is the mixing together into a fiction of both the objects that have aroused our emotions and our soul. The means by which it does this is suggestion: people are given the memory of something that they have never seen.]

This is the reason that he finds psychology and Naturalism pointless— they merely seek to reproduce in words what the world has already created in nature, whereas the Symbolists give infinitely more. Barrès is the least Symbolist of writers because he teaches that 'il faut *cultiver son moi*.' [one must *cultivate one's self*].[90] Hofmannsthal also paraphrased Morice's view of Jean Moréas: 'Moréas plutôt allégoriste que symboliste le symbolisme est une transposition dans un autre ordre de choses' [Moréas is more an allegorist than a Symbolist, Symbolism is transposing things on to a different plane]. Moréas was no Symbolist, according to Morice, because he wrote too directly or too allegorically, which is alien to the concept of the symbol. The text in Huret has 'un autre' in capital letters, and explains further, 'Moréas serait donc plutôt un allégoriste roman, comme les poètes du moyen âge' [Moréas is therefore more of a Romance allegorist, like the medieval poets; 88–9]. He affirms the need for a new poetic language ('une langue nouvelle—suprême' [a new and supreme language]) but objects to Moréas's attempts to renew French by returning to the Middle Ages and by experimenting with verse to produce lines of such length that they merely resemble rhythmic prose. Morice nails his colours to the mast of Symbolism as represented by Villiers de l'Isle-Adam, Mallarmé and Verlaine. In his *La Littérature de tout à l'heure* he includes a diagram not unrelated in style to Timms's 'Vienna Circles' but in the form of a pyramid emerging from a circle. Near the pinnacle are Villiers, Mallarmé, Verlaine and Rimbaud, and their ancestry is traced by means of a network of lines to Leconte de Lisle and Banville, Wagner, Baudelaire and Poe, Balzac, Chateaubriand and Goethe.[91]

The response that follows Morice is that of Henri de Régnier, and Hofmannsthal takes from it a list of names, rather in the manner of the book list culled from Barrès. These names— 'Paul Adam, Gustave Kahn, Quillard, Bernard Lazare, Fénéon, Dujardin'—are not followed up with explanation or quotation, and it is impossible to trace any effects they may have had on Hofmannsthal's own thinking or writing. The Symbolist school, for de Régnier, was thrown together by

[90] Ibid. 86. Hofmannsthal also notes the unusual idea, 'Biographie de Barrès par Moréas', which I cannot trace in Huret: it may be a misreading of a phrase about Barrès's article on Moréas.

[91] Charles Morice, *La Littérature de tout à l'heure* (Paris: Perrin, 1889), between pp. 240 and 241.

circumstance, consisting of all those new poets 'qui ne sentaient pas disposés à marcher servilement sur les traces des devanciers' [who did not feel disposed to tread humbly in the footsteps of those who have gone before], and who failed to find favour in any other grouping (91). When de Régnier claims to be a Symbolist, 'ce n'est pas—croyez-le bien,—par amour des écoles et des classements. J'ajoute l'épithète, parce que je mets du symbole dans mes vers' [believe me, it is not for any love of schools and classifications. I use the term because I put symbols into my poetry; 92–3]. Symbols have always been instinctively used in art, but the modern movement, according to de Régnier, 'fait du symbole la condition essentielle de l'art' [makes the symbol into the essential condition of art]. Hofmannsthal quotes the next sentence, slightly truncating it: 'on veut bannir de l'art ce qu'on appelle les contingences, les accidents du milieu d'époque, les faits particuliers' [they wish to banish from art what they call contingencies, the accidents of circumstances and period, particular facts; 93]. Interestingly, de Régnier draws attention to similar beliefs amongst writers in the United States, Belgium, England and Switzerland, '[qui] viennent à Paris chercher la bonne parole parce qu'ils sentent que c'est là que la crise est la plus aiguë et qu'elle doit aboutir' [come to Paris to find good writing because they sense that it is here that the crisis is most acute and that it must come to its conclusion]. When asked about the technicalities of verse, as Morice was, de Régnier insists on the need for complete freedom of choice—'qu'importe le nombre du vers, si le rhythme est beau?' [what does the number of syllables in the lines matter if the rhythm is beautiful?]. His mentors, whom he praises at the end, are also Verlaine, Mallarmé and Villiers de l'Isle-Adam.

The third response from amongst the Symbolists-Decadents that Hofmannsthal quotes from is Adrien Remacle's (102–8). Hofmannsthal notes Remacle as editor of the *Revue contemporaine* and the title of his own novel *L'Absente* is jotted down as is 'Fêtes galantes (mit Musik)', which refers to a play, where music and text are a conceived of as a gloss on Verlaine (107). The writers for Remacle's review include Rod, Caraguel, Morice, Wyzewa and Barrès, all of whom Hofmannsthal cites or quotes in his notes. Remacle's first observation is about the mingling of literary '-isms', quoting Zola's dictum that 'le romantisme est mort, mais nous en sommes encore pleins' [Romanticism is dead, but we are still saturated by it], and making the same point about Naturalism. Symbolism as a movement does not exist, he says, for if it is represented by passionate pilgrims, no one has yet seen two such

pilgrims on the road together, and he goes on to expound the irreconcilable differences between so-called Symbolists such as Morice and de
Régnier. Remacle, too, claims to be a Symbolist and his definition is
quoted in Hofmannsthal's notes: Symbolism is 'la recherche de
l'inconnu par le connu, du non humain par l'humain' [the search for
the unknown via the known, for the non-human via the human].
According to this definition, only he and Morhardt apparently count
as proper Symbolists. Only they satisfy the triple demand of Symbolism
that not a character, not a milieu and not a verb be included that is not
'représentatif d'entités'. Symbolism demands 'l'excellence de la forme,
et *exige* la vieille *croyance à l'être en soi*' [excellence of form and *requires* the
human being's old-fashioned belief in his 'self']—all of which have
been denied by modern scientific thinking (107). Amazingly, the roots
of Symbolism seem to lie in Taine, and Hofmannsthal quotes
Remacle's gratitude to him, '[qui] nous a jetés jusqu'au col dans
l'esthétique anglaise et les préraphaélites et qui est responsable avec
Wagner des songeries dites décadentes puis symboliques' [who has
flung us up to our necks into English aestheticism and the Pre-
Raphaelites, and who is responsible, with Wagner, for the fantasies
once called Decadent and now referred to as Symbolist]. Remacle's
other masters are Banville, Villiers de l'Isle-Adam, Verlaine and
Mallarmé, César Franck and Puvis de Chavannes.

René Ghil, according to Huret, is head of the 'école évolutive-
instrumentiste' (noted by Hofmannsthal), which is explained as a
group 'qui professe à la fois une philosphie et une théorie d'art' [which
professes both a philosophy and a theory of art; 108]. Huret is slyly
sceptical of Ghil, who believes he has an exhaustive and definitive
formula for art, and quotes sections of a long letter he has received and
which is scornful of the Symbolists' achievements. Ghil cites
Mallarmé, Verlaine and Moréas as the chief exponents of Symbolism
but rages against Moréas's lack of method and the paucity of
Mallarmé's published works. The bulk of the article contains an
exposé of Ghil's own scientific theories of the musicality of poetry.
None of this is noted by Hofmannsthal, not even the long list of
recommended reading. He is clearly not interested.

There is one reference in Hofmannsthal's notes to the next
response, Maeterlinck's, and that is the note to Van Lerberghe's *Les
Flaireurs*, not mentioned elsewhere in the *Enquête*. For this reason, and
because of Hofmannsthal's familiarity with Maeterlinck's early
dramas, it seems safe to assume that he read this section. Much of it is

devoted to a walk that Huret took around Paris with Maeterlinck and a Flemish socialist, but the last few pages represent the most sustained reflection on the nature of the symbol in the whole book. Maeterlinck distinguishes between two types of symbol. First there is 'le symbole *a priori*; le symbole, de *propos délibéré* [qui] part de l'abstraction et tâche de revêtir d'humanité ces abstractions' [the *a priori* symbol, the symbol of deliberate intention, which starts from abstraction and attempts to dress these abstractions in a cloak of humanity; 124]. The prototype is identified as Goethe's *Märchen*. The second type 'serait plutôt incon-scient, aurait lieu à l'insu du poète, souvent malgré lui, et irait, presque toujours, bien au-delà de sa pensée: c'est le symbole qui naît de toute création géniale d'humanité' [is more unconscious, taking place with-out the poet's knowing, often despite him, and almost always moving beyond his own thoughts: this is the symbol that is born out of every human work of genius; 124–5]. Maeterlinck finds its prototypes in Shakespeare and Aeschylus. True symbols arise from within works of art; those works which arise from symbols will be allegorical. The poet's power comes not from what he constructs deliberately and con-sciously, but 'en raison de ce qu'il parvient à fair exécuter par les autres, et par l'ordre mystérieux et éternel de la force occultesse des choses' [by reason of what he manages to have put into practice by others and by the mysterious, eternal order of the deeply hidden power of things]. There follows then the passage about the passive role of the poet in this process quoted below.[92] With regard to those who have influenced him, Maeterlinck is generous but singles out Villiers de l'Isle-Adam, Van Lerberghe, Mallarmé, Verlaine and Barrès amongst recent and contemporary French writers, Swinburne, Rossetti, Burne-Jones and William Morris in England, and Edgar Allan Poe for his poems and tales. Most of all he owes a debt to Shakespeare (129).

Hofmannsthal's notes resume with a quotation from the article on Verlaine of whom he records merely 'antithèse de brutalité et de grace [*sic*], d'ironie farouche' [the contrast of brutality and grace, of fierce irony]—a compressed and distorted version of Huret's personal note on his conversations with the great poet: 'A chaque instant, dans les conversations de Verlaine, on est surpris et ravi par ces antithèses imprévues de brutalité et de grâce, d'ironie gaie et d'indignation farouche' [in conversation with Verlaine one is constantly surprised and delighted by these unexpected contrasts of brutality and grace, of light-hearted irony and fierce indignation; 67]. This is how Verlaine

---

[92] Huret, *Enquête*, 126, and below, p. 137.

proceeds; he is incapable of logically connected conversation. The only other reference to Verlaine in the notes is to *Sagesse*. His response is full of anger and pathos, he bangs his fist on the table and exclaims, 'ils m'embêtent, à la fin, les cymbalistes! eux et leurs manifestations ridicules!' [in the end they annoy me, these Cymbalists, them and their ridiculous 'events'!]. The arguments and debates annoy him, similarly the desire to return to the Renaissance rather than to the seventeenth or eighteenth centuries, to La Fontaine (called the originator of *vers libre*) or Chénier, seems misguided. Rimbaud has already achieved the novelties that most of the Symbolists attempt just as Villon had anticipated Ronsard—'je m'en fous de Ronsard!' [I don't give a damn about Ronsard!]. Above all, he despises too liberal an attitude to verse: 'moi, j'ai élargi la discipline du vers, et cela est bon; mais je ne l'ai pas supprimée! Pour qu'il y ait vers, il faut qu'il y ait rythme. A présent on fait des vers à mille pattes!' [me, I have relaxed the restricted discipline of verse, and that is good; but I have not suppressed it entirely! If you want verse, you have to have rhythm. At the moment people are writing lines with a thousand (metrical) feet]. And this is profoundly un-French.

Finally there are a few notes on the Parnassians, mostly from the response of Catulle Mendès, who is just as negative about literary schools—'c'est horripilant!' [it is exasperating! 288]. He claims that the Parnassians have no theory, no particular aesthetic, merely a friendly respect for the variety of each other's work. He defends the Symbolists from their attackers, but because young people should not be attacked rather than because he approves of their claims to have invented a completely new sense of beauty (291). Fundamentally, all poets are Symbolists, all novelists Naturalists and Psychologists. He is sceptical of the claim that Symbolists have invented a verse form where the unity of the strophe is 'plutôt psychique que syllabique, et variable en nombre et en durée selon les nécessités musicales' [more psychic than syllabic, variable in the number of feet and in length according to the demands of musicality], and which he compares to a violinist trying to play a piece of music without bar lines and time signature. Technically, he is strongly on the side of tradition and resists any attempt to systematize sound patternings since plenty of excellent effects have already been achieved by Hugo and Leconte de Lisle (not to mention himself). Above all he remonstrates against the rumour that the Parnassians are impassive and serene: this is not evident in Sully Prudhomme or de Hérédia, 'ce mangeur de rubis et de chrysoprases

... pas chez Coppée ... pas chez Dierx, ce rêveur et cet attendri' [the eater of rubies and chrysoprase, and not in Coppée or Dierx, the tender dreamer]. He continues, 'ça n'est pas chez Banville non plus, ce poète débordant de joie, lyrique comme Orphée et terrible comme Balzac' [it is not evident in Banville either, a poet overflowing with joy, as lyrical as Orpheus and as terrifying as Balzac; 298]. An excerpted version of this defence finds its way into Hofmannsthal's notes.

Hofmannsthal's reading of Huret was extremely important. Despite the whirl of attacks and counter-attacks of the participants in the inquiry, Hofmannsthal successfully focused on the major trends. The sections he ignored—Naturalists, Neo-Realists, Independents and Theoreticians and Philosophers—represented attitudes he thought outdated or too obscure. The *Enquête* is divided between those who think Symbolism is something more or less inherent to all literature and that the movement is therefore a nonsense and those who see something special in modern Symbolists' work and thought. It is interesting that Hofmannsthal owes most to the responses of writers such as Morice, de Régnier and Maeterlinck, the most kindly and courteous, and that he has little patience with the venom that Ghil and Kahn spit so liberally. Those who try to identify some coherence in Symbolism focus again and again on the autonomy of literature, the importance of providing access to a world beyond the empirical, the role of suggestion, the importance of rhythm in Symbolist technique, the paramount importance of beauty and the vital role of the poet in forming, synthesizing and therefore communicating this beauty. There is much, too, that maintains the occult functions of poetry, its high seriousness and its mystery. Above all, the Symbolists' responses to the *Enquête* make very little of the self as a coherent experiencing identity, and shift the emphasis in poetry firmly on to the language and on to the role of the poet as medium.

The idea of Huret's contributors that the movement was anchored to something of timeless poetic validity is reflected in one of Hofmannsthal's jottings from an early notebook:

Symbolismus. Wahl der Eigennamen. Warum stilisiert Heine eine gewisse Liebes-stimmung durch Cleopatra, andere durch Judith oder deutsches Bauernmädchen? Geliebte = Vignette für ein Kapitel im Tagebuch unserer Stimmungen.

[*line dividing the two paragraphs*]

Symbolisten haben für etwas Selbstverständliches eine ... Formel gefunden.[93]

---

[93] *Nachlaß*, H VB 13.5; cf. *RA* iii. 317. The omission is in indecipherable shorthand, probably a single adjective.

[Symbolism. Choice of proper names. Why does Heine use Cleopatra to convey certain moods of love, and Judith or a German peasant girl for others? Beloved = a vignette for a chapter in the diary of our moods. Symbolists have found a formula for something self-evident.]

This note is on a leaf torn from a small notebook. The use of the words 'Symbolisten' and 'Symbolismus', and comparison of the handwriting with dated notes and essay drafts, suggest that these jottings were made no earlier than the end of 1891. They continue: 'Da ist immer: die neuen Künstler [*inserted*: die individuell neuen] sprechen von einer [?] principiell . . . von Kunst . . .', where the omissions are again tantalizingly in scribbled shorthand. One might reconstruct: 'einer principiell verschiedenen Auffassung von Kunst' [there is always: the new artists (the individually new ones) talk about a fundamentally different attitude to art]. Hofmannsthal seems to have intended to oppose to the appearance of novelty the deeper understanding of art's fundamental continuity.

Hofmannsthal wonders in this note about the association of certain moods and certain historical or typical persons. Even his earliest notes draw a distinction between the kind of poetry that uses such names and types as triggers for a common mood and poetry that is deliberately crafted to create a particular mood around a familiar motif—where the poetic has to be made rather than found. On 18 December 1890 he notes:

der Kultus der historischen Lokalitäten, der äußerlichen Analogie und der falsch genannten 'poetischen' Situationen: Mondnacht, ein alter Mann, der laut aus der Bibel liest . . . das ist vielleicht ein Genrebild, aber kein Gedicht, es sagt gar nichts. (*RA* iii. 316)

[the cult of historical localities, external analogies and what are wrongly called 'poetic' situations: moonlit night, an old man reading aloud from the Bible . . . that is perhaps good for genre painting but it isn't a poem, it doesn't say anything at all.]

There is therefore a difference between a true poem and circumstances that one casually calls 'poetic', just as a so-called tragic accident (one that is poignant or especially unfortunate) is not the same tragedy as that of *Hamlet* or *Macbeth*. Poetry stocked with 'off-the-peg' poetic situations, the note goes on, is, 'Poesie ohne Innerlichkeit, also gar keine Poesie' [poetry without inwardness, and therefore not poetry at all]. This is either Impressionism or what Musil calls *Kitsch* in an essay entitled 'Unfreundliche Betrachtungen':

Der Dichter X. wäre in einer noch etwas schlechteren Zeit ein beliebter Familienblatterzähler geworden. Er hätte dann vorausgesetzt, daß das Herz auf bestimmte Situationen immer mit den gleichen bestimmten Gefühlen antwortet. Der Edelmut wäre in der bekannten Weise edel, das verlassene Kind beweinenswert und die Sommerlandschaft herzstärkend gewesen. Es ist zu bemerken, daß sich damit zwischen den Gefühlen und den Worten eine feste, eindeutige, gleichbleibende Beziehung eingestellt hätte, wie sie das Wesen des Begriffs ausmacht. Der Kitsch, der sich so viel auf das Gefühl zugute tut, macht also aus Gefühlen Begriffe.[94]

[In an even worse age, writer X would have become a popular magazine storyteller. He would have presupposed that the heart always responds to certain situations with the same specific feelings. Nobility would have been noble in the old familiar way, an abandoned child pitiable, and the summer landscape uplifting. It should be noted that a fixed, unambiguous, immutable relationship would thereby have been established between feelings and words, determining the nature of the concepts. Kitsch, which attaches so much importance to feeling, thus makes concepts out of feelings.]

None the less, for Hofmannsthal 'Innerlichkeit' alone is equally unpoetic without form:

Schönheit der Form bannt und erhält den Stimmungszauber wie das Gefäß den Wein: ein Aphorisma, einst lebhaft gefühlt, kann uns unverständlich werden; die abgeschlossene Form soll es *organisch, lebensfähig* machen.[95]

[Beauty of form captivates and maintains the magic of the mood as a barrel does wine: an aphorism that was once keenly felt can become incomprehensible to us; perfected form can make it *organic, viable*.]

No amount of vividness of feeling is effective without a vessel in which to contain it. Indeed, in a striking Symbolist reversal of Romantic priority, the emotion is considered as good as stillborn without the *coup de pouce* given by the form—like a version of the roles of art and life in the Pygmalion myth, where Galatea comes to life by virtue of her perfectly sculpted form and not because of the sculptor's love. The Romantic priority of poetic sensibility has been altered in favour of poetic *form*. The note 'Poetae nascuntur, vielleicht, aber *schaffend* erkennen wir den Weg' [poets are born, perhaps, but we find the true path by *creating*] subordinates sensibility to creative activity.[96] But a slightly later note (9 November 1891) envisages poetry in a continuum with life in a markedly Romantic manner: 'Poeta nascitur! Dichter und

---

[94] Musil, *Gesammelte Werke*, ed. Adolf Frisé, 2 vols. (Reinbek bei Hamburg: Rowohlt, 1978), ii. *Prosa und Stücke, Kleine Prosa, Autobiographisches, Essays und Reden, Kritik*, 502.

[95] *RA* iii. 315; 27 Jan. 1890; my italics.

[96] 12 Dec. 1890; *RA* iii. 315; my italics.

Nicht-dichter scheiden ist gerade so unmöglich, wie die 7 Regenbogenfarben trennen' [a poet is born! To distinguish between poet and non-poet is as impossible as separating the seven colours of the rainbow; *RA* iii. 322], incredulous that one could ever imagine the poet distinguished from the world. As isolated critical statements without the formal context of an essay or a poem like 'Was ist die Welt?', these appear not so much ambivalent as inconsistent.

None the less, a note made on 13 July 1892 (*RA* iii. 348) pursues the issues in terms identified in its opening words—'die neue Technik' [the new technique]—as specifically Symbolist. Technique was an important aspect of the originality to which Hofmannsthal judged Symbolists had a claim and which is repeatedly raised in Huret's questions to the French writers. The phrase 'neue Technik' is used by Hermann Bahr to describe Symbolism in the essay (originally entitled 'Symbolismus', later 'Symbolisten') that he published on 18 June 1892 and in which he quotes two of Hofmannsthal's poems. 'Technik' is also the word Hofmannsthal uses to describe George's supreme mastery of Symbolism in a letter from this period.[97] 'Technik' also picks up some of the implications of the word 'Formel' in the first note, and it was generally Hofmannsthal's tendency, when discussing Symbolism, to prioritize expression over experience or the transcendentalism that Huret's *Enquête* sometimes conveys. The latter aspect was represented most vociferously by Moréas: 'la poésie symbolique cherche à vêtir *l'Idée* d'une forme sensible' [symbolic poetry seeks to clothe the *idea* in tangible form].[98] Here religious tone was the norm even where belief had been abandoned, for as Bourget pointed out in his essay on Baudelaire, there are '[d]es permanences de la sensibilité religieuse dans la défaillance de la pensée religieuse' [parts of religious sensibility that remain permanent even when religious thinking is lacking].[99] But this is one pole of Symbolism which Hofmannsthal, although aware of, largely disregarded, something which his June 1893 summary implies: 'der französische Symbolismus ist künstlerische Transfiguration der

---

[97] Quoted in Chapter 3 below, p. 151.

[98] *Un manifeste littéraire* in *Figaro littéraire*, 18 Sept. 1886. Reprinted in *Les Premières Armes du Symbolisme* in 1889. Quoted by Lehmann, *The Symbolist Aesthetic in France*, 66. There are many further examples in Michaud, *Message poétique*, whose appendix, *La Doctrine symboliste*, is an invaluable collection of otherwise often inaccessible Symbolist theoretical writing. Cf. esp. 728 (Ghil, *Le Symbole*), 731–2 (Stuart Merrill's *Credo*), 735–6 (Paul Adam's *L'Art symboliste*), 744–6 (Georges Vanor, recalling Augustine and St Cyril), and 753 (Albert Mockel, George's acquaintance, in *Propos de littérature*). Cf. also Huret, *Enquête*, 148 (Saint-Pol-Roux) and Gide's *Traité du Narcisse* (see below, pp. 134–7).

[99] Bourget, *OC*, i. 6.

Wirklichkeit, der englische Hinausflüchten in ein Traumland' [French Symbolism is the artistic transfiguration of reality, English Symbolism is an escape into a dream-world].[100] Hofmannsthal was concerned with techniques for transfiguration, not primarily with transcendentalism.

The 'neue Technik' note goes on to quote Amiel's dictum 'tout paysage est un état de l'âme' [every landscape is a condition of the soul]—and since a parallel note from April 1892 reads 'Symbolismus: "Un paysage est un état de l'âme" (Amiel)', it is clear that the new technique to which Hofmannsthal refers in July is Symbolism.[101] However, the July note (written on headed notepaper from the bank where his father worked) was substantially copied from a diary note made on 21 May 1891, shortly after Hofmannsthal met Bahr and during the time he was working on his review of Amiel's *Fragments d'un journal intime*.[102] Reworking and copying on to fresh sheets suggest that Hofmannsthal was particularly interested in the subject-matter, most probably preparing an essay.[103] The first part of the note reads as follows:

Die neue Technik.

Amiel: 'Tout paysage est un état de l'âme.' Das heißt auch: jede Sensation findet ihren feinsten und eigensten Ausdruck nur in einem bestimmten Milieu; erste Liebe ist eine hellgrüne Frühlingslandschaft zwischen weißen Gardinen durchgesehen (Jean Paul); Ungeduld eine Landschaft ganz aus Metall mit heißer vibrierender Luft (Manier des Baudelaire); unbestimmte Sehnsucht das Rauschen der Bäume und das unbestimmte Wehen der Nacht (Eichendorff); es gibt namenlose Stimmungen, die man nur durch ein Bild suggerieren kann: die Stimmung der klaren hohen Berge (Zarathustra), der stillen Zimmer, der feucht kalten Gewölbe (Maeterlinck, E. T. A. Hoffmann).[104]

[100] *RA* iii. 365. An exception can be found in the Biese review, quoted below.

[101] *RA* iii. 344. Srdan Bogosavljević refers to both of these notes and complains 'Einmal wird Amiel als Kronzeuge für den Symbolismus, das zweite Mal als Gewährsmann für die Berechtigung der impressionistischen Technik zitiert, ohne daß eine solche Vermengung von verschiedenen Stilmitteln irgendwie problematisiert wird': 'Der Amiel-Aufsatz. Zum Dilettantismus- und Décadence-Begriff des jungen Hofmannsthal', in Wolfram Mauser (ed.), *Hofmannsthal-Forschungen*, ix (Freiburg i.Br.: Hofmannsthal-Gesellschaft, 1987), 231–2, n. 5. The 'neue Technik' note, however, is exactly such a problematization and cannot accurately be summarized as impressionistic: Hofmannsthal evidently saw *état de l'âme* as a component of Symbolism and proceeds to investigate how this was so.

[102] The note from 21 May 1891 is in *Nachlaß*, H VII 2. It fits between the paragraph beginning 'Der beste Kritiker' and 'Es ist sonderbar, zu bemerken', *RA* iii. 329–30, the omission not noted in that edition. The Amiel essay appeared on 15 June 1891; cf. *RA* i. 106–17, esp. 113 (where the dictum is quoted again). Very little is altered between May 1891 and July 1892, except that the names do not occur in the earlier version.

[103] These notes may be linked to the 'Drahtgestell für ein Essay' on Symbolism that he sent in the letter in which he quotes himself and Verlaine as Symbolists, and whose last two pages only are preserved. See below, p. 151.

[104] *RA* iii. 349; 13 July 1892.

[The new technique. Amiel: 'every landscape is a condition of the soul.' That also means that every sensation only finds its finest and most characteristic expression in a particular milieu; first love is a pale green spring landscape seen through white net curtains (Jean Paul); impatience is a landscape entirely of metal with hot, trembling air (Baudelaire's style); indeterminate longing is the rustling of the trees and the indeterminate wafting of the night (Eichendorff); there are nameless moods that one can suggest in an image, the mood of clear high mountains (Zarathustra), of quiet rooms, of the damp, cold vault (Maeterlinck, E. T. A. Hoffmann).]

Hofmannsthal analyses the 'new technique' in terms that at first look as if he is committing the fallacy he identified in 1890 as the 'Kultus...der aüßerlichen Analogie' [the worship of external correlative] and that Musil called *Kitsch*, that is, simply labelling a mood with a name or an atmosphere. Just like Proust's names, which operate as mnemonic distillates of complex emotional associations, in Hofmannsthal's note the mood is prior to the expression and suggests its own capturing in a landscape. Far from suggesting that landscape and mood are permanently interchangeable (that the situation of rustling trees at night, for instance, epitomizes longing and always will), Hofmannsthal's addition of an author's name to the examples in the 'neue Technik' note (first love, impatience, longing), invites us to see each example as an acknowledgement that the mood's need for expression has found its best response in a particular verbally constructed instance. Without writing it, the correspondence between 'Stimmung' and 'Milieu' is not made. This is a strongly Symbolist idea, presupposed by all of Verlaine's 'Paysages tristes', for example, and central to Gide's *Traité du Narcisse*—although expressed more directly in the preface to the second edition of his *Voyage d'Urien*:

Une émotion naît. Comment?—peu importe; il suffit qu'elle soit. L'*être* chez elle comme chez tous est le besoin de se manifester. Me comprendrez-vous si je dis que *le manifeste vaut l'émotion, intégralement?* Il y a là une sorte d'algèbre esthétique; émotion et manifeste forment l'équation; l'un est l'équivalent de l'autre. Qui dira *émotion* dira donc *paysage*; et qui dit *paysage* devra donc connaître *émotion*.[105]

[An emotion is born. How? It does not matter, it is enough that it exists. *Being* for the emotion, just like for everything else, is the need to manifest itself. Would you understand me if I said that *the manifestation is perfectly equivalent to the emotion?* There is here a sort of aesthetic algebra; emotion and manifestation make the equation;

---

[105] André Gide, *Romans, récits et soties: Œuvres lyriques*, ed. Maurice Nadeau et al. (Paris: Gallimard, 1958), 1464. This was first published in the Dec. 1894 edition of *Mercure de France*, so Hofmannsthal may very well have seen it then.

one is the equivalent of the other. If you say *emotion* you say *landscape* at the same time; if you say *landscape* you will know the *emotion*.]

This is a version of what Hofmannsthal expressed as 'Sein und Bedeuten ist eins' [being and meaning are the same; *RA* iii. 391]. The idea of aesthetic algebra, finally, has its origin in Baudelaire's 'adaptation mathématiquement exacte' [a mathematically exact adaptation] that is characteristic of metaphor.[106]

'Stimmung' is modulated to 'Zustand' in the next paragraph of Hofmannsthal's 'neue Technik' note, and the condition is added that a poetic response to material should embrace it wholly and utterly:[107]

Definition der Poesie bei Hebbel:
Vollendetstes Gedicht muß einen Zustand bis ins Tiefste ausschöpfen. (Poesie soll die dunkelsten Zustände durch *Melodien* lösen).
Die symbolistische Reaktion gegen die flache Epik kommt von lyrischen Grund-bedürfnissen her.
Unsere Klassiker waren nur Plastiker des Stils, noch nicht Maler und Musiker.
ὑπείπω—dicendo suggerere
ὑποτίθεσθαι—erraten lassen
[*new page*] Symbolistische Technik eine Unterstützung, wie die Instrumentation gegenüber symphonischen Gedanken, wie Bemalung bei Holzskulpturen, reine Farben gegenüber Zeichnung.
    Photographie—Naturalismus
verzichten auf die Mitwirkung der Suggestion (der Farbe), welche sie durch Genauigkeit ersetzten wollen.[108]

[Definition of poetry in Hebbel: the most perfect poem must delve fully into a state (poetry should dissolve the darkest states with *melodies*). The Symbolist reaction against banal epic derives from fundamental lyric necessities. Our classic authors were merely stylistic sculptors, not yet painters and musicians. ὑπείπω—to suggest by saying, ὑποτίθεσθαι—to make one guess. Symbolist technique is a support, as instrumentation is for symphonic thoughts, as colour is on wooden sculptures, pure colours for drawing. Photography—Naturalism reject the co-operation of suggestion (colour), which wants to replace it with precision.]

This brings out very clearly the two angles from which Hofmannsthal saw Symbolist poetry, its essentially traditional nature and its historical function in re-establishing tradition after the un-poetic deviation of Naturalism. This second, historical role, however, is seen primarily as

[106] Baudelaire, *OC*, ii. 133.
[107] The same point is made in a poem from early Feb. 1893, 'Epilog zu den lebenden Bildern', linking mood and symbol as its expression: 'Doch was ein jeder ist, das ist er ganz; | Ganz *einer* Stimmung athmendes Symbol' (*SW* i. 40).
[108] *RA* iii. 349 (layout altered to conform with the manuscript, *Nachlaß*, H VB 2.1ᵃ⁻ᵇ).

a matter of support; the implication is that the substance of the poetic tradition has not changed in the lyric revival. Its origin is revealed in the definition of poetry that Hofmannsthal chooses, which is not from a Symbolist manifesto nor even from one of Baudelaire's theoretical essays, but the Romantic definition by Hebbel quoted at the beginning of this chapter: 'die lyr. Poesie soll das menschliche Gemüth im Tiefsten erschließen, sie soll seine dunkelsten Zustände durch himmel-klare Melodien lösen, sie soll es durch sich selbst berauschen und erquicken.' Hofmannsthal introduces a slightly different emphasis, for Hebbel's metaphors of 'erschließen' and 'lösen' suggest that the condi-tion lies in readiness, waiting to be released, whereas Hofmannsthal's 'ausschöpfen' implies that it needs to be drawn out more actively. The difference perhaps betrays anxiety over the pressing need for poetry to resume its old functions rather than quiet confidence in its power. Nevertheless, the belief in Symbolism as the carrier of something archetypally poetic, Symbolism's reaction against bland epic as a resurfacing of 'lyrische Grundbedürfnisse', is an idea that will persist in Hofmannsthal's understanding, as a note from March 1893 makes clear: '"Symbolismus" Form des künstlerischen Grundtriebes, des Triebes, dem Geschaffenen die letzte Deutlichkeit, den göttlichen Hauch des Lebens, zu geben (la chair im "Œuvre")' ['Symbolism' a form of fundamental artistic necessity, the urge to give what has been created its final clarity, give it the divine inspiration of life (flesh in the 'Work'); RA iii. 357]. The reference to the Œuvre is perhaps to Mallarmé's projected Livre, and both the conviction that the created world is lifeless without art and the desire to vivify are central interests of the Symbolists.

Hofmannsthal proceeds to expand on the phrase 'symbolistische Reaktion', by distinguishing the new French technique first from those of the German classics, and then from Symbolism's most immediate target, Naturalism. The phrase 'Unsere Klassiker waren nur Plastiker des Stils, noch nicht Maler und Musiker' was most probably George's, and thus the judgement of a Symbolist-in-spirit.[109]

[109] It occurs in speech marks at the end of a note on George from Dec. 1891 (RA iii. 340). The distinct presence of Hebbel behind this section of the 'neue Technik' note raises the possibility that this quotation is of his diaries. There are several passages there and in his reviews of poetry that make similar points, but neither this quotation nor even a close approximation to it has proved traceable. Many of Novalis's notes hover round the same themes: 'Musik—Plastik, und Poësie sind Synonymen' (ii. 572), for example; a long fragment comparing and contrasting 'Mahler' and 'Musiker' (ii. 573–5), followed by the note 'Durch-dringung von Plastik und Musik' (ii. 575); another contrasting 'Plastiker' and 'Musiker' (iii. 383). There is also the assertion in Heinrich von Ofterdingen that 'Überhaupt können die Dichter

An article by Saint-Antoine in *Ermitage* of June 1894 entitled 'Qu'est-ce que le Symbolisme?' makes exactly the same point:

L'expression musicale est toujours en quelque sorte symbolique, l'expression plastique ne l'est jamais. Le symbolisme est étranger à l'art plastique parce qu'il est aussi indépendant que possible de la réalité; il ne prend à la nature que les éléments formels de son œuvre; sa raison d'être est l'idée qu'il personnifie.[110]

[Musical expression is always in some sense symbolic, plastic expression never is. Symbolism is alien to the plastic arts because it is as independent of reality as it is possible to be. It only takes from nature the formal elements of its production; its *raison d'être* is the idea that it expresses.]

According to this view, the contribution of recent French poetry to the plasticity of German verse is to have added the same power of suggestion that certain types of music and painting possess. The importance of suggestion is underlined by the two Greek verbs in the 'neue Technik' note: both confirm the function of indirect expression as a means of attaining a subjacent truth.[111]

The idea that Symbolism is a form of 'Unterstützung' is odd: at first it suggests something incidental to the main structure, important perhaps but not part of it. The analogies from music and painting attribute to 'symbolistische Technik', however, the function of giving body to a basic shape—changes in instrumentation bringing out the multiple suggestive possibilities of a musical subject, colour adding warmth to the contours of a wooden statue. Neither instrumentation nor colour exists independently of the shapes to which they are added, and thus suggestion, far from being incidental, comes to represent something essential and transforming. It is important, however, that what Hofmannsthal here calls 'Symbolist technique' is a modification of an idea found in a distinctly pre-Symbolist source, again Friedrich Hebbel. Hebbel's diary notes 'Das Instrumentiren in der Musik ist, wie das Coloriren in der Malerei' [instrumentation in music is like colour in painting].[112] Klein's article on George in the *Blätter* quotes Novalis

nicht genug von den Musikern und Malern lernen' (i. 286), but no precise source for the phrase in speech marks is traceable in Novalis either—although the fragments cited here would confirm what I suppose to be George's judgement that German classical authors write with more plasticity than music.

[110] Michaud, *Message poétique*, 750.

[111] Both mean in a general sense 'to suggest': the first has overtones of the deliberate creation of nuance, insinuation or hinting at concealed significance; the second is an Aristotelian word concerning the relationship between what is on the surface and what underlies it.

[112] Hebbel, *Tagebücher*, i. 399 (28 Oct. 1839; entry 1787).

making a similar comparison: 'Die poesie im strengen sinn scheint fast die mittelkunst zwischen den bildenden und tönenden künsten zu sein. sollte der takt der figur, der ton der farbe entsprechen?' [poetry in the strictest sense seems to be almost the mid-point between the plastic arts and music. Might musical time correspond to shape? musical sound to colour?].[113]

The reference to 'reine Farbe' towards the end of the 'neue Technik' note is clearer when one adduces other notes. One made soon afterwards and headed 'Franz Stuck', begins with the phrases 'Suggestions-geheimnis. das Verschleierte, wie durch einen Nebel' [the secret of suggestion. Being veiled, as if through a mist],[114] and this may be what Hofmannsthal has in mind in the 'neue Technik' note. On the same page is a jotting that starts 'Technik. a. Böcklin b. die Praeraphaeliten', and includes under Böcklin the following *Steigerung*: 'das Blau, pene-trante Farben [die Meerfrauen] blaues Blau, Seele des Blau' [blue, penetrating colours [sea colours of the sea] blue blue, the soul of blue]. Both here and in the July note there is a stress on the intensity of colour—'reine Farbe' and 'blaues Blau'—with intensity leading to the revelation of the essence of the colour, and thus to a form of symbolism.[115]

In the 'neue Technik' note Symbolism is distinguished from Naturalism, or in visual terms the photographic approach to art: Naturalism dispenses with suggestion (here equated with use of colour) in favour of precision (or use of line), whereas suggestion is one of the defining characteristics of Symbolism, as the Huret inquiry, Mallarmé's and Morice's contribution in particular, emphasized most strongly.[116] Baudelaire famously launched a tirade against the substitution of photography for art in the *Salon de 1859*. He trenchantly affirmed that 'l'industrie photographique était le réfuge de tous les peintres manqués, trop mal doués ou trop paresseux' [the photographic industry was the refuge of all the failed painters who were insufficiently gifted or too lazy], and that enthusiasm for it demonstrates blindness or stupidity, linking this directly to the other arts: 'chez nous le peintre naturel, comme le poète naturel, est presque un

---

[113] Klein, 'Über Stefan George', 47.
[114] *Nachlaß*, H VII 4.35. Datable to Nov./Dec. 1892.
[115] For a much fuller context, linked to the poem 'Wolken', see Andreas Thomasberger, *Verwandlungen in Hofmannsthals Lyrik: Zur sprachlichen Bedeutung von Genese und Gestalt* (Tübingen: Niemeyer, 1994), 64–9.
[116] Morice's *La Littérature de tout à l'heure* ends with 'Commentaires d'un livre futur' and the importance for this of suggestion.

monstre. Le goût exclusif du Vrai . . . étouffe le goût du Beau' [in our society the natural painter and the natural poet are almost monsters. A taste exclusively for Truth . . . stifles a taste for Beauty].[117] Hofmannsthal makes a link with the literary tradition with the remainder of the colour note (headed 'Franz Stuck'), which reads:

Maeterlinck: die traurig dämmernden Teiche; die Märchenprinzessin; die opalinen Augen, das unheimlich Schöne.
[*new page*] 'symbolistische Schule'
die Franzosen mit den scheuen Symbolen der flüchtigen Fledermaus des phantastischen Fauns, der alten verblichenen Seide, der dämmernden Teiche.[118]

[Maeterlinck: the melancholy twilit pools, the fairy-tale princess, the opaline eyes, the uncannily beautiful. 'Symbolist School'. The French with their timid symbols, such as the flitting bat, the fantastic faun, old faded silk, twilit pools.]

The reference to the bat is probably to Baudelaire's 'Spleen', where 'l'Espérance, comme une chauve-souris, | S'en va battant les murs de son aile timide' [Hope, like a bat, flies away, striking the walls with its timid wing]—especially as 'scheu' in Hofmannsthal's note matches the 'timide' of Baudelaire's poem.[119] The faun is Mallarmé's,[120] and Maeterlinck's pools are from *Pelléas et Mélisande.*

The faun—'Personifikation gewisser täppisch boshafter Triebe in uns' [personification of certain clumsily malicious instincts within us; *RA* iii. 356]—was almost an archetype for Symbolism, depicted by Franz von Stuck in *Fighting Fauns* in 1889. In a review for the *Wiener Literatur-Zeitung* Hofmannsthal noted Stuck's irresistible need to move away from wittily interpreted allegories and lose himself in the mysterious naivety of fairy tales.[121] He summarizes: 'So entstand eine Landschaftsmalerei voll phantastisch sinnlicher Lyrik' [thus a style of landscape painting was developed that was full of fantastically sensuous poetry]. The review is worth quoting at some length, since it brings the discussion of the 'neue Technik' note and its related jottings full circle:

Das 'Schummerige, Farbenträumerische' einer gewissen Abendstunde zog ihn

[117] Baudelaire, *OC*, ii. 618 and 616.
[118] *Nachlaß*, H VII 4.35. This note was altered slightly and used in a letter to George after a reference to Rodenbach and editors of Symbolist periodicals (*BW*, 50). Another note, *Nachlaß*, H VII 5.10 (Dec. 1892), links the 'Prinzessinnen' with Maeterlinck and the English Pre-Raphaelites.
[119] Baudelaire, *OC*, i. 75. If this is so, this reference would confirm that Hofmannsthal thought of Baudelaire as a Symbolist.
[120] 'L'Après-midi d'un faune', Mallarmé, *OC*, 50–3.
[121] 'Franz Stuck', written in 1893 but published 17 Jan. 1894: *RA* i. 529–33 (531).

besonders an. Jener Abendstunde, wo die Dinge ihr Körperliches verlieren und bebenden voll dunkler Farbe gesogenen Schatten gleich in die feuchte Luft gewebt erscheinen. . . . Neben dieser Abendstunde liebt Stuck den grellen heißen Tag; hinter den in Sonnenlicht gebadeten Strand legt er dann gern einen Streifen Meeres von jenem eigentümlich penetranten Blau, das Böcklin gefunden hat. . . . Zur Staffage seiner phantastischen Landschaft, gleichsam als lebendiges Symbol ihres lyrischen Gefühlsinhaltes, nimmt Stuck jene von Böcklin überlieferten, von der Antike schon völlig losgebundenen Fabelwesen: Zentaur und Zentaurin, Faun und Paniske. Sie erlauben ein Reflektieren der Stimmung ohne Sentimentalität.[122]

[He was particularly attracted by the dimness and colourful dreaminess of a certain evening hour. That evening hour where things lose their tangibleness and appear to be woven into the damp air like trembling shadows drenched in dark colours. Apart from this evening hour Stuck loves the glaring heat of the day. Behind the beach bathed in sunlight he likes to put a strip of sea in that peculiarly penetrating blue that Böcklin discovered. To decorate his fantastic landscape, to serve almost as living symbols of its lyrical emotional content, Stuck takes male and female centaurs, fauns and pan figures, the fabulous creatures handed down by Böcklin and completely divorced from their classical origins. They permit a reflection of the mood without any form of sentimentality.]

This passage is obviously a reworking of the 1892 note on colour, and throughout both notes and essay the poetic and the visual intermingle.[123] The flexible use of the words 'Lyrik' and 'lyrisch', the recurrence of 'Symbol' or 'symbolisch' in both contexts, the appearance of the faun as the motif of Stuck and of 'die Franzosen'—all these provide a thorough illustration of the maxim 'tout paysage est un état de l'âme' in the two contexts of poetry and painting. It was central to Hofmannsthal's understanding of Symbolism, but there is always a suggestion that, unlike Gide's Narcissus, he was concerned less with the pure correspondence of mood and scene than with a personal 'Gefühlsinhalt' to be expressed.

One of the Greek words for suggestion quoted in Hofmannsthal's

---

[122] *RA* i. 531–2. A passage in Remer's 'Symbolisten' article comparing Böcklin with Laforgue makes a series of very similar points: 'hier wie dort jene trunkene Phantasie, die sich gleichsam an ihrer eigenen Allmacht berauscht hat, hier wie dort jene tolle Unmöglichkeit der Personen und Landschaften, die geschildert werden, hier wie dort jene seltsam neue Farbengebung, die sich wie mit glühendem Eisen den Sinnen des Lesers oder Zuschauers einätzt. . . . Es scheint fast, als bilde die Phantasie bei gewissen Künstlernaturen einen zweiten Gesichtssinn, der sie eine andere Welt sehen läßt, als wir sie mit unserem prosaischen Auge wahrnehmen, aber mit der gleichen Bestimmtheit, der gleichen Wahrheit und Natürlichkeit': Remer, 'Die Symbolisten', 394.

[123] The 'Märchenprinzessin' appears a little later in the review, and the 'opaline [unheimliche Satans-]augen' feature in one of the longer sections omitted in this quotation. There are other overlaps in the essay from notes adjacent to the one quoted.

'neue Technik' note recurs in a note of March 1893 that explicitly refers back to the 'Begriff der "Grundstimmung" einer künstlerischen Individualität' [concept of the 'fundamental mood' of artistic individuality] with which Hofmannsthal was concerned in 1891 and 1892:

1. Was jeder ist, projiziert er nach außen: Wille zur Erkenntnis, zum Leben, zur Macht etc. Was jeden am deutlichsten beseelt, dünkt ihm, die Welt zu beseelen. 2. Kritik und Symbolik, die beiden sich ergänzenden Kugelschalen a) Kritik ist Ausdruck des Verständlichen, in abstracto Darstellbaren an der eigenen Individualität, insofern man nur *diese* inneren Besitztümer, wo sie sich an anderen finden, lebendig erfaßt und hervorhebt.

b) Symbolik, der Rest, der nicht aufgeht, der Keimboden der reinen Subjektivität pflegt in Symbolen, Andeutungen (ὑπειπεῖν, suggerieren) ausgedrückt zu werden, einer Art persönlichen Musik, eben der 'Grundstimmung'. (*RA* iii. 357)

[(1) What a person is, he projects outwardly: the will to insight, to life, to power, etc.. What most distinctly animates an individual seems to him to animate the world. (2) Criticism and Symbolism, two halves of a whole. (*a*) Criticism is the expression of the elements of one's individuality that can be understood, that can be represented *in abstracto*, in as far as one only seizes upon and emphasizes these particular inner riches when they are discovered in others. (*b*) Symbolism is the rest that cannot be expressed; the seedbed of pure subjectivity is usually expressed in symbols, suggestions (ὑπειπεῖν, to suggest), a kind of personal music specifically of the 'fundamental mood'.]

The note ends with the passage on ' "Symbolismus" Form des künstlerischen Grundtriebes' quoted above. At the heart of this idea is 'reine Subjektivität', 'persönliche Musik', the self *tout pur*. 'Symbolik' and 'Kritik' are paired mechanisms of self-expression, realizing the individual's need to communicate his relationship with the world. This relationship is as intimate as it possibly could be, in that the characteristics that inspire the world are seen as a projection of those that inspire the self. The symbols and suggestions that convey the essence of identity are directly opposed to 'Kritik', which can communicate only the aspects of the self that are accessible to reason and abstract formulation. 'Symbolik' is thus vital to the adequate presentation of the essential self.

The purest examples of the use of suggestion in Symbolist technique can be found in Verlaine. His 'Ariette oubliée V' from the *Romances sans paroles* was quoted by Hofmannsthal himself as essentially characteristic of Symbolism:

Le piano que baise une main frêle
Luit dans le soir rose et gris vaguement,
Tandis qu'avec un très léger bruit d'aile
Un air bien vieux, bien faible et bien charmant
Rôde discret, épeuré quasiment,
Par le boudoir longtemps parfumé d'Elle.

Qu'est-ce que c'est que ce berceau soudain
Qui lentement dorlote mon pauvre être?
Que voudrais-tu de moi, doux Chant badin?
Qu'as-tu voulu, fin refrain incertain
Qui vas tantôt mourir vers la fenêtre
Ouverte un peur sur le petit jardin?[124]

[The piano that a frail hand is kissing gleams vaguely in the pink and grey evening, whilst with the very slight sound of a wing-beat a tune quite old, quite weak, quite charming, discreetly prowls, as if startled, through the boudoir that has long been perfumed by Her. What is this sudden cradle that slowly cossets my poor being? What do you want of me, sweet and playful Song? What did you want, delicate, hesitant refrain, which will soon die towards the window that is open a little on to the little garden?]

Contours are smudged with pastel colours and mysterious light; 'vaguement', 'incertain' and 'faible' add further indistinctness. The certainties of extension are reduced, as the apparently spatial 'vers' in the penultimate line constructs as much imaginatively with 'mourir' as practically with 'vas'; 'par' in line 6 is consummately vague, with none of the clarity that, say, 'dans', 'autour de' or 'le long de' would have contributed. The perceiving self is distilled to its impersonal essence, 'mon pauvre être', and there are no other identities involved—*Elle* is absent, leaving only a perfume, and it is quite unclear that anyone is actually *playing* the piano whose music, part of the verse itself as much as anything else, suffuses the scene. And yet even though identity is renounced, it would be easy to extend the analysis into the dimension of what the poem might symbolize—a relationship is suggested by the cradle, for example, even though this is actually a metaphor for a feeling, not a real object.

Where poets such as Mallarmé invoked suggestion in their reflections on poetry, it was without Hofmannsthal's Romantic focus on subjectivity. On 12 June 1891 Hofmannsthal noted, 'Wir malen nie ein Ding, sondern immer den Eindruck, den ein Ding in uns macht: das Bild eines Bildes' [we never paint a thing, instead we only paint the

---

[124] Verlaine, *OPC*, 193.

impression that a thing makes within us, the image of an image; *RA* iii. 332]. Mallarmé had recently made much of a closely related dictum, 'peindre non la chose, mais l'effet qu'elle produit' [paint not the thing but the effect that it produces]. This was a phrase coined to express *in nuce* his new poetics in a letter to Cazalis of October 1864.[125] He developed the idea at length in several other places, including his reply to Huret's *Enquête*:

Nommer un objet, c'est supprimer les trois-quarts de la jouissance du poëme qui est faite de deviner peu à peu: le *suggérer*, voilà le rêve. C'est le parfait usage de ce mystère qui constitue le symbole: évoquer petit à petit un objet pour montrer un état d'âme, ou, inversement, choisir un objet et en dégager un état d'âme, par une série de déchiffrements.[126]

[to *name* an object is to suppress three-quarters of the enjoyment of the poem that is made to divine little by little: *suggest* it, that is one's dream. This is the perfect practice of the mystery that is the symbol: evoking an object little by little in order to show a condition of the soul, or, conversely, choosing an object and releasing from it a condition of the soul via a process of deciphering.]

The passage became current—Saint-Antoine quotes it in his 'Qu'est-ce que le Symbolisme?' in 1894, for example. Mallarmé here provided a clear definition of Symbolism, accessible to Hofmannsthal, in terms of opposite but complementary processes of suggestion and graded deciphering.[127] But whilst Mallarmé's *état d'âme* floats without any reference to an individual, Hofmannsthal's similar statement attaches the impression suggested to a perceiving consciousness, 'den Eindruck, den ein Ding *in uns* macht'. When he wrote of 'Symbolismus im weiten Sinn' [Symbolism in its extended sense] later, in March 1894, he defined it in terms of just such a personal dynamic: 'die unein-gestandenen Seelenvorgänge, die ins Kunstwerk eingewebt werden' [the unacknowledged spiritual processes that are woven into a work of art; *RA* iii. 380].

This process of weaving the mind and the work of art together is akin to the genesis of metaphor:

Das Entstehen des metaphorischen Ausdruckes ist ein geheimnisvolles Ding: der Anschauung eines Vorgangs substituiert sich plötzlich unwillkürlich die Anschauung eines andern nur in der Idee verwandten Bildlicheren, Körper-licheren. . . . Einfluß der Sprache auf das Denken.—Sprache ist überhaupt nur

---

[125] Mallarmé, *Correspondance*, i. 137.
[126] Huret, *Enquête*, 60; Mallarmé, *OC*, 869.
[127] 'Chiffre' is the term picked up in *Das Gespräch über Gedichte*; see below, pp. 304–5.

Bild. Manche erstarrt wie Hieroglyphen, haben nur Münzwert, manche lebendig, wirken direkt auf die Nerven.[128]

[A metaphorical expression arises in a mysterious way: the contemplation of one process is suddenly and involuntarily replaced by the contemplation of another, more pictorial, more tangible one that is related only on the level of ideas. Influence of language on thought.—Language consists only of images. Some that are ossified, like hieroglyphs, only have token value, others are alive and directly affect the nerves.]

Metaphor arises by an unconscious 'slippage' between an abstract process and a related, more concrete one. This can only take place within a world where 'metaphysische und physische Probleme' are '2 Erscheinungsformen desselben Dings' and where inner and outer worlds are identical but 'auf einer anderen Stufe der Phänomenalität' [metaphysical and physical problems are two manifestations of the same thing, on a different phenomenological level; *RA* iii. 369]. The Romantic roots of such thinking were pointed out by Thorel, in his article of September 1891: 'tous les phénomènes de la vie physique et de la vie morale ne sont que des manifestations différentes d'un principe unique' [all the phenomena of the psychological and moral life are only different manifestations of a single principle].[129] Although Hofmannsthal can hardly have read it, Nietzsche's *Über Wahrheit und Lüge im aussermoralischen Sinn* treats closely related questions, and in similar terms. Nietzsche maintains that truths are illusions that we treat as if they were real, 'Metaphern, die abgenutzt und sinnlich kraftlos geworden sind, Münzen, die ihr Bild verloren haben und nun als Metall, nicht mehr als Münzen, in Betracht kommen' [metaphors that are worn out and spent sensuously, coins that have lost their faces and are now only treated as metal, no longer as coins].[130] Truth consists merely of obeying the particular metaphorical convention in force: 'wahrhaft zu sein, das heißt die usuellen Metaphern zu brauchen, also moralisch ausgedrückt: von der Verpflichtung, nach einer festen Konvention zu lügen, herdenweise in einem für alle verbindlichen Stile zu lügen' [to be truthful means using the conventional metaphors, or in moral terms, lying for reasons of duty and according to a fixed convention, all lying in exactly the same way, sheep-like]. Metaphor is the source of conceptualization: 'die Illusion der künstlerische

[128] *RA* iii. 360; May 1893.
[129] Jean Thorel, 'Les Romantiques allemands et les Symbolistes français', *Entretiens politiques et littéraires*, 3.18 (Sept. 1891), 101.
[130] Nietzsche, *Werke in drei Bänden*, ed. Karl Schlechta (Munich: Hanser, 1955), iii. 314.

Übertragung eines Nervenreizes in Bilder [ist] wenn nicht die Mutter, so doch die Großmutter eines jeden Begriffs' [the illusion that one is artistically transforming sensations of the nerves into images is if not the mother then the grandmother of all concepts].[131] Humanity consists in the ability to build these metaphors into systems, and establish a hierarchical structure that would be impossible if direct and unstructured perception were the norm:

Im Bereich jener Schemata nämlich ist [es] möglich, . . . eine neue Welt von Gesetzen, Privilegien, Unterordnungen, Grenzbestimmungen zu schaffen, die nun der andern anschaulichen Welt der ersten Eindrücke gegenübertritt als das Festere, Allgemeinere, Bekanntere, Menschlichere und daher als das Regulierende und Imperativische.[132]

[On the level of those schemes it is possible to create a new world of laws, privileges, hierarchies and boundaries that is opposed to the other, visible world and appears more solid, more universal, more familiar, more human and therefore the one that regulates and determines things.]

Much of the imagery and vocabulary of Hofmannsthal's note is very similar to Nietzsche's essay, and the rather enigmatic 'Einfluß der Sprache auf das Denken' is perhaps more comprehensible after reference to this parallel. The comparison with Nietzsche, however, is important as much because of the differences in their thinking as because of similarities: Hofmannsthal still has faith in the validity of the relationship between 'Nervenreiz' and metaphor. Where Nietzsche maintains that 'selbst das Verhältnis eines Nervenreizes zu dem hervorgebrachten Bilde ist an sich kein notwendiges' [even the relationship between the stimulation of a nerve and the image that arises from it is not a necessary relationship],[133] and that it becomes accepted as causal only by dint of its millionth repetition over generations, Hofmannsthal is concerned to affirm a real correspondence between personal perception and expression.

The point is reinforced in his review of the literary historian Alfred Biese's *Philosophie des Metaphorischen* (published in March 1894), when it shifts from critique of the book written to an evocation of the book that the title made Hofmannsthal imagine:

Ich erwartete eine Philosophie der subjektiven Metaphorik; eine Betrachtung des metaphernbildenden Triebes in uns und der unheimlichen Herrschaft, die die von uns erzeugten Metaphern rückwirkend auf unser Denken ausüben—andererseits der unsäglichen Lust, die wir durch metaphorische Beseelung aus toten Dingen

---

[131] Nietzsche, *Werke in drei Bänden*, 315.   [132] Ibid. 314–15.   [133] Ibid. 317.

saugen. Eine hellsichtige Darstellung des seltsam vibrierenden Zustandes, in welchem die Metapher zu uns kommt, über uns kommt in Schauer, Blitz und Sturm: dieser plötzlichen blitzartigen Erleuchtung, in der wir einen Augenblick lang den großen Weltzusammenhang ahnen, schauernd die Gegenwart der Idee spüren, dieses ganzen mystischen Vorganges, der uns die Metapher leuchtend und real hinterläßt. (*RA* i. 192)

[I was expecting a philosophy of subjective metaphors, a discussion of our urge to create metaphors and of the uncanny influence that the metaphors we create then have on our thinking—or a consideration of the ineffable joy that we derive from lifeless things because of their revivification via metaphor. I expected a perceptive depiction of that strangely agitated condition in which metaphors come to us, come *upon* us indeed, with a shudder, a bolt of lightning and a clap of thunder— of that sudden flash of illumination in which we sense for a moment the vast coherence of the world, and, trembling, feel the presence of the Idea, of the whole mystical process that the metaphor truly and brilliantly vouchsafes to us.]

The process whereby a metaphor is created is tense (the review says 'vibrierend', the note on metaphor mentions the effect of language on the nerves) and sudden ('plötzlich' is common to both descriptions); it is also independent of conscious control, for it either comes to or upon us (review), or simply occurs whilst we are watching (note). Hofmannsthal's faith in the expressive power of metaphor is encapsulated in the word 'real', alien to Nietzsche's sceptical account. It is nearer to the faith in essential truths articulated by Mallarmé's definition of the function of poetic language:

Je dis: une fleur! et, hors de l'oubli où ma voix relègue aucun contour, en tant que quelque chose d'autre que les calices sus, musicalement se lève, idée même et suave, l'absente de tous bouquets.[134]

[I say, 'a flower', and, from out of the oblivion where my voice casts all outlines, in as much as something other than the known calyces, there rises musically the very, the sweet idea, the absence of all perfume.]

But this locates the power in the language itself, and dispenses altogether with the mediating mind of the personal observer. Hofmannsthal's view shares elements with Rilke's, who wrote to Clara describing the process of observing:

Das Anschauen ist eine so wunderbare Sache, von der wir so wenig wissen; wir sind mit ihm ganz nach außen gekehrt, aber gerade wenn wirs am meisten sind, scheinen in uns Dinge vor sich zu gehen, die auf das Unbeobachtetsein sehnsüchtig gewartet haben, und während sie sich, intakt und seltsam anonym, in uns

---

[134] Mallarmé, *OC*, 857 (the preface to Ghil's *Traité du verbe*); later in *Crise de vers*, *OC*, 368.

vollziehen, ohne uns,—wächst in dem Gegenstand draußen ihre Bedeutung heran, ein überzeugender, starker—ihr einzig möglicher Name, in dem wir das Geschehnis in unserem Innern selig und ehrerbietig erkennen, ohne selbst daran heranzureichen, es nur leise, ganz von fern, unter dem Zeichen eines eben noch fremden und schon im nächsten Augenblick aufs neue entfremdeten Dinges begreifend—Mir geht es jetzt oft so, daß irgendein Gesicht mich so anrührt; am Morgen, z.B., . . . man hat schon viel Sonne gehabt ganz früh, eine Menge Helligkeit, und wenn dann plötzlich im Schatten in einer Gasse ein Gesicht einem hingehalten wird, so sieht man, unter dem Einfluß des Kontrastes, sein Wesen mit solcher Deutlichkeit (Deutlichkeit der Nuancen), daß der momentane Eindruck sich unwillkürlich zum symbolischen steigert.[135]

[Gazing is such a wonderful thing, and one we know so little about. In gazing we are completely turned outwards, but at the very moment when we are most outward-turned things appear to happen within us that have waited longingly until they are unobserved, and whilst these things happen within us, without us, perfectly and strangely anonymously—their significance grows in the object outside, a convincing, strong name, their only possible name, in which we blissfully and reverently recognize what is happening within us, without being able to touch it, understanding it very softly, quite remotely, under the sign of a thing that was strange to us a moment ago and will be made strange again in the very next moment.—It often happens that a face affects me in this way; in the morning, for example, one has had so much sunshine in the early morning, a lot of brightness, and when suddenly a face in a street is stuck in front of one, then, under the influence of the contrast, one sees its essence with such clarity (the clarity of nuances) that the momentary impression involuntarily becomes symbolic.]

Both Hofmannsthal and Rilke describe the rise of parallel significance simultaneously within the self and externally to it, suddenly and forcefully. Both give glimpses of something beyond the empirical, either 'den großen Weltzusammenhang', 'die Gegenwart der Idee' or 'sein Wesen'; Hofmannsthal's impression is 'leuchtend und real' and Rilke's has 'Deutlichkeit'. What Hofmannsthal describes as metaphorical, Rilke designates symbolic; Hofmannsthal does not clearly distinguish between these.

The interpenetration of one's self and the world is fundamentally Romantic in tenor, cognate with Keats's emptying of his self into the sparrow. A more immediate and slightly differently angled source, however, for both Hofmannsthal and Rilke, was Baudelaire's *Les Paradis artificiels*, to which Hofmannsthal refers in a note from mid-

---

[135] Rainer Maria Rilke, *Briefe 1906–1907*, ed. Ruth Sieber-Rilke and Carl Sieber (Leipzig: Insel, 1930), 214; letter of 8 Mar. 1907. The similarity of this description to Novalis's quoted above, p. 78 ('Auf alles, was der Mensch vornimmt . . .') is striking.

1892, actually headed 'De Quincey'.[136] *Les Paradis artificiels* is Baudelaire's response to, and analysis and adaptation of, De Quincey's *Confessions of an English Opium-Eater*, after his own experiments with hashish. Even though the ostensible subject of the work is the effect of hallucinogenic drugs, Baudelaire explicitly states that the heightening of the senses and the synaesthetic perceptions they bring about is perfectly natural: 'tout cerveau poétique, dans son état sain et normal, conçoit facilement ces analogies' [any poetic brain, in its healthy, normal state, easily conceives such analogies].[137] He describes his intoxication:

Il arrive quelquefois que la personnalité disparaît et que l'objectivité, qui est le propre des poètes panthéistes, se développe en vous si anormalement, que la contemplation des objets extérieurs vous fait oublier votre propre existence, et que vous vous confondez bientôt avec eux. . . . L'oiseau qui plane au fond de l'azur *représente* d'abord l'immortelle envie de planer au-dessus des choses humaines; mais déjà vous êtes l'oiseau lui-même.[138]

[It happens sometimes that your personality disappears and that an objectivity, which is the peculiarity of pantheist poets, develops in you so abnormally that contemplating external objects makes you forget your own existence, and that you are soon mingled in with them. The bird soaring high in the sky at first *represents* an immortal desire to soar above merely human concerns, but then soon you are the bird itself.]

What is for most the product of artificial stimulation is for the poet a natural circumstance: the exchange of self and object contemplated. The personality of the poet is but a medium for effecting the correspondence. Baudelaire makes no distinction between symbol, allegory, analogy and correspondence, and the process he describes is complementary with Hofmannsthal's account of the condition in which metaphoric correspondence takes place. What distinguishes them both from Romantic soul-sharing is the priority given to form in initiating the process: an innate love of form and colour is what stimulates Baudelaire's perceptions, 'la sinuosité des lignes est un langage

---

[136] *RA* iii. 348. He had noted De Quincey's name once before in connection with Baudelaire and Poe (cf. *SW* xxxi. 7 and 249). The note seems to date from late Dec. 1891, and consists of jottings inspired by his reading of Gautier's essay on Baudelaire.

[137] Baudelaire, *OC*, i. 419. Cf. Pichois's note to the effect that *Les Paradis artificiels* are 'non le message adressé par un drogué à des drogués, mais le livre écrit par un poète pour tous ceux qui considèrent que la seule vraie drogue, la drogue absolue, est la Poésie, et le seul problème, sa naissance et sa connaissance' (ibid., 1358). The analogy is made in *Le Spleen de Paris*, too: 'de vin, de poésie ou de vertu, à votre guise. Mais enivrez-vous' (ibid. 337).

[138] Ibid. 419–20.

définitivement clair où vous lisez l'agitation et le désir des âmes' [the curve of the lines is a perfectly clear language where you can read the turbulence and aspiration of people's souls].[139] Hofmannsthal's June 1892 note on *Les Paradis artificiels* is followed by another, related, observation that confirms his receptiveness to its ideas: 'Ihre Theorie'—presumably referring to De Quincey and Baudelaire—'es muß Klänge, Worte, Farbenverbindungen geben, die in uns Dinge erwecken, gegen die alles Irdische sinnlos und des Erhaltens unwert erscheint' [their theory: there must be sounds, words, combinations of colours that arouse things within us against which everything earthly appears to be senseless and not worth preserving; *RA* iii. 348]. Form is what gives rise to the symbolic.

The note on metaphor quoted above arose in connection with a series of jottings headed 'Dialoge über die Kunst' made at some point in 1893. Although the plan was never carried out, the skeleton allows a glimpse of the stage which his thinking about the nature and function of art had reached by this time, and adds a further dimension to those already discussed. Six dialogues were planned, the first on beauty, the second on the philosophical justification for an artistic life, and the third on the 'Kunst und Kritik' couple. The other sections were sketched as follows:

IV. Die Kunst als Äußerung des Machtstrebens. . . . Als Beispiel des Unvollkommenen, vielleicht höchst Vollkommenen Hermann Bahr. Unvollkommen, da er viel von sich an das Leben verliert; vollkommen insofern als vieles Rohe und Gemeine vielleicht eine Hieroglyphenschrift, die seiner Seele Wunder erzählt. . . .

V. Eklektizismus und Originalität in uns gemischt. Unsere Kunst eine nachschaffende. Wir wohnen in verlassenen Zyklopenbauten, die wir ausgehöhlt haben: Maeterlinck . . . Böcklins Mythologie.

VI. Hereindämmern einer anderen Weltanschauung. Sehnsucht danach ('Midas Garten', Preislied Tannhäuser im Venusberg), Furcht davor; Furcht vor dem Leben: Turgenjew 'Visionen' [= *Prizraki*].[140]

[IV. Arts as the expression of a craving for power. As an example of the imperfect, perhaps of the most perfect, Hermann Bahr. Imperfect in that he loses much of

---

[139] Baudelaire, *OC*, i. 430.

[140] *RA* iii. 360. Not included in *SW* xxxi. although other so-called 'platon[ische] Dialoge' are. The text of these notes is therefore taken from *RA* iii in comparison with *Nachlaß*, H IVB and H VB: the block of notes appended to this scheme in *RA* iii. 360–1 does not appear as a continuous block in the manuscripts. The editors have collated at least ten separate sections and offered them as a gloss to the scheme, not always in the same order that they appear in Hofmannsthal's notes. The six dialogue subjects, however, are given in *RA* iii exactly as in the manuscript.

himself to life; perfect in so far as much of his coarseness and vulgarity is perhaps a cipher that relates the miracles of his soul. V. Eclecticism and originality are mixed in us. Our art is an imitative art. We are living in the abandoned caves of the cyclopes, which we have hollowed out: Maeterlinck. Böcklin's mythology. VI. The gradual dawning of a different world-view. Longing for it ('Midas Garden', Tannhäuser's hymn of praise in the Venusberg), Fear of it, fear of life: Turgenev, 'Visions').]

The art to be described in these dialogues is one that operates within the Romantics' harmonious and unified world, and with their sense of its mystery. The mystique is part of the justification of art, as one of the supplementary notes states: 'Dichterische Produktion [ist] das Weben in einer keimenden, formentauschenden Gedankenwelt, einem mystischen Geheimdienst zu vergleichen' [poetic production is weaving in a burgeoning world where forms are exchanged, comparable with a secret, mystic service; *RA* iii. 361]—which is an echo of the 'Dienst des Orpheus' note. Poetic form is said to reflect the spiritual harmony of the world: 'Form hinterläßt Harmonie, . . . gibt eine Ahnung der kosmischen Harmonie, befriedigt kosmogonische Triebe' [form begets harmony, gives an intimation of the cosmic harmony, satisfies cosmogonic urges].

   This vocabulary is also highly Romantic—'Hieroglyphen' echoes Novalis, for example—but it is not only Romantic. Vanor in *L'Art symboliste* writes of the poet as one knowing the language to interpret the world, one who will decipher and explain its hieroglyphs.[141] The name Maeterlinck, perhaps also Bahr, and the reference to Hofmannsthal's self-designated Symbolist poem 'Mein Garten' confirm the suggestion that conception is associated with Symbolism, too. Whatever the Romantic elements, Hofmannsthal is conscious that the art of his generation is epigonal, 'eine nachschaffende', and that originality is a problem in the wake of strong talents. Beings of powerful, mythical stature built caves in which to dwell, and now the Cyclopes are dead, modern literature has recycled their structures. The somewhat utilitarian or mechanistic overtones of the image match those already noted in 'Formel' and 'Technik', both of which suggest at their most extreme that Symbolism merely repackaged a body of ideas and assumptions about literature in a convenient new way.

   The same indebtedness of Symbolism to Romanticism is evident in an image that occurs frequently in the nineteenth century and which

---

[141] Quoted in Michaud, *Message poétique*, 746.

was picked up several times by Hofmannsthal. The pervasive image of the crystal or prism is also an index of a change in priorities from organic to inorganic and the idea that it is the formal qualities of poetry that effect spiritual significance. In his survey of the genesis of German theories of Symbolism, Ernest Stahl makes the point briefly that it contrasts with the mirror, an integrative image for identity, but it appears in many of the key texts he cites. Grillparzer used it to explain symbolism:

Das symbolische der Poesie besteht darin, daß sie nicht die Wahrheit an die Spitze ihres Beginnens stellt, sondern, bildlich in allem, ein *Bild* der Wahrheit, eine Inkarnazion derselben, die Art und Weise wie sich das Licht des Geistes in dem halbdunkeln Medium des Gemüthes färbt und bricht.[142]

[The symbolism of poetry consists in not setting truth at the sharpest point of its beginning, but setting it figuratively in everything, an *image* of truth, an incarnation of it, the way in which the light of the spirit is coloured and split in the semi-darkness of the human temperament.]

The prism is the human temperament, and poetic symbolism is anchored to it. One could add to Stahl's examples the hero's statement in *Heinrich von Ofterdingen*, 'Die Menschen sind Krystalle für unser Gemüt' [people are crystals for our souls].[143] As faith in the stability of 'Gemüt' declined, the image was transferred to the work of art, which had the function of reconstituting a totality. A crystal is perhaps an ideal image for a certain type of Symbolist art and for the realm that this art reflects, suggests, or creates. It transforms light by refracting and dividing, yet may focus the spectrum into a single ray, and as such it manipulates diversity within unity. It is not opaque, yet is not as transparent as plain glass. Its purity and beauty suggest simplicity, yet it owes its fascinating clarity to a complex, rigid structuredness. But despite its beauty and structure, crystal is only a medium, and a mineral, not an organic form.

The crystal is one of the imagistic cruxes of André Gide's *Le Traité du Narcisse*, the 'Théorie du Symbole' of another member of Mallarmé's

---

[142] Franz Grillparzer, *Sämtliche Werke*, ed. August Sauer and Reinhold Backmann (Vienna: Schroll, 1909–48), ii.10: *Tagebücher und literarische Skizzenhefte 4*, 149, no. 3202 (diary note, late 1836 or perhaps 1837). Schiller also uses it in *Theosophie des Julius*. Herder in 1774 had used another image for broken light, the rainbow ('Empfindung ist ein Farbenspiel des Regenbogens'); Goethe, too, in the first scene of *Faust II*. Despite their differences, both these authors are concerned with human faculties and the capacity of the self to experience life, either directly or as an 'Abglanz'. See Stahl, 'Symbolist Theories', 307–9 and 316.

[143] Novalis, *Schriften*, i. 280.

circle for the *mardis* in the Rue de Rome.[144] Narcissus has been described as the one myth with which Symbolism has enriched the world.[145] The *Traité* is a classic statement of the Symbolists' intense self-awareness and of the poet's function: 'il se penche sur les symboles, et silencieux descend profondément au cœur des choses' [he leans over the symbols and silently descends deep into the heart of things]. Narcissus' self-contemplation reveals, 'résorbées, les générations humaines qui passent' [absorbed within him, the passing of human generations], the permanent presence of the poetic tradition within Symbolism. It is simultaneously a search for identity. As the poet departs in search of the shapes with which he wishes to surround his soul, he is confronted by uniformity: 'toujours les mêmes formes passent; l'élan du flot, seul les différencie' [it is always the same forms that are passing, only the momentum of the river differentiates them]. He feels that all worldly manifestations are rushing towards a lost, primal form, and that the poet alone is able to give the unifying Idea its own form, 'veritable enfin, et fatale,—paradisiaque et cristalline' [real at last, and fatal—paradisiacal and crystalline]. The poet's recreation in the work of art is another crystal:

Car l'œuvre d'art est un cristal—paradis partiel où l'Idée refleurit en sa pureté supérieure; où, comme dans L'Éden disparu, l'ordre normal et nécessaire a disposé toutes les formes dans une réciproque et symétrique dépendance . . . où les phrases rythmiques et sûres, symboles encore, mais symboles purs, où les paroles, se font transparentes et révélatrices.

[For the work of art is a crystal—a partial paradise where the Idea blossoms again in its higher purity; a place where, like in the lost Eden, the normal, necessary order has arranged all forms in reciprocal and symmetrical interdependence . . . where speech and rhythmic, confident phrases, still symbols but pure symbols, make themselves transparent and revelatory.]

The Romantic ideal of participation with the whole world is still present, but organic unity has vanished, the emphasis now being not on permanent participation but on transience, and on the capacity primarily of form in art to render it possible at all. Gide's ideal of symbolism is Christ's passion, but perfect symbolization fails to occur because at the moment of His death someone thinks not of the Idea but

---

[144] Gide, *Romans, récits et soties*, 1–12. It was published on 1 Jan. 1892 in *Les Entretiens politiques et littéraires*, a journal founded by Henri de Régnier and Francis Vielé-Griffin to give voice to Symbolist ideas. Hofmannsthal may well have read it but there is no evidence that he did.

[145] Lehmann, *The Symbolist Aesthetic in France*, 114 (and cf. 229).

of himself. That self-awareness, the search for personal identity, thwarts the goal of Symbolism is a lesson from which Hofmannsthal might have profited.

A concern for the self and its position in the world was articulated by Hofmannsthal in the early 1890s using just this image. He noted in January 1891 that during the Mass he felt an 'Ahnung einer latenten Harmonie aller Formen erhalten in Zauberformeln, die Verbindung von Zeit, Ort, Zahl und Ton verlangen' [an intimation of the latent harmony of all forms preserved in magic formulae that demand the linking of time, place, number and tone; *RA* iii. 320]. In the poetry into which he simultaneously converted this perception, the *Ghasel* 'In der ärmsten kleinen Geige liegt die Harmonie des Alls verborgen' (*SW* ii. 44), the image chosen to convey language's power to express such a harmony is that of the crystal: 'In dem Wort, dem abgegriff'nen, liegt, was mancher sinnend suchet: | Eine Wahrheit, mit der Klarheit leuchtenden Krystalls verborgen' [in the hackneyed word lies what many are pensively seeking: a truth, hidden with the clarity of a brilliant crystal]. Hofmannsthal ends the poem with the regret that 'Unsern Blicken ist Vollkomm'nes seit dem Tag des Sündenfalls verborgen' [perfection has been hidden from our eyes since the day of the Fall], repeating 'verborgen' for the fifth time and shifting its meaning. The crystal is an intimation of that lost paradise, as nostalgic for Romantic security as it was in Gide's 'Théorie du Symbolisme'.

As the image recurs in Hofmannsthal's diaries, the nostalgia is gradually identified as one for the stability of the self. In January 1891, in connection with the *Ghasel*, it follows another assertion of perfect unity:

Nie habe ich so tief wie jetzt den Zusammenhang in allem, was ich lese, gefühlt und verstanden, daß wir alles Vergangene auf Gegenwärtiges, Fremdes auf Verwandtes, ja Verwandtes auf Persönliches auslaufen lassen können und müssen; ich glaube, Farben sind verschieden gebrochenes Licht, so wären auch alle Verschiedenheiten der Erscheinungswelt nur verschieden klar erkannte Seiten einer Wahrheit. (*RA* iii. 320–1)

[Never have I felt and comprehended so deeply as now the connectedness of everything that I read, that we can and must allow everything past to run on into the present, likewise the strange into the familiar, even the familiar into the personal; I think that as colours are light broken up differently, so all the differences of the world of appearances are only sides of a single truth perceived with different clarity.]

In the same vein he noted in December 1893, 'es gibt nur eine Wahrheit, aber verschiedene Brennpunkte, in die sich ihre Strahlen sammeln lassen, verschiedene imaginäre Zentren des Daseins' [there is only one truth, but there are various foci in which its rays are collected, various imaginary centres of existence; *RA* iii. 369], but here the idea is reversed, the prism focusing rather than refracting light. The single truth emits prismatically split light, which, because of its essential unity, can be reconstituted in poetry. As in Gide's *Traité*, again, another of the crystalline structures that both dissipates and collects is the self, and it is here, early in 1891, that the attractions of the image begin to transmute into dangers:

Wir erscheinen uns selbst als strahlenbrechende Prismen, den andern als Sammellinsen (unser Selbst ist für uns Medium, durch welches wir die Farbe der Dinge zu erkennen glauben, für die andern etwas Einförmiges, Selbstfärbiges). (*RA* iii. 329)

[We seem to ourselves to be refracting prisms, to others as converging lenses (our Self is for us a medium through which we think we recognize the colour of things, for others it is something monotonous, with a colour of its own).]

From within, the self is perceived as a prism that breaks down the components of stimuli; from outside it is apparently a unifying medium, and the individual is perceived as coherent or solid. The phrase 'unser Selbst ist für uns Medium' pre-empts Eliot's similar phrase in 'Tradition and the Individual Talent' by twenty-eight years: famously Eliot wrote that 'the poet has, not a "personality" to express, but a particular medium, which is only a medium and not a personality, in which impressions and experiences combine in peculiar and unexpected ways'.[146] Maurice Maeterlinck had made an almost identical point in his response to Huret's *Enquête*:

Le Poète doit, me semble-t-il, être passif dans le symbole, et le symbole le plus pur est peut-être celui qui a lieu à son insu et même à l'encontre de ses intentions; le symbole serait la fleur de la vitalité du poème.[147]

[It seems to me that the poet must be passive in the symbol, and the purest symbol is perhaps the one that takes place without the poet's knowing and even despite his intentions; the symbol would be the flower of the poem's vitality.]

Hofmannsthal gave an extreme example of what it was for the artist to be purely a medium in his second essay on D'Annunzio. This artist's

[146] Eliot, *Selected Prose*, 27–8.
[147] Huret, *Enquête*, 126. Maeterlinck has already distinguished the deliberate, or 'allegorical' symbol (e.g. those in *Faust II*, and Goethe's *Märchen*) from those of this type.

primary repertory of images and signs is not something as so real and concrete as nature or humanity, but the world of art. D'Annunzio derives a heightened existence

von einer durch das Medium der Kunst erfaßten Sinnlichkeit und von einer an den Büchern von Edgar Poe, Dostojewsky und Taine oder an den Traktaten über die Seele von Origenes oder Bernhard von Clairvaux entfachten Gier, die Seelen der Menschen leben zu spüren. Für alle diese Einflüsse war sein Geist nicht einfach ein gutes, sondern ein ganz wundervolles, raffiniertes Medium: aus den Bildern trug er nicht etwa Äußerlichkeiten mit sich, sondern der Seelenzustand, den die Gebärden der gemalten Menschen oder die Farbennuancen der gemalten Lippen, Haare, Blumen und Bäume in sich tragen, schlägt manchmal aus den Schwingungen seiner Verse geheimnisvoll auf. (*RA* i. 199)

[from a sensuality that is grasped via the medium of art and from a greedy desire to feel people's souls living that has been fed with the books of Edgar Allan Poe, Dostoevsky and Taine or with treatises on the soul by Origen or Bernard of Clairvaux. His spirit was not only a good medium for all these influences, but a quite miraculous and refined medium: he did not carry with him merely superficialities taken from the pictures, but sometimes from the vibrations of his verses there opens out the very condition of the soul that is contained in the gestures of the painted figures or the delicate colours of the painted lips, hair, flowers and trees.]

Where this leaves D'Annunzio himself is not clear; his action is that of medium rather than creator, and he is evidently one of those individuals, described in the Amiel review, 'welche die Leiden der Zeit leiden und die Gedanken der Zeit denken' [that suffer the sufferings of the time and think its thoughts; *RA* i. 106], the philosophical equivalent of a primitive tribal sin-eater.

For Hofmannsthal the passivity of the medium was characteristic not only of poetry but of man's whole manner of experiencing: 'Erleben: in uns, wie durch ein unkörperliches Medium hindurch, realisieren sich Ideen' [experience: ideas are realized in us, as if through an intangible medium; *RA* iii. 381], he wrote in March 1894. The loss of self that it implies is greeted with regret, as it causes 'das Unreale, überwiegend Symbolische an unserer Lebensweise. Was wir tuen, bedeutet meistens nur, *ist* nicht' [the unreal, the overwhelmingly symbolic nature of our lives. What we do usually only has meaning, not *being*], noted on 20 June 1893 (*RA* iii. 364). Later that year we read something very similar: 'Den Empfindungen soll man sagen: Du scheinst nicht, du erinnerst nicht, du verkündest nicht, du *bist*; sonst kommt man um den Inhalt des Lebens' [one should say to sensations: You do not seem, you do not remind, you do not proclaim, you *are*;

otherwise you are robbed of the content of life; *RA* iii. 371]. The transitive verbs, even the intransitive but copulative *scheinen*, are rejected in favour of the one verb that focuses directly on the essence of existence. 'Das Symbolische' and 'bedeuten' here are negative terms that have lost the positive connotations they had when, for example, Schelling explained mythological symbolism with the same distinction between essence and significance: 'Die Bedeutung ist [in der Mythologie] zugleich das Sein selbst, übergegangen in den Gegenstand, mit ihm eins. Sobald wir diese Wesen etwas bedeuten lassen, sind sie selbst nichts mehr' [in mythology, meaning is simultaneously also being, passed into the object, one with it. As soon as we permit these things to mean something, they are themselves nothing].[148] In *Das Gespräch über Gedichte* from 1903 this condition will be reinstated, and by 1894 or 1895—when Hofmannsthal maintains 'Sein und Bedeuten ist eins: folglich ist alles Seiende Symbol' [being and meaning are the same: therefore everything that is, is a symbol; *RA* iii. 391]—the symbolic is strong again, but in the early 1890s Hofmannsthal is highly ambivalent about the term, which often designates a failure to achieve the unity of self and world.

One of the strongest advocates of such passivity, and an important influence on a disintegrative view of poetic creation for Hofmannsthal, was Decadence. Romantic literature depicted a reality authenticated by the experience of a reliable identity, even if experience and its poetic expression required the identity to be sacrificed; Symbolist writers put their language in place of an experiencing self, the contours of which had been dissolved by poetic practice since Baudelaire, and sought rather to bring reality into being by poetic and linguistic construction. Huret confounds Symbolist and Decadent, and there is evidence that Hofmannsthal was not always able to make a distinction, although he attempted to do so. Writing in 1899, Arthur Symons was to see Decadence as a temporary measure until 'something more serious [had] crystallized' in Symbolism.[149] Huysmans was the prophet of Decadence, it was analysed by Bourget (who included a 'Théorie de la Décadence' in the first volume of his *Essais de psychologie contemporaine*) and reported by Bahr and Ola Hansson. Huysmans's hero, Des Esseintes, 'lives through the Baudelairian voyage of experience without the transcendental vision that gives the repeated renewal of the

---

[148] *Sämmtliche Werke* (1859), v. 411. Quoted by Stahl, 'Symbolist Theories', 314.
[149] Arthur Symons, *The Symbolist Movement in Literature* (New York: Dutton, 1958), 4. First published in 1899.

journey its signficance'.[150] He takes aestheticism to an extreme and creates for himself an artificial world of carefully arranged lights, smells, hot-house plants, Redon's pastels and music. Bourget's analysis of Decadence was of a combination of inadequacy in willpower and a deliberate inattention to morality, and Bahr saw him as the decisive stage in the abandonment of Naturalism, the point at which the focus definitively shifted from the outside world to the inner self. 'Sie wollen *modeler notre univers intérieur*' [they wish to 'mould our inner universe'], he wrote in his essay on 'Die Décadence'.[151] He highlights the Decadent attention to vague mood rather than personal feeling or thought, their over-sensitive nerves, their preference for the sensationally exceptional or merely artificial. Bahr is also sensitive to the fact that elements of the Decadents' psychological interest are derived directly from Naturalism.[152]

In Hofmannsthal's view, Decadence was also an intermediary style, a style of decomposition before a recomposition could take place in Symbolism: 'Decadenz: das Auseinanderfallen des Ganzen; die Theile glühen und leuchten; die Leidenschaften geniessen sich' [Decadence: the disintegration of the whole; the parts glow and shine; the passions enjoy each other].[153] In his diary notes he quotes the same point from one of its recent sources, Bourget's essay on Baudelaire:

un style de décadence est celui où l'unité du livre se décompose pour laisser la place à l'indépendance de la page, où la page se décompose pour laisser la place à l'indépendance de la phrase, et la phrase pour laisser la place à l'ind. du mot.[154]

[a Decadent style is one where the unity of the book disintegrates to give way to the independence of the page, where the page disintegrates to give way to the independence of the sentence, and the sentence to give way to the independence of the word.]

As if completing the rhetorical figure of chiasmus, Nietzsche's analysis of Decadence focuses on the same features:

Das Leben [wohnt] nicht mehr im Ganzen. Das Wort wird Souverain und springt aus dem Satz hinaus, der Satz greift über und verdunkelt den Sinn der Seite, die

[150] Robinson, *French Literature in the Nineteenth Century*, 167–8.

[151] Bahr, *Studien*, 20.

[152] Cf. Bahr, 'Die Krisis der französischen Naturalismus', reprinted in *Die Überwindung des Naturalismus* (1891).

[153] 20 Mar. 1893, *Nachlaß*, H VII 17.112ᵇ (a part of the note for this date incompletely given in *RA* iii. 343).

[154] Dec. 1892; *Nachlaß*, H VII 4.37, quoting Bourget, *Œuvres complètes: Critique I*, 15–16.

Seite gewinnt Leben auf Unkosten des Ganzen—das Ganze ist kein Ganzes mehr.[155]

[Life is no longer resident in the whole. The word is sovereign and leaps out of the sentence, the sentence takes over and obscures the sense of the page, the page takes on life at the expense of the whole—the whole is no longer a whole.]

But the poetic assumptions Hofmannsthal inherited from Romanticism, and which imbued his view of Symbolism, are anti-Decadent, shot through with a desire to validate the poetic principle articulated by Baudelaire as 'vaporisation et centralisation du moi'.

This is echoed in Hofmannsthal's own formulation, in a note from 1893 or 1894, of what he expects of poetry: '2 heilige Arbeiten: das Auflösen und das Bilden von Begriffen: letzteres heißt, einen Zauber üben, Gott näher werden. Dienst des Orpheus' [2 sacred tasks: the dissolving and composing of concepts: the last is to practise magic, to become closer to God. The service of Orpheus; *RA* iii. 373]. Both dissolving and composing are sacred tasks, but composition is the function of poetry and the service to Orpheus. Hofmannsthal's thinking here is closely analogous to Baudelaire's conception of the imagination in the *Salon de 1859*:

Mystérieuse faculté que cette reine des facultés! . . . Elle est l'analyse, elle est la synthèse. . . . C'est l'imagination qui enseigne à l'homme le sens moral de la couleur, du contour, du son et du parfum. Elle a créé, au commencement du monde, l'analogie et la métaphore. Elle décompose toute la création, et, avec les matériaux amassés et disposés suivant les règles dont on ne peut trouver l'origine que dans le plus profond de l'âme, elle crée un monde nouveau.[156]

[How mysterious the queen of our faculties is! She is both analysis and synthesis. It is the imagination that teaches man the moral sense of colour, shape, sound and smell. When the world was new she created analogy and metaphor. She disintegrates all of creation and with the material amassed and arranged according to the rules whose origin is only to be found in the depths of the soul, she creates a new world.]

Godlike, the imagination deconstructs in order to reconstruct, and its creature-servants are analogy and metaphor, the stuff of poetry. The dual action is fundamental to Baudelaire's conception of art, and recurs frequently under different forms. The *Salon de 1859* again has, 'tout l'univers visible n'est qu'un magasin d'images et de signes auxquels l'imagination donnera une place et une valeur relative; c'est

[155] From 'Der Fall Wagner', Nietzsche, *Werke*, ii. 917.
[156] Baudelaire, *OC*, ii., 620–1

une espèce de pâture que l'imagination doit *digérer* et *transformer'* [the whole universe is only a storehouse of images and signs to which the imagination will assign a place and a relative value; it is a kind of food that the imagination must *digest* and *transform*].[157] Hofmannsthal attempts to remain faithful to this kind of vision, although the notes quoted above suggest that it was sometimes difficult.

In addition, several of the notes and essays from the early 1890s use words such as 'anempfinden' [to feel inauthentically *or* vicariously] and 'sich aneignen' [to appropriate for oneself] in the context of the individual's relation to his intellectual tradition. 'Resultate unseres Kulturzustandes', Hofmannsthal wrote on 22 January 1891, 'wir schildern ohne zu sehen, urteilen ohne zu verstehen, denken ohne eigenes Bewußtsein . . . werden es noch dahin bringen, an anempfundenen Wunden zu sterben' [results of our cultural condition, we depict without seeing, judge without understanding, think without having our own consciousness . . . will even manage to die of vicarious wounds; *RA* iii. 320]. Initially, and ironically, he associated this attitude with what he called 'Baudelairismus', defined in his review of *Die Mutter* as 'die Darstellung des Angelebten', the attempt, 'fremde, angefühlte Empfindungen künstlerisch [zu] gestalten' [the depiction of things lived vicariously, the attempt to give artistic form to alien, second-hand sensations], and associated with post-Romantic poetry in general.[158] This is certainly a view of Baudelaire obscured by Huysmans or the like, and the 'Anempfindungsvermögen' has been explored as one of the components of Hofmannsthal's understanding of Dilettantism and Decadence mediated via Amiel and Bourget and analysed by Nietzsche.[159] Despite the pedigree, the problem was genuinely Hofmannsthal's own from time to time. He was often extremely pessimistic about the possibility in his generation of genuinely personal thought or feeling, since humanity tends in its confusion to seize upon a repertoire of ready-made forms of expression:

---

[157] Baudelaire, *OC*, ii., 627; my italics. Very similar ideas recur in the essay *L'Œuvre et la vie de Delacroix* of 1863, ii. 746–53; the passage just quoted is repeated verbatim on ii. 750.

[158] *RA* i. 102–3. Cf. Hans Steffen, 'Hofmannsthals Übernahme der symbolistischen Technik', in Reinhold Grimm and Conrad Wiedemann (eds.), *Literatur und Geistesgeschichte*, (Berlin: E. Schmidt, 1968), 272–3. It is true that at this point, before meeting George, Hofmannsthal's use of terms such as 'Baudelairismus' and 'Dekadenz' is unstable, and that 'Hofmannsthal lehnt den Inhalt dieser Dichtungen ab'. But the assertion '[er] hat das poetologische oder Formproblem offenbar gar nicht erkannt' (273) is false.

[159] Cf. Srdan Bogosavljević, 'Der Amiel-Aufsatz', 207–35; Ulrich Schulz-Buschhaus, 'Der Tod des "Dilettanten"', who concludes: 'Auch die Abrechnung mit dem "Anempfindungsvermögen" . . . entbehrt bei Hofmannsthal . . . nicht des Anempfundenen' (187).

Unserm unklaren Gedanken bietet sich, da wir mit Anempfundenem und Anerzogenem erfüllt sind, sofort eine fertige Ausdrucksform; wir sprechen ihn biblisch oder philosophisch aus, rhetorisch oder plaudernd, im Stile Goethes, Schopenhauers... wir geben ihm die beinahe richtige Form, aber nur beinahe; es bleibt immer ein Rest, der nicht aufgeht, eine Lüge. Also gehören auch die Gedanken, die wir selbständig ahnen, gar nicht uns, denn wir sehen sie unbewußt durch das angeeignete Medium eines anderen, und der andere in uns spricht sie aus. Die Menschen sind also nur abgeschwächte Umbildungen der großen Geister, die in ihnen weiterdenken, ihre Lebensgedanken variieren. Daher die vielen unnützen Bücher.[160]

[Because we are so imbued with inauthentic feelings and behaviour, our unclear thinking immediately has a ready-made form of expression available; we express it biblically, philosophically, rhetorically or chattily, in the style of Goethe or Schopenhauer, we give it nearly the right form, but no better than nearly; there is always something left over, part of the equation that does not fit, a lie. Therefore the thoughts that we have for ourselves are also not properly ours, because we perceive them unconsciously, through the borrowed medium of someone else, and that someone else in us utters them. People are therefore only diluted versions of the great spirits that think on in them and vary their life thoughts. That is the reason for all the useless books.]

The note is a clear statement of the problem of literary influence— 'große Geister' might correspond to Harold Bloom's 'strong poets'— and in this light the analysis of D'Annunzio's writing appears as ambiguous as Hofmannsthal's assessment of Bahr in the review of *Die Mutter*.[161] Such examples could be multiplied many times over to confirm that Hofmannsthal, if nostalgic, had an acute awareness of the changes that had taken place in the literary tradition.[162]

Hofmannsthal's broader statements on poetics bear the signs of Modernism, concern with the reliability of subjective perception, scepticism about identity, and anxiety about sustaining literary originality. Symbolist poetry took steps to deal with these, by reducing the presence of the self and allowing suggestivity to operate autonomously,

---

[160] *RA* iii. 324–5; Mar. 1891.

[161] It is interesting that the failure of the modern artist to match exactly his models is described in moral terms as 'eine Lüge', and that he writes of thoughts and feelings with the verb 'gehören': these terms will recur in Hofmannsthal's reviews of George and Vielé-Griffin and the context to 'Manche freilich'.

[162] More so than many scholars would have us believe. Hoppe argues that 'die Auflösung des Ichs in eine Reihe von Kostüm-Ichs' (*Hofmannsthal*, 80) is a series of purely stylistic *Aneignungen*, unsupported by true critical awareness. Literature, he implies, is not investigated for its own qualities but merely appropriated for the game of writing; *Literatentum* is evacuated by Hoppe of the component of *Literaturwissenschaft* of which in fact Hofmannsthal was very early a master.

as the examples from Verlaine and Mallarmé have indicated. That Hofmannsthal was clear on the shifts in self-expression that had taken place is confirmed by a note from November 1892 on Baudelaire: 'Von dem Pathos der Romantik zu der cynisch resignierten Attitüde des Baudelaire ist derselbe Übergang wie vom ersten Ausbruch des Zornes zur höhnischen Kälte bei einem betrogenen und in heissen Hoffnungen enttäuschten Mann' [the transition from Romantic pathos to the cynically resigned pose of Baudelaire is the same as that from the first explosion of rage to scornful iciness in a man deceived and disappointed in his fervent hopes].[163] The progression from uncontrolled emotion to ironically distanced self-possession is an apt summary of the poetic development. But Hofmannsthal's statements on Symbolism treat not this aspect but only the technique, and however much he may have espoused the idea that the poet is only a medium, repeatedly his description of mood, suggestion and metaphor allows a hankering after selfhood to be detected beneath. Whilst working on *Ascanio und Gioconda* in mid-1892, Hofmannsthal had noted 'symbolist[ische] Technik' next to a passage from Otto Ludwig's *Shakespeare-Studien* that reads 'Phantasie ist das eigentliche Werkzeug des Dichters; wenn der Mensch das Spiel der Phantasie, wie es Gedanken- und Gefühlsfolgen begleitet, fixieren könnte, so würde dies das unmittelbarste Gedicht geben' [the imagination is the poet's true tool; if man could fix the play of imagination as it attends upon trains of thought and emotion, this would produce the most immediate kind of poem; *SW* xviii. 389]. But the capturing of suggestions before they evaporate into the profanely non-poetic atmosphere is in many respects profoundly un-Symbolist, and only a rigorous distinction of technique and substance could tolerate the label 'symbolistische Technik' for something so Romantically inspired. Mallarmé's prescription runs thus:

L'œuvre pure implique la disparition élocutoire du poëte, qui cède l'initiative aux mots, par le heurt de leur inégalité mobilisés; ils s'allument de reflets réciproques comme une virtuelle traînée de feux sur des pierreries, remplaçant la respiration perceptible en l'ancien souffle lyrique ou la direction personnelle enthousiaste de la phrase.[164]

---

[163] *Nachlaß*, H VII 4.33. This, like the 'Baudelairismus' remark in the Bahr essay some eighteen months earlier, still bears in its vehemence the strong imprint of Bourget's analysis—not from the Baudelaire essay itself, perhaps, but from the intensification of Bourget's hostility to Decadence in later essays on Turgenev and Amiel (cf. Schulz-Buschhaus, 'Der Tod des "Dilettanten" ', 185).

[164] *Crise de vers*; Mallarmé, *OC*, 366.

[A pure work implies the disappearance of the poet as speaking voice, who surrenders the initiative to the words that are mobilized by the clash of their unequalness; they are inflamed by mutual reflections like a virtual trail of lights on precious stones, replacing real respiration with the ancient inspiration of lyric poetry or the keen personal direction of the phrase.]

This denies the relevance of 'Gedanken- und Gefühlsfolgen'. To try to use Symbolist technique as a means of regaining identity was therefore apparently to use a tool evolved for an alien purpose.

The tension of self-forgetting and the reconstruction of identity in poetry is not irresolvable in post-Romantic poetry, and Hofmannsthal's problems were partly his own and not only those of his time. Rilke, for instance, inherited the Romantics' openness of identity and proclaims it in violent imagery. In the last poem in part I of *Die Sonette an Orpheus* the maenads tear the poet limb from limb and his voice is distributed to the world: 'Schließlich zerschlugen sie dich . . . während dein Klang noch in Löwen und Felsen verweilte | und in den Bäumen und Vögeln' [finally they crushed you, whilst your sound still lingered in lions and rocks and in the trees and birds]. But the reintegrative capacity of poetry is simultaneously invoked: as the maenads howled, Orpheus drowned their noise in 'Ordnung', characteristic of poetic language, especially of the sonnet. In a poem full of paradoxes, the essential message is cognate with the Romantic view that losing the self is the prerequisite of finding poetry: '*nur* weil dich reißend zuletzt die Feindschaft verteilte | sind wir die Hörenden jetzt' [it is *only* because enmity finally ripped and divided you that we are now the hearing ones].[165] Yet the vigour of the images also represents confidence in the ultimate stability of the self. It is no coincidence that the last words of Rilke's *Sonette an Orpheus* are firmly 'Ich bin'—I am. They occur in a poem about transformations, where the poet's dissolution is celebrated as he is enjoined to become the wine he drinks and the space in which he exists. Yet the tercets charge him to be the 'Sinn' of his senses' 'seltsame Begegnungen' [the sense of his senses' strange meetings], a single meeting point as well as the many manifestations, and if he is to represent motion to contrast with the still earth, he is also to offer a solid *point de repère* to the flowing water.[166]

The first line of this poem, 'Stiller Freund der vielen Fernen' [silent friend of the many distances], whilst expressing a familiar general idea, more specifically echoes Hofmannsthal's 'lautloser Bruder aller Dinge' [soundless brother of all things] from the speech *Der Dichter und diese Zeit*

---

[165] Rilke, *Sämtliche Werke*, i. 748; my italics.   [166] Ibid. 770–1.

(1906). The passage in fact continues with an echo of Keats's chameleon poet: 'das Wechseln seiner [des Dichters] Farbe ist eine innige Qual: denn er leidet an allen Dingen, und indem er an ihnen leidet, genießt er sie. Dies Leidend-Genießen, dies ist der ganze Inhalt seines Lebens' [the changing of the poet's colour is a deeply felt torture, for all things cause him suffering, and as he suffers because of them, he enjoys them. This suffering-enjoying is the sum content of his life; *RA* i. 67]. But Keats's letter contains no trace of suffering, and his poetical character 'lives in gusto', as Rilke's did; yet Hofmannsthal repeatedly stresses the negative component of the pair. Margaret Jacobs points out that the letter to Gruss of 1907 also contains a parallel 'misinterpretation' of the chameleon image. Hofmannsthal complains of a 'sonderbare, fast unheimliche seelische Beschaffenheit, diese scheinbar alles durchdringende Lieblosigkeit und Treulosigkeit' [strange, almost uncanny composition of the soul, this seemingly all-pervasive lovelessness and faithlessness] that is poetic openness, whereas Keats refers to a condition of 'general love and participation'.[167] But this was not so much a detail misread as the failure of Hofmannsthal's whole poetic approach to grasp the joy and 'gusto' of Romantic self-annihilation, motivated as it was by a profound anxiety that the self, once cast loose, might never be recoverable. That this was at least as much a product of Hofmannsthal's time as of his own poetic constitution is indicated by a striking detail from Rudolf Kassner's essay on Keats, published in 1900. He quotes from a letter to the George Keatses of February 1819 (228, mistranslating it slightly) in which John complains of indolence. Kassner adds:

Er fühlt sich selbst wie ein Gedicht, wie die Nymphe möchte er sein und gleich der Blume, von der er singt. Er stilisiert sich selbst:

> Mir ist, als wär' ich doppelt, könnte selber
> Mir zusehen, wissend, daß ich's selber bin . . .[168]

[He feels himself to be a poem, he wishes to be like the nymphs and the flower of which he writes. He is stylizing himself: 'I feel as if I were doubled, as if I could observe myself, knowing that it is I who do so.']

This is an awkward mixture of original Keats and a Keats filtered through *fin-de-siècle* sensibility—for the suggestion that Keats feels as if he were himself a poem is Kassner's own, and to read participation in

---

[167] Margaret Jacobs, 'Hugo von Hofmannsthal: *Das Bergwerk zu Falun*', in F. Norman (ed.), *Hofmannsthal: Studies in Commemoration* (London: Institute of Germanic Studies, 1963), 73.
[168] Kassner, 'John Keats', 47.

the natural world as stylization is more reminiscent of Hofmannsthal than authentically Keatsian. The lines quoted are in fact from Hofmannsthal's *Die Frau im Fenster* (*SW* iii. 105, ll. 33–4), and if they seem superficially appropriate to Keats's self-contemplation, their wistfulness and the insecurity implied in the need to find one's self as a reflection in a pool confirm their true origin as Hofmannsthal's words. They are followed, after all, by 'Ich glaube, so sind die Gedanken, die | ein Mensch in seiner Todesstunde denkt' [I think these are the kind of thoughts that a man thinks at the hour of his death].

Richard Exner quotes an extract from a letter that evidently replies to a reproach made by Hofmannsthal's father and appears to recognize the dangers of jumping on bandwagons, inviting us to believe that he avoided them: 'Ärgere Dich nicht über Symbolismus. Ich weiß ganz gut, wo ich hin gehöre und bin gleichweit von charge d'atelier wie von bourgeoisisme entfernt' [do not fret about Symbolism. I know perfectly well where I belong and am as far from being part of an entourage as I am from bourgeois conventionality].[169] Exner, writing about the previously impenetrable 'Lebenslied', says that he failed to avoid the danger in at least this one instance: 'ein solches Gedicht [ist] unter allen früheren und späteren des Autors dem Symbolismus am verwandtesten. Der symbolische Impuls ließ . . . den Dichter seinen Text verschlüsseln' [of all the author's poems, early or late, this is the one most closely related to Symbolism. The Symbolist impulse drove the poet to encode his text].[170] But obscurity is not the defining characteristic of Symbolist verse, even if it was often the outcome of too heavy a reliance on the capacity of language to suggest.[171] By locating the Symbolists' originality too exclusively in a somewhat formulaically conceived 'Technik', Hofmannsthal suppressed the more discomfiting elements of change. The desire to regain a Romantic self-confidence and to attach his own poetry to the solidity of that tradition would perhaps have been inherently problematic for any poet. But a view of the new situation of poetry uninhibited by Romantic nostalgia would have been a more promising starting-point for Hofmannsthal than the laming attempt to use as his model a Symbolism read so one-sidedly.

---

[169] Undated. Richard Exner, *Hugo von Hofmannsthals 'Lebenslied'* (Heidelberg: Winter, 1964), 23.

[170] Ibid. 22–3.

[171] Exner warily quotes Musil to the effect that the deciphered poem would be less beautiful than the incomprehensible text he knew (ibid. 22). Merely the suggestion that 'Lebenslied' is in fact a *Schlüsselgedicht* removes it from the realm of Symbolist verse, which knows no such potential certainties.

Chapters 3 and 4 will deal in more detail with Hofmannsthal's appro-priation of Symbolist techniques and forms, and the consequences involved for the self, but the examples of Hofmannsthal's critical reflections in this chapter cast doubt on whether his particular under-standing of Symbolism was fully integrated into his more sophisticated thinking about poetry in general, and this is at least the first stage of succumbing to the danger of 'charge d'atelier'.

3

'SYMBOLISMUS: MEINE DEFINITIONEN': EARLY POEMS AND THE PRESENCE OF STEFAN GEORGE

Hofmannsthal's interest in Symbolism did not begin with Stefan George's arrival in Vienna in December 1891, and was not confined to the few days either side of Christmas when they met most frequently. His diary for 28 May 1891 reports a conversation with Gustav Schwarzkopf, Hermann Bahr, Heinrich von Korff and Julius Kulka in the Café Griensteidl:

Ein Bericht über einen Symbolistenabend in Paris bringt uns auf Maeterlinck; Bahr erzählt den Inhalt der Aveugles; Schwarzkopf nennt das meisterhafte Skizzen in neuer Form, kann es aber kein Stück nennen, weil das Publikum es nie soweit bringen werde, leugnet, dass es ... Dichter gebe, die beim Schreiben nur an sich und hundert auserwählte Menschen, gar nicht ans Publikum dächten; Bahr und ich: die für hundert schreiben, giebts gewiss.[1]

[A report of a Symbolism evening in Paris brings us on to Maeterlinck. Bahr tells us the content of *Les Aveugles*; Schwarzkopf says it is a set of expert sketches in a new form but cannot call it a play since the public would never accept it as such; he denies that there are poets who think only about themselves and a hundred select others when they are writing and never about the public; Bahr and I say that there are certainly people that write for a hundred.]

The high exclusivity of the Symbolist ideals was clearly common currency for the young Hofmannsthal and his friends well before the end of December. But it was at that time that Hofmannsthal sought most urgently to articulate for himself and for others his understanding of the concept, which in the hands of critics such as Bahr was highly unstable, but which was for Hofmannsthal of great importance. Hans Steffen reports that in an unpublished letter from this period Hofmannsthal 'bezeichnet sein Erlebnis als ein "symbolistisches Experiment"' [called his experience a 'Symbolist experiment'].[2]

On 27 December 1891 Hofmannsthal read aloud to Schnitzler, Salten, Bahr and Ferry Bératon poems by himself and George that

---

[1] *Nachlaß*, H VII 17.76[b] and *SW* ii. 296–7.
[2] Steffen, 'Hofmannsthals Übernahme der symbolistischen Technik', 273.

he presented as Symbolist works, and it appears that he read them in order to *define* Symbolism. Schnitzler noted the event in his diary and remarked that opinions were divided: 'Ueber den Symbolismus. Bahr und Loris sprachen. Loris las Gedichte Stefan George's und eigne vor, die getheilten Eindruck hinterließen' [about Symbolism: Bahr and Loris talked. Loris read aloud poems by Stefan George and some of his own, which left a mixed impression].[3] On 19 December Hofmannsthal had noted 'das Gespräch über die andere Kunst' [the conversation about the other form of art] with George; the day afterwards he received and read his *Hymnen*; Hofmannsthal discussed Baudelaire, Verlaine, Mallarmé and others on the 21st, in the Café Griensteidl; on Christmas Eve there was a discussion with George of *L'Ermitage*. Then the initiative seems to have passed to Bahr, for the same diary entry records conversations with Bahr and the one-word note 'Symbolistenstreit' [Symbolist debate].[4] It is possible that this word refers to Jules Huret's *Enquête sur l'évolution littéraire* and the debate out of which it arose.[5] Perhaps the more likely interpretation, however, is that it refers to the debate about Symbolism that was current among the *Jung Wien* circle, possibly that single evening's discussion after the reading *chez* Schnitzler which left 'getheilten Eindruck', or to the longer-lasting debate around Christmas 1891.

That a debate about the nature of Symbolism did take place is confirmed by a note headed 'Bahr über Symbolismus meine Definitionen' [Bahr on Symbolism, my definitions; *SW* i. 134], which again implies that there had been some disagreement. A degree of reconciliation seems to have been reached by June 1892, for at the end of his essay on 'Symbolismus' (published on 18 June 1892), Bahr quotes 'Mein Garten' and 'Die Töchter der Gärtnerin', 'gleichsam als handliche Schulbeispiele' [as if by way of handy textbook examples] to show 'das Wesentliche der Symbolisten' [what is essential about the Symbolists].[6] Editing *Der Tod des Tizian*, Klaus-Gerhard Pott summarizes these events to give the context of the playlet's genesis, and he suggests that the reading at Schnitzler's flat led 'zu Bahrs späterer, außerordentlich negativer Reaktion in seinem am 18. Juli [*sic*] 1892 erscheinenden Aufsatz "Symbolismus"' [to Bahr's later, extraordinarily negative

---

[3] Schnitzler, *Tagebuch 1879–1892*, 358–9. The fact that Bahr and Hofmannsthal 'spoke'—perhaps gave a short paper—reinforces the idea that the poems were read in support of a programmatic definition of Symbolism.

[4] H VII 9.32. Cf. *RA* iii. 340–1 and *SW* ii. 288 (which is clearer).

[5] Suggested by Spahr, 'Hofmannsthals Aufzeichnungen zu Jules Hurets *Enquête*', 431.

[6] 'Symbolismus', *Die Nation*, 9.38: 577; also in *Studien*, 31–2.

reaction in his essay 'Symbolism' that appeared on 18 July 1892].[7] The misprint in the date is trivial, but the account of Bahr's essay as 'extraordinarily negative' is more seriously wrong. Bahr is extremely positive, sees Symbolism as a natural development of poetry, and is very careful to distinguish between its handling by true poets (amongst whom he counts Hofmannsthal) and its debasement by mere virtuosi. The most negative remark in the essay is that Symbolism is *perhaps* inherently inclined to overvalue technique. Whatever their original differences, Bahr and Hofmannsthal ended up on the same side in the 'Symbolistenstreit'.

In the note headed 'meine Definitionen', Hofmannsthal lists the poems under debate, those by himself being as follows:

'Ghasel' [= probably 'Für mich'; October 1890]
'Werke' [= 'Werke sind totes Gestein'; begun May/June 1891?; final versions 20 and 21 January 1892]
'Lehre' [date unknown; see below]
'Midas Garten' [= 'Mein Garten'; 22 December 1891]
'Wolken' [begun March 1891; completion date unknown]
'der Prophet' [26 December 1891]
'die Töchter' [= 'Die Töchter der Gärtnerin'; drafted on 25 December 1891]
'Stille' [22 December 1891][8]

He also listed seven of the eighteen poems that constitute Stefan George's *Hymnen*: 'Der Infant', 'Nachthymne' (followed by two exclamation marks), 'Im Park', 'Weihe', 'Strand', 'Verwandlung' (for 'Verwandlungen') and 'Nachmittag'. Hofmannsthal links himself with George and identifies another of his poems as Symbolist in the draft of a letter, ending with a flourish,

Voilà! Ich hoffe Sie werden mit diesem Drahtgestell für ein Essay auskommen, wenn nicht, werde ich Ihnen zur Verfügung stehen. Nur bitte, wenn Sie fertig sind, geben Sie mir diese Notizen zurück, weil ich sie umgeformt selber einmal brauchen kann.

Und eins: falls Sie überhaupt Namen nennen, bitte vergessen Sie den Stefan George nicht, der wirklich am meisten die Technik hat und auch persönlich die deutsche an die französische Bewegung bindet.[9]

---

[7] *SW* iii. 333. Ingeborg Beyer-Ahlert's remark in the FDH exhibition catalogue, ed. Lüders, is perhaps the source: she, too, notes that 'Bahrs äußerst negativer Aufsatz *Symbolismus* erschien am 18.7.1892 [*sic*]' (p. 17).

[8] *Nachlaß*, H VA 46.1 (quoted in *SW* I, 134 and in its original format in *SW* iii. 333 n. 4).

[9] *Nachlaß*, H I 53.6. See also Steven P. Sondrup, 'Three Notes on Symbolism by Hugo von Hofmannsthal', *Modern Austrian Literature*, 9.2 (1976), 4. The addressee is unknown, since only pages 5 and 6 of the letter have been preserved. Sondrup's view is that the tone implies that

[Voilà! I hope this skeleton essay will suffice for you, if not I am at your disposal again. I would ask you only that you return these notes to me when you are finished with them, because I can use them myself sometime in a different form. One more thing: if you are intending to name names at all, please do not forget Stefan George, who is the one who most thoroughly possesses the technique and is also a personal link between the German movement and the French.]

The poems cited are Verlaine's 'Le piano que baise', from the 'Ariettes oubliées' of *Romances sans paroles*,[10] and Hofmannsthal's 'Vorfrühling'. Of the poems by Hofmannsthal listed in these sources, 'Für mich', 'Lehre' and 'Der Prophet' were not published at all during his lifetime. Of the poems listed above, only 'Vorfrühling' was included in any edition of poetry compiled by Hofmannsthal himself. Very few were ever even intended for an edition: only 'Für mich', 'Wolken' and 'Der Prophet' were planned for inclusion in the joint edition with Kessler in 1905.[11]

Sondrup, publishing these notes for the first time, thinks that 'taken as a group Hofmannsthal's poems are not particularly distinguished in an artistic sense' whilst George's treat the same themes 'in a more subtle, highly refined form'.[12] But a more detailed analysis is necessary to establish both what Hofmannsthal saw as the characteristic features of Symbolism and his attitude towards it at this point, when his interest was most overt and most concentrated. A comparison of these poems with those exchanged by Hofmannsthal and George at this time reveals not only the specific Symbolist features of the poems and the extent to which Hofmannsthal's interest was coloured by personal relations, but also the manner in which the relationship was interpreted, by Hofmannsthal at least, with reference to criteria derived from Symbolist literature.

Some of the poems listed in Hofmannsthal's 'Symbolismus' note seem to have been selected for the sake of their typical contemporary imagery. 'Strand' is replete with the imagery that was soon to be diluted into the paraphernalia of *Jugendstil*—swans, expanses of waves, a moss-circled pool, the pollen of plants in the wind—but it has a delicacy and elegance of execution characteristic of the early George. The second stanza asks us to turn

the intended recipient was someone close to Hofmannsthal, but since he signs not Hugo, or even Hofmannsthal, but 'Loris' this is unlikely, and youth would permit him such a magisterial tone to anyone.

[10] See above, pp. 124-5.
[11] See *SW* i. 444-7. The 1907 Insel edition put an end to this plan.
[12] Sondrup, 'Three Notes', 2-3.

Zu weihern grün mit moor und blumenspuren
Wo gras und laub und ranken wirr und üppig schwanken
Und ewger abend einen altar weiht!
Die schwäne die da aus der buchtung fuhren ·
Geheimnisreich · sind unser brautgeleit.[13]

[to pools, marshy green with traces of flowers, where grass and leaves and tendrils sway in luxuriant tangles, and eternal evening consecrates an altar! The swans that came from the bay over there, mysteriously, are our bridal procession.]

There is a characteristic Georgean mystique about the setting, both stated simply in 'geheimnisreich' and more subtly evoked by imagery and the careful diction. The language deliberately has some very concentrated and obtrusive phonetic patterns: the poem begins with a torrent of alliterative 'w's, 'O lenken wir hinweg von wellenauen! | Die · wenn auch wild im wollen . . .' [O let us turn away from fields of waves, which, even if they are wild and demanding], and the third line of the stanza quoted above achieves a peculiar solemn effect as all the words except the last begin with vowel-sounds. Nevertheless, the poem scarcely questions its borrowed subject-matter, and does not seek to remould it substantially.

'Im Park' also seems to have been chosen primarily for its characteristic vocabulary and setting:

Rubinen perlen schmücken die fontänen·
Zu boden streut sie fürstlich jeder strahl·
In eines teppichs seidengrünen strähnen

Verbirgt sich ihre unbegrenzte zahl.
Der dichter dem die vögel angstlos nahen
Träumt einsam in dem weiten schattensaal..

Die jenen wonnetag erwachen sahen
Empfinden heiss von weichem klang berauscht·
Es schmachtet leib und leib sich zu umfahen.

Der dichter auch der töne lockung lauscht.
Doch heut darf ihre weise nicht ihn rühren
Weil er mit seinen geistern rede tauscht:

Er hat den griffel der sich sträubt zu führen.[14]

[Rubies and pearls decorate the fountains, every ray of light casts them imperiously to the ground and their incalculable number is hidden in the silky green strands of a carpet. The poet, whom the birds approach fearlessly, is dreaming alone in the vast room of shadows . Those who witnessed the awakening of that

---

[13] George, *Werke*, i. 17.   [14] Ibid. 10.

blissful day have hot sensations, intoxicated by the soft sounds, and bodies long to embrace each other. The poet also hearkens to the enticement of the sounds. But today their melody may not touch him because he is communing with his spirits: he has the pen that is straining to take the lead.]

It is suffused with the Symbolists' stock-in-trade. The figure of the poet is constructed as a dreaming magus, seated at the centre of an artificial world of gemstones, in communion with the spirits that inspire him and positively itching to command. The natural scene is in complete subjection. The grass is transfigured by the cut gemstones, whose colours are projected by the light playing through them and through the water in the fountain. The birds, too, are in thrall to the poet, and his attention is deliberately withdrawn from the outside world as he hearkens to his spirits. The moment evokes in the onlookers a feeling of passionate intoxication.

The world created is a wish-world, as it were of Mallarmé's *cénacle* conducted in a Verlainean landscape of languor and half-tones. Compare the scene of the latter's 'En sourdine', which also eroticizes landscape:

> Calmes dans le demi-jour
> Que les branches hautes font,
> Pénétrons bien notre amour
> De ce silence profond.
>
> Fondons nos âmes, nos cœurs
> Es nos sens extasiés,
> Parmi les vague langueurs
> Des pins et des arbousiers. . . .
>
> Et quand, solennel, le soir
> Des chênes noirs tombera,
> Voix de notre désespoir,
> Le rossignol chantera.[15]

[Calm in the half-light of the high branches, let us penetrate our love with this profound silence. Let us melt our souls, our hearts and our ecstatic senses amongst the vague languors of pines and arbutus. . . . And when, solemnly, the evening falls from the black oaks, the nightingale will sing, the voice of our despair.]

George's poem associates tense new sexuality with the brightness of dawn; Verlaine's uses the approach of dusk to evoke a sexual ecstasy that is slowed down and experienced almost through a drugged haze. But the use of the outside world as the expression of eroticism is

---

[15] Verlaine, *OPC*, 120.

common to both. George is unwilling to leave it to speak for itself: he merely calls it 'jener wonnetag' rather than trusting it to be one; and he merely states that it intoxicates, and that the witnesses of the dawn 'empfinden'. Verlaine uses imperatives inviting action for the immediate future, 'pénétrons, fondons', but the languid music of the verse leaves no doubt that the time is the present. Despair emerges from sexual saturation, as he knows it will. And the nightingale is no mere prop to express the next emotion in an arbitrary series: it is the natural and inevitable consequence of falling night in the lovers' woods. George places a poet within his scene, resistant to its charms, and the physical, sexual daybreak is a foil to the poet's austere calling— communion with incorporeal spirits for the creation of poetry. Placing the poem in the context of the title of the collection, the poem is a *Hymne* in the sense that it celebrates the circumstance in which hymns are themselves composed rather than any of the traditional objects of praise.

Although George's use of the familiar material of Symbolism in 'Im Park' in fact leads to a rather different sort of poetry from that of his models, he is close to incurring Mallarmé's censure for having 'listed' rather than 'created'. In his response to Huret's *Enquête*, Mallarmé complained:

L'enfantillage de la littérature jusqu'ici a été de croire, par exemple, que de choisir un certain nombre de pierres précieuses et en mettre les noms sur le papier, même très bien, c'était *faire* des pierres précieuses. Eh bien! non! La poésie consiste à *créer* . . . si, véritablement, les pierres précieuses dont on se pare ne manifestent pas un état d'âme, c'est indûment qu'on s'en pare.[16]

[The childish naivety of literature hitherto has been to believe, for example, that to choose a certain number of precious stones and put their names on paper, even very nicely, is to *make* precious stones. No indeed! Poetry consists in *creating* . . . and if in truth the precious stones with which we adorn ourselves have no soul, then we are adorning ourselves inappropriately.]

Hofmannsthal's choice of this poem indicates that it is in part the *repertoire* of images, motifs and techniques from his French influences by which he is seduced.

The transformations that are presented by 'Verwandlungen' are due solely to shifts in sense-perceptions. Colour, touch, weight, heat, light and sound all modulate. The poem does not present a scene whose mood changes, or a relationship, or a time; rather there is first

---

[16] Mallarmé, *OC*, 870; Huret, *Enquête*, 62–3.

the mood, without identifiable location, but with symbolic potential. It
begins thus:

> Abendlich auf schattenbegleiteten wegen
> Über brücken den türmen und mauern entgegen
> Wenn leise klänge sich regen:
>
> Auf einem goldenen wagen
> Wo perlgraue flügel dich tragen
> Und lindenbüsche dich fächeln
> Herniedertauche
> Mit mildem lächeln
> Und linderndem hauche![17]

[In the evenings, on paths in shadow, over bridges towards the towers and walls,
when quiet sounds begin to stir: on a golden chariot where you are carried by
pearly grey wings and fanned by the limes, dive downwards with a gentle smile and
soothing breath!]

This pattern is repeated twice more in the poem: the first three lines of
each section rhyme, but on a different sound from verse to verse; the
final words of the next six lines are identical in each verse. As the poem
develops, the morning-mood of the first three lines turns to midday
and then to evening, and shadows give way first to sunlight and then to
darkness. The golden chariot becomes silver then steely; the pearl-grey
wings turn into light green mirrors and then into blocks of lava; the
limes become foamy threads and blazing clouds; the gentle smile turns
joyful and then wild; and the breath that initially soothes becomes a
caress and then scorches. The last lines in particular show how these
structures of repetition maintain a constant tension between the transformations and their origin:

> . . . grell lohe wolken dich fächeln
> Herniedertauche
> Mit wildem lächeln
> Und sengendem hauche!

[you are fanned by brightly blazing clouds, dive downwards with a wild smile and
scorching breath!]

The constant element of each line does not remain obviously appropriate to the attribute, which changes. The process of transformation
is itself symbolized through the preservation of a shadow of the
original formulation behind each new manifestation: although the

[17] George, *Werke*, i. 14–15.

final sections are more violent and threatening, the substance of the poetic structure is preserved and the elements in the later versions that have changed are not permitted to efface that original structure entirely. It is the arrangement of the words that is crucial to this achievement, not the concepts to which they refer, and George is here approaching the Symbolist ideal of a 'poésie pure' in which language itself contains the meaning rather than the things to which language refers.

The letter that George sent to Hofmannsthal in December 1891, declaring his affection, 'ein hoffen—ein ahnen—ein zucken—ein schwanken—o mein zwillingsbruder' [hoping—suspecting—trembling—vacillating—O my twin!],[18] quotes his own poem 'Der Infant'. Given the high profile of literature in this relationship, we can assume that he was inviting Hofmannsthal to pick up the echo:

> Bei schild und degen unter fahlem friese
> Mit weissem antlitz lächelt der infant
> In dunklem goldumgürtetem oval.
> Nicht lang im damals unberührten saal
> Ein zwillingsbruder: kühle bergesbrise
> Sie war ein allzu rauher spieltrabant.[19]

[With shields and swords beneath a faded frieze, the Infante smiles, pale-faced in the dark, gold-framed oval. There was a twin in that room, then untouched, but not for long: the cool mountain breeze was too rough a playmate.]

'Ein zwillingsbruder' in 'Der Infant' refers to the living face from which the portrait of the *Infante* was made. Their relationship between the two, crudely, is that of art and life, and in George's poem the living-but-transient are subordinate to the dead-but-lasting. It is the image that begins and the image that has the twin brother, and the privileging of the artistic over the 'real' is a characteristic Symbolist emphasis. The royal child exists now only 'im goldumgürtetem oval', in a museum hall that was once his home and in which he played with the green and rose-coloured silk ball that seems to have been preserved in the picture. The real child did not grow up—as those who surround him in the museum as pictures on the walls grew up—and life has ceded to the immortality of art. Unlike his real-life twin, susceptible to the smallest breeze, the *Infante* in the picture has moments of freedom and sublimity when the elfin maid roughly plays ball with him. Hence the poet's interpretation of the picture-child's smile, a supposition that the *Infante*

---

[18] George, *BW*, 13; undated.   [19] George, *Werke*, i. 20–1.

will not regret his never having reached manhood ('dass er zum *finstern mann nicht aufgeschossen*'). Had he lived, the sword and shield that now surround him as part of the room's decoration beneath the frieze would probably have been real weapons.

The phrase 'O mein zwillingsbruder' in George's letter may thus refer to one who, if not a child, was still only 17 (and incidentally the age at which the *Infante* Don Baltasar Carlos in the picture was to die).[20] He was perhaps seen as the living counterpart to George's frozen prince in art, and the reference may have been a warning against wanting to 'grow up' and become independent too soon. Hofmannsthal certainly saw the possibility of identifying himself with 'Der Infant', as the Page in the prologue to the fragment *Der Tod des Tizian* makes explicit:

> Da blieb ich stehn bei des Infanten Bild—
> Er ist sehr jung und blaß und früh verstorben...
> Ich seh ihm ähnlich—sagen sie—und drum
> Lieb ich ihn auch...
> Und wenn es ringsum still und dämmrig ist,
> So träum ich dann, ich wäre der Infant,
> Der längst verstorbene traurige Infant...[21]

[I stopped by the painting of the Infante—he is very young and pale and died young. I am said to be like him, and that is why I love him. And when it is quiet and the light is dim around me I dream that I am the Infante, the poor long-dead Infante.]

The notes to this passage in the Critical Edition mention Arnold Böcklin's portrait of the young Graf Karl Salm from 1879 and its striking resemblance to Hofmannsthal as a young man.[22] This may be the portrait Hofmannsthal has in mind here (it was once hung in Vienna). Hofmannsthal's homage to George in 'Einem, der vorübergeht' was also originally to have included a reference to such a picture, and one of the stanzas of the draft reads 'Du warst wie das Bild, wie das

---

[20] The poem has been shown to represent Don Baltasar Carlos (1629–46), the first-born son of Philip IV of Spain and Elisabeth of Bourbon, painted by Velázquez in 1632 at the age of 2½ years. The room in which the poem places the painting is probably the Panteón de los Infantes in the Escorial, completed in 1888, one year before George's visit there. George could have discovered all the facts about the Infante and the building from Carl Justi, *Diego Velasquez und sein Jahrhundert* (Bonn: Verlag Friedrich Cohen, 1888), ii. 127–40 and 235–44. See Jörg-Ulrich Fechner, 'Erfahrungen spanischer Wirklichkeit in frühen Gedichten Stefan Georges', *Castrum Peregrini*, 138 (1978), 62–76.

[21] *SW* iii. 39, ll. 15–24. He acknowledges it in a letter to George as 'ein bekanntes Detail' (George, *BW*, 30).

[22] See *SW* iii. 390 and Jürgen Wißmann, 'Zum Nachleben der Malerei Arnold Böcklins', in *Arnold Böcklin 1827–1901: Ausstellung im Kunstmuseum Düsseldorf* (1974), 31–2.

alte | Das wo im Dunklen hängt' [you were like the picture, like the old picture that is hanging somewhere in the dark].[23] The echoes between the various poetic texts make it clear that the poem 'Der Infant' was certainly as important here as any real picture. Yet Hofmannsthal could only contemplate playing the role that George had imaginatively conceived for him in a dream: the effete pupils of Titian are not the true heirs of their vigorous master, and if Hofmannsthal played the role at all, it was as a Prince destined not to take his father's crown. The resonances of the irony in his use of the image are too complex to permit one to decide with certainty whether this was a situation he viewed with wry contentment—the inheritance being one he did not desire—or whether it represents a wistful premonition of never inheriting poetic power.

'Der Infant' is one of a pair of poems headed 'Bilder', and the other, 'Ein Angelico', was originally dedicated to Albert Saint-Paul, George's mentor and guide through the salons and cafés of Symbolist Paris in 1889. 'Der Infant' reaches a little further back into the French tradition, in being a variant of the *transposition d'art* poem practised by Gautier and the Parnassians. It does not share their aesthetic of *l'art pour l'art*, however. Neither does it share the tentativeness and delicacy of another possible subtext, Mörike's 'Auf eine Lampe', which has similarities of both scene and theme. The tension between living, breathing children and their freezing in artistic form governs both poems, for the child's most blissful and most perfect moments are experienced in play and *dis*play rather than in what one might crudely call his function as a human being, and the latter is irrelevant to the lamp's value, too. In 'Der Infant' that distance from flesh-and-blood existence is plainly preferable, however, and Mörike makes no such suggestion. 'Seligkeit' in 'Auf eine Lampe' is the expression of the object's being so perfectly what it is, whereas for George 'Seligkeit' is the result of dreaming, the child's becoming briefly and insubstantially something that he is not.

The substance—if it can properly be called that—of George's dream-world is the dignified luxury of the Symbolists' world: silk, gold, crystal, oak, carefully selected colours. Pristine and costly, they are adorned with light and shadow of a Verlainean delicacy. The child's face shining from the dark frame that none the less has the lustre of gold, with the glitter of the chandeliers and the twinkling interchange of pink and green, have the same effect of subduing and simultaneously

---

[23] *SW* ii. 283; see also Rieckmann, '(Anti-)Semitism and Homoeroticism', 219.

intensifying emotion as the pale decors of the *Fêtes galantes* or the 'Ariettes oubliées'. The rich word-music performs a parallel function: there is an exceptional alliterative concentration of *b, d, f, g, m* and *n*, together with bright and dark vowel sounds shimmering in an acoustic mosaic. It all contributes to a sense of expectancy in the poem that seems at first at odds with its subject—a finished painting and a dead child. Structurally, too, eagerness dominates reflection, since the dream is the last element, introduced by the last line of the second section with a colon, which impels the reader over the natural ending of the stanza.

This tingling sensation in a poem about a dead child is to the non-Symbolist's ear unsettling, even perverse or perverted. There is a similar semi-sensual charge that oppresses Hofmannsthal's 'Die Stunden!'. But thrill is fundamental to the Symbolists' aesthetic, and it derives from a series of paradoxical combinations. In the case of the *Infante*, a privileged and isolated royal child, it depends on a combination of vulnerability and prestige. Mallarmé's swan in 'Le vierge, le vivace et le bel aujourd'hui' is magnificent but trapped in exile; Hérodiade is both princess and victim; so many of Verlaine's landscapes are set at 'l'heure exquise'[24] with its overtones of expectation and pain. All these poets most frequently attach a sexual frisson to their paradoxes, produced by both heightened sensations and the pain of sadness that accompanies them.

Another of the poems by George that Hofmannsthal designated Symbolist, 'Nachmittag', is positively masochistic in its association of uniqueness and pain. It opens with the line 'Sengende strahlen senken sich nieder' [scorching rays descend] and the insistent alliteration and the threefold repetition of the line match the beating of the sun's rays. The first longer section of the poem evokes a dangerous, unpeopled scene of scorched flowers and dry wells:

> Und dem Einsamen der mit entzücken sie fühlt
> Der des gemaches duftender kühle entfloh
> Gegenglut für zerstörende gluten suchend
> Stetig sie auf scheitel und nacken scheinen
> Bis er rettender schwäche erliegen darf
> Hingleitend bei eines pfeilers fuss.[25]

[And they shine constantly on the head and the neck of the solitary, who feels them with delight, who left the fragrant cool of his room in search of an ardour to

---

[24] 'The exquisite hour', from 'La Lune blanche' in *La Bonne Chanson* (Verlaine, *OPC*, 146).
[25] George, *Werke*, i. 12.

counter his destructive ardours; they shine until he may succumb to a saving weakness, slipping to the floor at the foot of a pillar.]

There is no moral context for this, as there is for example in *Der Tod in Venedig* when Gustav von Aschenbach (also called 'der Einsame'), crushed by the heat, 'auf den Stufen der Zisterne . . . sich niedersinken [ließ] und lehnte den Kopf an das steinerne Rund' [on the steps of the well he sank to the ground and leaned his head against its stone rim], also amongst balconied palaces in a southern city.[26] George's lone hero actively seeks pain to counterbalance pain, deliberately exhausts himself, and enjoys the sun's flagellant effect. To be the bearer of such troubles, it is suggested, both enables the pleasure and necessitates the pain. The pain is exquisite, in the full etymological sense of the word 'sought out', and since the whole poem is concerned with the feeling, there is no room for the explanatory context that the wider structures of Mann's novella permit and demand.

Baudelaire provides a model, most readily in the famous 'Une charogne' but elsewhere also:

> De ce ciel bizarre et livide,
> Tourmenté comme ton destin,
> Quels pensers dans ton âme vide
> Descendent? réponds, libertin.[27]

[What thoughts come down to your empty soul from this strange and pallid sky, as tormented as your destiny? Answer, libertine!]

More important, his attitude of self-torment throughout *Les Fleurs du mal* was formative for a generation of poets after him. 'Nachthymne' shares this tradition, makes it more explicit and greedily seeks out the Symbolists' paradoxes. In this case it is the paradox of self-deprecation and self-aggrandizement. The speaker is waiting to be a sacrifice to a nameless Lord called 'der Eine', with vivid blue eyes like the gems in an oriental statue, who disdains to take cognizance of him much less look kindly upon the supplicant. His nervousness of the subject is erotically overlaid with longing for mortification and subjugation:

> Bin ich so ferne schon von opferjahren?
> Entweiht mich süsses lüsten nach dem tode
> Und sang ich nicht zu dröhnenden fanfaren
> Der freudenliebe sonnen-ode?

---

[26] Thomas Mann, *Gesammelte Werke* (Frankfurt a.M.: S. Fischer, 1960), viii. 521.
[27] Baudelaire, 'Horreur Sympathique', *OC*, i. 77.

Geruhe du nur dass ein kurzer schimmer
Aus deiner wimper brechend mich versehre:
Des glückes hoffnung misst ich gern für immer ·
Nach deinem preise schlöss ich meinen psalter
Und spottete dem schatten einer ehre
Und stürbe wertlos wie ein abendfalter.[28]

[Am I already so far from the age of sacrifice? Am I desecrated by the sweet lust for death, and did I not sing the joyous Ode to the Sun to resounding fanfares? Grant only that a brief shimmer from your eye might scorch me: I would gladly sacrifice the hope of happiness for ever, I would close my psalter after praising you and scorn the honour of a shadow and die as worthlessly as a moth.]

The speaker refers overtly to his self-denial, but in the context of the previous lines (where the poet remembers the election of 'ein jüngling angeglüht von frommem feuer' [a youth inflamed with the fire of piety] to be a pure sacrifice for the ancient gods), the effect is less self-abasement than self-promotion. The last line states that the speaker would die 'wertlos', but given the strong subtext of Goethe's 'Selige Sehnsucht' here—where the butterfly in the flame is exhorted, 'stirb und werde' [die and be transformed]—there is a double edge to the image in George's poem. 'Der Eine' may be a god, but he may also be the poet's lover. The exquisite immoderation of the speaker's request for a brief glance from beneath his lover's eyelash to be permitted to scald him is close to the language of the Metaphysicals' love poetry, and has many resonances in the paradoxical Platonic love treatises of the Italian Renaissance. Hofmannsthal's double exclamation mark in the list is perhaps partly a response to the thrilling and shocking combination of passion and religiosity.

A hymnic tone again evokes the processes of poetry in 'Weihe'. There are traces here of a response to a poem by Rimbaud, 'Aube', from the *Illuminations*.[29] It evokes the young poet's pursuit of the goddess/dawn and his temporary but sublime possession of her. The chase takes place during the ambiguous early hours between night and day; the goddess's veils are erotically stripped off, and the final embrace concludes with orgasmic exhaustion as they sink into sleep. When the speaker awakes—he is called 'l'enfant' ironically, since the poem is about a first sexual experience—his innocence is lost and the hour has matured to the glare of midday. 'Weihe', too, invokes the descent of the veiled goddess to the mature *Du*, although she is not as

[28] George, *Werke*, i. 17.
[29] See also below, pp. 328–38, for Hofmannsthal's response to this poem.

elusive as Rimbaud's and yields herself willingly as a blessing. George closes with the satisfaction of the lover; Rimbaud leaves his subject trembling with the anticipation that comes of having merely tasted bliss. The difference is perhaps due to temperament, and perhaps due to the relative positions of the poets in the tradition: Rimbaud was creating it, George responding to its achievements. The condition in which blessedness is achieved has already been described in stanza 4, and in peculiarly Symbolist terms:

> Schon scheinen durch der zweige zackenrahmen
> Mit sternenstädten selige gefilde ·
> Der zeiten flug verliert die alten namen
> Und raum und dasein bleiben nur im bilde.[30]

[Already blissful climes with starry cities are shining through the jagged frame of the twigs, the fleeting passage of time is leaving behind the old names, and space and being remain only in the image.]

The initiation, or as a French translation of selected George poems from 1941 has it, 'ordination',[31] is a kind of baptism in the raging river, an intoxication of the senses by wind, water, trees, light and elfin music. The first three stanzas build the onslaught to the point where reality slips away and vision supervenes. Then the subject is offered the Elysian vista of star-cities, where traditional names are abandoned, and space and being exist only in images: 'raum und dasein bleiben nur im bilde'. The French translation is more explicit and explanatory, rendering the line 'La Forme et L'Être morts revivent dans l'Image' [dead form and being relive in the image]. 'Nun bist du reif' [now you are ready] is the judgement that opens the next verse, and the poetic subject achieves union with the veiled goddess.[32]

The magic point where nomenclature is lost is the magic point that poetry should construct, according to Mallarmé:

A quoi bon la merveille de transposer un fait de nature en sa presque disparition vibratoire selon le jeu de la parole, cependant, si ce n'est pour qu'en émane, sans la gêne d'un proche ou concret rappel, la notion pure? . . .

Au contraire d'une fonction de numéraire facile et représentatif, comme le traite d'abord la foule, le Dire, avant tout, rêve et chant, retrouve chez le poëte, par nécessité constitutive d'un art consacré aux fictions, sa virtualité.

[30] George, *Werke*, i. 9.
[31] *Stefan George: Choix de poèmes*, trans. Maurice Boucher (Paris: Aubier, 1941), i: *Première Période 1890–1900*, 57.
[32] 'Auf der Terrasse', also from *Hymnen* is even more obviously a response to 'Aube': 'Triumph! du bist es· aus dem abendrote | Getauschter blicke las ich meine trauer· | Doch treu bekennend kamst du selber bote | Und stolz war unsres bundes kleine dauer' (i. 19).

Le vers qui de plusieurs vocables refait un mot total, neuf, étranger à la langue et comme incantatoire, achève cet isolement de la parole.[33]

[What is the use of the miracle of transposing a fact of nature into something that almost constitutes its disappearance into vibration according to the way the words operate, if it is not so that its pure essence can emanate from it, without the hindrance of any near or concrete recollection. Far from having a simple, representative function as a token, as the common herd initially suppose it to have, the Word primarily dreams and sings and finds in the poet its virtuality, because of the way an art devoted to fictions is necessarily constituted. The line of verse, which builds out of a series of vocables a complete word, new to language, strange to it, and as if in incantation perfects the isolation of the word.]

This is from the famous preface to René Ghil's *Traité du verbe* (Paris, 1886) which George cannot have missed, considering its fame, his acquaintance with Mallarmé and his presence in Paris shortly afterwards.[34] These paragraphs, it is almost certain, helped to formed George's poetic thinking: they illuminate his claim in 'Weihe' that a point is reached when the conversion of reality into virtuality takes place, where space and being survive only in the Image. Mallarmé claimed it was the Word that achieved this transposition; but he said so most explicitly in a critical preface and not a poem, in a context in which—even given Mallarmé's peculiarly difficult and dense critical writing style—explanation was in order. 'Weihe' implies that the transition is achieved with intoxication, and to an extent the poem inebriates with its images, rhythms and sounds. But the abandon is not so great that the fourth stanza quoted above cannot simply state that the condition is reached within the poem itself.

For a poet there is a difficulty inherent in being programmatic after the event. It is true that Baudelaire's 'Le Voyage' can also be read as a programmatic poem, but it comes at the end of *Les Fleurs du mal* and when read in this context derives the energy for its leap into 'l'Inconnu' from the collection itself. It reads as something like a battle-cry, not a set of instructions. 'Weihe' not only introduces a collection, which position enhances its programmatic function, but its poetic credo is also borrowed, and its epigonal character is even reinforced as the echo of Rimbaud is recognized. George was a more overtly confident writer than Hofmannsthal, and had experienced Symbolism at first hand in Paris, yet so conscious an attempt to perpetuate its practices and theoretical tenets makes it difficult to avoid the impression that the

---

[33] Mallarmé, *OC*, 857–8.
[34] Hermann Bahr mentions it in his essay 'Die Décadence' in *Studien*, 21.

poems are not in the fullest sense original and strong. Hans Steffen maintains that Hofmannsthal's early poems, those written before meeting George, are clearly distinguished from the poetry that was written after this meeting.[35] The analyses that follow of Hofmannsthal's own Symbolist poems written both before and after making his acquaintance will indicate that the distinction is not so sharp (and in particular that the impoverishment detected by Steffen in Hofmannsthal's use of imagery is illusory). Nevertheless, they will show that George's influence was considerable, effectively establishing a further level of indebtedness that makes itself clearly felt in Hofmannsthal's poems.

In the diary notes that chart the events of December 1891, the record of 'das Gespräch über die *andere* Kunst' was made at about the same time as the notes identifying Hofmannsthal's own poems as Symbolist. From the outset Hofmannsthal seems to have been undecided about whether Symbolism was best assimilated into his own repertoire or kept under observation as a foreign phenomenon. Nevertheless, not only is 'Mein Garten', in Bahr's opinion, a sonnet that 'enthält, rein und deutlich, den ganzen Symbolismus und es enthält nichts, das nicht Symbolismus wäre', it was also published for the first time as a pendant to Bahr's essay on Symbolism, and therefore appeared to the public as if it had been written especially for this context.

> Schön ist mein Garten mit den gold'nen Bäumen,
> Den Blättern, die mit Silbersäuseln zittern,
> Dem Diamantenthau, den Wappengittern,
> Dem Klang des Gong, bei dem die Löwen träumen,
> Die ehernen, und den Topasmäandern
> Und der Volière, wo die Reiher blinken,
> Die niemals aus den Silberbrunnen trinken...
> So schön, ich sehn' mich kaum nach jenem andern,
> Dem andern Garten, wo ich früher war.
> Ich weiß nicht wo... Ich rieche nur den Thau,
> Den Thau, der früh an meinen Haaren hing,
> Den Duft der Erde weiß ich, feucht und lau,
> Wenn ich die weichen Beeren suchen ging...
> In jenem Garten, wo ich früher war... (*SW* i. 20)

[My garden is beautiful, with its golden trees, its leaves that tremble with silvery rustling, the diamond dew, gates with their coats of arms, the sound of the gong at which the bronze lions dream, and its topaz-coloured meanders, the aviary where

---

[35] Steffen, 'Hofmannsthals Übernahme der symbolistischen Techik', 271.

the herons gleam and never drink from the silver fountain. It is so beautiful that I hardly long now for the other garden where I used to be. I don't know where it was. I can only smell the dew, the dew that used to hang in my hair, I remember the smell of the earth, damp and warm, when I used to go and pick the soft berries, in that garden where I used to be.]

Hofmannsthal wrote to George of this poem and 'Die Töchter der Gärtnerin' that although of little importance, 'wenig bedeutend', they had to stand in for George's own verse until he authorized public debate: 'sonst . . . giebt es in Deutschland kaum irgendwo für die neue Technik [= Symbolismus] characteristische Verse' [otherwise there are hardly any poems in Germany that are characteristic of the new technique].[36] 'Mein Garten' is also perhaps a response to one of George's own poems, 'Mein garten bedarf nicht luft und nicht wärme', from *Algabal*. Although this collection had not appeared in print by then, George will certainly have read or shown Hofmannsthal many of the poems that went into it.[37]

The garden in Hofmannsthal's poem is claimed as 'mein', suggesting some strength of affinity between speaker and place. Yet there are two gardens, and the one described with deceptive simplicity in the opening phrase is the lesser of the two in the speaker's emotional estimation. The artificial garden is a Fabergé creation of jewels and precious metals: the trees are golden, the fountain silver; the dew is of diamonds, the curves of the stream are topaz; even the rustling of the trees is silvery. The heron never drinks from the fountain because neither the water nor the bird is real, and in this glittering landscape the dreams of the bronze lions are lulled by the tremor of the gong. It is obvious why the poem was originally entitled 'Midas Garten'.

'Schön ist mein Garten' is a very emphatic opening, however, and the suggestions of too-much-protesting as 'so schön' is repeated are confirmed by the traitorous 'kaum'. 'Hardly longing' is rather coy, and the speaker's love for his artificially created environment is not perfect. The visual and aural sensations of the first seven lines anticipate the intenser touching and smelling that replace them in the second section (the two enmeshed across the traditional octave/sestet break). Here the dew is scented and felt in the hair, the speaker's mounting enthusiasm communicated in the repetition of 'den Thau' across the line-end. Whilst 'feucht und lau' and 'weich' are the natural attributes of a real experience in time (remembered as part of an early-morning feeling), the gold and jewels in the first part were inhumanly perfect

---

[36] George, *BW*, 30.   [37] See also *SW* i. 133–4.

and durable; the only reference to time was 'niemals', which denies it. In the second part the verse also softens phonetically: the bright 'a' sounds of 'Diamant', 'Klang', 'Mäandern' cede to the darker 'a's of 'Garten' and 'Haaren', while a preponderance of taut sibilants and affricatives ('Silbersäuseln', 'zittern') and plosives ('blinken' and 'trinken') gives way to nasal and velar consonants ('hing', 'ging', 'jenem', 'weichen'). There is no doubt where the sympathies of the *Ich* really lie.

Some of the more general similarities of this poem with Symbolist verse will become apparent as the rest of the poems from Hofmannsthal's 'Symbolismus' group are analysed, but strong overlaps with Mallarmé's *Hérodiade* are immediately evident.[38] All the elements of Hofmannsthal's gardens are prefigured in *Hérodiade* and they function in a structure whose basic scheme is also shared. The themes of the 'Scène' are massive: subjectivity and integrity; the definition and preservation (or destruction) of the self *vis-à-vis* the world; the place of beauty, art, sensuality and humanity in the struggle to attain transcendence and oneness. This weight of significance is absent from Hofmannsthal's poem except as a pale shadow, but his use of Mallarmé's imagery transmits something of the same concerns into the poem. The key tension in *Hérodiade* is between natural and artificial, and it is articulated in a symbolic network combining both the virgin Hérodiade and the landscape in which she walks. Hérodiade has walked invulnerable through a den of lions:

> Sous la lourde prison de pierres et de fer
> Où de mes vieux lions traînent les siècles fauves
> . . . et je marchais, fatale, les mains sauves,
> Dans le parfum désert de ces anciens rois: . . .
> Je m'arrête, rêvant aux exils, et j'effeuille,
> Comme près d'un bassin dont le jet d'eau m'accueille,
> Les pâles lys qui sont en moi, tandis que . . .
> . . . à travers ma rêverie, en silence,
> Les lions, de ma robe écartent l'indolence.

[Beneath the heavy prison of stones and iron where the tawny centuries of my ancient lions drag on and I walked, fateful, my hands intact, in the deserted perfume of those former kings. I stop, dreaming of the exiles, and as if close to a basin whose fountain welcomes me, I strip the pale lilies that are within me, whilst through my reverie, in silence, the lions push aside the indolence of my dress.]

[38] Mallarmé, *OC*, 44–8.

Her immortality and integrity is in her virginity, symbolized by the metallic perfection of her hair:

> Je veux que mes cheveux qui ne sont pas des fleurs
> A répandre l'oubli des humaines douleurs,
> Mais de l'or, à jamais vierge des aromates,
> Dans leurs éclairs cruels et dans leurs pâleurs mates,
> Observent la froideur stérile du métal.

[I want the locks of my hair, which are not flowers for spreading the oblivion of human pain, but made of gold, forever untouched by scent, in their cruel lightning bolts and in their dull paleness, to observe the sterile coldness of metal.]

She rejects the nurse's suggestion that she is waiting for a lover, shuns her kiss, and refuses to be anointed with perfume. Touch and smell, which Hofmannsthal's poetic *Ich* embraced in memory, arraign Hérodiade's self-contained, self-reflective poise. She exists narcissistically, in gardens denuded of humanity:

> Oui, c'est pour moi, pour moi, que je fleuris, déserte!
> Vous le savez, jardins d'améthyste . . .
> Ors ignorés, . . .
> Vous, pierres où mes yeux comme de purs bijoux
> Empruntent leur clarté mélodieuse, et vous
> Métaux qui donnez à ma jeune chevelure
> Une splendeur fatale et sa massive allure!

[Yes, it is for me, just for me that I bloom, deserted! You know this, gardens of amethyst, forgotten golds, you, stones from which my eyes like pure jewels take on their melodious brightness, and you, metals which lend to my young hair a fatal splendour and its massive allure!]

She is alone, and everything around her is a mirror in which she is icily reflected, 'Hérodiade au clair regard de diamant' [Hérodiade with the bright diamond gaze]. Despite this sharpness, when she looked in her own mirror, she was unable to see herself as a clear image—'Je m'apparus en toi comme une ombre lointaine' [I appeared in you like a distant shadow]—and she has to be reassured for the imperfect vision of her memories by the Nurse's promise that she is beautiful.

Beauty is where Hofmannsthal's poem begins, and his poetic speaker also perceives himself as a shadow, distant in time. Even though 'Mein Garten' is less intense, the beauty it begins to evoke is like Hérodiade's beauty in Mallarmé's poem in that both are a function of *un*natural nature, the garden and the virgin's hair described in terms of metals and precious stones. Artificiality for Mallarmé is cognate with

poetry, and his goal—summarized in the notorious 'le monde est
fait pour aboutir à un beau livre' [the world is made to culminate in a
beautiful book][39]—is, via art, to transcend contingent reality to arrive
at a form of spiritual sublimation. This is an ascetic and intimidating
task. There is indeed something fearful about Hérodiade's beauty, for
she frightens both her Nurse and herself; horror at her immaculate
hair leads to the wishful reflection, 'si la beauté n'était la mort . . .' [if
only beauty were not also death]. But her beauty is also fascinating:
'j'aime l'horreur d'être vierge' [I love the horror of being a virgin], she
says, and in her the Romantic *femme fatale* is introverted and superimposed on the Narcissus myth. The development within Hofmannsthal's poem from the anxiously trembling musicality of its early lines to
its sympathy with the ordinary human senses of touch and smell is an
instinctive reaction against the Mallarméan demands of art. The skill
of the first section suggests that he gave the imitative impulse a fair
chance, but the importance of artificiality in his sources was not able
to outweigh his instinctive reluctance to accept their fundamental
inhumanity.

Hofmannsthal may not have read the poem, although it is likely that
he did. Since its publication in *Le Parnasse contemporain* (1871) and in
Poésies (1887), the 'Scène' had attracted some attention, and it was
amongst the manuscript copies that George made whilst in Paris.[40]
Mallarmé was by July 1891 already a familiar name, as the note
'Mallarmé: jedes Buch hat einen dreifachen Sinn' [Mallarmé: every
book has a threefold meaning] suggests.[41] *Die Blätter für die Kunst* were to
feature his work in the fifth issue, drawing attention to 'die biblische
wildheit der *Herodias*' and 'ihren mattbraunen nackten leib . . . nur mit
einigen singenden edelsteinen geschmückt' [the biblical wildness of
Hérodiade and her dull brown naked body decorated only with a few
resonant precious stones].[42] The status of *Hérodiade* is in any case such
that it 'sets the *décor* and introduces the principal vocabulary' of the
Symbolist period (and if 'introduces' is not quite accurate, since
Hérodiade's 'monotone patrie' [monotonous country] has its direct

[39] Ibid. 872. From the response to Huret's *Enquête*.
[40] See Boehringer, *Mein Bild*, i. 212. For George's 1905 translation of the 'Scène' (*Werke*, ii.
419–24) and its influence on *Algabal*, cf. Ursula Franklin, 'Two German Poets "Autour
d'Hérodiade": A Spark of Heine and a Georgean Afterglow', in Will L. McLendon (ed.),
L'Hénaurme Siècle (Heidelberg: Winter, 1984), 181–6.
[41] *RA* iii. 336. This might refer to the famous *tiers aspect* that Mallarmé claims is characteristic of Symbolist writing: Mallarmé, *OC*, 365 ('Crise de vers').
[42] 'Dichterköpfe: III: Mallarmé', *Blätter für die Kunst*, 1.5 (1893), 134–7 (p. 136). The author-
ship of this article is not certain; it may have been written by George.

ancestor in the 'enivrante monotonie | Du métal, du marbre et de l'eau' [the intoxicating monotony of metal, marble and water] of Baudelaire's 'Rêve parisien', then the exaggeration is in the right spirit).[43] What Hofmannsthal saw as Symbolist in 'Mein Garten' was chiefly the artificial landscape as subject-matter, and merely to use the constitutive imagery of Symbolism is to enter into the field of its questions and presuppositions. By starting with the unreal landscape in 'Mein Garten', Hofmannsthal is referring directly to the movement. His nostalgia for the natural elements of the garden 'wo [er] früher war' may be interpreted in several ways. First, it may be nostalgia for life itself, a realm beyond any art—which is the line of argument initiated by Richard Alewyn's revisions of the previously dominant tendency to view Hofmannsthal merely as an aesthete. It may also be seen in more purely literary terms as a nostalgia for the Romantics' poetic presentations of identity, when the experiences of an identifiable *Ich*, with dew in its hair, had not been superseded by a surrogate form of experience in which the self does not appear at all. Finally, there is the possibility of a response—probably unconscious at this stage—against George's poem, which begins, 'Mein garten bedarf nicht luft und nicht wärme | Der garten den ich mir selber erbaut | Und seiner vögel leblose schwärme | Haben noch nie einen frühling geschaut' [my garden does not need air and heat, the garden that I constructed for myself, and the lifeless flocks of its birds have never seen springtime]. The structure of Hofmannsthal's poem is a deliberate rejection of this vision, since he builds in the suggestion of a turn away from his own artificial landscape and feels compelled to recall the other, the natural garden, 'wo ich früher war'.

'Die Töchter der Gärtnerin' also registers the implication made in *Hérodiade* that the perfection of an artificial landscape means the death of the self. It is structured, like 'Mein Garten', with the contrast of two sorts of nature, but begins with the soft and welcoming:

> Die eine füllt die großen Delfter Krüge,
> Auf denen blaue Drachen sind und Vögel,
> Mit einer lockern Garbe lichter Blüthen:
> Da ist Jasmin, da quellen reife Rosen
> Und Dahlien und Nelken und Narzissen..
> Darüber tanzen hohe Margeriten
> Und Fliederdolden wiegen sich und Schneeball

---

[43]   Wallace Fowlie, *Mallarmé* (London: Dobson, 1953), 134.

Und Halme nicken, Silberflaum und Rispen..
Ein duftend Bacchanal...
Die andre bricht mit blassen feinen Fingern
Langstielige und starre Orchideen,
Zwei oder drei, für eine enge Vase..
Aufragend, mit den Farben die verklingen,
Mit langen Griffeln, seltsam und gewunden,
Mit Purpurfäden und mit grellen Tupfen
Mit violetten, braunen Pantherflecken
Und lauernden verführerischen Kelchen,
Die tödten wollen.. (*SW* i. 22)

[One of them is filling the large Delft jugs that have dragons and birds on them with a loose sheaf of pale flowers: there is jasmine, ripe roses and dahlias and carnations and narcissi shoot forth, and above them dance marguerites, and clusters of lilac sway and Guelder roses and grasses nod, and silvery down and panicles . . ., a fragrant bacchanal . . . The other daughter is breaking stiff, long-stemmed orchids with her pale, fine fingers, two or three of them, for a narrow vase . . . standing tall with colours that fade away, with long styles, strange and contorted, with purple threads and bright spots, with violet, brown leopard patches, and sly, seductive calyces, that aim to kill . . .]

The threats in the second half are presented as a list, each element dependent on 'mit' much as they were with the list of datives in 'Mein Garten'. But where the characteristic Symbolist technique of synaesthesia was more subtly employed in the earlier poem ('Silbersäuseln', 'Diamantenthau'), here it is more forced, for 'mit den Farben die verklingen' is more a recipe than an effect. The wholesome and the sinister are opposed in a thorough series of contrasts: the large Delft jugs against the thin vases for few flowers; 'locker' and 'licht', blue and silver against 'gewunden', 'violett', 'braun' and 'grell'; 'tanzen', 'wiegen' and 'nicken' against 'brechen' and 'starr'; the unselfconscious Bacchanalia against the cunning of 'verführen'. Hofmannsthal seems to have taken to heart George's complaints about lack of plasticity in the style of German-language poetry, and this poem thrives on the love of listing and the palpability of polysyllables.

These latter flowers are, literally, 'les fleurs du mal'. As in 'Mein Garten' it is the contrast that makes the flowers symbolic, rather than anything intrinsic to them. 'Kelche die töten wollen' is a threat that commands attention only because of the suggestiveness of this elaborate network of contrasts. The threat is again from Symbolism, as the type of imagery chosen implies. A further clue is given in the nature of the verbs in the two sections: after the initial transitive verb 'füllt', the first daughter's creative input is diminished and intransitive verbs 'quellen', 'tanzen' and 'nicken', or the reflexive 'sich wiegen' take over. Nature governs its own movement in this case. The flowers arranged by the second daughter, however, do not move: she *breaks* them, submits them to her aesthetic will, constrains them in a narrow vase where they lurk. The subjugation of natural self-expression to artistic form has resonances on the poetological level, and they are confirmed by comparison with other works. On the other side of the sheet on which Hofmannsthal wrote the fair copy of 'Die Töchter der Gärtnerin' is 'Der Prophet', which ends with the powerful line 'Und er kann tödten, ohne zu berühren.'[44] The two poems were finished within a day of each other, which further encourages a superimposition of the two challenging final lines and the reconstruction of Hofmannsthal's understanding of 'tödten':

> In einer Halle hat er mich empfangen
> Die rätselhaft mich ängstet mit Gewalt
> Von süßen Duften widerlich durchwallt.
> Da hängen fremde Vögel, bunte Schlangen.
>
> Das Thor fällt zu, des Lebens Laut verhallt
> Der Seele Athmen hemmt ein dumpfes Bangen
> Ein Zaubertrunk hält jeden Sinn befangen
> Und alles flüchtet, hilflos, ohne Halt.
>
> Er aber ist nicht wie er immer war,
> Sein Auge bannt und fremd ist Stirn und Haar.
> Von seinen Worten, den unscheinbar leisen
> Geht eine Herrschaft aus und ein Verführen
> Er macht die leere Luft beengend kreisen
> Und er kann tödten, ohne zu berühren. (*SW* ii. 61)

[He received me in a great hall that in a mysterious way frightens and threatens me, filled with disgusting sweet scents. Strange birds hang there, and many-coloured snakes. The door slams shut, the sound of life dies away, the breathing of the soul is constricted by a dull fear, a magic potion freezes all my senses, and everything seems to be rushing away, helplessly, unstoppably. Yet he is not as he used to be. His look is spellbinding and his brow and hair are exotic. His words, inconspicuous and quiet, convey dominance and seductiveness. He makes the empty air spin stiflingly, and he can kill without touching.]

[44] *SW* ii. 61. Even here Hofmannsthal seems to have taken his phrases from another: Hoppe plausibly identifies the source as 'Zaubernden Augen voll Götterblicken, | Gleich mächtig zu tödten und zu entzücken', from a poem by Wieland and referring to Goethe: cf. Hoppe, 'Der Prophet: Hofmannsthals Gedichte an Stefan George', *Neue Zürcher Zeitung* (Fernausgabe), 3 Feb. 1974, 51.

The close atmosphere evoked matches the feeling of constriction in 'Die Töchter der Gärtnerin'; it is most obviously present in the Hall in which, according to the poem, George greeted Hofmannsthal, and which has something in common with the grandiose settings of Symbolist writers such as Huysmans and Villiers de l'Isle Adam. 'Der Duft', which in 'Mein Garten' was on the side of the living world, has multiplied to 'süße Dufte'—so many that their sweetness is sickly and potentially as stifling as the scent that kills Albine in Zola's *La Faute de l'abbé Mouret*. At the end of the poem, however, it is George's *words* that threaten to suffocate and can kill without touching, and touch was established in 'Mein Garten' as a sign of humanity. The gesture of the slammed door spawns the notion of life dying away as if it were the echo of the noise; then the suggestions of a throat tight with fear are transferred to the soul. With these two metaphorical expressions the sinister emanations of the Prophet's dwelling are anchored in the recognizable, physical world. If the magic potion might in other circumstances seem to be a prop inappropriately borrowed from a fairy-tale wizard, it carries here not superstitious shallowness but mythological seriousness.

The place is irrationally and darkly threatening, a scene from Edgar Allan Poe evoked in Symbolist conciseness. Its master has somehow succumbed to the magic, for he has changed. Whether George did change, or whether Hofmannsthal's perceptions had shifted as his anxiety grew, is a moot point. In either case, however, Hofmannsthal has condensed into his poem an expression of terror at the power of the Prophet's words. They share with the flowers in 'Die Töchter' the quality of seductiveness: it is as if Hofmannsthal is willing himself not to be seduced into writing poetry in a manner that allows the equation of beauty and death.

Both poems may refer in more and less cryptic fashion to the person of George, but the notes for 'Die Töchter der Gärtnerin' (containing almost all the important details and imagery) were made in June 1891, before their meeting, and thus confirming the view suggested in 'Einem, der vorübergeht' and elsewhere that the propensity for Symbolism predated his acquaintance with George. The note dated 10 June suggests that Hofmannsthal's intentions with his fatal flowers were more than biographical, and that they refer to poetry in general:

Künstler sind wie die Orchideen: sie berauschen die Insecten durch ihren Duft, *(1)* tauchen sie in fremde durchscheinende Farben . . . *(2)* locken sie in ihren leuchtenden *(1)* dunkel *(2)* Kelch und saugen *(1)* sie zu Tod *(2)* ihnen den Saft aus.[45]

[Artists are like orchids: they intoxicate the insects with their fragrance, (1) immerse them in strange translucent colours (2) entice them into their shining (1) dark (2) calyx and suck (1) them to death (2) their juices dry.]

It is the method of art to intoxicate and seduce. The flowers arranged by the Gardener's daughters may, like the gardens in the previous poem, be symbolic of the pulls of life and art. Hofmannsthal must have wished that it were so simple: another entry for the same day reads 'Menschen führen einander durch ihre Seelen wie Potemkin die Kaiserin Katharina durch Taurien' [people lead each other through their souls as Potemkin did the Empress Catharine through his province; *RA* iii. 332]. The business of personal interaction seems also to be based on deception and seduction.

If a personal preoccupation with George is very narrow, the note referring to 'Künstler' is rather general. A specifically French background to these thoughts is implied by a jotting made on 16 June, four days after the prose note to 'Die Töchter' and the Potemkin note:

'Des Esseintes': Homer in malvenfarbiges mattes Leder gebunden, geschöpftes Papier, am Rücken: 'Li Roman de Troies' und 'Li Roman d'Ulysse'. Ein weiß-goldener Rokokobeichtstuhl als Toilettentisch.[46]

['Des Esseintes': Homer bound in matt mauve leather, hand-made paper, on the back: *Li Roman de Troies* and *Li Roman d'Ulysse*. A white-gold rococo confessional as a dressing table.]

Des Esseintes is the hero—if that is the proper word—of Joris-Karl Huysmans's *A rebours*, an onslaught of decadence, containing forests of precious stones, luxuriant colours and hymns to Baudelaire and Mallarmé (sections of *Hérodiade* are quoted in chapter XIV). Des Esseintes is obsessed with combining artificially the perfumes of exotic flowers, an exaggeration of a Baudelairean topos. Huysmans was also a strong influence on George's *Algabal*: the final poem of 'Im Unterreich,' for example, has perhaps borrowed its coal-trees and lava fruits from a passage in chapter I of *A rebours* describing table decorations. George takes the dandy's whim more seriously than it was intended and makes of the dead decor a programme for Heliogabalus' conversion of sterility into art.[47]

[45] *SW* i. 142, corrections and substitutions indicated in the manner of the Critical Edition.

[46] *RA* iii. 333 (spelling after *Nachlaß*, H VII 2.124).

[47] See George, *Werke*, i. 47; Huysmans, *A rebours* (Paris: Mercure de France, 1977), 90; Mennemeier, *Literatur der Jahrhundertwende*, ii. 58–9.

The motif of dangerously seducing or enticing nature that appeared in 'Mein Garten' and 'Die Töchter' is also found in the poem 'Lehre'. The precise date of the poem is unknown, but there is much that speaks for including it amongst the poems written in December 1891 or January 1892 under the influence of George and French Symbolist verse:

Weile weile hier am Wege und ich will zum Teich hernieder
Wo der Wind mit den Lianen plätschert in der Fluth der braunen
Wo die schattenhaft[en] Blumen [dunkel] duften, Nacht Gefieder
Durch die Zweige huscht und Hexen kichern mit versteckten Faunen

Lass' ich will zum Teich hernieder wo die fiebernden Mimosen
Ihre Fäden bebend schlingen um die blinden tauben Bäume
Auf dem grünen Moor[e] liegen weiß und rein, die Wasserrosen
Aus dem braunen Moor[e] athmen sehnsuchtsschwere, bange Träume

Kalter Schauer und Tollheit wohnen hässlich in dem Feuchten
Blinde Thiere todte Wurzeln die zu keinem Traume taugen
Träume sind in dir Mimosen Faune die dich jenseits deuchten
Bunte Wunder in die Dämmrung weben ahnend deine Augen. (*SW* ii. 59)

[Linger, linger here on the path and I shall go down to the pool where the wind splashes about with the lianas in the brown flood waters where the shadowy flowers are darkly fragrant, night feathers darts through the branches and witches giggle with hidden fauns. Leave me, I want to go down to the pool where the feverish mimosas nervously wind their tendrils around the blind, deaf trees, on the green moor lie the waterlilies white and pure, anxious dreams laden with longing breathe out of the brown moor. Cold shuddering and madness dwell wretchedly in the dampness, blind animals dead roots that are fit for no dream, dreams are within you, mimosas, fauns that thought you were dead, your eyes prophetically weave colourful miracles into the twilight.]

The details of the scene around the pool are threatening: the water is muddy, the flowers dark and shaded, the noises of the night suggesting hidden witches and fauns, the trees clasped in the grip of lianas. Yet both the beginning of the first verse and the beginning of the second make it clear that the pool is somehow enticing the speaker away from a companion on the road—reminiscent of a similar enticement in George's 'Strand'. The companion in 'Lehre' seems to want to hold the speaker back, since he cries 'Lass'' and has to repeat his wish to leave the path. Perhaps the companion is a figment: the *Du* that surfaces in the last verse ('Träume sind in dir', 'deine Augen') is not necessarily another person, surely not to be identified with the person to whom the repeated 'weile' is addressed, and may be aimed at the speaker himself. The most one can say with any certainty is that there is a tension between a desire to experience the horrors of the pool and the need to resist that desire.

'Lehre' stands under the shadow of Poe, one of Symbolism's most important ancestors. There is an entry in Hofmannsthal's diary for sometime at, or just after, the end of August 1891 which reads,

E. A. Poe. die feuchte moorige Mulde, wo im *(1)* Schatten *(2)* Dunkel Nacht-schatten wachsen, Violen und blinde bebende Mimosen, die *(1)* nach *(2)* mit zitternden Fäden nach dem Licht tasten.[48]

[E. A. Poe. The damp boggy hollow, where in the (1) shadow (2) dark deadly night-shade grows, and violets and blind, nervous mimosas that feel for the light (1) after (2) with trembling tendrils.]

Poe's stories were of exceptional importance in the development of Symbolism after they were translated by Baudelaire.[49] More than to borrowed details, it is to the American's techniques of imaginative magnification that Hofmannsthal is most indebted, making fissures in the rational and breaking it apart by filling them with the products of the imagination. Not identified, as was Poe, but present nevertheless behind at least one image of 'Lehre', is Mallarmé, another of Poe's translators. There is something of Mallarmé's 'L'Azur' in the gloomy atmosphere of Hofmannsthal's pool:

> Brouillards, montez! Versez vos cendres monotones
> Avec de longs haillons de brume dans les cieux
> Qui noiera le marais livide des automnes
> Et bâtissez un grand plafond silencieux!
>
> Et toi, sors des étangs léthéens et ramasse
> En t'en venant la vase et les pâles roseaux,

[48] *Nachlaß*, H VII 9.4ᵃ (*SW* ii. 278).
[49] See P. Mansell Jones, 'Poe, Baudelaire and Mallarmé: A Problem of Literary Judgement', and 'Poe and Baudelaire: The "Affinity" ', both in *The Background of Modern French Poetry* (Cambridge: Cambridge University Press, 1951), 38–58 and 59–68; James R. Lawler, *Edgar Poe et les poètes français* (Paris: Julliard, 1989), 145–6; Léon Lemonnier, *Edgar Poe et les poètes français* (Paris: Éditions de la Nouvelle Revue Critique, 1932), especially 203–25; Louis Seylaz, *Edgar Poe et les premiers symbolistes français* (Lausanne: La Concorde, 1923), 73–86 and 145–66; Manfred Durzak, *Zwischen Expressionismus und Symbolismus: Stefan George* (Stuttgart: Kohl-hammer, 1974), 30–4 and 34–43. Durzak's assertion, following Wilson, *Axel's Castle*, 17, that Poe's influence was overwhelmingly from his theory rather than his writings is questionable. Poe's images, scenes and atmospheres contributed towards a distinct sensibility that the French and Germans have traditionally estimated more than the Anglo-Saxon world. For an informative account of Poe's influence on Decadent literature in another context, see Raymond Furness, 'Trakl and the Literature of Decadence', in Walter Methlagl and W. E. Yuill (eds.), *Londoner Trakl-Symposion* (Salzburg: Müller, 1981), 85–91.

Cher Ennui, pour boucher d'une main jamais lasse
Les grands trous bleus que font méchamment les oiseaux.[50]

[Rise up, mists! Pour your dull ashes into the skies with long tatters of fog that will drown the pallid swamp of autumns, and build a great silent ceiling! And you, Dear Ennui, climb out of the hellish ponds, and as you go pick up the vase and the pale reeds so as to plug untiringly the great blue holes made mischievously by the birds!]

Both poems share a sense of the hostility of nature and the motif of picking flowers for a vase recalls Hofmannsthal's 'Die Töchter der Gärtnerin'. Most obviously, however, the Faun in 'Lehre' almost inevitably suggests Mallarmé's 'L'Après-midi d'un Faune' and when one considers that the giggling witches of 'Lehre' were whispering nymphs in the first draft, the echo is a little stronger. One of the drafts of *Der Tod des Tizian* from the same period makes an unambiguous reference to nymphs—'Badende Nymphen leuchten zwischen Lianen durch (oder sind es Schwäne)' [bathing nymphs gleam through the lianas (or are they swans)].[51] This suggests that 'Gefieder' in 'Lehre' may be a reference to the swan-nymphs of Mallarmé's poem, where 'une blancheur animale [ondoie] au repos' [an animal whiteness undulates at rest] and rises into 'ce vol de cygnes, non! de naïades' [a flight of swans, no! of naiads].[52] The transformation of nymphs into witches and the revision of white plumage to 'Nacht Gefieder' is an index of how Hofmannsthal felt threatened by the Symbolist's work. Gianino's speech in the prologue to *Der Tod des Tizian* registers equal anxiety when 'was da war, ist in mir in eins verflossen: | In *eine* überstarke schwere Pracht, / Die Sinne stumm und Worte sinnlos macht' [what was there has now melted within me into a unity, into a single overwhelming, heavy thing of splendour that dulls one's senses and makes one's words meaningless], where the last phrase is the most concrete suggestion that the anxiety is on one level literary.[53]

Considering the strong element of threat in 'Lehre', there is an odd note in the poem in the phrase 'sehnsuchtsschwere, bange Träume'. These may be echoes of the Faun's fantasies, but they also have something in common with Maeterlinck's melancholia. The exotic lianas, together with the waterlilies, suggest in fact a specific debt to 'Feuillage du cœur', from the *Serres chaudes* of 1891:

Sous la cloche de cristal bleu
De mes lasses mélancolies,

[50] Mallarmé, *OC*, 37.
[51] *Nachlaß*, E III 245.23 (N6 in *SW* iii. 249).
[52] Mallarmé, *OC*, 51.
[53] *SW* iii. 44, ll. 35–7.

Mes vagues douleurs abolies
S'immobilisent peu à peu:

Végétations de symboles,
Nénuphars mornes des plaisirs,
Palmes lentes de mes désirs,
Mousses froides, lianes molles.[54]

[Beneath the blue crystal dome of my weary melancholies, my vague extinguished pains are gradually immobilized: symbolic vegetation, doleful waterlilies of pleasure, slow palms of my desires, cold mosses, soft lianas.]

Hofmannsthal noted excerpts from this collection in his diary in 1892.[55] In this poem Maeterlinck begins with a personal sadness and moves to its exteriorization in the protected plants. Melancholy is cultivated as something rare and isolated; it loses its vigour and freezes or congeals. Then the correlation between symbol and emotion is extended to take into its interpretative range the symbolical activity itself. The phonetic echoes between 's'immobilisent' and 'symboles' suggest an analogy between the process of preservation and the process of symbolization—a symbol is itself a hot-house flower, tended and protected from the rough-and-tumble of straightforward discursive meaning.

In contrast, Hofmannsthal's plants are still bursting with malign energy. His process of symbolization is equally dynamic, being here one of cumulation and intensification. Where Maeterlinck chose his plant-symbols for their potential symbolic capacity and cultivated it by isolating them, Hofmannsthal allows the imagination to wallow, and as dreams rise as vapour from the swamp in line 8, so the symbolic potential of the scene rises from the imagination's secretions. These dreams are confused: they include blind animals and dead roots deemed unfit for dream as they yield no imaginative fruits ('taugen zu keinem Traume'); then the mimosas and the fauns are seen to be part of a dreamworld, too, but a part that the *Du* had thought belonged to a world beyond himself. The whole poem is, however, the product of a single fevered imagination (line 12), the external scene the symbol of an internal state. The import of the title is that this is a lesson both in the interpretation of the mind's movements and in how these are expressed or revealed in Symbolist poetry. The last line is a formulation of the poem's own function: the mind's eye has been weaving colourful marvels into the otherwise dim outside world.

The priority of the psyche over the outside world, and the tendency

---

[54] Maeterlinck, *Poésies complètes*, 109.   [55] *Nachlaß*, H VII 4.23–36. See above, p. 67.

to see the world as a repertory of forms expressive of human emotion are characteristic of French Symbolism in general, but a brief comparison with a poem by Verlaine will show more clearly some points of contact. 'Promenade sentimentale' from *Poèmes saturniens* also reflects the self's inner states in a walk by a pool, and also pulls the comparison to the surface:

> Le couchant dardait ses rayons suprêmes
> Et le vent berçait les nénuphars blêmes;
> Les grands nénuphars entre les roseaux
> Tristement luisaient sur les calmes eaux.
> Moi j'errais tout seul, promenant ma plaie
> Au long de l'étang, parmi la saulaie
> Où la brume vague évoquait un grand
> Fantôme laiteux se désespérant
> Et pleurant avec la voix des sarcelles
> Qui se rappelaient en battant des ailes
> Parmi la saulaie où j'errais tout seul
> Promenant ma plaie; et l'épais linceul
> Des ténèbres vint noyer les suprêmes
> Rayons du couchant dans ses ondes blêmes
> Et les nénuphars, parmi les roseaux,
> Les grands nénuphars sur les calmes eaux.[56]

[The setting sun emitted its last rays and the wind cradled the pale waterlilies; the great waterlilies between the reeds glowed sadly on the calm waters. I was wandering alone, walking my wound by the pond, amongst the willows where the vague mist looked like a great milky phantom in despair, weeping with the voice of the teal calling to each other and beating their wings amongst the willows where I was wandering alone, walking my wound; and the dense shroud of darkness came and drowned the last rays of the setting sun in its pale waves and the waterlilies, amongst the reeds, the great waterlilies on the calm waters.]

Calm waters indicate almost the opposite state to the one which Hofmannsthal's disturbed pool ultimately evokes, although 'wo der Wind mit den Lianen plätschert' near the beginning of 'Lehre' corresponds to some extent with 'le vent berçait les nénuphars'. Hofmannsthal's waterlilies breathe dreams heavy with longing, and Verlaine's willow grove breathes a mist that evokes a milky phantom that in turn weeps with the cry of the teal calling to each other as they beat their wings, matching the plumage that shushes through the twigs in 'Lehre'. Hofmannsthal's greatest debt to Verlaine is not the imagery but his technique of lulling the reader by his sinuous syntax into the

[56] Verlaine, *OPC*, 70–1.

state where landscape and psyche seem naturally to express each other, prominent in all the 'Paysages tristes'. The résumé above of the chain of effects from the willow grove suggests something of this fluidity. Verlaine's repetition of lines, or of elements from one line rearranged for another in different syntactic relations, is one important element of this effect in this and others of the 'Paysages tristes'. In 'Promenade sentimentale', 'les grand nénuphars entre les roseaux' in line 3 is the subject of the verb 'luisaient', whereas almost the same words in lines 15 and 16, 'les nénuphars, parmi les roseaux', are the object of 'noyer', the shift, although semantically important, being almost imperceptible.

'Lehre' has elements of this unsettling Verlainean fluidity and its descendant, a Mallarméan syntactic obscurity. There is a characteristically structured start, two wo-clauses dependent on 'Teich', echoed by a third in verse 2.[57] After a grammatically contextless 'Nacht' the disembodied 'Gefieder . . . huscht' is also dependent on 'wo'. 'Hexen kichern' must be, too, but since for the sake of the rhyme 'kichern' has been shifted to a position more suggestive of a main clause, the structure begins to tremble; the last line and a half of this verse have therefore a more paratactic effect. Lack of punctuation blurs the syntactic boundaries throughout: at first sight there is the possibility of an enjambement from line 6 to line 7, but it is cancelled by the verb 'liegen'—whose subject, 'Wasserrosen', is oddly separated by a comma from its clause, giving an effect of dislocation. That comma has further consequences, since at first it suggests waterlilies as a subject for 'athmen' (the clause spreading across lines 7 and 8 and leaving 'liegen' hovering; the lilies growing out of the brown marsh and producing dreams with their scent). But when 'Träume' arise there is doubt as to whether 'athmen' is transitive after all. There is even a hint that 'bange Träume' might be co-subject with 'Kalter Schauer und Tollheit' of 'wohnen'; 'sehnsuchtsschwere' would be suggestive as a noun, too, the object of 'athmen'. None of these ghostly syntactic rearrangements ultimately proves satisfying, but at first and even in later readings they hover and destabilize the ordering of the text as it stands. The poem is unfinished, and these may be details for Hofmannsthal to have tidied, but this version reflects a murkiness in Hofmannsthal's thinking that reflects his attitude to his material.

The physical environment of this poem, the swampy jungle grove, is

---

[57] See the 'Terzinen über Vergänglichkeit' for a similar structure, this time with a series of 'daß'-clauses (SW i. 45).

the imagistic precipitate of a form of 'Tollheit' that the syntactic incoherence has heightened. As a projection of a troubled psyche (real or imagined) using the growths of imagination in a tense external scene, 'Lehre' is perhaps an unexceptional example of a device often used. At first Hofmannsthal's poem seems to evoke little more than mere feverishness, and if closer attention reveals traces of its being more deliberate and constructed than the state of mind itself would suggest, its Symbolist context enhances the reading still further. It legitimizes a self-reflexive interpretation, for dreams are cognate with the imaginative manipulation of words in poetry. 'Träume sind in dir' is not accidentally similar to 'Du hast mich an Dinge gemahnet, | Die heimlich in mir sind' from 'Einem, der vorübergeht', and its other overlaps with 'Lehre' are equally instructive. George is identified with some of the components of the sinister landscape in which 'Lehre' takes place—'Du warst . . . der nächtige, flüsternde Wind'; the circumstances in which George's inspiration acts are also those in which the subconscious dreams of the *Ich* in 'Lehre' are precipitated, amid 'das Rufen der athmenden Nacht'; and whilst breathing is the action of night in 'Lehre', it is that of the soul in 'Der Prophet'. 'Der Traum' has become 'sehnsuchtsschwere, bange Träume'; and what was 'leises Zittern' in 'Einem, der vorübergeht' has been intensified to 'kalter Schauer und Tollheit'. This intensification perhaps constitutes grounds for regarding the poem as a development of 'Einem, der vorübergeht' and thus dating it after December 1891.

'Einem, der vorübergeht' identifies one of the conditions of receptiveness as the time 'wenn draußen die Wolken gleiten | Und man aus dem Traum erwacht'. The moment is elaborated upon in the poem simply entitled 'Wolken':

> Am nächtigen Himmel
> Ein Drängen und Dehnen:
> Wolkengewimmel
> In hastigem Sehnen.
>
> In lautloser Hast
> —Von welchem Zug
> Gebietend erfaßt?—
> Gleitet ihr Flug...
>
> Es schwankt gigantisch
> Im Mondesglanz
> Auf meiner Seele
> Ihr Schattentanz,

Wogende Bilder:
Kaum noch besonnen
Wachsen sie wilder,
Sind sie zerronnen.

Ein loses Schweifen..
Ein Halb-versteh'n..
Ein flüchtig-Ergreifen...
Ein Weiterwehn...

Ein lautloses Gleiten,
Ledig der Schwere,
Durch aller Weiten
Blauende Leere.[58]

[In the night sky there is an urging and a stretching: throngs of clouds in hasty long-ing. In soundless haste—grasped by what commanding pull?—their flight glides along. Their shadowy dance sways massively over my soul in the light of the moon, surging images: hardly thought out, they grow ever more wildly and trickle away. A loose roaming, a half-understanding, a fleeting grasp, a blowing on past, a soundless gliding, untroubled by weight, through the intense blue emptiness of every expanse.]

The first of the three manuscript versions of 'Wolken' preserved is dated 16 March (certainly 1891, before Hofmannsthal met Bahr and George); the second was probably written in late December 1891 around the time of the poetry reading at Schnitzler's house.[59] Steven Sondrup concludes of the differences that they show the effects of a more concentrated reading and discussion of Symbolism, resulting in a shift from directness in early drafts to allusiveness in the later versions.[60] Certainly the poem itself becomes more concentrated, and the final version is only about a third as long as the first drafts. What is now missing is the overt depiction of a situation in which the observing speaker looks up at the moving clouds, the speaker's explicit reflections on what the clouds suggest is absent from his own life. In one version the clouds actually begin to speak to the observer.[61] The symbolic

[58] This is the version in *SW* i. 23, but incorporates the correction of 'begonnen' to 'besonnen' in line 14 made by Andreas Thomasberger, *Verwandlungen*, 62 n. 7, after close scrutiny of the manuscripts.

[59] See *SW* i. 144–6 and Thomasberger, *Verwandlungen*, 58. But cf. also Sondrup, *Hofmanns-thal and the French Symbolist Tradition*, 60, referring to Eugene Weber, 'A Chronology of Hofmannsthal's Poems', *Euphorion*, 63 (1969), 294–7.

[60] For a very detailed exposition of the changes between the Mar. 1891 versions and those from December, see Thomasberger, *Verwandlungen*, 55–78.

[61] Thomasberger summarizes: 'Die Themen des Gedichts, besonders die Problematik einer Übereinkunft von Seele und Gestalt, eines entsprechenden Haltenkönnens des

suggestion in the final version is much less deliberate and obvious, and operates mostly via overlaps of literal and metaphorical language. 'Drängen und Dehnen' evoke clusters of clouds primarily through spatial suggestions; 'Dehnen' alone is less susceptible to more than physical or temporal interpretation, but 'Drang' has overtones of enthusiasm and non-physical energy which are picked up by the rhyme-word 'Sehnen'. Longing, strictly, only has an emotional component, but its spatial suggestions arise in connection with the movement of clouds on the night sky and because of the phonetic connections of 'Sehnen' with the other words.

'Hast' is transferred to the next stanza, and with it the accumulated interpretative range of the first. A personal, even ethical dimension is added with the word 'gebietend', so that a curiosity is stimulated as to the motivation, the governing impulses of the cloud movement (gusts of wind) and also of the mental vacillations. There is a slight tension between 'gebietend' and 'gleitet', the one strongly authoritative, the other more relaxed, which keeps this curiosity in play. 'Gebietend' only appears from the version of the poem written around the time of Hofmannsthal's acquaintance with George. Its power is transferred to 'gigantisch' to describe the effect of the projection of the night-sky scene on to the soul of the *Ich*. 'Schwanken' here combines literal and metaphorical dimensions, reflecting the instability of the cloud pictures of verse 4 and the mental inability to hold on to hopes and understandings. The metaphorical 'Ergreifen' returns to its physical roots whilst maintaining its intellectual suggestions, and in combination with 'Weiterweh'n' it picks up the tension that was noted between 'gebieten' and 'gleiten'.

As if to confirm this, 'Gleiten' introduces the next and last stanza, and the soul—or the clouds, perhaps—is given free flight into an infinity of blue sky. The repetition of 'lautlos' almost suggests silent cinema. It is as if the *Ich* is sitting in a darkened room (or, *mutatis mutandis*, Plato's cave) watching his own soul projected on to the ceiling, becoming lost in the contemplation of the free play of his own emotions. The dynamic aspect of the higher world that both contains and reflects the motions of the observer's soul is suggested by the neologistic participle-form of the adjective 'blau' that qualifies 'Leere'. Blue features importantly in notes on Symbolism that Hofmannsthal

---

Dynamischen, scheinen mit der kürzeren Reinschriftfassung noch mehr in die Sprache gebracht. Weg fällt die Strophe, die noch von Bildern, nicht in Bildern sprach' (ibid. 64).

made towards the end of 1892,[62] and its importance here has more than once been linked to Mallarmé's poem 'L'Azur', in which the infinite blue sky's 'sereine ironie . . . accable . . . le poëte impuissant qui maudit son génie' [serene irony overwhelms the powerless poet who curses his genius] and haunts him in perpetuity.[63] Characteristically, however, Hofmannsthal mutates the threat into a promise.

Throughout the poem the literal and the metaphorical swim into each other's territory, and these overlaps are the symbolism. It is impossible to imagine a pre-existing mood, and the changes that were made during the poem's genesis point less to such a sharp implied division between content (mood) and form than to a striving to make the poem more densely meaningful. Hans Steffen sees this poem as rich in elements of movement but poor in imagery, and suggests that the stanzas could be spun out endlessly and are ultimately 'untereinander austauschbar' [mutually interchangeable].[64] If any of this were true, it would produce an Impressionist poem of mood-evocation essentially focused on the depiction and perception of the outside world, rather than the carefully structured Symbolist poem that Hofmannsthal has written in which the language makes self and world mutually defining.

Of the other poems written in December 1891, 'Stille' partakes less completely than 'Mein Garten', 'Die Töchter' or 'Lehre' of the exotic imagery, but it has traces of the mirroring of two types of symbolic descriptions that the first two of these evinced. It is dominated by sensations of oppression:

> Trübem Dunst entquillt die Sonne
> Zähen grauen Wolkenfetzen..
> Hässlich ist mein Boot geworden
> Alt und morsch mit wirren Netzen.
>
> Gleichgetöntes Wellenplätschern
> Schlägt den Kiel (er schaukelt träge)
> Und die Flut mit Schaum und Flecken
> Zeichnet nach die Spur der Wege.
>
> Ferne vor dem trüben Himmel
> Schweben graziöse Schatten
> —Helles Lachen schallt herüber—
> Gleiten Gondeln flink die glatten

---

[62] See above, p. 121.

[63] Mallarmé, *OC*, 37–8. See Werner Kraft, 'Die Wolken', in *Augenblicke der Dichtung* (Munich: Kosel-Verlag, 1964), 278–81, and Thomasberger, *Verwandlungen*, 68–9.

[64] Steffen, 'Hofmannsthals Übernahme der symbolistischen Technik', 275, 276 and 278.

Fackeln haben sie und Flöten
Und auf Polstern: Blumen, Frauen..
Langsam tauchen sie mir unter
In dem Dunst dem schweren grauen..

Stürme schlafen dort im Dunste:
Kämen sie noch heute abend
Zischend auf die glatte Öde
Wellentreibend brausend labend! (*SW* i. 21)

[The sun pours forth from murky haze and tough grey shreds of cloud; my boat has become hideous, old and rotten with tangled nets. The even-toned splash of the waves strikes at the keel (it rocks sluggishly) and the frothy, blotchy waters show the traces of its wake. Far away before the murky sky gracious shadows hover—bright laughter echoes across—and smooth gondolas nimbly glide: there are torches and flutes, and on their cushions are flowers and women. Slowly they sink away from me in the heavy grey haze. Storms are sleeping there in the haze: if only they would come this evening, flitting across the smooth barrenness, driving waves before them, thundering, refreshing!]

The overwhelming grey of the scene cannot suppress the glimmer of something brighter, and there is a tension in almost all the images. Even though 'trüber Dunst' is placed strongly at the opening, the sun 'entquillt', implying some vigour. The third line describes change over time and implies that ugliness is not the natural state but a regretted *development*. The traditional topos of the 'Kahnfahrt' (its attendant suggestions of progress and discovery echoed in 'Spur der Wege') avoids being overwhelmed by gloom with 'Wellenplätschern'; this is to some extent neutralized by 'gleichgetönt', but not wholly; neither are the potential positive overtones of 'schaukeln' quite negated by 'träge'. It is from this set of tensions that the emotional plausibility of the bright laughter is derived, and the smoothly skimming gondolas are not *just* opposites of the sluggish boat.

The sense of loss and regret that the first two stanzas communicate cast the happy boating party into the realm of the imagination. It is the imagination that takes over when, after the shadows of the gondolas have been seen afar and sounds have been heard at some distance ('schallt herüber'), the detail of the cushions and flowers is sketched in. The approach of the gondolas is at least as much a mnemonic process, the surfacing of suppressed happiness, as it is of recalling or inventing a scene spatially. And the gloom in which they disappear is emotional as well as scenic. The storm emerges from the gloom in which the boating party was submerged immediately before and represents the frustration of an imperfect melancholy, one in which the elements of previous happiness are still present as hopes. The speaker's wish is that elemental turmoil will at least provide the relief of outburst. The gondolas, however, are ill-equipped for such violence and the optative 'kämen' that wishes the storm upon them desires also a form of retribution for their insouciance. Once more there are faint similarities here with Mallarmé, and the poem that follows 'L'Azur' in *Poésies*, 'Brise marine'.[65] There the masts of the ships are described as 'invitant les orages' [inviting the storms], and the whole evokes 'un Ennui, désolé par les cruels espoirs' [an ennui, devastated by cruel hope]. The last line—'Mais, ô mon cœur, entends le chant des matelots!' [but, O heart, listen to the song of the sailors]—can be applied to 'Stille' as an injunction to listen for the laughter of the gondoliers, similarly focusing the effects of the people outside on the poet's emotional centre. The next poem in *Poésies*, 'Soupir', also has points of contact with 'Stille'— in particular the wake of the boat, 'sur l'eau morte où la fauve agonie | Des feuilles . . . creuse un froid sillon' [on the dead water where the brown agony of the leaves digs a cold furrow], and both poems may have contributed to the tone and imagery-range of Hofmannsthal's. 'Stille' evokes a complex *état d'âme*, the confusions hinted at from the outset in 'mit wirren Netzen'. The objects referred to are barely painted in at all, and the network of their impressions constitutes the substance of the poem. Hofmannsthal's understanding of Symbolism at this point, if less spiritually demanding than Mallarmé's, is certainly congruent with it. There are suggestions, too, of Verlaine, in the choice of the gondolas (a change made in the *Reinschrift* from 'Barken'), and the echoes and shadows of the boating party are simultaneously distant echoes of the faded Watteau characters of the *Fêtes galantes*.

There could be little in greater contrast to 'Wolken' than 'Werke sind todtes Gestein', a sequence of three epigrammatic distichs couplets redolent of Weimar. The classical echoes are so strong that at first sight it hardly looks as if the poem can have anything like the relationship with Symbolism of the others on Hofmannsthal's list so far examined.

> 'Werke' sind todtes Gestein, dem tönenden Meißel entsprungen,
>   Wenn am lebendigen Ich meißelnd der Meister erschuf..
> 'Werke' verkünden den Geist, wie Puppen den Falter verkünden:
>   'Sehet, er ließ mich zurück, leblos, und flatterte fort'...

---

[65] Mallarmé, *OC*, 38. This poem was published in translation in the *Blätter für die Kunst*, 1.2 (1893), 55.

'Werke', sie gleichen dem Schilf, dem flüsternden Schilfe des Midas,
  Streuen Geheimnisse aus, wenn sie schon längst nicht mehr wahr... (*SW* ii. 68)

['Works' are dead stone that escaped from the sounding chisel when the master
created them, chiselling away at a living self. 'Works' proclaim the spirit, as the
chrysalis does the butterfly: 'See! he left me behind, lifeless, and fluttered away.'
'Works' are like the reeds, the whispering reeds of Midas, they strew secrets
around, even those that have not been true for a long time.]

The view of the work of art presented here looks very negative. The
word 'Werke' is in distancing, almost mocking, inverted commas on
every occasion, and this also suggests that Hofmannsthal might have
literary works in mind as well as works of art in general. They are the
dead product of the artist's processing of his living self, or the empty
chrysalis left behind when the living butterfly has flown away, or they
betray long out-of-date secrets. The second version of the poem, completed a day later on 21 January 1892, ends differently, and the last line
reads, 'Midas ist lange schon todt, aber es flüstert noch fort...' [Midas
is long dead, but they go on whispering]. This might imply that the
whispering of the reeds—the work's capacity for communication—is
even more pointless since the subject of the message is now long dead;
alternatively it might suggest that even after the death of the individual
art has the capacity to communicate.

A pentameter such as 'Wenn am lebendigen Ich meißelnd der
Meister erschuf' with the sound-play of 'meißeln/Meister/erschuf',
could almost have figured in the *Römische Elegien* alongside the famous
line 'Sehe mit fühlendem Aug', fühle mit sehender Hand' [I see with a
feeling eye, I feel with a seeing hand].[66] But 'das lebendige Ich' is a very
un-Goethean phrase: Goethe's fifth Roman Elegy celebrates the meeting of art and life with the poet tapping out hexameters on the woman's
naked back and appreciating the forms of statues as he appreciates the
woman's curves. He experiences and enjoys life, and hence art, without needing to reassure himself of his identity so emphatically.
Hofmannsthal's poem has none of this confidence, although the contrast with Goethe is particularly pertinent since Hofmannsthal's
metaphorical comparison of 'Werke' with Midas's reeds echoes the
twentieth of the *Römische Elegien* ('Zieret Stärke den Mann'). Here
Goethe is wondering in whom he can confide now that he is bursting
with enthusiasm for his new erotic vigour: neither men nor women will
do, and to declare himself to the craggy landscape is the pose of youth.
He has compared his secret to Midas's desire to hide his ass's ears, a

[66] Goethe, *Werke*, i. 160.

wish too energetic to be kept by the reeds, and finally decides, 'Dir, Hexameter, dir Pentameter, sei es vertrauet | Wie sie des Tags mich erfreut, wie sie des Nachts mich beglückt' [let me confide in you, hexameter, and you, pentameter, how she pleases me during the day, how she delights me at night].[67] None of Goethe's confidence is inherited with his metre, however, for Hofmannsthal is too much a product of an age that questions the status and function of art.

The idea of a work of art, a poem in particular, as an object chiselled from a strong, resistant material owes much to the Parnassians' cult of form:

> Oui, l'œuvre sort plus belle
> D'une forme au travail
>   Rebelle,
> Vers, marbre, onyx, émail.[68]

[Yes, the work emerges more beautifully from a form when worked on, verse, marble, onyx or enamel.]

But in this programmatic poem, entitled simply 'L'Art', Gautier speaks only of the medium, the words themselves, whereas for Hofmannsthal it is the self that is worked on by the sculptor's chisel. Gautier's concentration on form has as its end the preservation of the work of art itself, reminiscent in this context of George's painted *Infante*:

> Tout passe—L'art robuste
> Seul à l'éternité,
>   Le buste
> Survit à la cité.

[Everything passes—art alone is robust for eternity, the bust survives the city.]

Gautier's poem ends with an important stanza indicating that the function of form is to capture and preserve the artist's dream in perpetuity:

> Sculpte, lime, ciselle;
> Que ton rêve flottant
>   Se scelle
> Dans le bloc résistant!

[Sculpt, file, chisel, may your floating dream be sealed in the unyielding block.]

---

[67] Goethe, *Werke*, i. 173.
[68] Théophile Gautier, 'L'Art', from *Émaux et camées*, ed. Jean Pommier and Georges Matoré (Lille: Giard-Droz, 1947), 130.

But despite its end-position and the stress the idea receives as the culmination of the poem's development, the other thirteen stanzas are so loving in their attention to the work itself that the final and dominant impression is not of the artist's conception but of his material creation.

Some of this is captured in Hofmannsthal's couplets, especially in their second version. Even if the works are 'dead', they are at least solid; even if they represent the empty hull rather than the living body, they none the less 'verkünden den Geist', triumphantly announce its existence; they outlive their creator and can continue speaking after his death. But Hofmannsthal's 'Geist' is vulnerable without the prop either of Goethe's sensual enjoyment or of Gautier's love (equally if differently sensual) of solid verse. Goethe confided his feelings gladly to strong poetry; Gautier's art is 'fier et charmant', cast in bronze (stanza 6) and depicts gods and emperors (stanzas 7 and 12). The comparison is invited by the use of the chisel-and-stone image, but despite a grander gesture in that image, 'dem tönenden Meißel', Hofmanns-thal's quasi-theoretical statement on the functioning of art shows him in contrast as defensive.

Part of this defensiveness is explained—again in the specific context of Symbolism—by a closer investigation of the inverted commas that always enclose the word 'Werke'. The reading above places 'works' in opposition to 'life' or the artist, the poet himself. But a diary note from 28 May 1891 suggests another possible construction—it is the continuation of the record of the conversation about Maeterlinck and Symbolism quoted at the beginning of this chapter. The question had been whether it was possible for an author to write just for himself and a few initiates without thinking of the wider public. Hofmannsthal and Bahr both agreed that this was perfectly possible; Gustav Schwarzkopf was less than perfectly convinced:

Ich [Hofmannsthal] frage Schwarzkopf, warum denn Gericault für 3 Bilder 1000 Skizzen malen sollte, und der Schriftsteller nur 'Werke'. Bekomme 4 Antworten: 1.) verkaufen die Maler auch ihre Studien und Skizzen wie wirkliche Werke 2.) seien eine Menge unserer 'Werke' in der That nichts als Skizzen 3.) sei das wieder Kunst für Künstler 4.) skizziere der Schriftsteller eben in Gedanken. Bahr fände es sehr lehrreich, wenn man mehr skizzierte, etwa alle Kaffeehausbekannten bei einer Revolution; ich meine, man sollte von einem Psychologen verfasste Fragebogen ausfüllen. Korff wirft ein, dass wir einander zu wenig kennen, um einander richtig zu characterisieren. Streit. Bahr und ich stehen auf Seite der Halbbekanntschaft, der Anticipation, die andern wollen gründliches Studium.[69]

[69] *Nachlaß*, H VII 17.6^b / 77^a and *SW* ii. 297.

[I ask Schwarzkopf why Géricault made 1,000 sketches for 3 pictures when the writer only produced 'works'. I get 4 answers: (1) the painters sell their studies and sketches in the same way as finished works, (2) a good many of our 'works' are in fact no more than sketches, (3) this is just art for artists again, (4) the writer sketches in his thoughts. Bahr said he would find it very instructive if we sketched more, say, our circle of acquaintances from the Café during a revolution. Korff objects that we do not know each other well enough to capture each other's character properly. Debate. Bahr and I are in favour of imperfect acquaintance, of anticipation, the others want a more serious investigation.]

'Werke' here are opposed to 'Skizzen', the well-wrought, rounded, polished kind of art set against the fragmentary and the approximate—precisely the kind of work that the discussion has suggested Maeterlinck's plays represent. Of the four answers, the third merely brackets off the visual arts unhelpfully; the first and second both destabilize the notion of 'the finished work', and the fourth re-establishes its importance again, since the thoughts (the equivalent to the preliminary sketches) are unavailable. Hofmannsthal favours the responses that privilege insight into the processes of art or imaginatively project a picture from a few external details (the 'sketch' of the denizens of the Griensteidl in the event of a revolution, for example, based on only a partial acquaintance). Symbolism was just such an approximate art, inviting imaginative participation and eschewing the lapidary, although in the hands of practitioners such as Mallarmé, precision of form was more important than Hofmannsthal is concerned with here.

Hofmannsthal seems to have written 'Werke sind todtes Gestein' as a response to this conversation in May 1891, then written it out again, perhaps for public recitation, in the context of the 'Symbolistenstreit' in early 1892. Formulating it in the classical metre of elegiac distichs ironically contrasts with the point he is making. It also makes clear the extent to which Hofmannsthal is cut off from the two strong but very different traditions of Goethe and the Parnassians. It is a curious, somewhat confused and ambivalent poem, for if on the one hand Hofmannsthal is defending a kind of Symbolism, he is also unwilling to condemn the older traditions and allows their independently standing 'Werke' a degree of communicative power. There is an element of this view in Rimbaud's conception of poetry, too, although the emphasis is quite different. Rimbaud declares, 'la chanson est si peu souvent l'œuvre, c'est-à-dire la pensée chantée *et comprise* du chanteur' [the song is so rarely the work, that is to say the singer's thought, sung and understood].[70] His famous *lettres du voyant* postulate a view of artistic creation as happening independently of the individual conscious personality of the artist:

Car Je est un autre. Si le cuivre s'éveille clairon, il n'y a rien de sa faute. Cela m'est évident: j'assiste à l'éclosion de ma pensée; je la regarde, je l'écoute: je lance un coup d'archet: la symphonie fait son remuement dans les profondeurs, ou vient d'un bond sur la scène.[71]

[For 'I' is someone else. If the brass turns out to be a trumpet, it is not of its own doing. This is clear to me: I am present at the flowering of my thought; I watch it, I listen to it: I make a movement with the bow: the symphony stirs in the depths or leaps in a single bound on to the stage.]

There is a dimension to the self, according to Rimbaud, that merely observes the true activity of the subconscious creating self. But for Rimbaud, the artist is unimportant because only the song counts, whilst 'Werke' suggests that alongside the increasing instability of the self, Hofmannsthal is not confident of the inherent linguistic and structural strengths of the work of art and calls it 'todtes Gestein' and 'leblos'. His poetic identity has thus been robbed of almost all possibility of support, and there is nothing to withstand the buffets of tradition or transform their energy into original poetry.

Some of the responsibility must be laid at the door (the slammed door) of George personally. Related questions of poetic selfhood are raised by the poem on Hofmannsthal's list that dates from more than a year before, the 'Ghasel' written in October 1890. It is first on the list, which must indicate some certainty in Hofmannsthal's mind that its style and technique are vitally Symbolist. Its inclusion points to an early component of Hofmannsthal's understanding of Symbolism that has affinities with the Romantic idea of nature being a universal symbol, to be deciphered by the poet's magical capabilities, as in Eichendorff's famous poem, 'Schläft ein Lied in allen Dingen' [a song slumbers in all things]. Hofmannsthal's *Ghasel* speaks of the poet's special power to conjure magical properties from the apparently ordinary outside world:

Das längst Gewohnte, das alltäglich Gleiche,
Mein Auge adelt mir's zum Zauberreiche:
Es singt der Sturm sein grollend Lied für mich,
Für mich erglüht die Rose, rauscht die Eiche.
Die Sonne spielt auf gold'nem Frauenhaar

[70] Rimbaud, *Poésies*, 201.   [71] Ibid. 202.

Für mich,—und Mondlicht auf dem stillen Teiche.
Die Seele les' ich aus dem stummen Blick,
Und zu mir spricht die Stirn, die schweigend bleiche.
Zum Traume sag' ich: 'Bleib' bei mir, sei wahr!'
Und zu der Wirklichkeit: 'Sei Traum, entweiche!'
Das Wort, das Andern Scheidemünze ist,
Mir ist's der Bilderquell, der flimmernd reiche.
Was ich erkenne, ist mein Eigenthum
Und lieblich locket, was ich *nicht* erreiche.
Der Rausch ist süß, den Geistertrank entflammt,
Und süß ist die Erschlaffung auch, die weiche.
So tiefe Welten thu'n sich oft mir auf,
Daß ich d'rein glanzgeblendet zögernd schleiche,
Und einen gold'nen Reigen schlingt um mich
Das längst Gewohnte, das alltäglich Gleiche. (*SW* i. 10)

[Things that are long familiar, the same every day are made by my eye into a magic realm: the storm sings its rumbling song for me, the rose glows with passion for me, the oak rustles and the sun plays on women's golden hair, and moonlight on the silent pool,—for me! I can read someone's soul from its silent gaze, and a pale, silent brow speaks to me. I can say to the dream, 'Stay with me, be true!' and to reality, 'Be dream, vanish!' The word that is a mere external token to others is to me the richly flickering source of images. What I recognize is my property and what I cannot reach is sweetly enticing. Intoxication is sweet when it has been aroused by the magic potion, and soft relaxation, too, and such deep worlds often open up for me that I slip inside them, blinded by their magnificence, tentative, and a golden round-dance wraps around me things that are long familiar, the same every day.]

The poet is the conductor of an enormous symphony, or he is like Prospero, with the power to switch between dream and reality. There is even some overlap of imagery between 'Für mich' and Prospero's monologue abjuring magic:

> . . . to the dread rattling thunder
> Have I given fire, and rifted Jove's stout oak
> With his own bolt. (*The Tempest*, v. i)

Hofmannsthal's *Ich* in the 'Ghasel' is elated, confident and superior. Dumb humanity is an open book, for he reads the soul from the eyes, the mind from the forehead[72]—and in turn he has at his disposal the means to write the book with his fountain of images. The poem is structured to reflect this interactive relationship. The first line makes the world subject to the poet's imperious glance and lays it open to

---

[72] 'Zu mir spricht die Stirn' becomes 'fremd ist Stirn und Haar' in 'Der Prophet'.

receive his ennobling inspiration. Proceeding by a series of oppositions (ordinary/magical; sun/moon; dream/reality; common word/poetic image; familiar/alien and enticing) it presents the *Ich* as blinded by the richness of the world. Finally, the ordinary world is transformed into the *agent* of poetic inspiration, binding the poet into a dance. The first line is repeated as the last line, but where 'das längst Gewohnte, das alltäglich Gleiche' began as the object of 'adeln', it ends as the subject of 'schlingen', wrapping the poet into reciprocity with his world. The technique will have been familiar from Verlaine, in particular from 'Crépuscule du soir mystique' which performs the same circle with 'Le Souvenir avec le Crépuscule', taking thirteen lines to transform the subject-phrase into the object-phrase of the same sentence.[73]

'Für mich' was included on Hofmannsthal's list perhaps because magical penetration into the outside world derives from the linguistic articulation of the pairs of opposites, and there is a characteristically modern touch to the quasi-epiphanic revelations in the ordinary, 'das *längst Gewohnte*'. Nevertheless, the debt in the poem is clearly more to Romanticism than to Symbolism, which accounts for the confidence with which it instinctively lives. It is the earliest poem on Hofmannsthal's list, finished over a year before the 'Symbolistenstreit'. The other seven poems all show material similarities with the French Symbolist poets' work and outlook: the range of imagery is often the same and (with the exception of the earliest) there is a shared fascination with the idea of seduction that echoes both Mallarmé and Verlaine. Most important, there is a critical interest in the business of writing poetry and the function of art displayed by all the poems. The poems by George that Hofmannsthal identified as Symbolist manifest imagery, attention to the importance of sound, a conception of poetry as a priestly service, and the paradox of election and curse as simultaneous parts of the poetic vocation that are identifiably Symbolist in character. The implicit attitude to language and its transforming power, too, was learned in part from Mallarmé.

Like Hofmannsthal's own poems, George's indicate sometimes a deliberate, critical response to Symbolism, lacking the confidence of spontaneous transformation of the tradition. Although both share the distance of the latecomer, George's poems do not manifest Hofmannsthal's frequently overt anxiety towards Symbolism, suggesting that even at the height of his interest in the movement he felt the need to retreat from it, propelled by an instinct to preserve his poetic

[73] See above, p. 180.

identity. By way of conclusion, an examination of both his and George's responses to a poem by Baudelaire may illustrate how their different expectations of their relationship parallel their contrasting attitudes to Symbolism; at the same time it offers an answer to the question of how significant Hofmannsthal judged George's mediation of the French tradition to be. On 21 December 1891 Hofmannsthal sent George 'Einem, der vorübergeht', a poem that symbolizes the action of inspiration and which comments on George's role in bringing out Hofmannsthal's Symbolist interests:

> Du hast mich an Dinge gemahnet,
> Die heimlich in mir sind,
> Du warst für die Saiten der Seele
> Der nächtige, flüsternde Wind
>
> Und wie das rätselhafte,
> Das Rufen der athmenden Nacht,
> Wenn draußen die Wolken gleiten
> Und man aus dem Traum erwacht:
>
> Zu weicher blauer Weite
> Die enge Nähe schwillt,
> Durch Pappeln vor dem Monde
> Ein leises Zittern quillt ...[74]

[You have urged me to recognize things that are secretly present within me. You were the whispering wind at night for the strings of my soul. And like the mysterious calling of the living night, when the clouds are slipping past outside and you are waking from a dream: the narrow nearness swells into soft, blue distance, a gentle trembling bubbles up through the poplars before the moon.]

The process of inspiration is symbolized by the wind operating on the speaker as it does on an Aeolian harp, and drawing out its innate musical possibilities. The image of the Aeolian harp may be a modified echo, conscious or otherwise, of Saint-Pol-Roux's contribution to Huret's *Enquête*:

Dans la religion poétique, l'âme est une harpiste dont la harpe est le corps: harpe à *cinq* cordes. Pincez une seule corde, vous avez la voix dans le désert égoïste et partial: pincez les cinq, voici l'expansive charité, voici la symphonie. . . .
    Le poète se peut donc comparer, organiquement parlant, à une harpe

---

[74] *SW* ii. 60, 'erste Fassung'. This is one of the versions that Hofmannsthal sent to George on Monday, 21 Dec. 1891 (the other is almost identical except that some of the punctuation is altered and it is written without capital letters, *à la* George). The 'zweite Fassung' is the version Hofmannsthal entered in his diary.

supérieure s'adressant aux harpes moindres des peuples. Les vibrations de celle-là doivent éoliennement vitaliser celles-ci.[75]

[In the religion of poetry the soul is a harpist whose instrument is the body: a harp with five strings. Pluck a single string and you will have the partial, selfish voice in the desert: pluck all five and you have expansive charity, the symphony. The poet, therefore, can be compared, organically speaking, with a superior harp addressing itself to the lesser harps of the peoples. Its vibrations must set theirs into motion 'aeolianly'.]

For Hofmannsthal, the process of inspiration is unsettling ('heimlich', 'rätselhaft').[76] The initially substantive *Du* and *Ich* soon melt into shadows and abstracts beyond the speaker's control ('Weite', 'Nähe'); the process culminates in the last line in a disembodied trembling (whose?) perceived (by whom?) through the poplars. It is hard to identify the precise source of the fear: it may be fear of the *Du*, or nerves at what might be found within the self, for the revelation of deep private concerns is an intimidating rite of passage.

George had recently translated Baudelaire's 'A une passante' under the title 'Einer Vorübergehenden', and Hofmannsthal's original heading had been 'Einem Vorübergehenden', which suggests he knew both original and translation and had them in mind when writing.[77] This is confirmed by another text, the autobiographical fragment 'Age of Innocence' (February 1892), where Hofmannsthal quotes the last two lines of the Baudelaire poem and prefaces them with the remark, 'es geht immerfort die Wahrheit an uns vorbei, die wir vielleicht hätten verstehen können, und die Frau die wir vielleicht hätten lieben können' [the truth that we might perhaps have been able to comprehend is constantly passing us by, like the woman whom we might perhaps have been able to love].[78] He introduces this section, 'Kreuz-

---

[75] Huret, *Enquête*, 145.

[76] The image suggests an Aeolian harp but may in fact be a response to a passage in *Heinrich von Ofterdingen*: 'Es mag wohl wahr sein, daß eine besondere Gestirnung dazu gehört, wenn ein Dichter zur Welt kommen soll; denn es ist gewiß eine recht wunderbare Sache mit dieser Kunst. Auch sind die andern Künste gar sehr davon unterschieden . . . [in music] die Töne liegen schon in den Saiten, und es gehört nur eine Fertigkeit dazu, diese zu bewegen' (Novalis, *Schriften*, i. 209).

[77] Cf. *SW* ii. 282: the draft in question is 1H¹. Angelika Corbineau-Hoffmann, who investigates 'Vorübergehen' in a wider literary context as a characteristic 'Motif der Moderne' without following up Hofmannsthal's debt to Baudelaire, is probably right to regard the echo of Hugo's 'A un passant' as insignificant. See '". . . zuweilen beim Vorübergehen . . .": Ein Motiv Hofmannsthals im Kontext der Moderne', *Hofmannsthal-Jahrbuch*, 1 (1993), 240 n. 22.

[78] *SW* xxix. 20. There is another note headed 'XIX Jahrhundert' that has simply 'Baudelaire A une passante' at the end, after mentions of *Atala*, *Salammbô* and Pierre Loti (*Nachlaß*,

wege' or crossroads, with reflections on the endless possibilities of Fate
and the Greeks' apposite use of ' "Tyche", das Zufällig-Zugefallene'
['Tyche', the chance happening] to represent it. On 10 January 1892
Hofmannsthal excused his refusal to respond to George's pleas in the
latter's most overtly emotional letter with the words 'ich sehe keine
Schuld und kein Verdienst und keinen Willen der helfen kann, wo
Tyche rätselhaft wirkt' [I can see no guilt, no merit and no will that can
help when Tyche is acting mysteriously].[79] The same terms are used in
all the documents—a repetition of 'Tyche' in the prose passage and the
letter, 'rätselhaft' in the letter and the poem—and this suggests again
that Baudelaire's poem was a literary *point de repère* for Hofmannsthal's
understanding of his dealings with George.

Baudelaire presents the dramatic charm exercised by a brief,
unexpected encounter with a woman in mourning. She appears like a
flash of lightning in the confusion of the street, excites in the speaker a
'rebirth' or epiphanic self-revelation, and disappears forever without a
word, leaving the speaker to contemplate the painful emptiness of his
future. Lines 9–14 read thus:

> Un éclair... puis la nuit!—Fugitive beauté
> Dont le regard m'a fait soudain renaître,
> Ne te verrai-je plus que dans l'éternité?
>
> Ailleurs, bien loin d'ici! trop tard! *jamais* peut-être!
> Car j'ignore où tu fuis, tu ne sais où je vais
> Ô toi que j'eusse aimée, ô toi qui le savais![80]

[A flash of lightning, then night!—fugitive beauty whose glance has suddenly
renewed me, will I not see you again until eternity? Elsewhere, far away from here!
Too late! Never perhaps! For I do not know where you are running to, you do not
know where I am going, you whom I might have loved, you who knew that!]

George's translation of these lines changes their force somewhat:

> Ein strahl... dann nacht! o schöne wesenheit
> Die mich mit EINEM blicke neu geboren,
> Kommst du erst wieder in der ewigkeit?
>
> Verändert, fern, zu spät, auf stets verloren!
> Du bist mir fremd, ich ward dir nie genannt,
> Dich hätte ich geliebt, dich die's erkannt.[81]

H VB 8). It is on a scrap torn from a notebook, and to judge from the paper type dates from
Hofmannsthal's schooldays.

[79] George, *BW*, 14.
[80] Baudelaire, *OC*, i. 92.
[81] George, *Werke*, ii. 310.

[A beam of light, then night! O beautiful essence, you who have renewed me with a single glance, will you only return in eternity? Changed, distant, too late, lost forever! You are a stranger to me, you do not know my name, I could have loved you, you who knew that!]

George plays down the speaker's pain. He smooths out the rhythms at the beginning of the second tercet and neutralizes the desperate 'jamais' with the somewhat mannered 'auf stets'. Line 12 in George refers to *du*, in Baudelaire to *je*: in George's version it is the woman who is changed and out of reach, whereas in Baudelaire's original it is the speaker who will be in a distant time and place and who might never see her. 'Schöne wesenheit' is more calmly abstract than the intense 'beauté'; and 'fugitive' is missing altogether. Fleetingness is the defining characteristic of the experience Baudelaire evokes, and its omission renders the *presence* of the woman more of an unambiguous high-point than in the French poem. The tensions of Baudelaire's lyric speaker persist to the very last words: 'dich, die's erkannt' in George's poem almost says 'you passed by *because* you did not desire to return my love', whereas in Baudelaire 'ô toi qui le savais!' (with an exclamation mark inconceivable in the German) says 'you passed by *despite* seeing, and accepting, that I loved you'.[82]

'Einem, der vorübergeht' and Hofmannsthal's other references to *Tyche* give the impression that he was receptive to Baudelaire's treatment of the effects of chance in life, rather than of the persons involved in the chance encounter. George's translation of Baudelaire tends to personalize, and if the two German-speaking poets thought so differently about the potential stimuli of chance acquaintance, as is crystallized in their responses to Baudelaire's poem, it is small wonder that their friendship was troubled. Hofmannsthal was using the reference to Baudelaire implied in his title to warn George off; the poem itself is exactly what George first thought it was, an oblique statement that he was most valuable as a passing influence.[83]

[82] Trakl wrote a poem entitled 'Einer Vorübergehenden' in *c*.1909, also based on Baudelaire. The pain in this poem is shared by speaker and passer-by. Cf. Georg Trakl, *Das dichterische Werk* (Munich: Deutscher Taschenbuch Verlag, 1972), 150.

[83] George, *BW*, 2. Wendelin Schmidt-Dengler underestimates Baudelaire's effect on Hofmannsthal: noting the link between 'Einem, der vorübergeht' and 'A une passante', and the centrality of the motif of the night (which in Baudelaire is the *consequence* of the meeting, whereas in Hofmannsthal it operates as an *agent* of revelation), he concludes that Baudelaire is present 'als Symbolum, aber nicht als Anreger oder als Formengeber', which is only true to the extent that Hofmannsthal's poem is not based structurally on Baudelaire's. It is also inaccurate to say 'George hat die Absage erkannt, die ihm durch diesen Vergleich zuteil wurde.' See 'Französischer Symbolismus und Wiener Dekadenz', 74–5.

Andrian's notes for his contribution to Fiechtner's *Der Dichter im Spiegel der Freunde* state Hofmannsthal's attitude bluntly: 'Bewunderung für den Dichter u. Antipathie gegen den Menschen und Homosexuellen' [admiration for the poet and antipathy for the man and homosexual].[84] Whatever the difficulties in their personal relationship, the poet in George set in motion 'die Saiten der Seele' by stimulating Hofmannsthal's interest in Symbolism, but the interest was already present and there is no clear 'Übernahme der symbolistischen Technik' [adoption of the Symbolist technique] in December 1891, as Steffen holds. Hofmannsthal recalled in 1929,

daß die Begegnung von entscheidender Bedeutung war—die Bestätigung dessen, was in mir lag, die Bekräftigung, daß ich kein ganz vereinzelter Sonderling war, wenn ich es für möglich hielt, in der deutschen Sprache etwas zu geben, was mit den großen Engländern von Keats an sich auf einer poetischen Ebene bewegte und andererseits mit den festen romanischen Formen zusammenhing. . . . Ich fühlte mich unter den Meinigen,—ohne einen Schritt von mir selber weg tun zu müssen.[85]

[that the meeting was of decisive importance for me—the affirmation of what was within me, the confirmation that I was no isolated freak if I thought it possible that I might produce in German something that was on the same poetic level as the great English writers from Keats onwards and at the same time was consistent with solid Romance forms. I felt amongst friends,—without having to move an inch away from myself.]

This closely matches the suggestions of 'Einem, der vorübergeht' and seems not to have been distorted by time. Hofmannsthal's ambitions were substantial: to produce something comparable with the works of no less a writer than Keats, and to do so on behalf of the broader German poetic tradition. The recollection also highlights Hofmannsthal's need to *belong*; but the two impulses were scarcely compatible.

---

[84] From the unpublished *Tagebücher und Aufzeichnungen*, Deutsches Literaturarchiv, Marbach. Quoted by Rieckmann, *Aufbruch*, 76.

[85] Quoted from George, *BW*, 235–6.

4

THE CONSEQUENCES OF SYMBOLISM: HESITATIONS, PROBLEMS AND A SOLUTION

Certain features of a poet's work—images, preferred settings, character types, attitudes—recur frequently enough to be called characteristic. Before embarking on detailed analysis of selected poems from the early 1890s, it may be useful to identify, even somewhat schematically, some of these features in Hofmannsthal's verse.

The most powerful sensations in Hofmannsthal's verse are those derived from smell, often exotic, sometimes threatening, almost always intense: 'der Orchideen Duft'; 'Dies flüssig Gold heißt Gift und tödtet. | Wie gut es riecht'; 'ein Hauch verklärter Möglichkeiten. | Ein Morgen . . . Von kühlem Duft und Einsamkeit durchzogen'; 'dufterfüllte laue Schatten'; 'Von aller Liebe dufterfüllter Garten'; 'tannenduftiges Haar'; 'der Duft der Hyazinthen'; 'ein Duft von Wachs und Weihnachtsbäumen, | Und Moderduft von alten lieben Büchern'; 'der tiefe Duft von nächtigen Früchten'; 'der starke Duft der schwachen Frühlingsblumen'; 'deine Worte hatten einen Ton | So fremd wie Duft von Sandelholz und Myrrhen'—there are a hundred more examples.[1]

The hours in which Hofmannsthal finds greatest significance are those of evening. The clouds in 'Wolken' chase each other 'am nächtigen Himmel'; Hofmannsthal's sombre celebration of Grillparzer views the monument in the Volksgarten in the half-light, 'Es dämmert . . . Es ist dumpf und schwül. | Der Werktag geht zur Neige', and the evening is metonymically transferred to the man: 'so dämmern

---

[1] 'Gülnare', *SW* i. 11 (the fragrance of orchids); 'Das Mädchen und der Tod', *SW* ii. 79 (this liquid gold is poison and will kill. How good it smells); 'Leben', *SW* i. 28 (a breath of transfigured possibilities, a morning shot through with cool fragrances and loneliness); 'Idylle', *SW* iii. 59 (warm shadows full of fragrance, a garden filled with the fragrance of love); 'Weihnacht', *SW* I, 37 (hair smelling of fir trees); 'Ein Knabe', *SW* i. 58 (the scent of hyacinths); 'Prolog zu den lebenden Bildern', *SW* i. 38 (a fragrance of wax and Christmas trees, and the musty smell of beloved old books); 'Nach einer Dantelektüre', *SW* ii. 100 (the strong smell of fruit at night); 'Der Jüngling in der Landschaft', *SW* i. 65 (the strong smell of the tender spring flowers); 'Wir gingen einen Weg', *SW* i. 76 (the tone of your words was as strange as the smell of sandalwood and myrrh).

Augen, die der Tod umschleiert'. The love-poem 'Gülnare' starts when it is dark, when 'schimmernd gießt die Ampel Dämmerwogen um Dich her'. In 'Leben', life itself is at its most powerful in the evening: 'die Sonne sinkt den lebenleeren Tagen | Und sinkt der Stadt, vergoldend und gewaltig.' A poem from the *Nachlaß* entitled 'Sonne' opens 'Die Sonne ist *versunken*', preferring despite the promise of the title to evoke the continued glow of evening; and another about the first poetic stammerings of a young man begins by addressing 'Lichte Dämmerung der Gedanken' and, with Novalis, the free-soaring of creativity at night. A very large proportion of the poems written in the first five years of the so-called lyrical decade are set in the evening. Evening is often associated with Hofmannsthal's preferred season—not the most often invoked, which is spring—but the most suggestive, autumn, not the autumn of mists and mellow fruitfulness, but a dying autumn approaching winter. In the 'Ballade vom kranken Kind', the child's dying is set in an autumnal scene, 'rothgolden versank im Laub der Tag'; the falling fruit set the 'Ballade vom äußeren Leben' in autumn, too.[2]

Hofmannsthal wrote very few love-poems, and those he did write are about love itself rather than the woman as an object of the affection—'Frühe Liebe', for example, from the *Nachlaß*, where the beloved is allotted no more tangible attribute than 'Schönheit' (*SW* ii. 41). Comparing another, 'Mädchenlied', with its model, 'Gretchen am Spinnrad', one sees how all the emotion that makes Goethe's poem so painful has drained away, leaving only the rather mannered symbol 'Mein Schleier ist zerrissen.' Where Hofmannsthal writes of women, his evocations are macabre and bloodless, and usually concern adolescents rather than adults, as in 'Zuweilen kommen niegeliebte Frauen | Im Traum als kleine Mädchen uns entgegen.' In 'Die Stunden!', the silent contemplation of uninterrupted stretches of blue is equated with the comprehension of death, 'leicht und feierlich und ohne Grauen'. The same solemnity is, however, the immediate response of the small girls to the prospect of death. They are wide-eyed and '*sehr* blaß'—an

---

[2] 'Wolken', *SW* i. 23 (in the sky at night); 'Denkmal-Legende', *SW* i. 12 (it is growing dim, it is still and close, the working day is coming to an end, thus eyes grow dim that are veiled by death); 'Gülnare', *SW* i. 11 (the shimmering street lamp casts waves of twilight around you); 'Leben', *SW* i. 28 (the sun sinks on the days empty of life and on the city, mightily painting it in gold); 'Sonne', *SW* ii. 57 (the sun has sunk; my italics); 'Lichte Dämmerung der Gedanken', *SW* ii. 65 (pale half-light of one's thoughts; there are several echoes of Novalis in the four stanzas of the poem). 'Ballade vom kranken Kind', SW ii. 80 (red-gold, the sun sank in the leaves of the day); 'Ballade des äußeren Lebens', SW i. 44.

emphasis which suggests unnaturally or uncannily pale, as if their life blood has already seeped out into the trees and grass of line 9 before the chill of death comes upon them. The poem is based on the memory of a real child, and contains echoes of a description of her death written by a friend of Hofmannsthal's. She is here given the status of a type (since 'kleine Mädchen' is plural): in very special cases the understanding gained by distant meditation is achieved immediately and intensely by a dying person, whose knowledge is akin to the spiritual insight of a saint. Sainthood here is in turn equated with martyrdom, the gift of ignoring the immediacy of pain and death, and concentrating on the higher, eternal view where suffering is annulled. The paradox of a bloodless attitude to a bloody martyrdom is made possible by the mediating figure of the little girl. The agonies of the real-life Addah, who died of tuberculosis, have been filtered out, and death has been anaesthetized. The tendency is perpetuated in later work, too, as a sketch from 1897 makes clear: the title, 'Idylle: Schlafende' might suggest tenderness, but Hofmannsthal's jotting includes 'Mädchen: still wie auf ihrem eignen Sarkophag'.[3]

What makes such dry and emotionless poems the more striking is the musical fluency with which they are written. Music in Hofmannsthal's verse lulls and caresses: in 'Erlebnis' the transition from life to death is achieved 'mit einem tiefen Schwellen | Schwermütiger Musik'; the 'Epilog zu den lebenden Bildern' has 'so führt den Reih'n | Der Träum' in uns Musik mit leisem Locken | Und die Gedanken wandeln hintendrein'; 'süß-geheime, nie vernomm'ne Töne' fill the world in 'Was ist die Welt?'; it is in 'Zukunftsmusik' that 'Töne den Tönen sich zaubrisch gesellen'. Pan's flute-playing entices to life in 'Idylle' and in 'Leben' the awakening of the world occurs to the sound of flutes—in the prologue and epilogue 'Zu den lebenden Bildern', violins perform the same function.[4]

These features are not selected randomly. They match the following description very closely:

---

[3] 'Mädchenlied', SW ii. 82 (my veil has been rent); 'Zuweilen . . . ', SW i. 46 (now and then women who have never been loved appear in our dreams as little girls); 'Die Stunden!', SW i. 49 (easily, solemnly and without terror, *very* pale); 'Idylle', *SW* ii. 130 (girls: still as if on their own sarcophagus).

[4] 'Erlebnis', *SW* i. 31 (with melancholy music welling up from the depths); 'Epilog zu den lebenden Bildern', *SW* i. 39 (so music leads the dance of dreams in us with gentle enticement and thoughts follow on behind); 'Was ist die Welt?', *SW* i. 7 (sweet and mysterious sounds never heard before); 'Zukunftsmusik', *SW* ii. 49; 'Idylle', *SW* iii. 58; 'Leben', *SW* I, 28 (sounds link magically with sounds).

Ses sensations préférées sont celles que procurent les parfums, parce qu'elles remuent plus que les autres ce je ne sais pas quoi de sensuellement obscur et triste que nous portons en nous. Sa saison aimée est la fin de l'automne, quand un charme de mélancholie ensorcelle le ciel qui se brouille et le cœur qui se crispe. Ses heures de délices sont les heures du soir, quand le ciel se colore. . . . La beauté de la femme ne lui plaît que précoce et presque macabre de maigreur, avec une élégance de squelette apparue sous la chair adolescente . . .

Les musiques caressantes et languissantes, les ameublements curieux, les peintures singulières sont l'accompagnement obligé de ses pensées mornes ou gaies.

[His favourite sensations are those offered by perfumes because they stir up better than the others something sensuously obscure and sad that we harbour within us. His favourite season is the end of autumn, when a melancholy charm bewitches the sky as it clouds over and the pangs of the heart. The times he delights in are the evening hours, when the sky becomes tinged. He only admires female beauty when it is precocious and almost chillingly thin, with a skeleton's elegance perceptible beneath the adolescent flesh. His thoughts, whether sombre or happy, are accompanied by tender, languid music, by intriguing furnishings, striking paintings.]

Intriguing furnishings and striking paintings are less obviously hallmarks of Hofmannsthal's verse, although they are not absent: there is the unction in 'Lebenslied', rococo vases and fountains in the prologue to *Anatol*, tables of malachite supported by griffins, whole roast peacocks and pomegranates on violet-scented cushions in Death's banqueting hall, or snakes and strange birds framing the encounter with George.[5] The quotation is Paul Bourget's thumbnail sketch of Baudelaire's poetic world that can be found immediately after the piece from *Essais de psychologie contemporaine* that Hofmannsthal quoted in his diary.[6] One might take issue with some of the elements—particularly the account of the women who concern Baudelaire in *Les Fleurs du mal*—but this is not the point. The 'checklist' represents a *fin-de-siècle* view of Baudelaire, almost exactly contemporary with Hofmannsthal's own reception, and if it suppresses some of the more robust and energetic aspects, it does so under similar conditions to those that affected Hofmannsthal's intellectual and poetic development.

All of these elements are equally characteristic of the later Symbolists' work, and there are several more that one might want to add. In particular, Mallarmé picked up Baudelaire's fascination with the artificial, people caparisoned in gold and landscapes encrusted

---

[5] 'Lebenslied', *SW* i. 63; 'Prolog zu dem Buch "Anatol" ', *SW* i. 24; 'Das Mädchen und der Tod', *SW* ii. 79; 'Der Prophet', *SW* ii. 61

[6] Bourget, *Œuvres complètes: Critique 1*, 18–19.

with jewels. Verlaine had an interest in the exotic, but his legacy from Baudelaire is in music, the evening hour and the autumnal mood. To refer to Bourget's summary as a 'checklist' may seem cynical, but it has been suggested, plausibly, that Hofmannsthal's response to the repertoire of images that Symbolism offered was often somewhat mechanical, gesturing towards Symbolism rather than practising or enacting it. It has already been pointed out that the phrase 'Die Farben, die verklingen' in 'Die Töchter der Gärtnerin' was more a recipe for synaesthesia than the effect itself. Hans Steffen cites many poems where the word 'tausend' is used to create the sense of cumulation and notes, 'es kommt nicht zur Häufung verbrauchter Naturmetaphern, sondern zur Angabe ihrer Häufigkeit' [it becomes not the accumulation of worn-out nature metaphors but the statement of their frequency].[7] He distinguishes between the many poems that use the word 'soul' and those that evoke a soulscape or inner state without needing to label it thus. On the other hand, Andreas Thomasberger's analyses of the genesis of Hofmannsthal's poems suggest that Hofmannsthal was often concerned to counteract this and remove the 'statements', leaving the symbolic correspondences.[8] Bernhard Böschenstein notes a tendency towards deliberately refined vocabulary in 'Leben' and makes the important point that the grand gesture of its opening, 'einen Anspruch der Diktion ausdrückt, der nicht gedeckt scheint. . . . Dies ist eine durch George vermittelte symbolistische Verfahrensweise: der anspruchsvolle Tonfall meint, sich aus sich selber legitimieren zu können' [expresses a claim that seems not to be met. This is a Symbolist manner of writing mediated via George: the ambitious intonation believes it is its own justification].[9] The third stanza is a good example:

> Und alle Dinge werden uns lebendig:
> Im Winde weht der Athem der Mänaden
> Aus dunklen Teichen winkt es silberhändig
> Und die verträumten flüstern, die Dryaden
> In leisen Schauern sehnend und beständig
> Von nächtigen geheimnisvollen Gnaden
> Mit gelbem warmem Mond und stillem Prangen
> Und vieler Schönheit, die vorbeigegangen. (*SW* i. 28)

---

[7] Steffen, 'Hofmannsthals Übernahme der symbolistischen Technik', 271.
[8] See for example Thomasberger, *Verwandlungen*, 131.
[9] Bernhard Böschenstein, 'Hofmannsthal und der europäische Symbolismus', in Wolfram Mauser (ed.), *Hofmannsthal-Forschungen*, ii (Freiburg i.Br.: Hofmannsthal-Gesellschaft, 1974), 81.

[And all things come alive for us: the breath of the maenads blows in the wind, silver hands wave from the dark pools and the dreamy dryads whisper, longing but constant in gentle shivers, about dark, mysterious thoughts with a warm yellow moon and silent splendour and much beauty that once was.]

Böschenstein assesses the poem thus: 'programmatisch . . . defiliert eine Reihe von Motiven, die uns aus der Dichtung der Symbolisten bekannt sind, ohne daß sie hier aber eigentlich ausgeführt werden. Das Gedicht liest sich eher wie eine Anweisung zu einem Gedicht' [a row of motifs familiar from Symbolist poetry is paraded in front of us programmatically, without actually being enacted here. The poem reads like the instructions for a poem].[10] Böschenstein's conclusions from these observations are forcefully stated:

das heißt, daß Hofmannsthal den Stil der symbolistischen Dichtungsform nicht mit vollem Ernst übernommen, sondern als eine Möglichkeit für sich selber durchgespielt hätte; dabei macht die Reihung der einzelnen Bilder, die bewußt wie vorgeprägte Zitate herangezogen werden, deren programmatischen Charakter deutlich. Hofmannsthal schreibt nicht ein symbolistisches Gedicht, er schreibt über die Aufgabe, ein symbolistisches Gedicht zu dichten. Er gibt Regieanweisungen.[11]

[that means that Hofmannsthal did not adopt the style of Symbolist writings in full seriousness but tried it out as one possibility for his own work; the listing of the individual images, which are deliberately adduced like ready-made quotations, makes it evident that they are programmatic. Hofmannsthal does not write a Symbolist poem, he writes about the task of writing a Symbolist poem. He gives stage directions.]

This has for some time been the dominant view of Hofmannsthal's response to French Symbolism. However, it has already been shown to be less superficial than this, and the movement, the style, meant more to him than a repertoire of images to be handled with rhetorical ease and metrical skill. It is true that Symbolism was not fully assimilated into Hofmannsthal's poetry, and the previous chapter examined a number of points at which this was evident, even at the point when he was most dedicated to following the Symbolists' models. But the consequences of this interest, and the reasons for its problematic nature, have yet to be examined, and this is the sense of the analyses of the first poems to be read in this chapter, 'Erlebnis', 'Psyche' and the prose poems. Doubts about leaning so heavily on the techniques and

---

[10] Bernhard Böschenstein, 'Hofmannsthal und der europäische Symbolismus', in Wolfram Mauser (ed.), *Hofmannsthal-Forschungen*, ii, 81–2.
[11] Ibid. 82.

the fields of imagery and vocabulary that Bourget described as characteristically Baudelairean led to a deeper understanding of the implications of Symbolism, and, in 'Manche freilich' a very rare attempt to
incorporate a more resolute attitude to the problems of identity and
originality that Symbolism raised for Hofmannsthal.

Let us consider 'Erlebnis', written in July 1892 and first published in
George's *Blätter für die Kunst* in December of the same year:

> Mit silbergrauem Dufte war das Tal
> Der Dämmerung erfüllt, wie wenn der Mond
> Durch Wolken sickert. Doch es war nicht Nacht.
> Mit silbergrauem Duft des dunklen Tales
> Verschwammen meine dämmernden Gedanken
> Und still versank ich in dem webenden
> Durchsicht'gen Meere und verließ das Leben.
> Wie wunderbare Blumen waren da
> Mit Kelchen dunkelglühend! Pflanzendickicht,
> Durch das ein gelbrot Licht wie von Topasen
> In warmen Strömen drang und glomm. Das Ganze
> War angefüllt mit einem tiefen Schwellen
> Schwermütiger Musik. Und dieses wußt ich,
> Obgleich ich's nicht begreife, doch ich wußt es:
> Das ist der Tod. Der ist Musik geworden,
> Gewaltig sehnend, süß und dunkelglühend,
> Verwandt der tiefsten Schwermut.
>   Aber seltsam!
> Ein namenloses Heimweh weinte lautlos
> In meiner Seele nach dem Leben, weinte
> Wie einer weint, wenn er auf großem Seeschiff
> Mit gelben Riesensegeln gegen Abend
> Auf dunkelblauem Wasser an der Stadt,
> Der Vaterstadt, vorüberfährt. Da sieht er
> Die Gassen, hört die Brunnen rauschen, riecht
> Den Duft der Fliederbüsche, sieht sich selber,
> Ein Kind am Ufer stehn, mit Kindesaugen,
> Die ängstlich sind und weinen wollen, sieht
> Durchs offne Fenster Licht in seinem Zimmer—
> Das große Seeschiff aber trägt ihn weiter
> Auf dunkelblauem Wasser lautlos gleitend
> Mit gelben fremdgeformten Riesensegeln. (*SW* i. 31)

[The valley of twilight was filled with silver-grey fragrance, as when the moon
trickles through clouds. Yet it was not night. My dawning thoughts were mingled
with the silver-grey fragrance of the dark valley and silently I sank into the

transparent twisting sea and left life behind. What marvellous flowers were there, with darkly glowing calyces! A thicket of shrubs through permeated by a glowing red and yellow light like that of topazes. The whole was filled with melancholy music welling up. And I knew one thing, even though I do not understand it, I knew it none the less: that this is death. It has become music, with powerful longing, sweet and darkly glowing, akin to the deepest melancholy. But how strange! A nameless nostalgia for life wept silently in my soul, wept like one on a great ship with huge yellow sails on dark blue water, in the evening, sailing past the city, his native city. He sees the streets, hears the fountains playing, smells the fragrance of the lilac bushes, sees himself, as a child, on the bank, with a child's frightened eyes close to tears, sees light in his room through the open window—but the great ship carries him past, gliding soundlessly on the dark blue water with huge yellow sails of a strange shape.]

The narrative manner of 'Erlebnis' suggests that it is an account of a dream. The *Ich* seems to be speaking and not writing, engaging with a listener rather than a reader—setting the scene with a main clause, instinctively offering a comparison to help convey what it was really like, but realizing that the comparison suggests rationally that it was night, although this was not the case in the dream. Exclamations (ll. 9 and 17), incomplete sentences (ll. 9–11 and 28), a pause followed by a partial repetition ('an der Stadt, | Der Vaterstadt vorüber', ll. 22–3), details added piecemeal as if improvised (l. 26)—these are hallmarks of oral delivery, for which blank verse is ideally fluent. The lines 'Und dieses wußt ich, | Obgleich ich's nicht begreife, doch ich wußt es' display an overstated certainty accompanied by an awareness of an inability to justify this that are both characteristic of dream. The poem ends with the *Ich* caught up in the memory, repeating his words without elucidating, as if sinking back into sleep. 'Erlebnis' is not an evocation or an emotional response to an event: it is a not quite confident attempt to set out the memory of an unreal experience so that sense can be made of it; and as such it has a fragile, quizzical, even slightly anxious quality.

The imagined experience is of death, which takes place within a landscape where visual perception is obscured in twilight, and also hampered synaesthetically by an indeterminate perfume, since the olfactory 'Duft' is qualified by the visual 'silbergrau'. The landscape is also an *état d'âme*: its characteristics are transferred to the self both by the synaesthetic pair in the opening line and by the conspicuous repetition of 'dämmern' in line 5. The landscape of death is one of brightness and vigour: 'dringen, glimmen, glühen' replace 'sickern' and 'weben', the light streams out warmly and the colour 'gelbrot' contrasts strikingly with 'silbergrau'. Death is equated with music, as it is in *Der Tor und der Tod*,[12] and the intensity communicated by the setting is channelled into longing and melancholy. The insistence on 'ich wußt es' suggests that perception here is complete, even if it is not achieved through the senses; sensory perception is replaced here by a more absolute form of *knowing*, and knowledge seems to be effected through music.

A threshold has been crossed, and as the transition occurs, the *Ich* of the first section of the poem loses its solidity. 'Meine Gedanken verschwammen' and 'ich versank' are clear statements, with subjects and verbs unproblematically related. But in the second section the *Ich* is refracted through a series of abstractions and comparisons, gradually losing its fixed contours and becoming, as Baudelaire would say, 'vaporized'.[13] The subject of the first sentence in this part is 'ein Heimweh', weeping for life. Then a human being is introduced, but as a comparison, not in his own right. He is, therefore, either a memory or a creature of the imagination—'nostalgia for life wept *like* one who . . .'. The next sentence specifies this individual's sensory perceptions, 'sieht, hört, riecht', but has only illusory concreteness, since the 'er' that is its subject is still the remembered or imagined term of the comparison. 'He' takes on a certain independence in that main verbs are used to express his perceptions and actions, but 'he' is in fact only a personification of 'Heimweh', which was itself an abstraction of a component of the *Ich* after its death. This unstable imaginary self splits up and sees itself from a distance (across water) as a child on a far shore in whose eyes tears are welling up. Nostalgia for life is conveyed as comparable both to the nostalgia that one might feel deprived of home and one's secure 'Vaterstadt', and also to the nostalgia one might feel for one's lost childhood. The second sense is the consequence of the first, as the very word 'Vaterstadt' seems to have precipitated the vision of the child in the imagined psyche. 'Heimweh' encompasses both the loss of the security provided by a father and the loss of a child's innocence, and this emotional oxymoron is radically disorienting. It produces an internalized oedipal envy, the envy of the adult self for the child self, where the child (as the idiom has it) is father to the

---

[12] See *SW* iii. 69–71 and the letter-poem to Beer-Hofmann of 22 July 1892: 'traurig-schöne | Dunkelglühende Musik: der | Tod der Griechischen Tragödie' (*SW* ii. 77, ll. 69–71). Cf. Böcklin's *Self-Portrait with Death the Fiddler* (1872).

[13] Baudelaire, *OC*, i. 676. See also the poem 'L'Amour et le crâne' (i. 119–20), which enacts this dramatically.

man. Nothing can be done, however, and the ship with strange sails (heightening the sense of alienation from the familiarity of the 'Vater-stadt') carries 'him' past. The poem never returns to an *Ich*, which seems to have been prismatically split into too broad an imaginative spectrum to remain intact.

One possible interpretative key to this situation is offered by Eugene Weber's note to Hofmannsthal's reading matter at the time when 'Erlebnis' was written, late July 1892: the first volume of Stanisław Przybyszewski's *Zur Psychologie des Individuums*.[14] Przybyszewski uses similar imagery to Hofmannsthal's, describing the subconscious as a fathomless sea, or the womb of the Mother of Mothers, in a study of the structure of the creative identity, and one could apply the insights of psychopathology to Hofmannsthal via his poem. But 'Erlebnis' has literary resonances, too. The landscape of death has obvious ante-cedents in Symbolist poetry, jewel-encrusted, planted with threatening flowers, 'wunderbar . . . mit Kelchen dunkelglühend'—an echo of '[die] lauernden verführerischen Kelchen, | Die tödten wollen' and the literal 'fleurs du mal' of 'Die Töchter der Gärtnerin'. Leaving a state of confusion ('das Tal der Dämmerung', metonymically equated with 'meine dämmernden Gedanken'), Hofmannsthal enters the world of Symbolist poetry as he then understood it, identifying it as music—'de la musique avant toute chose', as Verlaine's 'Art poétique' demands,

> De la musique encore et toujours!
> Que ton vers soit la chose envolée
> Qu'on sent qui fuit d'une âme en allée
> Vers d'autres cieux.[15]

[More music, always music! Let your verse be the thing that has taken flight, that one feels is fleeing from a soul on its way to other skies.]

However, the literary subtext that most closely corresponds to the process described in 'Erlebnis' is the first paragraph of Gérard de Nerval's prose fantasy *Aurélia* (1855):

---

[14] Stanisław Przybyszewski, *Zur Psychologie des Individuums*, ii: *Chopin und Nietzsche* (Berlin: Fontane, 1892). Cf. *SW* i. 175.

[15] Verlaine, *OPC*, 326–7. Lene Mravlag compares ll. 6–19 to Verlaine, without explana-tion. Her interpretation is the very model of how to miss the point of Symbolism, which she understands unconvincingly here as the equation of certain sounds with movements and sensations: 'die abnehmende Helligkeit der Vokale . . . kann das Niedersteigen aus dem Nebel zum dunklen Tal symbolisieren'; she sees 'das Hervortreten des M-Lautes als Symbol für das Verbreiten und Verschwimmen': 'Der Symbolismus in Frankreich, der Symbolismus in Deutschland und Versuch einer Gegenüberstellung', Ph.D. thesis (Vienna, 1938), 77–8.

Le Rêve est une seconde vie. Je n'ai pu percer sans frémir ces portes d'ivoire ou de corne qui nous séparent du *monde invisible*. Les premiers instants du sommeil sont l'image de la mort; un engourdissement nébuleux saisit notre pensée, et nous ne pouvons déterminer l'instant précis où le *moi*, sous une autre forme, continue l'œuvre de l'existence. C'est un souterrain vague qui s'éclaire peu à peu et où se dégagent de l'ombre et de nuit les pâles figures, gravement immobiles, qui habitent le séjour des limbes. Puis le tableau se forme, une clarté nouvelle illumine et fait jouer ces apparitions bizarres: le monde des Esprits s'ouvre pour nous.[16]

[Dream is a second life. I have not been able to pass without quaking through the gates of ivory and horn that separate us from the *invisible world*. The first moments of sleep are the image of death; our thoughts are seized by a misty numbness and we cannot determine the precise moment where the *self*, in a different form, continues the business of existence. There is a dark underground passage that is gradually illuminated and where pale figures emerge from the shadows and the night, gravely still, inhabiting the dwelling place of limbo. Then the scene takes shape, a new light illuminates and enlivens these strange apparitions: the Spirit world is revealed to us.]

'Erlebnis' is narrated as a dream and its opening moments are identified as the image of death, characterized by a hazy feeling of sinking. The second part of the poem is exactly as Nerval describes, the continuation of the existence of the self in a different form, populated by pale, motionless figures. There is indeed the ghost of a tableau, dimly illuminated by the light of the lamp in the child's room—but crucially Hofmannsthal's tableau does not lead to the opening of the world of spirits. Nerval's Romantic dream is a visionary experience in which the self can explore its own existence through its oneiric alter egos and he ultimately derives his spiritual redemption from the autobiographical narration of dream and madness; Hofmannsthal's experience here is the very opposite, one of alienation and self-fragmentation.

The fate of the poetic *Ich* in the Symbolist landscape of 'Erlebnis' corresponds to the development in poetry that Symbolism represents most strongly, the loss of self-definition and the gradual recession of the self from verse; and Hofmannsthal's dream is a commentary on these processes. Mallarmé states the goal:

l'œuvre pure implique la disparition élocutoire du poète, qui cède l'initiative aux mots par le heurt de leur inégalité mobilisés; ils s'allument de reflets réciproques comme une virtuelle traînée de feux sur des pierreries, remplaçant la respiration

---

[16] Gérard de Nerval, *Œuvres*, ed. Albert Béguin and Jean Richer (Paris: Gallimard, 1960), i. 359.

perceptible en l'ancien souffle lyrique ou la direction personnelle enthousiaste de la phrase.[17]

And in Mallarmé's symbolic vocabulary, the state where poetic intentionality disappears and poetry becomes pure is referred to as 'Death': Mallarmé wrote to Cazalis in 1867, 'je suis parfaitement mort' [I am perfectly dead], and earlier to Aubanel, 'je suis mort' [I am dead],[18] explaining this death in poetic terms as the result of the detachment of a sensation from the self and its transfiguration in the poem, which he compares to fruit dropping from a tree.[19] Paul de Man describes this sense of dissociation in Mallarmé with another of the images that Hofmannsthal employs, the far bank of a river: 'death for Mallarmé means precisely the discontinuity between the personal self and the voice that speaks in the poetry *from the other bank of the river, beyond death.*'[20] The nostalgia expressed in the second half of 'Erlebnis' is directed towards a poetry in which the perceptions of the self are real: the *Er* sees the streets, hears the fountains playing, smells the perfume of the lilacs, and sees himself. The outside world and the self are mutually definitive. 'Heimweh' in 'Erlebnis' is for a Romantic poetry where such a relationship is still intact.

The retreat of the *Ich* in Symbolist poetry, as Hofmannsthal knew, is not attributable merely to the poet's discomfort within society, and therefore equivalent to a flight from life and the awkwardness of reality. In a note from June 1893 he distinguishes French Symbolism and its English counterpart thus, attributing the hypothesis to Bahr: 'der französische Symbolismus ist künstlerische Transfiguration der Wirklichkeit, der englische Hinausflüchten in ein Traumland' [French Symbolism is the artistic transfiguration of reality, English Symbolism is an escape into a dream-world; *RA* iii. 365]. The self formerly represented a natural world; when it absents itself the natural images are replaced with imagery derived from other poetry, which is what has happened in 'Erlebnis'. Yeats, in his introduction to the *Oxford Book of Modern Verse* in 1936, identifies the emblem of non-modern, representational poetry as the mirror. One might add to this that when the mirror ceases to reflect the external world and instead offers access to what Yeats calls 'the private soul' or the non-material world, it

[17] From 'Crise de vers', Mallarmé, *OC*, 366. See also above, pp. 145–5.

[18] Mallarmé, *Correspondance*, 240 and 222.

[19] Cf. Leo Bersani, *The Death of Stéphane Mallarmé* (Cambridge: Cambridge University Press, 1982), esp. 5–7.

[20] Paul de Man, 'Lyric and Modernity', in *Blindness and Insight* (London: Methuen, 1983), 181, my italics.

becomes the emblem of the modern.[21] The mirrored surface of Narcissus' river did not reflect his physical features so much as set up a symbolic correspondence. In a note from April 1893, opposing Artist and Dilettante, the former is not only identified as 'Künstler' but also called 'Kenner', a connoisseur of other art. He leans over the mirrored surface of the pool and his face is 'völlig durchgeistigt, ganz Sinn . . . Symbol des Inhalts (kein Totenkopf mehr zu spüren, nichts Materielles . . .)' [completely made spirit, wholly sense, the symbol of the content (the skull is no longer to be seen, there is nothing material); (*RA* iii. 381]. The landscape in which 'Erlebnis' is placed is borrowed from Symbolist poetry, represents Symbolism itself, and this is what death means: being within a poetry starved of the material that nourishes poetry, being a mere representation of a real self, and having to create new poetry out of old. The child is the living, breathing, old poetry; the adult self is made of the same flesh and blood but is dead— what it sees in the mirroring process is not even its real dead self, a solid 'Totenkopf', but a version of itself that was born out of a word in a poem, not real but 'ganz Sinn'.

M. H. Abrams's symbol for 'the constitutive, autonomous self' in Romantic poetry, 'the creative subjectivity that certainly looms large in romantic theory, as an analogous microcosm of the world of nature' is the lamp.[22] 'The light of that lamp is the self-knowledge of a consciousness, an internalized metaphor of daylight vision'. Hofmannsthal's dissociated *Er* perceives a light that is explicitly not daylight, and must be cast by a lamp in 'his' own room, the room 'he' had as a child. It is perceived as a memory of something distant and unattainable by an *Er* with virtually no identity. It is thus what de Man calls 'self-knowledge of a consciousness' represented by Hofmannsthal as childhood. Childhood becomes a symbol of the poet's origins in Romantic poetry, which are lost and have ceded to the less living verse that is Symbolist.[23]

July 1892 was a point at which Hofmannsthal's interest in Symbolism was particularly intense, and some further details will reinforce this interpretation of 'Erlebnis'. Within a week of completing the poem, Hofmannsthal had also written 'Psyche', at first glance also susceptible

[21] De Man, ibid. 170–1, quoting W. B. Yeats, 'Introduction' to *The Oxford Book of Modern Verse 1892–1935* (Oxford: Oxford University Press, 1936), p. xxxi.

[22] De Man, 'Lyric and Modernity', 171.

[23] Peter Michelsen interprets the poem, whose sentiments he contrasts with Romantic longing, as evincing 'Trauer über den Verlust der Wirklichkeit' and he reads the title ironically. It need not be ironic, however, if the whole is read as a poem about literary experience. See Michelsen, 'ABEND: Zu einigen Gedichten Hugo von Hofmannsthals', in *Zeit und Bindung* (Göttingen: Vandenhoeck & Ruprecht, 1976), 29–30.

of analysis in psychopathological terms, but this poem is also encircled by Symbolist or quasi-Symbolist influence. The title and motto— 'Psyche, my Soul'—are originally from Edgar Allan Poe's poem 'Ulalume':

> Here once, through an alley Titanic
> Of cypress, I roamed with my Soul—
> Of cypress, with Psyche, my Soul.[24]

Poe's stories were amongst the reading material for the summer Hofmannsthal listed ebulliently to Marie Herzfeld on 21 July, and he wrote in a letter to Elsa Bruckmann-Cantacuzène in February 1894, that he knows the verse, too: 'Von Poe . . . kenn' ich nur die Verse und einige phantastische Novellen, ich halte ihn für einen der großen Künstler, Artisten wäre besser, die einen unbegreiflich packen und sehr wenig *geben*' [I only know Poe's verse and a few fantastic stories, I consider him one of the great artists, or rather artistes, who are unbelievably gripping but *yield* very little].[25] Poe was also one of the names listed beside Baudelaire, Verlaine and Mallarmé in a note recording the conversation with George in December 1891 (*RA* iii. 340).

The more immediate source of the phrase for 'Psyche', however, was probably *Le Pèlerin passionné* by Jean Moréas, where it is used, in French, as the epigraph and the refrain for the 'Élégie troisième'.[26] Although the first edition is dated 1891, *Le Pèlerin passionné* had appeared in Paris at the end of December 1890 with immense *éclat* and interest from the Symbolist press, orchestrated by Moréas himself— who was the toast of the February banquet of *La Plume*—and was reviewed enthusiastically by Anatole France in *Le Temps* and Maurice Barrès in *Le Figaro*.[27] Huret notes in the introduction to his *Enquête* that it was 'réclamé, dans tous les sens du mot, par les Symbolistes-Décadents' [claimed/demanded/advertised in every sense of the

[24] *Collected Works of Edgar Allan Poe*, ed. Thomas Ollive Mabbott (Cambridge, Mass.: Belknap/Harvard University Press, 1969), i: *Poems*, 415–19.

[25] Herzfeld, *BW*, 28; letter of 21 July 1892. *Briefe 1890–1901*, 97, to Elsa Bruckmann-Cantacuzène; letter of 18 Feb. 1894.

[26] Moréas, *Le Pèlerin passionné* (Paris: Léon Vannier, 1891), 67–8; *Œuvres* (Paris: Mercure de France, 1923–6; repr. Geneva: Slatkine, 1977), i. 188–9. Hofmannsthal consistently has 'é' for the more usual 'è' in *Pèlerin*, which might suggest, in fact, that he read the first edition, since the word is spelt thus there.

[27] See Cornell, *The Symbolist Movement*, 101–3; John Davis Butler, *Jean Moréas: A Critique of his Poetry and Philosophy* (The Hague: Mouton, 1967), 71–5, who notes that the volume appeared before the cover publication date of 1891, but is not aware that Barrès's article in *La Plume* in Jan. 1892 is a reprint of the *Figaro* piece.

word by the Symbolist-Decadents]. Asserting its credentials as a work of Symbolist poetry, Moréas himself claims in the interview reprinted in this volume that the work 'rompt définitivement avec la période du symbolisme que j'appellerai de *transition*, il entre dans la phase *vraie* de la manifestation poétique que je rêve' [breaks definitively with the period of Symbolism that I shall call the *transition* period, it enters into the *true* phase of the poetic practice that I dream of].[28]

Le Pèlerin passionné will have appealed to Hofmannsthal both for its eclectic 'Stilverdrehungsmanie' and for its Symbolist imitations of Du Bellay and Ronsard as well as Verlaine and Baudelaire. It has been suggested also that Hofmannsthal was the author of two translations of poems by Moréas that appeared in *Die Blätter für die Kunst* (in December 1892), although this is unlikely.[29] Moréas was accused of being a mere *pasticheur*, and this is true of the 'Élégie troisième': not only does it employ Poe's technique of mournful repetition and refrain and his bleak landscape setting, but the twice-repeated line 'Et je lui dis, "N'est-ce pas?"' [and I say to her, 'Is it not so?'] is incomprehensible without reference to the dialogue between the self and Psyche in Poe's 'Ulalume'. In the American poem they traverse an imaginary 'ashen and sober' October landscape, designed by a poet and a painter, Auber and Weir, whose epithets are later transferred to the Body's heart. They see Astarte (Venus), promising warmth and love. Psyche mistrusts the pallor of Venus—indeed sobs in agony when the *I* will not flee, preferring to trust the message of hope and beauty that the planet seems to promise. They come upon the tomb of the beloved Ulalume, buried a year ago, and although at first dismayed, Body and Soul ask whether the friendly woodland ghosts have not called up the spectre of the planet (and therefore hope) to deflect the sadness at the loss of a loved one. The landscape of Moréas's Elegy is 'the Hell of the planetary souls' that Poe evokes in the last line of 'Ulalume', a scene of carnage and shame, which is viewed with heavy Romantic emotion. The voice in the poem seems to be asking, 'what is the point of being like these damned souls, caught up in regret and misery, never to be brought to paradise by anyone *else*? Was I not right to invoke for myself the spirit of hope instead?':

[28] Huret, *Enquête*, 74. Moréas also takes the opportunity also to assert the credentials of the Symbolists as a movement: 'ce sont ces *écoles* . . . qui renouvellent la création poétique' (ibid. 75).

[29] *Die Blätter für die Kunst*, 1.2: 60–1. The suggestion was made by Horst Weber (Herzfeld, *BW*, 71).

Et je lui dis, 'N'est-ce pas?' Et je lui dis
'Ah, ces damnés que chasse le regret,
En fleurs bénignes de Paradis
Qui jamais les mettrait,
Psyche, mon âme!'

[And I say to her, 'Is it not so?' And I say, 'Oh, these damned souls who are pursued by remorse, who would ever place them among the kindly flowers of Paradise, Psyche, my soul!']

Without the spectre of Venus remembered from Poe there is nothing to which to relate the question.

Hofmannsthal's poem consists of a similar dialogue between an enthusiastic and lively *Ich* and a tired, sorrowful Psyche. It begins with *points de suspension* and the word 'und', and reads as a continuation, possibly of the Moréas Elegy, possibly of 'Ulalume':

... und Psyche, meine Seele, sah mich an
Von unterdrücktem Weinen blass und bebend
Und sagte leise: 'Herr, ich möchte sterben,
Ich bin zum Sterben müde und mich friert.' (*SW* i. 32)

[and Psyche, my soul, looked at me, pale as I was and trembling with suppressed tears, and said quietly, 'Sir, I wish to die, I am tired unto death and I am cold.']

The Soul seems to be answering that the hope represented by Venus in 'Ulalume' is not enough to warm her, or that the spectacle of the mutilated and damned has triumphed. The response of the *Ich* is to offer Psyche a draught of warm life, consisting of a sensory extravaganza:

'Mit gutem, warmem Wein will ich Dich tränken,
Mit glühendem, sprühendem Saft des lebendigen,
Funkelnden, dunkelnden, rauschend unbändigen,
Quellenden, schwellenden, lachenden Lebens,
Mit Farben und Garben des trunkenen Bebens:
Mit sehnender Seele von weinenden Liedern
Mit Ballspiel und Grazie von tanzenden Gliedern,
Mit jauchzender Schönheit von sonnigem Wehen
Hellrollender Stürme auf schwarzgrünen Seen,
Mit Gärten, wo Rosen und Epheu verwildern,
Mit blassen Frauen und leuchtenden Bildern,
Mit fremden Ländern, mit violetten,
Gelbleuchtenden Wolken und Rosenbetten,
Mit heissen Rubinen, grüngoldenen Ringen
Und allen prunkenden, duftenden Dingen.'

['I will quench your thirst with good, warm wine, with the glowing, sparkling juice of living, glittering, darkening, rushing untamed, up-welling, swelling, laughing life, with colours and sheaves of drunken trembling: with a longing soul of weeping songs, with ball-games and the grace of dancing limbs, with rejoicing beauty of the sunny blowing of brightly rolling storms on black-green lakes, with gardens where roses and ivy grow wild, with pale women and shining pictures, with foreign lands, with purple and shining yellow clouds and beds of roses, with hot rubies, green-golden rings, and all manner of magnificent, fragrant things.']

This is what the speaker calls the living world, full of Dionysiac laughter and energy, colours, roses and ivy—and is rejected by Psyche as 'schal und trüb und todt' [shallow, dismal and dead]. One might object that if it is a living world, it is a 'composed' selection of elements which are strongly reminiscent of Böcklin's paintings—or more precisely, Böcklin's paintings as described by Hofmannsthal under the guise of Titian's in *Der Tod des Tizian* and later in the 'Prolog zu einem Totenfeier für Arnold Böcklin' added in 1901.[30] Böcklin was later to be championed by George as one of the last bastions of a pure, visionary art to be untouched by the degrading influences of the late nineteenth and early twentieth centuries. Hofmannsthal is more sceptical: according to Martin Stern, George believed in the restoration of an eternally valid classical-heathen form of humanity, but Hofmannsthal had doubts, experiencing the enchantment of Böcklin's pictures but without seeing any possibility of perpetuating this kind of art.[31] There are echoes of the 'elfentanz' in 'Weihe', and of Hofmannsthal's own poems, in particular of 'Die Töchter der Gärtnerin', as 'blasse Frauen' and 'violette, gelbleuchtende Wolken' recall the second daughter's 'blasse feine Finger', and the flowers she picks 'mit violetten, braunen Pantherflecken | Und lauernden verführerischen Kelchen, | Die tödten wollen' (*SW* i. 22). No wonder Hofmannsthal saw the art of Böcklin as ultimately unsatisfactory, and no wonder this vision of life is rejected by the Soul.

The alternative presented by the *Ich*—'mit wunderbar niever-nommenen Worten' [with marvellous words never heard before]—is a world revealed as the way to open the gates of dream, a fantastic descant on the image of the gates of horn and ivory invoked by Nerval:

> Mit goldglühenden, süssen, lauen
> Wie duftendes Tanzen von lachenden Frauen;

---

[30] See Martin Stern, 'Böcklin—George—Hofmannsthal', in Karl Pestalozzi and Martin Stern (eds.), *Basler Hofmannsthal-Beiträge* (Würzburg: Königshausen & Neumann, 1991), 91–2.
[31] Ibid. 93.

Mit monddurchsickerten nächtig webenden,
Wie fiebernde Blumenkelche bebenden;
Mit grünen, rieselnden, kühlen, feuchten
Wie rieselndes, grünes Meeresleuchten
Mit trunkentanzenden, dunkeln, schwülen
Wie dunkelglühender Geigen Wühlen;
Mit wilden, wehenden, irren und wirren
Wie grosser, nächtiger Vögel Schwirren;
Mit schnellen und gellenden, heissen und grellen
Wie metallener Flüsse grellblinkende Wellen...
Mit vielerlei solchen verzauberten Worten
Werf ich Dir auf der Träume Pforten. (*SW* i. 33)

[with gleaming gold, sweet, warm words, like the fragrant dancing of laughing women, with darkly moving words drenched in drops of moonlight, trembling like the feverish calyces of flowers, with green, drizzling, cool, damp words like the drizzling green glow of the sea, with drunkly dancing, dark, sultry words like the penetrating sounds of darkly glowing fiddles, with wild, fluttering, crazy, confused words like the whirring of great night-birds, with quick, shrill, hot, loud words like rivers of metal and dazzlingly flashing waves, with many such magical words I shall throw open for you the gates of dream.]

In the 'wie'-clauses, the persons, objects or natural phenomena are being compared to words: as in 'Erlebnis' the physical, the actual, is subordinated grammatically to the non-corporeal, and is thus distanced. There are some hints to Hofmannsthal's train of thought as he creates this world of words for Psyche, since 'metallener Flüsse' (echoed in line 55 by 'das Land von Metall') are identified in a note from 13 July as characteristic of the Baudelairean landscape: 'Ungeduld eine Landschaft ganz aus Metall mit heißer vibrierender Luft (Manier des Baudelaire)' [impatience is a landscape entirely of metal with hot, trembling air (Baudelaire's manner); *RA* iii. 348]. If the first landscape evoked to comfort the Soul (supposedly the landscape of life) was borrowed from George's verse, and thus in part at second-hand from Symbolist poetry, the other world is also of poetry, specifically of Symbolist poetry. Already in the lines above 'nächtige Vögel', 'wie fiebernde Blumenkelche bebende . . . kühle, feuchte . . . dunkle, schwüle [Worte]' are almost word-for-word echoes of the pool in 'Lehre', 'wo die schattenhaften Blumen *dunkel* duften, *Nacht Gefied*er | Durch die Zweige huscht . . . wo die *fiebernden* Mimosen | Ihre Fäden *bebend* schlingen' and where 'Kalter Schauer und Tollheit wohnen hässlich in dem *Feuchten*.'[32] Later lines of 'Psyche' add to the echoes: line

[32] *SW* ii. 59, my italics.

49, '[der] braune, vergessene *Teich*' [the brown, forgotten pool], lines 52–4, '[mit] *Schwülduftenden Blumen* und blassen Gesichtern; | Die Heimath der Winde, die nachts wild wehen | Mit riesigen *Schatten* auf traurigen Seen' [with flowers of sultry fragrances and pale faces, the home of the winds that blow wildly at night with vast shadows on sad lakes]. These, and 'das rauschende, violette Dunkel' [the rushing violet dark] of line 47, establish a double link with the first section of 'Psyche' and 'Die Töchter der Gärtnerin'. Fragmentary trial phrases and drafts for these and the last lines include 'das dämmernde Thal erf[üllt]' (a clear link to 'Erlebnis') and 'Die Larven des Fühlens die schattenhaft weben | Und unausgesprochen . . . im Unbewußten verbeben' [the masks of feeling that weave in shadows and tremble away without being uttered; *SW* i. 183]—almost a rewriting of the last line of 'Lehre', 'Bunte Wunder in die Dämmrung weben ahnend deine Augen.'

These overlaps clearly indicate that Hofmannsthal imagined these worlds as Symbolist poetry, that the words he proposes to spin for Psyche are a Symbolist poem. This conclusion is supplemented by a further overlap, in the words used to *introduce* the riotous and somewhat erotic pageant of vocabulary: 'mit wunderbar nievernommenen Worten' (l. 28). Two years previously 'nie vernomm'ne Töne' were invoked as what filled 'eine Welt für sich allein . . . begabt mit eig'ner, unentweihter Schöne'—the world of the programme sonnet 'Was ist die Welt?' (*SW* i. 7). There is another echo, as '[der] Trank, . . . | Der warmes Leben strömt durch alle Glieder' is 'guter, warmer Wein'— and the world/poem of the sonnet is also the source of 'Wein der Weisheit'. This sonnet, which has already been interpreted as a response to Baudelaire, evokes like 'Psyche' a world which is also a poem, and it would seem that the kind of poem that Hofmannsthal is envisaging two years later is a Symbolist poem.

There are two possible directions in which to proceed, once the extent of the overlaps between these works are recognized. Either Hofmannsthal is using the vocabulary and imagery almost at random, without their carrying a 'charge' from one context to the next; or one context affects our interpretation of the other, by virtue either of similarity or contrasts. The first case implies too cavalier an attitude to poetry to be plausible for Hofmannsthal, quite apart from its elimination of the possibility of subconscious echoes. The alternative approach was revealing when applied to Baudelaire's 'Correspondances', and is no less so for 'Psyche': it shows a shift in his attitude towards Symbolism, which reinforces the analysis of 'Erlebnis'. The Soul rejects both worlds. The conclusion added on 9 December 1893 is explicit:

> Da sah mich Psyche meine Seele an
> Mit bösem Blick und hartem Mund und sprach:
> 'Dann muss ich sterben, wenn Du so nichts weisst
> Von allen Dingen, die das Leben will.'[33]

[Then Psyche, my soul, looked at me with an angry expression and a stern mouth, and said, 'then I must die if you are so ignorant of all the things that life demands.']

A note from January 1894 explains exactly why Psyche rejects poetry:

> ... Psyche—ich.
> ihr Grundton: würd ich vom Rechten nur besessen
>   dann könnt ich aller Schwermut ledig werden
>   Was *(1)* mich verbrennt *(2)* mir im Inneren vergessen
>   Und *lebte* statt mich lebend zu geberden.[34]

[Psyche—me. Her fundamental tone: if I were only possessed by what is right, then I could shake off all the melancholy that consumes me / lies forgotten within me and could *live* instead of merely behaving like someone living.]

The conclusion that Symbolism is not life but playing at life, a counterfeit of a living soul, is an extension of the fear that 'Lehre' and 'Die Töchter der Gärtnerin' registered in the face of an art propounded by George. These were the poems Hofmannsthal saw as his own Symbolist works and the threat was identified with Symbolism. 'Psyche' and 'Erlebnis' have moved a stage further: unlike the earlier poems they no longer imitate Symbolist techniques and make them Hofmannsthal's own, betraying their fear as they do so (which was the manner in which the earlier poems operated) but now incorporate a consciousness that Symbolism is something *other*, and that to accept it or fall within its orbit means death. The Soul is cold and sick unto death as the poem opens, and is never given the wine of life she is promised. In a note from September 1892 Hofmannsthal took her to Hades with Faust, whom she has killed. Whilst Faust lies lifeless, Psyche sits 'mit ewig offenen Augen. | Der Kahn gleitet weiter; weiter | Geflüster der

---

[33] These additional lines merely articulate what is already clear, and hardly represent, as Vordtriede suggests, a decision about the effects of the garden to which Hofmannsthal came *later*. 'Offenbar war sich Hofmannsthal noch nicht ganz klar darüber, wie Psyche diese Lockung aufnehmen würde' (*Novalis und die französischen Symbolisten*, 85). Stern links these lines interestingly with Böcklin, 'Böcklin—George—Hofmannsthal', 92.

[34] *Nachlaß*, H VB 4.26. The Critical Edition (*SW* i. 186) dates this note 'vermutlich August 1892' but the manuscript is very clearly headed '4.1.94'.

Schatten am Ufer' [with eyes eternally open. The boat glides onwards; whispering of the shadows on the bank].[35] Although their positions are reversed, these are the same images as in 'Erlebnis', the eyes, the boat passing on, and the distant shore. The failure to fulfil Psyche's needs with poetry that provides life is associated with the experience of poetic death that 'Erlebnis' depicts.

Hofmannsthal's stance towards Symbolism in these poems is not, however, wholly negative and is best described as ambivalent. Both analyses have highlighted how there is a critical perspective on Symbolism built into the poems and that the consequences of writing Symbolist poetry are potentially dangerous. It is associated with the dissolution of the self, and with death. But the fact that Psyche rejects the poetry she is offered does not negate the enthusiasm with which it is offered; neither does the disintegrative experience that Symbolism proves to be in 'Erlebnis' cancel the sense of awe and respect for its power that the first section conveyed. The weeping of nostalgia is after all registered with some surprise—'Aber seltsam!'—and the poem does not resolve to learn from the experience and declare, like Hans Castorp, 'Der Mensch soll um der Güte und Liebe willen dem Tode keine Herrschaft einräumen über seine Gedanken' [for the sake of goodness and love, man should not grant death any dominion over his thoughts].[36]

No Symbolist poet's *œuvre* is complete without some experimentation with prose poetry. This is meant literally, not facetiously as one might remark that no modern pop star's career is complete without at least one film role, since although not invented by Symbolist writers, the genre flowered in their hands. In the lecture 'Making, Knowing and Judging', Auden succinctly makes the point that 'language is prosaic to the extent that "it does not matter what particular word is associated with an idea, provided that the association once made is permanent". Language is poetic to the extent that it does matter.'[37] In

---

[35] *Nachlaß*, H V B 10.61^b (*SW* i. 187). There is too little of the notes to allow firm conclusions, but they permit the speculative suggestion that Psyche kills Faust because she is bored. If Faust's traditional or at least Goethean striving bores her, might he not have been conceived as a Symbolist Faust? Other notes on this project (*SW* xviii. 60–2) support such a suggestion: there is 'kein eigentlich böser Geist δαίμον in Faust' and his servant is Pierrot, hero of Beer-Hofmann's 'Pantomime' that Hofmannsthal was to translate into French in Mar. 1893 (Beer-Hofmann, *BW*, 185–6) and of a planned prose poem (*SW* xxix. 397). It is at least a conception of Faust inspired by Decadence. For more details see Vilain, 'An Innocent Abroad', 81–3.

[36] Thomas Mann, *Gesammelte Werke*, iii. 686.

[37] W. H. Auden, 'Making, Knowing and Judging', in *The Dyer's Hand and Other Essays* (London: Faber, 1975), 35.

the prose poem new expectations of how language is made to matter are aroused as many of the traditional poetic devices are excluded: by taking away the technicalities of verse, emphasis is placed on the poetic as a quality in itself. It is precisely because language mattered so much, and because the central principle of Symbolist writing is the self-conscious attempt at the renewal of language and form, that an attempt to come to terms with this tantalizingly ambivalent genre was naturally integral to the Symbolists' range of writing.

Hofmannsthal's prose poetry has not been widely studied. Although the single prose poem in volume xxviii of the Critical Edition and the first twenty-one of the thirty-one texts under *Prosagedichte* in volume xxix were written between October 1892 and May 1894, most are published there for the first time, in 1978.[38] Some were included amongst the *Aufzeichnungen* by Herbert Steiner in 1959.[39] Some appeared in periodicals in 1957 and 1959. 'Gerechtigkeit' (included under *Erzählungen* in the ten-volume *Gesammelte Werke*) appeared shortly after Hofmannsthal's death in the *Neue Freie Presse* in 1929 and was placed by Steiner in the volume *Prosa I*.[40] Only 'Erinnerung' appeared at the time it was written, in 1924.[41] This partly accounts for the dearth of secondary literature on the prose poetry. Ulrich Fülleborn allots a few lines of his slender book *Das deutsche Prosagedicht* to Hofmannsthal's prose poems—calling them 'Musterstücke des Erzählgedichts in Prosa . . . ein interessanter Beitrag Hofmannsthals zum Jugendstil' [models of the narrative prose poem, an interesting contribution by Hofmannsthal to *Jugendstil*]; an article on Austrian prose poetry by Roger Bauer includes Hofmannsthal; Rolf Tarot analyses two prose poems and devotes a footnote to another; one chapter of Stefan Nienhaus's history of the prose poem in Vienna between 1895 and 1914 is devoted entirely to Hofmannsthal, as are two articles by Gotthart Wunberg and Ursula Renner.[42] Others, and indeed some of these

---

[38] Stefan Nienhaus expresses some well-founded doubts about what should not be included under the heading 'Prosagedichte' and what belongs with 'notes' or 'jottings'. A case in point is: 'Liebende, die einander nicht angehören, verbindet ein metaphysisches Band. Sie sind Vater u Mutter eines ungeborenen Kindes' (*SW* xxix. 230), and despite the heading 'Prosagedicht' this belongs amongst *paralipomena* rather than amongst the texts. The same is true *a fortiori* of the single word 'Salzburgerstrasse' (no. 15, xxix. 233).

[39] Nos. 6 (A 101), 8 (A 102), part of nos. 19 (A 103), 22 (A 115–16), and 24 (A 119–20) and no. 28 (A 128 and 130).

[40] No. 28, 'Geschöpf der Flut—Geschöpfe der Flamme', was published in *Botthege Oscure* in 1957; nos. 4, 'Traumtod', 19, 'Die Stunden' and 21, 'Intermezzo' were all published in the *Neue Rundschau* (1959), 363–9. See *EGB*, 672–3 and *SW* xxix. 398–9.   [41] Cf. *EGB*, 673.

[42] Ulrich Fülleborn, *Das deutsche Prosagedicht* (Munich: Fink, 1970), 54; Roger Bauer, 'Le Poème en prose autrichien de Baudelaire à Peter Altenberg', *Romanica Wratislavensia*, 36

scholars, do not treat the prose poems as a serious contribution to the genre.

Nienhaus applies techniques of close structural analysis to show how Hofmannsthal's prose texts enjoy an autonomy akin to that of the lyric poem, and that, despite a high degree of detail in his narrative, his is a poetics of suggestion and an expression of fundamental 'Sprachskepsis'. Nienhaus's meticulous analyses efficiently highlight the key details of each text, although interpretation within the context of Symbolist influence will suggest more differentiated possibilities within his general conclusion that the poems manifest the characteristic *fin-de-siècle* radical doubts about the capacities of language, the famous 'Sprachskepsis'. His view is that to refer these texts to the French tradition 'klärt kaum etwas, sondern verdeckt eher das Spezifische der deutschsprachigen Prosagedichte' [hardly clarifies anything, but tends rather to obscure the specificity of the German prose poems].[43] Since he locates an element of this specificity in the character of the literary scene in *fin-de-siècle* Vienna, however, to leave aside the French influence is to suppress an important dimension. Because the history of the prose poem in Germany is vestigial—Novalis's *Hymnen an die Nacht* being an exceptional high-point—both Hofmannsthal and Altenberg derived their conception of what the genre of the prose poem could offer primarily from their familiarity with the French tradition, and from Baudelaire in particular.

There had naturally been poetic prose in European literature for many generations: in the French tradition Chateaubriand and Sénancour made frequent use of characteristic strong rhythms of verse in unrhymed, uneven, non-end-stopped lines; Nodier's visionary exoticism becomes so concentrated in the prologue and epilogue to *Smarra* that the narrative turns into prose couplets; Nerval's mystical *Aurélia* metamorphoses at the end into a hymn to Paradise, a strophic treatment of Nerval's mystic and poetic ambitions. In Britain, the intensity of emotion and the heightened diction in Macpherson's Ossianic fragments added to their already poetic rhythms. In

(1991), 239–53; Tarot, *Hugo von Hofmannsthal*, 301–5 and 280; Stefan Nienhaus, *Das deutsche Prosagedicht im Wien der Jahrhundertwende* (Berlin: de Gruyter, 1986); Gotthart Wunberg, '"Ohne Rücksicht auf Inhalt, lauter venerabilia": Überlegungen zu den Prosagedichten Hugo von Hofmannsthals' and Ursula Renner, '"Die Tiefe muß man verstecken—wo? An der Oberfläche": Allegorisierung als Verfahren der Moderne in Hofmannsthals "Glück am Weg"', both in Jacques Le Rider (ed.), *Austriaca*, 37: *Modernité de Hofmannsthal* (Université de Rouen: 1993), 319–31 and 253–65.

[43] Nienhaus, *Das deutsche Prosagedicht*, 1.

Germany, Novalis and Jean Paul wrote what Emil Staiger calls 'eine Art Scheinprosa' [a kind of mock prose],[44] and Nietzsche's by turns fragmented and dithyrambic prose also kept up the momentum of the developing genre.

The prose poem proper originated with Aloysius Bertrand's *Gaspard de la nuit*, which was written in the late 1820s and early 1830s but not published until 1842, just after the author's death. These tense fragments of prose, inspired by the Romantics' revival of interest in the Middle Ages, E. T. A. Hoffmann's febrile imagination,[45] engravings of Brueghel amongst others, and possibly by Bertrand's own mental instability, were acknowledged by Baudelaire in the preface to *Le Spleen de Paris* as the texts that gave him the idea for his own formally hybrid works. The difference between the two writers' intentions was that, in his urge to attempt something analogous, Baudelaire wished to 'appliquer à la description de la vie moderne, ou plutôt d'*une* vie moderne et plus abstraite, le procédé qu'il [Bertrand] avait appliqué à la peinture de la vie ancienne' [apply to the description of modern life, or rather of *a* life that is modern and more abstract, the procedure that [Bertrand] had applied to the depiction of life in earlier times]. With the publication of Baudelaire's *Spleen de Paris* (as one work after his death in the 1869 *Œuvres*, but also sporadically in periodicals from 1855) the genre was *de facto* established. At almost exactly the same time Lautréamont's *Chants de Maldoror* began to appear, also perhaps influenced by Bertrand. The genre was picked up by Mallarmé, too, who wrote twelve 'Poëmes en prose' between 1864 and 1887, and by Huysmans in a volume entitled *Le Drageoir aux épices* (1874). In the mid-1870s Rimbaud wrote his *Illuminations*, most of which were published in *La Vogue* in 1886.

This summary of the history of the prose poem identifies no turning point when poetic prose, or 'prose rythmée' becomes a new genre. Yet by the Symbolist period it was certainly *regarded* as a separate genre. Suzanne Bernard's book, *Le Poème en prose de Baudelaire jusqu'à nos jours* (1959), is still the most thorough study, and she too is concerned to

[44] Emil Staiger, 'Andeutung einer Musterpoetik' in *Unterscheidung und Bewahrung: Festschrift für Hermann Kunisch* (Berlin: De Gruyter, 1961), 356; quoted by Fülleborn, *Das deutsche Prosagedicht*, 5.

[45] The subtitle is *Fantaisie à la manière de Rembrandt et de Callot*, which is probably derived from Hoffmann's *Fantasie-Stücke in Callots Manier* (1814–15). Bertrand's explicit intention was to establish a new genre of *prose*, as he stated in a letter to David d'Angers (18 Sept. 1837): '*Gaspard de la nuit* . . . où j'ai essayé de créer un nouveau genre de prose' (quoted by Barbara Z. Schoenberg, 'The Influence of the French Prose Poem on Peter Altenberg', *Modern Austrian Literature*, 22.3 (1989), 19).

establish it via analysis as a *distinct* genre, not a hybrid halfway between prose and verse, but a special poetic genre.[46] Baudelaire's dedicatory letter to Arsène Houssaye (published in *La Presse* in 1862) suggests that rhythm is one of the defining characteristics of the genre:

Quel est celui de nous qui n'a pas, dans ses jours d'ambition, rêvé le miracle d'une prose poétique, musicale sans rythme et sans rime, assez souple et assez heurté pour s'adapter aux mouvements lyriques de l'âme, aux ondulations de la rêverie, aux soubresauts de la conscience?[47]

[Who amongst us has not, in his most ambitious moments, dreamed of the miracle of poetic prose, musical without rhythm and rhyme, flexible and uneven enough to allow it to adapt to the lyrical movements of the soul, to the undulations of dream, to the shocks and starts of consciousness.]

Paradoxically in spite of the words 'sans rythme', which refer to formal metrical rhythmic structures (associated with rhyme in the traditional lyric poem), these phrases place rhythm, understood more broadly, at the centre of an evocation of an ideal language, following the rhythms of the mind and the soul. For the Symbolists, rhythm was frequently dominant in their accounts of the poetic—Mallarmé's definition of poetry quoted at the beginning of Chapter 2 also prioritizes rhythm: 'La poésie est l'expression, par le langage humain ramené à son rythme essentiel, du sens mystérieux des aspects de l'existence.' And Verlaine's major contribution to the development of poetry was also rhythmic, the popularization of the *vers impair*. Bernard shows by rhythmic analysis that prose poetry and free verse are quite separate genres, but the same techniques of analysis fail to establish a similarly clear distinction between prose poetry and 'prose rythmée'.[48] She is

---

[46] Suzanne Bernard, *Le Poème en prose de Baudelaire jusqu'à nos jours* (Paris: Nizet, 1959), 434. But see also Sonya Stephens, *Baudelaire's Prose Poems: The Practice and Politics of Irony* (Oxford: Clarendon Press, 1999), which appeared just as this study was going to press.

[47] Baudelaire, *OC*, i. 275–6. This question is embedded between his ambiguous reflections on his debt to Bertrand and his sense that he has ended up doing 'quelque chose (si cela peut s'appeler *quelque chose*) de singulièrement différent', which might suggest that he prefers not to count Bertrand as his proper ancestor, but regards the prose poem as his own invention, the product of his own aesthetic revolution and essentially connected with the modern world. He also implies that he is uncertain whether or not he *has* created a real thing at all. The difficulties of interpretation and the impossibility of assessing the degree of irony active in this dedicatory letter are analysed wittily by Barbara Johnson, *Défigurations du langage poétique* (Paris: Flammarion, 1979), 17–29. Henceforth, quotations from Baudelaire will usually be indicated by volume- and page-number in parentheses in the text.

[48] Bernard does not analyse this example, but W. B. Yeats's surgical restructuring of Walter Pater's famous Mona Lisa passage from *The Renaissance* in a *vers libre* version as the liminal poem to his edition of *The Oxford Book of Modern Verse 1892–1935* resulted in comparable 'mirrored' deformations to her fascinating restructuring of de Régnier's 'Le Vase': Bernard, *Le Poème en prose*, 413–15.

compelled to end her rigorous investigation with the statement that the former possesses 'une structure et une organisation d'ensemble, dont il nous reste à découvrir les lois: lois non seulement formelles, mais profondes, organiques' [an overall structure and organization whose laws we have still to discover: laws that are not only formal, but profound and organic].[49]

The concept that assists most in pinning down the elusive genre is autonomy, which partakes of both formal and non-formal characteristics, and moreover was one that the inventors of the prose poem's generic distinctiveness, the Symbolists, were concerned to promote. For the Symbolists, educated by Poe's theoretical work mediated by Baudelaire, the poem-component of the couple arouses expectations of brevity and self-containment: 'un long poème n'existe pas' [there is no such thing as a long poem], as Baudelaire translated from Poe's 'The Poetic Principle' (ii. 332). The fragments by Baudelaire and Bertrand called 'prose poems' enjoy the same self-contained autonomy as does a lyric poem. Bertrand's are arranged in stanza-paragraphs, sometimes with a refrain, while Baudelaire's are in the form of short continuous scenic narratives, tending in the direction of the story. Mallarmé's are sometimes as long as three or four pages, but each is a structured, closed unit. Rimbaud's *Illuminations* are sometimes modelled on sonnet form, sometimes arranged in looser stanza-paragraph style, sometimes a series of ejaculated visions, but they are always short and complete.

Baudelaire also pinpointed how the formal expectations of the 'prose' component of the name permit a more differentiated response to the primacy of rhythm:

Il est un point par lequel la nouvelle a une supériorité, même sur le poème. Le rythme est nécessaire au développement de l'idée de beauté, qui est le but le plus grand et le plus noble du poème. Or, les artifices du rythme sont un obstacle insurmontable à ce développement minutieux de pensées et d'expressions qui a pour objet la *vérité*. Car la vérité peut être souvent le but de la nouvelle, et le raisonnement, le meilleur outil pour la construction d'une nouvelle parfaite. C'est pourquoi ce genre de composition qui n'est pas situé à une aussi grande élévation que la poésie pure, peut fournir des produits plus variés. . . . De plus, l'auteur d'une nouvelle a à sa disposition une multitude de tons, de nuances de langage, le ton raisonneur, le sarcastique, l'humoristique, que répudie la poésie, et qui sont comme des dissonances, des outrages à l'idée de beauté pure. (ii. 329–30)

[There is a sense in which prose is superior even to the poem. Rhythm is necessary

[49] Bernard, *Le Poème en prose*, 434.

for the development of the idea of beauty, which is the greatest and most noble object of the poem. Well, the artifices of rhythm are an insurmountable obstacle to the detailed development of thoughts and expressions that has *truth* as its object. Truth may often be the object of the prose and reasoning may be the best tool for the construction of perfect prose. This is why that mode of composition, which is not on the same high level as pure poetry, may provide more varied products. In addition, the author of a novel has a multitude of tones and linguistic nuances at his disposition, the tone of reasoning, sarcasm, humour, which are repudiated by poetry and felt to be dissonances, offensive to the idea of pure beauty.]

Truth here is equivalent to representational precision in portraying what is, and is the province of prose, the short story in particular; beauty has a spiritual dimension and is the business of poetry. Baudelaire's preface to *Le Spleen de Paris* merges the two, using the rhythmic potential of narrative prose to convey the spiritual elevation characteristic of poetry. Only a short work is able to fulfil the conditions of poetry, 'l'Unité—je ne veux parler de l'unité dans la conception, mais de l'unité dans l'impression, de la *totalité* de l'effet' [unity—I do not mean the unity of conception but the unity of impression, the *totality* of the effect; ii. 332]. In the section of *L'Art Romantique* devoted to Victor Hugo and *La Légende des siècles*— which is 'le seul poème épique qui pût être créé par un homme de son temps pour des lecteurs de son temps' [the only epic poem that could have been created by a man of his time for readers of his own time]—Baudelaire writes that the poems are usually short, and that 'ceci est déjà une considération importante, qui témoigne d'une connaissance absolue de tout le possible de la poésie moderne' [this is already an important consideration that bears witness to an exact understanding of what is possible for modern poetry; ii. 140]. The question of a work's length was a vital part of the Symbolist aesthetic, 'which rejects nearly all the conditions by which the long poem exists',[50] and which led to the development of the prose poem. It is an aesthetic based on suggestion and evocation, and on a holistic concept of the work of art:

un poème ne mérite son titre qu'autant qu'il excite, qu'il enlève l'âme, et la valeur positive d'un poème est en raison de cette excitation, de cet *enlèvement* de l'âme. Mais, par nécessité psychologique, toutes les excitations sont fugitives et transitoires. Cet état singulier, dans lequel l'âme du lecteur a été, pour ainsi dire, tirée de force, ne durera certainement pas autant que la lecture de tel poème qui dépasse la ténacité d'enthousiasme dont la nature humaine est capable. (ii. 332)

[a poem only deserves to be called such in as much as it excites and carries the soul

---

[50] Frank Kermode, *Romantic Image* (London: Routledge & Kegan Paul, 1986), 117.

away, and the value of a poem is positive precisely by reason of the way it excites and carries the soul away. But it is a psychological necessity that all excitement is short-lived and transitory. This peculiar state into which the reader's soul has been so to speak pulled by force will certainly not last as long as it takes to read a poem that exceeds the extent to which human nature is capable of enthusiasm.]

He goes on to say that in bygone ages epic poems may well have been constructed out of a series of previously existing lyric poems, but that 'toute *intention épique* résulte évidemment d'un sens imparfait de l'art' [all epic intent clearly results from an imperfect sense of art]. A Symbolist poem must be autonomous, deriving its meaning from its internal symbolic relationships—the relationships of words by reason of both phonetic and semantic charge—rather than from its discursive meaning. Yeats criticized Pound's *Cantos* for aiming to be a long poem, and in a long poem these relationships are too stretched to be sustainable. Kermode explains his objections:

the ideograms of that poem are symbols . . . which seemed, because of their developed function in Chinese thought, to have some hope of holding together in a structure owing nothing to logic and connective discourse. In this way, and with the aid of music (a fugue has a structure but no discursive meaning) a long poem might be possible, whereas if it has to resort to continuous narrative or doctrine it becomes at best a series of short poems tediously bound together by prose. But the difficulties are enormous, in terms of precision and complexity of the symbolic relationships; and the finished product, eschewing all devices which we habitually recognize as establishing connections, may be nothing but a confused heap of words, with only the isolated detail to show how the artist has squandered his power.[51]

In a long poem the internal symbolic relationships are too stretched to be sustainable. Suzanne Bernard quotes a critic writing on the hundredth anniversary of the publication of Bertrand's *Gaspard de la nuit*, who uses the characteristic Symbolist image of the crystal to describe just this aspect of the genre: 'uni et serré comme un bloc de cristal et dans lequel se jouent cent reflets divers . . . une chose contractée dont les suggestions [sont] infinies' [unified and tightly organized like a block of crystal in which hundreds of varied reflections are playing, a compressed thing whose suggestions are infinite].[52]

The genre of the prose poem was needed in order that language's capacity to reflect the rhythms of the psyche (Baudelaire's 'multitude

[51] Frank Kermode, *Romantic Image*, 118.
[52] Edmond Jaloux, 'Le Centenaire du poème en prose', *Le Temps*, 25 Apr. 1942; Bernard, *Le Poème en prose*, 439.

de tons') be given fuller rein without losing the aesthetic and structural tautness that the form of the short lyric poem provides (the 'crystal' structure of reflections within a dense verbal matrix). It originates as a reaction against the constraints of verse but also against the diffuseness of prose narrative, seeking simultaneously a breaking of order and a reimposition of order in the form of artistic concentration. Baudelaire's oxymoronic critical pair 'vaporisation et centralisation', referring in its context to the self, could be applied here as well; so, too, could his description of the imagination, 'elle est l'analyse, elle est la synthèse' [it is analysis and synthesis alike] in 'Mon cœur mis à nu' (i. 676)—and finally Hofmannsthal's two sacred tasks, 'das Auflösen und Bilden von Begriffen' [dissolution and formation of concepts; *RA* iii. 373], fit the same pattern. This type of prose poem (which represents one of the two poles in Bernard's taxonomy of the genre, the 'poème artistique') is one version of this combination of impulses central to Symbolism and applicable to the individual psyche and the work of art. Even Rimbaud's visionary prose poems the *Illuminations* (the other pole, the 'poème anarchique'), which seek to dissolve the world by means of a radical restructuring of our perceptive habits, end up by recombining in the perception of a new reality. He, too, makes use of the sonnet structure, of repetition, incantation and echo to regroup poetically his explosive challenges to normality.

Hofmannsthal's access to the genre was threefold, via Bertrand, Baudelaire and Turgenev. He made two references to the first of these, the first a bold scribble in a notebook: 'Aloysius Bertrand: Gaspard de la Nuit' (*SW* xxxi. 7). After a short horizontal line there follows 'das Erwachen in finsterer Nacht mit sich ganz allein' [waking up quite alone on a dark night], in the same *ductus*. The note is not dated, but other details on this and surrounding pages suggest mid-1892.[53] The name and title might have come not from reading the book but from Baudelaire's introduction to *Le Spleen de Paris*—quoted also in Gautier's essay on Baudelaire that Hofmannsthal referred to on the previous page of the notebook.[54] The phrase after the reference does, however,

---

[53] *Nachlaß*, H VB, 2.28. These details include a note for a planned Platonic dialogue, references to Bahr, De Quincey and Baudelaire and to 'die Bacchantin' (*SW* xxxi. 7). On 21 June 1892 Hofmannsthal noted a plan for a Bacchus tragedy; later in June or early in July there are notes reading 'Dialoge in der Manier des Platon aus Athen' and 'De Quincey "Paradis artificiels"' and a note beginning 'Ihre Theorie' that seems to be a reference to Baudelaire's doctrine of correspondences (see *RA* iii. 345–8).

[54] Gautier, 'Charles Baudelaire', in *Souvenirs romantiques*, ed. Adolphe Boschot (Paris: Garnier, 1929), 337. See *SW* xxxi. 7 and *Nachlaß*, H VB 2.26.

suggest some kind of response to at least a cursory glance at the work. The second reference to Bertrand is merely the name *Gaspard* noted after the prose poem 'Liebende die einander nicht angehören' [lovers who do not belong to each other].[55] It may be significant also that George is known to have copied out seven of the nine poems in the first section of *Gaspard*.[56] Stuart Merrill, with whom George had become acquainted at dinners of *La Plume*, was particularly interested in the prose poem and had published an anthology in English translation in 1890 that included Bertrand.[57] George is likely to have passed on at least some elements of his familiarity to Hofmannsthal.

By the time he met George, however, Hofmannsthal was already enthusiastic about Turgenev's prose poems, *Stichotvoreniya v proze* (1878–83), and continued his interest until at least 1893, the poetic short story *Prizraki* being the 'Visionen' of the sixth Dialogue on Art mentioned in a notebook.[58] To judge by Marie Herzfeld's 1891 essay 'Die meist gelesenen Bücher', if Turgenev was by then 'ein wenig aus der Mode gekommen' [a little out of fashion], he had been required reading in the previous year.[59] Hofmannsthal came across the prose poems as part of a more general fascination with Turgenev in summer 1890, and noted in his diary for 5 July:

Turgenjew, 'Gedichte in Prosa'. Die Gedichte in Prosa, reine Lyrik, lose Gedanken, kleine Bilder, Allegorien. Ein Schimmer von Subjektivität über allem. Das Aufgreifen des Alltäglichen, die meisterhaften kleinen Naturskizzen erinnern an die Spätromantiker, die Stimmung von Eichendorff. (*RA* iii. 314)

[Turgenev, 'Poems in Prose'. The poems in prose, pure lyric, loose thoughts, little images, allegories. A shimmer of subjectivity over it all. Taking inspiration from everyday life, the masterful little sketches of nature, these remind one of the late Romantics, the mood of Eichendorff.]

---

[55] *Nachlaß*, H VB 123.1ª; *SW* xxix. 230. The *Nachlaß* note finishes with a reference to Laforgue's *Imitation de notre dame de la lune*, mentioned by Paul Remer in his article on 'Die Symbolisten' in *Die Gegenwart* on 14 June 1890 (394), and widely known, mostly by association with *Moralités légendaires*.

[56] Boehringer, *Mein Bild*, i. 209. George's reception is incidentally the only reference to Bertrand in Gsteiger, *Französische Symbolisten*, 72.

[57] Stuart Merrill, *Pastels in Prose: From the French* (New York: Harper & Brothers, 1890). Cf. Cornell, *The Symbolist Movement*, 65 and Saint-Paul, 'Stefan George et le Symbolisme français', 399.

[58] *RA* iii. 360. A note to *Prizraki* on the same sheet as the thirteenth prose poem catalogued in *SW* xxix. 232 (*Nachlaß*, H VB 10.124, probably 1893) records Hofmannsthal's interpretation: 'ein dumpfer gestaltloser Feind bedroht und ängstigt die den Dichter tragende Fee. Lebensangst. Zweifel an der *(1)* Berechtigung *(2)* Existenz der Kunst gegenüber dem Elend in der Welt.'

[59] Marie Herzfeld, 'Die meist gelesenen Bücher', *Wiener Literatur-Zeitung*, 2.8 (15 June 1891), 1. Also in Wunberg (ed.), *Das junge Wien*, i. 227.

He also formed the idea of writing 'eine Art lyrisches Prosatagebuch, etwa "Gedanken" oder "Eindrücke" oder "Träume" ' [a kind of lyric prose diary, to be called 'Thoughts', or 'Impressions' or 'Dreams']. Turgenev's 'fragmentary self-communings'[60] were mostly written between summer 1877 and summer 1880 and represented a new genre for Russian literature, immediately imitated, if not widely, and owing their formal stimulus to Baudelaire's prose poems. The collection is a mixture of moral vignettes that sentimentally exploit emotions such as pity, regret and patriotism in concentrated form, and allegorical situations, almost always explained at the end in the manner of a parable. Thus 'Two Rich Men' is a version of the parable of the Widow's mite; in 'The Last Meeting' the deathbed scene of friends shaking hands after a quarrel is explicitly interpreted as 'Death has reconciled us'; and 'A Visit', where the tiny butterfly-like woman is identified at the end as the Goddess of Fantasy.[61] Their settings are either the glorious Russian countryside or the depressing poorer quarters of towns, their characters most often peasants and beggars, lovers and the dying. The sleeper's dream or the dreamlike vision of daytime musing are typical introductory situations, *mne pochudilos* ('it seemed to me', 'I fancied'), a typical phrase leading into an allegory or symbolic turn of events. The landscape is always a mirror of the soul, with grief suggested in the chill of winter and exultation by clear blue skies.

Nothing came of the lyric diary, but by late 1892 Hofmannsthal himself had begun to write prose poems, and use the term to describe them. On the page in the notebook before the reference to Bertrand, after that to Gautier's essay, there is the note 'überhaupt Baudelaire, Prosagedichte' [Baudelaire generally, prose poems], and another note from 1892, mostly in shorthand and connected with the poem 'Die Rose und der Schreibtisch', also quotes Baudelaire.[62] Both Stefan Nienhaus and Ellen Ritter are of the opinion that Turgenev's prose poetry was more important than Baudelaire's in the formation of

[60] Frank Friedeberg Seeley, *Turgenev: A Reading of his Fiction* (Cambridge: Cambridge University Press, 1991), 316.

[61] Turgenev, *Dream Tales and Prose Poems*, trans. Constance Garnett (London: Heinemann, 1920), 289, 277–8 and 278–80.

[62] *Nachlaß*, H VB 12.28—little is legible other than 'Baudelaire sagt: ich werde morgen mit Ihnen reden wenn Sie fanierter sind' (*SW* xxix. 401) and the words 'lawn tennis'! The reference to Baudelaire in the Barrès essay of late 1891 also has 'parfümschwere Atmosphäre fanierter, künstlicher und seltener Dinge' (*RA* i. 123). Hofmannsthal's copy of Baudelaire's prose poems was *Petits Poëmes en prose—Les Paradis artificiels—par Charles Baudelaire* (Paris: Calmann-Lévy, [n.d.])—most probably the edition published in 1889.

Hofmannsthal's. They use the chronological priority of the Russian texts in Hofmannsthal's reading to justify this view.[63] However, despite his earlier knowledge of the Russian works Hofmannsthal did not feel inspired to attempt prose poetry himself until he had read Baudelaire's *Le Spleen de Paris*.[64] This altered his conception of the genre significantly and made it relevant to his own poetic development. By August 1893 Hofmannsthal noted of Turgenev's prose poems that what attracted him was their conciseness; he was pleased to have discovered a form of prose with no wastage of words, and where each phrase demanded the attention it would receive in a verse poem: 'die bloss angedeuteten Prosagedichte, er sagt ungeheur wenig überflüssiges' [the prose poems with bare suggestions: he says tremendously little that is wasted].[65] The note on the lyric diary, by contrast—made before reading Baudelaire—suggests that prose poetry under the dominant influence of Turgenev would have been along the lines of ' "Gedanken", "Eindrücke" oder "Träume" '.[66]

Baudelaire repeats in his prose poems the struggle of *Spleen* and *Idéal* that characterized *Les Fleurs du mal*, but frustration, dissatisfaction and friction dominate. They have a different thematic emphasis, but the modern sensibility of *Le Spleen de Paris* is most sharply distinguished from that of the verse collection by being rooted in contemporary Parisian life, just as Turgenev's Russia is constantly present in his prose poems. The possibility of escape for the Baudelaire of the prose poems is more remote than it was for the verse poet, because the place fled is more strongly established in the imagination. The location of

[63]   For Ritter's view, see *SW* xxix. 397, where the reading of Baudelaire is noted as an aside; Nienhaus, *Das deutsche Prosagedicht*, 142, in a footnote only ('Erst später beschäftigte sich Hofmannsthal mit Baudelaires "Petits Poèmes en Prose" '). Wunberg, rightly, is less convinced, suggesting that the importance of modern French literature to Hofmannsthal means that his prose poems may be nearer in spirit to Baudelaire's and even Rimbaud's than Turgenev's.

[64]   Dominique Jehl, in one of the very few studies of Hofmannsthal and Baudelaire, makes no mention at all of the prose poetry of either: 'Hofmannsthal und Baudelaire', in Mauser (ed.), *Hofmannsthal-Forschungen*, ix. Nienhaus is the only scholar to investigate the connection, and this only in his article 'Die "scharfe Spitze der Unendlichkeit" ', *Poetica*, 21 (1989), 84–97.

[65]   *SW* xxix. 397 (*Nachlaß*, H VB 10.124).

[66]   This assertion may, however, be very wide of the mark. See Walter Koschmal, *Vom Realismus zum Symbolismus: Zu Genese und Morphologie der Symbolsprache in den späten Werken I. S. Turgenevs* (Amsterdam: Rodopi, 1984), 158–83. Koschmal locates the Symbolist aspects of Turgenev's prose poetry partly in their tendency to relate intertextually to his other works, an aspect to which Hofmannsthal would have been particularly sensitive. He would have noted, too, Turgenev's evocations of landscapes in precious stones and jewels (a tendency parodied by Dostoevsky in *The Devils*). Turgenev's influence on Hofmannsthal needs further investigation (including, for example, the inspiration from *Prizraki* for 'Erlebnis', the Symbolist poems discussed in Chapter 3, and even *Das Bergwerk zu Falun*).

Baudelaire's poems in a clearly depicted contemporary urban environment constitutes a strength of attachment to the world from which escape is desired. It also means that the gestures of escape are more mental, more idealizing: significantly the first image of aspiration in the collection is not a journey but clouds. None of Hofmannsthal's poetry, verse or prose, inherits this urban basis; the nearest is Gianino's view of the city from afar in *Der Tod des Tizian* (*SW* iii. 45).

What will have been of importance for Hofmannsthal is the stimulus of *Le Spleen de Paris* as a more abstract model of contradictory aspirations and as a powerfully articulated reminder of the artist's agonies of ambivalence, the temptations and threats of the unified, correspondent world, and of the artist's struggle to represent it without being crushed by it. For Baudelaire in 'Le *Confiteor* de l'artiste', art is a struggle: 'L'étude du beau est un duel où l'artiste crie de frayeur avant d'être vaincu' [the study of beauty is a duel where the artist cries out in fear before being vanquished; i. 279]. It is a delight to contemplate the solitude, the silence and the incomparable chasteness of the blue, for these offer both a refuge from the rationalizing behaviour of ordinary life and the possibility of self-forgetting:

toutes ces choses pensent par moi, ou je pense par elles (car dans la grandeur de la rêverie, le *moi* se perd vite!); elles pensent, dis-je, mais musicalement et pittoresquement, sans arguties, sans syllogismes, sans déductions. (i. 278)

[all these things think through me, or I think through them (since in the grandeur of a dream the *self* is soon lost!); they think, I say, but musically and picturesquely, without quibbling, without logic, without deduction.]

But their intensity inevitably creates 'une souffrance positive' [a positive suffering] so that the artist is revolted by the depth, limpidity and the insensibility of the sea. These qualities threaten to overwhelm his existence, and the loss of the self is not really desirable, however 'irrémédiable' the existence of the self is sometimes perceived to be. The suffering they induce is positive in that it brings back the consciousness of the self that was threatened.

Le Spleen de Paris is specifically about poetry and the poet. This is demonstrated most clearly by poems that share the allegorizing tendency of Turgenev's prose poems. In 'Le Vieux Saltimbanque', for example, the figure of the acrobat is interpreted explicitly at the end: 'je viens de voir l'image du vieil homme de lettres qui a survécu à la génération dont il fut le brillant amuseur; du vieux poète' [I have just seen the image of the old man of letters who has survived the generation he entertained so brilliantly, the image of the old poet; i. 297]. One of the collection's fundamental themes (and one particularly relevant to Hofmannsthal, at least a poetic generation further removed from the Romantic source) is the function of the poet whose materials, the images and the techniques, belong to a past age. Hence the tension within the collection between the modern city world and the visions of totality. The poems thematize the ability of poetry to communicate both vision and its loss: in 'L'Invitation au voyage' the totality is glimpsed and an effective means of preserving this perception is desired:

Moi, j'ai trouvé mon *tulipe noire* et mon *dahlia bleu*.
   Fleur incomparable, tulipe retrouvée, allégorique dahlia, c'est là, n'est-ce pas, qu'il faudrait aller vivre et fleurir? Ne serais-tu pas encadrée dans ton analogie, et ne pourrais-tu pas te mirer, pour parler comme les mystiques, dans ta propre *correspondance*? (i. 303)

[Me, I have found my *black tulip* and my *blue dahlia*. Incomparable flower, the tulip that has been retrieved, the allegorical dahlia, that is where one should go to live and flower, is it not? Would you not be framed in your analogy, and would you not mirror yourself, to use the language of mystics, in your own *correspondence*?]

The impossible flowers, like the blue flower of the Romantics, are symbols of escape from surface reality and function poetically, by means of allegory, analogy and correspondence. The 'là' which is the ideal home of the flowers, is Cockaigne and the realm of art. The incantatory repetition of 'pays de Cockagne' and 'Oui, c'est là que . . .' spurs on towards this infinite realm, as does the enumeration of opulent details, the sun receiving its glory from the metals, stones and porcelains on which it shines. But at the end, 'mes pensées enrichies . . . reviennent de l'Infini vers toi' [my thoughts have been enriched and return from the Infinite towards you]—back to prosaic earth. The aspiration has in any case already been deflated ironically by the bathetic figure 'où tout est riche, propre et luisant, comme une magnifique batterie de cuisine' [where everything is rich, clean and gleaming, like a magnificent set of pots and pans; i. 302]. Even when the sought-after paradise is found, as in 'Déjà!', it is initially rejected as inferior to the journey over the sea towards it, that is in favour of aspiration itself:

je ne pouvais, sans une navrante amertume, me détacher de cette mer si monstrueusement séduisante, de cette mer si infiniment variée dans son effrayante simplicité, et qui semble contenir en elle et représenter par ses jeux, ses allures, ses colères et ses sourires, les humeurs, les agonies, et les extases de toutes les âmes qui ont vécu, qui vivent et qui vivront! (i. 338)

[I could not tear myself from this most monstrously seductive sea without distress and bitterness, from the sea that is so infinitely varied in its terrifying simplicity and which seems to contain within it and represent in its playful movements, its airs, its rages and its smiles, the humours, the agonies and the ecstasies of all the souls that have lived, who are living now and who will live in the future!]

It is almost grudgingly that the figure in the poem admits finally 'cependant c'était la terre' [nevertheless it was the land], but his enthusiasm grows quickly for its suggestive possibilities: 'c'était une terre riche et magnifique, pleine de promesses, qui nous envoyait un mystérieux parfum de rose et de musc, et d'où les musiques de la vie nous arrivaient en un amoureux murmure' [it was a rich and magnificent land, full of promise, conveying a mysterious perfume of rose and musk and whence the music of life came to us in an amorous murmur]. The imagination has already begun the same cycle of aspiration beyond the realm of immediate human emotion, with its noises and passions, towards the more abstract 'musiques de la vie' [musics of life]. This is the 'rhythmic' quality that Hofmannsthal's prose poems inherit from Baudelaire's: they are less intensely rhythmic in the narrower (prosodic) sense, but benefit greatly from models of variety in the extended sense of rhythm, language that follows 'les soubresauts de la conscience' of the letter to Houssaye (where 'con-science' is not the English 'conscience' but 'consciousness').

The stark oppositional structure of Hofmannsthal's first prose poem 'Die Rose und der Schreibtisch' has something of the allegorical about it that betrays a trace of Turgenev.[67] Even though, unlike many of the Russian poems, Hofmannsthal's allegorizing does not end simply with the key to an interpretation, Nienhaus wonders whether the binomial character of the text-structure, the way it falls into two parts that he feels are only loosely connected with each other, is one reason why Hofmannsthal never revised and published the piece. Many of Hofmannsthal's poems are antithetically structured, though, and this is unlikely to have been decisive in his neglect of the work. In any case, just as the oppositions in, for example, 'Psyche' are undermined, 'Die Rose und der Schreibtisch' is equally ambivalent:

---

[67] Nienhaus cites 'A Conversation', a witty fable of two mountains 'chatting' over thousands of years, reducing man's significance in the immensity of the natural world to a minimum (146 n. 12). In Hofmannsthal's prose poem, too, man is the subject of the conversation of inanimate objects.

Ich weiß, dass Blumen nie von selbst aus offnen Fenstern fallen. Namentlich nicht bei Nacht. Aber darum handelt es sich nicht. Kurz, die rothe Rose lag plötzlich vor meinen schwarzen Lackschuhen auf dem weissen Schnee der Strasse. Sie war sehr dunkel, wie Sammt, noch schlank, nicht aufgeblättert, und vor Kälte ganz ohne Duft. Ich nahm sie mit, stellte sie in eine ganz kleine japanische Vase auf meinem Schreibtisch und legte mich schlafen.

Nach kurzer Zeit muss ich aufgewacht sein. Im Zimmer lag dämmernde Helle, nicht vom Mond aber vom Sternlicht. Ich fühlte beim Athmen den Duft der erwärmten Rose herschweben und hörte leises Reden. Es war die Porzellanrose des alt-wiener Tintenzeuges, die über irgend etwas Bemerkungen machte. 'Er hat absolut kein Stylgefühl mehr,' sagte sie, 'keine Spur von Geschmack.' Damit meinte sie mich. 'Sonst hätte er unmöglich so etwas neben mich stellen können.' Damit meinte sie die lebendige Rose.[68]

[I know that flowers do not fall from open windows of their own accord. Especially not at night. But that is not what it is about. In short, the red rose suddenly lay just in front of my black patent leather shoes on the white snow of the street. It was very dark, like velvet, still slender, not open, and quite without fragrance because of the cold. I took it with me, put it in a tiny Japanese vase on my writing desk and went to bed. I must have woken up a short while later. My room was bathed in pale light, not the light of the moon but starlight. When I breathed I could feel the fragrance of the rose wafting towards me now that it had warmed up, and I heard muffled talking. It was the china rose of the old Viennese inkstand that was commenting on something. 'He has completely lost his sense of style,' it said, 'quite lost his good taste.' She was referring to me. 'Otherwise he could never have put something like that next to me.' She meant the real rose.]

Far from being a straightforward symbol of the natural world, the rose found in the street is cold and odourless like a glass decoration, its colour starkly contrasted with black and white in a manner that suggests artifice and construction—patent leather shoes are attributes of formal dress and ceremony—rather than a natural setting, and reminds the speaker of velvet (also richly artificial and associated with evening dress). It is subsequently treated partly as a work of art, set in a delicate Japanese vase on the desk, to function aesthetically for the *Ich* the following day when he sits down to write. The first paragraph has ostentatiously dismissed its function as a living rose ('nicht auf-geblättert', 'ganz ohne Duft'), isolated it in time as well as in space ('plötzlich'), then framed it artistically in a surround of contrasting colours, before placing it in a vase whose decorative style is highly stylized; finally it is assigned to a literary sphere, the desk. Hofmanns-

---

[68] *SW* xxix. 227. Quotations from the prose poems will first be given by volume- and page-numbers of the Critical Edition, thereafter by page- and line-numbers.

thal's aestheticizing treatment of his rose brings it back to a kind of life again, where it vies with a porcelain rose on the inkwell. The contrast is not so much 'Kunst versus Leben'[69] as between one kind of art and another, for there is in reality nothing in the poem that can truly be called living. The so-called living rose is a cut flower in a vase and will not survive long; it is 'erwärmt' rather than 'warm'. Most importantly, it derives its superiority over the gossipy, snobbish *altwienerisch* inkwell-rose from its artistic treatment. The aesthetic value of a starkly red rose in a delicately painted Japanese vase is enhanced also by association with 'dämmernde Helle' and 'Sternlicht', a deliberately poeticized scene.

The rose may have fallen from a window into the street, but on another level it has fallen into the hands of a poet or into a poem, and the gesture of isolating it from its origins in the opening lines is the poet's gesture of appropriation. The rose appropriated is given style— *pace* the porcelain rose—and the process whereby this happened is the process of poetic composition. The replacement of living value by aesthetic value in a poem, which is the process that has been enacted in these two paragraphs, is the goal of Symbolism. The gesture of the first few lines, making the provenance of the rose into a subject for the reader's speculation and then dismissing it as irrelevant to the matter in hand, is important. Like it or not, roses have symbolic capacity and a history of symbolic meaning, and it is a natural impulse to attribute to a rose symbolic possibilities. The gesture of cutting off, 'darum handelt es sich nicht' does not stop that, but establishes it as a pole of contrast with what is about to happen. A similar situation to the one Hofmannsthal describes occurs in Turgenev's 'The Rose', where the speaker finds a rose on the garden path, also at night, the flower 'bright red even through the mist'.[70] However, he knows it is from the dress of the woman who recently ran from the room to her lover. Hofmannsthal may be suggesting that his rose has such a history as a symbol of passion, but whether or not he has Turgenev in mind, and *because of* rather than despite the disclaimer 'darum handelt es sich nicht', the first sentences establish the object's capacity to suggest and intrigue. By cutting off speculation, the *Ich* deflects attention from the rose's meaning in its old context and guides it on to the nature of the rose itself and to new surroundings. In Turgenev's poem the rose is sacrificed to passion and flung unceremoniously into the fire, its death expressing

[69] Nienhaus, *Das deutsche Prosagedicht*, 143.
[70] Turgenev, *Dream Tales and Prose Poems*, 273–5.

high romantic emotion. Hofmannsthal has taken away any romantic context and replaced it with a depiction of revivified symbolic capacity: mannered, constructed, artificially set up in a framework of contrasts, it is unclear *what* the rose symbolizes, but certain that it is powerfully capable of symbolism. That is, on one level, its 'life', and the last line is not simply naive. Another of Turgenev's prose poems focuses on the symbol of the rose: 'Somewhere, sometime, long ago, I read a poem. It was soon forgotten . . . but the first line has stuck in my memory—"How fair, how fresh were the roses..." ' This line is repeated throughout the poem in ironic counterpoint to the physical decline of the speaker and as a medium for the surfacing of his memories of youth, themselves in ironic contrast with his present wretchedness. The poem is a demonstration of how the emotion of life is articulated by literature, a notion to which Hofmannsthal was highly sensitive.

There is an air of almost naive simplicity about Hofmannsthal's second prose poem, 'Gerechtigkeit', written on 26 May 1893 (*SW* xxix. 228–30). The narrative style is like that of an old-fashioned fairy tale, and the combination of this with the severe title leads one to expect a straightforward moral allegory, much like one of Turgenev's prose poems.[71] The speaker is sitting in a colourful garden and is joined by a large dog and 'ein junger blonder schlanker Engel' [a young, blond, slender angel] wearing steely blue armour and carrying both sword and dagger. The gardener's child is also in the garden playing, and asks the Angel about his beautiful shoes, to be told that they are made from a piece of the cloak of the Mother of God. The speaker feels uplifted by the mere thought that the Angel will speak to him, too, 'denn auf den einfachen Worten, die über seine Lippen sprangen, lag ein Glanz, als dächte er dabei an ganz etwas anderes, dächte verschwiegen und mit unterdrücktem Jubel an paradiesische Glückseligkeiten' [for there was a lustre on the simple words that passed his lips, as if he were thinking of something completely different, thinking discreetly and with suppressed rejoicing about the bliss of paradise]. Greeting the Angel, the speaker is frightened by its dark blue, almost threatening eyes, and the 'unheimliches metallisches Blinken' [the uncanny metallic sparkle] of its golden hair. The Angel asks sternly, 'hochmütig, fast verächtlich', ' "Bist du ein Gerechter?" ' [arrogantly, almost scornfully, 'Are you just?'] and when the *Ich* of the poem blusters about being 'nice' or 'good', repeats the question in the tone of a great lord repeating simple

---

[71] Rolf Tarot writes of its 'verkrampfte Allegorisierung' (*Hugo von Hofmannsthal*, 303).

orders to a servant and begins to draw the sword. The *Ich* is afraid and his faculty of comprehension fails him entirely. Eventually he manages to say that he has little understanding of life but is sometimes overcome by a strong feeling of love which gives him a sense of communion with all things, and then he thinks he is just. At such times he has complete understanding of everything, 'von allem das tiefste Wesen, und alle Regungen des Menschen' [the deepest essence of everything and all the stirrings of humanity]. Stopped in his tracks by a sense of overwhelming inadequacy, he sees the Angel looking at him disdainfully. The Angel turns to go, saying, 'Gerechtigkeit ist alles . . . Wer das nicht begreift, wird sterben' [justice is all important, whoever does not understand that, will die], and disappears down the hill, followed by the dog.

The poem is less an investigation into the moral content of the *concept* 'Gerechtigkeit' than a questioning of the communicative power of the *word*. The enumeration of contrasting colours in the garden scene, especially the metallic ones or those described in comparison with precious stones, is one of the characteristic devices of Symbolist poetry that Hofmannsthal found most arresting and imitated, and the Angel is 'einer von den schlanken Pagen Gottes' [one of God's slender pages], redolent of the slightly languid elegance of George's figures. The Angel, his dog and the artificially sculpted landscape are linked by repetitions of vocabulary, and all are elements of a heightened, unnatural, poeticized world. The Angel is addressed simply by the Child, who appears suddenly, the narrator having been so fascinated by the park and the Angel that he has not mentioned it. The Angel and the Child communicate simply and effectively; the Child clearly does not feel in awe as the narrator does; it makes no attempt to interpret the Angel's account of the origin of its shoes and merely repeats the simple fact that they are beautiful. Like the child in the poem 'Weltgeheimnis', this Child possesses the innocent sense of oneness with its world that is the prerequisite for perfect understanding. When the speaker is asked by the Angel, 'Bist du ein Gerechter?' (229, 37) he cannot answer coherently. The Angel is 'streng', his tone 'hochmüthig, fast verächtlich'; 'in seinen Worten war ein Schatten von . . . herrische[r] Ungeduld' [in his words there was a tinge of peremptory impatience; 230, 2–3], and when the *Ich* fails to respond adequately, 'ein hochmüthiges Lächeln verzog [des Engels] schmalen Lippen' [an arrogant smile came over the angel's tight lips; 230, 21]. One might add, without changing the effect, 'Sein Auge bannt und fremd ist Stirn und Haar. | Von seinen Worten, den unscheinbar leisen | Geht eine Herrschaft aus und ein Verführen | Er macht die leere Luft beengend kreisen' (*SW* ii. 61) from 'Der Prophet', describing Stefan George. The challenge emanates from an Angel associated via imagery and tone with a specific background. This is represented not so much by the person of George—who by May 1893 has lost most of the affective force he once had—as by the rigour of the poetic tradition he mediated. The question 'Bist du ein Gerechter?' is less of an enquiry into the ethical state of the narrator than a test to see whether he is in a condition to understand and articulate this understanding meaningfully, a form of linguistic self-possession.

The result of the confrontation, however, is the terrified paralysis of the narrator: 'ich versuchte ihn zu begreifen, aber es gelang mir nicht; mein Denken erlosch, unfähig den lebendigen Sinn des Wortes zu erfassen; vor meinem inneren Aug stand eine leere Wand' [I attempted to understand him, but I could not; my capacity for thought was extinguished, and I could not grasp the real meaning of the word; there was a blank wall before my inner eye; 230, 6–8]. It is not the concept that is unintelligible, but the word that fails to communicate it; the word will not communicate to one fundamentally out of harmony with the context from which it comes, and this context, in poetic terms, is the Symbolist tradition. The parallels with the situation described in the Chandos Letter of 1902 are obvious, and the later text even clearly echoes some of the formulations of the prose poem: 'es gelang mir nicht, [die Menschen und ihre Handlungen] mit dem vereinfachenden Blick der Gewohnheit zu erfassen' [I could not grasp the people and their actions in that habitual manner that makes everything less complex; *SW* xxxi. 49] is closely based on one of the phrases quoted above. As the next chapter will indicate, the world of the Chandos Letter and its pendant, *Das Gespräch über Gedichte*, are intimately concerned with the production and Symbolist aesthetics of the early 1890s.

A further dimension of significance is revealed by the contrast between the material of the narrator's answer to the challenging question and the description he has already provided of the landscape. He answers nervously at first, but then more fluently:

Ich habe so wenig vom Leben ergriffen . . . aber manchmal durchweht mich eine starke Liebe und da ist mir nichts fremd. Und sicherlich bin ich dann gerecht: denn mir ist dann, als könnte ich alles begreifen, wie die Erde rauschende Bäume herauftreibt und wie die Sterne im Raum hängen und kreisen, von allem das tiefste Wesen, und alle Regungen der Menschen. . . . (230, 9–15)

[I have understood so little of life, but sometimes I am possessed by a strong feeling of love and then I understand everything. And I am certainly just then, because I feel I could grasp everything, the way the earth pushes forth rustling trees, the way the stars hang and orbit in space, and above all I grasp the profoundest essence of everything and all the stirrings of humanity.]

This is a perfectly reasonable answer to the question of whether or not the speaker is 'gerecht'. It describes fleeting, epiphanic moments in which the perfect comprehension that the Angel requires is achieved. But since he is cut off by the scorn in the Angel's gaze, it is not because he has failed to understand 'Gerechtigkeit', but because the description he offers is of 'die Liebe' and above all, the innermost essence of mankind. He has recourse to direct natural sensations, and is penetrated by the belief that the evidence of his senses—the rustling of the trees, the sight of the stars, and (synaesthetically) the breeze of love—is reliable. His answer is a restatement of Romantic confidence in the harmony of the world and its participation in the definition of his self. There is no suggestion that perceiving such harmony is the first step towards a higher world; on the contrary it is an enthusiasm for the coherence of this one. For the Symbolist Angel, this is not enough: 'der Blick sagte deutlich: "Was für ein widerwärtiger hohler Schwätzer!" ' [his face clearly said, 'What a revolting, shallow chatterer!'; 230, 18–19], contrasting two types of communication, the supposedly empty babble and the silent but eloquent glance of the Angel. The inadequacy that the *Ich* feels in the face of the Angel, who has now invested communicative force both in the single word 'gerecht' and in silence, is not the realization of his moral or conceptual shallowness but of the inappropriateness of his means of expression and its preconditions.

The final paragraph of the prose poem restates the superior integration of the Angel with his surroundings by repeating the linguistic elements that established it, and confirms the aesthetic unity of the poem by an effect of mirroring, or more exactly of chiasmus, for the dog initially preceded the Angel and at the end leaves behind him. The Angel's elegant golden-haired figure, clad in dark armour and an emerald-green beret, vanishes 'in's Unsichtbare' [into the Invisible; 230, 29–31], and thus to the territory inhabited by the Symbolists, 'L'inconnu', 'l'infini' or 'l'invisible'. Hofmannsthal's attitude to this is ambivalent: on the one hand the figure of the Angel and what he stands for is not only impressive but beautiful; but on the other the narrator's simple faith is beautiful too. This positive component is made even clearer when the description of the Angel is compared with a note that Hofmannsthal made in his diary in November 1892 about Lili Schalk: 'sie erinnert an irgendeinen der Engel des Mantegna, der schlanken Pagen Gottes, mit goldblondem Haar und stahlblauem Harnisch' [she reminds me of one of Mantegna's angels, God's slender pages with golden hair and steely blue armour].[72] The Angel's progress towards 'das Unsichtbare' is characterized by fluctuations in his visibility— 'wurde unsichtbar . . . tauchte dann wieder auf' [became invisible, then re-emerged; 230, 25–6]—rather as the language demanded by the Symbolists is a mixture of clarity and obscurity. Finally, he jumps from the world into the beyond 'mit einem Satz', where the double valency of 'Satz' as 'bound' or 'sentence' (in what is also the last sentence of the poem) is unavoidable.

The most problematic aspect of the poem 'Gerechtigkeit' is in the clash of two kinds of rhetoric in the mouth of one speaker. The Angel has been conjured into existence by the linguistic facility of the *Ich* narrator, who then describes his own failure in precisely the same area (a problem all too familiar in studies of the Chandos Letter). What resolves the contradiction is the difference in status between the description of the Angel and the reply that the *Ich* is called upon to make. The point at which the narrator's language was seen to fail was where it became engaged with morality, that is to say with an evaluative demand not previously placed on it. What has to be evaluated is the self. Whether the challenge is to be just, honest, loving or generous is immaterial: the question asked is 'Bist *du* gerecht?' and the response attempts to deflect responsibility away from the self. 'Manchmal durchweht mich eine starke Liebe', 'da ist mir nichts fremd' and 'mir ist dann . . .' are the phrases with which the speaker justifies 'sicherlich bin ich dann gerecht' [sometimes I feel a strong love blow through me; then nothing is alien to me; I feel then; I am certainly just then; 230, 10–12]. His instinct is to define himself in terms of his world, for each of these phrases grammatically subordinates *ich* into *mir* or *mich*, locating the initiative elsewhere. The Symbolist's language must be adequate and expressive of everything including the self, and the Angel's challenge reveals how this is not true of the *Ich* writing the prose poem. Hofmannsthal feels instinctively that he does not have the

---

[72] *SW* xxix. 403. Cf. also Wunberg, 'Ohne Rücksicht auf Inhalt', 321.

confidence of a Mallarmé or a George and dramatizes his failure before the challenge of Symbolism.

The prose poem in this instance, perhaps because of its idiosyncratic generic situation, has proved to be an opportunity for Hofmannsthal to introduce a firmer *Ich* than has been possible in the Symbolist-influenced lyric, where it tends to retreat or dissolve altogether. Both Turgenev and Baudelaire offer models of poems with first- or third-person narrative which gives scope for a degree of characterization offering roundedness and strength to the *Ich*. 'Das Glück am Weg' (*SW* xxviii. 7–11) does the same: although it is thought to have been written just after 'Gerechtigkeit' in June or July 1893, it is based on Hofmannsthal's journey to the south of France with Dubray in September 1892, and the *Ich* enjoys therefore not only the support and space for development afforded by prose but also a grounding in real experience. Nienhaus points out that the status of this text as a prose poem is debated.[73] In the paperback edition of Hofmannsthal's works it is published under *Erzählungen*; the Critical Edition rather fudges the matter, since 'Das Glück am Weg' is on its own in the volume entitled *Erzählungen 1*, being the only putative prose poem whose publication was sanctioned by Hofmannsthal himself. It is unlike the rest, therefore, and not in the volume devoted to prose from the *Nachlaß*, namely *Erzählungen 2* (which is subdivided, with a special section for *Prosagedichte*). Herbert Steiner assigned the text to *Prosa I*, amongst the critical essays. Given the degree to which the genre is dependent for its existence on authorial intention, however, I take as decisive Hofmannsthal's note made in 1893 in which 'Glück am Weg' features in a list headed 'Prosagedichte' (*SW* xxix. 397). But there is other evidence, too, since unlike the short story the prose poem shares with the contemporary lyric poetry a concentration of verbal, lexical and morphological echoing, modulation and repetition, its musicality, and often also a heightening of diction.[74]

'Das Glück am Weg' was written about a month after 'Gerechtigkeit' and although it begins much the same way, locating the speaker ('Ich saß . . .', I sat), is initially more like a Mediterranean adventure story than a fairy tale. The speaker is sitting on the deck of a ship sailing out to sea, looking back and preserving a mental picture of the coastline that has now vanished, still smelling the sand and the roses. Three dolphins leap out of the water, entertaining him—in two

[73] Nienhaus, *Das deutsche Prosagedicht*, 140 n. 3.
[74] Nienhaus (ibid. 154–62) discusses some of these features.

striking and incongruous comparisons—like jesters during a procession or 'betrunkene, bocksfüßige Faune vor dem Wagen des
Bakchos' [drunken, cloven-hoofed fauns before Bacchus' cart]. He
almost expects to see Neptune rising from the waves with his conch-
chariot and horses of foam, not a dull painted figure but 'unheimlich
und reizend, wie das Meer selbst, mit reicher Anmut, frauenhaften
Zügen und Lippen, rot wie eine giftige rote Blume' [uncanny and
charming, like the sea itself, full of grace, with feminine features and
lips red like a poisonous red flower]. A ship appears on the horizon,
evidently on its way to Toulon, and the narrator fetches his telescope.
Magnified, the ship is almost uncannily close, and he sees a young
blonde woman lying in a deckchair, with her eyes closed. He observes
her when she sits up, staring ahead of her, and has a sudden intimation
that he knows her: 'Es quoll in mir auf, wie etwas Unbestimmtes,
Süßes, Liebes und Vergangenes' [something indeterminate, sweet,
most dear and long-gone welled up within me]. He tries to imagine
where he has seen her—as a child, in the theatre, riding in the Prater,
a certain boudoir, but cannot place the memory of 'diese schmächtige,
lichte Gestalt und die blumenhafte müde Lieblichkeit des kleinen
Kopfes und darin die faszinierenden, dunklen, mystischen Augen'
[this slight, pale figure and the weary, flower-like charm of her little
head and her fascinating, dark, mystical eyes]. The thought that he
does not know her after all leaves the speaker with a desolate feeling of
inner emptiness apparently quite disproportionate to the situation: 'es
war mir, als hätte ich das Beste an meinem Leben versäumt' [I felt that
the best of my life had passed me by]. But he realizes that he does know
her, not in the way that one normally knows people, but with an
instinctive knowledge associated with music, poetry, and certain evening moods. This instinctive knowledge includes images of their communication in a special, perfect language, her special pose, which
would occur—had already occurred—many times. In one pose 'lag
für mich eine Unendlichkeit von Dingen ausgedrückt: eine ganz
bestimmte Art, ernsthaft, zufrieden und in Schönheit glücklich zu sein'
[there was expressed for me an infinity of things: a quite particular
manner of being serious, satisfied and happy in her beauty]. Looking
across at the woman on the deck, the narrator seems to see her shake
her head, and the ships begin to draw apart again, and it is as if his life
itself is slipping away. He watches in helpless terror as she climbs down
a ladder into the cabin until she has quite disappeared. The departure
of the Angel down the hill in 'Gerechtigkeit' was carefully described:

first its legs vanishing from view, 'dann die Hüften, endlich die dunkel-gepanzerten Schultern, das goldene Haar und das smaragdgrüne Barett' [then the hips, finally the shoulders in dark armour, the golden hair and the emerald green beret]. The descent of the woman into the cabin is lingered over in the same way, and he watches 'wie . . . der grüner Gürtel verschwand, dann die feinen Schultern und dann das dunkelgoldene Haar' [as the green belt disappeared, then her delicate shoulders and then her dark golden hair]. It is as if she has been laid into a grave, sealed with a stone and covered in grass. As the ship sails away the speaker's attention is caught by the golden putti holding its name-plate on which is written 'La Fortune'.

Despite its grounding in real experience, 'Das Glück am Weg' has much in common with 'Erlebnis' and other poems by Hofmannsthal. The connection is apparent first in echoes of phrase and formulation, as in this sentence near the end, for example: 'es war einfach, als glitte dort mein Leben selbst weg . . . und zöge langsam, *lautlos gleitend* seine tiefen, langen Wurzeln aus meiner schwindelnden Seele' [it was simply as if my life were slipping away over there . . . and was slowly, *silently slipping*, pulling its deep, long roots from my giddy soul].[75] There are similarities here, too, with 'Manche freilich', in the phrase 'bei den Wurzeln des verworrenen Lebens' [at the roots of life in its confusion] and in the sensation of giddiness beneath the falling stars. The links are evident from the outset: sitting on the deck of a ship in the Mediterranean, the speaker is lulled, as in 'Erlebnis', by the impression of a scent, perhaps an illusion, but apparently 'der feine Duft . . . der doppelte Duft der süßen Rosen und des sandigen, salzigen Strandes' [the fine fragrance . . . the double fragrance of the sweet roses and the sandy, salty beach; 7, 8–9]; after seeing three dolphins and imagining their place being taken by Neptune in a chariot with Nereids and Tritons (like the statues in Versailles), the vision fades and a dark patch is visible on the horizon—'[ein] fremdes Schiff' [a strange ship].

Es war, wie wenn man durchs Fenster in ein ebenerdiges Zimmer schaut, worin sich Menschen bewegen, die man nie gesehen hat und wahrscheinlich nie kennen wird; aber einen Augenblick lang belauscht man sie ganz in der engen dumpfen Stube, und es ist, als ob man ihnen da unsäglich nahe käme. (8, 10–15)

[It was like when you look through the window into a ground-floor room where there are people moving that you have never seen before and will probably never know; but for a single moment you listen intently to them in the small, stuffy room and you feel as if you are ineffably close to them there.]

[75] 10, 29–31, my italics.

The defamiliarization of the self that 'Erlebnis' gradually enacts is treated here as a *fait accompli*, and 'Das Glück am Weg' registers a longing for reunion, experienced as a sudden epiphanic flash of kinship: the vessel, however, is still alien, as are the 'fremdgeformte Riesensegeln' of the verse poem. However, after at first failing to establish that he knows the woman, the *Ich* of the prose poem (which the reference to the Prater and the setting in the Mediterranean compel us to associate with Hofmannsthal's biographical identity) manages to re-establish the continuity that 'Erlebnis' dissolved into two alien selves, separated by water, and he does so initially with the same agent that effected the dissolution in the verse poem, namely music.

Dann fiel mir ein: Ja, ich kannte sie, das heißt, nicht wie man gewöhnlich Menschen kennt, aber gleichviel, ich hatte hundermal an sie gedacht, Hunderte von Malen, Jahre und Jahre hindurch

   Gewisse Musik hatte mir von ihr geredet, ganz deutlich von ihr, am stärksten Schumannsche; gewisse Abendstunden auf grünen Veilchenwiesen, an einem rauschenden kleinen Fluß, darüber der feuchte, rosige Abend lag; gewisse Blumen, Anemonen mit müden Köpfchen . . . gewisse seltsame Stellen in den Werken der Dichter, wo man aufsieht und den Kopf in die Hand stützt und auf einmal vor dem inneren Aug' die goldenen Tore des Lebens aufgerissen scheinen. (9, 15–20)

[Then I remembered: yes, I knew her, that is, not in the sense in which one normally knows people, but no matter, I had thought about her a hundred times, hundreds of times, for years and years. Certain pieces of music spoke to me of her very clearly, Schumann in particular; certain times of the evening in green meadows of violets, by a little rushing river over which the humid, rosy evening hung; certain flowers, anemones with weary heads, certain peculiar passages in the works of the poets when you look up and rest your head in your hands and suddenly the golden gates of life are flung open before your inner eye.]

The Romantic scenes being evoked are important to Hofmannsthal as indicators of the force of a *literary* tradition—the golden gates of life yet again recall Nerval's use of the Homeric images for dream—and he repeats the introductory phrase with its metaphor of language, 'alles das hatte von ihr geredet' [all that spoke to me of her].

   The relationship the *Ich* imagines with the girl on the distant ship is envisaged as sudden and complete: 'solche Dinge *begreift* man nicht: man weiß sie plötzlich' [you do not *comprehend* such things, you just *know* them all of a sudden; 9, 31]. It will be conducted in a perfect language:

ich wußte noch viel mehr; ich wußte, daß ich mit ihr eine besondere Sprache reden würde, besonders im Ton und besonders im Stil: meine Rede wäre leichtsinniger,

beflügelter, freier, sie liefe gleichsam nachtwandelnd auf einer schmalen Rampe dahin; aber sie wäre auch eindringlicher, feierlicher, und gewisser seltsame Saitensysteme würden verstärkend mittönen.
Alle diese Dinge dachte ich nicht deutlich, ich schaute sie in einer fliegenden, vagen Bildersprache. (9, 32–9)

[I knew much more, I knew that I would speak a particular language with her, particular in its tone and in its style: I would speak less deliberately, with more élan, more freely, and my words would run as if sleepwalking along a narrow gangway; but I would speak, too, more insistently, more solemnly, and certain peculiar arrangements of strings would sound along with me in support. I did not think all these things clearly, I saw them in a rapid, indistinct language of images.]

Language is re-expressed not only with the familiar musical metaphor, but spatially as a run towards the beloved, and visually as 'Bildersprache'. Out of the memories of past knowledge of the girl (all in the past and pluperfect tenses) has grown a new language, specially fitted to the circumstance, suddenly complete and perfect in the way that Hofmannsthal's account of metaphor describes the achievement of metaphoric correspondence as a sudden matching of word and situation.[76] The vision is expressed in the tense of unrealized future possibilities, the conditional. The enumeration of its details brings the ship closer, though it is still described as 'fremd': 'In dem Augenblick war uns das fremde Schiff recht nah; näher würde es wohl kaum kommen' [In that moment the strange ship was really close; it would probably not be able to come any closer; 10, 1–2]. Within the last clause are poised the realization of the vision and acceptance of its failure, for it expresses both satisfaction that the ship is so close and an implicit recognition that however close that is, like the asymptote it will never actually be reachable.

Previously, through the telescope, the girl perceived was a young blond woman, wearing little pale-coloured shoes and a moss-green belt (8, 19–21). Having envisaged the language in which the vision of the girl will be realized, the speaker knows more about her,

ihre Bewegungen, die Haltung ihres Kopfes, das Lächeln, das sie haben würde, wenn ich ihr gewisse Dinge sagte. Wenn sie auf der Terrasse säße, . . . dann würde sie mit einer undefinierbaren reizenden kleinen Pose die Schultern wie frierend in die Höhe ziehen und mich mit ihren mystischen Augen ernst und leise spöttisch von oben herab ansehen. (10, 3–12)

[her movements, the way she holds her head, the smile she would give when I said certain things to her. If she sat on the terrace, she would raise her shoulders in an

[76] See above, pp. 126–7.

indefinable, charming little gesture, as if she were cold, and look down at me with her mystical eyes, seriously and gently mocking.]

Like the dying child in the *Terzinen* 'Die Stunden!', for example, who is likened to a saint (*SW* i. 49), she seems in her perfection to reproach the observer: 'da war mir, als ob sie leise, mit unmerklichem Lächeln den Kopf schüttelte' [I felt as if she were gently shaking her head and smiling imperceptibly; 10, 24–5]. And indeed, as if in response, the ships begin to part company: 'es war einfach, als glitte mein Leben selbst weg . . . nichts zurücklassend als unendliche, blöde Leere' [it was simply as if my life itself were slipping away, leaving nothing behind but a stupid, infinite vacuum].[77] The same word, 'unendlich', is used both of the sensations of fulfilment and of the experience of crushing loss, for infinity has the same ambivalence in Hofmannsthal's thinking as it does in Baudelaire's, and as it was manifested in his 'Le *Confiteor* de l'artiste'.

The vacuum that is produced when the girl's ship departs is created by the loss of the dream of perfect communication. The *Ich* had had a vision of complete correspondence (expressed in the absolutist use of 'wissen': 'ich *wußte* ihre Bewegungen' and 'man *weiß* [solche Dinge] plötzlich') and it has disappeared leaving nothingness behind, the equivalent of Baudelaire's *gouffre*. The characteristics that Hofmannsthal enumerates to describe the gradual withdrawal of the vision are those that he has consistently associated with Symbolist poetry:

Stumpf, gedankenlos aufmerksam sah ich zu, wie sich zwischen sie und mich ein leerer, reinlicher, emailblauer, glänzender Wasserstreifen legte, der immer breiter wurde. In hilfloser Angst sah ich ihr nach, wie sie mit langsamen Schritten schlank und biegsam eine kleine Treppe hinabstieg, wie Ruck auf Ruck in der Luke der grüne Gürtel verschwand, dann die feinen Schultern und dann das dunkelgoldene Haar. (10, 33–9)

[I watched leadenly, thoughtlessly attentive, as an empty, pristine, enamel-blue, sparkling strip of water came between her and me and became wider and wider. Helpless with fear, I watched her go down a little stairway, treading slowly, slender

---

[77] 10, 29–32. The poise and profundity evoked in this description have much in common with the figures who sit with the Sibyls and Queens in 'Manche freilich', on thrones aloft, 'wie zu Hause, | Leichten Hauptes und leichter Hände' (*SW* i. 54). They too look down on 'manche' below; they have within them an infinity of existences, like the Mona Lisa, upon whose head 'all the ends of the world are come' (cf. below, p. 259), just as in the pose of the girl on the ship 'eine Unendlichkeit von Dingen [lag] ausgedrückt' (10, 17). In the prose poem, the *Ich* also looks across at the girl: 'dabei sah ich ununterbrochen *hinüber*' (10, 22–3; my italics); in 'Manche freilich' the same word (not entirely unproblematic in its context) is used: 'ein Schatten fällt von jenen Leben | In die anderen Leben *hinüber*' (my italics).

and supple, watching as the green belt disappeared jerkily into the hatch, and then her delicate shoulders and then her dark golden hair.]

For the *Ich* it is as if the girl so lovingly evoked has been laid amongst the dead, 'gar nichts konnte sie mehr für mich sein' (11, 3). To say 'she could mean absolutely nothing more to me now' is an odd way of describing the death of one's beloved; it focuses on her usefulness or her function rather than on any emotions that might be aroused. But since she represents a branch of the poetic tradition, the expression is appropriate, for Symbolism was envisaged at this point as functional, a tool with which to develop a more expressive poetic language.

The poem almost enacts a scene from Hofmannsthal's Symbolist-associated past, as the passing of ships in the sun strongly echoes the complex of ideas around Baudelaire's sonnet 'A une passante', Hofmannsthal's poem to George, and the reference to ' "Tyche", das Zufällig-Zugefallene' in 'Age of Innocence' in 1891 and 1892.[78] The narrator of 'Glück am Wege' has encountered someone in whom the entire meaning of his existence is concentrated, someone, in Baudelaire's phrase, 'dont le regard m'a fait soudainement renaître'. The image of burial at the end of the prose poem closes off all possibility of ever seeing the woman again, except, again in Baudelaire's phrase, 'dans l'éternité'. Hofmannsthal complained to Beer-Hofmann that in print 'Das Glück am Weg' was 'schattenhaft, unkörperlich, saftlos, leblos' [shadowy, insubstantial, dry, lifeless], which is hardly surprising.[79] The moment of epiphanic self-revelation that the narrator has experienced is over and will not recur on earth. George's imaginative translation of the penultimate line is equally appropriate, 'Du bist mir fremd, ich ward dir nie genannt': 'das fremde Schiff' in 'Glück am Weg' approaches 'recht nah; näher würde es kaum kommen'.[80] A few lines before the reference to 'Tyche' in 'Age of Innocence' Hofmannsthal writes of his young alter ego, 'er empfand plötzlich eine Sehnsucht danach, in fremde Zimmer hineinzuschauen und fremde Menschen fühlen zu fühlen' [he suddenly felt an urge to look into strange rooms and feel strange people feeling; *SW* xxix. 20], which anticipates both the image of the child seeing 'durchs offene Fenster Licht in seinem Zimmer' in 'Erlebnis' and more exactly in 'Glück am Weg' the narrator's comparison of looking through the telescope to looking 'durchs Fenster in ein ebenerdiges Zimmer' and seeing people he has

---

[78] See above, pp. 195–7, Baudelaire, *OC*, i. 92–3, *SW* ii. 60 and *SW* xxix. 20.
[79] Beer-Hofmann, *BW*, 19; letter of 4 July 1893.
[80] George, *Werke*, ii. 310.

never met and will never meet. The prose poems are tied in very firmly
to the issues of the early verse poems.[81]

Given these intertexts, one might expect the name of the ship on
which the woman was carried to be 'Tyche', but in the very last words
of the poem it is identified as 'La Fortune', which is closely related.
Nienhaus identifies the striking repetitions of the words 'Glück'
and 'glücklich' in the description of how the pose of the young girl
guaranteed the 'Glück' of the narrator, and thus establishes the
metonymical equation of girl and vessel.[82] He interprets the recession
of the ship Fortune, however, as the loss of the narrator's ability to
make concepts meaningful, the debunking of the narrator's naive trust
in being able to bring about and maintain an experience of happiness.[83] Tarot, too, interprets the ship's name as 'die Hoffnung auf ein
Finden des Glücks im Schicksal' [the hope of finding happiness in
fate], relying on the double meaning of the ship's name, the French
word 'Fortune', as *fortuna/ Geschick*.[84] This leaves open the question of
what an experience of 'Glück' might constitute. The experience whose
loss is described by the *Ich* is the successful appropriation of a recent
poetic tradition for the purposes of more perfect communication. Like
the Chandos Letter, though, there is a paradoxical ambiguity about
this loss since it is in a sense recaptured by the poem: the inability to
maintain a 'fortunate' or perfectly correspondent relationship between
Ich and girl is permanently enshrined in the prose poem that describes
its failure. He has achieved a communicative 'fliegende, vage Bildersprache' and whatever he might say about being left 'stumpf' or
'gedankenlos', the death of the vision has not left him inarticulate.
What is most effectively articulated is the 'hilflose Angst' that the
subject feels at the prospect of loss, and not the loss itself.

The last of Hofmannsthal's prose poems is 'Erinnerung' from 1924
and thus written at a point well beyond the chronological confines of
this study. None the less, it should be examined briefly here because it
is almost explicitly a reflection on the mode of writing practised in 'jene
Jugendtage' [the days of my youth] to which the first line refers.[85]

[81] Cf. Renner, 'Die Tiefe muß man verstecken', 253–65, an excellent commentary
that situates Hofmannsthal's prose poem in the context of Nietzsche and Stendhal and develops the interpretation of the Baudelaire echoes. Hofmannsthal's modernistic revaluation
of the stylistic device of allegory should also be seen in the context of his interest in
Symbolism, however.
[82] Nienhaus, *Das deutsche Prosagedicht*, 158.
[83] Ibid. 160.
[84] Tarot, *Hugo von Hofmannsthal*, 305.
[85] *EGB*, 454. All quotations from this poem are from *EGB*, 454–5. Cf. Nienhaus's

Even writing at a distance of some thirty-five years, Hofmannsthal's memories take him back in the same vocabulary as 'Erlebnis', 'Psyche', and the early prose poems such that he lands 'in einem geisterhaften Raum, in dessen dunkelglänzender Fülle die Seele badet' [a spectral room, in whose darkly shining opulence the soul can immerse itself].[86] The room is barely delimited—'Raum' means both 'room' and 'space'—its walls merely 'angedeutet als ein Etwas, das ein geräumiges Innen von einem mit düsterem Glanz hereindrohenden Außen trennt' [hinted at as something that separates a spacious interior from an outside that threatens to break in with sombre brilliance]. He sees, therefore, his early experiences as distinct, but not sharply so—certainly not as sharply cut off as the Chandos Letter implies. And these years are threatened by what lies outside them, something sombrely splendid—like the weight of past literary tradition. The occupants of the room that is Hofmannsthal's past are shadows:

wer weiß auch, ob es durchaus sterbliche Wesen sind, deren Gegenwart dieses gedämpfte harmonische Durcheinanderwogen bildet, oder ob nicht seine eigenen Emanationen gleich abgelösten Spiegelbildern mit dem einzelnen Gaste wandeln und durch die Gegenwart dieser Genien jene eigentümlich reichen Gruppen entstehen, gleich Bündeln von Masken, Garben farbigen Wassers oder erleuchteten Kandelabern, von deren Anblick dem Auge in diesem Raum so wohl wird.

[and who knows if the beings whose presence is formed by this muffled harmonious mingling are quite mortal beings, or whether his own emanations are walking with the only guest like reflections released from their mirrors, and through the presence of these genies are formed those peculiarly rich groups, like bundles of masks, sheaves of colourful water or blazing candelabra at the sight of which the eye derives a feeling of comfort here in this room.]

The first alternative evokes mortal—that is, impermanent—figures produced from the harmony of the atmosphere itself; the second conjures up figures like independently existing reflections of oneself surrounding the one occupant of the room, the illusion of crowds and groups arising from projections of one's own psyche. The images used

comment, ' "Erinnerung" ist auch zu verstehen als späte Reflexion des Autors aufs eigene Dichten' (*Das deutsche Prosagedicht*, 170), which seems to imply that the other prose poems are not reflections of this nature. His later article on the various contexts, including *Andreas*, in which Hofmannsthal uses the quotation from Baudelaire that appears towards the end of 'Erinnerung' (see below) does not extend this point significantly: the prose poem is 'als späte Formulierung [des] Ideals poetischen Sprechens als des einzig wahren und realistischen . . . zu lesen' (Nienhaus, ' "Scharfe Spitze" ', 96).

[86] Although Hofmannsthal insists that the experience of memory is not like the experience of death, the imagery suggests a comparison: cf. 'Erlebnis', ll. 6–9 (*SW* i. 31).

for the groups confirm the impression of instability and artificiality: bundles of masks instead of real faces; sheaves of coloured water that only exist for the moment they are perceived in the fountain before falling away; the collected light of the branches of a candelabrum. There is no core or permanent unity to any of these. The question that Hofmannsthal implies is whether what populated his early years was the genuine product of harmonious totality or the insubstantial creation of his own self-image. The latter possibility is evoked in the language he used to associate with Symbolist poetry.

None of the beings in the space is wholly alien to the remembering *Ich*, and a mere scrap of conversation is enough to bring back to him its whole context. He paraphrases his own poetry (the *Terzinen* 'Über Vergänglichkeit') to describe his relationship to them, who are 'so vertraut und fremd wie mein Selbst' [as familiar and strange as my own self], an oxymoron characteristic of Hofmannsthal in the early 1890s. They are proud, and 'Stolz' is seen as being in reality 'grenzenlose Hingabe an das Unbekannte' [boundless abandonment to the unknown], which has a familiar duality of control and abandon. The attitude of the figure from 1924 is tolerant and indulgent: he detects in their pride 'die Verlorenheit ihres Ichs in der Größe ihres Traumes, und der unstillbare Durst nach dem Schönen' [the disorientation of their self in the vastness of their dream, the unquenchable thirst for beauty], the latter his artistic *raison d'être* during his first creative decade, the former its greatest threat. His conclusion, 'sie gleichen Dämonen, und sie sind es' [they are like demons, they *are* demons], is immediately mitigated to 'es sind lauter junge Menschen' [they are just young people]. Such attitudes and categories for interpreting the world are the province of youth, and 'tout comprendre, c'est tout pardonner'. The demons, however, were powerful at the time.

The stateliness of the tone and the self-control with which Hofmannsthal both performs a memory of a past and evokes the mechanisms of the act of remembering give way in the fourth paragraph to a slight quickening of enthusiasm as nostalgia grows: 'aber es ist der reichste Raum den ich jemals betreten habe oder betreten werde' [but it is the richest room I have ever been in or will ever be in]. There is a beautiful description of its light, that also echoes early poetry:

Das Licht, das ihn erfüllt, ist das Licht des Morgens, aber ohne die Naivetät, die dem irdischen Morgen eignet: es ist als hätte dieser Morgen im voraus den Abend verzehrt; sein Glanz ist ahnungsvoll, und seine Schatten sind wissend.

[The light that fills it is the light of morning, but without the naivety that is characteristic of the earthly morning: it is as if this morning had already consumed the evening; its brilliance is portentous, and its shadows are knowing.]

The image of the night devouring morning is the reverse of the image Hofmannsthal used in *Ad me ipsum* to interpret the last line of 'Ballade des äußeren Lebens', 'Und dennoch sagt der viel, der "Abend" sagt' [and whoever says the word 'Evening' says a great deal none the less]. *Ad me ipsum* adds the gloss, 'Den Hesperos lassen die Alten alles zusammenführen was die Eos trennt' [the ancients said that Hesperos brought back together what Eos divided],[87] where the evening is said to reconcile the divisions of the day. But the irony, and the significance of the integrative symbolic effect of 'Abend', is that the evening star and the morning star are the same. Youth, in Hofmannsthal's 'Erinnerung', has precociously devoured the maturity of evening, for it has swallowed the whole of an older tradition—and risked losing its identity in the process. But the risk is that generation's distinguishing glory: 'ungleich jenem andern Saal, dessen Wände sterbliche Wesen umschließen, ist es gerade die Ungesichertheit, welche diesen so verherrlicht' [unlike that other room, whose walls are surrounded by mortal beings, it is precisely insecurity that so dignifies this one].

The fifth and sixth paragraphs concentrate the sense of threat that mounts around the occupants of the remembered room of youth. Nienhaus identifies the source of the danger: it is already contained within the room itself, since there is nothing that the room/space (of the dream and of art) cannot subsume into itself—by virtue of its emptiness.[88] The threat is simultaneously from outside and from inside, the danger of being *too* receptive to external stimuli, and the core of selfhood is targeted. 'Jeder fühlt sie [die Drohung] wie die Spitze einer Lanze, sein Herz suchen' [everyone feels the threat aiming at his heart, like the point of a lance; *EGB*, 455]. But as the lance is identified with a quotation from Baudelaire's 'Le *Confiteor* de l'artiste' as infinity, 'die scharfe Spitze der Unendlichkeit' [the sharp point of infinity], threat becomes triumph. Source and new context of this quotation are criss-crossed with oxymoron and paradox. Baudelaire writes of concentration and extension: 'il est de certaines sensations délicieuses dont le vague n'exclut pas l'intensité; et il n'est pas de pointe plus acérée que celle de l'Infini' [there are certain delicious sensations whose vagueness does not preclude intensity; there is no sharper point

---

[87] *RA* iii. 609. Cf. *SW* i. 44.   [88] Nienhaus, *Das deutsche Prosagedicht*, 169.

than that of infinity; i. 278]. Hofmannsthal modulates this into vulnerability and confidence, leaving open the final question of whether such
confidence is justified or not:

> die Drohung [geht] jäh über in eine Erfüllung von fast unerträglicher Herrlichkeit,
> und wen sie, 'die scharfe Spitze der Unendlichkeit', in diesem geisterhaften
> Morgenkampf getroffen hat, dem hat in dem langen Kampf, der nun anhebt, der
> Richter den höchsten Kranz weder zu geben noch zu weigern. Er trägt ihn.—
> Unverdient?—um welchen Blutpreis erkauft?—das ist sein Geheimnis.

[the threat suddenly modules into fulfilment of an almost unbearable magnificence, and whoever is pierced in this spectral morning combat by the 'sharp point
of infinity' will neither be given nor refused the highest garland in the long battle
that is just now beginning. He already wears it.—Undeservedly?—acquired at
what bloody price?—that is his secret.]

The couple 'Drohung/Herrlichkeit', like the 'Stolz/Hingabe' pair, is
only a slight modulation of the 'Gefühl von Herrschaftlichkeit und
Abhängigkeit' of Hofmannsthal's 1895 letter to Beer-Hofmann. Either
both elements are simultaneously present and inseparable, or judgement on whether the triumph of one component is justified is withheld.
The 'Blutpreis' that may or may not have been paid is the integrity of
the self.[89]

It has been a consistent characteristic of Hofmannsthal's poetry,
verse and prose, to incorporate a hermeneutic dimension of reflections
on the literary climate in which he was writing, *pace* Gotthart Wunberg's view that the prose poems are 'eine Leere Form eigentlich'—
'"Bedeuten" tun sie nicht; sie wollen nicht signifikant sein. Sie sind,
was sie sind' [an empty form—they do not 'mean'; they do not wish to
be significant. They are what they are][90] Hofmannsthal's concerns
about its effects on his originality, and his 'Erinnerung' make this clear,
from the opening paragraph onwards. The quotation from Baudelaire's prose poem indicates that 'jene Jugendtage' are linked in
Hofmannsthal's mind with the influence of French poetry and the
need to come to terms with the problems its presuppositions created. It
is probably true that 'sein "Lieblingswort", das "Unendliche", hat der
"Neuromantiker" Hofmannsthal nicht etwa von der deutschen
Romantik, sondern vom französischen Symbolismus gelernt' [the
'Neo-Romantic' Hofmannsthal did not learn his 'favourite word', 'the

---

[89] It may also be an echo of the sacrifice passage in *Das Gespräch über Gedichte*, *SW* xxxi. 80–1.
See Chapter 5 below.

[90] Wunberg, 'Ohne Rücksicht auf Inhalt', 322 and 320.

infinite', from German Romanticism but from French Symbolism],[91] and infinity was both enticing and threatening. Hofmannsthal's poetic temperament did not permit him anything as demonstrative as a Baudelairean 'cri de frayeur', but it may be, as it perhaps was for Baudelaire, too, that the abandoning of verse is itself a gesture towards admitting failure. His prose poems evoke the dangers and temptations of his own poetic situation, and tend on the whole to warn against pursuing the Symbolist path. The verdict that 'Erinnerung' implies is open: looking back without the context of the 'hilflose Angst' with which the speaker in 'Das Glück am Weg' greets the disappearance of the mysterious woman perhaps even implies that the stimulus of Symbolism is in 1924 recognized as having contributed to the formation of an independent and stable self, and that the fear did not swamp but build it, although at the point at which the earlier prose poems were written, 1893, no such serenity was possible.

The early verse poems analysed in Chapter 3 were experiments with Symbolist imagery that revealed not a Symbolist's confidence in casting loose language from identity in order to create access to a spiritually transfigured harmonious universe, but dissatisfaction with the artificial worlds thus created and a Romantic's nostalgia for real experience. The prose poems reflect at a greater distance from the rhetoric of such Symbolist verse its capacity, or rather failure, to enshrine subjective truths reliably, and the anxiety that consequently characterizes the self's relationship with both real and artistic worlds. 'Manche freilich' also belongs to this group of poems. It is a sustained reflection on the issues of identity they raise, links them to the questions of intertextual borrowing and artistic originality that have been hovering in the Symbolist climate since Baudelaire, and does so using image-complexes derived not only from past poetry but in particular from recent French poetry and from George. It also represents one of the very points at which Hofmannsthal's lyric poetry manages to convert its disintegrative influences into an assertion of integration that carries some conviction.

The poem was finished in February 1896, shortly before it was sent to George for publication in *Die Blätter für die Kunst* at the end of March. Although 'Manche freilich' is usually dated from the summer of 1895, and thus outside the period in which Hofmannsthal was most interested in Symbolism, this is not an unshakeable *terminus a quo* for the

<hr />

[91] Nienhaus, ' "Scharfe Spitze" ', 84. 'Lieblingswort' is taken from Alewyn, *Über Hugo von Hofmannsthal*, 169 n. 68.

poem's conception. When Hofmannsthal gave away his first manuscript in the 1920s he wrote, 'ganz zufällig kam mir dieser kleine Zettel
in die Hand—das kann nichts Anderes sein als die erste Niederschrift
des Gedichts "Manche freilich" *aus meinem 19ᵗᵉⁿ Lebensjahr.* Vielleicht
macht Ihnen Spaß, es zu behalten' [quite by chance this little sheet of
paper came into my hand—it must be nothing other than the first
written version of the poem 'Manche freilich' from my 19th year.
Perhaps it would amuse you to keep it].[92] But Hofmannsthal's nineteenth year was 1892–3, which suggests there was some confusion: the
version enclosed already contained clear echoes of Knackfuß's biography of Michelangelo read in July 1895 (not before, since it was first
published in 1895) and cannot have been written down earlier.[93]
Hofmannsthal's memory seems not to have been quite precise: either
this *is* the first written version, misdated in recollection; or it has been
mistaken for a version, since lost, actually dating from 1892–3. And at
a distance of thirty years Hofmannsthal may in any case have meant
his twentieth year, 1893–4. Confusions notwithstanding, however,
Hofmannsthal's retrospective glance at 'Manche freilich' associates
the poem with a period some time before 1895–6. There are echoes,
too, of Walter Pater in 'Manche freilich', and although Hofmannsthal
began reading Pater seriously early in 1894, after Elsa Bruckmann-
Cantacuzène sent him *The Renaissance* and *Imaginary Portraits* on 27
January, a diary entry from December 1892 suggests that Pater had
been familiar for over a year.[94] This, too, responds to the hint in the late
letter to look further back than summer 1895 and place at least the conception of the poem, if not an early draft, in 1893. The final text reads
as follows:

> Manche freilich müssen drunten sterben,
> Wo die schweren Ruder der Schiffe streifen,
> Andre wohnen bei dem Steuer droben,
> Kennen Vogelflug und die Länder der Sterne.

[92] My italics. I am grateful to the late Dr Rudolf Hirsch for this quotation. The letter concerned is unavailable for consultation in full, and no further details are accessible. Although
the present study represents some advances of thinking and even changes of heart since the
article 'Wer lügt, macht schlechte Metaphern' (*Deutsche Vierteljahrsschrift für Literaturwissenschaft
und Geistesgeschichte*, 65 (1991), 717–54) appeared (the point at which Pater is thought to have
become influential is here advanced somewhat, for example), several passages are retained in
modified form. These are passages important for the context in which 'Manche freilich' is
here presented, and which was only sketched in the earlier article.

[93] Cf. Hoppe, *Hofmannsthal*, 36–7; Vilain, 'Wer lügt', 745–6.

[94] Cf. *SW* iii. 482. For a fuller exposition of the significance of Pater for 'Manche freilich',
see Vilain, 'Wer lügt', 730–41, and for suggestions of modifications to this, see Rizza, *Kassner
and Hofmannsthal*, 61.

Manche liegen immer mit schweren Gliedern
Bei den Wurzeln des verworrenen Lebens,
Andern sind die Stühle gerichtet
Bei den Sibyllen, den Königinnen,
Und da sitzen sie wie zu Hause,
Leichten Hauptes und leichter Hände.

Doch ein Schatten fällt von jenen Leben
In die anderen Leben hinüber,
Und die leichten sind an die schweren
Wie an Luft und Erde gebunden:

Ganz vergessener Völker Müdigkeiten
Kann ich nicht abtun von meinen Lidern,
Noch weghalten von der erschrockenen Seele
Stummes Niederfallen ferner Sterne.

Viele Geschicke weben neben dem meinen,
Durcheinander spielt sie alle das Dasein,
Und mein Teil ist mehr als dieses Lebens
Schlanke Flamme oder schmale Leier. (*SW* i. 54)

[Some, it is true, must die down below where the heavy ship's oars ply, whilst others live above by the wheel, know the flight of birds and the lands of the stars. Some lie forever with heavy limbs down at the roots of life in its confusion, others have their seats with the Sibyls, the Queens, and sit there, at home, with heads and hands light and unburdened. But a shadow falls from the first lives across on to the others' lives, and the lightly burdened are bound to those weighted down as they are to air and earth. I cannot shift the weariness of quite forgotten peoples from my eyelids, nor can I keep the silent falling of distant stars from my terrified soul. Many fates are woven next to mine, existence mixes them all up, and my part is more than the slender flame or narrow lyre of this life.]

The first verse of 'Manche freilich' is structured by the opposition of 'Manche' and 'andre' on a vertical axis established by 'drunten' and 'droben'. This axis is superimposed on the concrete image of a classical galley, where 'manche' are those condemned to spend their lives rowing the ship in the dark of the hull until they die there, and 'andre' are such as the captain and crew, on deck in the open air. Significantly, both below and above are described with interdependent images: propulsion (oars) and navigation ('Vogelflug' and the stars) are both indispensable for efficient progress. But both 'Vogelflug' (in the sense of auspices) and 'Länder der Sterne' also point to a consciousness of something beyond the contingency of present existence, and the inevitable death of those below marks the absence of such a consciousness.

Verse 2 uses the same structural pillars and develops the implied contrast between lightness and heaviness, 'schweren Gliedern' balancing 'leichten Hauptes und leichter Hände'. Literal heaviness and lightness are augmented by sensations of difficulty and ease, passivity and alertness, and the complete notion 'heaviness of limb' carries psychic associations of depression as well as suggestions of physical massiveness. The image of '[die] Wurzeln des verworrenen Lebens' economically uses a transferred epithet to extend this sense of the equivalence of physical and psychic states, for the force of 'verworren' is shared between the visual picture of tangled roots and the intellectual-emotional assessment of a confused life. The parallels in the last line of this verse, however—repeated adjective, alliteration and rhythm—encapsulate the balanced interdependence of mind and body in a formal equilibrium.

The beings associated with lightness are both feminine, 'Sibyllen' and 'Königinnen', and they unite associations of increased perception, knowledge and authority. The Sibyls were prophetesses of the ancient world, sources of obscure but significant pronouncements, an acknowledgment here of an important dimension of life not universally or immediately accessible. Their juxtaposition with 'Königinnen' identifies this dimension as one of dignity, a suggestion confirmed by the note of imperious ease in 'leichten Hauptes und leichter Hände'. There is, however, a touch of instability. Reinhold Grimm contends that 'wie zu Hause' means *as if* they were there at home, or in other words that they are therefore precisely *not* at home there by right, but permanently endangered and exposed to the whims of the higher powers.[95] It is perhaps unnecessary to insist: the phrase is of its nature potentially ambiguous, hovering between security and insecurity. The unease it suggests is all the subtler for its necessary ambiguity.

Where the first verse had a clear vertical line notionally linking the sequence 'drunten—droben—Vogelflug—Sterne', the second is augmented by a horizontal plane. Its vertical axis ('gerichtet', reinforced by the contrast between 'bei den Wurzeln' and the implications of 'highness' in 'Königinnen') is crossed by the horizontal established in the word 'liegen'. The bare vertical structure of the metaphor's vehicle is filled out with a second dimension, which anticipates the complexity

[95] Grimm, 'Das einzige Gesetz und das bittere: Hofmannsthals "Schicksalslied"', in Benjamin Bennett et al. (eds.), *Probleme der Moderne* (Tübingen: Niemeyer, 1983), 161.

that verse 3 introduces into the spiritual tenor. It is at this stage, however, fundamentally an upward-looking structure: each verse repeats the sequence low-to-high and ends on a positive image.

The shadow that falls in verse 3 falls in a definite direction, from those below on to those above. 'Jene' must pick up 'manche' (those below) and 'andere', consistent with its use so far, those on the open deck or sitting amongst the Sibyls and Queens. But the vertical axis is ignored in favour of the horizontal, for 'hinüber' is not 'hinauf'. Those at the source of the shadow are distanced from a possible narrating figure by the use of 'jene', whilst any intimacy with those above is precluded by calling them 'andere'. It is wholly *un*clear where the observer is to be found, and indeed so far there has not been an identity in the poem to hold any position from which to observe or speak. There has been a concentration of words and images denoting relative positions in space but nothing, until the 'ich' of the next verse (line 16), to which the reader can confidently relate that space.

Lines 13 and 14 exacerbate the subtle sense of disorientation: 'Und die leichten sind an die schweren | Wie an Luft und Erde gebunden.' The key notion here, 'binden und gebunden werden', or reciprocal commitment, is one of the foundations of Hofmannsthal's view of a fulfilling life, first formulated by Death in *Der Tor und der Tod* as 'man bindet und man wird gebunden' [one binds and one is bound; *SW* iii. 72]. Here it is ostensibly again a notion of straightforward stability and clear definition. But the *form* of this comparison withholds stability. The skeleton can be rendered thus: 'The light are bound to the heavy as [the light are bound] to air-and-earth.' This is an appeal to elemental dependence, for life presupposes air to breathe and a place to stand, and the implication is that the link of 'die leichten' to 'die schweren' is one of the same order of natural necessity. However, this demonstration of the interpenetration of opposites calls upon an unstable term of comparison. Air and earth are themselves a contrastive pair of weightlessness and weight, and make themselves felt as such because the force of the binary oppositions that have so far structured the poem is so pervasive—and paradoxically they thereby undermine the original, apparently categorical antagonism. Even if the general sense of the *difference* of supposed opposites is not obscured, their clarity is deliberately reduced. Hofmannsthal has been very careful not to allow his opposites to freeze: by elevating the adjectives 'leicht' and 'schwer' into substantives with a capital letter, he would have fixed them more firmly into incompatible factions. As it stands, they remain dependent on their common antecedent noun, 'Leben', which permits of no such over-simplification.

The colon at the end of the third verse is eloquent. A stage has been set and we are waiting for the entrance of a performer. The general critical view of the effect of this colon follows Wolfgang Kayser, namely that the poem is in two parts, the colon being the place where they pivot; the first part focuses on the world of the others, the second on the world of the speaking voice.[96] But this separates too sharply the *Ich* and the others, and neglects a development within what he calls the first section. It is perhaps more helpful to abandon the view of a simple duplex structure in favour of a triplex one: verses 1 and 2 set up and offer extensions of a basic contrast, verse 3 proposes a revision of the apparently simple polarity, and verses 4 and 5 relate the revision to an individual consciousness. Each section ends with a two-line phrase introduced with *und*. The middle verse is isolated both by the 'doch' that begins it and by the occurrence of the *und*-cadences at the end of it and of the previous verse. This triplex structure would account for the drawing-out effect produced by the presence of two extra lines on the second verse (9–10): they seem to be claiming space for a distinct idea to round itself off.

The reason for the revision that the middle stanza articulates is that a polarized view of the types of human consciousness is inadequate to account for the individual case about to be described. The *Ich* of verse 4 is one of the overshadowed 'andere Leben'. It is sensitive to things beyond the immediate boundaries of the self, but, unlike the 'andre' of verses 1 and 2, is not characterized by upward-striving images. Rather, it is oppressed by a weight dragging from below, and cowers before attack from above. The subject describes itself in very negative terms as being *un*able to *relieve* itself of *other* nations' tiredness. Moreover, the abstract state of *Müdigkeit* is, in a very Verlainean move, made plural as if it were a concrete count-noun, which has the paradoxical effect of increasing its intangibility. And these tirednesses are those of completely forgotten peoples no longer conceived of as having direct relation to the self. That which is beyond, in space or time, is felt as a pressure, a psychic influence expressed in physical terms (consistent with the 'leicht/schwer' complex) acting upon the eyelids. The familiar Hofmannsthalian word 'Schwere' is not used, but it is clearly the sensation evoked, and is reminiscent of Bourget's *taedium vitae* in

---

[96] Wolfgang Kayser, *Das sprachliche Kunstwerk* (Berne: Franke, 1948), 319.

the essay on Baudelaire, 'le ver secret des existences comblées' [the secret worm of overburdened lives].[97]

The *Ich* in the poem is reluctant to assume the burden of this 'composite consciousness', for this inheritance is here somehow problematic. The sensation of heaviness evoked in connection with the limbs of those below is now transferred to the *Ich*, which is forced to acknowledge them as a component of its identity. The implications of verses 1 and 2 were that 'Schwere' characterized an absence of further sensitivity, that the privilege of light lives was an unproblematic awareness of a spiritual dimension. 'Schwere' now seems to be the unavoidable consequence of precisely that sensitivity whose riches tend to stifle any independently existing core of selfhood. This is linked with the besetting problem of aestheticism. The kind of open consciousness that the poem ambivalently describes risks shutting itself off from the pressure of life to enjoy its own sensitivity selectively.

Line 18 adds a note of terror to the languor already evoked. With the lines 'Noch weghalten von der erschrockenen Seele | Stummes Niederfallen ferner Sterne' the direction of the poem has completed a change: the upward sense of the first two verses levelled out in verse 3 and has now turned sharply down. Where the stars of verse 1 were attractive testimonies to a finer consciousness, those of verse 4 are its frightening, even violent, oppressors. Where they were the objects of familiarity in line 4 ('kennen'), they are now emphatically impersonal, for the phonetic link of 'fern' and 'Sterne' is obtrusive. The other distinguishing component of the first constellation image ('Länder') has been modulated into 'Völker', which now has a negative effect conveyed by its qualifiers, and the suggestions of conviviality with the Sibyls are replaced by the discouraging and anonymous 'stumm'.

The individual has been approached from two perspectives. A bird's-eye view of the extremes of human consciousness was inadequate to express the complexity of the individual's spiritual composition, but a view from within completes the picture. The effect is curiously circular: the vaunted sensibility of some individuals distinguishes them from others, but exposes them to sensations analogous to the oppression felt by those others. There is a revival of individual distinction in the last verse, but it is pervaded by the firmly established sense of difficulty and oppression accompanying the realization that a sensitive soul must accept a legacy ranging far beyond the ostensible span of his own experience and duration. The eventual reaffirmation

---

[97] Bourget, 'Charles Baudelaire', in *Œuvres complètes: Critique 1*, 9.

of self-distinction is all the more impressive because we are conscious of the effort required.

The vertical again gives way to the horizontal in line 19 with 'neben'. The plurality of 'viele Geschicke' is juxtaposed with the individuality of 'das meine', but simple lateral proximity is augmented by the idea of interaction, first in the word 'weben', and then in 'durcheinander'. The source of interaction—the reason, in fact, why the simple opposition was inadequate to describe the circumstances of the sensitive—is 'das Dasein', a force operating on each individual life but greater than all of them. Against existence in general, existence in particular ('Leben') is relativized. It is because the lives of the sensitive are part of 'Dasein' that they can be susceptible to the effects of contact with others' lives evoked in verse 3. The notion of community, then, is the source of the oppression registered in verse 4.

The 'schlanke Flamme' and 'schmale Leier' in line 22 are the only internal evidence there is to define what 'dieses Leben' means, and thus the only method of assessing the significance that the phrase 'mein Teil ist mehr' claims.[98] Considering the suggestions of lines 19 and 20 alone, the readiest interpretation is that 'dieses Leben' derives its significance from being part of a greater whole ('Dasein') and that line 22 is merely a self-deprecating description of the physical span of existence. This would, however, represent a surprising *volte-face* after verse 4, where the doubts registered in the sensation of 'Schwere' appear to preclude locating significance solely in community. The alternative is the assertion of independent individual significance where the life referred to in line 21 would be a life at the mercy of other lives, 'composite consciousness'. But to introduce into an interpretation a new, transcendent element of self-assertion in tension with the totality perhaps runs counter to the implications of the 'und' that begins line 21. It is not 'doch' or 'aber', and although this does not necessarily suggest that the last two lines merely expand the previous two, it may preclude the unmotivated introduction of a new value. There is no alternative but to see what the last line suggests and work backwards.

At the end, fire at last joins the other three elements (earth, air and water) in 'Manche freilich', and it arrives not just as fire but as flame. Flame can suggest much, but an attempt to make sense of the image in the context of this poem might concentrate on the following aspects. It represents energy but also inconstancy, instability, and movement. Its

---

[98] External manuscript evidence, too, focuses attention on the last line. Cf. Vilain, 'Wer lügt', 727–8.

boundaries flicker, it has no stable relationship with space, and seems to be struggling to find its own contours. Its visual aspect is one of constant redefinition. It is most certainly there, but has no substance of its own, and seems to be pulled and teased by invisible forces, the victim of their tensions. The adjective 'schlank' highlights its lack of assertiveness, its frailty and perhaps the imminence of extinction, but also its *dis*tinction, its elegance and beauty. Seen thus, the flame is an effective representation of tension, the uneasy interrelationship of opposing forces.

'Leier' is a very different case from its partner. It is an emblem said to have been invented by Mercury and given by him to Apollo. As Apollo's and Orpheus' mythological attribute it is the emblem of poetry. Poetry, even if produced on an object so materially insignificant as a lyre, represents a possibility that the rapidly stilled vibrations of the lyre-strings are nevertheless the source of something greater than themselves. The lyre, then, symbolizes the potential of life not circumscribed by its physical span. The life of the *Ich* is likened to this instrument because the gap between its sensibility and that of 'andre' is the equivalent of the lyre's difference from the inanimate materials that make it up. The adjective 'schmal' is as double-edged as 'schlank', for although life is certainly brief, its brevity is of no consequence in considering its value.

Although the phonetic similarity of the adjectives 'schmal' and 'schlank' reinforces the similarity of the attributes of the two, the images are not synonymous: the flame symbolizes the tensions that compose consciousness; the lyre symbolizes the weakness of the object itself in comparison with its power for more extensive and durable significance. The 'oder' that stands between the flame and the lyre in line 22 is not a mark of mutual exclusivity or interchangeability but an acknowledgement of the necessary multiplicity of perspective faced by a sensitive soul. Thus the images do not force a choice between the two directions in which the phrase 'dieses Leben' points, but owe their existence and meaning to them both. 'Dieses Lebens . . . schmale Leier' defines life as physically short, with potential for greater significance, and 'dieses Lebens schlanke Flamme' encapsulates the definition of life that takes account of the multiple forces acting upon it.

'Dieses Leben', however, is the lesser half of a comparison with 'mein Teil'. It is a lesser pole by no means scorned, and it is because of the positive components of the two images in the last line that the assertion of any greater worth does not necessitate an appeal to some unspecified external values that would clash with the use of 'und' in line 21. The tension and potential that the two images together represent are the products of the tensions of the poem and make possible the affirmation of 'mein Teil ist mehr'. 'Mein Teil' means individual significance itself, and this is derived from tension that has been recognized and exploited, and potential realized—in the manner of the 'Centrumsgefühl, ein Gefühl von Herrschaftlichkeit *und* Abhängigkeit' of the letter to Beer-Hofmann.[99] To be greater than life, it is implied, necessitates being part of it. The lot of the *Ich* is to be simultaneously of life and more than life, to be within life and above it, which is why it is simultaneously blessed with the serenity of 'andre' and burdened with their receptiveness to the ills of 'manche'. Being *aware* of participation in a wider context is the true superiority of the sensitive soul. The progress of the poem has neither effaced the distinction between 'manche' and 'andre' nor confirmed their initial incompatibility, but dissected that distinction, revealed its (and their) underlying tensions and recomposed these in the dynamic symbols at the end.

Wolfgang Kayser refuses to use the word 'symbol' here, which he feels is meaningless, and calls the flame and the lyre 'emblems';[100] Franz-Norbert Mennemeier agrees, describing the *Ich*-figure in the last lines as 'durch emblematische Wortfiguren gleichsam auf Klassikerart geschmückt' [decorated with emblematic word figurations as if in the classical manner].[101] Hofmannsthal was quite explicit about resisting this line of reading in 'Bildlicher Ausdruck' (1897), complaining of a 'falsche Anschauung . . . als seien die Bilder—Metaphern—etwas allenfalls Entbehrliches, dem eigentlichen Stoff, aus welchem Gedichtetes besteht, äußerlich Aufgeheftetes' [a false view, as if the images—metaphors—were something dispensable, something merely stuck on to the outside of the real substance that poems are made of; *RA* i. 234]. Hofmannsthal's images are symbols in the Symbolists' sense of being precipitates of the tensions of the whole poem. Distinct from many characteristic Mallarméan symbols because they point to no transcendent, 'more real' reality than human

---

[99] Beer-Hofmann, *BW*, 47–8; my italics. Cf. 'Ein Knabe' (14 Feb. 1896), whose second verse reads: 'Doch alle seine Tage waren so | Geöffnet wie ein leierförmig Tal, | Darin er *Herr zugleich und Knecht zugleich* | Des weißen Lebens war und ohne Wahl' (*SW* i. 58, my italics).

[100] Kayser, *Das sprachliche Kunstwerk*, 317. He is in good company, however, since Gabriel in *Das Gespräch über Gedichte* is also repelled by the banality of the word 'Symbol' (*SW* xxxi. 80); cf. p. 304.

[101] Mennemeier, 'Gesellschaftliches bei Hugo von Hofmannsthal', in Joachim Bark (ed.), *Literatursoziologie* (Stuttgart: Kohlhammer, 1974), ii. 191 n. 19.

consciousness, they are nevertheless neither static, ready-made tags (emblems), nor are they familiar symbols inserted into the poem but deriving their charge of significance from a wider cultural context (as, say, a rose might). Like Baudelaire's swan, for example, Mallarmé's clown or Verlaine's autumnal scenes, they are significant because composed of the suggestions and relationships of the material within the poem, and almost of those alone, yet resisting deconstruction into those components.

Hofmannsthal effectively offered an interpretation of his symbols in *Der Dichter und diese Zeit* (1906), where a particularly concentrated passage echoes the phrases and ideas of the poem:

[Dem Dichter] ist die Gegenwart in einer unbeschreiblichen Weise durchwoben mit Vergangenheit: in den Poren seines Leibes spürt er das Herübergelebte von vergangenen Tagen, von fernen nie gekannten Vätern und Urvätern, verschwundenen Völkern, abgelebte Zeiten; sein Auge, wenn sonst keines, trifft noch—wie konnte er es wehren?—das lebendige Feuer von Sternen, die längst der eisige Raum hinweggezehrt hat . . . Was ein Mensch ist, ein lebendiger, der die Hände gegen ihn reckt, das ist ihm, nichts Fremderes, der flimmernde Sternenstrahl, den vor dreitausend Jahren eine Welt entsandt und der heute das Auge ihm trifft, und im Gewebe seines Leibes das Nachzucken uralter, kaum mehr zu messender Regung. (*RA* i. 68)

[For the poet, the present is intertwined with the past in an indescribable manner: in the pores of his body he can feel the inherited life of past times, of distant ancestors whom he has never met, of vanished peoples, worn-out ages; his eye, if no one else's, is still met by the living fire of stars long since subsumed into icy space—how could he prevent it? What a human being means to him, a living being stretching out his hands towards him, is meant just the same, no less, by the flickering beam of light from a star that was emitted by a different world three thousand years ago and reaches the eye today, and the same is meant in the very texture of his body by the last throes of an ancient movement that may hardly even be measured now.]

A poet's sensitivity is clearly one that could appropriately be described by the characteristics of the *Ich*, and the poem would show how the creative ability marking the poet's distinction is only of value if the poet is aware that his privilege, far from being located in a cut-and-dried difference from lesser mortals, is derived from his necessary intimate connection with them. This is in fact very different from the implications of a noticeably similar idea and formulation near the end of Gide's *Traité du Narcisse*, where Narcissus (identified with the poet), 'penché sur l'apparence du Monde, sent vaguement en lui, résorbées, les générations humaines qui passent' [leaning over the image of the world, feels vaguely absorbed within him, the passing of human generations].[102] For Gide, more deeply imbued with the Mallarméan ethic of the poet's irreducible distance from society, the myth of the boy in love with himself is the best context in which to express the hermetic action of symbols. Hofmannsthal's poem constitutes a rejection of this ethic; and for him, whatever compliments he might make to the equally aloof George in the review 'Gedichte von Stefan George' written in early 1896, such a stance is inimical to poetry.

Many of the constituent images of 'Manche freilich', like those of 'Correspondances', are echoes from other works. I have analysed elsewhere a variety of the subtexts perceptible behind the images of the poem, but it will be necessary to recapitulate briefly on some of these so as to provide a context for others of more particular relevance to Hofmannsthal's recent interest in Symbolism. Of the key symbols at the end, the flame has characteristics perhaps suggested by an image in one of Vielé-Griffin's love-poems, 'Vous si claire', from the collection *Joies*: 'Vous gracieuse comme une flamme | Et svelte et frêle de corps et d'âme' [you, gracious as a flame, and slender, frail, in body and soul].[103] The image, one element in a man's catalogue of compliments to his lover, makes explicit the aspects of fragility and grace embraced by the flame in 'Manche freilich', and its qualifier, 'schlank', is almost an exact translation of 'svelte'. Vielé-Griffin's comparison incorporates both physical and spiritual dimensions: 'svelte' can refer strictly only to the woman's body; 'frêle' retains this reference but expands the possible associative range into the non-material; 'de corps' activates the physical potential of the image, and keeps the spiritual suspended, to be picked up again finally by 'd'âme'. The woman's response in Vielé-Griffin's dialogue is to call her lover 'Vous mon poème' [you, my poem]: in the model, the poetic metaphor, like the flame, is merely one of a series of hypotactically juxtaposed redefinitions of the beloved, an Impressionist touch without the interpretative resonance that I shall suggest self-as-poem has in 'Manche freilich'. Hofmannsthal may have borrowed elements from the poet he so sharply condemned, but he has annexed them completely.

The notion of slenderness is seized and similarly exploited from another source. 'Schlank' and 'schmal' in the last line of 'Manche

---

[102] Gide, *Traité du Narcisse*, 11.

[103] Francis Vielé-Griffin, *Poèmes et Poésies* (Paris: Mercure de France, 1895), 99. Cf. Bernhard Böschenstein, 'Wirkungen des französischen Symbolismus auf die deutsche Lyrik der Jahrhundertwende', *Euphorion*, 58 (1964), 377–80, for George's debt to Vielé-Griffin.

freilich' were borrowed from George's 'An Phaon', from *Das Buch der Hirten- und Preisgedichte*, and when he quotes the relevant lines in the George review, Hofmannsthal in effect explains why he took over the pair of adjectives:

Wie lieblich schweißt dieser Vers
                An den schmalen Flüssen,
                Schlanken Bäumen deiner Gegend
die Erinnerung an eine Seele und eine Landschaft zusammen'. (*RA* i. 217–18)

[How delightfully these lines—'By the narrow rivers and slender trees of the places round you'—weld together the memory of a soul and a landscape.]

The lines were for Hofmannsthal a memorable example of symbolic correspondence between inner and outer worlds, and the incorporation of the adjectives is a semi-private acknowledgement of that memory. They have a function within 'Manche freilich' and no knowledge of George is required for the fulfilment of this function. Nevertheless they are the nearest to deliberate quotation that is to be found in the poem: the quotation is not so much of an idea elegantly expressed by someone else, but of a poetic *technique* already practised. Hofmannsthal instantly consolidates his point in the review by adding 'und wie *schlank* drücken ein paar andere Zeilen die Flüchtigkeit der Begegnungen aus und ihren nachbebenden Zauber'[and how slenderly a few other lines express the fleetingness of the meetings and the magic that lingers after them].[104] The word 'schlank' is one of the points at which soul and landscape coincide in George, and Hofmannsthal now uses the word to describe the poetic process of establishing this coincidence, adding another dimension.

Hoppe identifies Paul Bourget as another influence on the ideas in 'Manche freilich'. In a poem called 'L'Espace' Bourget almost quotes the famous fragment by Pascal that Pater cites in the Pico della Mirandola essay, 'Le silence éternel de ces espaces infinis m'effraie' [the eternal silence of those infinite spaces frightens me]. Bourget's lines are, 'Merveilleux univers sourd à l'homme qui pense, | Ton espace infini m'épouvante' [marvellous universe, deaf to the thinking man, your infinite space terrifies me], and 'l'homme qui pense' is a another reference to Pascal, to what he saw as the definitive quality of man's distinction: 'L'homme n'est qu'un roseau . . . mais c'est un roseau pensant' [man is only a reed, but he is a thinking reed].[105] Both

---

[104] *RA* i. 218; my italics.
[105] Hoppe, *Hofmannsthal*, 37; Bourget, *La Vie inquiète* (Paris: Lemerre, 1875), 79; Walter

Pater's reflections and Paul Bourget's verses owe their illustrative and constitutive imagery to Pascal. The terror in lines 17–18 of 'Manche freilich' was originally that of Pascal's man without God, and became Bourget's. This dual impetus transforms it into Hofmannsthal's own. Much of the imagery of the rest of 'L'Espace' is similar to Hofmannsthal's, but it is all transmuted into quite distinct sensations. Bourget's fear derives from isolation and loneliness: the heavens, deceptively attractive, in fact ignore him whereas Hofmannsthal suffers because his stars seek to crush him. The next poem in the collection, 'A Léon Claudel', may also have been in Hofmannsthal's mind—proclaiming, for example, 'Toute l'humanité n'est qu'un seul être immense' [the whole of humanity is but a single immense being]. These two consecutive poems are at least as likely to have stimulated Hofmannsthal as 'Après une lecture de Sully Prudhomme' suggested by Hoppe.[106]

Hofmannsthal certainly read Bourget's essay on Baudelaire, and it is probable, given his great interest in Turgenev, that he read his appreciation of the Russian's works in the same series, *Essais de psychologie contemporaine*. In this the image of the flame is used in a context strikingly like that adumbrated in 'Manche freilich', as a summary of the discussion of unity within diversity, and its characteristics match those of Hofmannsthal's:

A ce frémissement de l'humanité retrouvée par delà les analyses, à cette sympathie profonde même dans la mise à nu de la misère humaine, à ce don des larmes conservé jusqu'au bout, vous reconnaissez la présence constante, chez Tourguéniev, de la flamme divine de l'amour. Il est si difficile de la garder intacte, cette flamme réchauffante et tremblante, à travers les dégradations de l'existence moderne![107]

[In this quivering of humanity that you sense beyond mere analyses, in this profound sympathy even when human misery is exposed, in this gift of tears that you keep until the very end, you will recognize the constant presence in Turgenev of the divine flame of love. It is so difficult to keep intact this warming, trembling flame, through the degradation that is modern existence.]

'Il est si difficile de la garder intacte' might be the message of 'Manche freilich', and the calm determination with which Hofmannsthal insists on the success of the undertaking matches what is perhaps Bourget's

Pater, *The Renaissance: Studies in Art and Poetry*, The Library Edition of the Works of Walter Pater (London: Macmillan, 1910), 41–2; Pascal, *Pensées*, 201 and 200.

[106] Hoppe, *Hofmannsthal*, 37. The suggestion is repeated in *SW* i. 263, where the poem is quoted in full (repeating, incidentally, Hoppe's accidental omission of 'purs' in line 4, and adding another misprint in line 11).

[107] Bourget, 'Ivan Tourguéniev', in *Œuvres complètes: Critique 1*, 438–9.

own subtext, Baudelaire's 'Élévation', the poem immediately before 'Correspondances' in *Les Fleurs du mal*:

> Envole-toi bien loin de ces miasmes morbides;
> Va te purifier dans l'air supérieur,
> Et bois, comme une pure et divine liqueur,
> Le feu clair qui remplit les espaces limpides.
>
> Derrière les ennuis et les vastes chagrins
> Qui chargent de leur poids l'existence brumeuse,
> Heureux celui qui peut d'une aile vigoureuse
> S'élancer vers les champs lumineux et sereins.[108]

[Take flight far beyond these morbid miasmas; go and purify yourself in the upper air, and drink, like a pure, divine liquor, the bright fire that fills the limpid spaces. Beyond the worries and huge sorrows that hazy human existence is burdened with, happy is he who can launch himself with a vigorous wing-beat towards the calm fields of light.]

Consciously or not, the three authors seem to be moving within the same intellectual space, furnished with closely similar images: Baudelaire's 'miasmes morbides' and 'ennui' match Bourget's 'misère humaine'; Baudelaire's vision of serene paradise corresponds to the dignified realm of Hofmannsthal's Sibyls and Queens; both poets' worlds carry the vast weight of others' worries; all three imagine the flame of integrity burning purely through the spaces that have otherwise terrified. Baudelaire's hope is a 'feu clair', whereas Hofmannsthal's is a 'schlanke Flamme', but then Baudelaire is part of Hofmannsthal's problem of integrity and the Austrian is bound to lack the confidence in originality.

Another possible stimulus for the depressing elements in the images of humanity in 'Manche freilich' is a letter from Gabriel Dubray that Hofmannsthal received on the evening of 2 September 1893. The specific occasion for the letter is not clear, but Dubray is in sombre mood:

Ne concevez de cette faiblesse putride des hommes ni trop de rancœur contre eux ni trop d'orgueil pour vous. Au fond nous ne valons pas grand' chose ni les uns ni les autres. Vous verrez pis que ce qui vous arrive en ce moment. Insensiblement vous en arriverez où j'en suis. Ce ne sont pas les hommes que je méprise: c'est la condition humaine, chose vile. Les hommes . . . mon Dieu, ce sont des compagnons de chaîne dans ce bagne qu'on appelle l'existence. Je les plains et moi avec eux.[109]

---

[108] Baudelaire, *OC*, i. 10.
[109] Copied into Hofmannsthal's diary, *RA* iii. 366; *Nachlaß*, H VII 4.100.

[Do not derive from man's putrid weakness too much rancour towards them or too much pride for yourself. None of us is worth much, at bottom. You will see worse things than you are experiencing at this moment. Without knowing it you will reach the stage that I am at. I do not despise mankind, but the human condition, a vile thing. Mankind, my God, mankind is your fellow prisoner in the chain gang that we call existence. I pity mankind and me with it.]

The image of being fellow prisoners in a chain gang is striking in rela-tion to the galley image of 'Manche freilich'. Equally, Dubray makes it clear that individual human beings are not what overwhelms him, but that the human condition itself is problematic. Most interesting is Hofmannsthal's comment, 'Dies ist die Stellung der Dichter zum Leben' [this is the attitude of the poet towards life], and he adds references to Goethe's *Die Mitschuldigen* and to Victor Hugo's poem from *Les Voix intérieurs*, 'Après une lecture de Dante', where 'das Inferno des Dante als Dämonologie der eigenen Seele des Dichters aufgefaßt wird' [Dante's *Inferno* is seen as the demonology of the very soul of the poet].

The tensions of the *Ich* in 'Manche freilich' relate not only literally to the psychological state of the author in his human context, but metaphorically to the integrity of the poem *vis-à-vis* the literary world of its sources. Borrowings must be seen to have their own function in the new text independently of (but possibly parallel to) their function in the old, but it is the functioning of the new text that defines its identity. To sense vaguely, as Narcissus did, that other literature is 'résorbée' within him, is an impossible position for Hofmannsthal, whose con-sciousness of his predecessors was more problematic than Gide's at that point. Hofmannsthal's treatment of the images and ideas from the wide range of subtexts shows how in this case the new poetry has been encouraged and not lamed, but the relationship is precarious. Those elements which would seem to be most at risk, borrowed phrases and images, mark the degree of Hofmannsthal's success in finding his own poetic manner and from this point of view the twenty-two lines of 'Manche freilich' clearly constitute the successful winning of an 'indi-vidual identity' for the new poem. They display what Hofmannsthal said George's poetry possessed, 'einen eigenen Ton . . . was in der Poesie und mutatis mutandis in allen Künsten, das einzige ist, worauf es ankommt und wodurch sich das Etwas vom Nichts, das Wesentliche vom Scheinhaften, das Lebensfähige vom Totgeborenen unter-scheidet' [a voice of its own, which in poetry, and *mutatis mutandis* in all the arts, is the only thing that matters and that separates something from nothing, the essential from the incidental, the strong from the still-born].[110] This identity suffers the pressure of other, earlier works of literature, and it requires a flexible but very resilient individuality to resist being entirely swallowed by their formations and formulations. Read from this metaphorical perspective, where 'mein Teil' is a claim to individual significance not of a personal speaker but of the poem itself (and 'Leben' not life but a metaphor for the world of literature), 'Manche freilich' can be seen to be aware of having successfully exploited the tensions of the literary context that produces and thus in part defines it, in order then to transcend the limitations of that definition.

Perhaps the most important series of borrowings in 'Manche freilich', however, are those detectable from Hofmannsthal's own prose poem, 'Das Glück am Weg'. The sensations of confusion detected in verse 2 of the verse poem are prefigured by the sentence 'es war einfach, als . . . zöge [mein Leben] langsam, lautlos gleitend seine tiefen, langen *Wurzeln* aus meiner *schwindelnden Seele*' [it was simply as if my life were slowly, silently slipping, pulling its deep, long roots from my giddy soul],[111] where 'lautlos gleitend' is itself an echo of the penultimate line of 'Erlebnis'. The Sibyls and Queens of 'Manche freilich' seem to inherit the poise and profundity of the young blond woman, the poise of her head, and the manner in which she would raise 'mit einer undefinierbaren reizenden kleinen Pose die Schultern wie frierend in die Höhe . . . und mich mit ihren mystischen Augen ernst und leise spöttisch von oben herab ansehen' [her shoulders in an indefinable, charming little gesture, as if she were cold, and look down at me with her mystical eyes, seriously and gently mocking; *SW* xxviii. 10, 3–12]. In the essay on Pico della Mirandola from *The Renaissance*, Pater dwells on the significance of the shut eye, thus:

> The word *mystic* has been usually derived from a Greek word which signifies *to shut*, as if one *shut one's lips* brooding on what cannot be uttered; but the Platonists themselves derive it rather from the act of *shutting the eyes*, that one may see the more, inwardly. Perhaps the eyes of the mystic Ficino . . . had come to be thus half-closed.[112]

It is possible that this is a common source for both the image 'Ganz vergessener Völker Müdigkeiten | Kann ich nicht abtun von meinen

---

[110] *RA* i. 214. Cf. in this context the vocabulary of 'lügen' and 'gehören' in the note from Mar. 1891 quoted above, p. 143, in connection with Hofmannsthal's reception of Decadence.

[111] *SW* xxviii. 10, 29–31; my italics.

[112] Pater, *The Renaissance*, 37.

Lidern' and the woman's 'mystische Augen' in 'Das Glück am Weg'. Both the figures in 'Manche freilich' and the lady in the prose poem carry echoes of Pater's description of the Mona Lisa, upon whose head 'all the ends of the world are come', just as in the pose of the girl on the ship, 'eine Unendlichkeit von Dingen [lag] ausgedrückt' (*SW* xxviii. 10, 17). Hofmannsthal may also have noted a reference to the painting in Bourget's Baudelaire essay:

Charles Baudelaire fait flotter un vague halo d'étrangeté autour de ses poèmes, persuadé, comme l'esthéticien du *Corbeau*, qu'il n'est de beauté qu'un peu singulière . . . L'impression est comparable à celle que l'on ressent en présence des figures peintes par Léonard, avec ce modelé dans la dégradation des teintes qui veloute de mystère le contour du sourire.[113]

[Charles Baudelaire causes a vague halo of strangeness to float around his poems, believing, like the aesthetic theorist of *The Raven*, that there is no beauty unless it is a little peculiar. . . . The impression is comparable to the one you have in the presence of figures painted by Leonardo, with that relief in the shading off of the colours that envelops the contours of the smile in mystery.]

The woman's smile, referred to later as '[das] unmerkliche Lächeln' [the imperceptible smile; 10, 24], may itself be an echo of one of these sources. Echoes such as these reinforce the suggestion that 'Manche freilich' was conceived sometime in 1893, possibly contemporaneously with the prose poem. 'Das Glück am Weg' seems also to have served as a source for *Das Märchen der 672. Nacht*, which contains the following sentence: 'sehr viel von ihrem Reiz [lag] darin, wie die Schultern und der Hals in demütiger kindlicher Grazie die Schönheit des Hauptes trugen, des Hauptes einer jungen Königin' [much of her charm lay in the modest, childlike grace with which her shoulders and neck carried the beauty of her head, the head of a young queen; *SW* xxviii. 2]. It overlaps significantly with images in the extract beginning 'die Haltung ihres Köpfes' quoted above.[114]

The last examples of phrases borrowed from the 1893 prose poem deal with the nature of the language used:

Ich wußte, daß ich mit ihr eine besondere Sprache reden würde, besonders im Ton und besonders im Stil: meine Rede wäre leichtsinniger, beflügelter, freier, sie liefe gleichsam nachtwandelnd auf einer *schmale* Rampe dahin; aber sie wäre auch eindringlicher, feierlicher, und *gewisse Saitensysteme* würden verstärkend mittönen.[115]

[113] Bourget, 'Charles Baudelaire', in *Œuvres complètes: Critique 1*, 4.
[114] For parallels between *Das Märchen* and 'Manche freilich', see Vilain, 'Wer lügt', 725–6.
[115] *SW* xxxviii. 9, 32–7; my italics.

And then, as the lady disappears into the ship, 'mit langsamen Schritten *schlank* und biegsam . . . als hätte man sie in einen *schmalen* kleinen Schacht gelegt', the speaker watches with increasing anxiety. In his review of George's *Hirten- und Preisgedichte*, Hofmannsthal used phrases from 'Manche freilich' and simultaneously echoed the prose poem. The people in George's verse

scheinen freier, leichten Hauptes und leichter Hände, behender und lautloser ihr Atem, minderes Gewicht auf ihren Augenlidern. Wir erkennen unser Dasein in ihnen wieder . . . Man wird an jene glücklichen Bewohner entfernter Gestirne erinnert, die aus leichterem und feinerem Stoff vermutet werden.[116]

[seem freer, with heads and hands light and unburdened, their breathing quicker and more silent, with less weight on their eyelids. We recognize our own existence in them. We are reminded of the fortunate inhabitants of distant stars whom we suppose to be made of lighter and finer material.]

The whole partakes of 'eine beflügelte Stimmung' [an inspired mood], in which 'das Widerwärtigste und der feinste Reiz scheinen . . . durcheinander zu liegen' [the most disagreeable things and the most delicate charm seem to be mingled together; *RA* i. 200]. The speech evoked in the prose poem, 'leichtsinniger, beflügelter, freier' [less deliberately, with more élan, more freely], the woman's 'reizende kleine Pose', 'die komplizierte und feine Gefallsucht der Seele' [charming little pose, the complicated and delicate vanity of the soul], and the thoughts 'mit einer sicheren, ruhigen Anmut' [with secure, calm grace] are related.

There are further, conscious echoes of the verse poem in the review, as Hofmannsthal defines weak poetry as the kind that would be written by one 'an [d]em die Welt mit *verworrenen Auspizien* zerrt' [who feels the tug of the world with its confused auspices].[117] Furthermore, Hofmannsthal's concluding paragraph contains the assertion,

Die Zeit wird sich begnügen, aus den *schlanken* tyrannischen Gebärden, aus den mit *schmalen* Lippen sparsam gesetzten Worten, aus dieser *leichtschreitenden hochköpfigen* Menschlichkeit . . . einen seltsamen Reiz zu ziehen.[118]

[Our age will be content to derive a peculiar charm from the slender, tyrannical gestures, from the words uttered sparingly by narrow lips, from this race of beings who walk easily with their heads held high.]

---

[116] *RA* i. 220–1; my italics. The review was begun on or soon after 24 Jan. 1896, and published in *Die Zeit* on 21 Mar..
[117] *RA* i. 219; my italics.
[118] Ibid. 221, my italics.

They associate the poem very closely with the reflections in the review on what constitutes original poetry and its conclusion that only 'die angeborene Königlichkeit eines sich selbst besitzenden Gemütes' [the innate nobility of a temperament at one with itself] will be capable of strong writing. A month or so before finishing 'Manche freilich' and writing the review of George, Hofmannsthal criticized Francis Vielé-Griffin's poetry for failing to satisfy this crucial criterion: 'Es ist, als ob er die Dinge, von denen er redet, nie angerührt hätte, nie wirklich ihren Geruch gerochen . . . nie wirklich ihren Geschmack geschmeckt' [it is as if he had never touched the things of which he speaks, never really smelt their smell, never really tasted their taste; *RA* i. 203], reminding one of Baudelaire's critique of the professors of aesthetics whose methodology 'a oublié la couleur du ciel, la forme du végétal, le mouvement et l'odeur de l'animalité' [has forgotten the colour of the sky, the shape of plants, the movement and the smell of things animal].[119] Second-hand impressions not properly accommodated in the prison of the soul cannot be passed off as first-rate poetry. He has been too strongly influenced by Verlaine:

Die Gegenwart einer sehr starken künstlerischen Individualität wirkt auf schwächliche schöne Geister wie der gefährlichste chemische Feind, treibt ihr Hohles blähend auf und läßt es nach kurzem Glühen als materia vilis elend niederfallen. Man muß sehr gut geboren sein, um die Existenz eines so komplexen und verführerischen Künstlers, als Verlaine ist, zu ertragen, ohne von ihr unterworfen zu werden. Herr Vielé-Griffin scheint mir dem nicht entgangen zu sein. (*RA* i. 203)

[The presence of a very strong artistic individual temperament has an effect on weaker spirits like that of the most dangerous chemical attack, it inflates their hollowness and swells it up, then lets it collapse miserably again after a brief glow of energy into *materia vilis*. One must be very well born to tolerate the existence of so complex and seductive an artist as Verlaine without being subjugated by him. M. Vielé-Griffin seems not to have escaped this danger.]

'Hohles' and 'materia vilis' are taken up in the George review as 'scheinhaft und gemein'. Vielé-Griffin's failure is to be dishonest,

[119] Baudelaire, *OC*, ii. 577. Elsewhere in the *Salon de 1859* Baudelaire ridicules the aesthetic precept that runs as follows: 'L'artiste, le vrai artiste, le vrai poète, ne doit peindre que selon qu'il voit et qu'il sent. Il doit être *réellement* fidèle à sa propre nature. Il doit éviter comme la mort d'emprunter les yeux et les sentiments d'un autre homme, si grand qu'il soit; car alors les productions qu'il nous donnerait seraient, relativement à lui, des mensonges, et non des *réalités*.' Although at first sight this appears to be in flat contradiction to Hofmannsthal's sentiments in the Vielé-Griffin review, it is a tirade against banal realism and on behalf of the strengths of the imagination. Borrowed sentiments are acceptable if imaginatively reprocessed.

succumbing to the temptation to adopt another's style and being crushed by it. The review thus makes explicit critically thoughts that the poem had already adumbrated poetically.

The overlaps between these texts and the prose poem are less concentrated, yet striking all the same. They associate the poetological dimensions of Hofmannsthal's thinking at this period with his concerns about the effect and effectiveness of Symbolism in the first three years of the decade. In 'Das Glück am Weg' what was lost was the relationship between girl and *Ich*; Symbolist language was associated there with this failure, because it did not fulfil the promise dreamt of earlier, the finding of a 'besondere Sprache' for perfect communication. 'Manche freilich' echoes that dream, the rush of speech along the 'schmale Rampe' and the contribution of 'gewisse seltsame Saitensysteme'; it establishes also a symbolic use of language that does capture the tensions of the relationship between the *Ich* and its surroundings, psychic, poetic and traditional, as if giving Symbolism more profoundly understood a second chance.

The greater profundity of understanding consists in abandoning the images and artificiality of Symbolist rhetoric, in order to concentrate on the nature of the symbol itself. This desire had been present for some time alongside the experimentation with Symbolist language, for of the two sacred tasks of poetry, 'das Auflösen und das Bilden von Begriffen' (*RA* iii. 373), the second is equivalent to the formation of the symbols in 'Manche freilich', and 'Dienst des Orpheus', the traditional bearer of the lyre. Rilke seems to have appreciated the difficulties for a poet to achieve the task of recomposition, as the third of the *Sonette an Orpheus* implies:

> Ein Gott vermags. Wie aber, sag mir, soll
> ein Mann ihm folgen durch die schmale Leier?
> Sein Sinn ist Zwiespalt. An der Kreuzung zweier
> Herzwege steht kein Tempel für Apoll.[120]

[A god can do it. But tell me, how am I, a man, to follow him through the narrow lyre? Its meaning is division. There is no temple to Apollo at the crossroads of two heart-paths.]

The reference to 'Manche freilich' was certainly conscious since Rilke's dedicatory copy of the Sonnets to Hofmannsthal bears the inscription 'Im Einsehn der "schmalen Leier" ' [in acknowledgement of the 'narrow lyre']. The sonnet continues in phrases that suggest an

---

[120] Rilke, *Werke*, i. 732.

appreciation of the link of poetry and psyche made in 'Manche
freilich':

> Gesang, wie du ihn lehrst, ist nicht Begehr,
> nicht Werbung um ein endlich noch Erreichtes;
> Gesang ist Dasein. Für den Gott ein Leichtes

[Song, as you taught it, is not desire, not the wooing of something finite and already
reached. Song is existence. Easy for the god]

—although for mankind, or for Hofmannsthal at least, not so simple.

5

TAKING STOCK: *DAS GESPRÄCH ÜBER GEDICHTE*

On 24 March 1894 Hofmannsthal's review of a book by Alfred Biese entitled *Philosophie des Metaphorischen* was published in the *Frankfurter Zeitung*. It is a characteristically ambivalent review, beginning with a raised eyebrow of surprise:

Die unlängst erschienene 'Philosophie des Metaphorischen' von Alfred Biese geht von einer sonderbaren Voraussetzung aus: es gebe in Deutschland Leute, die den metaphorischen Ausdruck für einen willkürlich gewählten Schmuck der Rede, eine geistreiche Erfindung der Schriftsteller hielten und denen man erst beweisen müsse, es sei dem nicht so, es sei ganz im Gegenteil das Metaphorische eine primäre Anschauung zu nennen, das eigentliche innerste Schema des Menschengeistes, und die Metapher die wahre Wurzel alles Denkens und Redens. (*RA* i. 190)

[Alfred Biese's recent book *The Philosophy of Metaphor* works from a strange premiss, namely that there are people in Germany who think that metaphorical expression is an arbitrarily selected speech-decoration, a writer's entertaining invention, and that one must first persuade these people that this is not the case and that metaphor is on the contrary to be regarded as a form of primary expression, the most real, most intimate pattern of the human spirit, the true root of all thought and speech.]

Hofmannsthal can barely imagine that such a heresy exists and that a book such as Biese's should be necessary. But in his view its fundamental premisses are at least accurate and for good measure he quotes the maxim of Goethe's that is one of the intellectual pillars on which the book appears to be based:

Alles, was wir Erfinden, Entdecken im höheren Sinne nennen, ist eine aus dem Innern am Äußern sich entwickelnde Offenbarung, die den Menschen seine Gottähnlichkeit vorahnen läßt. Es ist eine Synthese von Welt und Geist, welche von der ewigen Harmonie des Daseins die seligste Versicherung gibt.[1]

[Everything that we call invention or discovery in the highest sense of the word is a revelation from within us developing on the outside, a revelation that permits mankind a sense of his kinship with the divine. It is a synthesis of world and spirit, which gives the most blissful confirmation of the eternal harmony of existence.]

---

[1] A slightly truncated quotation from *Maximen und Reflexionen* no. 364 (Goethe, *Werke*, xii. 414).

'Harmonie des Daseins' is a phrase that Hofmannsthal will have noted in 1894 with both approval and apprehension. But he is soon disappointed: the book turns out to be a catalogue of past metaphors, 'eine Sammlung herrlicher Gedichte' [a collection of marvellous poems; *RA* i. 191], with many excerpts from the Greek philosophers and the Church Fathers, which is not what he had hoped for. The book that the title promised to one of Hofmannsthal's cast of mind was

eine Philosophie der subjektiven Metaphorik; eine Betrachtung des metaphern-bildenden Triebes in uns und der unheimlichen Herrschaft, die die von uns erzeugten Metaphern rückwirkend auf unser Denken ausüben,—andererseits der unsäglichen Lust, die wir durch metaphorische Beseelung aus toten Dingen saugen. Eine hellsichtige Darstellung des seltsam vibrierenden Zustandes, in welchem die Metapher zu uns kommt, über uns kommt in Schauer, Blitz und Sturm: dieser plötzlich blitzartigen Erleuchtung, in der wir einen Augenblick lang den großen Weltzusammenhang ahnen, schauernd die Gegenwart der Idee spüren, dieses ganzen mystischen Vorganges, der uns die Metapher leuchtend und real hinterläßt.[2]

[a philosophy of the subjective use of metaphor, a consideration of the urge that we have to form metaphors and of the uncanny power that the metaphors we have created exercise retroactively on our thought—on the other hand it is a consideration of the ineffable pleasure that we derive from dead things by animating them with metaphor. A clear-sighted depiction of the peculiarly trembling state in which metaphor comes to us, comes upon us in a shower, a flash of lightning, a tempest: this sudden flash of illumination in which we sense for a moment the great continuity of the world and feel with a shiver the presence of the Idea, the whole mystical event that metaphor leaves behind, brilliant and real.]

In other words, he was looking for a book that discussed the relationship between language and perception, the means whereby the Symbolists' conception of a unified cosmos can be not only communicated to readers but created within the mind of the writer. The language of this review reveals how thoroughly Hofmannsthal was immersed in the outlook of the Symbolists: he is searching for a book about correspondences of all kinds.

The critic in Hofmannsthal soon gives way to the poet, who starts sketching a slim little volume, the book he would himself have written:

Man müßte eine anspruchslose und wenig pedantische Form wählen. Etwa den platonischen Dialog . . . Zwei oder drei recht moderne junge Menschen, unruhig,

---

[2] *RA* i. 192. The vocabulary and ideas here are from the same field as the section omitted from the Goethe quotation: 'Alles, was wir Erfinden, Entdecken . . . nennen, ist die bedeutende Ausübung, Betätigung eines originalen Weltgefühles, das, im stillen längst ausgebildet, unversehens, mit Blitzesschnelle zu einer fruchtbaren Erkenntnis führt.'

mit vielerlei Sehnsucht und viel Altklugheit; und auf den Boden der großen Stadt müßte man sie stellen, der aufregend bebt und tönt wie Geigenholz . . . im Volksgarten an einem Juniabend. Weiße Kastanienblüten und blaßrote liegen auf dem Weg, und daneben leuchtet smaragdgrün das dichte kühle Gras. (*RA* i. 192)

[One would have to choose an unpretentious and unpedantic form. A Platonic dialogue, say. Two or three really modern young people, restless, with all sorts of longings and much precociousness; and they would have to be set on the ground in a large city, a ground quivering and echoing like the wood of a violin . . . in the 'Volksgarten' on a June evening. White and pale red chestnut blossom covers the path and beside it, radiant in emerald green, the lush, cool grass.]

Not satisfied with suggesting a new content, Hofmannsthal instinctively adumbrates the form and sets the scene, an artificial landscape littered with the bright jewel-colours of the Symbolists, picking up not only the 'heiße vibrierende Luft' characteristic of Baudelaire (*RA* iii. 348), but also elements from a review of the *Moderner Musenalmanach* for 1893 (published on 1 February of that year) in which Hofmannsthal mentions for the first and only time Albert Giraud's *Pierrot Lunaire*, 'das morbide und hübsche Buch eines französischen Symbolisten' [the pretty but morbid book of a French Symbolist]. He notes,

dieser Pierrot hat die Mondsucht eines hysterischen Künstlers von heute, er hat seine vibrierende Empfänglichkeit für Chopinsche Musik und Martergedanken, für Geigenspiel, für grelles Rot und 'heiliges' sanftes Weiß. Er sitzt im Café und phantasiert über die grünlichgelben gefährlichen Wolken des Absinth. Er leidet an der Kunst und nennt die Verse 'heilige Kreuze, dran die Dichter stumm verbluten.' (*RA* i. 171)

[this Pierrot has an addiction to the moon characteristic of today's hysterical artists, he has their quivering receptiveness for the music of Chopin and for the thoughts of torture, for violin music, for bright red and 'holy' soft white. He sits in the cafe and fantasizes over the dangerous greenish-yellow clouds of absinthe. Art makes him suffer and he calls poetry the 'holy cross on which poets bleed silently to death'.]

All these scenes have elements in common, too, with the description of the garden in 'Gerechtigkeit'.

In the Biese review there follow details of a decadent park with marble and gold ornamentation, a red sky and the distant prospect of gold-green and copper-red cupolas through the dusk,

Und einer sagt vielleicht: 'Wie schön ist das! Wie lebendig, erfaßbar, wie wirklich! Wie schön ist Schönheit!' . . . Aber endlich, getroffen von so viel Schönheit, müssen diese jungen Menschen anfangen, von Kunst zu reden, wie die Memnonssäulen tönen müssen, wenn das Licht sie trifft. Und sie sind ja 'innerlich so voll Figur', so

durchtränkt mit Metaphorischem, so gewohnt, ihre Seele unter seltsamen Gleichnissen anzuschauen, ihren Lebensweg mit drohenden und lockenden apokalyp-
tischen Gestalten zu umstellen. (*RA* i. 193)

[And one of them perhaps says, 'How lovely that is! How alive, how real, how
genuine! How beautiful beauty is!' . . . But eventually, struck by so much beauty,
these young people inevitably begin to talk about art, just as the columns of
Memnon always sound when light hits them. And they are 'internally so full of
figuration', so saturated in metaphor, so used to looking at their souls in the light of
curious parables and surrounding the path of their lives with threatening and
enticing apocalyptic figures.]

Such people, according to Hofmannsthal, are the proper persons to
philosophize about metaphor. But the book produced would be 'ein
ganz unwissenschaftliches Buch, eher ein Gedicht, eine bebende
Hymne auf Gottweißwas, als eine ordentliche Abhandlung' [a completely unscientific book, more a poem, a quivering hymn to Heaven-
knows-what than a serious treatise; *RA* i. 193].

The first direct reference to what was to become *Das Gespräch über
Gedichte* is in a letter to George from 1898, in which Hofmannsthal
expresses his hope of writing an essay about 'die mit Genuß
gewonnene Einsicht in die wundervolle Einheitlichkeit der mitsam-
men das "Jahr" bildenden Gedichte' [the pleasurably won insight into
the marvellous consistency of the poems that together make up the
'Year'].[3] Hofmannsthal makes explicit the aim of such an essay,
aiming to extend his 1896 review of George's poetry, which he says
only really dealt with the *Das Buch der Hirten- und Preisgedichte*, by adding
commentaries on the *Sagen und Sänge* and *Das Buch der Hängenden Gärten*.
Yet *Das Gespräch*—a dialogue between Gabriel and Clemens, two
modern young men 'mit vielerlei Sehnsucht und viel Altklugheit' [with
all sorts of longing and plenty of early maturity]—clearly has deeper
roots in the Biese review. Clemens almost quotes from it, saying
directly, or naively, of a poem describing a landscape if not exactly,
'Wie schön ist das', then at least 'Es ist schön.'[4] This and the link back
to the 1896 George review and its discussion of poetological problems
suggest that the substance of the plan may be attitudes formed somewhat earlier than 1898.

The writing of *Das Gespräch über Gedichte* was not begun until June
1903, in Cortina; the remaining notes were completed in Grundlsee in

[3] George, *BW*, 137; letter of 13 Oct. 1898, referring to *Das Jahr der Seele*. Ellen Ritter sees the
earliest origins of *Das Gespräch über Gedichte* in this letter (*SW* xxxi. 316–17).

[4] *SW* xxxi. 74, 30. Henceforth references for quotations from this volume of the Critical
Edition will usually be by page- and line-numbers in parentheses in the text.

the second week of July; the draft and a fair copy were made in Rodaun before publication in *Die Neue Rundschau* in February 1904. Later that year it came out in book form together with *Über Charaktere im Roman und im Drama*, in a series edited by Georg Brandes. It thus dates from *after* Hofmannsthal's crisis of language and what is usually interpreted as a farewell to lyric poetry in *Ein Brief*, and suggests therefore that, even if very few poems were published after the Chandos Letter, the break was in an important sense not really as decisive as it is usually thought to be. Very soon after publishing *Ein Brief* Hofmannsthal was making plans to publish a collection of his poems, and it is also out of these discussions that the dialogue on poetry arises. He and Stefan George met in Munich in the second week of February 1903, and Hofmannsthal drew up a list of the poems for a luxury edition (*BW*, 180). As usual, the project seems not to have been regarded with equal enthusiasm by both poets, at least not after the initial discussions. A residual suspicion of George, or just a healthy wariness of making artistic decisions in haste, persuaded Hofmannsthal to take this list away with him and thereby deprive George of the initiative. In any case, Hofmannsthal dropped the subject and had to be prompted to take it up again: A letter from George written in May 1903 is insistent that the book appear in the autumn and that Hofmannsthal send the list—just as it is—immediately (*BW*, 184). He clearly felt the project slipping away and had not the tact to accept that Hofmannsthal's eagerness was waning.

Hofmannsthal had already sent a letter to George expressing his frustration in the clearest terms:

Von München zurückgekommen, trieb ich das gesammte Manuscript so wie *jene widerwärtige Liste* es enthielt, auf und suchte mich mit aller Kraft guten Willens mit dem Gedanken abzufinden, es werde demnächst ein Band da liegen, der *diese* Gedichte als ein geschlossen sein wollendes enthielte—und dieser Gedanke erfüllte mich mit einem Zorn, dessen Heftigkeit auch jetzt, nach Monaten nur schlummert, nicht erloschen ist. Ich will diesen Band nicht.[5]

[On my return from Munich I got hold of the whole manuscript as it is outlined in *that repulsive list* and tried with all the goodwill I could muster to come to terms with the thought that a volume would soon be ready, containing *these* poems, claiming to be complete—and this thought filled me with a rage whose vehemence even now, after months, is only slumbering and has not been extinguished. I do not want this volume.]

[5] George, *BW*, 185; my italics.

He writes that he had only agreed to make a list in the first place to show some goodwill, but that he respects his own best poems too much to dilute them with inconsequential works, 'Nichtigkeiten', mixing wine with washing-up water, as he puts it. This view now prevails, and Hofmannsthal would like to wait,

und wären es Jahre und Jahre, bis eine Stunde wieder, und wäre es die Stunde der größten Schmerzen, noch ein paar Tropfen von gleicher Stärke dazuträufelt, und dann einmal das Buch daraus machen, meinethalben auf dem Todtenbett es daraus machen, das rein ist, das mit einem Menschen, den das Vermischte ekelt, in den Garten darf—wie ein Band Keats, wie ein Band Goethe, wie ein Band von Ihnen! (*BW*, 186)

[and even if it were for years and years, until a time came, even a time of the greatest pain, that could add a trickle of a few drops of the same strength, and then make them into a book, do so on my deathbed for all I care, but a book that is pure, could be carried into a garden by someone who hates adulterated mixtures—like a volume of Keats, of Goethe, like one of yours!]

Hofmannsthal was perhaps not so much angry as fractious; he had been ill in April and was still suffering from the depressive after-effects of a minor operation. Eventually he gave in and allowed George to publish twelve poems, as *Ausgewählte Gedichte*, in the Verlag der Blätter für die Kunst, Berlin, 1903.

Illness notwithstanding, however, Hofmannsthal's reservations and objections were perfectly reasoned and were based on the same sense of dissatisfaction with his own writing that is registered in the Chandos Letter. He refused, for example, to contribute to the *Blätter*, saying, 'Ich konnte bei mehrmaligen Versuchen nicht weiter kommen als zu dem nicht schönen Gefühl, breiten Massen von Worten, in Colonnen formiert, einsam gegenüberzustehen' [after trying several times I could not proceed beyond the ugly feeling that I was standing alone in front of broad masses of words, formed up into columns; *BW*, 186]. But the end of the letter is hopeful, and Hofmannsthal is already thinking of his adaptation of *Elektra*. The bridge between frustration—both at George's request and at his own inability to compose—and anticipation was made not simply by the physical remedies he proposes to try to assuage his illness, 'Milch, Luft, Gebirge' [milk, air, mountains]. Immediately following his confession of helplessness before the task of forming the now strange medium of words, he added a note of confidence in his ability to read: 'Aber ich bin langsam im Genießen. Das schöne Buch "Entrevisions" von Lerberghe, das ich seit 4 Jahren besitze, fängt nun auf einmal an, sich mir zu erschließen' [but I enjoy things only gradually. Lerberghe's beautiful book *Entrevisions*, which I have had for four years, is now suddenly beginning to reveal itself to me; *BW*, 186]. In June Hofmannsthal wrote similarly of one of George's own volumes: 'Seltsam, daß ich das "Jahr der Seele" schon 1898 einen Sommer auf dem Land mithatte und nun erst zu sehen anfange, wie viel, wie unerschöpflich viel es enthält' [odd that I had *The Year of the Soul* with me in the country as long ago as 1898 and am only now beginning to see how much it contains, how inexhaustible it is; *BW*, 192].

As Hofmannsthal recovered, his irritation faded and he outlined *Das Gespräch über Gedichte* to George:

So hat mich vorigen Monat das 'Jahr der Seele' . . . aus einer schlimmeren Zeit in eine bessere hinübergeleitet. Ich habe einen Dialog, das Wesen und den Genuß der kurzen Gedichte, die man die lyrischen nennt, behandelnd, angefangen und lege ihm mehrere Ihrer Gedichte unter, beginne geradezu mit einer Reihe des 'Jahr der Seele'. . . . Ich hoffe nicht vieles zu übersehen, was sich zu diesem Thema, mehr in Metaphern als in dürren Terminologien, sagen läßt. (*BW*, 194)

[Last month *The Year of the Soul* helped me move from a rather bad period into a better one. I have begun a dialogue about the nature and the enjoyment of the short poems that we call lyric poems and have put in several of your poems, beginning in fact with a series from the *Year of the Soul*. I hope not to miss out much that can be said about this topic, more in metaphors than in dry jargon.]

He goes on to mention the 1896 review again and to reiterate his disappointment at not having written then on the *Sagen* and *Hängende Gärten*. His aim in the early 1890s had been to produce for German literature something poetically comparable to the achievements of Keats in English, and the present critical plan to write a definitive essay on lyric poetry is in a sense no less grand. The desire to compose criticism in metaphors rather than dry jargon is also important: I have already suggested that the network of texts around 'Manche freilich' implies that poetic language is the truest form in which poetry criticism can be expressed.[6] In his early poetry, too, Hofmannsthal's metaphors had been expressive of both personal and poetological considerations, and if the extent and scope of the reflections in *Das Gespräch über Gedichte* are unusually broad, the critical dialogue is the mirror of his previous activity rather than anything fundamentally new.

The extent to which the dialogue is rooted in the lyrical decade is confirmed in several ways that one might describe as 'external' to the

[6] In the reversal of Hofmannsthal's dictum from the George review as 'wer gute Metaphern macht, lügt nicht', Vilain, 'Wer lügt', 754.

published work. First, there are the other fictional dialogues and letters
that were written in the same period. *Ein Brief*, which dates from
August 1902, is the most obvious, but it is too well known and too
thoroughly debated to permit of much original detailed analysis in this
study. It is important to *Das Gespräch über Gedichte* in that, however else
it may be interpreted, and whether or not it is seen to deny its own
scepticism by virtue of its linguistic polish and lucidity, it documents a
crisis of language. The theme is a substitute persona's decision not to
continue with literary activity because he is overwhelmed by the chasm
between word and meaning (45, 5). The letter is not simply 'the explanation of why [Hofmannsthal] had to give up writing lyric poetry',
although it is true that after 1902 he wrote very little verse.[7] The works
that Chandos now feels unable to write include *tractati* and essays,
which Hofmannsthal was continuing to produce, and projects such as
the *Apophthegmata* and *Nosce te ipsum* that correspond to Hofmannsthal's
own in later years.[8] Yet as the analysis of *Das Gespräch über Gedichte* will
imply, *Ein Brief* does in an important sense articulate the 'symbolischer
Tod' [symbolic death] of Hofmannsthal's early works that Alewyn
claims.[9] Some of its links with the very early 1890s have already been
pointed out: when Hofmannsthal sent George the typescript, he was
thanked for his 'zweifachen Brief' [twofold letter] implying that he
received the homage to Lord Bacon as equivalent to a gesture in his
direction.[10] Boehringer points out parallels of phrase and image

---

[7] *Hofmannsthal: Selected Essays*, ed. Mary Gilbert (Oxford: Blackwell, 1955), 155.

[8] For a balanced summary of the confessional and fictional elements in Chandos, see
W. E. Yates, 'Hofmannsthal and the Renaissance or: Once more unto "Ein Brief"',
Publications of the English Goethe Society, NS 61 (1990–1), 110–11. Tarot seeks to counteract a
previous tendency to identify Chandos too simply with Hofmannsthal and leans towards the
opposite extreme (*Hugo von Hofmannsthal*, 380–2). Bennett centres the debate again ('Werther
and Chandos', *Modern Language Notes*, 91 (1976), 557–8). Morton fascinatingly investigates the
plans that Chandos had made for future works and links them to Hofmannsthal's situation
and the paradox of how eloquent is Chandos's falling silent ('Chandos and his Plans', *Deutsche
Vierteljahrsschrift*, 62 (1988), 385–96). Whatever the differences between Chandos and
Hofmannsthal, however, Daviau's attempts to refute the 'irrige Anschauung' that *Ein Brief* is
a reflection of its author's *Sprachkrise* are ultimately far from convincing ('Hugo von
Hofmannsthal, Stefan George und der *Chandos-Brief*: Eine neue Perspektive auf Hofmannsthals sogenannte Sprachkrise', in Karl Konrad Polheim (ed.), *Sinn und Symbol: Festschrift
für Joseph P. Strelka zum 60. Geburtstag* (Berne: Lang, 1987), 229). His article contains many
inaccuracies and exaggerations, not least the claim that '[es gibt] keinen Nachweis dafür, daß
George Hofmannsthal wirklich beeinflußte' (234).

[9] Alewyn, *Über Hugo von Hofmannsthal*, 181, cited by H. Stefan Schultz, 'Hofmannsthal and
Bacon: The Sources of the Chandos Letter', *Comparative Literature*, 13 (1961), 3.

[10] George, *BW*, 175; letter of 25 Dec. 1902; cf. Schultz, 'Hofmannsthal and Bacon', 2. *Pace*
Daviau ('Hofmannsthal, George und der *Chandos-Brief*', 230), it has several times been
suggested that the Chandos Letter may have been written with George in mind; cf. also

between Hofmannsthal's letters to George of 13 October 1896 and 13 October 1898 and the Chandos Letter.[11]

Much more striking as evidence that the dialogues of 1902–3 are anchored in the lyrical decade are the echoes of 'Manche freilich' and the related poetological reflections of the 1896 George review that are traceable in what may be called the partner-dialogue to *Das Gespräch*. This is *Über Charaktere im Roman und im Drama*, published as the second in the *Unterhaltungen über literarische Gegenstände* in the 1904 volume in which *Das Gespräch* first appeared in book form. It takes the form of a conversation between the Austrian orientalist Baron Joseph Hammer-Purgstall and Honoré de Balzac and is a fictional expansion of a meeting that actually took place in 1835. The dialogue was conceived in June 1902 and written in mid-December of the same year. Its theme is the relationship between individual experience and its expression in art, not only drama and the novel, but implicitly, too, in poetry.

The earliest sketch for the piece includes a statement on the dramatist's craft made not only using an image familiar from a decade before, but picking up reflections on the nature of poetry, too: 'Der Dramatiker muss die vermischten Charaktere des Lebens zerlegen wie der Bergcrystall das Licht zerlegt' [the dramatist must separate the mixed characters of life as the rock crystal separates light; 270, 15–16]. Balzac regrets his failure in the theatre, and attributes it to the illegitimate attempt to make of himself a dramatist, which he essentially is not:

Ich wollte etwas finden, was ich nicht in mir trug. Ich wollte eine Unehrlichkeit begehen, eine der versteckten großen Unehrlichkeiten. Es liegt im Wesen der meisten Schriftsteller, dergleichen Unehrlichkeiten in Masse zu begehen . . . Eine Kunstform gebrauchen und ihr gerecht werden: welch ein Abgrund liegt dazwischen! . . . Mögen andere die Formen vergewaltigen, ich für mein Teil, ich weiß, daß ich kein Dramatiker bin. (30, 19–29)

[I wanted to find something that I did not carry within me. I wanted to commit an act of dishonesty, one of the great, secret acts of dishonesty. It is in the nature of

Alewyn's comment: 'Wenn immer der junge Hofmannsthal Gerichtstag hielt über sich selbst, dann nahm der Ankläger das scharfe Profil Georges an. Manchmal werden solche innere Gespräche aufgezeichnet. Dann entsteht der "Brief des Lord Chandos"' ('Hofmannsthal und Stefan George', in Fiechtner (ed.), *Der Dichter im Spiegel der Freunde*, 295–6). Walter Perl suggests that Andrian is the subject of the letter (*Andrian und die Blätter*, 133): for a full discussion of this proposition, echoed by other scholars, see Klieneberger, 'Hofmannsthal und Leopold Andrian', 626–7.

[11] George, *BW*, 113 and 256 (and, less convincingly, 136 and 262), cited by Schultz, 'Hofmannsthal and Bacon', 2.

most writers to commit many such acts of dishonesty. To use an artistic form and to do it justice: what a chasm lies between these things! Others may do violence to forms, but I for my part, I know that I am no dramatist.]

The vocabulary of dishonesty, the notion of truth to one's self, even the formula 'ich für mein Teil', all echo the considerations surrounding the composition of 'Manche freilich'. Hofmannsthal's Balzac claims not to believe in character in the way that Shakespeare did; he sees not rounded human beings but individual 'allotropic' incarnations of essential powers or fates. For the artist Frenhofer of *Le Chef d'œuvre inconnu*, the outside world is 'die Schale eines ausgegessenen Eies' [the shell of an egg that has been eaten; 35, 5], which is an image of delusion as evocative as the more famous 'modrige Pilze' [musty mushrooms] in *Ein Brief*. Dramatic characters interact and share experiences; but Balzac insists that, for him and his figures, 'es gibt keine Erlebnisse, als das Erlebnis des eigenen Wesens' [there are no experiences other than the experience of one's own nature; 32, 4–5]—which despite the ostensible subject of the dialogue, is a lyric focus.

The extended metaphor used by Balzac to explain his contention is a modern form of the classical galley image from 'Manche freilich', a steam ship. He asks Hammer-Purgstall to recall journeys made on a steamer, thinking of the figure who will have emerged in the evening from the engine room below, standing for a while 'oben . . . um Luft zu schöpfen' [on deck, to catch some air]. When we are told that the stoker whom Balzac conjures up 'warf ein paar scheue, fast schwachsinnige Blicke auf die schönen und fröhlichen Passagiere der ersten Kajüte, die auf Deck waren, sich an den Sternen des südlichen Himmels zu entzücken' [cast a few timid, almost idiotic glances towards the beautiful, happy passengers from the first-class cabins, who were on deck to delight in the stars of the southern skies], the faint echoes become unmistakably strong.[12] They are clearly deliberate, for a few lines further two lovers are evoked watching 'das Hinstürzen unermeßlich ferner Sterne' [the plummeting of immeasurably distant stars]. The 'droben/drunten' opposition of the poem (those up on deck or those down with the oars), is modulated in the dialogue into the contrast between first-class passengers and boiler-room hands; the stoker's sorties for air are interpreted as representing the forays made by an

---

[12] Michèle Pauget fascinatingly links the image of the stoker to three scenes in *Ein Brief*, those of Crassus and the lamprey (53–54), the water beetle (41, 38–40) and the mother rat (51, 18–26): *L'Interrogation sur l'art dans l'œuvre essayistique de Hugo von Hofmannsthal: Analyse de configurations* (Frankfurt a.M.: Peter Lang, 1984), 351–3.

artist into the ordinary human community. Just as in 'Manche freilich' there is no clear value-division between the two poles here either, and 'dieses Geschöpf ist nicht ärmer, als die droben auf dem Deck' [this creature is not poorer than those on deck above]. By way of proof Balzac proceeds to evoke the combination of ecstasy and agony in the writer's existence, and his ability (or destiny, for he uses the word 'geschickt' ambiguously to mean 'able' or 'fated') to see himself as the distillation of the whole world's trials, 'in das Auf und Nieder aller menschlichen Seelen das Spiegelbild ihrer eigenen Ekstasen und Abspannungen hinzudeuten' [to see in the ups and downs of all human souls the mirror image of their own moments of ecstasy and weariness; 33, 25–7]. This, too, can be read as an interpretation of 'Manche freilich' and of the tensions of the flame in the last line. The images of flame and fire take over somewhat later in the dialogue as Balzac tries to convey the problems of self-expression:

ich weiß, daß jede menschliche Existenz, die der Darstellung wert ist, sich selbst verzehrt und, um diesen Brand zu unterhalten, aus der ganzen Welt nichts als die ihrem Brennen dienlichen Elemente in sich saugt, wie die Kerze den Sauerstoff aus der Luft auffrißt. (36, 13–17)

[I know that every human existence worthy of depiction devours itself and, in order to feed this fire, sucks in from the whole world nothing but the elements that will serve its own combustion, as the candle devours the oxygen from the air.]

His characters, he says, are so self-obsessed that they are unable 'das in der Welt zu sehen, was sie nicht mit dem Flackern ihres Blickes in die Welt hineinwerfen' [to see in the world those things that they are not themselves casting into the world with the flickering of their gaze; 36, 31–3]. The image was evidently at the forefront of Hofmannsthal's mind during the second half of 1902 and in 1903. Notes for a fictional conversation between a young European and a Japanese nobleman contain a related reference: 'In uns ist eine heilige Flamme. In euch ein dämonisch flackerndes Feuer' [in us there is a holy flame. In you there is a demonically flickering fire; 41, 16–17].

In *Über Charaktere im Roman und im Drama*—set in the 1830s—Balzac predicts that a crisis will take place around 1890 in the form of a fatal tendency amongst over-sensitive writers to buckle under the 'symbolische Gewalt auch unscheinbarer Dinge' [the Symbolic power even of nondescript things] and of a developing inability 'sich mit dem existierenden Worte beim Ausdruck ihrer Gefühle zu begnügen' [to content themselves, when they are expressing their feelings, with a word that already exists; 33, 33–6]. This is clearly a reference to the situation in Vienna in the 1890s, to Hofmannsthal's own circumstances at that time and its crisis in 1902. Balzac's speeches lurch ambiguously between predictions of this type and the description of his own works, such that the theme of Balzac's inability to write drama continually evokes Hofmannsthal's renunciation of lyric. Balzac argues that for the figures that people his works in the 1830s there is no such thing as experience—'es gibt für sie keine Erlebnisse darum, weil es überhaupt keine Erlebnisse gibt' [there are no experiences for them because there *are* no experiences at all; 36, 34–5]—and that therefore, by the last decade of the century, one will no longer understand 'was wir mit dem Wort "Erlebnis" haben sagen wollen' [what we wanted to say with the word 'experience'; 37, 9–10].

Yet as Hofmannsthal writes this in 1902 he is perfectly well aware that he has himself published a poem under this very title a decade before. But the experience evoked there is very different from what Balzac would have wanted to understand by the word. Behind the mask of the French novelist, Hofmannsthal is not only summarizing the literary development of his century, but doing so in personal terms, raising the questions that most radically affected his poetry in the early 1890s, self-sacrifice and loss of identity. He does so, too, with the images of that period, artificial flowers and metallic forms, because the reason why there is no such thing as 'experience' is, according to Balzac,

weil das Innere des Menschen ein sich selbst verzehrender Brand ist, ein Schmerzensbrand, ein Glasofen, in welchem die zähflüssige Masse des Lebens ihre Formen erhält, entzückend blumenhafte, wie die Stengelgläser der Insel Murano, oder heldenhafte, von metallischen Reflexen funkelnde, wie die Töpfereien von Derutta und Rhodus. (36, 36–7, 2)

[because the interior of man is a self-consuming fire, a fire of pain, a glass-furnace in which the viscous mass of life receives its forms, delightful flower forms, like the long-stemmed glasses of the island of Murano, sparkling with metallic reflections like the pottery of Derutta and Rhodes.]

The delicate image of the flame from 'Manche freilich', used to capture the fragile balance of individual identity, has ceded in 1902 to the violence of a kind of hell-fire. It is the kind of fire that produces stylized lives expressed in works of art, but it is emphatically not one that will produce a personal experience. The peculiar optic that allows Hofmannsthal to cast his Symbolist memories in the form of a prediction by a disillusioned Romantic confirms the impression already registered above, in the analyses of his poems in Chapters 3 and 4, namely that Romanticism is present within his writing as a permanent reproach to the disintegrative tendencies of the brand of Symbolism he inherited. Balzac is particularly bitter: not even the experiences of disappointment and loss of illusion inevitably undergone by more self-conscious later generations will constitute a definable 'Block' of experience; they will be reduced to tiny particles and scattered as dust into the deep well of the soul (37, 2–7). Hofmannsthal's skill at manipulating his overlaid perspectives is revealed by the allusion to the experiences of Lucien de Rubempré in Balzac's own novel, *Illusions perdues*, where the hero's precariously constructed social identity is indeed pulverized as each apparently solid experience is revealed as a sham.

There is a dimension of 'Manche freilich' that registers the difficulties inherent in creating an original poem because of the strength and weight of past literature, and this is also present in *Über Charaktere*, via an equally complex stratification of Symbolist, Classical and Romantic layers of reference. Goethe is cited by Balzac as the equivalent of one of the dæmons that constitute his characters; he represents the inhibiting effect of a complete literary personality on a less secure talent: 'Aber der ganze Mensch, aber der ganze Dichter, aber das ganze Wesen!' [but the whole man, the whole poet, the whole nature!] exclaims Balzac in horror and admiration (37, 29–30):

sein Auge muß unheimlicher gewesen sein als das Klingsors, des Magiers, unheimlicher als das Merlins, von dem es heißt, es habe wie ein bodenloser Schacht in die Tiefen der Hölle geführt, unheimlicher als das der Medusa. *Er konnte töten*, dieser ungeheure Mensch, mit einem Blick . . . er konnte eine Seele töten und dann sich abwenden, als ob nichts geschehen wäre.[13]

[his eye must have been more uncanny than that of Klingsor the magician, more uncanny than Merlin's, of which it is said that it led like a bottomless shaft into the depths of hell, more uncanny than the Medusa's. *He could kill*, this monstrous man, with a single glance, he could kill a soul and then turn away as if nothing had happened.]

Goethe, the murderer of Kleist's soul according to Balzac, is compared explicitly to Novalis's magus and implicitly to Stefan George, whose glance, in 'Der Prophet', could cast a spell and who could kill without touching. These lines themselves may have been taken from a poem by

[13] *SW* xxxi. 37, 30–8; my italics.

Wieland that refers to Goethe.[14] That Hofmannsthal's is referring
most pointedly to literature and not to real personality is established
most unambiguously at the very end of the dialogue. Balzac exclaims
of Goethe,

O ich sehe ihn, und welch ein schauderndes Entzücken, ihn zu sehen. Dort sehe
ich ihn, wo er lebt, wo sein Leben ist: in den dreißig oder vierzig Bänden seiner
Werke . . . Denn es kommt darauf an, die Schicksale dort zu sehen, wo sie in
göttlicher Materie ausgeprägt sind. . . . Goethes Schicksal [steht] in seinen
Werken.

Die Schicksale dort lesen, wo sie geschrieben sind: das ist alles. Die Kraft haben,
sie alle zu sehen, wie sie sich selber verzehren, diese lebenden Fackeln. Sie alle auf
einmal zu sehen, gebunden an die Bäume des ungeheuren Gartens, den ihr Brand
allein beleuchtet: und auf der obersten Terrasse stehen, der einzige Zuschauer,
und in den Saiten der Leier die Akkorde suchen, die Himmel, Hölle und diesen
Anblick zusammenbinden. (38, 19–39)

[Oh, I can see him, and what a thrilling delight it is to see him. I can see him where
he lives, where his life is: in the thirty or forty volumes of his works. For it is a
question of seeing people's fates where they are made distinct in divine matter.
Goethe's fate is in his works. Reading fates where they are written, that is all that
matters. To have the power to see them all devouring themselves, these living
torches. Seeing them all at once, bound to the trees of the monstrous garden
illuminated only by their flames: standing on the uppermost terrace as the only
spectator, seeking in the strings of the lyre the chords that bind together heaven,
hell and this spectacle.]

Hofmannsthal has already interpreted his updated image from
'Manche freilich' in terms that identify the artist with the stoker or
oarsman from 'drunten'; here, with an unmistakable reprise both of
the flame and of the lyre, he implies that the position of insight is
amongst those 'droben'—on a terrace rather than on deck this time,
but looking down at the agony of the living torches in the garden.[15]
Flame and lyre are no longer conjoined in the same place, as they were
at the end of 'Manche freilich', but the two are nevertheless mutually
illustrative. The flame denotes deliberate sacrifice of the self, but the
reintegration of heaven and hell, the watchers and the sufferers, the
self-conscious and the self-sacrificial, takes place by means of the lyre of
poetry. Poetry here is the combination of self-sacrifice and self-awareness, a paradoxical and even somewhat perverse mixture of sharp pain

[14] Cf. *SW* xxxi. 273, 4–12 and above, p. 172.
[15] This is also perhaps an echo from Hebbel: 'Wo Menschen, | Die man mit Hanf
umwickelt und mit Pech | Beträufelt hatte, in den Gärten nachts | als Fackeln brannten'
(*Herodes und Mariamne*, IV. iv).

and cool observation. There is a similar perversity in Lord Chandos's memory of the poisoned rats, which is an illustration of what he paradoxically calls 'jene *sanft und jäh* steigende Flut göttlichen Gefühles' [that flow of divine feeling that rises both gently and steeply].[16] And again, it is perpetuated also in simultaneity of 'etwas Quälendes und Erlösendes' [something torturous and redemptive] in the remembered story, noted in the first publication of *Der Dichter und diese Zeit*, of the lion-tamer who deliberately poisons his lions.[17] This speech, too, is full of echoes of 'Manche freilich', including one that appears only a few lines before this story is related, evoking 'die schwächste Flamme eines eigenen Daseins' [the weakest flame of one's own existence; *RA* i. 70].

Given the proximity of *Über Charaktere im Roman und im Drama* to the anxieties that gave rise to *Ein Brief*, it is unsurprising that it should revolve as much round the functions of lyric poetry as around the conditions of the genres advertised in its title.[18] The dialogue makes substantial reference to images and thought that date back to the period when Hofmannsthal's lyric writing was at its height. It raises the question of the relationship of 1890s poetry to the tradition as an outpouring of retrospective anxiety over the stability of individual identity; the lyre and the flame, which I have suggested are for Hofmannsthal the incarnations of successful symbolization, recur in a more vehement context that seems to indicate an almost desperate clinging to the positive memories they represent. Yet the appearance of only tenuously held control that the dialogue gives—the tone of some of Balzac's speeches is as awkwardly shrill as the prose of the Chandos Letter is conspicuously moderate and crafted—may account for Hofmannsthal's striking lack of concern with the fate of *Über Charaktere*. He even permitted the astonishing misprint 'Hammer-Gurgwall' to go uncorrected in all editions of his *Prosaische Schriften*.[19] The reasons may lie in the dialogue's proximity to *Ein Brief* and the desire to avoid associations of frustration and pain, but they are equally likely to be found in his unwillingness to confront again a piece of work

[16] *SW* xxxi. 50, 35–6; my italics.

[17] *RA* i. 70–1, referring to Hermann Bang's *Fratelli Bedini*. Cf. Robertson, 'Sacrifice', 22–3, for several other related examples, all sharing the paradoxical mixture of a kind of ecstasy with pain.

[18] In fact, such was Hofmannsthal's continuing obsession with the lyric genre, proximity is not always a necessary condition for this kind of generic subterfuge. Cf. my ' "Stop All the Clocks": Time and Times in the "Vienna Operas" of Hofmannsthal and Strauss', in John R. P. McKenzie and Lesley Sharpe (eds.), *The Austrian Comic Tradition: Studies in Honour of W.E. Yates* (Edinburgh: Edinburgh University Press, 1998), 198–201.

[19] Cf. *SW* xxxi. 26.

that betrays creative anxieties not merely on the level of the subject-matter but in the images and the style, too, written and published so quickly as to suggest impulsiveness. Be this as it may, both *Über Charaktere* and *Ein Brief* constitute the immediate context for *Das Gespräch über Gedichte*, and the former, together with other external evidence, associates the dialogue with Hofmannsthal's own early poetry and its difficulties.

In a manner not strictly external, but still before the dialogue proper begins, the rootedness of *Das Gespräch über Gedichte* in the thinking and practice of the early 1890s is made evident again.[20] Its epigraph is a passage on poetry from Hebbel's correspondence with Elise Lensing, which recalls Hofmannsthal's attempts under the heading 'die neue Technik' to understand Symbolism in terms of its relationship with the established tradition: 'Es leben jetzt, die wenigen ausgenommen, die selbst im Lyrischen etwas hervorbringen, keine fünf Menschen in Deutschland, welche über diese zartesten Geburten der Seele ein Urteil hätten' [apart from those few who are productive in the domain of the lyric, there are not five people in Germany who have an opinion on these most delicate offspring of the soul].[21] There is an irony here: Hofmannsthal had by the time he quoted this almost withdrawn from amongst those, 'die selbst im Lyrischen etwas hervorbringen', and although this was not the exclusive focus of *Ein Brief*, he was aware that it represents at least one component of the letter's 'confessional' dimension. Yet by being Hofmannsthal's first sustained exegesis of symbolism in poetry, the 1903 dialogue makes a statement that significantly relativizes the crisis of 1902, reaffirming faith in the ability of language to express the subtleties of the soul. Even if he has

[20] Relatively little has been written on *Das Gespräch über Gedichte*, and almost nothing on its connections with the early 1890s. Studies include Penrith Goff, 'Hugo von Hofmannsthal: The Symbol as Experience', *Kentucky Foreign Language Quarterly*, 7 (1960), 196–200 and 'Hugo von Hofmannsthal and the Aesthetic Experience', *Papers on Language and Literature*, 4 (1968), 414–19; J. H. Reid, ' "Draussen sind wir zu finden . . .": The Development of a Hofmannsthal Symbol', *German Life and Letters*, 27 (1973–4), 35–51; Margit Resch, *Das Symbol als Prozeß bei Hugo von Hofmannsthal* (Königstein/Ts.: Forum Academicum, 1980); Pauget, *L'Interrogation sur l'art*, 358–408; Robertson, 'Sacrifice'. The most rigorous and stimulating studies are by Robertson, looking at connections with works from 1903 onwards, and Pauget, concerned with links between this dialogue and other near-contemporary works. Reid, although taking his title from the text, in fact understands it as a summary of Hofmannsthal's development from lyric to drama and devotes only a few lines to *Das Gespräch*. Goff's articles focus exclusively on the symbol as experience; Resch devotes only two pages to *Das Gespräch* and claims, 'der Dichter hat [das symbolische Erlebnis] nirgends zusammenhängend als ein Ganzes dargestellt' (5).

[21] *SW* xxxi. 74, 2–5; Friedrich Hebbel, *Sämtliche Werke*, iii/i: *Briefe 1829–1839*, 283.

effectively abandoned the use of the lyric form for himself, he feels the need to establish its more general validity from a critical perspective. The epigraph is ostensibly an expression of frustration at the inadequacies of contemporaries' appreciation of poetry. Hofmannsthal may have intended it to be read as a delicate declaration of support for George, whose poems form the subject-matter of the first few pages, offering wry comfort in the implication that with genius it was ever so. A letter from Hofmannsthal to Oscar Bie indicates that Clemens was at one stage to have echoed 'wie wenige' and picked up the lament of the epigraph: 'In wem aber wird ein Sinn lebendig, der über alle Sinne ist? in wie wenigen, Gabriel, in wie furchtbar wenigen?' [in whom, then, is a meaning beyond all meanings made living? In how few, Gabriel, in how terribly few?].[22] Its original context (identified in the first publication in *Die Neue Rundschau*, but not when the dialogue was issued in book form) suggests that it may also have wider resonance in more theoretical terms. Hebbel's complaint was specifically about the inability of his contemporaries to restrain their eagerness for content—'das *Was*' or the *what*—and concentrate instead on asking 'nach dem *Wie*, worauf es doch allein ankommt' [about the *how*, which alone is what matters].[23] Hebbel was no Symbolist, yet his explicit emphasis on the relative functions of form and content in the communication of his essential qualities makes him in a general but important sense a precursor:

wenn vielleicht das Gelinde, das sanft Verschwimmende, welches den letzten Eindruck meiner Productionen bezeichnen mag, an Hölty erinnert, so geht dies (und das bedeutet einen bedeutenden Unterschied) bei mir aus einer Nothwendigkeit der *Form* hervor, indem meines Erachtens die Stimme der Dichtkunst, mag sie nun besingen, was sie will, immer melodisch und rein seyn muß, während es bei Hölty aus dem *Stoff* entspringt.[24]

[if the mildness, the soft blurring that may be said to characterize the final impression of what I write, if this is perhaps reminiscent of Hölty, then for me—and this is an important difference—this derives from a *formal* necessity, in that in my opinion the voice of poetry, whatever it celebrates, must always be melodious and pure, whilst in Hölty it derives from the *material*.]

Thoughts such as these, in particular the role of musicality—the

---

[22] Hofmannsthal, *Briefe 1900–1909*, 129; letter of 9 Oct. 1903. Cf. also *SW* xxxi. 337, 19–21. This passage was to have followed the quotation of Van Lerberghe's 'Sur le seuil' and a poem by George.

[23] Hebbel, *Briefe*, 283—an anticipation of the Marschallin's 'Doch in dem *Wie*, da liegt der ganze Unterschied' (*SW* xxiii. 37).

[24] Hebbel, *Briefe*, 284.

'himmelklare Melodien' that Hebbel refers to in the letter to Elise Lensing to which Hofmannsthal referred in July 1892 and which is quoted at the beginning of Chapter 2[25]—characterized Hofmannsthal's analysis of Symbolism in the early 1890s, where stress on technique was felt to constitute Symbolism's claim to originality.

Again before the dialogue gets under way, there is another clear echo of the lyrical decade. When Gabriel opens the discussion by drawing attention to a book of verse he has laid aside for his friend, Clemens assumes it is by Keats. Clemens evidently *expects* Keats, and the name is almost a reflex response to the word 'Gedichte'. The reaction has first a practical function, establishing a sense that the two characters have some vestiges of independent existence, and that rather than being merely a tract of poetic theory, arbitrarily separated and articulated into two voices, the dialogue relates to their broader experience of poetry and a continuum of discussion. But Keats was also one of the early influences that Hofmannsthal retrospectively identified as having informed his earliest poetic development, and it seems that he originally intended to quote a whole poem in *Das Gespräch*.[26] These references to Hebbel and Keats are subtle internal indicators that the dialogue has as its subtext an earlier period in Hofmannsthal's creative life and is deliberately and specifically retrospective, and later, when Clemens asks to hear Hebbel's 'Sie seh'n sich nicht wieder', he asks for it not by name but as 'ein anderes [Gedicht], das du früher gerne hattest' [another poem, which you used to like; 78, 26–7].

Gabriel responds to Clemens's enquiry by establishing the frame of reference as German poetry—'Nein, es sind deutsche Gedichte. Sie bilden eine Einheit, so sind sie angeordnet' [no, they are German poems. They form a unity, they are arranged like that; 74, 9–10]— identifying his book as George's *Jahr der Seele*. George was, of course, the catalyst for Hofmannsthal's attention to Symbolism, but introducing his collection now in the curious and very pointed way that Hofmannsthal does, with a sudden and apparently unmotivated reference to Keats, suggests that this association is still important to him in 1903; it constitutes in effect a reference to the tensions between Romantic and Symbolist conceptions of poetry and identity that dominated the early 1890s. It is a prefiguration, too, of the ambition to which Hofmannsthal confessed in the letter to Walther Brecht, his

---

[25] *RA* iii. 349; Hebbel, *Briefe*, 401; cf. above p. 74.
[26] Cf. *SW* xxxi. 323, 29; *RA* iii. 620.

early determination to create for German literature works of the stature that Keats's held for the English poetic tradition and the importance George had in encouraging him (*SW* iii. 387). Of the components of Gabriel's reply, only 'deutsch' is an obviously contrasting feature, but 'Einheit' and 'angeordnet', too, mark a distinction from the more general 'Band Gedichte'. They reinforce the Keats–George tension, thus also the Romantic–Symbolist, by drawing attention to an additional degree of constructedness in the later poet, itself an aspect of his concern for the priorities of art and the artificial over direct Romantic personal responsiveness.

Clemens's innocence and apparent naivety are an ironic device, not fully hiding Hofmannsthal's attempt to manipulate the reader's view of literary history. The wisdom of simplicity—'es ist schön. Es atmet den Herbst' [it is beautiful, it exudes autumn]—is supplemented by a gesture towards refuting the kind of criticism that Symbolist poetry used to receive in the 1890s: pointing out that it is technically inaccurate to attribute the blue to the clouds themselves rather than to the sky between, Clemens is nevertheless pleasantly intrigued by it and the 'bold' collocation 'unverhofftes Blau' [unhoped for blue]. Even sympathetic essayists such as Rudolf Lothar and Stephan Waetzold had felt a kind of embarrassed need to acknowledge the criticisms of Symbolism's opponents whilst defending it: Lothar writes in mock condescension, anticipating Clemens's naivety, that the Symbolists'

hervorragendstes Merkmal war die Unverständlichkeit. Man mochte ihre Verse . . . noch so oft lesen und wieder lesen, das klang seltsam, bisweilen sogar schön, sehr schön am Ohr vorbei, aber ein Sinn war absolut nicht zu entdecken.[27]

[most outstanding characteristic was incomprehensibility. One could read and reread their poems again and again, they sounded peculiar to the ear, sometimes even beautiful, very beautiful, but there was absolutely no meaning to be discovered in them.]

Waetzold defends Verlaine's 'Chanson d'automne' from the charge of being 'lächerlich und unfranzösisch . . . weil es keinen "Sinn" gibt' [ridiculous and un-French, because there is no 'meaning'], and with almost as pedantic a query as Clemens's objection to the location of blue in the sky—'was haben die Geigen mit dem Herbste zu thun?' [what have violins to do with autumn?].[28] But by invoking the supposed approbation of Goethe for George's daring phrases,

---

[27] Rudolf Lothar, *Kritische Studien zur Psychologie der Litteratur* (Breslau: Schottländer, 1895), 29–30; cited by Gsteiger, *Französische Symbolisten*, 67.

[28] Waetzold, 'Paul Verlaine', 175.

Hofmannsthal simultaneously disarms such quibbles through Clemens and makes the point that underlying both modern and canonical poetry there is a shared sense of the poetic.

By 'modern' here one should understand 'Symbolist'. Clemens's deceptively simple statement 'es ist schön' captures what for the Symbolist Charles Morice was the essence of poetry: 'la poésie n'a pas d'autre essentiel et naturel objet que la beauté' [the only essential and natural object of poetry is beauty]—as Hofmannsthal noted from Huret's *Enquête* in 1892.[29] Morice was only one of many who held this belief, and their dominant local source for such thoughts was certainly Baudelaire: 'le principe de la poésie est, strictement et simplement, l'aspiration humaine vers une beauté supérieure' [the principle of poetry is, strictly and simply, human aspiration towards a higher form of beauty].[30] Yet this is also borrowed, indeed translated directly from Edgar Allan Poe's essay, 'The Poetic Principle': 'this Principle itself is, strictly and simply, the Human Aspiration for Supernal Beauty.'[31] Hofmannsthal's notes for *Das Gespräch* include several extracts from this essay, in English, and he will have absorbed Poe's argument that poetry consists of '*The Rhythmical Creation of Beauty*' with the aim of attaining to a higher, more spiritual level of reality analogous to the Platonic idea.[32] In his notes, Hofmannsthal quoted one of the key passages:

thus when by Poetry or by Music the most entrancing of the Poetic moods we find ourselves melted, into tears, we weep then through a certain petulant impatient sorrow at our inability to grasp now, wholly, here on earth, at once and for ever, those divine and rapturous joys of which, *through* the poem, we attain to but brief and indeterminate glimpses.[33]

Another jotting for *Das Gespräch über Gedichte* reads, 'über diese Welt hinaus: (Gedanken von Poe)' [out beyond this world (thoughts from Poe); 324, 29]. This refers to the poem 'The Bridge of Sighs' by Thomas Hood, quoted in 'The Poetic Principle', which speculates on the desperate need of a suicide to be 'Anywhere, anywhere | Out of the World!'[34] Hofmannsthal will also have recognized it from Baudelaire's prose poem with these lines as its title.[35]

   [29] Cf. above, p. 106.
   [30] Baudelaire, *OC*, ii. 334, quoted again in the 1859 essay on Gautier (ibid. 114).
   [31] Poe, 'The Poetic Principle', in *Essays and Reviews*, ed. G. R. Thompson (New York: Literary Classics of the United States, 1984), 92.   [32] Ibid. 78.
   [33] Ibid. 77; quoted by Hofmannsthal, *SW* xxxi. 325, 20–4.
   [34] Poe, 'The Poetic Principle', 89.
   [35] Baudelaire, *OC*, i. 356–7.

It cannot be coincidental either that the poems by Stefan George that Hofmannsthal cites in *Das Gespräch* are in so many respects characteristic of Symbolism as he understood it in the 1890s. The first poem, for example, 'Komm in den totgesagten Park', even if it is the opening poem of a collection published as late as 1897, is imbued with Symbolist imagery and outlook: nature is subjected to art (most obviously in the imperious phrase 'tot*gesagt*er Park', as if the saying has caused the dying), the imagery is of pools and fading roses, and there is a strong sense of colour ('unverhofftes Blau', 'das tiefe Gelb, das weiche Grau', 'Purpur', 'das grüne Leben' [unhoped for blue, deep yellow, soft grey, purple, verdant life]). The same is true of the other poems quoted: the iron lilies, from 'Wir werden heute nicht zum Garten gehen' freeze nature into art,[36] and the shivering birds that drink rain-water from the hollow vases in the same poem might be conscious echoes of Hofmannsthal's own Symbolist poems 'Mein Garten' ('wo die Reiher blinken, | Die niemals aus den Silberbrunnen trinken' and 'Die Töchter der Gärtnerin'.[37] George's phrase 'trinken . . . | Vom Regen aus den hohlen Blumenvasen' [drink of the rain from the hollow flower vases] may echo 'Wie schwerer Honig aus den hohlen Waben' [like heavy honey from the hollow combs], the last line of 'Ballade des äußeren Lebens' (*SW* i. 44)—especially since the last lines of the same poem also echo Hofmannsthal's 'Ballade'. These lines— 'Und blicken nur und horchen, wenn in Pausen | Die reifen Früchte an den Boden klopfen' [and only look and listen when in silent moments the ripe fruits fall with a thud on the ground]—are closely related in rhythm, imagery and structure to 'Und süße Früchte werden aus den herben | Und fallen nachts wie tote Vögel nieder' [and sweet fruits develop from the tart ones and fall to the ground at night like dead birds].[38]

By evoking the autumn, all these poems reproduce in Amiel's sense an *état d'âme*. Clemens says simply, 'es ist der Herbst' [it is the autumn; 75, 5–6], and by being so intensely autumn it can also correspond to a state of mind, that Gabriel formulates as 'mehr als ein Herbst' [more than an autumn; 76, 2]. This, too, has Romantic ancestry: Novalis writes in *Die Lehrlinge zu Sais*, expressing a similar sense of dual significance, 'wenn man echte Gedichte liest und hört, so fühlt man einen inneren Verstand der Natur sich bewegen, und schwebt, wie der

---

[36] George, *Werke*, i. 124; *SW* xxxi. 75, 7.
[37] *SW* i. 20 and 22; cf. also above, pp. 165–74.
[38] 'Wir schreiten auf und ab im reichen flitter', George, *Werke*, i. 122; 'Die Ballade des äußeren Lebens', *SW* i. 44.

himmlische Leib derselben, *in ihr und über ihr zugleich'* [when you read and listen to real poems you feel an inner sense of nature move, and like its heavenly body you float *in it and above it at the same time*].[39] However, when Gabriel says that the seasons and landscapes are 'nichts als die Träger des *Anderen'* [merely the bearers of the Other; 76, 3–4], Hofmannsthal points to the mystical dimension of Symbolism, echoing another of Charles Morice's statements that he copied down in 1892: 'le symbolisme est la transposition dans un AUTRE ordre de choses' [Symbolism is transposition into another, a different order of things].[40] But then Gabriel appears to take back this suggestion. His long speech (76, 5–28) is a complex distillation of ideas from Symbolism and from Novalis that perhaps better than any other single paragraph of Hofmannsthal's writing encapsulates the anxieties he felt at the Symbolists' distance from their Romantic ancestors. He describes first a 'Verfassung des Daseins' [a state of being] as a prelude to an exposition of how poetry functions, but the comparison is implicit throughout. He begins thus:

Sind nicht die Gefühle, die Halbgefühle, alle die geheimsten und tiefsten Zustände unseres Inneren in der seltsamsten Weise mit einer Landschaft verflochten, mit einer Jahreszeit, mit einer Beschaffenheit der Luft, mit einem Hauch? (76, 5–8)

[Are not feelings, half-feelings, all the most secret and profound circumstances of our inner being bound up in the strangest way with a landscape, with a season, with a certain something in the air, with a breath of wind?]

Again this echoes Hebbel and Hofmannsthal's summary of Hebbel in July 1892: 'Definition der Poesie bei Hebbel: Vollendetstes Gedicht muß einen Zustand bis ins Tiefste ausschöpfen (Poesie soll die dunkelsten Zustände durch Melodien lösen).'[41] Gabriel's 'Die . . . tiefsten Zustände unseres Innern' echo Hebbel's prescription that poetry must delve into 'einen Zustand bis ins Tiefste'; 'geheim' is a modulation of 'dunkel' in 'die dunkelsten Zustände', which musicality in verse is charged to release; even 'verflochten' reads as a response to the 'lösen' of the definition Hofmannsthal noted in 1892 as part of the 'neue Technik' note on Symbolism. But whether or not its vocabulary is derived from Hebbel's definition of poetry, Gabriel's evocation might well describe Heinrich von Ofterdingen's relationship with nature, even if the expression here has more delicacy and less confidence than Novalis's evocations of Heinrich's sensibility. The

---

[39] Novalis, *Schriften*, i. 84; my italics.
[40] Quoted from Huret, *Enquête*, 88.
[41] *RA* iii. 349; 13 July 1892. For Hebbel's original, cf. above, p. 74.

second part of *Die Lehrlinge zu Sais* makes a similar point: 'es ist ein geheimnisvoller Zug nach allen Seiten in unserm Innern, aus einem unendlich tiefen Mittelpunkt sich rings verbreitend' [deep inside us we are mysteriously drawn in all directions by a force that spreads in circles from an infinitely deep centre].[42] According to Gabriel, the self is so intimately tied to the sights, smells and sounds of the ordinary outside world—'eine gewisse Bewegung, mit der du von einem hohen Wagen herabspringst; eine schwüle sternlose Sommernacht; der Geruch feuchter Steine in einer Hausflur' [a certain movement with which you jump down from a high carriage, a close, starless night in summer, the smell of damp stones in the hallway]—the phrase that apparently struck Kafka when he first read the dialogue[43]—and 'das Gefühl eisigen Wassers' [the feeling of icy water; 76, 8–10], and the sense that one's 'ganzer innerer Besitz [ist] mit den Wurzeln ihres Lebens festgewachsen' [everything within one is firmly intertwined with the roots of their lives; 76, 12–15]. These are all examples reminiscent of the ephiphanic objects evoked in *Ein Brief* (51, 35–40). To cut off these experiences would make one's 'Aufschwünge',' Sehnsucht', 'Trunkenheiten' shrivel and die, 'zwischen den Händen zu nichts ver[gehen]' [exaltations, longing, intoxications, fall away to nothing in one's hands; 76, 17]. The image of existence turning insubstantially to dust is a familiar fear from the lyrical decade.

Gabriel's summary of the implications of the interpenetration of self and world is this:

Wollen wir uns finden, so dürfen wir nicht in unser Inneres hinabsteigen: draußen sind wir zu finden, draußen. Wie der wesenlose Regenbogen spannt sich unsere Seele über den unaufhaltsamen Sturz des Daseins. Wir besitzen unser Selbst nicht: von außen weht es uns an, es flieht uns für lange und kehrt uns in einem Hauch zurück. (76, 17–22)

[If we wish to find ourselves, we must not delve into our interior being: it is outside that we are to be found, outside. Like the insubstantial rainbow our soul arches over the unstoppable headlong fall of existence. We do not possess our Self: it is blown towards us from outside, it flees away from us for long periods of time and returns in a single breath.]

The subtexts are positively jostling for space behind these few phrases. The rainbow recalls Faust's rejuvenation, the image he uses of the waterfall, 'von Sturz zu Sturzen [wälzend]' [pouring down in torrent after torrent], and his assertion of the necessity and power of

---

[42] Novalis, *Schriften*, i. 85.
[43] See Max Brod, *Über Franz Kafka* (Frankfurt a.M.: S. Fischer, 1974), 46.

symbolism, 'Am farbigen Abglanz haben wir das Leben' [we have life in its colourful reflection].[44] To explain the significance of 'Abglanz', Erich Trunz refers to a passage in *Versuch einer Witterungslehre*: 'das Wahre, mit dem Göttlichen identisch, läßt sich niemals von uns direkt erkennen, wir schauen es nur im Abglanz, im Beispiel, Symbol' [truth, which is identical with the Divine, can never be perceived by us directly, we can see it only in its reflection, in the example, in the symbol].[45] Gabriel's use of 'Hauch' is also a Goethean echo: in his notes for *Das Gespräch* Hofmannsthal quotes Goethe's 'Spruch', 'Bilde, Künstler! Rede nicht! | Nur ein Hauch sei dein Gedicht' [make forms, O artist! Do not talk! Let your poem be only a breath of air][46]—in the light of which, the return of one's self as 'ein Hauch' suggests that poetry is the medium. Later in the note Hofmannsthal writes 'ein Hauch ist ein Gedicht und als solches heiligste Handlung' [a breath of air is a poem and as such the most sacred of acts; 326, 3], confirming that he has preserved his conception of poetry as 'heilige Arbeit' [a sacred task; *RA* iii. 373]. In *Über Charaktere im Roman und im Drama*, Balzac accuses Goethe of being able to destroy 'mit einem Hauch seines Mundes' [with a breath from his mouth; 37, 35], also perhaps a reference to poetry. The Critical Edition suggests that Hofmannsthal knew Hebbel's sonnet 'Was ist ein Hauch?' (318, 7–21), which celebrates the power of subtle suggestion and sensations intimated rather than strongly felt: in a state of heightened perception, the dying may derive much greater delight from 'ein kühler Hauch' [a cool breath] than anything felt by those who really pick flowers.[47] Finally, another sketch for *Das Gespräch* uses the same image to indicate the symbolic action of poetry: 'Die Menschen müssen "poetisch" werden durch die Erfahrung des Lebens: wie alles entgleitet, nur an den Worten haftet. Wie die Gegenwart unwirklich, die durch einen Hauch vermittelte Nicht-gegenwart wirklich ist' [mankind must become 'poetic' through its experience of life, of how everything slips away, is caught only on words. Just as the present is unreal, so the not-present communicated

---

[44] Goethe, *Werke*, iii. 149. Hofmannsthal's 'Sturz des Daseins' was originally 'Sturz des Lebens' (*Nachlaß*, H VB 66.5; not recorded in *SW* xxxi).

[45] Goethe, *Werke*, xiii. 305; cf. ibid. iii. 538.

[46] Ibid. i. 325 ('Sprüche'); cf. Hofmannsthal, *SW* xxxi. 325.

[47] Note 9 ('Ein Hauch aber ist so viel'; 326, 15–20) reinforces the suggestion that Hebbel's poem was in Hofmannsthal's mind. There are also phrases in this poem besides its opening words, and a strong rhythmic similarity, that suggest an influence on Hofmannsthal's sonnet 'Was ist die Welt?' (*SW* i. 7). The idea that a light suggestion may be an intimation of something more significant or more powerful beyond is common to both poems.

by a breath is real; 326, 36–327, 2]—which is effectively a statement of the theory of *correspondances*.

Hofmannsthal has therefore used or quoted 'Hauch' in three related ways: to indicate how sensations in the outside world correspond with our inner selves ('die tiefsten Zustände unseres Inneren . . . mit einem Hauch [verflochten]'; 76, 6–8); to describe the manner in which one registers a sense of one's self as communicated by the outside world ('unser Selbst . . . kehrt uns in einem Hauch zurück'; 76, 21–2); and as a metaphor for the poem itself. The superimposition of these layers both gives the symbol density and provides a basis for what will follow, the evocation of the loss of self and the simultaneous formation of the poetic symbol in the sacrifice. A note from January 1892 associates this with Stefan George: 'Wort ist der Windhauch, der an die Saiten der Seele schlägt, berauschende Wirkung der Lectüre, einzelne Schwingungen und Chor' [the word is a breath of wind that strikes the strings of one's soul, the intoxicating effect of reading, individual vibrations and the ensemble].[48] Another, from early 1893, explicitly links this with Symbolism: ' "Symbolismus" Form des künstlerischen Grundtriebes, des Triebes, dem Geschaffenen die letzte Deutlichkeit, den göttlichen Hauch des Lebens, zu geben (la chair im "Œuvre").'[49]

The formulation 'draußen sind wir zu finden' records both an affirmation of aspects of Novalis's writing and the establishment of an important distinction between his and Hofmannsthal's poetic thinking. On one level it states an openness of identity that is comparable to Novalis's presentation of Heinrich and of the Apprentices' participation in the world. Yet on many occasions Novalis insists that the proper perspective is the reverse of Hofmannsthal's:

Wir träumen von Reisen durch das Weltall: ist denn das Weltall nicht in uns? Die Tiefen unsers Geistes kennen wir nicht.—Nach Innen geht der geheimnisvolle Weg. In uns, oder nirgends ist die Ewigkeit mit ihren Welten, die Vergangenheit und Zukunft. Die Außenwelt ist die Schattenwelt.

Mich führt alles in mich selbst zurück. . . . Mich freuen die wunderlichen Haufen und Figuren in den Sälen, allein mir ist, als wären sie nur Bilder, Hüllen, Zierden, versammelt um ein göttlich Wunderbild, und dieses liegt mir immer in Gedanken.

---

[48] *Nachlaß*, H VB 12.57; *SW* ii. 286.

[49] *RA* iii. 357. See above, p. 119. Pauget's reference to 'le jeu avec le mot "souffle" ' (*L'Interrogation sur l'art*, 367) does not perhaps do justice to Hofmannsthal's deliberate and subtle metaphorical manipulation here. She makes the point (371) that 'Hauch' is a translation of πνευμα and thus etymologically links these dimensions with divine inspiration and a human being's breathing, thus implicitly echoing Hofmannsthal's early note.

Keine Unruhe treibt sie [die Dichter] nach außen. Ein stiller Besitz genügt ihnen und das unermeßliche Schauspiel außer ihnen reizt sie nicht selbst, darin aufzutreten.[50]

[We dream of journeying through space: is space not within us? We do not know the depths of our spirit.—The mysterious path leads inwards. Eternity with its own worlds, past and future, is within us, or nowhere. The external world is a world of shadows.]

[Everything leads me back within myself. . . . The wondrous heaps and figures in the rooms delight me, but I feel as if they were only images, shells, decorations, collected around a miraculous divine image, and this is always in my thoughts.]

[Poets are not driven outwards by any form of restlessness. They are satisfied with quiet self-possession, and the vast drama outside them does not stimulate them to take part in it themselves.]

Although the last quotation describes activity in the world rather than a mystical participation in nature, it articulates most clearly the difference between Hofmannsthal and Novalis. The Romantic writer's poets 'possess themselves', enjoy 'ein stiller Besitz'—'gehören sich selbst' in the idealist terms of Hofmannsthal's 1896 George review (*RA* i. 219)—whereas for Gabriel the opposite is true: 'wir besitzen unser Selbst nicht' (76, 20–21). A secure sense of self-possession is the prerequisite for Novalis's 'Weg nach Innen', and for him, the opening out of the self brings one back to the self. Hofmannsthal noted from Bruno Wille's introduction to the 1899 edition of Novalis by Meißner, 'Wir sollen alles in ein Du, ein zweites Ich verwandeln; nur dadurch erheben wir uns selbst zum großen Ich' [We should transform everything into a You, a second I, for only by doing so will we elevate our own selves to the level of a great I; 324, 15–16], but such goals are inconceivable for Gabriel. 'Unser Selbst!', he exclaims, 'Das Wort ist solch eine Metapher' [our Self! the word is such a metaphor; 76, 22–3]: the world is the vehicle of the metaphor, but the tenor is fatally elusive.

Clemens notes that this kind of dissipated self, the absence of an essential nature beneath superficial external characteristics, must make it hard for one to write a drama or condemn a murderer (76, 32–5)—and indeed structured mutual interaction, or a capacity for moral judgement, which these require, presuppose a much more controlled sense of self. In these two examples, the relationship of *Das Gespräch über Gedichte* to the two most important near-contemporary

[50] From, respectively, *Blüthenstaub* (Novalis, *Schriften*, ii. 418–19), *Die Lehrlinge zu Sais* (i. 81) and *Heinrich von Ofterdingen* (i. 266–7).

essays, *Ein Brief* and *Über Charaktere im Roman und im Drama*, is crystal-lized. Lord Chandos in the former is unable to reproach his daughter for a lie, since 'die mir im Munde zuströmenden Begriffe plötzlich eine so schillernde Färbung annahmen und so ineinander überflossen, daß ich den Satz, so gut es ging, zu Ende haspelnd . . . das Kind allein ließ' [the concepts that flowed into my mouth suddenly began to shimmer and flow into each other such that, stammering to the end of the sentence as well as I could manage, I left the child alone; 49, 5–7]. The crisis of expression is linked to a crisis of identity, in turn associated with the lack of confidence that a moral system needs. The *point de départ* for Balzac in the other dialogue is his inability to write drama, consequent upon his view of character—that there is no such thing as a unified personal individual.

Such freedom, however, is ideally suited to lyric poetry, whose activity is to gather the self from 'die ganze ungeheuere unerschöpf-liche Natur' [nature as a whole, monstrous, inexhaustible; 76, 38–9]. It is, says Gabriel, an Ariel-figure, ranging beyond humanity, yet ulti-mately in the service of humanity, bringing back 'nichts anderes . . . als den zitternden Hauch der menschlichen Gefühle . . . beladen . . . mit einem ungeheuren aber einem menschlichen Gefühl' [nothing other than the trembling breath of human feelings, laden with a monstrous, but human feeling; 77, 7–16]. This is the sense of Gabriel's second long speech: in expansively poetic and symbolic phrases he develops the paradox of limited unlimitedness, the central paradox of the symbol in Symbolism. There are suggestions of Nietzsche's Zarathustra as well as of Ariel, of *Faust*,[51] and perhaps an echo of Act V, scene i of *A Midsummer Night's Dream*:

> The poet's eye, in a fine frenzy rolling,
> Doth glance from heaven to earth, from earth to heaven;
> And, as imagination bodies forth
> The forms of things unknown, the poet's pen
> Turns them to shapes, and gives to airy nothing
> A local habitation and a name.

Found by the poet's eye and formed by his pen, the natural objects of poetry are limitless in their variety, but united to humanity by language. The progression of the speech suggests that the connection between 'die enge Kammer unseres Herzens' [the narrow chamber of

---

[51] Even down to the clipped demonstrative in 'dies Schauspiel in sich saugen' (77, 14) which recalls 'Welch Schauspiel! Aber ach! ein Schauspiel nur!' (Goethe, *Werke*, iii. 22) and repolarizes it positively.

our heart; 76, 37–8] and 'unerschöpfliche Natur' is linguistic formulation.

Clemens, the tool of Hofmannsthal's Socratic irony, makes the mistake of conceiving of language as a kind of substitution code: 'sie setzt eine Sache für die andere' [it sets one thing in the place of another; 77, 23]. This corresponds more to Goethe's definition of allegory than to truly poetic language: 'Die Allegorie verwandelt die Erscheinung in einen Begriff, den Begriff in ein Bild, doch so, daß der Begriff im Bilde immer noch begrenzt und vollständig zu halten und zu haben und an demselben auszusprechen sei' [allegory transforms appearances into a concept, the concept into an image, but in such a way that the concept may always be contained within the image, restricted and complete, and may be expressed with it].[52] But Gabriel's outlook is essentially that of a Symbolist, where 'die Poesie . . . fieberhaft bestrebt ist, die Sache selbst zu setzen' [poetry is feverishly striving to give us the very thing itself; 77, 26]. Clemens was nearer the mark when he said of George's poem, 'es ist der Herbst' (75, 5–6), simply using the verb 'to be'. His conviction that it is the nature of language itself, a particular symbolic language, that effects the correspondence between self and world represents for Hofmannsthal both a relativization of the Chandos-crisis and a decisive advance beyond Romantic participation with the world into Symbolist re-creation of it. Gabriel makes certain that the word 'Symbol' is not misunderstood in a casual sense that would make it virtually the equivalent of 'Vergleich', or comparison (77, 36–7), and thereby performs the kind of revaluation of the term that the French Symbolists strove for. Yet the simile he chooses to express it is borrowed from the activity of the will-o'-the-wisps in Goethe's *Märchen*: out of every image of the world poetry sucks

sein Wesenhaftestes, so wie jene Irrlichter in dem Märchen, die überall das Gold herauslecken. Und sie tut es aus dem gleichen Grunde: weil sie sich vom dem Mark der Dinge nährt, weil sie elend verlöschen würde, wenn sie dies nährende Gold nicht aus allen Fugen, allen Spalten in sich zöge.[53]

[52] *Maximen und Reflexionen*, 750; Goethe, *Werke*, xii. 471; see also above, pp. 87–8, for the parallel definition of the symbol.

[53] *SW* xxxi. 77, 31–5. Hofmannsthal's critical comments on the *Märchen* can be found in his introduction to the volume of Goethe's 'Opern und Singspiele' (*RA* i. 443–4). He draws implicitly the same distinction between 'eine Sache für die andere setzen' and 'die Sache selbst setzen': 'das "Märchen" . . . worin die Elemente des Daseins tiefsinnig spielend nebeneinander gebracht sind und eine undeutbare innere Musik aus schönen Bildern und Lebensbezügen entsteht, deren Deutung aber auch das Gemüt nicht verlangt, da es sich an der Harmonie des Vorgestellten völlig zur Genüge ergötzt. Dieses "Märchen" hat Novalis eine *erzählte Oper* genannt' (443).

[its essential nature, like the will-o'-the-wisps in the fairy tale that suck out the gold everywhere. And it does so for the same reason, because it is nourished from the very marrow of things, because it would be miserably extinguished if it did not draw into itself this nourishing gold from every nook and cranny.]

Simultaneously, this insistence upon the essence, the marrow of things, suggests that Hofmannsthal has come to terms with Symbolism's true inheritance of Romanticism, and that it is the activity of language that will counteract the sense of self-fragmentation or self-dissipation. At this point, however, Gabriel breaks the tension of his impassioned defence of poetic language, saying he thinks he is boring Clemens (77, 38), and creating a pause for the import to sink in. Clemens is so captivated, though, that he wishes to continue the discussion; theory gives way to case-study again with a poem from the section 'Sieg des Sommers' in *Das Jahr der Seele*.

Hearing this poem Clemens is moved once again to exclaim how beautiful it is, and how perfectly, or purely and simply, it expresses 'einen grenzenlosen Zustand' (78, 18). Yet again, the image of the boundary is used: the subject-matter of poetry 'hat keine Grenzen' (77, 16); poetry is 'in ihrem Wesen . . . begrenzt' (77, 17), yet may express 'einen grenzenlosen Zustand' [a boundless state; has no boundaries; restricted in its essence; a boundless state]. One word thrust into different but closely juxtaposed contexts loses its stability without becoming meaningless, and it is by means of just such tantalizing para-doxes that Symbolism operates. Gabriel repeats Hebbel's definition of poetry as the articulation of 'einen Zustand des Gemütes' [a state of one's own nature; 78, 21], and he, too, adds a paradox, that of motion within a state: 'nur diese [Gedichte] können *das Spiel* der Gefühle zeigen' [only these poems can show the play of feelings].[54] This again parallels the central paradox of the symbol, which represents the uni-versal in the particular or the infinite in the finite. That poetry func-tions thus is the very justification of its existence[55]—which implies that, despite the Chandos Letter, Hofmannsthal is satisfied that he has over-come the existential angst he registered in 1893: 'Zweifel an der Existenzberechtigung der Kunst gegenüber dem Elend der Welt' [doubts about the justification of the existence of art in the face of the wretchedness of the world; *RA* iii. 363].

[54] *SW* xxxi. 78, 24; my italics.
[55] 'Existenzberechtigung': the reading of both the MS (*Nachlaß*, H VB 66.9) and the first publication. The Critical Edition follows the version published in *Prosa I* (1907) with 'Berechtigung ihrer Existenz' (78, 21–2).

When Clemens wanted to explain symbolism as the substitution of one thing for another, Gabriel reacted vehemently and exclaimed, 'welch ein häßlicher Gedanke!' [what an ugly thought! 77, 24]. Even after reading Hebbel's 'Sie seh'n sich nicht wieder', Clemens has not fully grasped the explanation and almost makes the same mistake again: 'Und diese Schwäne? Sie sind ein Symbol? Sie bedeuten—' [And these swans? Are they a symbol? They mean—; 79, 16–17]. He wants to use the verb 'bedeuten' transitively, to use it, in fact 'um eine Sache für die andere zu setzen', but Gabriel interrupts, more gently than the last time, and intercepts the object, leaving the transitive potential of the verb dramatically suspended. The dialogue is not merely a convenient formal peg upon which to hang a treatise; it allows Hofmannsthal to inject such interactive exchanges, and in this case creates thereby a 'cliff-hanging' sense of enormous possibility not only perfectly appropriate to the subject-matter but essential to its articulation. Since the symbol does not permit of explanation, for the uninitiated a sense of the value of being rationally inexplicable must be created—a sense by definition beyond discursive communication. The swans *mean*, in the sense that they have great significance beyond their mere natural existence, and to convey this Gabriel is reduced to tautology: 'sie bedeuten hier nichts als sich selber: Schwäne' [they mean nothing other than themselves: swans; 79, 20]. The author, however, can be confident that the inadequacies of this account have already been rendered insignificant by the gesture of interruption, a different level of communication.

Gabriel's explanation of the swans' role reveals the extent to which Romantic preconceptions have now been integrated into Hofmannsthal's Symbolist thinking. They are described as 'die eigentlichen Hieroglyphen, . . . lebendige geheimnisvolle Chiffern, mit denen Gott unaussprechliche Dinge in die Welt geschrieben hat' [the true hieroglyphs, living, mysterious ciphers with which God has inscribed ineffable things in the world; 79, 27–9]. The passage is redolent of Novalis once more, in particular the 'große Chiffernschrift' [great symbolic script] described in the opening of *Die Lehrlinge zu Sais*, or nature seen as the product of 'der eigentliche Chiffrierer' [the one true symbolizer].[56] The vocabulary is also Baudelaire's, however, and became a staple of Symbolist manifestos. By 1903, after completing his *Habilitationsschrift*, Hofmannsthal will certainly have read Baudelaire's essay on Hugo, in which the correspondent world of nature is evoked

---

[56] Novalis, *Schriften*, i. 70 and 99.

in order to arrive at 'cette vérité que tout est hiéroglyphique' [the truth which says that everything is hieroglyphic].[57] Vanor's *L'Art symboliste* of 1889 explains that the world is a book, and that the poet 'en déchiffrera et en expliquera les hiéroglyphes' [will decipher and explain its hieroglyphs].[58] But for Hofmannsthal the symbols are indecipherable. Gabriel maintains that, although images are written in and with language, 'es sind Chiffern, welche aufzulösen die Sprache ohnmächtig ist . . . du wirst keine Gedankenworte, keine Gefühlsworte finden, in welchen sich die Seele jener, gerade jener Regungen entladen könnte, deren hier ein Bild sie entbindet' [they are ciphers that language is incapable of solving . . . you will find no conceptual words, no emotional words in which the soul can unload those very stirrings that are here born into an image; 80, 1–5]. His terminological irritation—'wie gern wollte ich dir das Wort "Symbol" zugestehen, wäre es nicht schal geworden, daß mich's ekelt' [how I should like to concede you the word 'symbol', if it had not become so shallow that it disgusts me; 80, 5–7]—both echoes the debates of the Symbolists themselves and puts them into perspective by recognizing that it was the wrangling of French writers and critics in the 1880s that conclusively debased the term. It is also an acknowledgement of a stage in Hofmannsthal's development when he was interested enough in the term to discuss it with his friends and imitate the verse it described.[59]

Hofmannsthal returns to the images of his early verse to exemplify how symbols may be appreciated: 'dem Kind ist alles Symbol, dem Frommen ist Symbol das einzig Wirkliche und der Dichter vermag nichts anderes zu erblicken' [for a child, everything is a symbol, for the religious man the symbol is the only truth, and the poet is incapable of perceiving anything else; 80, 9–10]. A poet's heightened insight had been a constant theme since the Romantics, and the unselfconsciously percipient innocence of the child is a familiar topos, illustrated in 'Weltgeheimnis', 'Ein Knabe', 'Ballade des äußeren Lebens' and many other of Hofmannsthal's poems. Religious terminology for poetic practice was commonplace, and Hofmannsthal had long considered poetry as a sacred task. Despite Clemens's surprise at the sudden shift of focus from poet to divine (80, 11–12), spiritual openness,

[57] Baudelaire, *OC*, ii. 133.
[58] Quoted from Michaud, *Message poétique*, 746.
[59] Even Gabriel's word 'Hieroglyphen', despite its pedigree beyond the Symbolists' squabbles, is regarded ambivalently by Hofmannsthal. In the 1893 notes for 'Dialoge über die Kunst' it is used negatively: 'Sprache ist überhaupt nur Bild. Manche, erstarrt wie Hieroglyphen, haben nur Münzwert, manche lebendig, wirken direkt auf die Nerven' (*RA* iii. 360).

childhood and poetry, the conditions in which symbolic perception is possible, all have in common the deliberate forgetting of one's self. This forms the basis for Gabriel's next long speech, perhaps the best-known passage from the dialogue, which takes the idea of sacrifice literally in order to convey the concept of poetic self-abandonment. Despite the shift from an often abstract and always aesthetically stylized language to more intense and violent imagery than is usually associated with Hofmannsthal, this will remain the function of the discussion of the sacrifice.

The scenario that Gabriel sketches is the situation of primitive man, largely without the burden of self-consciousness, and wholly without that of tradition, who enjoys a marvellously high degree of sensuousness (80, 20) and responds to a strong emotional conviction of the need to placate the gods. His instinctive awareness of a spiritual dimension is communicated via the forces of nature, 'die Wellen des Gießbaches und das Geröll der Berge' and '[die] fürchterliche Stille des Waldes' [the swelling of the mountain torrent and the boulders in the mountains, the terrifying silence of the forest; 80, 23–5]. The man's receptiveness to the symbolic transference of his sense of responsibility to the animal is created physically, by the frightening experience of the dark, by the warmth of the fleece and the animal's blood, then by the twitching of the knife and the animal's death-groans. The combination of cumulated, acute physical sensation with great intensity of emotion comes to constitute the man's own death: 'er muß, einen Augenblick lang, in dem Tier gestorben sein' [he must, for a moment, have died in the beast; 81, 2–3]. It is a kind of self-annihilation, real only in poetic terms but real none the less. It is true that 'Gabriel insists that this was a real experience'[60]—'einen Augenblick lang [war] wirklich sein Blut aus der Kehle des Tieres gequollen' [for a moment it was really his blood flowing from the beast's throat; 81, 28–9]—but necessary also to define the sense in which he means real, and poetry for Gabriel and Hofmannsthal is 'wirklich'.

The story of the birth of the symbol in sacrifice that now follows intrigues many commentators. René Wellek surely misses the point when he complains of Hofmannsthal's fanciful account, saying 'man glaubt nicht an diese Fiktion und versteht nicht, was sie eigentlich beweisen soll' [we do not believe this fiction and we do not understand what it is supposed to prove].[61] The account is not given as an article of

[60] Robertson, 'Sacrifice', 21.
[61] René Wellek, 'Hofmannsthal als Literaturkritiker', *Arcadia*, 20 (1985), 69.

faith but as an example of what it attempts to evoke, a symbol. Hofmannsthal's technique throughout *Das Gespräch über Gedichte* is to exemplify rather than rely on discursive language to explain, and the story of the sacrifice is not intended to be a *history* of the origins of symbolism so much as the provision of a suggestive new perspective on the *nature* of the symbol. Ritchie Robertson gives a detailed account of how the theme of sacrifice in *Das Gespräch* recurs 'almost obsessively in Hofmannsthal's writings between about 1903 and 1912', and convincingly refutes Wellek's accusation of its unintelligibility.[62] If one approaches the dialogue from the direction of Hofmannsthal's works and thought *before* 1903, the sense that it 'becomes perplexing . . . when Gabriel derives the poetic symbol from sacrifice' is reduced.[63] The intensity of emotion that Gabriel calls participation in the sacrificial death of the animal is certainly gruesome, but it is not any more perplexing than Keats's claim 'I am . . . annihilated' or Rilke's evocation of the dismemberment of Orpheus by the maenads at the end of the first part of the *Sonette an Orpheus*.[64] It is the equivalent of what Rilke announced in that sonnet, for the primitive man in the dialogue enjoys 'eine bewölkte lebenstrunkene *orphische* Sinnlichkeit' [a cloudy, *orphic* sensuousness that is drunk on life].[65]

The essential explanation of Hofmannsthal's procedure here is already contained in his notes for the first of the 'Dialogues on Art', 'Beschäftigung mit der Schönheit':

Das Entstehen des metaphorischen Ausdruckes ist ein geheimnisvolles Ding: der Anschauung eines Vorgangs substituiert sich plötzlich unwillkürlich die Anschauung eines anderen nur in der Idee verwandten Bildlicheren, Körperlicheren.[66]

This note might have been amongst the *paralipomena* to the dialogue itself, so precisely does it anticipate *Das Gespräch*. The sacrifice is exactly such a 'more bodily' illustration of the process of symbolization described hitherto in more abstract terms. It is 'in der Idee verwandt', in essence the same thing, not Gabriel's detested substitution of one thing for another, but the substitution of a new perspective, as the repetition of 'Anschauung' demonstrates. The transference of

[62] Robertson, 'Sacrifice', 19.
[63] Ibid. 20.
[64] Keats, *Complete Poems*, 158; Rilke, *Sämtliche Werke*, i. 748, cf. also above, pp. 85 and 145. It is nevertheless sacrifice of identity rather than death that is at issue (cf. in contrast Pauget, *L'Interrogation sur l'art*, 377–9).
[65] *SW* xxxi. 80, 21; my italics.
[66] *RA* iii. 360; May 1893. See above, p. 126.

significance (which is what symbolization consists of) takes place suddenly and briefly, lasting only 'einen Augenblick lang' and 'für die Dauer eines Atemzugs' [a moment long, for the duration of a breath].[67] The correspondence of the animal's death with his own devotion constitutes a great and mysterious truth (81, 5).

The Biese review of 1894 contains the first thoughts of how *Das Gespräch* might be structured, as a conversation between young people, and a diary note from the same period indicates that elements of the somewhat gory subject-matter may already have been present at that period:

Ich bin ein Dichter weil ich bildlich erlebe.

Das Leben erobern, mit dem Leben *fertig werden*, in sich fertig werden, den Dingen ihre Seele abgewinnen, in ihre Blutwärme untertauchen, aus ihnen mit den naiven Augen ihrer Liebe herausschauen: das ist zugleich alle Poesie (ποίησις). (*RA* iii. 382)

[I am a poet because I experience in images. To conquer life, to *deal with life*, to deal with oneself, to take over the souls of things, to be submerged in their blood-warmth, to look out from them with the naive eyes of their love: that is the whole of poetry, too.]

There is an unsettling progression here from the clinical and distancing 'fertig werden' to the empathetic warmth of blood, and this suggests some uneasy tensions in Hofmannsthal's thinking about poetry. But the important link of naivety and poetry is made, and the suggestion 'Blutwärme' is developed and echoed literally in the finished dialogue ('blutwarm' and 'das warme Blut', 80, 34–5). But more precisely even than this, the very image Hofmannsthal chose to illustrate his theory of the symbol in 1903 may derive from his very earliest reading. Robertson suggests that the account of sacrifice in *Das Gespräch* was possibly suggested by Erwin Rohde's description of the sacrificial priests of ancient Greece in *Psyche*.[68] But the core was surely two consecutive reflections in Hebbel's diary for 15 December 1839:

Formen heißt Gebären.—Warum is *Thierschmerz* nicht poetisch? Weil der Schmerz des Thiers mit dem Daseyn Eins wird, weil das Thier, das z.B. an einem Fieber leidet, nur ein lebendiges Fieber ist.

Dichten heißt, sich ermorden.[69]

---

[67] *SW* xxxi. 80, 37 and 81, 8. The phrase 'einen Augenblick lang' is insistently repeated three times. For a very similar use of repetition to make a related point, cf. Vilain, ' "Stop all the Clocks" ', 188 and 193.

[68] Robertson, 'Sacrifice', 27.

[69] Hebbel, *Tagebücher*, i. 411; fragments 1837–8.

[To form means to give birth.—Why is an *animal's* pain not poetic? Because the pain of the animal becomes one with existence, because the animal that has a fever, say, is merely a living fever. | To write poetry is to murder oneself.]

Hebbel denies that mere animal pain can be poetic because there is no self-consciousness and we perceive the pain merely as part of the animal's physical existence, with no *poetic* significance for the observer who has not in any way formed, shaped or created it. True poetry, in contrast, is defined as '*sich* ermorden', when the sensations are both caused and felt by the self; not only has there to be a self to annihilate, but the process has to be recreated in a formal structure. Hofmannsthal combines the two statements in his conception of the symbol, suggesting how the observer identifies with the animal's pain for a brief moment. To object that this identification is not real, or that no empirical test will identify the blood gushing to the floor as human rather than ovine, is to trivialize the meaning of 'wirklich'. This represents, incidentally, a distinct shift of emphasis from the similar moments of epiphanic realization and participation so famously evoked in the Chandos Letter—themselves, like the theme of the sacrifice, anticipated in their subject-matter a full decade earlier by a diary note from July 1891 that reads 'Details sollen sein wie jener Blitz bei Dickens, bei dessen Licht man "harrows and ploughs left alone in the fields" sah' [details should be like that flash of lightning in Dickens, in whose light they saw 'harrows . . .'].[70] In *Ein Brief* there is a similar example of an animal's pain, when Chandos recalls the episode of the poisoned rats dying in agony in a cellar. There Chandos states the achievement of participation or identification—'Alles war in mir' [everything was within me; 51, 4]—but there is no suggestion that this experience is symbolic and thus the basis for future literary creation; quite the reverse.

When Gabriel says that the condition of the participation of man in the suffering of the beast, and thus of symbolism, is that 'wir und die Welt nichts Verschiedenes sind' [we and the world are not distinct from each other], Clemens confesses that there is something strange and disquieting in that thought (82, 1–3). Gabriel in contrast has achieved a serenity that Clemens has not found, and that Hofmannsthal in the 1890s had not found, although all the elements for the insight were present. He finds 'etwas unendlich Ruhevolles. Es ist das

---

[70] *RA* iii. 334. 'Harrows and ploughs left out in fields' is a phrase from chapter 42 of *Martin Chuzzlewit*, probably the source of the image of the harrow in *Ein Brief*.

einzig Süße, einen Teil seiner Schwere abgehen zu *sehen*, und wäre es
nur für die mystische Frist eines Hauches' [something infinitely peaceful. It is the sweetest thing to *see* oneself relieved of a part of one's heaviness, even if only for the mystical duration of a breath]—where one
should remember Hofmannsthal's multiple understanding of 'Hauch',
and perhaps also see in 'einen Teil seiner Schwere abgehen' an echo of
'Manche freilich', of 'Wolken' or 'Ein Traum von großer Magie'.[71]
There is a balance achievable in the writing of a poem that prevents the
permanent annihilation of self about which even Baudelaire evinced
nerves. The dramatization of the process of symbolism in self-sacrifice
in *Das Gespräch* seems fully Romantic: as he prepared the dialogue,
Hofmannsthal noted Novalis's 'Poesie löst fremdes Dasein im eigenen
auf' and 'Alle Bezauberung geschieht durch partielle Idenfitication mit
dem Bezauberten, den ich so zwingen kann, eine Sache zu sehen, zu
glauben, zu fühlen, wie ich will' [poetry dissolves other existences into
one's own; all forms of enchantment occur via a partial identification
with the person enchanted, which I can force to see, believe and feel as
I want him to].[72] As Gabriel suddenly shifts to describing the action of
words, he reveals the modern or Symbolist aspect of the process.
Words achieve the same 'Bezauberung' when they are uttered, 'um
der Worte willen . . . um der magischen Kraft willen, welche die Worte
haben, unseren Leib zu rühren' [for the sake of the words, of the magic
power that words have to move us physically; 81, 21–3]. The transition
is not explained, but it is clear that the magic consists in linguistic un-
selfconsciousness or the sheer joy of utterance without anxiety about
significance or origin. It is language's 'orphische Sinnlichkeit' [orphic
sensuousness]—rhythm and musicality above all—that enables it to be

---

[71] *SW* xxxi. 82, 4–6; my italics. The Critical Edition has the curious 'abgeben zu sehen',
which is also the reading in Steiner's edition: Hugo von Hofmannsthal, *Prosa II* (Frankfurt
a.M.: S. Fischer, 1951), 92. Schoeller corrects it to 'abgegeben' (*EGB*, 504), presumably to
restore the grammatical sense. The MS, *Nachlaß*, H VB 66.15, supports the reading
'abgehen'. The relevant line from 'Wolken' is in the last verse, 'ledig der Schwere' (*SW* i. 23),
an echo reinforced by Clemens's comparison of George's 'Gemahnt dich noch' (78, 3–14)
with 'eine freie leichte kleine Wolke' (78, 17); of the magician in 'Ein Traum' Hofmannsthal
writes 'An ihm sah ich die Macht der Schwere enden' (*SW* i. 52). This 'relief from weight' is a
necessary component of the 'Steigerung des Selbst' noted in *Ad me ipsum* (*RA* iii. 606) in connection with this poem, and continues to be associated with Hofmannsthal's conception
of the symbol in one of the notes to the planned drama *Pentheus* made in 1914: 'Um die
Ödipussage symbolisch zu nehmen, muss man die Schwere, die *Möglichkeit* des eigentlichen
Geschehens mit Gewalt um ihr Gewicht bringen . . . symbolisch, d.h. gleichzeitig leicht und
schwer' (*SW* xviii. 57).

[72] *SW* xxxi. 323, 31–4. Taken from the introduction to Wille's edition of Novalis's
Sämmtliche Werke.

symbolic in the full sense, and it was this aspect that Hofmannsthal strove to reproduce in the early 1890s. Hofmannsthal is now implicitly reflecting on the conditions for his previous failure, conscious that he wrote too rarely 'um der Worte willen'.

Pauget and Robertson have shown how the apparently tangential evocations of poems from the *Greek Anthology* and by Goethe during the dialogue in fact illustrate the action of the symbol.[73] Gabriel's account of the poems, 'ostensibly confined to their literal meaning, brings out the eroticism which the fruit, the wine-press and the other objects in the poems symbolize'[74]—even though Clemens supposed these poems to be merely beautiful, but 'ohne [des Symbols] schwüle Bezauberung' [without the sultry enchantment of the symbol; 82, 10]. Notes for *Der Tod des Tizian* show that Hofmannsthal had been interested in the same themes, with equally erotic overtones, in Swinburne's work since 1891: he quotes from 'At Eleusis', 'a lordly vine whose grapes bleed the red heavy blood of soft swoln wine'.[75] But it is the form that most closely links the Greek poems with Hofmannsthal's early poetic preoccupations. He describes them in a note as 'durchs Alter zu Edelstein erkalteten Gedichte' [poems that age has petrified into precious stones], and the jewel image is explained thus: 'Edelsteine wirken gleich als 2te Potenz als symbolisch gewordene Naturproducte' [precious stones have an immediately intensified effect, like works of nature that have become symbolic; 323, 7–8]. Again, in the context of Hebbel's swans and Goethe's equation of the poem and the 'Hauch', Hofmannsthal notes 'mehr als Zustände: die Schwäne das Symb. für Menschen 2ter Potenz. Das Symbolische "Edelsteine", diese antiken Gedichte sind für uns Gebilde, nicht *geredet*' [more than states: the swans are the symbol of intensified mankind. The symbolic, precious stones, these classical poems are for us an object, and not *spoken*; 325, 30–3]. The swans were poetic symbols of man, and precious stones are symbols of poetry itself, picking up a charge they held for the Symbolists.

The amethyst (82, 24) is quoted from the *Anthology*, but when Gabriel likens the poems to beautiful shallow onyx and jade drinking bowls (83, 30–1), and extols the 'geformter Gedanke' [moulded thought] that is a poem, and how it '[verzehnfacht] den Glanz des Lebens in sich wie die

---

[73] Pauget, *L'Interrogation sur l'art*, 394–5; Robertson, 'Sacrifice', 21. Hofmannsthal had known the *Greek Anthology* for some time; there is a reference to it in 'Französische Redensarten' (1897), *RA* i. 238.

[74] Robertson, 'Sacrifice', 21.

[75] *SW* iii. 328; cf. also iii. 403–4.

Perlen den feuchten Schimmer der nackten Haut in sich saugen und zehnfach widerstrahlen' [multiplies the brilliance of life in us ten times, as pearls absorb the damp shimmering of naked skin within themselves and radiate it ten times as strongly; 84, 21–3], Hofmannsthal's own imagination is at work. The vocabulary of French Symbolism and of his and George's early imitations of it resurfaces, encouraged no doubt by echoes raised by the pomegranate and the shining grapes (82, 17–19). These details are taken from a poem by Philippus in the *Anthology*, but must have reminded Hofmannsthal of Mallarmé's 'L'Après-midi d'un faune' given him in manuscript by Stefan George in January 1892. The Faun sucks the sweetness from the grapes and blows into their empty skins, and, 'avide d'ivresse, jusqu'au soir . . . regarde au travers'; as he eats pomegranates, too, 'chaque grenade éclate et d'abeilles murmure' [made eager by drunkenness, looks through them until the evening; each segment explodes and buzzes with bees].[76] The whole evocation of the *Anthology* lives through the opulent and lyrical, almost lush detail characteristic of Symbolist writing. It proceeds by associations of shape and colour rather than logic: the 'schöne Muscheln mit rosigem Mund' [beautiful mussel-shells with pink mouths; 83, 29–30] conjured up to describe one poem—not a detail from it—give the shape for the shallow drinking bowls (83, 30–1); ornamental drinking vessels are magnified into copper basins; the basins of fountains filled to the edge with water become the river-water under the arch of a bridge (83, 33) and this provides the curve for the 'geschwungenes Joch der pflügenden Stiere' [the curved yoke of the ploughing oxen; 83, 34]. The poems are indeed treated as jewels, piled up in Hofmannsthal's prose and scattering their light brilliantly.

It is easy to forget at this point that the speaker is the usually less confident Clemens as he moves on to refer with facility to the *West-östlicher Divan*. Gabriel pulls him up with a compliment on his comparison of thought with precious stones, and develops the theme of their inspirational potential. He reminds Clemens that man is 'reicher an Gedanken, als der endloser Meeresstrand an Muscheln. Was uns Not tut, ist der Hauch' [richer in thoughts than the infinite sea-shore is in shells. What we need is the breath of inspiration; 85, 2–3]—in other words the transfiguring power of poetic form. Gabriel's warning to Clemens may perhaps be understood as Hofmannsthal's own somewhat rueful retrospective reproach to himself: he collected the stones

[76] Mallarmé, *OC*, 51–2.

but was not consistently or sustainedly able to produce the 'Hauch' that would have made it truly Symbolic poetry, or poetry with life. His own early work was often to the inspired products of a powerful identity as Pygmalion's lifeless stone statue was to the breathing Galatea, finely and lovingly made, beautiful even, yet consisting still of an inanimate material because the product of a craftsman rather than an inspirational creator.

There follows, to finish the dialogue, an evocation of Goethe's poetry that seems to introduce a further category of symbolic writing. The early poems are described using Goethe's own image: 'die Lieder seiner Jugend sind nichts als ein Hauch' [the songs of his youth are nothing but a breath; 85, 20]. 'Nichts als' is less deprecating than it first appears, for each of these poems is pure,

der entbundene Geist eines Augenblicks, der sich aufgeschwungen hat in den Zenith und dort strahlend hängt und alle Seligkeit des Augenblickes rein in sich saugt und verhauchend sich löst in den klaren Äther. (85, 20–4)

[the liberated spirit of the moment, which has lifted itself high in the sky and is hanging there, brilliantly, absorbing purely into itself the whole blissful moment before breathing out and dissolving into the clear ether.]

Gabriel again uses images of precious stones to characterize this type of poem, brilliant but capturing only a fleeting moment or temporary condition. For Gabriel, it is inconceivable that a set of such poems, however fine, could be the summit of what a man such as Goethe achieved: 'meinst du wirklich, er habe immer und immer den geformten Gedanken ans Licht der Sonne gehoben wie eine gestielte Schale aus Sardonyx und Chrysopras?' [do you really think he was for ever and ever lifting the moulded thought up to the light of the sun like a long-stemmed bowl of sardonyx and chrysoprase?].[77] He quotes 'Selige Sehnsucht', a poem that has perhaps been associated with George and Symbolism since 1891 (as a stimulus for the last line of George's 'Nachthymne', 'Und stürbe wertlos wie ein abendfalter'), and contrasts the jewels of Goethe's youth with the kind of poem he occasionally wrote in old age, looking deep into the significance of life rather than holding it up to the light and watching it sparkle. To express this, Gabriel uses images first met in 'Welgeheimnis', therefore giving the thoughts a strong association with the young Hofmannsthal as well as the older Goethe:

---

[77] SW xxxi. 85, 28–31 (where the last word is misprinted as 'Chrysopas').

die Gedichte seines Alters sind zuweilen wie die dunklen tiefen Brunnen, über
deren Spiegel Gesichte hingleiten, die das aufwärts starrende Auge nie wahr-
nimmt, die für keinen auf der Welt sichtbar werden als für den, der sich
hinabbeugt auf das tiefe dunkle Wasser eines langen Lebens. (85, 24–8)

[the poems of his old age are often like a deep, dark well over whose surface faces
slip past that the upwardly staring eye never perceives, that are visible to no one in
the world except one bending over the deep, dark water of a long life.]

In the 1894 poem, the deep well guards the secret of the world; a man
leans over, comprehends and almost at once loses his insight; only a
child, '[das sich] auf dessen dunklen Spiegel bückt' [who leans over its
dark surface], is capable of keeping hold. By 1903—astonishingly, if
one considers that Hofmannsthal was himself then only 29 years old—
the same privileged insight, expressed with many of the same words
and images, is the preserve of the mature, the experienced, even the
old, which gives Hofmannsthal's perspective on his early lyric a strong
sense of irrecoverable distance.

   This is perhaps not a different kind of symbolism so much as a
different quality, the realization that, with age, what there is to symbolize will be more significant. If the self is a metaphor, as Gabriel suggested, then the tenor sought by the poetic vehicles will be weightier
than for the self of youth. In the rhythms of 'was niemals da war, nie
sich gab, jetzt ist es da, jetzt gibt es sich, ist Gegenwart, ist mehr als
Gegenwart' [what was never there, never happened, now it is there,
now it is happening; 86, 21–2], Hofmannsthal echoes Goethe's own
most famous statement of symbolism, the 'Chorus Mysticus' of *Faust II*,
'Alles Vergängliche ist nur ein Gleichnis' [everything transient is but a
parable].[78] What Goethe's late poetry symbolizes is the infinite profundity of his life, illuminated like the night sky in a poetic moment of
vision. There are few such poems, but is it not marvellous

daß es Zusammenstellungen von Worten gibt, aus welchen, wie der Funke aus
dem geschlagenen dunklen Stein, die Landschaften der Seele hervorbrechen, die
unermeßlich sind wie der gestirnte Himmel, Landschaften, die sich ausdehnen im
Raum und in der Zeit, und deren Anblick abzuweiden in uns ein Sinn lebendig
wird, der über alle Sinne ist. (86, 35–41)

[that there are arrangements of words from which the landscapes of the soul break
forth like a spark from a stone when it is struck, landscapes that are immeasurable
like the star-studded sky, landscapes that stretch far away in space and time, and
the spectacle of which, when we gaze upon it, awakens in us a sense that is far
beyond all senses.]

[78] Goethe, *Werke*, iii. 364.

Gabriel is mixing his metaphors, since he has earlier stated that the profundity of Goethe's late poetry is to be found only by looking inwards to the world, through the mouth of the well, and that no upward-looking eye will perceive such truths. None the less, the final words of the dialogue, in the present tense, are a subtle but firm statement of his and Hofmannsthal's faith that poetry of this magnificent type is still possible: 'Und dennoch entstehen solche Gedichte' [and none the less, such poems are written; 86, 41]. The echo from 'Ballade des äußeren Lebens' is unmistakable. There, in 1894, the line 'Und dennoch sagt der viel, der "Abend" sagt' (*SW* i. 44) was an affirmation, in the face of the transience evoked in the larger part of the poem, that language could still be meaningful.

Hofmannsthal originally intended to continue the dialogue after this point with an example of a modern poem. Gabriel was to quote a poem by a Belgian Symbolist poet, prose poet and dramatist, a schoolfriend of Maeterlinck called Charles Van Lerberghe.[79] The note that records Hofmannsthal's intention to include a poem by Keats also notes Van Lerberghe's 'Sur le seuil', from *Entrevisions*, the volume he had mentioned to George and from which he had also intended to quote an example in *Die Briefe des Paulus Silentiarius*.[80] The poem begins thus:

> Le rêve de son âme enfin se réalise,
> Et c'est une adorable et soudaine surprise.
> Il s'arrête ravi, tremblant, extasié:
> Toute l'aube confuse est pleine de rosiers.
> Un monde merveilleux et bleuissant émane
> D'un brouillard de lumière et d'ombre diaphane;
> D'étranges floraisons pâles, des chants d'oiseaux,
> Des nappes de parfums, des transparences d'eaux,
> Des gerbes de rayons et des grappes touffues
> De chrysoprases et d'améthystes fondues.[81]

[At last the dream of his soul is realized, and it is a sudden, adorable surprise. He stops, delighted, trembling, in ecstasy: the entire bewildered dawn is full of rosebushes. A marvellous, blue-tinged world is emanating from a mist of light and diaphanous shadow; strange pale blossoms, birdsong, sheaves of light and dense clusters of chrysoprase and melting amethyst.]

[79] A note from 1907 refers to 'Maeterlinck und Lerberghe (= die sinnlichen Atome der Angst, der Beklommenheit)', *RA* iii. 489.
[80] Cf. *SW* xxxi. 60, 3, George, *BW*, 186 and above, pp. 280–1.
[81] *SW* xxxi. 329–30. First published in Charles Van Lerberghe, *Entrevisions* (Brussels: Lacomblez, 1898), 55–6.

The first draft of *Das Gespräch über Gedichte* quotes 'Sur le seuil' in full. It is obviously wholly germane to the issues of the dialogue—and its title, meaning 'On the Threshold', is yet another example of the use of the boundary image that has been so striking. But to have quoted this at or near the end of *Das Gespräch über Gedichte* might have been to have added a rather weighty pendant to a moving argument about the superior insight attained by Goethe's poems of old age. A Symbolist poem, full of precious stones, colours, roses and trembling half-memories *à la* Verlaine—and such a long poem, too—might have seemed something of an anticlimax after the succinct, controlled beauty of 'Selige Sehnsucht'. Yet it was not merely an afterthought. Plans for the dialogue indicate that it was to be contrasted or compared with 'Das Keltern' from the *Greek Anthology*;[82] the 'améthystes fondues' echo the Greek poem translated as 'Der Liebeszauber' and the chrysoprase is anticipated in the finished text. Van Lerberghe describes what amounts to a moment of symbolization in Hofmannsthal's sense, as, in the face of the beauties of the dawn, the soul of the speaker mingles with their divinity in a timeless moment. This is the loss of selfhood that occurs in perfect correspondence with the outer world and which culminates in knowledge of the essence of things: 'il pressentit le monde et connut l'avenir' [he felt the world in advance and knew the future]. Love enters the world not as an individual instance of reciprocal feeling but as the absolute, the quintessence of the emotion. In the last two lines, 'L'ardente flèche d'or de l'invisible archer | L'a tué de son vol avant de le toucher' [the invisible archer's burning golden arrow has killed him in its flight without touching him]: Cupid's golden arrow kills without touching because in the heightened existence that is this symbolic state, time and place give way to simultaneity and the arrow's release becomes its hitting home.

'Sur le seuil' was to have been followed by a poem by George, possibly from *Lieder vom Traum und Tod*, and the two poets were clearly closely associated in Hofmannsthal's mind. Furthermore, 'Sur le seuil' was the very poem calculated to remind him most of these associations. The phrase 'le tue . . . avant de le toucher' will inevitably have conjured up 'Der Prophet' and their situation in the early 1890s when Hofmannsthal's interest in Symbolism in its narrow sense, that of certain modes of recent French poetry, had not been properly assimilated. The 1903 dialogue is a statement on how Symbolism is possible without abandoning all hold on one's identity, of how the linguistic

[82] Cf. *SW* xxxi. 341, 23–35.

structures of poems, provided that they express a human temperament, can achieve a reconstruction of the identity willingly sacrificed.
'Die poetische Macht in uns, das poetische Vermögen', Hofmannsthal
noted in preparations for *Das Gespräch*, is 'die synthetische Kraft' [the
poetic power within us, the poetic capacity is the power of synthesis;
324, 18–19]. The idea is familiar from his earliest notes, but it is
significant that its restatement in 1903 is à propos of others' poetry,
made in conjunction with a decision *not* to quote a Belgian Symbolist
poem. Nevertheless, the prominence of poems by George with such
strong Symbolist features, and Hofmannsthal's frequent use of such
motifs in the prose text, show that Hofmannsthal did not reject the
Symbolist phase entirely. His stress on the function of language and the
privilege of poetic construction in Symbolism show that he has not
taken refuge entirely in nostalgia for its Romantic origins.

6

POSTSCRIPT AND CONCLUSION: HOFMANNSTHAL AND RIMBAUD

There is a name glaringly absent so far from this survey of Hofmannsthal's reception of French Symbolist poets, that of Arthur Rimbaud. Rimbaud is nowadays commonly placed alongside Verlaine and Mallarmé as one of the three most important representatives of French Symbolist poetry, arguably the most radical and inspirational of them all. 'Le Bateau ivre' and 'Voyelles' are two of the most famous, most frequently anthologized and most influential of the poems ever gathered together under the heading of Symbolism. Yet Hofmannsthal seems either not to have known of Rimbaud's work or to have ignored it. Rimbaud is absent, for example, from the list of 'Maler und Musiker' that George contrasted with the 'Plastiker des Stils' in his important conversation with Hofmannsthal on 21 December 1891—which is doubly surprising, since Rimbaud had died only six weeks before, and, as is often the case, had been the subject of a sudden rush of articles, reviews, homages, retrospectives and appreciations in the French literary press. There is apparently no mention of this anywhere in Hofmannsthal's works, notes or correspondence, and a rumour (current in the 1960s) that the poem 'Der Schatten eines Todten fiel auf uns' was written to commemorate Rimbaud has been comprehensively dispelled.[1] There is no review devoted to Rimbaud's work, nothing in any of Hofmannsthal's letters from the 1890s marking a passing enthusiasm, no stylistic idiosyncrasies, not even a brief note to record a striking phrase or a point of difficulty. Whilst Hofmannsthal's admiration for Verlaine is regularly attested during this period, and whilst his rather more distant regard for Mallarmé surfaces in notes and a relatively frequent use of images from some of Mallarmé's work, especially in the lyrical dramas, Rimbaud is never singled out in any context that would suggest his importance as an influence on Hofmannsthal's writing.

[1] The suggestion was made by Hilde Burger, 'Hugo von Hofmannsthal: Anordnung einer Ausgabe seiner "Frühesten Schriften"', *Neue Rundschau*, 73.4 (1962), 608, and by Étienne Coche de La Ferté, *Hugo von Hofmannsthal*, Poètes d'aujourd'hui, 115 (Paris: Seghers, 1964), 85. The poem was written in Feb. 1891, eight months before Rimbaud died. See also Sondrup, *Hofmannsthal and the French Symbolist Tradition*, 59.

In a sense this is not surprising. Rimbaud was not generally regarded as a Symbolist in the 1890s. He did not merit a chapter in Huret's 1891 *Enquête sur l'évolution littéraire*—either alongside the 'Symbolistes et Décadents' like Mallarmé and Verlaine (although he is mentioned *by* Verlaine), or under any other heading for that matter—and where he was known at all he tended to be viewed rather as *hapax legomenon*, too individual even to be classified. His association with Symbolism is even now not uncontested: he did not participate in any of the public debates that accompanied the establishment of Symbolism as a literary movement, and his poetic originality was so explosive and far-reaching that the label 'Symbolist' is more than usually inadequate when applied to his work. Whilst he was well enough known as a phenomenon, the nature of his poetic achievement was not then appreciated nearly so distinctly as it is now.

Despite his being a contemporary of Verlaine and a precursor of Mallarmé, Rimbaud's poetry was not as widely known in the early 1890s as that of the other two poets. German and Austrian reception of Rimbaud in the 1890s concentrated largely on the myth of the precocious talent or 'gamin génie', Rimbaud's status as a social outsider, and on incidents in his biography—the affair with Verlaine in the early 1870s, the incident in Brussels during which a drunken Verlaine shot Rimbaud in the wrist and was sentenced to two years' hard labour, and Rimbaud's abandonment of poetry and subsequent career as a gun runner and slave-trader in Africa.[2] The publication in 1897 of a biography by his brother-in-law Paterne Berrichon exacerbated this tendency towards biographical prurience.[3]

The only two clear references to Rimbaud in Hofmannsthal's works occur in 1912 and 1929. The latter is in 'Einige Worte als Vorrede zu St.-J. Perse "Anabasis"', where Rimbaud's name is included amongst

---

[2] See Clemens Sokal, 'Paul Verlaine, der Dichter der Décadence: I', *Beilage zur Allgemeinen Zeitung*, 7 Apr. 1892 (Supplement no. 83), 2; Arthur Eloesser, 'Arthur Rimbaud', *Monatsschrift*, 2 (1898), 522–3; Paul Ernst, 'Rimbaud', *Magazin für Litteratur*, 69 (1900), 822 and 882; Paul Wiegler, 'Verlaine's Prosaschriften', *Die Wage*, 4 (1901), 635; Gsteiger, *Französische Symbolisten*, 47, 103, 105 and 148. A trace of the horror with which some of the more scandalous biographical information was received is perhaps detectable in a little volume on French Symbolism published in 1923, where Rimbaud's date of birth is twice given as 1851 rather than 1854: Rimbaud's precocious flight from sleepy Charleville in Belgium to the turbulence of Paris is thus decorously set in his nineteenth year rather than accurately in his fifteenth: Helmut Hatzfeld, *Der französische Symbolismus*, Philosophische Reihe 73 (Munich: Rösl, 1923), 84.

[3] Despite its polemic stance, Étiemble's monumental study clearly shows the decisive and distortive effect of Berrichon's early biography: *Le Mythe de Rimbaud*, i: *Genèse du mythe, 1869–1949* (Paris: nrf, 1954); ii: *Structure du mythe* (Paris: nrf, 1952).

the major writers who shaped the development of French poetic language in the nineteenth century:

vor Mallarmé gehen Baudelaire und Rimbaud, und der majestätische Fluß, die geheime Polyphonie des einen sowie das wilde Durchbrechen der Ordnungen bei dem andern, bei beiden ist es ein Sich-Annähern an den Bereich der Musik, das sie als Brüder zu Mallarmé stellt. Denn dieser war ja schon fast ebensosehr Musiker als Dichter: kompositorisch ist zwischen ihm und Debussy kaum ein Unterschied zu erkennen. (*RA* iii. 145)

[Mallarmé is preceded by Baudelaire and Rimbaud, by the majestic flow, the secret polyphony of the one, and the wild shattering of traditional structures by the other. In both poets it is a gradual approach towards the realm of music that makes them co-equal with Mallarmé. The latter was almost as much a musician as he was a poet, in matters of composition there is hardly any difference recognizable between him and Debussy.]

The importance Hofmannsthal attributes to the musical dimension of poetic language associates this comment firmly with the views he developed during his years of experimentation with Symbolism. None the less, the whole is the comment of a critic, and an unremarkable retrospective summary, rather than a gesture of acknowledgement from one poet to another—as the same words might have been read in the early 1890s. In isolation, this indicates no more than that Hofmannsthal was properly aware of the significance of Rimbaud in the history of European poetry.

The earlier reference is an episode in one of Hofmannsthal's travel essays. The summer and autumn of 1912 were partly spent writing up part of an account of a journey made with Harry Kessler and Aristide Maillol to Greece in April and May 1908. Published in 1917 as 'Der Wanderer', this is part 2 of the *Augenblicke in Griechenland*. During a ride from the Monastery of St Luke to Chaeronea, the first two or three hours were spent in conversation with Kessler, conjuring up the ghosts of 'unsre Freunde'. The most powerful evocation is of the dying Rimbaud—a 'friend' in the loosest sense, that of sympathetic fellow human being—but for all the intensity of feeling displayed, Rimbaud is treated merely as a personal, phenomenal irruption into history, not as a source of poetic inspiration. There is a short reference to his writing:

Aber seine Briefe, ein Wort einmal kalt und groß, andre Worte wie blutend, sein Tagebuch, die wenigen, mit nichts zu vergleichenden Gedichte, alle aus einem einzigen Jahr seines Lebens, dem neunzehnten, und die er haßt, verachtet, in Stücke reißt, wo er sie findet, bespeit, die Fetzen mit Füßen tritt. (*EGB*, 611)

[But his letters, a word sometimes cold and grand, other words almost bleeding, his diary, those few incomparable poems, all written in a single year of his life, his nineteenth, hated by him, despised, ripped to shreds, spat on when he comes across them, their scraps trodden underfoot.]

Most of Rimbaud's poems were in fact written between the ages of 15 and 19, so this slightly exaggerates the brevity of Rimbaud's poetic career, conforming to the sensationalist tendencies of contemporary Rimbaud reception. Both this and the 1929 reference will be examined in more detail below.

The passage from *Augenblicke in Griechenland* suggests that by 1912 Hofmannsthal was familiar with all Rimbaud's available work, although it is impossible to judge when he began reading it. The earliest of Hofmannsthal's two Rimbaud editions preserved in the Freies Deutsches Hochstift is from 1895; the second is from 1912.[4] But he may very well have been aware of some of the poems that appeared in journals such as *La Vogue* during the mid-1880s, perhaps even of the collection including both *Les Illuminations* and *Une saison en enfer* that was published at the end of 1891.[5] This was the first time the general public could have read *Une saison en enfer*—which may be what Hofmannsthal refers to as the 'Tagebuch', since there is no diary proper in existence.[6]

Despite the lack of overt acknowledgement, however, Rimbaud is undoubtedly 'present' in Hofmannsthal's literary background from the early 1890s, and there are a few signs that his work was known at least by reputation. Stefan George knew Rimbaud's early poetry well from his time in Paris. Amongst the poems that he copied out then are seventeen by Rimbaud, including 'Le Bateau ivre', 'Après le déluge', 'Les Chercheuses de poux' from *Poésies* and four 'Enfance' poems from *Illuminations*.[7] But whether George failed to expatiate enthusiastically on Rimbaud at that point in 1891, or whether Hofmannsthal did

[4] Arthur Rimbaud, *Poésies complètes avec préface de Paul Verlaine et notes de l'éditeur* (Paris: Léon Vanier, 1895). It is not in fact 'complete': the first edition that could reasonably claim this was the Mercure de France edition of 1898. *Œuvres de Arthur Rimbaud. Vers et prose. Revues sur les manuscrits originaux et les premières éditions. Mises en ordre et annotées par Paterne Berrichon. Poèmes retrouvés. Préface de Paul Claudel* (Paris: Mercure de France, n.d. [1912]).

[5] Arthur Rimbaud, *Poèmes. Les Illuminations. Une saison en enfer. Notice par Paul Verlaine* (Paris: Vanier, 1892). A few copies have 1891, but most are dated 1892.

[6] The first edition of *Une saison en enfer*, Rimbaud's own, was made in 1873 but was not distributed; most of the copies printed were only discovered in 1901. *Les Illuminations* appeared in 1886 (Publications de 'La Vogue') in a limited edition of 200. The letters Hofmannsthal knew may have been Berrichon's edition, *Lettres de Jean-Arthur Rimbaud: Égypte, Arabie, Éthiopie* (Paris: Société du 'Mercure de France', 1899).

[7] Boehringer, *Mein Bild*, i. 214.

not register any of the references because they were so unfamiliar, is impossible to judge.

By July 1892, however, something of the phenomenon of 'audition colorée' associated with Rimbaud's 'Sonnet des voyelles' had certainly filtered through to Hofmannsthal. In a letter to Carl August Klein, George's collaborator on the *Blätter für die Kunst*, he suggests submitting 'Reflexionen über technische Fragen, Beiträge zur Farbenlehre der Worte und ähnliche Nebenprodukte des künstlerischen Arbeitsprozesses' [reflections on technical matters, contributions to the theory of the colour of words and other side-products of the artistic process].[8] He may have had in mind the following passage from Hermann Bahr's essay 'Die Décadence', commenting on recent poets' innovations:

Die Töne werden gesehen, Farben singen und Stimmen riechen. Die Alten behaupten, dass das keine Errungenschaft, sondern bloss eine Krankheit sei, welche die Aerzte *l'audition colorée* nennen—'das farbige Gehör', sagen die Aerzte, ist eine Erscheinung, die darin besteht, dass auf den Reiz eines einzigen Sinnes hin zwei verschiedene Sinne zugleich thätig werden oder mit anderen Worten, dass der Ton einer Stimme oder eines Instrumentes sich in eine charakteristische und zwar immer in dieselbe Farbe umsetzt. So geben gewisse Personen eine grüne, rothe oder gelbe Farbe jedem Laute, jedem Tone, der an ihr Ohr schlägt. Genau ebenso, vollkommen nach der Schilderung der Aerzte, sagt Rhené [*sic*] Ghil, dass jeder Vokal seine Farbe hat, dass das *a* schwarz, das *e* weiss, das *i* roth, das *u* grün, das *o* blau ist; dass die Harfen weiss, die Geigen blau, die Flöten gelb und die Orgeln schwarz klingen; dass das *o* Leidenschaft, das *a* Grösse, das *e* Schmerz, das *i* Feinheit und Schärfe, das *u* Räthsel und Geheimniss und das *r* Wildheit und Sturm mitteilt. Das ist die Poetik der Décadence.[9]

[Sounds are seen, colours sing and voices are scented. The ancients maintained that this is not an achievement but merely an illness that is called 'hearing in colours' by doctors—a phenomenon that consists of two different senses being activated by a single sense-stimulus, or in other words, of the tone of a voice or an instrument being converted into a characteristic colour, always the same one. Thus certain persons associate a green, a red or a yellow colour with a given sound or tone that they hear. In just the same way, and fully in accordance with what the doctors say, René Ghil maintains that every vowel has a colour, that *a* is black, *e* is white, *i* red, *u* green and *o* blue, that harps sound white, violins blue, flutes yellow and organs black, that *o* communicates passion, *a* greatness, *e* pain, *i* finesse and precision, *u* mystery and enigma and *r* wildness and storminess. This is the poetics of Decadence.]

8 George, *BW*, 25.
9 Hermann Bahr, *Studien*, 21–2; originally in *Die Nation*, 8.40 (4 July 1891).

The reference to Ghil is footnoted to his *Traité du verbe avec avant-dire de Stéphane Mallarmé*, and synaethesia is here elaborated into an extended poetical system.

In the early 1890s the words 'Farbenlehre der Worte' would also have suggested the famous Rimbaud sonnet. It begins, 'A noir, E blanc, I rouge, U vert, O bleu: voyelles' [A black, E white, I red, U green, O blue: vowels][10]—the same combinations as described in Bahr's essay. Although Hofmannsthal need never have read 'Voyelles' to have come across the idea, the sonnet was widely quoted and discussed and it is likely that he knew it. It is, for example, the first poem quoted by Verlaine in the Rimbaud article of *Les Poètes maudits*; Verlaine also cites Rimbaud in Huret's *Enquête* as having achieved all the so-called 'nouveautés' of the 'cymbalistes' decades before them.[11] In the same volume Charles Henry calls Rimbaud's thoughts on colour 'des intuitions de génie qui vont au cœur de tout être cultivé' [the intuitions of a genius that will go straight to the heart of any cultivated person].[12] Stephan Waetzold's 'Paul Verlaine, ein Dichter der Décadence' mentions a certain Arthur Rimbaud, 'der die Vokale . . . deutete' [who interpreted the vowels],[13] and Clemens Sokal focuses on the sonnet in his *Allgemeine Zeitung* article of April 1892, calling it '[das] zierlich gedrechselte, halb scherzhaft, halb ernst gemeinte Sonett . . . ein Kraftstück jugendlichen Reformatorentums' [the daintily composed sonnet, half joking, half serious . . . a masterpiece of youthful reforming zeal].[14] Max Nordau bases his irritated case against Rimbaud's supposed stupidity and madness in *Entartung* on the often-cited sonnet 'Les Voyelles'.[15] Finally, Charles Morice, in *La Littérature de tout à l'heure* that Hofmannsthal noted in connection with Huret's *Enquête*, devotes several pages to it and to Ghil's naive literal interpretation of it.[16]

We know that Rimbaud was also the subject of talk in Hofmannsthal's circle at this time, and that his poetry was linked with Hofmannsthal's:

---

[10] Rimbaud, *Poésies, Une saison en enfer, Illuminations*, 78–9.

[11] Huret, *Enquête*, 69.

[12] Ibid. 416 Rimbaud is mentioned twice more in Huret, by Gustave Kahn as 'un très grand poète qu'on oublie' (402) and by Charles Vignier as one of the originators of irregular verse (102).

[13] Waetzold, 'Paul Verlaine', 177; Gsteiger, *Französische Symbolisten*,108.

[14] Sokal, 'Paul Verlaine', ii. 14 Apr. 1892 (No. 84), 4; Gsteiger, *Französische Symbolisten*, 49.

[15] Nordau, *Entartung*, i. 247.

[16] Morice, *La Littérature de tout à l'heure*, 319–21.

Arthur Rimbaud mit seiner 'audition colorée' (die vom Physiologen Ernst Brücke wissenschaftlich und von J.-K. Huysmans in 'A rebours' künstlerisch umfassend dargestellt wurde), Rimbaud, für uns neu, guckte durch, wenn Loris—und nicht er allein, aber keiner so tief poetisch wie er—den Zusammenhang von Ton und Farbenempfindungen, den Ausdrucksinhalt bloßer Klänge, bloßer Farben, das Gruppieren und fast tonleitermäßige Anordnen und Abtönen von Farben zu interessanten Wichtigkeiten gestalten wollte.[17]

[Arthur Rimbaud with this 'hearing in colours' (treated in depth scientifically by the physiologist Ernst Brücke and artistically by J.-K. Huysmans in *A rebours*), Rimbaud, who was new to us, peeked through when Loris—and not only him, but no one as profoundly poetically as him—wished to represent as interesting and significant the relationship of sound and colour-sensations, the expressive content of mere sounds, mere colours, the taxonomy, the arrangement in almost musical scale-like fashion, and the distinction of colours.]

These are part of Marie Herzfeld's recollections after her first meeting with Hofmannsthal on 16 March 1892. The currency of 'audition colorée' was wide. The contribution of Saint-Pol-Roux to Huret's *Enquête* circles around the idea, emphasising the integration of 'saveur, parfum, son, lumière, forme' [taste, perfume, sound, light, form] in the poem.[18] A Dr Jules Millet presented a thesis on the topic to the Faculty of Medicine at Montpellier in 1892 which cites Rimbaud's sonnet in full.[19] Nordau cites another recent scientific work on the subject, *L'Audition colorée: Étude sur les fausses sensations secondaires physiologiques* published in Paris in 1892 by F. Suarez de Mendoza.[20] And Bahr refers in a note to the passage quoted above to 'J. Baratoux, *Le Progrès médical*, 10. Dec. 1887.' The idea is by 1897 so completely a part of modern thinking on French poetry that Rimbaud's sonnet and Ghil's *Traité* are completed confused.[21]

Synaesthesia has a long history, but Herzfeld does suggest that Rimbaud was known as a specific source of contemporary interest in the subject, the author of what would become the locus classicus. It was

---

[17] Marie Herzfeld, 'Blätter der Erinnerung', in Fiechtner (ed.), *Der Dichter im Spiegel seiner Freunde*, 52.   [18] Huret, *Enquête*, 145.

[19] See Étiemble, *Le Mythe de Rimbaud*, ii. 83.

[20] Ibid., i. 249. Fascinatingly, Victor Hugo, the subject of Hofmannsthal's doctoral thesis, had made a comment very similar in import to Rimbaud's sonnet, but many years before: 'Ne penserait-on pas que les voyelles existent pour le regard presque autant que pour l'oreille, et qu'elles peignent des couleurs? On les voit. A et I sont des voyelles blanches et brillantes. O est une voyelle rouge. Et EU sont des voyelles bleues. U est la voyelle noire.' Hofmannsthal cannot have known it, since it was first published in 1950. See Etiemble, *Le Mythe de Rimbaud*, ii. 84.

[21] Anna Brunnemann, 'Die französische Lyrik der Gegenwart', *Monatsschrift für neue Literatur und Kunst*, 1 (1897), 180–1.

also a fundamental feature of Symbolist poetry. There is no doubt that Hofmannsthal was aware of the poetic possibilities of synaesthesia almost from the outset of his career, but as so often with his assimilation of the techniques of Symbolist poetry, it remained to some extent self-conscious and imitative. The poem 'Gülnare' (December 1890) synaesthetically encircles the oriental Queen with 'die Melodie der Farben' [the melody of colours; *SW* i. 11]; 'Die Töcher der Gärtnerin' (25 December 1891) notes '[die] Farben die verklingen' [the colours that die away; *SW* i. 22]—but these are metaphors rather than symbolic correspondences. The same is true of an often-quoted sentence from a letter from Hofmannsthal to Herzfeld:

Ich habe die Empfindung, das Ihnen bei dieser Aufzählung [a book list] ist, als hätte ich hübsche und bunte Farben aufgezählt: matt gold, lapis-blau, mauve, silberlila, feuilles mortes, moosgrün, blaß corail, u. so f.[22]

Again this is a commentary rather than the poetic practice of synaesthesia or 'audition colorée', and represents a critical distance that is quite characteristic of Hofmannsthal's approach to Symbolism at this period. Rimbaud is present in the background, but too strange, his poetry too little assimilated for him to be of more than passing interest.

This certainly corresponds with the general German-language reception of Rimbaud of the time. Public interest did not really start to grow until about 1899 with Karl Klammer's translations in *Pan*, Emil Rudolf Weiß's in the *Wiener Rundschau* (1900). Stefan George published his translation of 'Voyelles' in 1905. Something like a renaissance began in 1907 with the publication of Klammer's condensed German version of Paterne Berrichon's 1897 biography and twenty-five poems in translation, with an introduction by Stefan Zweig. Zweig's preface was also published in *Die Zukunft* in February 1907 and heralded Rimbaud as a prophet, a meteoric figure, coeval with Nietzsche, responsible for introducing a Germanic element into French poetry.[23] The translation was reviewed enthusiastically in *Die Frankfurter Zeitung* and *Das Literarische Echo* in 1908—'Le Bateau ivre' and 'Voyelles' were singled out for greatest attention, and Rimbaud's influence on French Symbolism was judged to be immense. 1908 also saw the first substantial article devoted entirely to Rimbaud in the German press since Eloesser. Rudolf Kurz published a two-part study in *Die Gegenwart* in September, referring to Klammer's translations of the poetry and

---

[22] Herzfeld, *BW*, 28; cf. also p. 65.

[23] Arthur Rimbaud, *Leben und Dichtung, übertragen von K. L. Ammer. Eingeleitet von Stefan Zweig* (Leipzig: Insel, 1907); Stefan Zweig, 'Arthur Rimbaud', *Die Zukunft* (23 Feb. 1907), 303–5.

Berrichon's biography, reproducing Klammer's translations of 'Sensation' and 'Fleurs' as well as George's of 'Voyelles' (from *Zeitgenössische Dichter*), as well as devoting some extended attention to the problem of 'audition colorée'.[24] Kurz's conclusion was that 'die moderne Lyrik in Frankreich die beginnende in Deutschland, steht in seinem Zeichen' [modern lyric poetry in France, and the new lyric in Germany, stands under its aegis]. Hofmannsthal's own affinities with the French Symbolists were also embraced by the Rimbaud revival, and in 1908 Josef Hofmiller wrote of 'Ein Gedicht in Blankversen, "Erlebnis" überschrieben, das sich wie eine Übersetzung aus dem Französischen des Artur Rimbaud liest' [a poem in blank verse, called 'Erlebnis', that reads as if it were a translation from the French by Arthur Rimbaud].[25]

A further external association of Hofmannsthal and Rimbaud, at about the same time, comes from the unexpected quarter of the utopian socialist Gustav Landauer. Hofmannsthal seems to have corresponded with Landauer between 1905 and 1907, and had read his *Skepsis und Mystik* at least twice by April 1904. Landauer was a passionate defender of Hofmannsthal: the end of *Skepsis und Mystik* heralds him, with Stefan George, Richard Dehmel and Alfred Mombert, as the literary embodiment of Fritz Mauthner's critique of language—perhaps to Mauthner's horror, as he says himself— quoting extensively from the Chandos Letter. He distinguishes 'rhetorical' poetry, in which musicality is the instrument by which words and concepts are communicated to us, from the new poetry, since Goethe, Novalis and Brentano, where 'Worte und Begriffe das Instrument [sind], das uns zur Musik führt,—zum Rhythmus, zum Unsagbaren, das in uns einschwingt und uns mitschwingen laßt' [words and concepts are the instrument that leads us to music, to rhythm, to the ineffable that resonates within us and causes us to resonate with it]. This and an 'Auflösen alles Realen im Elemente des Traums' [a dissolution of everything that is real in the element of dream] is Hofmannsthal's great contribution to literature.[26] Landauer even risked his friendship with Fritz Mauthner over Hofmannsthal, for

[24] Rudolf Kurtz, 'Arthur Rimbaud', *Die Gegenwart*, 74 (19 Sept. 1908), 184–6 and (26 Sept. 1908), 202–5.

[25] Josef Hofmiller, 'Hofmannsthal', *Süddeutsche Monatshefte*, 5.1 (Jan. 1908), 12–27, cited from *Hofmannsthal im Urteil seiner Kritiker*, 166. The two poems really only have the image of the ship in common, and Sondrup's comparison in *Hofmannsthal and the French Symbolist Tradition*, 82–3, is not persuasive.

[26] Gustav Landauer, *Skepsis und Mysik. Versuche im Anschluß an Mauthners Sprachkritik* (Berlin: Egon Fleischel & Co., 1903), 150–1.

in an essay on Mauthner's foreword to an edition of part of Walter
Calé's *Nachlaß*, Landauer defended Hofmannsthal against charges of
epigonism and Decadence. Calé, according to Landauer, represents a
type not so much 'frühreif' as 'scheinreif', not so much preciously
mature as deceptively mature, Decadent in that he wrote 'in vollen-
deter Form, in runder Abgeschlossenheit, in großer Zivilisation, in
einer fertigen Eleganz' [with formal perfection, rounded self-containment, great civilization and polished elegance]. Young city-dwelling
writers of Jewish origin are particularly prone to this form of Decadence, he suggests. Even writers of genuine talent or true genius seem
sometimes to have to pass through this stage: 'als Beispiele fallen mir
Rimbaud und Hofmannsthal ein':

Hofmannsthal begann als früher Jüngling unter dem Namen Loris seine tiefen,
geisterfüllten Gefühle mit einer Fertigkeit, einer Ruhe, einer sanften Reife des
Tons auszusprechen, die alle Welt in Erstaunen setzte, manche aber ängstigte.
Auch in seiner Jugend war etwas wie Alter. Aber er ist durch dieses Alter hindurch-
gekommen und hat hinter ihm noch einmal Jugend gefunden und ist nun als eine
große Natur in erstaunlicher Steigerung und Wachstum begriffen. . . . Anders ging
es mit Rimbaud: fast noch als Kind dichtete er im erstaunlichen Tone der
Vollendung, kam in den Bannkreis Verlaines und erlebte an ihm Unmäßiges und
Tragisches, an dem auch sehr Starke hätten zugrunde gehen können. Über ihn
kam die Männlichkeit und die Gärung in einer völligen Abkehr von allem
Dichten, aller Kunst, aller Gestaltung in totem Material; mit Ekel wandte er sich
von allen Worten und allem Wortähnlichen ab und wurde in Afrika ein Händler
und Abenteurer großen Stils.[27]

[Hofmannsthal and Rimbaud come to mind as examples: Hofmannsthal began as
a mere youth, under the name Loris, to express his profound, intelligent feelings
with a degree of polish and calm, with a gentle maturity of tone that amazed the
whole world, but frightened some. Even in his youth there was something reminiscent of old age. None the less, he got through this feeling of old age and found
youth once more, and is now a great individual in the process of astonishing
improvement and growth. It was different for Rimbaud. Still almost a child he
wrote poems with a quality of astonishing perfection, came under Verlaine's
influence and had excessive and tragic experiences with him that might have
brought even strong men to destruction. He was overwhelmed by masculinity and
ferment and turned completely away from all forms of writing, art or creativity in
dead materials. He turned in disgust from words and anything resembling words
and became a trader in Africa and an adventurer on a grand scale.]

[27] Gustav Landauer, 'Walter Calé', *Das Blaubuch*, 2.1 (3 Jan. 1907), 14–17. Cited from
'Hugo von Hofmannsthal und Gustav Landauer. Eine Dokumentation. Mit dem Brief-
wechsel Hofmannsthal–Landauer und Landauers Essays über Hofmannsthal', ed. Norbert
Altenhofer, *Hofmannsthal Blätter*, 19/20 (1978), 52–3.

Norbert Altenhofer suggests that Landauer implies here a preference for Rimbaud's development, which fulfilled the potential implicit in the Chandos Letter that Landauer so much admired.[28] His relationship with Hofmannsthal was certainly more distant from this point on. This is in fact the period at which the only really clear echoes of Rimbaud in Hofmannsthal's work are to be discerned. They are of the poem 'Aube', published as part of *Illuminations* in *La Vogue* in 1886:

> J'ai embrassé l'aube d'été.
>
> Rien ne bougeait encore au front des palais. L'eau était morte. Les camps d'ombres ne quittaient pas la route du bois. J'ai marché, réveillant les haleines vives et tièdes, et les pierreries regardèrent, et les ailes se levèrent sans bruit.
>
> La première entreprise fut, dans le sentier déjà empli de frais et blêmes éclats, une fleur qui me dit son nom.
>
> Je ris au wasserfall blond qui s'échevela à travers les sapins: à la cime argentée je reconnus la déesse.
>
> Alors je levai un à un les voiles. Dans l'allée, en agitant les bras. Par la plaine, où je l'ai dénoncée au coq. A la grand'ville elle fuyait parmi les clochers et les dômes, et courant comme un mendiant sur les quais de marbre, je la chassais.
>
> En haut de la route, près d'un bois de lauriers, je l'ai entourée avec ses voiles amassés, et j'ai senti un peu son immense corps. L'aube et l'enfant tombèrent au bas du bois.
>
> Au réveil il était midi.[29]

[I have embraced [or 'kissed'] the summer's dawn. Nothing was yet moving before the façades of the palaces. The water was dead. The patches of shadow were not leaving the road through the forest. I walked, waking the warm, living breaths, and the stones watched, and the wings rose noiselessly. The first activity, in the path already full of fresh, pale brilliance, was a flower that told me its name. I laughed at the blond waterfall that ruffled its hair through the pine trees, and on the silvery summit I recognized the goddess. Then I lifted her veils one by one. In the avenue, waving my arms. Across the plain where I denounced her to the cockerel. In the city she fled through the belfries and the domes, and running like a beggar on the marble embankments I chased her. At the top of the road, near to a laurel wood, I surrounded her with her piles of veils, and I felt a little her vast body. The dawn and the child fell at the foot of the wood. On awakening, it was midday.]

In seven paragraphs, mostly in prose but beginning and ending with perfect octosyllabic lines of verse, 'Aube' is an explanation of the startling claim in the first line, of how the speaker managed to embrace the summer dawn. He begins with the evocation of the moment just before

---

[28] 'Hofmannsthal und Landauer', 54.   [29] Rimbaud, *Poésies*, 178.

daybreak, where the magical world of the palaces is still dark, in shadow and still, with the immobility and chill of death. The *je* walks through the scene like a sorcerer, enlivening it, giving it breath and warmth so that even the minerals are endowed with vision. He is greeted by a single flower which has been given the gift of language and tells him its name. The mood is expansive and cheerful, even sexual as he laughs at the blond waterfall, 'qui s'échevela', brilliantly anthropomorphized with the image of ruffling its hair as if just awakening and getting up. This is the central point of the poem and it is where the speaker sees the goddess on the silvery pinnacle.

The association of the goddess with the dawn sets the poem firmly into the context of the literary tradition of dawn poetry—examples in nineteenth-century French literature range from Hugo's 'Le Matin' and 'Aube' to Lamartine's 'Hymne du matin', Baudelaire's 'Élévation' and Verlaine's 'Avant que tu ne t'en ailles'— albeit without a trace of conventionality.[30] It is as if Rimbaud is showing us this tradition in a split second of stillness, only to strip it of its layers, lifting the veil of poetic utterance from the topos in order to approach its living, breathing substance. He chases the dawn energetically through the street and across the countryside—where this goddess is ironically not announced *by* the cock-crow, as dawn usually is, or *de*nounced *at* the cock-crow, as Christ was, but denounced *to* the cockerel—and into the town. He is reduced to the level of the beggars on the river banks, a far cry from his vivifying power in the magical world of the palaces with which the poem began. He captures her near the laurels: laurel is the leaf for the crown of Apollo and thus of the poet himself. Apollo also pursued Daphne, but unsuccessfully, as she was turned into a laurel tree by her mother, the Earth, which anticipates the slenderness of Rimbaud's victory here, for although the *je* surrounds her with her veils and touches her, it is only fleetingly and the sense of fulfilment is deflated, almost sexually, by collapse. And when the poet, now a child, wakes it is noon, the sun is high and the goddess is gone. 'Aube' charts the poet's aspirations for purity and the union with nature and if it ends

[30] Hugo, *OP*, i. 460 and ii. 108–9; Alphonse de Lamartine, *Œuvres poétiques complètes*, ed. Maxim-François Guyard, Bibliothèque de la Pléiade (Paris: Gallimard, 1963), 298–304; Baudelaire, *OC*, i. 10; Verlaine, *OPC*, 145. See also K. Alfons Knauth, 'Formen französischer und italienischer Morgenpoesie: Tradition und Transformation in Rimbauds "Aube"', *Arcadia*, 14 (1979), 271–91. The end of Baudelaire's poem is especially close in imagery and idea to Rimbaud's: 'Heureux celui qui peut d'une aile vigoureuse | S'élancer vers les champs lumineux et sereins; | Celui dont les pensers, comme des alouettes, | Vers les cieux le matin prennent un libre essor, | —Qui plane sur la vie, et comprend sans effort | Le langage des fleurs et des choses muettes!'

with emptiness, it is the emptiness that is contingent upon fulfilment, rather in the manner of 'post coitum omne animal triste'.

This poem lies behind Stefan George's 'Weihe', the opening poem of *Hymnen*, albeit in adapted form. The last two stanzas are as follows:

> Nun bist du reif · nun schwebt die herrin nieder ·
> Mondfarbne gazeschleier sie umschlingen ·
> Halboffen ihre traumesschweren lider
> Zu dir geneigt die segnung zu vollbringen:
>
> Indem ihr mund auf deinem antlitz bebte
> Und sie dich rein und so geheiligt sah
> Dass sie im kuss nicht auszuweichen strebte
> Dem finger stützend deiner lippe nah.[31]

[Now you are ready, now the mistress floats downwards, moon-coloured gauzes surround her, her eyelids, heavy with dreams, are half-open and inclined towards you so as to perfect the blessing as her mouth trembled on your countenance, and as she saw you pure and so sanctified that she did not seek in her kiss to evade the finger that supported her near to your lips.]

Where Rimbaud had a goddess, George has merely 'die herrin', but she too has the capacity to bring George's protagonist the blessing he searches for. Characteristically he manages to keep hold of his conquest, and the kiss that Rimbaud's poem gives as the most fleeting contact is here reciprocated by the woman. It is a moment of purification and spiritual elevation all the same.

'Aube' seems also to have caught Hofmannsthal's attention, for in 1906 he published an essay entitled 'Vorspiel für ein Puppentheater' in *Die Neue Rundschau* that reads in part as a response to it.[32] The prologue is set in a woodland clearing and presents a poet on a familiar walk but overwhelmed by a sudden new sense of belonging to nature. For the first time here in his ecstasy he feels as if he could drink in the place, 'diese ganze Sonnenwelt und dann zusammensinken, mein Inneres nach außen gekehrt wie ein umgestülpter Handschuh' [this whole world of sun and then collapse, my interior facing outwards like a glove turned inside out]. He wants to embrace nature: 'meines Wesens Inhalt, mein Ich tropft hinweg wie eine zu weiche Kerze, und darüber zehrt wie eine durchsichtige, wütende, stille Flamme ein Du, ein unsichtbares Du!' [the content of my being, my self is dripping away like too soft a candle, and above it like a transparent, furious, silent

---

[31] George, *Werke*, i. 11.
[32] *Neue Rundschau*, 17.10 (1906); first published in book form in *Vorspiele* (Leipzig: Insel Verlag, 1908); quoted from *D* iii. 485–90.

flame, is sustained a You, an invisible You]. It is as if he can transform himself into an eagle and fly to the stars, wrapping the whole world around him like a great cloak. Everything before this moment was like sleepwalking through life and he is willing to abandon his mere earthly existence, trusting innocently like a child who is being kidnapped, and demands an answer from the great 'Du'. With mounting frustration and excitement he senses the approach of the goddess of eternal nature for his embrace—but is greeted instead by a toothless old crone, whom he apostrophizes as the goddess in disguise, expecting at any moment that she will be transformed Papagena-like into a beautiful angel, come to real life like Galatea. Their conversation is difficult, not to say comic, owing to the woman's deafness, but the Poet feels that her lack of enthusiasm is a message, rather like the Erdgeist's in *Faust*, to seek communion not with nature but with something less elevated, more appropriate to his own status, with mankind. He exclaims 'o Welt!, Welt!'—but she hears only 'Geld' [O world! world!—gold]; he speaks of 'die Seele fremd'—and she hears instead 'A Hemd?' [the soul alien—a shirt] and becomes impatient to go. As he watches her leave—'als ob sie eine junge Prinzessin wäre' [as if she were a young princess]—the Poet again has a vision of the world within him, like a mine 'in dessen tiefen dunklen Schächten sich tausend Leben rühren: alle Besonderheiten und Geheimnisse meines Blutes rinnen zusammen zu Gestalten und Figuren' [in whose deep dark shafts thousands of lives stir: all that is special and secret in my blood runs together into shapes and figures]. He feels within the strong emotions of all sorts of people, the devout, the peasant, the bourgeois, the thief, and the child. Following the old woman's tracks, 'die mir glühen wie Karfunkel im grünen Grund' [that shine at me like carbuncles in the green ground], he performs in the imagination a leap from one dream-world into another, 'der heißt Menschenwelt und -leben' [which is called the human world and the human life]. As he turns to the audience, he conjures up the potential new worlds that will arise on the stage as often as the cuckoo-calls that have accompanied the prologue as a comic descant. That his examples—Caspar Hauser, Faust and Helena, Leda, Genofeva—are mostly already literary suggests that the new art he is offering is to harness older artistic exemplars to effect the transportation.

The gesture of embrace is central to both Rimbaud's and Hofmannsthal's texts. '[Ich] möchte an die Erde mich drücken, meine Arme um einen Baum schlingen' [I wish to press myself to the earth, wrap my arms around a tree], is the Poet's desire, 'ich fühle dich: meine Sinne alle mit entzückter Stärke umarmen dich zuvor!' [I can feel you: all my senses embrace you in anticipation with delighted strength]— which is reversed in 'soll ich meine Kleider von mir werfen, und darf ich dafür die ganze Welt als meinen Mantel um mich schlagen?' [shall I cast my clothing from me, and might I instead wrap the whole world around me like my cloak?], echoing first the removal of the veils in Rimbaud and the subsequent reverse gesture, 'je l'ai *entourée* avec ses voiles'. The sexual overtones of 'Aube' are picked up in the Poet's nervous excitement and his ambivalent desires: 'mach mich so schamlos und so keusch wie sie, so nackt und so bekleidet' [make me as free of shame and as chaste as she is, as naked and as clothed]. Again like the speaker in 'Aube', the Poet's relation to the fulfilment he seeks in nature is defined in terms of both revelation and concealment.

The object of desire in both works is characterized as a goddess: the veiled goddess of dawn is revealed as such in the central word in Rimbaud's poem and she is 'die Nieentschleierte, . . . die Göttin selber, die ewige Natur' [the never-unveiled, the goddess herself, eternal nature] in Hofmannsthal. While the *je* of 'Aube' chases, the Poet in the prologue feels pursued, but both processes concern the instilling of life by the speaker into his surroundings. The Poet cries 'ich küsse die Nieentschleierte ins Leben' [I shall kiss the never-unveiled one into life], but the entry of the old woman immediately deflates his creative pretensions and stands in stark contrast to Rimbaud's passionate and defiant opening statement, 'J'ai embrassé l'aube d'été' (where 'embrasser' means both 'kiss' and 'embrace'). Whereas Rimbaud's subject does instil life into the things he passes, his progress accompanied by an increase in light, Hofmannsthal's is a Poet, striving to animate in words. His failure is indicated by the comic discrepancy between the verbal tapestry he generates and the reality of the old woman. 'Ich fühle dich: meine Sinne alle mit entzückter Stärke umarmen dich zuvor!' is a never-to-be-fulfilled premonition of success. The phrases 'j'ai embrassé' and 'j'ai senti un peu son immense corps' themselves nearly 'embrace' Rimbaud's poems, and even if the success is partial, it is real. Rimbaud is not able to hold on to his conquest, for at midday the goddess of dawn will have vanished, but fleeting immediacy was what he sought, the capacity to enjoy the neither/nor moment at dawn rather than permanent communion.

As he touches the goddess, Rimbaud's *je* becomes a child, suggesting the rebirth of innocence and perfect unselfconscious awareness.

Hofmannsthal's Poet also compares himself to a child as he seeks the embrace, a child lured into the woods by wayfarers, the movement of whose hands to throttle him he innocently interprets as a request for flowers. But the threat of strangulation dramatically raises the reader's awareness of the child's vulnerability and of the threats inherent in communion with the natural world. They are deflected completely—comically and accidentally—as the Poet changes his focus towards humanity. Whether or not 'Aube' was a conscious model for the first part of his prologue, Hofmannsthal has shown the kind of triumphantly unashamed self-fulfilment that Rimbaud represents as a pale shadow. Where Rimbaud's Symbolist poem strives for the ideals of purity and self-forgetting, the same desires in Hofmannsthal—in part also with the same scenic details, the waterfall representing the constant, bubbling flow of life, for example—are held at a distinct ironic distance. What is put in their place is a more modest sense of self-abandonment, the same kind that is represented by 'Manche freilich', and yet again with some discreet echoes of that poem's formulations as the Poet describes the woman's departure: she is carried like a princess on a small boat that moves into the shadow cast by the mountain being climbed by people singing, echoing the relationship of 'manche' and 'andere' from the earlier poem; the Poet is struck as 'von ganz vergessenen Leuten regt sich ein Bewußtsein' [from people quite forgotten there stirs a consciousness].[33] The flame that the Poet senses surrounding him as he searches for the great 'Du' is 'eine durchsichtige, wütende, stille Flamme' [a transparent, furious, silent flame]; he feels this is his 'Sternstunde' and aspires to touch a star, but will have his dreams channelled differently. The *Ich* of 'Manche freilich' that is eventually reconciled to itself is characterized by the reverse of both these images, a slender flame and the weight of the stars.

The influence of 'Aube' does not end with the 'Vorspiel für ein Puppentheater', for it surfaces in one of Hofmannsthal's last major lyric poems, 'Vor Tag' from 1907:

> Nun liegt und zuckt am fahlen Himmelsrand
> In sich zusamm'gesunken das Gewitter.
> Nun denkt der Kranke: 'Tag! Jetzt werd ich schlafen!'
> Und drückt die heißen Lider zu. Nun streckt
> Die junge Kuh im Stall die starken Nüstern

---

[33] Cf. Karl Pestalozzi, 'Hofmannsthals Schwierigkeiten mit Dramenschlüssen', *Hofmannsthal Forschungen*, 7 (Freiburg i.Br.: Hofmannsthal-Gesellschaft, 1983), 100: 'die Anspielung . . . auf "Manche freilich . . . " ist unüberhörbar.'

Nach kühlem Frühduft. Nun im stummen Wald
Hebt der Landstreicher ungewaschen sich
Aus weichem Bett vorjährigen Laubes auf
Und wirft mit frecher Hand den nächsten Stein
Nach einer Taube, die schlaftrunken fliegt,
Und graust sich selber wie der Stein so dumpf
Und schwer zur Erde fällt. Nun rennt das Wasser
Als wollte es der Nacht, der fortgeschlichnen, nach
Ins Dunkel stürzen, unteilnehmend, wild
Und kalten Hauches hin, indessen droben
Der Heiland und die Mutter leise leise
Sich unterreden auf dem Brücklein: leise,
Und doch ist ihre kleine Rede ewig
Und unzerstörbar wie die Sterne droben.
Er trägt sein Kreuz und sagt nur: 'Meine Mutter!'
Und sieht sie an, und: 'Ach mein lieber Sohn!'
Sagt sie.—Nun hat der Himmel mit der Erde
Ein stumm beklemmend Zwiegespräch. Dann geht
Ein Schauer durch den schweren alten Leib:
Sie rüstet sich, den neuen Tag zu leben.
Nun steigt das geisterhafte Frühlicht. Nun
Schleicht einer ohne Schuh von einem Frauenbett,
Läuft wie ein Schatten, klettert wie ein Dieb
Durchs Fenster in sein eigenes Zimmer, sieht
Sich im Wandspiegel und hat plötzlich Angst
Vor diesem blassen übernächtigen Fremden,
Als hätte dieser selber heute Nacht
Den guten Knaben, der er war, ermordet
Und käme jetzt die Hände sich zu waschen
Im Krüglein seines Opfers wie zum Hohn,
Und darum sei der Himmel so beklommen
Und alles in der Luft so sonderbar.
Nun geht die Stallthür. Nun ist auch Tag. (*SW* i. 106–7)

[Now the storm lies and twitches on the pale horizon, drained of energy. Now the sick man thinks, 'The day is here! Now I shall be able to sleep!' and closes his feverish eyes. Now the heifer in the byre stall flares her firm nostrils in search of cool spring air. Now in the silent wood the tramp gets up unwashed from his soft bed of last year's leaves and with an impudent gesture throws the nearest stone at a pigeon [*or* dove] that flies away, still befuddled from sleep, and he is himself shocked at how dully and heavily the stone falls to earth. Now the water hastens on, as if it were trying to rush after the darkness that has slipped away, indifferently, wildly and with a breath of cold, whilst above it the Saviour and his Mother converse quietly, quietly on the little bridge: quietly, but their little talk is eternal and indestructible like the stars above. He is carrying his cross and says only, 'Mother!', and looks at her and she replies, 'Oh, my dear son!'—Now the sky [*or* heaven] has a silent, oppressive dialogue with the earth. Then a shudder passes through its heavy old body: it is stirring itself to live the new day. Now the eerie morning light is rising. Now a barefoot figure slips from a woman's bed, runs like a shadow, climbs like a thief through the window into his own room, sees himself in the mirror and is suddenly afraid at the sight of this pale, sleepy stranger, as if last night this man had murdered the good lad that he had been, and was now coming to wash his hands scornfully in his victim's basin, and that is why the sky is so apprehensive, why everything in the air is so strange. Now the byre door is opened. Now the day is here.]

This poem, too, is about the hour that precedes morning yet is no longer night, and corresponding to this temporal indeterminacy, its framework is the word 'nun', ten times repeated. Between the first and the last there is clearly a progression, for the dying storm and the day-break are not the same moment, but it is hard to say at first exactly which 'nun' marks the turning-point, although there is such a point in fact. 'Aube' is the same point, just before 'aurore', and Rimbaud's poem traces a similar sequence from 'rien ne bougeait' to the final embrace, the point when dawn comes and simultaneously disappears. For Hofmannsthal, however, the point before sunrise is not just chronologically ambiguous. The heavens are 'beklommen' because of the muggy atmosphere created by the storm; the sick man greets the day exceptionally as a time for sleep because the atmosphere during the night has been too oppressive for his sensibilities, enhanced by ill-ness; the dumb creatures of the countryside sense the same change. Something out of the ordinary has disturbed the normal climate.

It takes some effort to engage with the new day: the tramp is at least as sleepy as the pigeon or the dove he tries to kill and is surprised at how heavily the stone falls, as if the night that is rapidly vanishing had sus-pended the usual effects of weight and gravity and the stone would fly like the bird. But the stone's thud brings the tramp up short, reminds him of himself, as it were, and of what he has attempted: the word 'frech' suggests transgression, that the object is 'eine Taube', the symbol of peace and reconciliation and of the Holy Spirit, gives it a sin-ful dimension. Erwin Kobel draws a comparison with a passage from Hofmannsthal's *Das kleine Welttheater* in which the Young Man wakes up and throws his horse's bridle at some birds, killing two chickens and a quail:

Sonderbar
War mir die Beute, und der Traum umschwirrte mich so stark,
Daß ich den Brunnen suchte und mir beide Augen so schnell
Mit klarem Wasser wusch; und wie mir flüchtig da
Aus feuchtem Dunkel mein Gesicht entgegenflog,
Kam mir ein Taumel so, als würd ich innerlich
Durch einen Abgrund hingerissen, und mir war,
Da ich den Kopf erhob, als wär ich um ein Stück
Gealtert in dem Augenblick. (*SW* iii. 139)

[My kill seemed odd and the dream was buzzing so insistently in my head that I sought out the well and quickly washed my two eyes with clear water. And as my own face suddenly looked up at me for a moment from the damp darkness I felt giddy, as if inside I were being pulled through a chasm, and when I raised my head I felt as if I had aged a little in that moment.]

The Young Man was formerly brought to the knowledge of his innate sinfulness by such moments of reflection, but now that he has known love is made happy by them. Kobel then links the figure of the tramp with Rimbaud himself:

Der Landstreicher ist stärker ins Böse verstrickt als der junge Herr des *Kleinen Welt-theaters*. Es ist eine Gestalt, die auf Rimbaud vorausdeutet, wie er von Hofmanns-thal wenig später, im zweiten Teil der *Augenblicke in Griechenland*, dargestellt wird: als einer, 'der mit übermenschlicher Kraft sein Selbst zusammenkrümmt wie einen Bogen, den umbarmherzigsten Pfeil von der Sehne zu schicken', und der doch, indem er nach Hause begehrt, schon ein Besiegter ist.[34]

[The tramp is more intimately implicated in evil than the young man in the *Little Theatre of the World*. He is a figure that anticipates the Rimbaud that Hofmannsthal depicts a while later in the second part of the *Moments in Greece*: he is someone 'who used superhuman force to concentrate his Self like a bow to shoot the pitiless arrow from the string', and who is none the less already vanquished because he wishes to return home.]

The alienation that the tramp in 'Vor Tag' both senses and embodies is present in the stream, too, flowing quickly as if to follow the night into the past, 'unteilnehmend' and cold. It lacks all the usual connotations of the babbling brook, and invites no empathy between humanity and nature. It is starkly contrasted with the conversation between Christ and the Virgin imagined on the wayside cross scene which consists essentially of the evocation of eternal sympathy and love. The

---

[34] Erwin Kobel, 'Magie und Ewigkeit: Überlegungen zu Hofmannsthals Gedicht "Vor Tag"', *Jahrbuch der Deutschen Schiller-Gesellschaft*, 21 (1977), 361, referring to *Augenblicke in Griechenland*, *EGB*, 611–12.

temporal setting of the poem, always 'nun', out of time as if in a perpetually suspended moment before daybreak, also has a perspective on eternity, and it is this that seems to shake the earth into action. The simple conversation between Christ and the Virgin reveals a context of shared love that is echoed in the conversation between the sky and the earth which results in the earth pulling herself together to experience the new day and abandoning her previous indifference. The 'nun—nun—nun' sequence now has a sense of progression rather than stasis: the earth has made up its mind, so the eerie morning light begins to lift in consequence, and so the shadowy figure leaves the woman's bed.

The identity of this figure is deliberately allowed to emerge only gradually, and in familiar Hofmannsthalian fashion he appears impersonally at first, 'einer', then runs 'wie ein Schatten', climbs into his room 'wie ein Dieb', sees himself in the mirror and is so disconcerted that the reflection appears to be of a pale stranger. Furthermore, it is as if this other person has murdered his former self during the night. It is clearly an identity in a moment of flux, perhaps not as attenuated as in 'Erlebnis'—with which Hofmannsthal linked 'Vor Tag' in a note for *Ad me ipsum* (*RA* iii. 602)—but none the less deliberately destabilized. The reason is that the figure has returned from his first sexual experience, has crossed a Rubicon that has forever separated him from his childhood innocence and the prelapsarian state of purity that children in Hofmannsthal's poetry often represent. There is something cruelly final about this experience, communicated by the suggestions of crime. Not only does the figure climb through the window to his own room like a thief, but he feels guilty, as if he has murdered his former self and returned to revel mockingly in the crime by washing his hands in the victim's own basin. He is no longer 'der gute Knabe' and this transition is stated as the reason for the atmospheric disturbance that the early part of the poem evoked: 'darum sei der Himmel so beklommen | Und alles in der Luft so sonderbar.' The man in the poem is now fully self-conscious, startled into full awareness of his self by the strangeness of his own reflection. Likewise the poem has admitted to itself the reasons for the conditions of its descriptive opening. Both realizations break the spell that the 'nun—nun—nun' sequence created, the byre door is opened and day begins in earnest. Timelessness and simultaneity have been replaced, not without some violence, by the operation of time.

There are many respects in which 'Vor Tag' reads as a response to 'Aube'. Structurally both poems 'embrace' a heightened, significant moment: Rimbaud's seven-paragraph structure culminates centrally with the vision of the goddess on the silvery summit in paragraph 4; Hofmannsthal's poem has its turning-point in a comparable meeting of natural and divine roughly halfway through—at the 'nun' of line 22 following the dash. 'Aube' sets up a tension by announcing its end in its beginning; 'Vor Tag' less overtly sets up a similar tension by describing the effects of 'Beklommenheit' and leaving the explanation of its cause until the very end. Neither poem is at all explicit about the progression of time: there is only the word 'alors' in Rimbaud's, at the beginning of the fifth paragraph, and Hofmannsthal's only clear indication of temporal change is 'dann' in line 23. Both poems therefore manage to combine the suspension of time that characterizes that peculiar morning hour with the subtle indication of progression. Both poems awaken a dead or dying landscape into life, Hofmannsthal's storm 'liegt und zuckt' in its death-throes, the water in Rimbaud's shadowy world is dead. Both also use the precarious balance that exists between pre-dawn and day to symbolize the breaking of a suspended perfection with the realization of a momentous event, Rimbaud's 'au réveil il était midi' exposing the transitoriness of the union with the dawn-goddess but simultaneously confirming the sense of fulfilment, Hofmannsthal's 'und nun ist auch Tag' marking the definitive break of his subject from his past and the loss of a natural unity for the sake of a sexual union. The two protagonists share some characteristics, too: Rimbaud's is seen 'courant comme un mendiant', Hofmannsthal's 'klettert wie ein Dieb', and the experience of both is linked to the state of childhood.

None of this amounts to proof that Hofmannsthal was inspired by Rimbaud at this phase in his life, or that 'Aube' is a model for 'Vor Tag', but the congruities of theme, image and structure are substantial, and the manner in which Hofmannsthal's two works shy away from Rimbaud's confidence is perfectly in accord with his response to Symbolism between the early 1890s and *Das Gespräch über Gedichte* in 1903. In both the 'Vorspiel für ein Puppentheater' and 'Vor Tag' Hofmannsthal rejects the perfect, self-contained experience evoked by Rimbaud's 'Aube' and the aspiration towards the spiritual absolute which it conveys, and favours instead something rather more down-to-earth. The prologue does offer the audience a dream-world but one of drama, not that of mystical communion. The poem is about an intimate moment of transition in the composition of a personal identity. It associates this intimately with a landscape very much in the manner of the Symbolists' *état d'âme* but without any of the paraphernalia of the Symbolist poems by which he was most influenced in the 1890s.

Hofmannsthal may himself have associated Rimbaud's brief, youthful poetic career with his own early productive phase and its painful close. On the journey in May 1908 between the Monastery of St Luke and Chaeronaea recorded in *Augenblicke in Griechenland*, it seems that it was Kessler who brought up the subject of Rimbaud:

Wir sprachen vom Reisen, vom Wandern, von der Mühsal des Wanderns. Ich erzählte von Rimbaud, wie er als Junge ohne Geld, oft hungernd und obdachlos, von Frankreich durch Deutschland und Österreich nach dem Orient gewandert sei, wunderbare Geste des Genies, das daran verzweifelte, sich auszudrücken, Van Gogh war nah daran, ähnlich zu verzichten.[35]

[We were talking of travel, of journeying, of the tribulations of walking. I recounted how Rimbaud, when he was a penniless boy, often starving and with nowhere to stay, walked from France, through Germany to the East, the marvellous action of a genius who despaired of being able to express himself. Van Gogh came close to giving up in the same way.]

Hofmannsthal had been extremely moody during their visit to Greece, indeed had been for some while so tense as to be apparently on the verge of a breakdown. Later that day he talked to Kessler about his own writing, explaining, 'bei ihm [Hofmannsthal] sei die Produktivität ein seltener Glücksfall, aber wenn sie eintrete, ein unbeschreiblicher Glückszustand' [productivity for him was a rare chance, but when it happened it produced a condition of indescribable happiness]. Kessler seems pleased to have recognized,

dass sehr viel von Hofmannsthals scheinbarer Launenhaftigkeit, Nervosität, Aufgeregtheit von einem intimen Drama, von einem Ringen nach Produktivität, einer Angst vor irgendwelcher plötzlich hereinbrechenden endgültigen Impotenz, kommt.[36]

[that much of Hofmannsthal's apparent moodiness, nervousness and excitability derives from a private drama, from a struggle for productivity, from a fear that impotence might suddenly and permanently set in.]

Certainly Hofmannsthal's difficulties with lyric poetry were overcome in 'Vor Tag'. It may be that at a distance of more than fifteen years from his first Symbolist-inspired poetry, and now that the tortured

[35] Kessler, diary entry for 10 May 1908. Quoted from Werner Volke, 'Unterwegs mit Hofmannsthal. Berlin—Griechenland—Venedig. Aus Harry Graf Kesslers Tagebüchern und aus Briefen Kesslers und Hofmannsthals', ed. Werner Volke, *Hofmannsthal-Blätter*, 35/36 (1987), 83.

[36] Ibid. 84–5.

wrestling for productivity that Kessler described is no longer primarily concerned with lyric poetry, an encounter with a supremely successful example of another's tortured poetic genius released a brief moment of lyric productivity in Hofmannsthal.

The difficulties seemed to Hofmannsthal to have lain in his mastery of rhythm, as he wrote to Rudolf Borchardt in 1912:

Mir ist als würde ich wieder im Lyrischen productiver werden . . . Aber ich fühle mich mit dem Rhytmischen im Unklaren . . . Der 'siebente Ring' Georges . . . Miltons kleinere Gedichte und der Keats—zwischen diesen Wegweisern nach verschiedenen Gebieten rhytmischer Möglichkeiten fühle ich mich ein wenig pendeln.

[I seem to be producing more lyric poetry again, but I feel uncertain about rhythm. George's *The Seventh Ring*, Milton's shorter poems and Keats—I feel myself veering slightly between these pointers to various areas of rhythmic possibility.]

He is writing a series of poems in blank verse about the seven ages of Man, to be called 'Lebenspyramide', and adds that in the light of these,

hier scheint mir meinem früheren Gebrauch etwas allzu weibliches fließendes anzuhaften, allzu viele enjambements u.s.f. offenbar flüchtete ich damals zur strengen Terzine und ähnlichen Gebilden, um dem zu entgehen—Georges Vers in den Zeitgedichten ist der Gegenpol—aber mir selber ist in der Zwischenzeit in dem einen Gedicht 'Vor Tag', glaub ich, etwas gelungen, rein instinctmäßig, das, scheint mir, zwischen beiden steht.[37]

[I now think that there was something too feminine and flowing about my earlier practice, that there were too many enjambements etc., and then I was obviously taking refuge in strict Terzinen and other such forms in order to escape it—George's verse in the 'Zeitgedichte' (the first section of *The Seventh Ring*) is the opposite pole—but in the meantime, in the one poem 'Before Daybreak', I managed something, purely instinctively I think, that lies between the two extremes.]

Rhythmically, 'Vor Tag'—in fluent blank verse throughout—is certainly confident and fluent, although it is full of the enjambements that Hofmannsthal thought were too frequent in his early verse. Much later Rimbaud is associated with the same rhythmic confidence:

Ihnen allen [Mallarmé, Baudelaire, Rimbaud, Claudel, Valéry] geht es darum . . . die lyrische Inspiration aus dem Innern der Sprache selbst zu erneuern. Das kreative Individuum . . . wirft sich in die Sprache selbst und sucht in ihr die Trunkenheit der Eingebung sich zu verschaffen und neue Zugänge ins Leben sich

---

[37] 'Hugo von Hofmannsthal: Unbekannte Briefe', *Jahrbuch der Deutschen Schiller-Gesellschaft*, 8 (1964), 24–5; letter of 3 Aug. 1912. Quoted in *SW* i. 418–19.

zu erschließen, gemäß jenen Ahnungen der Sinne, wenn sie sich von der Herrschaft des wachen Verstandes losreißen. Dies ist, dies war immer die lateinische Annäherung an das Unbewußte: sie geschieht nicht im halbträumerischen Sich-Verschwelgen des germanischen Geistes . . . sondern durch ein heftiges Sich-Hinüberwerfen, einen Taumel: durch ein Durcheinanderschütteln der Objekte, ein Brechen der Ordnungen. Es sind Saturnalien des Geistes. Neue Reflexe tauchen auf vor fast brechenden Augen, es ist eine Verjüngung ohnegleichen, ein eigentliches Mysterium. Hier führt auch ein Weg von dem 'Bateau ivre' des Rimbaud zu den frühesten Versen Stefan Georges: beiden ist das gemein, was der Römer mit dem Wort 'incantatio' umschrieb: die dunkle und gewaltsame Selbstbezauberung durch die Magie der Worte und die Rhythmen. (*RA* iii. 145–6)

[They are all concerned . . . to renew lyric inspiration from within language itself. The creative individual . . . flings himself into language itself and tries to bring about there the intoxication of inspiration, to unlock new ways into life, following those intimations of the senses when they have freed themselves from the dominance of watchful reason. This is, this was always the Latin way of getting at the unconscious: it does not happen in the half-dreamlike dissipated revelry of the Germanic spirit . . . but by means of a massive upheaval of the self, a frenzy, or by shaking things up, breaking traditional structures apart. These are spiritual saturnalias. New reflexes emerge before one's very eyes and make them pop out, there is an incomparable sense of rejuvenation, a true mystery. There is here a path between Rimbaud's 'Drunken Boat' to the earliest verse of Stefan George: they both have in common what the Romans called 'incantatio', the dark and powerful enchantment of the self through the magic of words and rhythms.]

Rimbaud's 'Bateau ivre', even if it is named late in this passage, is clearly the poem that inspired it. Hofmannsthal does not write coincidentally of 'the drunkenness of inspiration', and the idea of casting oneself into language, as if into water, picks up the key line, 'je me suis baigné dans le Poème | De la Mer' [I have bathed in the Poem of the Sea].[38] But despite Hofmannsthal's insistence on the phrase 'Brechen der Ordnungen', in both the passage quoted above and that from the same essay on Saint-John Perse quoted earlier in this chapter, it is not the wild and iconoclastic aspects of Rimbaud's poetic revolution that he identifies as an impetus to the German poetic tradition in the person of George, but the music and the rhythm he so confidently practises. He focuses rather on the element of *incantatio*, musically working oneself into a state of enhanced perception, and thus even at this late stage—1929—on the same element so crucial to the Symbolist aesthetic that George identified in conversation in December 1891.

---

[38] Rimbaud, *Poésies*, 94.

Originality is not a new concern. An allegorical reflection by Choerilus of Samos laments the difficulties of finding a distinctive place for one-self in the wake of past achievements:

Blessed indeed the man who was skilled in song in those days, a 'servant of the Muses' when the meadow was still undefiled! Now, when everything has been portioned out and the arts have reached their limits, we are left behind in the race, and one looks everywhere in vain for a place to drive one's newly yoked chariot.[39]

It would be depressing and not a little absurd now to think that the arts had really 'reached their limits' by the fifth century BC, but there could hardly be a more dramatic illustration that there is nothing specifically modern about the problem. It has been avoided over and over again, and far from being inhibitive, literary tradition may act in so challenging and provocative a way as to spawn the very originality that at other times it threatens to stifle. The action of tradition may be reassuring, too. Rilke thought of it thus, and wrote of it to Clara in terms uncannily reminiscent of Hofmannsthal's poetry:

Ach, wir rechnen die Jahre und machen Abschnitte da und dort und hören auf und fangen an und zögern zwischen beidem. Aber wie sehr ist, was uns begegnet, aus einem Stück, in welcher Verwandschaft steht eines zum anderen, hat sich geboren und wächst heran und wird erzogen zu sich selbst, und wir haben im Grunde nur *dazusein*, aber schlicht, aber inständig, wie die Erde das ist, den Jahreszeiten zustimmend, hell und dunkel und ganz im Raum, nicht verlangend, in anderem aufzuruhen als in dem Netz von Einflüssen und Kräften, in dem die Sterne sich sicher fühlen.[40]

[Oh, we count up the years and divide them here and there into periods and stop and start again and hesitate between the two. But how much of a piece everything is that we come across, what a close relationship one thing has to another, has been born, grows up and is brought up to become itself, and we really only have to *be there*, simply and insistently of course, in the way that the earth is there, in accord with the seasons, light and dark and whole in space, not needing to take comfort in anything but the network of influences and forces in which the stars feel safe.]

The *und*-clauses at the beginning of that passage recall Hofmannsthal's 'Ballade des äußeren Lebens'; the opposition of light and dark, the prospect of the entirety of space, and above all the images of the stars and the net seem drawn from 'Manche freilich', either directly or via the speech *Der Dichter und diese Zeit*, first published in March 1907.

The sentiment Rilke expresses is very different from the usual level

---

[39] Quoted from *A Hellenistic Anthology*, selected and ed. Neil Hopkinson (Cambridge: Cambridge University Press, 1988), 1.

[40] Rilke, *Briefe 1906–1907*, 395; letter of 19 Oct. 1907.

of Hofmannsthal's literary confidence. Hofmannsthal started out with the ambition to provide poetry in German of the power and status of Keats's in English, yet attempted to put this hope into practice by focusing on a very different kind of poetry. The extreme self-consciousness of Symbolism combined with Hofmannsthal's own extraordinarily active literary receptiveness to produce poetry too clearly aware of its own status as imitative, which sometimes made it derivative. The sheer quantity and repetition of borrowed imagery and phrases must cast doubt on whether in the poetry most directly influenced by Symbolism Hofmannsthal found what might be called an authentic lyric voice. The anxieties of the early verse poems and the constant intertextual pulls of the prose poetry are not appropriately characterized with Rilke's relaxed image of resting in a network of influences, although an urgent desire, 'Verlangen', for just such a security can be felt throughout Hofmannsthal's early work.

Das Gespräch über Gedichte encapsulates the confusions; it and Hofmannsthal's responses to Rimbaud seem to ask why it was ever necessary to develop an aesthetic that prefers the frozen, the metallic or the anorganic to the living and breathing. Hofmannsthal tries to force the symbol of the 'Hauch' to correspond to 'Edelsteine', to make it symbolize poetry by using the precious stone as an inter-mediary correlative for both, and as one is carried away by the often impassioned language of the dialogue, one may temporarily accept the equation. But even through the haze of subtexts and metaphors, com-parisons with Ariel and the sacrifice of a beast, it is phrases that evoke natural phenomena that carry the greatest conviction—Gabriel's 'gewisse Bewegung, mit der du von einem hohon Wagen abspringst; eine schwüle sternlose Sommernacht; der Geruch feuchter Steine in einer Hausflur; das Gefühl eisigen Wassers, das aus einem Lauf-brunnen über deine Hände sprüht' [certain movement with which you jump down from a high carriage, a close, starless night in summer, the smell of damp stones in the hallway, the feeling of icy water from a fountain bubbling over your hands; *SW* xxxi. 76]. It is most probably only accidental that 'sternlos' in the second example appears specifi-cally to repudiate the 'stummes Niederfallen ferner Sterne' of 'Manche freilich' and all the psychic weight of inherited tradition that the image stood for there. Nevertheless, the natural and tangible sensations are savoured in *Das Gespräch* in a way that amounts to such a repudiation.

The dialogue ends with a tribute to Goethe and with Hofmanns-thal's thinking better of citing a Symbolist poem, and this reveals where his allegiance lies. The tradition itself was not inherently too strong for modern poets; nor is a large range of influences necessarily damaging, although it will always be potentially dangerous and difficult. Rilke knew how to cope with the condition that Hofmannsthal found himself in, and his answer was to trust that the poet's self will quietly work on the stimuli it receives:

Verse sind nicht, wie die Leute meinen, Gefühle (die hat man früh genug),—es sind Erfahrungen. Um eines Verses willen muß man viele Städte sehen, Menschen und Dinge, man muß die Tiere kennen, man muß fühlen, wie die Vögel fliegen . . . Und es genügt auch noch nicht, daß man Erinnerungen hat. Man muß sie vergessen können, wenn es viele sind, und man muß die große Geduld haben, zu warten, daß sie wiederkommen. Denn die Erinnerungen selbst *sind* es noch nicht. Erst wenn sie Blut werden in uns und nicht mehr zu unterscheiden von uns selbst, erst dann kann es geschehen, daß in einer sehr seltenen Stunde das erste Wort eines Verses aufsteht in ihrer Mitte und aus ihnen ausgeht.[41]

[Poetry is not feelings, as people think it is—you have those quite early enough—it is experiences. To make a line of verse you have to see many cities, people and things, you have to be familiar with animals, you have to feel how the birds fly. And it is not enough to have memories. You have to be able to forget them if there are lots of them, and you must have enough patience to wait for them to return. Memories are not in themselves enough. Only when they become part of our bloodstream, no longer distinguishable from our selves, only then is it possible, in a very rare moment, for the first word of a poem to stand up in the midst of them and move beyond them.]

Yet again the imagery is reminiscent of Hofmannsthal, this time of *Das Gespräch über Gedichte* itself and the momentary loss of self in the sacrifice.

The letter sent by Hofmannsthal to Richard Beer-Hofmann in 1895 with which this study began describes the necessity of setting up 'Potemkin villages' on which the self can concentrate for stability, lest it should be overwhelmed by a multiplicity of irreconcilable influences: 'Es handelt sich freilich immer nur darum ringsum an den Grenzen des Gesichtskreises Potemkin'sche Dörfer aufzustellen, aber solche an die man selber glaubt.' Perhaps that very task was flawed. The process described in the letter is uncannily similar to one described by Huysmans in *A rebours*:

Le tout est de savoir s'y prendre, de savoir concentrer son esprit sur un seul point, de savoir s'abstraire suffisamment pour amener l'hallucination et pouvoir substituer le rêve de la réalité à la réalité même.[42]

---

[41] Rilke, *Die Aufzeichnungen des Malte Laurids Brigge*, in *Werke*, vi. 25–7.
[42] Huysmans, *A rebours*, 103.

[The thing is to know how to go about it, to know how to concentrate one's mind on a single point, to know how to abstract oneself sufficiently to bring about a hallucination and to be able to substitute a dream of reality for reality itself.]

Hofmannsthal certainly knew this passage; if he had missed it in his reading of the novel, he would have seen it translated by Hermann Bahr in the essay entitled 'Die Décadence'.[43] The processes of both Huysmans's Des Esseintes and Hofmannsthal in his letter have in common the deliberate suspension of reality through a psychological artifice and the erection of a hallucinatory world in its place. But Hofmannsthal was no Decadent, not even in 1891. Huysmans's hero advocates the complete substitution of dream for reality, the construction of an artificial alternative to real life: 'la nature a fait son temps; elle a définitivement lassé, par la dégoûtante uniformité de ses paysages et de ses ciels, l'attentive patience des raffinés' [nature has had its day, because of the disgusting uniformity of its landscapes and its skies it has definitively tried the patience of cultivated people]. Hofmannsthal specifically guards against this, being 'zu kritisch um in einer Traum-welt zu leben, wie die Romantiker', and his device is a temporary measure, a makeshift for the purposes of self-preservation within the real world, and not an escape hatch out of it. Hofmannsthal certainly achieved this, as Das Gespräch indicates, although it was despite the Symbolist phase, and perhaps at the cost of a longer career as a lyric poet. The admiration for Goethe that stands out from Das Gespräch, especially the poetry of his old age, and the enthusiasm for which sensations from the natural world are invoked as the substance of poetry, represent both an acknowledgement of the importance of Symbolism and the realization that it was ultimately a substitute, a dummy aesthetic that had previously overlaid and stifled Hofmanns-thal's more genuine Romantic leanings.

[43] Bahr, Studien, 23.

BIBLIOGRAPHY

I MANUSCRIPT SOURCES

Houghton Library, Harvard University, Cambridge, Massachusetts, *Nachlaß* of Hugo von Hofmannsthal, bMS Ger 147–8.

2 PRINTED SOURCES

Primary Sources

Hofmannsthal

HOFMANNSTHAL, HUGO VON, *Sämtliche Werke*, ed. Rudolf Hirsch et al. (Frankfurt am Main: S. Fischer, 1975–).
i: *Gedichte 1*, ed. Eugene Weber (1984).
ii: *Gedichte 2: Aus dem Nachlaß*, ed. Andreas Thomasberger and Eugene Weber (1988).
iii: *Dramen 1*, ed. Götz Eberhard Hübner, Klaus-Gerhard Pott and Christoph Michel (1982).
xviii: *Dramen 16: Fragmente aus dem Nachlaß*, ed. Ellen Ritter (1987).
xxviii: *Erzählungen 1*, ed. Ellen Ritter (1975).
xxix: *Erzählungen 2: Aus dem Nachlaß*, ed. Ellen Ritter (1978).
xxxi: *Erfundene Gespräche und Briefe*, ed. Ellen Ritter (1991).
—— *Gesammelte Werke in 10 Einzelausgaben*, ed. Bernd Schoeller with Rudolf Hirsch (Frankfurt am Main: Fischer Taschenbuch, 1979–80).
Dramen III: 1893–1927 (1979).
Dramen VI: Ballette, Pantomimen, Bearbeitungen, Übersetzungen (1979).
Erzählungen, Erfundene Gespräche und Briefe (1979).
Reden und Aufsätze I: 1891–1913 (1979).
Reden und Aufsätze II: 1914–1924 (1979).
Reden und Aufsätze III: 1925–1929. Aufzeichnungen 1889–1929 (1980).
—— *Selected Essays*, ed. Mary E. Gilbert (Oxford: Blackwell, 1955).
—— 'Über Gedichte: Ein Dialog', in *Unterhaltungen über literarische Gegenstände*, ed. Georg Brandes (Berlin: Bard, Marquardt, 1904), 1–32.
—— *Briefe: 1890–1900*, [ed. Heinrich Zimmer] (Berlin: S. Fischer, 1935).
—— *Briefe: 1900–1909* (Vienna: Bermann-Fischer, 1937).
—— 'Briefe an Freunde', ed. H[erbert] St[einer], *Merkur: Deutsche Zeitschrift für europäisches Denken*, 9.2 (1955), 964–70.
—— and ANDRIAN, LEOPOLD VON, *Briefwechsel*, ed. Walter H. Perl (Frankfurt am Main: S. Fischer, 1968).

—— [and BAHR, HERMANN], *Neue Rundschau*, 59 (1948), 215–28.

—— and BEER-HOFMANN, RICHARD, *Briefwechsel*, ed. Eugene Weber (Frankfurt am Main: S. Fischer, 1972).

—— [and BIE, OSCAR], in 'Aus der Werkstatt der Neuen Rundschau 1890–1917', *Neue Rundschau*, 72 (1961), 548–58.

—— and BORCHARDT, RUDOLF, *Briefwechsel*, ed. Marie-Luise Borchardt and Herbert Steiner (Frankfurt am Main: S. Fischer, 1954).

—— 'Unbekannte Briefe. Mitgeteilt von Werner Volke', *Jahrbuch der Deutschen Schiller-Gesellschaft*, 8 (1964), 19–32.

—— and DEHMEL, RICHARD, 'Briefwechsel 1893–1919', ed. Martin Stern, *Hofmannsthal-Blätter*, 21/22 (1979), 1–130.

—— and GEORGE, STEFAN, *Briefwechsel zwischen George und Hofmannsthal*, 2nd, extended edn. (Düsseldorf: Küpper-Bondi, 1953).

—— and HERZFELD, MARIE, *Briefe an Marie Herzfeld*, ed. Horst Weber (Heidelberg: Stiehm, 1967).

—— and KARG VON BEBENBURG, EDGAR, *Briefwechsel*, ed. Mary E. Gilbert (Frankfurt am Main: S. Fischer, 1966).

—— and KESSLER, HARRY GRAF, *Briefwechsel 1898–1929*, ed. Hilde Burger (Frankfurt am Main: Insel, 1968).

—— —— 'Unterwegs mit Hofmannsthal. Berlin–Griechenland–Venedig. Aus Harry Graf Kesslers Tagebüchern und aus Briefen Kesslers und Hofmannsthals', ed. Werner Volke, *Hofmannsthal-Blätter*, 35/6 (1987), 50–104.

—— and LANDAUER, GUSTAV, 'Hugo von Hofmannsthal und Gustav Landauer. Eine Dokumentation. Mit dem Briefwechsel Hofmannsthal–Landauer und Landauers Essays über Hofmannsthal', ed. Norbert Altenhofer, *Hofmannsthal-Blätter*, 19/20 (1978), 43–72.

—— and MAETERLINCK, MAURICE, 'Hugo von Hofmannsthal–Maurice Maeterlinck: Zwei unveröffentlichte Briefe', ed. Hilde Burger, *Neue Rundschau*, 73 (1962), 314–19.

—— and SCHMULJOW-CLAASSEN, RIA, *Briefe, Aufsätze, Dokumente*, ed. Claudia Abrecht, Marbacher Schriften 18 (Stuttgart: Cotta in Kommission, 1982).

—— and SCHNITZLER, ARTHUR, *Briefwechsel*, ed. Therese Nickl and Heinrich Schnitzler (Frankfurt am Main: S. Fischer, 1964).

Other

AESCHYLUS, *Äschylos: Deutsch in den Versmaßen der Urschrift*, trans. J. J. C. Donner, 2nd edn. (Berlin: Langenscheidt, 1892).

AMIEL, HENRI-FRÉDÉRIC, *Fragments d'un journal intime*, ed. Edmond Scherer, 2 vols., 9th edn. (Geneva: Georg, 1905).

ANDRIAN, LEOPOLD VON, *Der Garten der Erkenntnis*, ed. Walter H. Perl (Frankfurt am Main: S. Fischer, 1970).

—— *Leopold von Andrian und die Blätter für die Kunst*, ed. Walter H. Perl (Hamburg: Verlag Dr Ernst Hauswedell, 1960).

ANDRIAN, LEOPOLD VON, 'Leopold von Andrian über Hugo von Hofmannsthal. Auszüge aus seinen Tagebüchern', ed. Ursula Renner, *Hofmannsthal-Blätter*, 35/6 (1987), 3–49.

—— *Correspondenzen: Briefe an Leopold von Andrian 1894–1950*, ed. Ferruccio delle Cave (Marbach am Neckar: Deutsche Schiller-Gesellschaft, 1989).

BAHR, HERMANN, *Zur Kritik der Moderne: Gesammelte Aufsätze: Erste Reihe* (Zurich: Schabelitz, 1890).

—— *Die Überwindung des Naturalismus, als zweite Reihe von 'Zur Kritik der Moderne'*, (Dresden: Pierson, 1891).

—— *Studien zur Kritik der Moderne* (Frankfurt am Main: Rütten & Loening, 1894).

—— *Renaissance: Neue Studien zur Kritik der Moderne* (Berlin: S. Fischer, 1897).

—— *Selbstbildnis* (Berlin: S. Fischer, 1923).

—— *Zur Überwindung des Naturalismus: Theoretische Schriften 1887–1904*, ed. Gotthart Wunberg, Sprache und Literatur 46 (Stuttgart: Kohlhammer, 1968).

—— *Prophet der Moderne: Tagebücher 1888–1904*, ed. Reinhard Farkas (Vienna: Böhlau, 1987).

—— *Tagebücher, Skizzenbücher, Notizhefte*, ii: *1890–1900*, ed. Mortiz Csáky (Vienna: Böhlau, 1996).

BAUDELAIRE, CHARLES, *Œuvres complètes*, ed. Claude Pichois, 2 vols., Bibliothèque de la Pléiade (Paris: Gallimard, 1975–6).

BORCHARDT, RUDOLF, *Gesammelte Werke in Einzelbänden*, ed. Marie-Luise Borchardt (Stuttgart: Klett-Cotta, 1957–90).

BOURGET, PAUL, *La Vie inquiète. Poèmes* (Paris: Lemerre, 1875).

—— *Poésies*, 2 vols. (Paris: Lemerre, [1885–7]).

—— *Œuvres complètes: Critique 1: Essais de psychologie contemporaine* (Paris: Plon, 1899).

GAUTIER, THÉOPHILE, *Émaux et camées*, ed. Jean Pommier and Georges Matoré (Lille: Giard-Droz, 1947).

—— *Souvenirs romantiques*, ed. Adolphe Boschot (Paris: Garnier, 1929).

—— *Poésies complètes de Théophile Gautier*, ed. René Jasinski, enlarged edn., 3 vols. (Paris: Nizet, 1970).

GEORGE, STEFAN, *Werke: Ausgabe in zwei Bänden* (Düsseldorf: Küpper-Bondi, 1958).

—— *Die Blätter für die Kunst*, founded by Stefan George, ed. Carl August Klein (Berlin: Verlag der Blätter für die Kunst, 1892–1919; photomechanical reprint, ed. Robert Boehringer: Munich: Küpper-Bondi, 1968).

GIDE, ANDRÉ, *Le Traité du Narcisse*, in *Romans, récits et soties: Œuvres lyriques*, ed. Maurice Nadeau et al., Bibliothèque de la Pléiade (Paris: Gallimard, 1958).

GOETHE, JOHANN WOLFGANG VON, *Werke: Hamburger Ausgabe in 14 Bänden*, ed. Erich Trunz (Munich: Beck, 1981).

GRILLPARZER, FRANZ, *Sämtliche Werke*, Historisch-kritische Gesamtausgabe im Auftrag der Bundeshauptstadt Wien, ed. August Sauer and Reinhold Backmann (Vienna: Schroll, 1909–48), ii.10: *Tagebücher und literarische Skizzenhefte 4*.

HEBBEL, FRIEDRICH, *Sämtliche Werke*, Historisch-kritische Ausgabe, ed. Richard Maria Werner (Berlin: Behr, 1904).

ii: *Tagebücher*, 4 vols.

iii/i: *Briefe 1829–1839*.

HÖLDERLIN, FRIEDRICH, *Sämtliche Werke und Briefe*, ed. Günter Mieth (Munich: Hanser, 1970).

HUGO, VICTOR, *Œuvres poétiques*, ed. Pierre Albouy, Bibliothèque de la Pléiade, 3 vols. (Paris: Gallimard, 1964–74).

HURET, JULES (ed.), *Enquête sur l'évolution littéraire* (Paris: Charpentier, 1891); new edn., with notes and a preface by Daniel Grojnowski (Vanves: Thot, 1982).

HUYSMANS, JORIS-KARL, *A rebours* (Paris: Charpentier, 1884; repr. Paris: Mercure de France, 1977).

KASSNER, RUDOLF, 'John Keats', in *Englische Dichter* (Leipzig: Insel, 1920), 43–60, first published in *Die Mystik, die Künstler und das Leben: Über englische Dichter und Maler im 19. Jahrhundert* (Leipzig: Diederichs, 1900), 95–115.

KEATS, JOHN, *The Complete Poems*, ed. John Barnard (Harmondsworth: Penguin, 1973).

—— *Letters of John Keats: A Selection*, ed. Robert Gittings (Oxford: Oxford University Press, 1987).

KESSLER, HARRY, 'Henri de Régnier', *Pan*, 1.4 (1895), 243–9.

KRAUS, KARL, 'Die demolirte Litteratur', in *Frühe Schriften 1892–1900*, ed. J. J. Braakenburg, 2 vols. (Munich: Kösel, 1979), ii: *1897–1900*, 277–97.

LAMARTINE, ALPHONSE DE, *Œuvres poétiques complètes*, ed. Maxim-François Guyard, Bibliothèque de la Pléiade (Paris: Gallimard, 1963).

MAETERLINCK, MAURICE, *Poésies complètes*, ed. Joseph Hanse (Brussels: La Renaissance du Livre, 1965).

—— *Théâtre*, 4 vols. (Brussels: Lacomblez, 1908).

MALLARMÉ, STÉPHANE, *Œuvres complètes*, ed. Henri Mondor and G. Jean-Aubry, Bibliothèque de la Pléiade (Paris: Gallimard, 1945).

—— *Correspondance*, ed. Henri Mondor and L. J. Austin, 10 vols. (Paris: Gallimard, 1959–85).

MANN, THOMAS, *Gesammelte Werke* (Frankfurt am Main: S. Fischer, 1960).

MORÉAS, JEAN, *Le Pélerin passionné* (Paris: Léon Vannier, 1891).

—— *Œuvres* (Paris: Mercure de France, 1923–6; repr. Geneva: Slatkine, 1977).

MORICE, CHARLES, *La Littérature de tout à l'heure* (Paris: Perrin, 1889).

MUSIL, ROBERT, *Gesammelte Werke*, ed. Adolf Frisé, 2 vols. (Reinbek bei Hamburg: Rowohlt, 1978), ii: *Prosa und Stücke, Kleine Prosa, Autobiographisches, Essays und Reden, Kritik*.

—— *Tagebücher*, ed. Adolf Frisé, 2 vols. (Reinbek bei Hamburg: Rowohlt, 1976).

NERVAL, GÉRARD DE, *Œuvres*, ed. Albert Béguin and Jean Richer, 2 vols. (Paris: Gallimard, 1960).

NIETZSCHE, FRIEDRICH, *Werke in drei Bänden*, ed. Karl Schlechta (Munich: Hanser, 1955).

NORDAU, MAX, *Entartung*, 2 vols. (Berlin: Duncker, 1892).

NOVALIS, *Schriften: Die Werke Friedrich von Hardenbergs*, ed. Paul Kluckhohn and

Richard Samuel, 5 vols., 2nd extended edn. (Stuttgart: Kohlhammer, 1960–88).

PASCAL, BLAISE, *Pensées*, in *Œuvres complètes*, ed. L. Lafuma, Édition Intégrale (Paris: Seuil, 1963).

PATER, WALTER, *The Renaissance: Studies in Art and Poetry*, The Library Edition of the Works of Walter Pater (London: Macmillan, 1910; originally published as *Studies in the History of the Renaissance*, 1873).

POE, EDGAR ALLAN, *Collected Works of Edgar Allan Poe*, ed. Thomas Ollive Mabbott (Cambridge, Mass.: Belknap/Harvard University Press, 1969), i: *Poems*.

—— *Essays and Reviews*, ed. G. R. Thompson (New York: Literary Classics of the United States, 1984).

RILKE, RAINER MARIA, *Sämtliche Werke*, ed. Rilke-Archiv and Ruth Sieber-Rilke, with Ernst Zinn, 7 vols. (Frankfurt am Main: Insel, 1955–97).

—— *Briefe 1906–1907*, ed. Ruth Sieber-Rilke and Carl Sieber (Leipzig: Insel, 1930).

RIMBAUD, ARTHUR, *Poésies, Une saison en enfer, Illuminations*, ed. Louis Forestier, 2nd, rev. edn. (Paris: Gallimard, 1984).

SALTEN, FELIX, *Geister der Zeit: Erlebnisse* (Berlin: Paul Zsolnay, 1924).

SCHNITZLER, ARTHUR, *Tagebuch 1879–1892*, ed. Werner Welzig et al. (Vienna: Verlag der Österreichischen Akademie der Wissenschaften, 1987).

—— *Tagebuch 1893–1902*, ed. Werner Welzig et al. (Vienna: Verlag der Österreichischen Akademie der Wissenschaften, 1989).

—— *Tagebuch 1903–1908*, ed. Werner Welzig et al. (Vienna: Verlag der Österreichischen Akademie der Wissenschaften, 1991).

—— *Arthur Schnitzler–Hugo von Hofmannsthal: Charakteristik aus den Tagebüchern*: *Hofmannsthal-Forschungen*, iii, ed. Bernd Urban with Werner Volke (Freiburg i.Br.: Hofmannsthal-Gesellschaft, 1975).

TURGENEV, IVAN, *The Novels of Ivan Turgenev*, trans. Constance Garnett, Library edition, 17 vols. (London: Heinemann, 1920–2), x: *Dream Tales and Prose Poems* (1920).

VALÉRY, PAUL, *Œuvres*, ed. Jean Hytier, Bibliothèque de la Pléiade, 2 vols. (Paris: Gallimard, 1957–60).

VERLAINE, PAUL, *Œuvres poétiques complètes*, ed. Y.-G. Le Dantec, rev. Jacques Borel, Bibliothèque de la Pléiade (Paris: Gallimard, 1962).

VIELÉ-GRIFFIN, FRANCIS, *Poèmes et poésies* (Paris: Mercure de France, 1895).

VILLIERS DE L'ISLE-ADAM, PHILIPPE-AUGUSTE, *Axël*, ed. Pierre Mariel, Littérature et tradition 1 (Paris: La Colombe, 1960).

YEATS, W. B., 'Introduction', in *The Oxford Book of Modern Verse 1892–1935* (Oxford: Oxford University Press, 1936), pp. v–xlii.

ZWEIG, STEFAN, *Die Welt von Gestern: Erinnerungen eines Europäers* (Stockholm: Bermann-Fischer, 1944; repr. Frankfurt am Main: Fischer Taschenbuch, 1970).

3 Secondary Sources

ABRECHT, CLAUDIA, 'Hofmannsthals "Weltgeheimnis" und *Die Lehrlinge zu Sais* des Novalis', *Hofmannsthal-Blätter*, 16 (1976), 201–8.

ADORNO, THEODOR W., 'George und Hofmannsthal: Zum Briefwechsel', in *Prismen: Kulturkritik und Gesellschaft* (Frankfurt am Main: Suhrkamp, 1955), 232–82.

ALEWYN, RICHARD, *Über Hugo von Hofmannsthal*, 4th extended edn., Kleine Vandenhoeck-Reihe 57, 57a, 57b (Göttingen: Vandenhoeck & Ruprecht, 1967).

ALT, PETER-ANDRÉ, 'Hofmannsthal und die "Blätter für die Kunst"', in Klaus Deterding (ed.), *Wahrnehmungen im Poetischen All: Festschrift für Alfred Behrmann zum 65. Geburtstag* (Heidelberg: Winter, 1993), 30–49.

AUDEN, W. H., 'Making, Knowing and Judging' (1956) in *The Dyer's Hand and Other Essays* (London: Faber, 1963; repr. 1975), 31–60.

AUSTIN, LLOYD JAMES, *L'Univers poétique de Baudelaire: Symbolisme et symbolique* (Paris: Mercure de France, 1956).

BALAKIAN, ANNA, *The Symbolist Movement: A Critical Appraisal* (New York: New York University Press, 1977).

BAREA, ILSE, *Vienna: Legend and Reality* (London: Secker & Warburg, 1966).

BARKER, ANDREW W., '"Der große Überwinder": Hermann Bahr and the Rejection of Naturalism', *Modern Language Review*, 78 (1983), 617–30.

BAUER, ROGER, *Das Treibhaus oder der Garten des Bösen: Ursprung und Wandlung eines Motivs der Dekadenzliteratur*, Abhandlungen der Geistes- und Sozialwissenschaftlichen Klasse, Akademie der Wissenschaften und der Literatur, 1979/12 (Wiesbaden: Steiner, 1979).

—— 'Gänsefüßchendékadence: Zur Kritik und Literatur der Jahrhundertwende in Wien', *Literatur und Kritik*, 191/2 (1985), 21–9.

—— 'Le Poème en prose autrichien de Baudelaire à Peter Altenberg', *Romanica Wratislavensia*, 36 (1991), 239–53.

—— 'Deux "Décadents" inattendus: Édouard Rod et J. H. Rosny vus par Hermann Bahr', in *Les Songes de la raison: Mélanges offerts à Dominique Jehl* (Berne: Lang, 1995), 408–17.

BÉGUIN, ALBERT, *L'Âme romantique et le rêve: Essai sur le romantisme allemand et la poésie française* (Paris: Corti, 1946).

BERNARD, SUZANNE, *Le Poème en prose de Baudelaire jusqu'à nos jours* (Paris: Nizet, 1959).

BERNER, PETER, BRIX, EMIL, and MANTL, WOLFGANG (eds.), *Wien um 1900: Aufbruch in die Moderne* (Munich: R. Oldenbourg Verlag, 1986).

BERSANI, LEO, *The Death of Stéphane Mallarmé* (Cambridge: Cambridge University Press: 1982).

BIANQUIS, GENEVIÈVE, *La Poésie autrichienne de Hofmannsthal à Rilke* (Paris: Presses Universitaires, 1926).

—— 'Hofmannsthal et la France', *Revue de littérature comparée*, 27 (1953), 301–18.

BLOCK, HASKELL M., 'Hugo von Hofmannstahl [*sic*] and the Symbolist Drama', *Transactions of the Wisconsin Academy of Sciences, Arts and Letters*, 48 (1959), 161–78.

BLOOM, HAROLD, *The Anxiety of Influence: A Theory of Poetry* (New York: Oxford University Press, 1973).

—— 'Walter Pater: The Intoxication of Belatedness', *Yale French Studies,* 50 (1974), 163–89.

—— *Poetry and Repression* (New Haven: Yale University Press, 1976).

BOEHRINGER, ROBERT, *Mein Bild von Stefan George,* 2 vols., 2nd extended edn. (Düsseldorf: Küpper-Bondi, 1968).

BÖSCHENSTEIN, BERNHARD, 'Wirkungen des französischen Symbolismus auf die deutsche Lyrik der Jahrhundertwende', *Euphorion,* 58 (1964), 375–95.

—— 'Hofmannsthal und der europäische Symbolismus', in Wolfram Mauser (ed.), *Hofmannsthal-Forschungen,* ii (Freiburg i.Br.: Hofmannsthal-Gesellschaft, 1974), 73–86; repr. with minor changes as 'Hofmannsthal, George und die französischen Symbolisten', in *Arcadia,* 10 (1975), 158–70 and in *Leuchttürme: Von Hölderlin zu Celan: Wirkung und Vergleich* (Frankfurt am Main: Insel, 1977), 224–46.

BOGOSAVLJEVIĆ, SRDAN, 'Der Amiel-Aufsatz. Zum Dilettantismus- und Décadence-Begriff des jungen Hofmannsthal', in Wolfram Mauser (ed.), *Hofmannsthal-Forschungen,* ix: *Hofmannsthal und Frankreich* (Freiburg i.Br.: Hofmannsthal-Gesellschaft, 1987), 207–35.

BOWIE, MALCOLM, *Mallarmé and the Art of Being Difficult* (Cambridge: Cambridge University Press, 1978).

BRADBURY, MALCOLM and McFARLANE, JAMES (eds.), *Modernism 1890–1930* (London: Pelican, 1976).

BRINKMANN, RICHARD, 'Hofmannsthal und die Sprache', *Deutsche Vierteljahrsschrift für Literaturwissenschaft und Geistesgeschichte,* 35 (1961), 69–95.

BRIX, EMIL and WERKNER, PATRICK (eds.), *Die Wiener Moderne: Ergebnisse eines Forschungsgespräches der Arbeitsgemeinschaft Wien um 1900 zum Thema 'Aktualität und Moderne'* (Vienna: Verlag für Geschichte und Politik and R. Oldenbourg Verlag, 1990).

BROCH, HERMANN, 'Hofmannsthal und seine Zeit: Eine Studie', in Paul Michael Lützeler (ed.), *Kommentierte Werkausgabe* (Frankfurt am Main: Suhrkamp, 1974–81), xi/i: *Schriften zur Literatur 1: Kritik* (1975), 111–75.

BROMBERT, VICTOR, ' "Le Cygne" de Baudelaire: Douleur, souvenir, travail', in *Études Baudelairiennes 3: Hommage à W. T. Bandy* (Neuchâtel: Éditions de la Baconière, 1973), 254–61.

—— *Victor Hugo and the Visionary Novel* (Cambridge, Mass.: Harvard University Press, 1984).

BRÜCKLER, SILKE, 'Hugo von Hofmannsthal und Maurice Maeterlinck' (unpublished doctoral thesis, University of Würzburg, 1953).

BURCKHARDT, SIGURD, 'The Poetry of Hugo von Hofmannsthal', *Hudson Review,* 14 (1961), 474–80.

BURGER, HILDE, 'French Influences on Hugo von Hofmannsthal', in W. P. Friedrich (ed.), *Comparative Literature 2: Proceedings of the Second Congress of the ICLA,* University of North Carolina Studies in Comparative Literature 24 (Chapel

Hill: University of North Carolina Press, 1959), 691–7.

—— 'Hofmannsthal: Ses relations avec la Belgique et la Suisse', *Revue de littérature comparée*, 36 (1962), 369–76.

—— 'Marie-Gabriel Dubray (1846–1915): Professeur de français de Hofmannsthal', *Études danubiennes*, 2.1 (1986), 49–62.

BUTLER, JOHN DAVIS, *Jean Moréas: A Critique of his Poetry and Philosophy* (The Hague: Mouton, 1967).

CASTLE, EDUARD (ed.), *Deutsch-Österreichische Literaturgeschichte. Ein Handbuch zur Geschichte der deutschen Literatur in Österreich-Ungarn*, iv: *1890–1918* (Vienna: C. Fromme, 1927).

CHASTEL, EMILE, *Hermann Bahr: Son Œuvre et son temps: De l'enfance à la maturité* (Lille: Champion, 1977).

CLAUDON, FRANCIS, *Hofmannsthal et la France*, European University Studies, Series XVIII: Comparative Literature 21 (Berne: Peter Lang, 1979).

CORBINEAU-HOFFMANN, ANGELIKA, ' "... zuweilen beim Vorübergehen ...": Ein Motiv Hofmannsthals im Kontext der Moderne', *Hofmannsthal-Jahrbuch*, 1 (1993), 235–62.

CORNELL, KENNETH, *The Symbolist Movement* (New Haven: Yale University Press, 1951).

CULLER, JONATHAN, 'Intertextuality and Interpretation: Baudelaire's "Correspondances" ', in Christopher Prendergast (ed.), *Nineteenth-Century French Poetry* (Cambridge: Cambridge University Press, 1990), 118–37.

CURTIUS, ERNST ROBERT, 'Zu Hofmannsthals Gedächtnis', in *Kritische Essays zur europäischen Literatur* (Berne: Franke, 1950; pbk edn., Frankfurt am Main: Fischer Taschenbuch, 1984), 158–71.

DAVIAU, DONALD, 'The Misconception of Hermann Bahr as a "Verwandlungskünstler" ', *German Life and Letters*, 11 (1957–8), 182–92.

—— 'Hermann Bahr's *Nachlaß*', *Journal of the International Arthur Schnitzler Research Association*, 2/3 (1963), 4–27.

—— 'Hermann Bahr and Decadence', *Modern Austrian Literature*, 10.2 (1977), 52–100.

—— *Der Mann von Übermorgen: Hermann Bahr 1863–1934* (Vienna: Österreichischer Bundesverlag, 1984).

—— 'Hugo von Hofmannsthal, Stefan George und der *Chandos-Brief*: Eine neue Perspektive auf Hofmannsthals sogenannte Sprachkrise', in Karl Konrad Polheim (ed.), *Sinn und Symbol: Festschrift für Joseph P. Strelka zum 60. Geburtstag* (Berne: Peter Lang, 1987), 229–48.

DAVID, CLAUDE, 'Hofmannsthals Frankreich-Bild', *Arcadia*, 5 (1970), 162–75.

—— 'Hofmannsthal als Leser des französischen Schrifttums', in Wolfram Mauser (ed.), *Hofmannsthal-Forschungen*, 9: *Hofmannsthal und Frankreich* (Freiburg i.Br.: Hofmannsthal-Gesellschaft, 1987), 9–18.

DIERSCH, MANFRED, *Empiriokritizismus und Impressionismus: Über Beziehungen zur Philosophie, Ästhetik und Literatur um 1900 in Wien*, Neue Beiträge zur Literaturwissenschaft 36 (Berlin: Rütten & Loening, 1973), 127–45.

DIERSCH, MANFRED, 'Vereinsamung und Selbstentfremdung als Lebenserfahrung Wiener Dichter um 1900' repr. in Viktor Žmegač (ed.), *Deutsche Literatur der Jahrhundertwende* (Königstein: Athenäum etc., 1981), 81–106.

DURZAK, MANFRED, *Der junge Stefan George: Kunsttheorie und Dichtung*, Zur Erkenntnis der Dichtung 3 (Munich: Fink, 1968).

—— *Zwischen Expressionismus und Symbolismus: Stefan George*, Sprache und Literatur 89 (Stuttgart: Kohlhammer, 1974).

DUTHIE, ENID, *L'Influence du symbolisme français dans le renouveau poétique de l'Allemagne: Les Blätter für die Kunst de 1892 à 1900* (Paris: Champion, 1933).

ELIOT, T. S., *For Lancelot Andrewes* (London: Faber, 1928; new edn. 1970).

—— *Selected Prose*, ed. John Hayward (Harmondsworth: Penguin, 1953; repr. Peregrine, 1963).

ETIEMBLE, *Le Mythe de Rimbaud*, i: *Genèse du mythe, 1869–1949* (Paris: nrf, 1954); ii: *Structure du mythe* (Paris: nrf, 1952).

—— *Le Sonnet des voyelles: De l'audition colorée à la vision érotique* (Paris: Gallimard, 1968).

EXNER, RICHARD, *Hugo von Hofmannsthals 'Lebenslied'* (Heidelberg: Winter, 1964).

FABER DU FAUR, CURT VON, 'Stefan George et le symbolisme français', *Comparative Literature*, 5 (1953), 151–66.

FAIRLIE, ALISON, *Baudelaire: Les Fleurs du mal*, Studies in French Literature 6 (London: Arnold, 1960).

FECHNER, JÖRG-ULRICH, 'Erfahrungen spanischer Wirklichkeit in frühen Gedichten Stefan Georges: Zum Verständnis von "Als durch die dämmerung jähe", "Verjährte fahrten II" und "Der infant"', *Castrum Peregrini*, 138 (1978), 52–76.

FIECHTNER, HELMUT, 'Hofmannsthal und Frankreich', *Literatur und Kritik*, 135 (1979), 260–75.

FISCHER, JENS MALTE, 'Dekadenz und Entartung: Max Nordau als Kritiker des Fin de siècle', in Roger Bauer et al. (eds.), *Fin de Siècle: Zu Literatur und Kunst der Jahrhundertwende*, Studien zur Philologie und Literatur des neunzehnten Jahrhunderts 35 (Frankfurt am Main: Klostermann, 1977), 93–111.

—— *Fin-de-siècle: Kommentar zu einer Epoche* (Munich: Winkler, 1978).

FOWLIE, WALLACE, *Mallarmé* (London: Dobson, 1953).

FRANKLIN, URSULA, 'The Quest for the Black Flower: Baudelairean and Mallarméan Inspirations in Stefan George's *Algabal*', *Comparative Literature Studies*, 16 (1979), 131–40.

—— 'Two German Poets "Autour d'Hérodiade": A Spark of Heine and a Georgean Afterglow', in Will L. McLendon (ed.), *L'Hénaurme Siècle: A Miscellany of Essays on Nineteenth-Century French Literature* (Heidelberg: Winter, 1984), 175–86.

FRIEDRICH, HUGO, *Die Struktur der modernen Lyrik: Von Baudelaire bis zur Gegenwart* (Hamburg: Rowohlt, 1956).

FÜLLEBORN, ULRICH, *Das deutsche Prosagedicht* (Munich: Fink, 1970).

FURNESS, RAYMOND, 'Trakl and the Literature of Decadence', in Walter Methlagl and William E. Yuill (eds.), *Londoner Trakl-Symposion*, Trakl-Studien 10 (Salzburg: Müller, 1981), 82–95.

FURST, LILIAN, *Romanticism in Perspective* (London: Macmillan, 1969).

—— *Counterparts: The Dynamics of Franco-German Literary Relationships, 1770–1895* (London: Methuen, 1977).

GLENN, JERRY, 'Hofmannsthal, George and Nietzsche: "Herrn Stefan George | einem, der vorübergeht"', *Modern Language Notes*, 97 (1982), 770–3.

GNÜG, HILTRUD, *Entstehung und Krise lyrischer Subjektivität: Vom klassischen lyrischen Ich zur modernen Erfahrungswirklichkeit* (Stuttgart: Metzler, 1983).

GOFF, PENRITH, 'Hugo von Hofmannsthal: The Symbol as Experience', *Kentucky Foreign Language Quarterly*, 7 (1960), 196–200.

—— 'Hugo von Hofmannsthal and the Aesthetic Experience', *Papers on Language and Literature*, 4 (1968), 414–19.

GORCEIX, PAUL, 'Sur la rencontre de Hermann Bahr avec le symbolisme franco-belge', in *Les Songes de la raison: Mélanges offerts à Dominique Jehl* (Berne: Lang, 1995), 273–88.

GRAY, MARY O. R., 'Hugo von Hofmannsthal and Nineteenth Century French Symbolism', Ph.D. thesis (Trinity College, Dublin, 1951).

GRIMM, REINHOLD, 'Zur Wirkungsgeschichte Maurice Maeterlincks in der deutschsprachigen Literatur', *Revue de littérature comparée*, 33 (1959), 535–44.

—— 'Das einzige Gesetz und das bittere: Hofmannsthals "Schicksalslied"', in Benjamin Bennett et al. (eds.), *Probleme der Moderne: Studien zur deutschen Literatur von Nietzsche bis Brecht: Festschrift zum 65. Geburtstag von Walter Sokel* (Tübingen: Niemeyer, 1983), 143–64.

GSTEIGER, MANFRED, *Französische Symbolisten in der deutschen Literatur der Jahrhundertwende (1896–1914)* (Berne: Franke, 1971).

HAMANN, RICHARD, and HERMAND, JOST, *Impressionismus*, Deutsche Kunst und Kultur von der Gründerzeit bis zum Expressionismus 3, 2nd edn. (Berlin: Akademie-Verlag, 1966).

HAMBURGER, MICHAEL, *Reason and Energy: Studies in German Literature* (London: Routledge & Kegan Paul, 1957).

—— 'Hofmannsthals Bibliothek: Ein Bericht', *Euphorion*, 55 (1961), 15–76.

HEANEY, SEAMUS, '"The Fire i' the Flint": Reflections on the Poetry of Gerard Manley Hopkins', *Proceedings of the British Academy*, 60 (1974), 413–29.

—— 'The Interesting Case of Nero, Chekhov's Cognac and a Knocker', in *The Government of the Tongue: The 1986 T. S. Eliot Memorial Lectures and Other Critical Writings* (London: Faber, 1988), pp. xi–xxiii.

HIRSCH, RUDOLF, *Beiträge zum Verständnis Hugo von Hofmannsthals*, ed. Matthias Mayer (Frankfurt am Main: S. Fischer, 1995).

HOBOHN, FREYA, *Die Bedeutung französischer Dichter in Werk und Weltbild Stefan Georges (Baudelaire, Verlaine, Mallarmé)* (Marburg a.Lahn: N. G. Elwert, 1931), rep. Kölner Romanistische Arbeiten, ed. Leo Spitzer, 3 (New York: Johnson Reprint

Corporation, 1968).

HOFFMANN, PAUL, *Symbolismus*, Deutsche Literatur im 20. Jahrhundert 2 (Munich: Fink, 1987).

HOLZER, RUDOLF, *Villa Wertheimstein: Haus der Genie und Dämonen. Mit unveröffentlichten Briefen und Tagebuch-Aufzeichnungen*, Österreichische Reihe 118/20 (Vienna: Bergland, 1960).

HOPPE, MANFRED, *Literatentum, Magie und Mystik im Frühwerk Hugo von Hofmannsthals*, Quellen und Forschungen zur Sprach- und Kulturgeschichte der germanischen Völker, NS 28 (Berlin: de Gruyter, 1968).

—— 'Der Prophet: Hofmannsthals Gedichte an Stefan George', *Neue Zürcher Zeitung* (Fernausgabe), 3 Feb. 1974, 51–2.

HOUGH, GRAHAM, *The Last Romantics* (London: Duckworth, 1949).

HOWE, PATRICIA, 'Hofmannsthal and Keats', in W. E. Yuill and Patricia Howe (eds.), *Hugo von Hofmannsthal (1874–1929): Commemorative Essays* (London: University of London, 1981), 21–34.

JACOBS, MARGARET, 'Hugo von Hofmannsthal: *Das Bergwerk zu Falun*', in F. Norman (ed.), *Hofmannsthal: Studies in Commemoration* (London: University of London Institute of Germanic Studies, 1963), 53–82.

JEHL, DOMINIQUE, 'Hofmannsthal und Baudelaire', in Wolfram Mauser (ed.), *Hofmannsthal-Forschungen*, ix: *Hofmannsthal und Frankreich* (Freiburg i.Br.: Hofmannsthal-Gesellschaft, 1987), 117–33.

JOHNSON, BARBARA, *Défigurations du langage poétique* (Paris: Flammarion, 1979).

—— '*Les Fleurs du mal armé*: Some Reflections on Intertextuality', in Harold Bloom (ed.), *Stéphane Mallarmé*, Modern Critical Views (New York: Chelsea House, 1987), 211–27.

JONES, P. MANSELL, 'Poe, Baudelaire and Mallarmé: A Problem of Literary Judgement', in *The Background of Modern French Poetry: Essays and Interviews* (Cambridge: Cambridge University Press, 1951), 38–58.

—— 'Poe and Baudelaire: The "Affinity"', in *The Background of Modern French Poetry: Essays and Interviews* (Cambridge: Cambridge University Press, 1951), 59–68.

KAYSER, WOLFGANG, *Das sprachliche Kunstwerk: Eine Einführung in die Literaturwissenschaft* (Berne: Franke, 1948).

KERMODE, FRANK, *Romantic Image* (London: Routledge & Kegan Paul, 1957; repr. 1986).

KLIENEBERGER, H. R., 'Hofmannsthal and Leopold Andrian', *Modern Language Review*, 80 (1985), 619–36.

—— *George, Rilke, Hofmannsthal and the Romantic Tradition*, Stuttgarter Arbeiten zur Germanistik 259 (Stuttgart: Heinz, 1991).

KNACKFUß, H., *Michelangelo*, Künstler-Monographien 4 (Bielefeld: Velhagen & Klasing, 1895; 9th edn., 1907).

KNAUTH, K. ALFONS, 'Formen französischer und italienischer Morgenpoesie: Tradition und Transformation in Rimbauds "Aube"', *Arcadia*, 14 (1979), 271–91.

KOBEL, ERWIN, 'Magie und Ewigkeit: Überlegungen zu Hofmannsthals Gedicht "Vor Tag" ', *Jahrbuch der Deutschen Schiller-Gesellschaft*, 21 (1977), 352–92.

KOSCHMAL, WALTER, *Vom Realismus zum Symbolismus: Zu Genese und Morphologie der Symbolsprache in den späten Werken I. S. Turgenevs*, Studies in Slavic Literature and Poetics 5 (Amsterdam: Rodopi, 1984).

KOVACH, THOMAS A., *Hofmannsthal and Symbolism: Art and Life in the Work of a Modern Poet*, American University Studies, Series III: Comparative Literature, 18 (New York: Peter Lang, 1985).

KRAFT, WERNER, *Augenblicke der Dichtung: Kritische Betrachtungen* (Munich: Kosel-Verlag, 1964).

KUNA, FRANZ, 'The Expense of Silence: Sincerity and Strategy in Hofmannsthal's Chandos Letter', *Publications of the English Goethe Society*, NS 40 (1970), 69–94.

LANDAUER, GUSTAV, *Skepsis und Mystik. Versuche im Anschluß an Mauthners Sprachkritik* (Berlin: Egon Fleischel & Co., 1903).

LAUSTER, MARTINA, *Die Objektivität des Innenraums: Studien zur Lyrik Georges, Hofmannsthals und Rilkes*, Stuttgarter Arbeiten zur Germanistik 113 (Stuttgart: Heinz, 1982).

LAWLER, JAMES R., *Edgar Poe et les poètes français*, Conférences, essais et leçons du Collège de France (Paris: Julliard, 1989).

LEAKEY, FELIX W., *Baudelaire and Nature* (Manchester: Manchester University Press, 1969).

—— 'The Originality of Baudelaire's "Le Cygne": Genesis as Structure and Theme', in E. M. Beaumont et al. (eds.), *Order and Adventure in Post-Romantic French Poetry: Essays Presented to C. A. Hackett* (Oxford: Oxford University Press, 1973), 38–55.

LEHMANN, A. G., *The Symbolist Aesthetic in France 1885–1895* (Oxford: Blackwell, 1968).

LEMAÎTRE, JULES, *Les Contemporains: Études et portraits littéraires*, 7 vols. (Paris: Lecène & Oudin, 1885–99).

LEMONNIER, LÉON, *Edgar Poe et les poètes français* (Paris: Éditions de la Nouvelle Revue Critique, 1932).

LE RIDER, JACQUES, 'Between Modernism and Postmodernism: The Viennese Identity Crisis', trans. Ralph Manheim, in Edward Timms and Ritchie Robertson (eds.), *Austrian Studies*, i: *Vienna 1900: From Altenberg to Wittgenstein* (Edinburgh: Edinburgh University Press, 1990), 1–11.

—— *Modernité viennoise et crises de l'identité* (Paris: Presses Universitaires de France, 1990).

—— *Hugo von Hofmannsthal: Historicisme et modernité*, Perspectives Germaniques (Paris: Presses Universitaires de France, 1995).

LEWIS, HANNA B., 'Hofmannsthal, Shelley, and Keats', *German Life and Letters*, 27 (1973–4), 220–34.

LLOYD, ROSEMARY, *Baudelaire's Literary Criticism* (Cambridge: Cambridge University Press, 1981).

LLOYD, ROSEMARY, *Mallarmé: Poésies*, Critical Guides to French Texts 42 (London: Grant & Cutler, 1984).

MAN, PAUL DE, 'Lyric and Modernity', in *Blindness and Insight: Essays in the Rhetoric of Contemporary Criticism*, 2nd edn., revised (London: Methuen, 1983), 166–86.

—— *The Rhetoric of Romanticism* (New York: Columbia University Press, 1984).

MAYER, MATTHIAS, ' "Intérieur" und "Nature morte": Bilder des Lebens bei Maeterlinck und Hofmannsthal', *Études Germaniques*, 46 (1991), 305–24.

MEESSEN, H. J., 'Stefan Georges *Algabal* und die französische *Décadence*', *Monatshefte für Deutschunterricht*, 39 (1947), 304–21.

MENNEMEIER, FRANZ NORBERT, 'Gesellschaftliches bei Hugo von Hofmannsthal', in Joachim Bark (ed.), *Literatursoziologie* (Stuttgart: Kohlhammer, 1974), ii. 181–91.

—— *Literatur der Jahrhundertwende*, Germanistische Lehrbuchsammlung 39, 2 vols. (Frankfurt am Main: Peter Lang, 1985–8).

MEWS, SIEGFRIED, 'Information and Propagation: A German Mediator of "Weltliteratur" in the Late Nineteenth Century', *Revue de littérature comparée*, 42 (1968), 50–75.

MICHAUD, GUY, *Message poétique du symbolisme* (Paris: Nizet, 1947; repr. 1961).

MICHELSEN, PETER, 'ABEND: Zu einigen Gedichten Hugo von Hofmannsthals', in *Zeit und Bindung: Studien zur deutschen Literatur der Moderne* (Göttingen: Vandenhoeck & Ruprecht, 1976), 25–39.

MILCH, WERNER, 'Hugo von Hofmannsthal' (unpublished thesis, [n.p.], [1938(?)]).

MOCKEL, ALBERT, 'Quelques Souvenirs sur Stefan George', *Revue d'Allemagne*, 2 (1928), 385–96.

MORTON, MICHAEL, 'Chandos and his Plans', *Deutsche Vierteljahrsschrift für Literaturwissenschaft und Geistesgeschichte*, 62 (1988), 385–96.

MRAVLAG, LENE, 'Der Symbolismus in Frankreich, der Symbolismus in Deutschland und Versuch einer Gegenüberstellung', Ph.D. thesis (Vienna, 1938).

MÜLLER, KARL JOHANN, *Das Dekadenzproblem in der österreichischen Literatur um die Jahrhundertwende, dargelegt an Texten von Hermann Bahr, Richard von Schaukal, Hugo von Hofmannsthal und Leopold von Andrian* (Stuttgart: Heinz, 1977).

NAUMANN, WALTER, 'Hofmannsthals Verhältnis zur Tradition', *Deutsche Rundschau*, 85 (1959), 612–25.

NAUTZ, JÜRGEN P., and VAHRENKAMP, RICHARD, *Die Wiener Jahrhundertwende* (Vienna: Böhlau, 1993).

NEUMANN, GERHARD, 'Proverb in Versen oder Schöpfungsmysterium? Hofmannsthals Einakter zwischen Sprach-Spiel und Augen-Blick', *Hofmannsthal-Jahrbuch*, 1 (1993), 183–234.

NIENHAUS, STEFAN, *Das deutsche Prosagedicht im Wien der Jahrhundertwende: Altenberg—Hofmannsthal—Polgar*, Quellen und Forschungen zur Sprach- und Kulturgeschichte der germanischen Völker, NS 85 (Berlin: de Gruyter, 1986).

—— 'Die "scharfe Spitze der Unendlichkeit": Bedeutungen eines Baudelaire-Zitats im Werk Hugo von Hofmannsthals', *Poetica*, 21 (1989), 84–97.

OCKENDEN, RAY, 'Stefan George and the Heritage of Romanticism', in Hanne Castein and Alexander Stillmark (eds.), *Deutsche Romantik und das 20. Jahrhundert: Londoner Symposium 1985* (Stuttgart: Hans-Dieter Heinz, 1986), 41–59.

PAUGET, MICHÈLE, *L'Interrogation sur l'art dans l'œuvre essayistique de Hugo von Hofmannsthal: Analyse de configurations* (Frankfurt am Main: Peter Lang, 1984).

PAUL, LOTHAR, 'Subjektivität. Geschichtliche Logik in lyrischer Gestalt. Hugo von Hofmannsthal: "Manche freilich" ', in Christa Bürger et al. (eds.), *Naturalismus / Ästhetizismus* (Frankfurt am Main: Suhrkamp, 1979), 139–61.

PERL, WALTER H., *Das lyrische Jugendwerk Hugo von Hofmannsthals*, Germanische Studien 173 (Berlin: Dr Emil Ebering, 1936).

—— 'Leopold von Andrian, ein vergessener Dichter des Symbolismus, Freund Georges und Hofmannsthals', *Philobiblon* (Dec. 1958), 302–9.

—— 'Visionen der Jugend: Leopold Andrian und der literarische Symbolismus', *Neue Zürcher Zeitung* (15 Nov. 1966), 28.

—— 'Der österreichische Symbolismus 1890–1900', *Duitse Kroniek*, 23 (1971), 133–43.

POR, PETER, 'Paradigmawechsel: Der gemeinsame Anfang von George, Hofmannsthal und Rilke', in *Der Körper des Turmes: Essays zur europäischen Literatur von Schiller bis Valéry* (Frankfurt am Main: Peter Lang, 1988), 145–81.

PRAWER, S. S., *German Lyric Poetry: A Critical Analysis of Selected Poems from Klopstock to Rilke* (London: Routledge & Kegan Paul, 1952).

PRAZ, MARIO, *The Romantic Agony*, trans. Angus Davidson, 2nd edn. (Oxford: Oxford University Press, 1951; reissued 1970).

RASCH, WOLFDIETRICH, *Die literarische Décadence um 1900* (Munich: Beck, 1986).

RAYMOND, MARCEL, *De Baudelaire au surréalisme* (Paris: Corti, 1947; repr. 1985).

REID, J. H., ' "Draussen sind wir zu finden . . .": The Development of a Hofmannsthal Symbol', *German Life and Letters*, 27 (1973–4), 35–51.

RENNER, URSULA, ' "Die Tiefe muß man verstecken—wo? An der Oberfläche": Allegorisierung als Verfahren der Moderne in Hofmannsthals "Glück am Weg" ', in Jacques Le Rider (ed.), *Austriaca*, 37: *Modernité de Hofmannsthal* (Rouen: Université de Rouen, 1993), 253–65.

RESCH, MARGIT, *Das Symbol als Prozeß bei Hugo von Hofmannsthal*, Hochschulschriften: Literaturwissenschaft 48 (Königstein/Ts.: Forum Academicum, 1980).

—— (ed.), *Seltene Augenblicke: Interpretations of Poems by Hugo von Hofmannsthal*, Studies in German Literature and Culture 40 (Columbia, SC: Camden House, 1989).

RIECKMANN, JENS, 'Narziss und Dionysos: Leopold von Andrians *Der Garten der Erkenntnis*', *Modern Austrian Literature*, 16.2 (1983), 65–81.

—— *Aufbruch in die Moderne: Die Anfänge des Jungen Wien: Österreichische Literatur und Kritik im Fin de Siècle* (Königstein/Ts.: Athenäum, 1985).

—— 'Zwischen Bewußtsein und Verdrängung: Hofmannsthals jüdisches Erbe', *Deutsche Vierteljahrsschrift für Literaturwissenschaft und Geistesgeschichte*, 67 (1993), 466–83.

RIECKMANN, JENS, '(Anti-)Semitism and Homoeroticism: Hofmannsthal's Reading of Bahr's Novel "Die Rotte Korah" ', *German Quarterly*, 66 (1993), 212–21.

RIZZA, STEVE, *Rudolf Kassner and Hugo von Hofmannsthal: Criticism as Art*, Tübinger Studien zur deutschen Literatur 16 (Frankfurt am Main: Peter Lang, 1997).

ROBERTSON, RITCHIE, 'The Theme of Sacrifice in Hofmannsthal's *Das Gespräch über Gedichte*', *Modern Austrian Literature*, 23.1 (1990), 19–33.

ROBINSON, CHRISTOPHER, *French Literature in the Nineteenth Century* (Newton Abbot: David & Charles, 1978).

ROSSBACHER, KARLHEINZ, *Literatur und Liberalismus: Zur Kultur der Ringstraßenzeit in Wien* (Vienna: J. & V. Edition, 1992).

—— 'Warum schrieben sie? Dichtende Nicht-Dichter in einem Wiener Familienverband des 19. Jahrhunderts. Diskretes Schreiben in Lebenskrisen. Ein inspiratives Milieu für den jungen Hofmannsthal?', *Sprachkunst: Beiträge zur Literaturwissenschaft*, 27.2 (1996), 218–38.

RYAN, JUDITH, 'Die "allomatische Lösung": Gespaltene Persönlichkeit und Konfiguration bei Hugo von Hofmannsthal', *Deutsche Vierteljahrsschrift für Literaturwissenschaft und Geistesgeschichte*, 44 (1970), 189–207.

SAINT-PAUL, ALBERT, 'Stefan George et le Symbolisme français', *Revue d'Allemagne et des pays de langue allemande*, 13/14 (1928), 397–405.

SALZMANN, KARL H., ' "Pan": Geschichte einer Zeitschrift', in Jost Hermand (ed.), *Jugendstil* (Darmstadt: Wissenschaftliche Buchgesellschaft, 1971), 178–208; originally in *Archiv für die Geschichte des Buchwesens*, 1 (1958), 212–25.

SAUL, NICHOLAS, 'Hofmannsthal and Novalis', in G. J. Carr and Eda Sagarra (eds.), *Fin de siècle Vienna: Proceedings of the Second Irish Symposium in Austrian Studies* (Dublin: Trinity College, 1985), 26–62.

SCHEICHL, SIGURD PAUL, 'La Place des revues et journaux dans la vie littéraire à Vienne', in François Latraverse and Walter Moser (eds.), *Vienne au tournant du siècle* (Paris: Albin Michel, 1988), 333–57.

SCHLAWE, FRITZ, *Literarische Zeitschriften 1885–1910* (Stuttgart: Metzler, 1961).

SCHMIDT-DENGLER, WENDELIN, 'Französischer Symbolismus und Wiener Dekadenz', in Mark Ward (ed.), *From Vormärz to Fin de Siècle: Essays in Nineteenth-Century Austrian Literature* (Blairgowrie: Lochee Publications, 1986), 73–89.

SCHNITZLER, OLGA, *Spiegelbild der Freundschaft* (Salzburg: Residenz Verlag, 1962).

SCHOENBERG, BARBARA Z., 'The Influence of the French Prose Poem on Peter Altenberg', *Modern Austrian Literature*, 22.3 (1989), 15–32.

SCHORSKE, CARL E., *Fin-de-Siècle Vienna: Politics and Culture* (New York: Knopf, 1980; repr. New York: Vintage, 1981).

SCHULTZ, H. STEFAN, 'Hofmannsthal and Bacon: The Sources of the Chandos Letter', *Comparative Literature*, 13 (1961), 1–15.

SCHULZ-BUSCHHAUS, ULRICH, 'Der Tod des "Dilettanten": Über Hofmannsthal und Paul Bourget', in Michael Rössner and Birgit Wagner (eds.), *Aufstieg und Krise der Vernunft: Komparatistische Studien zur Literatur der Aufklärung und des Fin-de-siècle* (Vienna: Böhlau, 1984), 181–95.

SCOTT, CLIVE, *A Question of Syllables: Essays in Nineteenth-Century French Verse* (Cambridge: Cambridge University Press, 1986).

—— *The Riches of Rhyme: Studies in French Verse* (Oxford: Clarendon Press, 1988).

—— *Vers Libre: The Emergence of Free Verse in France 1886–1914* (Oxford: Clarendon Press, 1990).

SEELEY, FRANK FRIEDEBERG, *Turgenev: A Reading of his Fiction*, Cambridge Studies in Russian Literature (Cambridge: Cambridge University Press, 1991).

SEYLAZ, LOUIS, *Edgar Poe et les premiers symbolistes français* (Lausanne: Imprimerie La Concorde, 1923).

SIMONIS, ANNETTE, 'Hofmannsthal und die englische Tradition—Rezeption und Adaptation englischsprachiger Literatur in den Schriften Hugo von Hofmannsthals', *Arcadia*, 30 (1995), 286–302.

SIOR, MARIE-LUISE, 'Stefan George und der französische Symbolismus', Ph.D. thesis (Giessen, 1932).

SOERGEL, ALBERT, *Dichtung und Dichter der Zeit: Eine Schilderung der deutschen Literatur der letzten Jahrzehnte*, 5th edn. (Leipzig: Voigtländer, 1911).

SOMMERHAGE, CLAUS, *Romantische Aporien: Zur Kontinuität des Romantischen bei Novalis, Eichendorff, Hofmannsthal und Handke* (Paderborn: Schöningh, 1993).

SONDRUP, STEVEN P., *Hofmannsthal and the French Symbolist Tradition*, Utah Studies in Literature and Linguistics 4 (Berne: Herbert Lang, 1976).

—— 'Three Notes on Symbolism by Hugo von Hofmannsthal', *Modern Austrian Literature*, 9.2 (1976), 1–9.

SPAHR, ROLAND, 'Hugo von Hofmannsthals Aufzeichnungen zu Jules Hurets *Enquête sur l'évolution littéraire*', *Wirkendes Wort*, 45 (1995), 428–33.

STAHL, ERNEST L., 'The Genesis of Symbolist Theories in Germany', *Modern Language Review*, 41 (1946), 306–17.

STAMM, ULRIKE, *'Ein Kritiker aus dem Willen der Natur': Hugo von Hofmannsthal und das Werk Walter Paters*, Epistemata: Reihe Literaturwissenschaft 213 (Würzburg: Königshausen & Neumann, 1997).

STEFFEN, HANS, 'Hofmannsthals Übernahme der symbolistischen Technik', in Reinhold Grimm and Conrad Wiedemann (eds.), *Literatur und Geistesgeschichte: Festgabe für Heinz Otto Burger* (Berlin: E. Schmidt, 1968), 271–9.

STEINER, HERBERT, 'A Note on "Symbolism"', *Yale French Studies*, 9: *Symbol and Symbolism* ([1952]), 36–9.

STEPHENS, SONYA, *Baudelaire's Prose Poems: The Practice and Politics of Irony* (Oxford: Clarendon Press, 1999).

STERN, MARTIN, 'Böcklin—George—Hofmannsthal', in Karl Pestalozzi and Martin Stern (eds.), *Basler Hofmannsthal-Beiträge* (Würzburg: Königshausen & Neumann, 1991), 89–94.

STERNBERGER, DOLF, 'Jugendstil: Begriff und Physiognomik', in Jost Hermand (ed.), *Jugendstil* (Darmstadt: Wissenschaftliche Buchgesellschaft, 1971), 27–46; originally in *Neue Rundschau*, 2 (1934), 255–71.

STIERLE, K., 'Hugo von Hofmannsthals "Manche freilich"—ein Paris Gedicht?',

Études Germaniques, 45 (1990), 111–29.

STILLMARK, ALEXANDER, 'The Significance of Novalis for Hofmannsthal', in Hanne Castein and Alexander Stillmark (eds.), *Deutsche Romantik und das 20. Jahrhundert: Londoner Symposium 1985* (Stuttgart: Hans-Dieter Heinz, 1986), 61–83.

—— 'Time and Symbol: Yeats and Hofmannsthal as Exponents of Lyrical Drama', in Paul Kirschner and Alexander Stillmark (eds.), *Between Time and Eternity: Nine Essays on W. B. Yeats and his Contemporaries Hofmannsthal and Blok* (Amsterdam: Rodopi, 1992), 97–119.

STOUPY, JOËLLE, 'Hofmannsthals Berührung mit dem Dilettantismusphänomen: Ergänzende Bemerkungen zur Begegnung mit Paul Bourget', in Wolfram Mauser (ed.), *Hofmannsthal-Forschungen*, ix: *Hofmannsthal und Frankreich* (Freiburg i.Br.: Hofmannsthal-Gesellschaft, 1987), 237–64.

STREIM, GREGOR, ' "Die richtige Moderne": Hermann Bahr und die Formierung der literarischen Moderne in Berlin', *Hofmannsthal-Jahrbuch*, 4 (1996), 323–59.

SYMONS, ARTHUR, *The Symbolist Movement in Literature*, introd. Richard Ellmann (London: Constable, 1899; repr. New York: Dutton, 1958).

SZONDI, PETER, *Das lyrische Drama des Fin de siècle*, ed. Henriette Beese (Frankfurt am Main: Suhrkamp, 1975).

TAROT, ROLF, *Hugo von Hofmannsthal: Daseinsformen und dichterische Struktur* (Tübingen: Niemeyer, 1970).

THOMASBERGER, ANDREAS, *Verwandlungen in Hofmannsthals Lyrik: Zur sprachlichen Bedeutung von Genese und Gestalt*, Untersuchungen zur deutschen Literaturgeschichte 70 (Tübingen: Niemeyer, 1994).

TIMMS, EDWARD, *Karl Kraus: Apocalyptic Satirist: Culture and Catastrophe in Habsburg Vienna* (New Haven: Yale University Press, 1986).

—— 'Die Wiener Kreise: Schöpferische Interaktionen in der Wiener Moderne', in Jürgen Nautz and Richard Vahrenkamp (eds.), *Die Wiener Jahrhundertwende: Einflüsse, Umwelt, Wirkungen* (Vienna: Böhlau, 1996), 128–43.

URBACH, REINHARD, 'Hermann Bahrs Wien', *Literatur und Kritik*, 199/200 (1985), 404–8.

VANHELLEPUTTE, MICHEL, 'Hofmannsthal und Maeterlinck', in Wolfram Mauser (ed.), *Hofmannsthal-Forschungen*, i (Freiburg i.Br.: Hofmannsthal-Gesellschaft, 1971), 85–98.

VERBEECK, LUDO, 'Scheidewege am Jahrhundertbeginn: Zu Hofmannsthal und Kafka', in Roger Goffin, Michel Vanhelleputte and Monique Weyembergh-Boussart (eds.), *Littérature et culture allemandes: Hommages à Henri Plard* (Brussels: Éditions de l'Université de Bruxelles, 1985), 271–82.

VILAIN, ROBERT, ' "Wer lügt, macht schlechte Metaphern": Hofmannsthal's "Manche freilich . . ." and Walter Pater', *Deutsche Vierteljahrsschrift für Literaturwissenschaft und Geistesgeschichte*, 65 (1991), 717–54.

—— 'An Innocent Abroad: The Pierrot Figure in German and Austrian Literature at the Turn of the Century', *Publications of the English Goethe Society*, NS 67 (1997), 69–99.

—— '"Stop All the Clocks": Time and Times in the "Vienna Operas" of Hofmannsthal and Strauss', in John R. P. McKenzie and Lesley Sharp (eds.), *The Austrian Comic Tradition: Studies in Honour of W.E. Yates*, Austrian Studies 9 (Edinburgh: Edinburgh University Press, 1998), 185–201.

VIVIER, ROBERT, *L'Originalité de Baudelaire* (Brussels: Palais des Académies, 1926; repr. 1952).

VOLKE, WERNER, *Hugo von Hofmannsthal mit Selbstzeugnissen und Bilddokumenten*, Rowohlts Monographien 127 (Reinbek bei Hamburg: Rowohlt, 1967).

VORDTRIEDE, WERNER, 'Direct Echoes of French Poetry in Stefan George's Works', *Modern Language Notes*, 60 (1945), 461–8.

—— *Novalis und die französischen Symbolisten: Zur Entstehungsgeschichte des dichterischen Symbols*, Sprache und Literatur 8 (Stuttgart: Kohlhammer, 1963).

WAIS, KURT, *Mallarmé: Dichtung—Weisheit—Haltung* (Munich: Beck, 1952).

—— 'Stefan George und Stéphane Mallarmé: Zwei Dichter des Abseits', in Werner Paul Sohnle (ed.), *Stefan George und der Symbolismus: Eine Ausstellung der Württembergischen Landesbibliothek* (Stuttgart: Württembergische Landesbibliothek, 1983), 156–82.

WEISSTEIN, ULRICH, 'Impressionism', in *Encyclopedia of Poetry and Poetics*, enlarged edn. (London: Macmillan, 1975), 381–2.

WELLEK, RENÉ, 'The Concept of Romanticism in Literary History', in *Comparative Literature*, 1 (1949), 1–23, 147–82.

—— 'The Term and Concept of Symbolism in Literary History', in *Discriminations: Further Concepts of Criticism* (New Haven: Yale University Press, 1970), 90–121.

—— 'Hofmannsthal als Literaturkritiker', *Arcadia*, 20 (1985), 61–71.

WHITE, J. J., 'A Reappraisal of the Treatment of Aestheticism in Hugo von Hofmannsthal's *Der Tod des Tizian*', *New German Studies*, 2 (1974), 31–47.

WILSON, EDMUND, *Axel's Castle: A Study of the Imaginative Literature of 1870–1930* (New York: C. Scribner's Sons, 1931).

WILSON, JEAN, *The Challenge of Belatedness: Goethe, Kleist, Hofmannsthal* (Lanham, Md.: University Press of America, 1991).

WINKLER, MICHAEL, 'Hofmannsthal, George, and Poems by Baudelaire: "Herrn Stefan George | einem, der vorübergeht"', *Modern Austrian Literature*, 16.2 (1983), 37–45.

WISCHMANN, ANTJE, *Ästheten und Décadents: Eine Figurenuntersuchung anhand ausgewählter Prosatexte der Autoren H. Bang, J. P. Jacobsen, R. M. Rilke, und H. von Hofmannsthal*, Europäische Hochschulschriften 18.58 (Frankfurt am Main: Peter Lang, 1991).

WOLTERS, FRIEDRICH, *Stefan George und die Blätter für die Kunst: Deutsche Geistesgeschichte seit 1890* (Berlin: Bondi, 1930).

WUNBERG, GOTTHART, *Der frühe Hofmannsthal: Schizophrenie als dichterische Struktur* (Stuttgart: Kohlhammer, 1965).

—— '"Ohne Rücksicht auf Inhalt, lauter venerabilia": Überlegungen zu den Prosagedichten Hugo von Hofmannsthals', in Jacques Le Rider (ed.), *Austriaca*,

37: *Modernité de Hofmannsthal* (Rouen: Université de Rouen, 1993), 319–31.

YATES, W. E., 'Erinnerung und Elegie in der Wiener Literatur 1890–1913', *Literatur und Kritik*, 223/4 (1988), 153–69.

—— 'Hofmannsthal and the Renaissance or: Once more unto "Ein Brief"', *Publications of the English Goethe Society*, NS 61 (1990–1), 99–118.

—— *Schnitzler, Hofmannsthal, and the Austrian Theatre* (New Haven & London: Yale University Press, 1992).

—— *Theatre in Vienna: A Critical History 1776–1995* (Cambridge: Cambridge University Press, 1996).

ZIOLKOWSKI, THEODORE, 'James Joyces Epiphanie und die Überwindung der empirischen Welt in der modernen deutschen Prosa', *Deutsche Vierteljahrsschrift für Literaturwissenschaft und Geistesgeschichte*, 35 (1961), 594–616.

4 Bibliographies, Indexes, Catalogues, Compilations and Other Research Compendia

BARRE, ANDRÉ, *Le Symbolisme*, ii: *Bibliographie de la poésie symboliste* (Paris: Jouve, 1911; repr. New York: Franklin, [n.d.]).

ERKEN, GÜNTHER, 'Hofmannsthal-Chronik: Beitrag zu einer Biographie', *Literaturwissenschaftliches Jahrbuch der Görresgesellschaft*, NS 3 (1962), 239–313.

EXNER, RICHARD, *Index Nominum zu Hugo von Hofmannsthals Gesammelten Werken*, Repertoria Heidelbergensia 1 (Heidelberg: Stiehm, 1976).

FIECHTNER, HELMUT (ed.), *Hugo von Hofmannsthal: Der Dichter im Spiegel der Freunde*, 2nd extended edn. (Berne: Franke, 1963).

GREVE, LUDWIG, and VOLKE, WERNER (eds.), *Jugend in Wien: Literatur um 1900: Katalog der Jahresausstellung 1974*, 2nd edn. (Marbach am Neckar: Deutsches Literaturarchiv, 1987).

HADAMOWSKY, FRANZ (ed.), *Ausstellung Hugo von Hofmannsthal: Katalog* (Salzburg: Amt der Salzburger Landesregierung, 1953).

KOCH, HANS-ALBRECHT, *Hugo von Hofmannsthal*, Erträge der Forschung 265 (Darmstadt: Wissenschaftliche Buchgesellschaft, 1989).

—— AND UTE, KOCH, *Hofmannsthal-Forschungen*, iv: *Hugo von Hofmannsthal: Bibliographie: 1965–1976* (Freiburg i.Br.: Hofmannsthal-Gesellschaft, 1976).

LÜDERS, DETLEV (ed.), *Hugo von Hofmannsthal: 'Gedichte und Kleine Dramen': Ausstellung im Freien Deutschen Hochstift* (Frankfurt am Main: Freies Deutsches Hochstift, 1979).

MAYER, MATTHIAS, *Hugo von Hofmannsthal*, Sammlung Metzler 273 (Stuttgart: Metzler, 1993).

MICHAUD, GUY, *La Doctrine symboliste (documents)* (Paris: Nizet, 1947).

NEUMANN, PETRA (ed.), *Wien und seine Kaffeehäuser. Ein literarischer Streifzug durch die berühmtesten Cafés der Donaumetropole* (Munich: Heyne, 1997).

SOHNLE, WERNER PAUL (ed.), *Stefan George und der Symbolismus: Eine Ausstellung der Württembergischen Landesbibliothek* (Stuttgart: Württembergische Landesbibliothek, 1983).

SONDRUP, STEVEN, AND INGLIS, CRAIG M., *Konkordanz zu den Gedichten Hugo von Hofmannsthals* (Provo, Ut.: Brigham Young University Press, 1977).

WEBER, EUGENE, 'A Chronology of Hofmannsthal's Poems', *Euphorion*, 63 (1969), 284–328.

WUNBERG, GOTTHART (ed.), *Hofmannsthal im Urteil seiner Kritiker* (Frankfurt am Main: Athenäum, 1972).

—— (ed.), *Das junge Wien: Österreichische Literatur- und Kunstkritik 1887–1902*, 2 vols. (Tübingen: Niemeyer, 1976).

INDEX TO HOFMANNSTHAL'S WRITING

GENERAL INDEX

References are included to most proper names cited in the text. This includes passing references by Hofmannsthal in notes or diary entries, since they are evidence of his voracious and eclectic reading habits and many of these references are not otherwise easily tracked down.